ENCYCLOPEDIA OF
ANCIENT MESOAMERICA

ENCYCLOPEDIA OF
ANCIENT MESOAMERICA

Margaret R. Bunson and Stephen M. Bunson

Facts On File, Inc.

AN INFOBASE HOLDINGS COMPANY

Encyclopedia of Ancient Mesoamerica

Facts On File, Inc.
11 Penn Plaza
New York NY 10001

Library of Congress Cataloging-in-Publication Data

Bunson, Margaret.
Encyclopedia of Ancient Mesoamerica / Margaret R. Bunson and Stephen M. Bunson.
p.   cm.
Includes bibliographical references and index.
ISBN 0-8160-2402-2
1. Indians of Mexico—Encyclopedias.   2. Indians of Central
America—Encyclopedias.   3. Mexico—Antiquities—Encyclopedias.
4. Central America—Antiquities—Encyclopedias.   I. Bunson,
Stephen.   II. Title.
F1219.B932   1996

972—dc20   95-13085

Facts On File books are available at special discounts when purchased in
bulk quantities for businesses, associations, institutions or sales
promotions. Please call our Special Sales Department in New York at
212/967-8800 or 800/322-8755.

Jacket design by Cathy Hyman

Printed in the United States of America
VB VC 10 9 8 7 6 5 4 3 2 1

This book is printed on acid-free paper.

For Roland and Nancy.

CONTENTS

ACKNOWLEDGMENTS

There are a number of individuals to whom a special debt is owed for their kind assistance in the preparation of this volume. Among them are the following: Professor Katherine Schreiber and the anthropology department of the University of California, Santa Barbara; Professor Mark Schlenz; Jane Freeburg of Companion Press; the staffs of several libraries, especially of UCSB; and Deirdre Mullane, the original editor of this book. A special appreciation is given to Jeffrey Golick, senior editor at Facts On File, for his enthusiasm and patience.

PREFACE
HOW TO USE THIS BOOK

The names, places and languages of Mesoamerica are difficult to master, and readers interested in the various cultures and historical eras may find them daunting. The rich and colorful history of the region, however, as well as the unique individuals who emerged as leaders in their particular eras or domains will compensate for the difficulty of the languages. Some cultures, in fact, are absolutely fascinating, and the architectural and artistic achievements in Mesoamerica offer spectacular adventures for the arm-chair explorer.

The sections devoted to various regions of Mesoamerica will introduce geographic, geologic and historical details. The various agricultural, architectural, artistic, ceramic, cosmological, religious, trade and warfare entries on Mesoamerica as a whole will provide a portrait of the region in general and will serve to open the way to an understanding of the specific cultures.

These specific cultures, such as the Aztec (Mexica), Olmec, Maya and Toltec, are also discussed in detail. The various sites, leaders, pantheons and religious ceremonies and other aspects of life in Mesoamerica are cited alphabetically, with cross-referencing. Charts for historical timetables, caves, lakes, rivers, cultures, sites and cultural phases will provide readily accessible references as well.

The Maya, for example, are explained in many different entries. Their slow rise to power in their own domains, their departure from regions threatened by natural or man-made disasters, their decline and mysterious exodus from some regions are all discussed. Under separate entries, referred to in the general section on the Maya, the graceful cities of the Maya are detailed as to architectural remains, artistic achievement, population, politics and the like. The rulers of the various city-states also are described and given their historical significance. The same sort of treatment is given to other cultures.

A GUIDE TO PRONUNCIATION

Vowels are pronounced as in Spanish:

a as in father
e as in they
i as ee in knee
o as in most

When *u* precedes another vowel, it is pronounced as the English *w*, except it is silent after *q*.

Consonants are pronounced as in Spanish, except

c is always hard
x is pronounced as the English "sh"
k is a glottalized "c"
q is a consonant similar to "k" but pronounced in the back of the mouth for some Maya words
ch is a glotallized "tz"
dz is a glottalized "tz"
h is silent in Spanish, soft-sounding in Maya
tl is almost silent at the end of Nahuatl words

In Maya, the stress is on the last syllable. In Nahuatl, the stress is usually on the next-to-last syllable.

Maya

Uaxactun - wah-shak-*toon*
Chichen Itza - chee-chain-ee-*tsah*

Yaxchilan - yash-chee-*lahn*

Nahuatl

Teotihuacan - tay-oh-tee-*wah*-khan
Quetzalcoatl - kay-tshal-*koh*-ahtl.

MESOAMERICAN HISTORICAL ERAS	
PERIOD	**DATE**
Paleo-Indian Period	11,000–7000 B.C.
Incipient Agricultural Period (Archaic)	7000 to 2000/2500 B.C.
Formative Period	
Early	2000/1600–900 B.C.
Middle	900–300 B.C.
Late	300 B.C.–A.D. c. 250/290
Classic Period	
Early	C. A.D. 1/250–600
Late	A.D. 600–900
Post-Classic Period	
Early	A.D. 900–c. 1200/1250
Late	C. A.D. 1200/1250–1521 (Spanish Conquest)

CHRONOLOGICAL TABLE

PERIOD	MEXICO	MAYA LANDS	ELSEWHERE
Paleo-Indian Period 11,000–7000 B.C.	Tlapacoya Mammoth Kills Ajuereado Tepexpan Man Iztapan	Mamon Emergence	Siberian hunters Nile shelters Mid-Eastern trade Saharan rock art
Incipient Agriculture Period 7000–2500/2000 B.C.	Tehuacan Tamaulipas Oaxaca growth Chalco growth Durango growth Desert Culture Nayarit San Jose Mogote	Proto-Maya First pottery Belize settlements	Ubaid Mesopotamia European longhouses Caribbean growth Nile cattle herded Uruk in Mesopotamia Pyramids at Giza
Early Formative Period c. 2000–1600–900 B.C.	Tlatilco culture Guerrero growth Jalisco culture Izapa culture Ocos culture Olmec emerge	Early pottery Huaxtec emerge Swasey in Belize Puuc settlements Lacandon Maya Yucatec Maya	Babylon in power Mycenaeans rise Egypt's New Kingdom Shang Dynasty in China European horses domesticated
Middle Formative Period 900–300 B.C.	Olmec La Venta Monte Alban Tabasco culture Monte Negro Tarasca culture	Lowland centers Bonampak built Yucatan sites Chicanel built Maya write Chichen Itza	Assyrian Empire Greeks colonize Olympic started Buddha lives Socrates teaches Carthage rebuilt
Late Formative Period 300 B.C.–c. A.D. 250/290	Teotihuacan Remojada Cuicuilco Tres Zapotes San Lorenzo Zapotec	Kaminaljuyu Ocos Quiche Maya Tikal Chicanel art	Alexander the Great Celts roam Europe Confucius in China Pharos Lighthouse (Alexandria) Library at Alexandria
Early Classic Period c. A.D. 1/250–600	Cholula growth Teotihuacan a power Chalchihuites in Mexico Chalco culture Zacatenco culture	Acanceh started Becal started Palenque built Quirigua built Copan started Bonampak built Jaina culture	Julius Caesar slain Roman Empire Han Dynasty in China Dead Sea Scrolls written
Late Classic Period 600–900 A.D.	Xochicalco Zacateca culture Teotihuacan falls	Palenque Quintana Roo	Byzantine Empire Rise of Islam Nara in Japan Ghana rise in Africa
Early Post-Classic Period 900–1200–1250 A.D.	Toltec in Tula Aztec arrive Zapotec Xochimilco	Seibal continues Puuc culture	Vikings in Newfoundland Seljuk Turks Mongols in China Normans in Britain
Late Post-Classic Period c. 1200–1250–1521	Aztec in power Acolhua Tepanec	Kukulcan cult Mayapan League	Gothic cathedrals Marco Polo travels Turks take Constantinople

A

ABAJ TAKALIK An important city located in the Pacific coastal region on the slopes of the Chiapas Mountains in Guatemala, on the present site of Santa Margarita and San Isidro Piedra Parada. This city, unfortified, dates to the Late Formative Period (300 B.C.–A.D. 250/290) or perhaps earlier. It is considered to be a true link between the Olmec and Maya civilizations, reflecting certain Izapa influences. The site is noted for the many Olmec statues recovered there, including a figure carved into a boulder. In all, more than 200 monumental stone pieces were discovered in Abaj Takalik's ruins. Most of these indicate an advanced understanding of artistic proportions and dimensional aspects of design. Colossal monuments, some weighing several tons, many life-size forms and other sculptures were carved from andesite boulders believed to have been quarried in the nearby Tuxtla Mountains.

Stelae recovered from Abaj Takalik include a human figure carved in basalt. Rectangular and square frame designs were also used. In the center of some sculpted pieces the Olmec U-shape serves as a cartouche (a royal or divine name plaque), and dragons flank the individual scenes. The cartouche was fashioned by incorporating the tail of the double-headed serpent into the design. A human head is depicted in one of the serpent's mouths. An innovation in Abaj Takalik sculpture is the portrayal of socks and sandals on the feet of the various personages represented. (See IZAPA.)

ABASALO A cultural development in the Tamaulipas Sequence in the Sierra de Tamaulipas region dating to the Paleo-Indian Period (11,000–7000 B.C.). The groups extant in the Abasalo era initiated agricultural techniques and also hunted and gathered food. Scrapers, points, mortars and other tools were used at the Abasalo site, as in other associated locales. (See MESOAMERICAN CERAMICS AND CULTURAL DEVELOPMENTS.)

ABEJAS PHASE A cultural development in the Tehuacan Valley of Mexico, dating to the Incipient Agriculture Period of Mesoamerica (7000–c. 2000/2500 B.C.). Pit houses were constructed by the Abejas residents and may have been used only on a seasonal basis. These houses were erected on river terraces and beside caves, where subterranean levels could be incorporated into the structures. Some families inhabited the caves as well. Year-round habitation has been documented, particularly in later eras, when agriculture had become a steady occupation for those living there. Crops raised at Abejas sites include squashes, beans and maize, kept in storage pits during certain times of the year. The Abejas groups also bred dogs, as companions or as a food source. Stoneware and obsidian for tools were produced. (See TEHUACAN SEQUENCE for details; see also MESOAMERICAN CERAMICS AND CULTURAL DEVELOPMENTS.)

ACALAN A province in the region of the Candelaria River Basin in the Yucatan Peninsula, the home of the Chontal Maya. The name means "canoe" in the Chontal language. Acalan's capital was Itzamkanac, dedicated to the Maya deity, Itzamna. The province was composed of coastal lowlands and islands along the ocean shore. Original settlements in Acalan were erected on naturally elevated tracts of land, with canals used for travel and transportation. Part of the vast Maya trade system in the Late Post-Classic Period (A.D. 1200/1250–1521), Acalan had factories and production centers and imported products that were delivered via the Chontal water routes. The province remained an independent part of the Maya confederacy throughout its history. An account by one Apoxpalon from Acalan details how the Chontal Maya elected their chiefs, based on trading experience. (See APOXPALON; MAYA GROUPS, CHONTAL.)

ACAMAPICHTLI The second Aztec (Mexica) ruler, whose name means "handful of reeds." He reigned from A.D. 1376 to c. 1391/1396, succeeding Tenoch, the priest-king who founded the capital of Tenochtitlan. Reportedly of Toltec descent, he went to Tenochtitlan from Azcapotzalco or Culhuacan, as the Aztec requested a Toltec noble to consolidate their claims to that once-powerful nation. One record states that Acamapichtli had an Aztec noble father and a mother of the royal Culhuacan line. He married a Culhuacan princess named Ilancueitl, who is recorded as having wielded considerable political power during his reign. Acamapichtli also wed 20 other local clan heiresses in order to associate himself with various political houses. Tenochtitlan benefited from his reign, as Acamapichtli initiated many building projects, including the development of the *chinampas*, the floating agricultural gardens seen frequently in Mesoamerican cultures. He also erected stone buildings and instituted religious rituals and festival observances. Laws and ordinances were also passed during his reign. In the service of Tezozomoc, the Tepanec king, Acamapichtli, as a vassal, led the Aztec in war against Tezozomoc's enemies.

ACANCEH A Maya city, located in the western part of the Yucatan Peninsula, now active as a capital and once called the "Howl of the Deer" or the "Deer Lament." Teotihuacan influences there indicate that Acanceh may have served as an outpost of that great center before assuming Maya allegiance and gaining prominence in the Early Classic Period (c. A.D. 1/250–600), surviving until the 15th century. Two major structures are visible today in Acanceh. One is a four-tiered pyramid facing a central plaza in the city. The pyramid has a central staircase with apron molding in the Peten (Putun) Maya style. Roughly cut stones cover the platform, which was originally covered with stucco. Sculptures and carved decorations adorned the uppermost level. The second major structure is the Temple of the Stucco Facade, built to honor Quetzalcoatl. An original, smaller building, probably a temple as well, forms the foundation of this vast monument. The original structure was filled with rubble and then incorporated into the present temple. The Temple of the Stucco Facade is believed to have been erected in the Later Formative Period (300 B.C.–c. A.D. 250/290). The carved stucco designs, which are actually stucco reliefs, depict humanized animals and birds, creatures seldom used in artistic architectural works. Each relief is bordered, thereby forming separate panels. The reliefs contain speech scrolls, thus providing the images with words, and glyphlike designs add more information. The facade of the temple is *talud-tablero* in style, an Olmec style of architecture using a base and a tabletop piece.

ACANTUN Maya spirits or demons, four in number, associated with religious traditions concerning the cardinal points of the earth, directions considered spiritually important in many Mesoamerican cultures. The *Acantun* played prominent roles in the Maya celebrations of the New Year. They served as the patrons of idols and religious carvings. These spirits are mentioned in the *Ritual of the Bacabs* and were associated with the Maya god Itzamna. (See *BACAB*; CARDINAL POINTS.)

ACAPULCO A port site on the coast of Guerrero, occupied in the Paleo-Indian Period (11,000–7000 B.C.) and inhabited even after the Aztec occupied the region in the reign of Ahuitzotl. Some old records list another Acapulco, a one-time city-state in the same area. It is possible that the modern resort of that name is neither of the original sites but is simply named after one of them.

ACATL The reed, a day sign used by the Aztec (Mexica) in their version of the *tonalpohualli*, the calendric system.

ACATLAN A section of the Aztec (Mexica) capital Tenochtitlan in the Valley of Mexico. The section was called "the place of the reeds," probably a reference to Lake Texcoco, the site of the capital. (See TENOCHTITLAN.)

ACATONALLI A ruler of the city-state of Xochimilco who took the throne in A.D. 1256. During his reign Acatonalli made Xochimilco the capital of the region. He also built temples and residential quarters and began the vast system of *chinampas*, the floating gardens for which Xochimilco is known.

ACCOMPAÑANTES Stone figures found on Zapotec sites, having no obvious purpose but used by architects as part of the overall design of monuments. Depictions of bats (symbols of fertility), the corn deity and a warrior figure with the head of a bird are considered *accompañantes*, or accompanying forms. (See ZAPOTEC ART AND ARCHITECTURE.)

ACHIOTLA A Tototepec site in the coastal area of Oaxaca in Mexico, mentioned in the traditional legends of that region. A unique tree grew in Achiotla, with rare and beautiful flowers and wondrous perfumes. An Aztec (Mexica) emperor (in some lists Motecuhzoma II) heard of Achiotla's tree and sent a delegation to the site to request samples of the bark and the flowers. The Tototepec refused, and the Aztec withdrew, returning soon after with a large army. Before an assembly of horrified citizens, the Aztec uprooted the tree, thereby killing it. The Tototepec, enraged, attacked the Aztec in retribution.

ACHITOMETL The ruler of Culhuacan, a city-state on Lake Texcoco, in power when the Aztec (Mexica) arrived in the region around A.D. 1319. The people of Culhuacan had entered the area after a brief alliance with the Toltec and were thus considered the rightful heirs to the Toltec culture in the region. Culhuacan also made an alliance with the Tepanec and other major groups. When the Aztec arrived, Achitometl allowed them to settle in a serpent-infested area, believing that the conditions there would compel the group to move on. The Aztec caught the snakes and roasted them, expressing their gratitude for such plentiful food supplies. When Achitometl asked the Aztec to fight as his vassals against the city-state of Xochimilco, in one of numerous regional wars, he did not provide them with weapons. They made their own, supposedly as instructed by their god Huitzilopochtli, and proved so ferocious in battle that Achitometl began to seek ways to rid himself of the newcomers. The Aztec, warned of the coming treachery, fled to Lake Texcoco's islands, which they transformed into their mighty capital, Tenochtitlan.

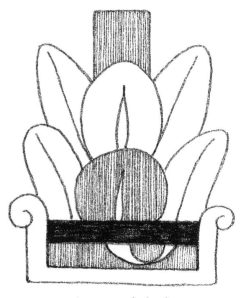

Aztec *acatl* glyph

A legend evolved from their flight. Supposedly the Aztec asked Achitometl for his daughter, a great beauty, so that she could become the bride of their god. He consented and attended a religious ceremony conducted by the Aztec. There he saw a priest wearing the skin of his daughter. She had been flayed in a ritual marrying her to the god. Enraged, Achitometl chased the Aztec into Lake Texcoco, thereby forcing them to launch what was to become their imperial destiny.

ACHUITLA The original home of the Mixtec people in the mountains of Oaxaca, called "the land in the clòuds." Mixtec traditions suggest that Achuitla and another site, Apoala, were where human beings were created, born from sacred trees. Achuitla is actually a region of caves and was the first domain of the four basic Mixtec groups.

ACOLHUA A group entering the Valley of Mexico around A.D. 1260, coming from Chicomoztoc, the legendary sacred ancestral home of the Nahual clans, including the Aztec (Mexica). Some records date their arrival to A.D. 1168, led by a chief named Huetzin. The first Acolhua capital was Coatlinchan, on the eastern shore of Lake Texcoco, but the original region inhabited by the group is given as Michoacan. In time the Acolhua established a rather large domain, including the city of Huexotla in the east. Eventually the Acolhua heritage influenced the entire area. Quinatzin, a descendant of Xolotl, the Chichimec ruler who had welcomed the Acolhua into the region, established Texcoco as his capital, absorbing other areas into his domain. Tezozomoc, the Tepanec ruler with ties to the Acolhua, fought Quinatzin's son, slaying him and thus setting the stage for the rise of Nezahualcoyotl in Texcoco.

ACOLNAHUACATL (Acolnahuatzin) A ruler of the Tepanec who founded the capital of Azcapotzalco c. A.D. 1230/1250. He was the grandson of the revered Tepanec ruler Matlaccoatl. The capital probably began as a colony of Teotihuacan, the dominant city of the region. The Tepanec, settling first on the western side of Lake Texcoco with the permission of the Chichimec ruler, Xolotl, populated Azcapotzalco and transformed it. Acolnahuacatl married one of Xolotl's daughters, a woman named Cuitlaxochitzin. She bore him a son, the powerful Tezozomoc.

ACOZAC A site dating to the Post-Classic Period (A.D. 900–1521) overlooking Lake Texcoco, the massive natural water reserve in the Valley of Mexico. Acozac is translated from the Nahuatl language as "in the Yellow Water." A small stepped pyramid was discovered on the site, designed with a platform and a wide frontal staircase. Occupied by one of the local cultures, Acozac was absorbed into the Aztec (Mexica) empire. It is believed to have served as a small ceremonial center.

ACTOPAN RIVER A waterway flowing through the central part of Veracruz, the domain of the Totonac. The Totonac city of Zempoala was established on the banks of the Actopan in the Late Post-Classic Period, A.D. 1200.

ACTUN A type of limestone cave used by the Maya in the western part of the Yucatan Peninsula and in Belize.

Most of these caves had freshwater sources, some quite deep in the earth. (See ACTUN BALAM.)

ACTUN BALAM A cave in southern Belize, used by the Maya for religious and ceremonial purposes. These rites continued in Actun Balam through the Post-Classic Period (A.D. 900–1521). It is believed that the Maya used Actun Balam and other caves for religious ceremonies after they abandoned their great ceremonial sites. (See CAVES.)

ACXOTEC A group that settled in the Chalco region of Mexico in the Early Formative Period (2000–900 B.C.) or even earlier. They are believed to have originated in the area around Tula. Traders and merchants, the Acxotec arrived in Chalco with their own market systems already established and introduced the local groups to these systems. They worshipped a deity called Acolactl Nahualtecuhtli.

"ADOLESCENT, THE" A remarkable statue of the god Quetzalcoatl, found in the Huaxtec city of Tamuin. In this statue the deity is depicted as the evening star, carrying his son on his back. (See HUAXTEC ART; TAMUIN; see also QUETZALCOATL.)

AGALTEPEC An island in Lake Catemaco in the central region of the Tuxtla Mountains in southern Veracruz. Volcanic in origin, the island is a companion to Tenaspi, a second mound. It was occupied between A.D. 900 and 1000. Olmec, Toltec and Totonac influences are evident in the ruins discovered on Agaltepec. Mounds as well as the remains of courts and plazas are visible.

AGRICULTURE See MESOAMERICAN AGRICULTURE.

AGUADA A small rainwater pond dug by the Maya in several regions or formed by natural processes. *Aguadas* were shallow and dependent upon rainfall. They were also vulnerable to silting and had to be cleaned out regularly. These ponds were part of the Maya agricultural resources, and remains of *aguadas* have been uncovered at Maya ceremonial sites. (See also *CENOTE*.)

AGUATECA A Maya site in the Peten (Putun) region (now modern Guatemala) drained by the Usumacinta River. The entire territory was dominated by Tikal in most historical eras. The city's nobles shared common ancestry and familial and social ties with Piedras Negras, another Maya city in the region. The ongoing conflicts between Tikal and other ceremonial centers involved Aguateca to some extent, but only a few records of the city and its rulers are available. Most of these record only local events.

AHAU CANEK An Itza-Maya ruler of the Itza capital of Tayasal, founded by that group in Maya territory after they were exiled from Chichen Itza. Ahau Canek, assuming the traditions and customs of the Yucatec Maya, shared power in Tayasal with his cousin, the high priest Kin Canek.

AH CACAU (Ah-Cacaw) Maya ruler of the city of Tikal, who took the throne in A.D. 682. He began a large building program in the city, laying out the North Acropolis

Ah Cacau of Tikal

He was buried in ceremonial robes with grave offerings of jewelry, including 180 pieces of jade, pottery and bone objects. Ceremonial reliefs adorn the tomb.

AH CANUL (1) A Mexica group who served as mercenary troops for the powerful Cocom dynasty of the Maya. When the Cocom were overthrown in their city of Mayapan in A.D. 1450, the Ah Canul were not exiled but provided with lands in the Yucatan. There they were assimilated into the regional population. In some records, Ah Canul refers to the region settled by these mercenaries. (See AH CANUL [2].)

AH CANUL (2) The domain of the Maya Canul clan in western Yucatan. This dynasty controlled many Maya ceremonial centers in the region.

AH CHAC MITAN CH'OC The Maya name for the planet Venus, translated as "he of the great stench" and associated with I Ahau on the Maya calendar. In some rituals Ah Chac Mitan Ch'oc was revered as the brother of the Maya god Itzamna and addressed as Xax Ek or Xaman Ek.

AH DZUN TITUL XIU Also called Napot Xiu in some records, the ruler of the Xiu clan in Mani, a region in northern Yucatan. He made a pilgrimage with his son Ah Ziyah Xiu and 40 servants, planning to take part in ceremonies in the *cenote* of Chichen Itza. En route Ah Dzun Titul Xiu asked permission of a local ruler, Nachi Cocom, to enter his territory. Ah Dzun Titul Xiu was lavishly honored by the Cocom for five days and nights and then murdered with his son and servants in an act carried out to avenge the death of a Cocom slain by one of Ah Dzun Titul Xiu's relatives.

AH KINCHIL A Maya god, called Kinich Ahau in the Yucatan, associated with the sun. Powerful Ah Kinchil played a vital role in Maya agricultural activities, which were the foundation for Maya prosperity. The name means "day lord," and in the Maya codices the god is described as somewhat malevolent toward humans, a possible allusion to the relentless nature of the sun in the tropics. In some regions Ah Kinchil was believed capable of taking the form of a jaguar at night, thus reflecting a mystical and mysterious nature. In other Maya traditions the god was believed to descend each night into Xibalba, the Maya underworld, where he was protected by his brother Usukunkyum from the evil spells of the earth god, Kisin (Cizin). In Altun Ha, a Maya city in Belize, Ah Kinchil was depicted in the largest Maya carved head ever found to have been worked in bold relief.

AH MUN Also called Yum Kaax, a Maya god of maize, usually depicted as a handsome young man, sometimes with maize sprouting from his head. He was symbolized by the Kan day glyph in inscriptions and was associated with God E in Maya codices. As the Lord of the Forests, Ah Mun was sometimes shown in combat with the god Ah Puch, or death.

and the Great Plaza. Ah Cacau also restored Tikal's prestige after the damage wrought upon the city by Caracol's ruler Kan II. In 695 Ah Cacau went to war against the Maya stronghold of Calakmul as an ally of Caracol. He took the ruler of Calakmul captive, along with many enemy warriors. As a result, Tikal's importance as a political entity in its own region was revived. A stela erected in A.D. 695 honors Ah Cacau for restoring Tikal after the previous decades of neglect and outside interference. Two pyramidal complexes of the city are also thought to have been built during Ah Cacau's reign. The tomb of Ah Cacau in Tikal is elaborate.

AH NAUM POT   A Maya ruler of the city of Cozumel, on the throne in A.D. 1527, when the Spanish arrived in the region. He greeted them courteously and allowed them to rest there before moving on.

AHPO HAI   A Maya noblewoman, the sister of Lord Pacal, the ruler of Palenque. A stucco head portraying Ahpo Hai was found in Pacal's tomb in the Temple of Inscriptions in Palenque. The carving is approximately 11 inches high and depicts a handsome, strong-featured woman.

AH PUCH   The Maya god of death, known also as God A in the Maya codices. Ah Puch is depicted as a figure with a death head, bony ribs and a spinal cord made visible by starvation. If shown clothed, the deity is covered with black spots, symbolizing the rotting of the flesh. Ah Puch presided over the lowest level of Xibalba, the Maya underworld. He fought both the gods Itzamna and Ah Mun, acting out the conflict of good over evil. The deity was associated with the owl, a bird that the Maya believed called their names to summon them to the grave.

AHUALACO (Ahualulco)   A site in western Mexico associated with the Jalisco culture. The small center had mounds and a rather large ceramic industry. After c. A.D. 150/200, the region came under the growing dominance of Teotihuacan. Shaft tombs were also discovered on the site.

AHUIATETEO   Five deities associated with excessive worldly pleasures worshipped by the Aztec (Mexica) and other cultures in the Valley of Mexico. The deities symbolized the misfortunes resulting from activities that were not moderated by religious observance and common sense, such as drinking, gambling and sex. Moderation was the ideal in the Aztec world. All of the Ahuiateteo bore the number five in their calendrical names, representing excessive amounts of *pulque* consumed by drunkards. The deities were also associated with the southern CARDINAL POINT. The deities were Macuilmalinalli—5 Grass, Macuilcuetzpalin—5 Lizard, Macuilcozcacuauhtli—5 Vulture, Macuiltochtli—5 Rabbit and Macuilxochitl—5 Flower.

AHUITZOTL   Aztec emperor succeeding Tizoc, ruling at Tenochtitlan from A.D. 1486 to 1502. His name means "water creature," and he was one of the most active warrior-emperors in Aztec history. Called the Great in some historical accounts, he began his reign by leading an army into Toluca to capture ceremonial victims for his coronation. He was a tireless campaigner whose ventures were recorded as cruel and successful. Ahuitzotl expanded his empire year after year, dedicating his conquests to the god Huitzito-pochtli.

He marched against Chiapas, capturing an area on the border of the Tarasca territory, west of the city of Tula. Ahuitzotl's armies attacked Alahuitzlan, a Chontal city, slaying or enslaving an estimated 40,000 there. His armies entered Guerrero on the Pacific coast and marched to the Isthmus of Tehuantepec.

The armies of Ahuitzotl were given free rein to loot the various regions, but because of protests made by the TRIPLE ALLIANCE and the local populations, he was forced to curtail

Aztec Ahuitzotl glyph

such traditional activities. When the people in the Soconusco region revolted against his demands for tribute Ahuitzotl attacked the region, marching as far as the border of modern Guatemala. Ahuitzotl encouraged colonization of the border regions of the Aztec empire, sending families into those areas adjoining the Tarasca and elsewhere in order to promote Mexica-ization.

Ahuitzotl's relations with the Zapotec were not as successful as his other endeavors. He gave his daughter Pelaxilla in marriage to the Zapotec king Cosihuesa. She was supposed to open the Zapotec lands to an Aztec invasion but allied herself instead with her husband and his people.

Despite his victories, Ahuitzotl was criticized for draining the treasury in order to mount military campaigns. He then sought to expand his empire through diplomacy.

The records of Tenochtitlan state that Ahuitzotl dedicated the Great Temple, the Templo Mayor, and presided over the building program started in AXAYACATL's reign. Thousands of political prisoners are said to have perished during the ritual dedication held in Tenochtitlan for the new temple. Ahuitzotl also built another temple at Tepoztlan in Morelos and added to the Malinalco ceremonial buildings, using the services of imported artisans.

AH ULIL   The ruler of Izamal, a Maya city, in A.D. 1194. His intended bride was stolen from him by the Itza Chac Ib Chac, the ruler of Chichen Itza, who seems to have been smitten with love. These lords did not battle personally over the woman. Another lord, Hunac Ceel, the ruler of Mayapan, turned the deed into a rallying cry and called for the overthrow of Chac Ib Chac. Chac Ib Chac was defeated in the campaign that followed. It was recorded that he was "trampled upon" and driven out of Chichen Itza. Hunac Ceel had Mexica support and intended to make Mayapan the chief city of the region and of his dynasty. Eventually he turned on Ah Ulil and Izamal was made a vassal city.

AH XUPAN   A Maya noble of the Xiu family who revolted against the dominant Cocom dynasty of Mayapan, traditional enemies of the Xiu. As a reason for the rebellion, Ah Xupan cited the fact that the Cocom were selling the Yucatan Maya to other nations as sacrificial victims or slaves. Ah Xupan and his allies overthrew the Cocom at Mayapan sometime in A.D. 1450.

AH ZUITAK TITUL XIU   The Maya nobleman who established the ceremonial site at Uxmal in northern Yucatan. He was a scion of the Xiu clan.

AH ZIYAH XIU   The ill-fated son of the Maya ruler of the Xiu clan of Mani who accompanied his father to Chichen Itza and was slain by Nachi Cocom. (See AH DZUN TITUL XIU.)

AJALPAN   A site in the Tehuacan Valley, dated from 1500 to 900 B.C. and associated with the agricultural development of the region. The Ajalpan site also represents a phase in the historical emergence of the area and is associated with the Tehuacan Sequence. It is believed that as many as 100 to 300 individuals organized in villages practiced agriculture. Male priests and religious observances were present, and the women were esteemed. Monochrome hematite red wares were produced, as well as *tecomates,* neckless jars. The people of this site and phase also decorated ceramics with rocker dentate stamps. (See TEHUACAN SEQUENCE for details.)

AJUEREADO COMPLEX   A site and cultural phase in the Tehuacan Valley, also a part of the Tehuacan Sequence, dating to at least 6000 B.C. The caves of this region were inhabited by hunter-gatherers who used the stable grasslands for food and prospered in the desertlike climate. Tools from the Paleo-Indian Period have been discovered here, but no burial sites have been found. (See TEHUACAN SEQUENCE for historical development.)

AKE   An important Maya Post-Classic (A.D. 900 to 1521) Period site covering more than two miles, located in the north-central part of the Yucatan Peninsula, and noted for its unique architect. The pyramid at Ake has a platform supported by 36 columns. It overlooks a plaza and has a stairway on its south face made of giant stone blocks, each over four feet long. The stairway measures 137 feet in width. The columns, 14 to 16 feet high, were fashioned out of drum-shaped and smaller stones. The plaza is bordered by smaller pyramids, one of which contains a *chultun,* a bottle-shaped chamber used as a pit or as a tomb in Maya temples. In the center of the plaza an uncarved stela was discovered. Ake may have had a protective wall at one time. Royal residences at the site lend an unusually vivid quality to the scene.

AKUMAL   A Maya settlement on the central coast of the northern Yucatan Peninsula dating to the Late Classic Period (A.D. 600–900). Probably a participant in the extensive Maya trade system, Akumal was built on a natural harbor. All that remains on the site is a small temple.

ALAHUITZLAN   A Chontal Maya city on the Apatzingan Plain, formed by the Tepalcatepec River in Michoacan. The Chontal (also called the Tequistlanteco) defended Alahuitzlan against the Aztec (Mexica) led by Emperor Ahuitzotl. These were "frontier" Chontal, Mexica-ized and distantly related to the Yucatan Chontal of the great Acalan region and who were respected as traders. The city fell to the Aztec, and reportedly thousands of Maya were slain or taken prisoner as sacrificial victims. There are some references to the fact that Alahuitzlan was fortified. (See CHONTAL (2) for details of this group.)

ALDAMA   A site in the gulf coastal lowlands marked by a large lava dome.

ALMAGRE PHASE   A cultural development associated with the Flacco Phase in the Tamaulipas Sequence in the Sierra de Tamaulipas, dating from 2200 to 1800 B.C. In this historical era agricultural production had increased by 20 percent, and an early form of maize has been found. Wattle-and-daub houses were constructed during this phase.

ALTAMIRA-BARRA CULTURE   A developmental phase existing from c. 1600/1400 to c. 1400/1300 B.C. in the region of Altamira on the Pacific coast in Chiapas near the Guatemalan border. Some Maya records date this culture to c. 1700 to 1500 B.C. in Guatemala and Chiapas. The region is flat and temperate, with rain forests and coastal swamps. Barra ceramics are important in the history of Mesoamerica, notable because they reflect continuing tradition as well as periodic innovations in style and design. The ceramics of the Altamira-Barra were sophisticated and unique in the Early Formative Period (2000/1600–900 B.C.). Consisting mainly of in-curved rim bowls, the vessels were incised and grooved, making them the earliest examples of such decorative style in the region. Altamira-Barra ceramics show some obvious affinities with those of Ecuador. Barra culture figurines predate the Ocos forms and probably the Oaxaca figures as well. They were recovered mostly in fragments. The people did not use obsidian, nor did they use *manos* and *metates,* grain grinding stones and platforms, initially. No evidence of public architecture has been found. The Altamira-Barra economy was based on manioc. The phase was also associated with burial mounds.

ALTAR DE SACRIFICIOS   A southern lowland Maya site on the Pasion River, south of Tikal, dated to the Classic Period (A.D. 1/250–900). Altar de Sacrificios occupied a strategic location in the vast Maya trade system because it was located on a main waterway. Temples and residential structures were constructed around a main plaza in the city. Several innovations are also evident at the site. The floors were formed from packed lime and ash, and the people appear to have been influenced by the Xe culture. The pyramidal platforms indicate that Altar de Sacrificios was a ceremonial center. Two burial sites have been found here,

Altar de Sacrificios glyph

suggesting that a social hierarchy existed. The funeral of one of these tomb owners drew Maya nobles from other cities, including Bird Jaguar from Yaxchilan. One altar gives a clear description of the event.

In earlier eras, the architecture of Altar de Sacrificios was influenced by the Olmec. A plaza complex, the largest in the region, was faced with shells and plaster. Stone masonry stairs were incorporated into the design. The city is believed to have served as the first ceremonial center in the west to employ the full Classical patterns of Maya civilization. Later the city was subordinate to Piedras Negras and Yaxchilan as a political power. The last dated monument on the site was erected in the late eighth century. Major public building projects ended, and Altar de Sacrificios continued with a ceramic industry connected to the site's trading tradition. Figurines and other wares recovered in the city include those made from Fine Orange and Fine Gray ceramics. Some of these wares reflect outside influence. Altar de Sacrificios was reported as being invaded sometime around A.D. 910. The Chontal Maya were located nearby.

ALTAR DESERT   Also known as El Gran Desierto, an arid region bordering a barren volcanic peak, Cerro Pinacate, in the Pacific coastal lowlands of Mexico.

ALTA VISTA   A Chalchihuites site in Zacatecas. A vassal of the city of Teotihuacan around A.D. 350, it was valued for its mines, which yielded malachite, cinnabar, hematite and rock crystals. Some 750 such mines have been located in the region. The site was a ceremonial center, constructed on a hill and having a colonnaded hall. Alta Vista also had a skull rack (*tzompantli*), which may have influenced the

Toltec at Tula, as the Toltec copied older art and religious forms. It is known that turquoise was brought to the city from the American New Mexico region. The turquoise was worked into mosaics and ornaments for trade in central Mexico. Alta Vista was abandoned around A.D. 900 as the nearby site called La Quemada grew in power. (See TURQUOISE ROAD.)

ALT CAUALO   Also called *Quiauitl eva,* an Aztec festival dedicated to the dams and dikes erected in Tenochtitlan, the Aztec capital, to protect the city in times of flood. Celebrated "when the tree rises," the festival honored agricultural processes as well. During the ritual, associated with the rain god Tlaloc, children were sacrificed on the deity's altars.

ALTOS CUCHUMATANES   A region in Guatemala that is an extension of the Chiapas highlands. The land is composed of steep crests and V-shaped basins and valleys. A distinctive feature of the topography is the *llano,* a grassy terrain with streams. (See CHIAPAS; GUATEMALA.)

ALTUN HA   A Maya site in the north-central region of Belize, called the Rockstone Pond. There is evidence of the Mamon culture in Altun Ha. Small by Maya standards, the city held as many as 500 buildings and covered over two square miles. The site was occupied as early as 200 B.C., although the ceremonial structures were erected a century later. An estimated 2,500 Maya lived in Altun Ha, with as many as 10,000 others farming and working in the surrounding region. The several separate ceremonial complexes of the site served the entire region, and were designed to accommodate gatherings from outside settlements.

A plaza in Altun Ha, part of this complex, was sunken in design. Three separate floors are evident in its construction. Entirely surfaced with plaster, the plaza was bordered by temples and other ceremonial structures. The Temple of the Green Tomb included a burial site dating to A.D. 550–600, the earliest such grave site there. The temple was named after the nearly 300 jade pieces discovered as offerings within it. The remains of a Maya codex were also discovered there. Facing a second plaza was the Temple of the Masonry Altars, the base of which contained mask panels, originally faced with stucco. A tomb in this building was the burial site for an important personage, evidenced by the large number of grave offerings, including ornaments, ceremonial flints, jade objects and the largest single piece of jade ever found in Mesoamerica, a carved head of the sun god, Ah Kinchil (Kinich Ahau). A second carved jade object found in the temple depicts a seated figure on one side and a glyph on the reverse. The Temple of the Masonry Altars appears to have undergone eight separate phases of construction. An altar once graced its summit. The *chultun* is believed to have been first dug in Altun Ha. The site reveals considerable evidence of Teotihuacan influence.

AMACUECA PHASE   A cultural development in the Zacoalco-Sayula archaeological zone in the Sayula Basin in southern Jalisco. Associated with the Autlan wares, the Amacueca Phase dates to the Formative Period (c. 2000/1600 B.C.–A.D. c. 250/290).

AMACUZAC RIVER   A tributary of the great Balsas River, which forms part of the system that defines the modern boundary between the Mexican states of Guerrero and Michoacan. The Amacuzac is in the northern Balsas system, fed by springs welling from the porous volcanic lavas of the plateau.

AMANALCO   A name meaning "the pool," a section of Tenochtitlan, the Aztec (Mexica) capital. The city was founded in A.D. 1325.

AMAPA   A Nayarit site on the Pacific coast that reflects evidence of an important ceramic industry. The people responsible for the industry progressed from crude petroglyphs to accomplished figures. Copper pieces, including pins, needles, knives and fish hooks, were found in Amapa. The site has over 200 mounds, dating to the Early Classic Period (c. A.D. 1/250–600). The villages of Amapa were built of wattle and daub, with thatched roofs. Amapa apparently was abandoned and then reoccupied. By c. A.D. 900/1200, the mounds had been completed and a ball court was provided for games. With the introduction of metallurgy in the region, Amapa's artisans became skilled and noted for their metal ornaments. Three separate periods of cultural development are evident here. The first was from A.D. 250 to 750. The second, noted for metalworking, was from A.D. 700 to 900. The last period dates from A.D. 900 to 1521. In the regional graves some 800 pieces of pottery were recovered, mostly orange and red-rimmed wares. Figurines, stone heads and axes were also found. (See NAYARIT.)

AMARANTH (*Amaranthus hybridus*)   A grain and pot herb popular in Mesoamerica and appearing as one of the earliest plants used. Amaranth remained in use throughout the historical eras of Mesoamerican development and is popular even today. Two species of amaranth were grown in some regions. Amaranth seeds were mixed with water to make a drink. During some eras amaranth was also used as an alternative crop when maize failed.

AMATITLAN LAKE   A water source near modern Guatemala City in Guatemala. Located near the Maya city of Kaminaljuyu, the lake served as a ceremonial site during some eras. Amatitlan has springs and fumaroles and a muddy bottom. Blackened vessels have been recovered from the lake.

AMATZINAC RIVER   A waterway in eastern Morelos, south of Popocatepetl Volcano. This river was a natural resource for the Olmec frontier city of Chalcatzinco in the Middle Formative Period, around 700 B.C., and perhaps even earlier.

AMIMITL   A deity worshipped in the city of Xochimilco in the Valley of Mexico. Amimitl was a patron of the vast canal and garden system of Xochimilco, as was the god Atlahuac.

ANALES DE CUAUHTITLAN   Also called the Codex Chimalpopoca, this document was composed by a Toltec for a Spanish governor, compiling a series of Toltec rulers.

This list differs from the one provided in the *Historia Tolteca-Chichimeca.* (See CODICES; see also TOLTEC GOVERNMENT.)

ANALES DE LOS XAHIL   See ANNALS OF THE CAKCHIQUELS.

ANNALS OF THE CAKCHIQUELS   A history of the Cakchiquel Maya of Guatemala, also called the *Memorial de Salada,* the *Memorial de Tecpan-Atitlan* or the *Anales de los Xahil.* The Cakchiquel, closely associated historically with the Quiche Maya, lived in the mountainous regions of the territory now called Guatemala. The annals concern the affairs of these Maya while under foreign domination. When completed, the history was kept by the Maya in the village of Solala, near Lake Atitlan. It was then given to the Franciscan friars of a nearby monastery for safeguarding. The document corresponds to the cosmological views expressed in the *Popol Vuh* and adds Maya myths. It also details the cruelty of the Spanish invaders. (See MAYA GROUPS, CAKCHIQUEL; QUIKAB.)

ANCESTORS, DIVINE   Deities significant in the creation myths essential to the religious beliefs of the various Mesoamerican cultures. The Divine Ancestors of the Maya were Xpiyacoc and Xmucane (Xpiyacoc's consort). Primordial beings, they instructed the creation deities in the task of fashioning human beings. Xmucane ground the maize from which the first humans were formed. The Maya Divine Ancestors are depicted in the Quiche Maya document, the *Popol Vuh.*

In the Nahual tradition, the Divine Ancestors were an aged couple, Oxomoco and Cipactonal. The Aztec (Mexica) and others believed that Cipactonal and his consort resided in a sacred cave and they were revered as the grandparents of the popular deity QUETZALCOATL.

APARICIO   A site of the Totonac culture located in the Sierra de Puebla region that gives some indication of Toltec influence. Aparicio was originally built according to Totonac architectural design, having temples, pyramidal platforms and friezes. The Totonac claimed a part in the building of the great pyramids in the city of Teotihuacan and were skilled architects, as the great temple at El Tajin so dramatically demonstrates. The site is also noted for a stela depicting the body of a decapitated ball player from which serpent heads emerge. The Totonac played the traditional Mesoamerican ball game, as did other Mesoamerican cultures, and they also conducted the *voladores,* a dance around a pole in which four men, representing the cardinal points of the earth, swing from ropes. (See TOTONAC ARCHITECTURE AND ART; TOTONAC.)

APATZINGAN PHASE   A cultural development in the Tepalcatepec Basin, a region of Michoacan, bounded by the Sierra mountains there. Apatzingan dates to the Early Classic Period (c. A.D. 1/250–600) or perhaps earlier. The sites associated with the phase contain evidence of habitation and stages of ceramic development. The Apatzingan Phase was preceded by both the Chumbicuaro and Delicias phases. Ceramics from the Apatzingan era include red-on-brown wares and plain ceramics in the shape of *ollas* and

Aztec eagle symbol

along with another site, Zacatenco, have been designated archaeological zones from which can be traced cultural and agricultural development in the region. Early nomadic groups entered Arbolillo and constructed wattle-and-daub houses, slowly initiating agricultural advancement and farming. Burial rituals included the wrapping of corpses as well as grave offerings. During the Formative Period (2000 B.C.–c. A.D. 250/290), Arbolillo increased in population but left no evidence of cultural innovation. As was true of Zacatenco, Arbolillo remained a farming community. Figures dating to this period, however, were hand-molded and then mass-produced. Childbirth scenes and mother and child figurines reflect the religious significance of the act of birth. In some records Arbolillo and Zacatenco are associated with the Ticoman Phase.

ARBOLILLO-ZACATENCO PHASE   A cultural development on the edge of Lake Texcoco in the Valley of Mexico, where lance points were fashioned from obsidian during the Formative Period (2000 B.C.–c. A.D. 250/290). Figurines of females wearing turbans and features formed by punching and filleting were uncovered from sites of this phase. The dead were buried in cemeteries and beneath house floors during this era. Some burial offerings date to this time.

ARCELIA   A site in Guerrero, Mexico, where a multistory structure was built out of adobe. This edifice has trapezoidal doorways, indicating a possible Peruvian influence in the region. Arcelia dates to the Post-Classic Period (A.D. 900–1521). The local groups of Arcelia are believed to be related to the Tarascan, although they have Quechua linguistic traits.

ARCHITECTURE, PUBLIC   See MESOAMERICAN ARCHITECTURE.

ARENAL   A subphase of the Miraflores cultural development, associated with the cities of Izapa and Kaminaljuyu. This subphase dates to the Middle Formative Period (900–300 B.C.).

AREVALO PHASE   A cultural development in the Isthmus of Tehuantepec during the Formative Period (2000 B.C.–c. A.D. 250/290), serving as a link between the gulf coast and the Pacific slopes of Guatemala. The people living in this region during this developmental phase left a cultural heritage and various sites, with evidence of habitation mounds and burned adobe fragments. The people camped in the open in undefended locations. The ceramics of the phase were of a high quality, reflecting advanced technique and skill in monochromes—red ware, buff ware, black ware and gray-brown wares—and bichromes—red or white on buff. Small hand-molded figurines were also recovered in Arevalo, as were clay stamps and hollow effigy whistles. *Tecomates* and red slip wares predominate. The Maya are associated with the Arevalo in the traditional Maya territories.

ARMERIA PHASE   A ceramic development in the Colima culture, dating to the Formative Period (2000 B.C.–c.

deep, unrimmed bowls with flaring sides. Some red-on-brown pieces, incised, were also recovered. A figurine has also been found. (See APATZINGAN PLAIN.)

APATZINGAN PLAIN   A natural geological formation in southern Michoacan associated with the Chumbicuaro Phase of the Late Formative Period (300 B.C.–c. A.D. 250/290) or perhaps later. The plain is formed by the Tepalcatepec River. It is also the site of the city of Alahuitzlan, the Chontal capital. (See APATZINGAN PHASE.)

APOALA   A mythical site called the homeland of the Mixtec nation in their records. Two sacred trees grew in Apoala and at a second site, Achuitla, one on each site, giving birth to the first Mixtec rulers, a male and a female.

APOCHQUIYAUHTZIN   The last ruler of the city-state of Xochimilco in the Valley of Mexico. He administered the city for the Spanish conquerors of the region.

APOXPALON   Also known as Paxbolonacha, a Chontal Maya merchant in the Acalan region who was elected as a regional ruler of Itzamkanac, the capital in the Candelaria River basin. His election demonstrates the Chontal system of raising established veterans of the trade system to high office in the Post Classic Period (A.D. 900–1521) and he was on the throne in A.D. 1525, noted by the Spanish. (See MAYA GROUPS, CHONTAL.)

APOZTLES   Sieves used by the Mixtec for washing impurities from maize before grinding. These sieves were recovered in a tomb in the city of Lachizaa.

ARBOLILLO   A site located on the shores of Lake Texcoco in the Valley of Mexico, dated c. 1350 B.C. Arbolillo,

A.D. 250/290). This culture flourished on the coast of western Mexico in the modern state of Colima.

ARROYO YAXCHILAN RIVER   A natural waterway in Chiapas, near the Maya site of Yaxchilan. The river's algae deposits are alluded to in the name of the Maya ceremonial center Yaxchilan, which translates as "green stones."

ART   See MESOAMERICAN ART.

ATASTA   A site believed to have been occupied by the Toltec at one time, located on the gulf coast near modern Ciudad Carmen. A figurine and pottery discovered in Atasta date to A.D. 1300–1500 and are Toltec in style and design. No ruins in Atasta have been documented to date.

ATEMOZTLI   An Aztec (Mexica) agricultural festival called "the coming of the water." The Aztec fasted before the festival and during the celebration made gifts of food and drink for the temples. Images of the rain god, Tlaloc, and his associates, the rain brewer dwarves, were honored during the ritual. (See DWARVES; *TLALOQUES*.)

ATEPEHUACAN, SAN BARTOLO   A site in the northeastern section of modern Mexico City where the remains of mammoth were unearthed in 1957. Partially destroyed in the ground before being recognized, the remains were discovered beside a cache of basalt and obsidian chips. Some potsherds were also discovered at the site. (See also TEPEXPAN; TEQUIXQUIAC.)

ATITLAN, LAKE   A water reserve in northwestern Chimaltenango, Guatemala, home to the Cakchiquel Maya and the site of their capital, Iximiche. Lake Atitlan, known as "the crowning glory of highland Guatemala," lies amid mountains and volcanoes; San Pedro, Toliman and Atitlan volcanoes rim the lake, which is nearly 1,600 feet deep and measures 11 by 8 miles.

ATIZAPAN   A name meaning "whitish water," a section of the Aztec capital, Tenochtitlan. The name is an obvious reference to Lake Texcoco, where the capital, founded in A.D. 1325, was located.

ATL   Water, the day sign used by the Aztec in their version of the *tonal-pohualli*, the calendrical system.

ATLAHUA   An Aztec deity, called the patron of fishing. Marine products were important to the Aztec (Mexica), who established their capital on Lake Texcoco in the Valley of Mexico. The god was called Atlahuac in Xochimilco, associated in that city-state with the deity Amimitl. (See AZTEC GODS.)

ATLAHUAC   A Xochimilco deity, patron of that city-state's canals and gardens along with the deity Amimitl.

ATLANTEAN (1)   Term describing a type of altar developed by the Olmec in San Lorenzo during the Early Formative Period (2000–900 B.C.). Atlantean altar tables were supported by carved figures.

Atlantean altar from Portrero Nuevo

ATLANTEAN (2)   Descriptive term for Toltec monuments called *telemones*, each 15 feet high, composed of four sections joined with mortise. These giant figures depict warriors, reflecting the preoccupation of the Toltec with the god Quetzalcoatl. The warriors are armed with the firebird breastplate of Quetzalcoatl, and their stylization enhances the geometric quality of the pieces. The headdresses, called *toques*, include rows of disks, probably representing the stars; they are also plumed. The swords of the *telemones* are attached to belts, and each figure carries a bag of copal, an incense used in religious ceremonies. The colossal Atlantean forms were once painted.

ATLATL   A Nahuatl word meaning "spear thrower," dating to the Paleo-Indian Period (11,000–7000 B.C.) when hunter groups began emerging in Mesoamerica. The *atlatl* was used to hurl percussion-chipped points or darts in hunting. The weapon was used for centuries; one is depicted on a Tula statue of the Early Post-Classic Period (c. A.D. 1/250–600). The Aztec (Mexica) introduced the *atlatl* into the Maya domain as well.

ATOYAC RIVER   A tributary of the great Balsas River system in the gulf coastal lowlands. The Atoyac drainage provided rich deposits of silt in the northern part of the Valley of Oaxaca, thereby giving rise to such major cultural developments as Monte Alban and the Zapotec. The Atoyac flows into the Pacific.

AUTLAN   (1) The name given to polychrome ceramic wares dating to the Formative Period (2000 B.C.–c. A.D. 250/290). Autlan wares are associated with the Amacueca Phase in southern Jalisco and with the Sayula Phase in Zacoalco-Durango. Shells and carved figurines dominate the wares recovered in the region.

AUTLAN   (2) A Nahuatl site in Jalisco, Mexico, dating to Early Formative Period (2000/1600–900 B.C.). The site is associated with the Colima culture.

AXALAPAZCOES   Cinder cones containing small lakes whose name translates to "containers of sand with water," found in the Valley of Mexico and in the Puebla Basin in the Mesa Central. Dry basins, called *xalapazcoes*, also were found in the region. (See MESOAMERICAN GEOGRAPHIC DIMENSIONS.)

AXAYACATL   The sixth Aztec (Mexica) emperor, he succeeded Motecuhzoma Ilhuicamina I and ruled from A.D.

1469 to 1481. Axayacatl was already a veteran soldier when he came to power at the age of 19. He began his reign by campaigning in the Isthmus of Tehuantepec, also attacking Guerrero, the Toluca and Puebla valleys, and positions on the gulf coast. Battling in the Toluca territories, Axayacatl fought hand-to-hand and was almost taken prisoner. Moquihuix, the ruler of Tlatelolco, the sister city of Tenochtitlan, used the 1472 death of Nezahualcoyotl, Axayacatl's valued counselor, as a pretext for ending the TRIPLE ALLIANCE. He was married to a sister of Axayacatl and is reported to have abused her. He also attempted a raid on Tenochtitlan, which was unsuccessful. Axayacatl ordered an immediate blockade of Tlatelolco in reprisal, and then he invaded the city. Moquihuix was thrown from the top of a pyramid in the battle, and the allies of the slain ruler, including the king of Xochimilco, were killed as well. Tlatelolco's people suffered acutely at Axayacatl's hands and the second-class status of that city and its population continued even after Axayacatl's death. Axayacatl's Tarascan campaigns, however, proved disastrous. He suffered a defeat in 1479 at the hands of a superior force of 50,000 Tarascans led by King Zuanga. Two other campaigns against the Tarascans also proved unsuccessful, and there is some speculation that Axayacatl received a battle wound that led to either his death or severe depression.

AYALA A phase of a cultural group called the Chalchihuite, who inhabited the region of the Sierra Madre Occidental in northern Mexico in the Early Classic Period (c. A.D. 1/250–600). The Ayala phase is dated from A.D. 450 to 700, and during that time the Chalchihuite developed uniform ceramic ware, including red-on-buff tripods, unadorned bowls and cloisonné decorations. Copper bells were also manufactured during this period.

AYAUHCIHUATL The daughter of the Tepanec king Tezozomoc (c. A.D. 1350) who was married to Huitzilihuitl, the Aztec ruler. She bore the heir, Chimalpopoca, and died in childbirth. She defended the Aztec when the Tepanec treated them harshly, begging her father for restraint.

AYOCUAN A poet and sage of the city of Huexotzinco, a Chichimec site in Puebla. He lived sometime around A.D. 1450. Ayocuan was popular throughout the region, acclaimed by his contemporaries.

AYOTLA PHASE A cultural development in the Valley of Mexico during the Formative Period (2000 B.C.–c. A.D. 250/290). The phase is associated with the Justo culture, dating to c. 1100 B.C. Ceramics of the Ayotla era include white-rimmed black ware and large, hollow doll figurines. The remains of this phase are evident in Ixtapaluca.

AZCAPOTZALCO A Tepanec capital city, called the Place of the Ant Hill of the People, established on Lake Texcoco. The site was inhabited as early as c. 3000/1500 B.C. and became a Tepanec stronghold in the reign of King Acolnahuatl, sometime around A.D. 1230/1250. The city had an earlier association with the Toltec and probably had been a colony of Teotihuacan before that time. Artisans were brought to the site to transform it into a beautiful capital. Azcapotzalco flourished during the reign of Tezozomoc, but

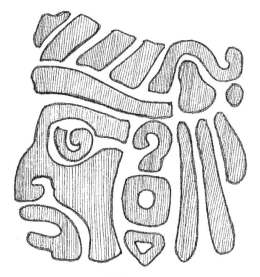

Tepanec seal from Azcapotzalco

it was put under siege during the reign of his heir, Mixtla. The Aztec (Mexica) and the members of the TRIPLE ALLIANCE slew Mixtla and destroyed the city in A.D. 1428.

AZTACALCO The western section of the Aztec (Mexica) capital of Tenochtitlan, called Beside the House of the Herons. Aztacalco was an urban district of the important metropolis on Lake Texcoco.

AZTATLAN A cultural complex in Sinaloa, the most northerly region of Mesoamerica, lasting until the Late Classic Period (A.D. 600–900). The Aztatlan Complex, which borders the American Southwest, charts the development in the region, reflecting the evolution of ceramics, trade routes and industrial complexes. The people here produced iron pyrite beads, onyx and alabaster vases, and other trade items. It was also part of the Turquoise Road, the vital merchant route from the American Southwest to central Mexico and beyond. (See SINALOA and TURQUOISE ROAD for details.)

AZTEC (MEXICA) The Aztec, who called themselves Mexica, were originally associated with the Chichimec, "the lineage of the dog," a confederation of groups that entered the Valley of Mexico, purportedly from a legendary site called the Land of the Seven Caves (Chicomoztoc), in the Late Classic Period (around A.D. 1300). The Aztec, or Mexica, were also called "the people whose face nobody knows," suggesting they were strangers to the region. Contemporaries describe them as tall, handsome and swarthy. According to tradition, Aztlan, or Place of the Herons, is the original home of the Aztec. Its actual location remains obscure; some scholars place it in Nayarit or in the northwestern part of the Valley of Mexico. In time, as a result of their religiously inspired destiny and their relentless military campaigns, alliances, marriages and pursuit of imperial power, the Aztec ruled from 5 to 7 million people, dominating as much as 125,000 square miles of Mesoamerica.

The Aztec records state that the group was the last Nahuatl-speaking group to leave Aztlan, sometime around A.D. 1100. Their journey to Chicomoztoc was long, taking

Aztec clay mask of Xipe Totec

them through fertile basins and desolate wildlands. Along the way, they built shrines to Huitzilopochtli ("Hummingbird-on-the Left" or "Blue Hummingbird-on-the Left"), a benevolent, rather personal deity honored throughout Aztec history. Under the rule of four priest-kings the god's sacred images and vessels were carried on the journey. The Aztec arrived in the heart of Mexico as the Toltec were in decline. Other city-states were competing for territory and consolidating their political positions.

Upon arrival, the Aztec appear to have divided into two groups, one going toward Malinalco and the other toward Coatepec, the Hill of the Serpent, near Tula. They celebrated the New Fire rituals there in 1163, remaining nearby until A.D. 1300, when they moved to Chapultepec. Exiled 15 years later, they returned, only to face a Tepanec assault in A.D. 1319. The surviving Aztec fled to Culhuacan. There, according to tradition, King Achitometl allowed them to live in a region infested by serpents. The Aztec killed the snakes and other creatures, ate them and thanked the king for providing such bounty. By this time the Aztec consisted of seven clans. Achitometl asked them to join him in his battle against Xochimilco, another city-state in the region, but he did not provide them with weapons. With the aid of their god Huitzilopochtli, the Aztec fashioned lances and shields and proved ferocious in battle. They also soon became knowledgeable about clothing, farming and building. Achitometl, alarmed by their ferocity and cleverness, began to plot the destruction of the Aztec. They were warned by allies, however, and fled into the marshes of Lake Texcoco. Legend describes this exodus in other terms. In this version, the Aztec request Achitometl's daughter, a great beauty, to serve as the bride of their god. Achitometl gave them his daughter and then went among them to attend a religious ceremony. The king discovered an Aztec priest wearing the skin of his daughter, as she had been flayed during her ritual marriage to the god. Horrified, he resolved to kill all the Aztec, and they fled into Lake Texcoco.

Lake Texcoco, called the Lake of the Moon, held a large island and a series of smaller islets. The Aztec, under the leadership of Tenoch, the priest-king of Huitzilopochtli, led the people to the main island. A sign was given to them en route, as the god had promised: An eagle landed on a cactus and devoured a serpent. Tenoch had predicted that such an omen would determine the site of the new Aztec capital.

He had also foretold the presence of a white willow and other signs. Tenochtitlan, the capital, was to be erected on the spot. The date of the founding is A.D. c. 1325 or 1345.

Tenoch ruled as priest-king for 25 years after Tenochtitlan's founding and is mentioned in the Codex Mendoza. When he died in A.D. 1376, the Aztec wanted to establish a legitimate dynasty acceptable to neighboring cultures. In order to do this, a ruler of Toltec lineage, the accepted royal house of the region, was necessary, although the Toltec Empire itself had collapsed. A man called Acamapichtli, born in either Azcapotzalco or Culhuacan or Coatlinchan, accepted the throne and married a Culhuacan princess of Toltec descent, called Ilacueitl. Acamapichtli, reportedly half Aztec by birth, accomplished much during his reign. He established a positive relationship with Tlatelolco, the Aztec city in Lake Texcoco adjoining Tenochtitlan.

Huitzilihuitl, the son of Acamapichtli, took the throne in c. A.D. 1391/96, ruling until c. A.D. 1415/17. An administrator and a military leader, he revived the religious and civil codes of law and welcomed outsiders to Tenochtitlan. The Aztec were vassals of the Tepanec during the time, and Huitzilihuitl married a Tepanec princess. Huitzilihuitl also purportedly had magical adventures in Cuernavaca and married a princess from that city who would become the mother of Motecuhzoma I.

Chimalpopoca, the son of Huitilihuitzl, became the Aztec ruler in c. A.D. 1415/17 but ruled for only a decade or so. During his brief reign, Tenochtitlan became a sophisticated stone city. Vital trade systems were begun, and the Aztec initiated the final stages toward achieving imperial rank. The murder of Chimalpopoca by Maxtla, the Tepanec king, was a turning point for the Aztec, who were ready to throw off the Tepanec yoke.

Itzcoatl, heir to the throne, negotiated the Triple Alliance, the confederation of the Aztec, the people of Texcoco, Tacuba and, later, other states. Maxtla was slain in his baths, and the Tepanec Empire was dismantled. Tlacaelel and Motecuhzoma supported Itzcoatl during his reign and were instrumental in the aggrandizement of Tenochtitlan.

Motecuhzoma Ilhuicamina I ruled from A.D. 1440 to 1469. He established the Aztec Empire, warring with Chalco for the territory. Motecuhzoma I also began the Great Temple in Tenochtitlan and defended the city during a plague of locusts in 1446. Floods ravaged the Aztec lands in 1449 and 1451, and there was an acute famine. Motecuhzoma then attacked Puebla and Tlaxcala and initiated the tradition of the Flower Wars, a style of battle adopted in order to gain sacrificial victims. Oaxaca, Zempoala and other regions were taken by the Aztec, with Motecuhzoma leading vast armies. His last campaign was in 1466.

Ruled by Axayacatl, Motecuhzoma's successor (A.D. 1469–1481), the empire grew to include Tlatelolco, which was united with Tenochtitlan. The Aztec Calendar Stone dates to Axayacatl's reign as well as the defeat of the Toluca and assaults on the Tarascan lands.

Tizoc was heir to Axayacatl, ruling from A.D. 1481 to 1486. The Stone of Tizoc dates to his reign, which ended abruptly, perhaps as the result of murder. Ahuitzotl then inherited the throne, ruling from A.D. 1486 to 1502; he is regarded as one of the great Aztec emperors. Demand for more human sacrifices for religious ceremonies resulted in

Aztec water goddess

more military campaigns and attacks. Ahuitzotl led his armies to the Guatemala border. In one ceremony, a dedication of the renovated Great Temple of Tenochtitlan, an estimated 20,000 to 40,000 died as victims to the gods. Ahuitzotl also moved Aztec families to the frontiers to colonize and transform the regions they hoped to win. His last campaign took place on the Guatemala border.

Motecuhzoma Xocoyotzin II assumed the throne in 1502 and was murdered by the Spanish in 1520. A military commander, he attacked several regions but also was able to absorb city-states and cultures by peaceful means. During his reign, Motecuhzoma II lost the counsel of Nezahualpili, the king of Texcoco, who had instilled in him a dread of the future by predicting the fall of the Aztec and the reappearance of Quetzalcoatl, the god. The Spanish were believed to be the embodiment of the prophecy. Motecuhzoma retired to his palace to await his doom. He is known to have had an aviary of exotic birds, and his name is associated with a legendary tree in Achiotla. (See all of the Aztec emperors under separate entries for details; see also FLOWER WARS.)

The lands occupied by the Aztec in the various stages of their development were subject to variations in climate, flora and fauna as well as in hydrogeography and geological formations. During the imperial period, the Aztec controlled lands from the Gulf of Mexico to the Pacific Ocean, from the Valley of Mexico to the border of Guatemala, including the Isthmus of Tehuantepec. (See AZTEC EMPIRE; MESOAMERICAN GEOGRAPHIC DIMENSIONS; see also TENOCHTITLAN.)

AZTEC AGRICULTURE An important socioeconomic aspect of Aztec life, tied to civic and religious activities, commanding its own deities and institutions. Agricultural practices were based on the solar calendar, and produce provided the principal means of sustenance for the people. The names of some months referred to the growing of crops, and the people held festivals associated with farming. The bulk of Aztec society, in fact, except for nobles and aristocrats, worked the land, and taxes were often paid in produce.

The ownership of Aztec land was divided into four major categories: *calpulli,* private estates, warrior lands and temple lands.

Calpulli. A form of "residential" ownership, with extensive holdings in a ward or district, normally containing schools, temples, patron deities and administrative offices. Some of the *calpulli* land was worked communally by men of the group to provide tribute to the temple. The remaining land was divided among local families. Ownership remained with the *calpulli,* however, and any assigned land that was not worked for more than two years reverted to the community at large. Produce was private property. In practice, the land passed from father to son, and if a line died out, the land again reverted to the *calpulli.*

Private Estates. Land belonging to the nobles or to the immediate family of the local ruler. It was presented to them as it had been to their ancestors for services to the state and generally was held by the family, inherited by later generations, or sold. The local peasants tied to this land, called *mayeque,* assisted in farming it.

Warrior Lands. Estates granted to Aztec warriors who had distinguished themselves in the acquisition of new territories for the empire. Parts of conquered regions were given to these warriors to hold in the name of the emperor. Estates of this nature passed from father to son, but they were true fiefs; should a warrior die childless, the land reverted to the state. Such holdings allowed the Aztec to imprint their own style on a region while creating a bastion of Aztec strength. Workers for the warrior estates normally were recruited from the local, conquered populations.

Temple Lands. Estates granted to the priests of the various temples, probably as a fief and worked by local populations or by workers imported for the purpose.

The Valley of Mexico, the home of the Aztec, was one of the most intensely utilized agricultural zones in all of Mesoamerica. A wide variety of cultivation systems was employed in the region, which offered a multitude of soil and climatic variations. These systems include *chinampas,* irrigation techniques, fallowing and the *milpas.* (See these under separate entries and under MESOAMERICAN AGRICULTURE.)

The Aztec, especially in the period of empire, grew or imported a large supply of agricultural products. The average Aztec, usually unable to afford meat, depended on a diversity of vegetables and fruits as well as fish for survival. Maize, the essential staple, was assigned divine attributes by the Aztec; thus it was associated with several deities. Traditional dishes were made out of maize, including corn loaves *(tlaxcalmimilli)*; tortilla *(quauhtlaqualli)*; dark tortilla *(tlaxcalpachalli)*; leafy, delicate tortilla *(tlacepoalli ilocalli)*; and various forms of tamale *(tamalli)*.

The nobility consumed maize products, usually as an accompaniment to turkey or some other meat. Other crops included:

amaranth	maguey
beans	mushrooms
cacao	peyote
carob	pumpkins
chia	squash
chili peppers	sweet potatoes
flowers	tomatoes

Game was scarce in the Aztec lands, but other Mesoamerican regions had large stocks of animals maintained for the hunt. The same held true for dogs, which were kept in herds, with the females kept as breeders and the males as sacrificial animals or as food. Several types of dogs were raised, including the ancestor of the modern Chihuahua. Turkeys were raised in flocks, and migratory and local birds and fowls were prized. Fish were plentiful, caught with hooks, nets and traps constructed out of fish scoops that were narrowed at one, baited end. The traps were supported in midstream by empty calabashes, gourds that kept the lines and the nettings secure. Like their hunting counterparts, fishermen prayed before commencing their tasks. The Aztec also relished the *axolotl*, a salamanderlike creature that thrived beside the *chinampas*, the "floating islands" used in agriculture. They also raised a stingless variety of bees, prized for their honey and their wax, in hives made out of tree trunks.

As was true in virtually every other aspect of Aztec life, agriculture was an essential part of the state religious ceremonies, which included prayers for rain, good crops and bountiful harvests. Prayers were recited as well at each stage of planting, sowing and harvesting. Some deities, such as Tlaloc, who was invoked throughout the year on many occasions for rain, were considered crucial to agriculture and were propitiated with frequent sacrificial offerings. Some of the gods associated with the various agricultural activities included:

Atlahua	Quetzalcoatl
Centeotl	Tlaloc
Chalchuihtlicue	Tlaloque-Tepictoton
Chicomecoatl	Tonacatecuhtli
Coatlicue	Xilonen
Mayahuel	Xipe Totec
Opochtli	Xochipilli

The agricultural monthly feasts that were important to the Aztec farming systems include *Alt cualo, Atemoztli, Etzalqualiztli, Hueytecuihuitl, Hueytozoztli, Ochpaniztli, Tepeihuitl, Tlaxochimaco* and *Tozoztontli.*

Aztec Chac Mul

AZTEC ARCHAEOLOGICAL SITES The cities or shrines that were built originally or absorbed by the Aztec during their period of imperial expansion. Such sites represent a diverse sampling of the ethnic cultures of Mesoamerica, as the Aztec armies ranged far and wide to conquer other cultures and their possessions. A partial list of the Aztec acquisitions includes:

Acolman	Mexicaltzinco
Atlacuihuayan	Mixcoatl
Atlapulco	Mixquic
Azcapotzalco	Otoncapulco
Calixtlahuaca	Popotlan
Chalco	Tenayuca
Chapultepec	Tepexpan
Chicoloapan	Tepeyacac
Chimalhuacan	Tepoztico
Cholula	Tepoztlan
Citlaltepec	Tetelco
Coatlinchan	Texcotzinco
Coyohuacan	Tezonipa
Coyoacan	Tezoyuca
Coyotepec	Tizapan
Cuauhtepec	Tizayucan
Cuauhtitlan	Tizitlan
Culhuacan	Tlacopan
Ecatepe	Tlalnepantla
Huehuetoca	Tlalpan
Huexotlan	Tlapacoya
Huipulco	Tlaxialtemalco
Huitzopochco	Tulpetlac
Iztacalco	Xilotepec
Iztahuacan	Xocotitlan
Iztapalapan	Yoaltepec
Ixtlan	Zapotitlan
Malinalco	

AZTEC ARCHITECTURE Influenced by the Toltec, Tepanec and the people of Texcoco, Aztec architecture relied on monumentality to promote the Aztec world view. The military might of the Aztec Empire was clearly demonstrated by massive structures, the creation of which required an ability to assemble vast human and material resources. Tenochtitlan, the capital, stood as a symbol of power and endurance, incorporating Toltec and other styles as well as some innovations. The Toltec city of Tula, for example, was looted by the Aztec when they were constructing Tenochtitlan, and they used Toltec monuments in their own capital.

At the same time, the Aztec introduced the double pyramid temple, for example the Templo Mayor, dedicated to the gods of rain and war, and their carved temples, even those embedded in rock, reflect an extraordinary architectural vibrance. Much of Aztec architecture, however, mirrors that of other Mesoamerica cultures. The use of geometric designs and the sweeping lines of their structures always served a basic purpose: to reflect religious tenets and to demonstrate the ultimate power of the state.

Some scholars have termed Aztec architecture "metropolitan," in that the builders were not concerned with outlying regions or with the ornamentation of existing structures but concentrated on the embellishment of Tenochtitlan and other major sites so that they could serve as symbols of the empire.

There is an innate sense of order and symmetry in Aztec buildings. They reflect as well an ability to utilize the natural resources available and to adapt them to the terrain. The capital, Tenochtitlan, certainly reflected its island base, with its causeways, dikes, canals and bridges. At MALINALCO, the Aztec integrated a temple into rock.

The use of bas-relief, plazas, platforms, walls and related forms, especially the massive representation of the Aztec deities, give evidence of the harmony of architectural ideals the Aztec absorbed during each period of development. The massive dimensions reflect the allied Aztec ability to design structures as stages for gigantic gatherings of local populations. It was reported that as many as 8,000 men danced in the plaza before the Great Temple of Tenochtitlan on certain feast days. The marketplace at Tlatelolco was reported to have held as many as 20,000 people on market days. According to the Spanish conquerors, the Aztec capital, the largest metropolis of the New World, rivaled the major cities of Europe.

AZTEC ART   The expression of ideals by the Aztec (Mexica) in a unique style that mirrored past civilizations and reflected the cosmological influence on the Aztec way of life. The Aztec art forms were imbued with an imposing sense of the divine. The Aztec excelled at anthropomorphic figures, in the representation of superhuman deities and in realistic depictions of humans and animals. Above all, Aztec art reflects an awareness of death in the midst of life, as well as the presence of cosmic forces at every level of human affairs. The depersonalization of Aztec art, almost ritualized in concept, stems from the Aztec view of worlds collapsing and humans serving merely as food for the gods. The severity of Aztec art reflects as well the sense of the militaristic ideals of the state, a code adopted by the various warrior groups. Those fallen in battle or in sacrifice were thus given the chance for immortality, and death was not something to be feared or regretted. Aztec art reflects these concepts with unique style and power.

Aztec sculpture mirrored not only Aztec traditions but those of past cultures, incorporating Toltec and Teotihuacan elements of style. Such sculpture had strong lines and relied on the inherent character of the stone used. Aztec sculpture always had a deep religious significance, incorporating symbols that were well known to priests of the various religious cults and to trained adepts of the temples and shrines. Their sculpture also could be narrative in function, relating or declaiming historical events for the benefit of the citizenry. The Stone of Tizoc, for example, commemorated the military prowess of Tizoc, an Aztec emperor who reigned briefly, relating not only his human activities but providing insight into his role as the representative of Huitzilopochtli, the patron deity of all the Aztec. The Aztec Calendar Stone, a circular disk weighing 24 tons, bears not only the prescribed religious symbols necessary for that particular form but offers a calendrical display carried out in a unique and compelling composition.

The magnificent stone sculptures depicting the various Aztec deities, such as Coatlicue, the Lady of the Serpent Skirt, are macabre by modern standards but assume a severe elegance and contain cosmic and religious themes at the same time. The serpent, employed in many Aztec sculptural forms, was adapted from the Toltec and depicted either feathered or plain. The Aztec also used the coiled serpent to produce beautiful images reflecting the sinuous charms of the creature and evoking its symbolic mysterious powers.

Hollow clay statuettes bearing a bell depicted the household deities of the Aztec, which were usually female. Solid statues, representing gods, warriors and temples, normally were molded forms. Incense burners, pipes and reed instruments were also produced. Popular among the Aztec was the *pintadera,* a seal used to stamp designs in paint on the human body, particularly during holy seasons of the year. Drums, scrapers and other objects served ornamental or practical purposes. In their sculpture, as in their ceramics, the Aztec were influenced by the artists of the Mixteca-Puebla region. Some reliefs placed on their religious monuments were similar to Mixtec designs and often bore the same precision of line and high style.

Aztec ornamentations were widely used, employing semiprecious stones, a tradition common among the Mixtec. Under their influence, Aztec artisans made exquisite ornaments from rock crystal, obsidian, turquoise, jet, jadeite, nephrite and other semiprecious materials. Gold and copper were used in many pieces, and the mosaic decoration on masks, shields and ritual objects became a hallmark of the Aztec.

Mosaic ornaments were popular, and these often had deep religious significance. Effigies of birds, fish and other animals sometimes were fashioned out of gold and silver. Mosaic ornaments were used for rituals on occasion, adorning large stone idols and wooden replicas of the gods within the various temples of Tenochtitlan. Turquoise was valued for these ornaments, and nobles and priests were allowed to wear them on certain ceremonial occasions. Most mosaics, however, were designed as adornments for crowns, scepters, shields, pectorals and headdresses as well as for ankle and arm bracelets. Wood was the common base for such mosaics, but bone, gold and silver were also used as matrices. The use of mosaic ornaments appears to have been a late development in Tenochtitlan, appearing just before the Spanish conquest. Vast numbers were sent to Europe, including the smaller, stone-encrusted varieties. Masks also were decorated with mosaics.

Ear, nose and lip plugs were produced; each had special symbols that signified the rank of the wearer. Some were worn during the coronation of Aztec rulers.

The Aztec highly prized feathers for headdresses, shields, costumes and fans. Designs and styles fashioned out of feathers marked the ranks and roles of the various military groups. Quetzal feathers were the most valued tribute demanded by the Aztec. Such feathers were incorporated into beautiful works of art, such as the feather headdress given to Cortez. (See FEATHER MURALS.)

The Aztec used paintings to adorn buildings and monumental sculpture in Tenochtitlan and other cities. Painting was closely associated with architectural style and with other art forms. Spanish chroniclers reported that Motecuhzoma's palace was a masterpiece of color and design. Surviving works reflect the masterful skill and quality of these Aztec decorative works. Mural paintings surviving in the Great Temple and in some other structures in the capital depict human figures in vivid colors. These personages are highly adorned, with many shades used to represent the richness of their attire. Tlaloc, the god of rain, was depicted in a vibrant combination of colors that represent his role on the earth and in the heavens.

As the Aztec developed their illustrative skills, they turned to pictorial manuscripts, such as the "Peregrination Painting" in the *Codex Boturini*, which depicts the journey of the Aztec to Tenochtitlan. Elaborately designed maps and codices provided historical, geographic and narrative accounts of events in Aztec history. Other subject matter included tribute accounts, calendrical systems and accounts of religious beliefs, censuses and ceremonies.

AZTEC ASTROLOGY   The system involving the observation of heavenly bodies and the interpretation of cosmic and universal laws as they affect human affairs. Aztec astrologers were religiously oriented as well as scientifically aware. The Aztec death-oriented culture was complemented by the calendric cycles and by the framework provided by the astrologers for religious divination. Aztec life revolved around shifting worlds and the use of human sacrifices as fuel for inexorable and eternal cosmic forces. Astrology thus had a definite purpose, associated with the calendars, that not only depicted the passage of time but provided people with cycles of events and cosmic truths.

Traditionally, Aztec astronomers studied heavenly bodies and their orbits and computed their positions throughout the year. They were involved only with the calendric and scientific aspects of the field, and were aware of the sun, moon, planets and stars. The astrologers recorded the heavenly movements, which provided keys to magic and divination. The Aztec calendar provided for traditional good or bad days, and the diviners, called *tlapauhqui*, made use of these in forecasting affairs. The magicians of the temples, called *nahualli*, also made use of the calendar and the astrological aspects of the Aztec religion. They believed that the future and one's individual role in the world could be ascertained by analyzing the time cycles and by performing the rituals associated with these cycles. The calendar was especially useful because it incorporated an astrological compendium of the ritual year. Each day had its own deity and was designated by name and by sacred number. Also, each day was associated with a 13-day group presided over by other deities. The name of the day was drawn from the number and sign, which could be categorized as bad, good or even neutral. Each day also had a partner or a so-called Lord of the Night, which also had a function representing good, bad or neutral aspects. These lords worked from noon until midnight in determining the destiny of the Aztec state as well as that of individuals. Divination based on this astrological calendar involved the interpretation of the significance of each day as it pertained to someone's birth, projects, marriages or political activities. A newborn child who was born on a luckless day, for example, was not named until a more propitious day arrived within the 13-day group. Not only were the events of life shaped by the days and their portents, but the very soul of an Aztec, called a *tetonal*, could be formed by these influences, which prompted individuals to take steps to offset bad days with good ones. The cardinal points of the earth—north, east, south and west—also were essential to astrological divination.

Comets, floods and plagues, all of which were visited on Tenochtitlan during the reign of Motecuhzoma I, always had been of great portent among the Aztec. Priests unable to explain the meaning of these natural events satisfactorily sometimes paid with their lives. Other, more skilled priests dared to make prophecies about future events, particularly as they concerned the better-known heavenly bodies. The sun, for instance, the most important celestial body, was vital to the continuation of the earth and of human beings. Sacrificial victims were called "the children of the sun" or "the messengers to the sun" and were given immortality because of their affiliation with this heavenly body. Venus, second only to the sun because of its position as the Morning Star, was important as well. According to Aztec calculations, Venus appeared at the heliacal rising every 584 days. Venus represented the god Quetzalcoatl and was thought to be extremely dangerous.

Astrological ceremonies conducted by the Aztec also involved the lighting of the New Fire, a ritual concerned with the passing of worlds or suns. (See NEW FIRE for details; see also AZTEC ASTRONOMY; AZTEC CALENDAR.)

AZTEC ASTRONOMY   The science of the stars and the study of the universe, important to the Aztec religious and cosmological endeavors and working hand in hand with the state-organized cult ceremonies. Astronomy as a science was utilized in the planning of festivities and in divination aspects of knowing the good or bad nature of the individual days of the year. Generally speaking, Aztec astronomy, when divorced from the religious aspects of Aztec life, was advanced, although the Aztec were not as sophisticated as the Maya in this regard. The actual systems employed by Aztec astronomers in their calculations and observances have not survived. All that is known about such endeavors is based on evidence gathered by later historians.

The best source for information concerning Aztec astronomical lore is the large dial made of stone, discovered in 1790 and called the Calendar Stone. The Aztec calculations of the hours of the day, solstices, equinoxes and the movement of the sun are clearly indicated in this vital work. The Aztec calendrical system, based on their scientific observances and calculations, was renowned in their own era, and even now it is considered one of the most complex in the world. Buildings, including observatories, offer secondary information about Aztec knowledge of astronomy. The Aztec also used illustrated maps, some of which depict eclipses, indicating that astronomers understood what eclipses were. In one map the moon is clearly shown covering the sun.

Just how much the Aztec knew about astronomy is debatable. Their achievements here were also colored by their religious beliefs and superstitions. This was evident in the *Tonalpohualli*, which included many divisions dedicated to priestly rituals as well as astronomical data. The Aztec did take note of the various constellations, but the full extent of their familiarity with the science has not been documented.

The Aztec Sky

Aztec views of astronomy reflected their cosmological and religious beliefs. The Aztec envisioned a world on many levels, both above and below the earth. Thirteen celestial levels usually are reported, although some records list nine or 12. The best extant documentation is in the illustrated *Codex Vaticanus 3738*. These levels include:

1. The moon and the clouds occupy this domain, which is the most easily observed.
2. Called the *citlalco*, the home of the stars, divided into two major groups: the *Centzon Mimixcoa* ("the innumerable ones of the north") and the *Centzon Huitnahua* ("the innumerable ones of the south").
3. The domain of the sun.
4. The domain of Venus, which was the goddess Uixtocihuatl, a deity belonging to the Tlaloc Complex.
5. The region in which the comets roamed.
6. Included in level 7, identified with the colors black and blue or possibly with green and blue.
7. United with level 6 and associated with the colors black and blue or with green and blue.
8. Known as *Iztapalnacayazan*, "the place where edges are of obsidian," the region in which storms are formed, and named for the sharp sides of the obsidian tools which made wounds.
9. The home of the gods.
10. The home of the gods.
11. The home of the gods.
12. Called the *Omeyocan*, the "Place of Duality."
13. Also called the *Omeyocan*.

Another list of Aztec sky levels, derived from such sources as the *Codex Vaticanus* and the *Historia de los Mexicanos por Sus Pinturas*, calculates the 13 heavens or levels from the earth, called *Tlaltipac*, reducing the Omeyocan level to one.

Aztec Astronomical Observations

Although they were not as sophisticated as the Maya in their astronomical observations, the Aztec did accumulate some knowledge of the science. Often these observations were tied to astrology, particularly as they related to the calendars, both the *Tonalpohualli*, the 260-day almanac year, and the *Xihuitl*, the 365-day year. Priests generally conducted the day-to-day observation of the heavens, although an interest in astronomy was not uncommon among the Aztec rulers. Motecuhzoma II, who reigned from 1502 to 1520, was notably absorbed in the study of astronomy. He was a recluse who was also a religious contemplative as well, taking a vital interest in the military and administrative offices.

In the celestial hierarchy the sun was dominant, followed by Venus, which was considered a manifestation of the god Quetzalcoatl, the time-honored deity of Mesoamerican cultures. Venus as the Morning Star, making its appearance in its heliacal rising every 584 days by Aztec calculations, was a significant celestial being.

The Pleiades were also observed as they crossed the meridian at midnight on certain nights, proof that the Fifth Sun, the world occupied by the Aztec, would not be destroyed. The Pleiades were vital to the New Fire rituals, conducted on the Hill of the Stars, near Colhuacan. Such observances allowed the Aztec to continue their tradition of service to the gods and their preoccupation with maintaining the health and stability of the world in which they found themselves. (See AZTEC CALENDAR; AZTEC COSMOLOGY; AZTEC PRIESTS AND RELIGION.)

AZTEC CALENDAR The system by which the Aztec recorded not only time but the cyclical aspects of the passing years relating to religious and cosmological views. Throughout Mesoamerica the various cultures were fascinated by time, and many developed complex chronological systems and cosmological theories to explain that concept. The ancient cultural development reached a new degree of intensity during the Aztec period, as time as a concept was paramount in the lives of the Aztec. Calendars were devised to establish certain basic points of reference in order to explain historical data and forecast natural events that might affect the community. Calendars were also employed in divination, used in ascertaining not only the state of the nation but the lives of individual Aztec as well. Three basic calendar systems had evolved in Mesoamerica from the Formative Period (2000 B.C.–c. A.D. 250/290). The Maya Long Count, a distinctive monthly calendar, was the first, followed by two others that the Aztec utilized and specialized for their religious needs: the *Tonalpohualli*, the divinatory calendar consisting of 20 named days in combination with the numbers one to 13, yielding 260 unique name and number combinations, and the *Xihuitl*, the chronological system of 365 days, divided into 18 months, with 20 days each and five (extra) epagomenal days, called *nemontemi*. The *Tonalpohualli* was produced in the *Tonalamatl*, the "Book of Days." Other groups also used the *Tonalpohualli*, with different names and divisions. This calendar may have been reserved mainly for astronomical or astrological purposes or for religious ceremonies and observances. Divination was a method of telling the future in association with the *Tonalpohualli*. The day signs provided for the calendar are:

Acatl—the reed   *Calli*—the house
Atl—water   *Cipachtli*—the alligator

Aztec Quetzalcoatl

Coatl—the snake, serpent
Cozcacuauhtli—the buzzard
Cuauhtli—the eagle
Ehecatl—the wind
Itzcuintli—the dog
Malinalli—the grass
Mazatl—the deer
Miquizitli—death

Ocelotl—the jaguar
Ollin—the movement
Ozomatli—the monkey
Quetzapalin—the lizard
Quiahutl—rain
Tecpatl—flint
Tochtli—the rabbit
Xochitl—the flower

The numbers one to 13, which always accompanied the day signs, were represented by dots in Aztec renditions. Older cultures had provided the bar-dot system for their own calendars. Also used in this system were distinctive signs called the Lords of the Day, the Lords of the Night and the Volatiles. The Lords of the Day and Night were accompanied by the Volatiles in the forms of birds. The Lords of the Night, possibly associated with the nine lower levels of the universe in Aztec cosmology, functioned after noon in some versions of the calendar. Each day of the calendar had a special patron as well.

In the arrangements of the calendar, the Aztec also assigned divine patrons for each 13-day group of numbers, starting with the number one. These numbers, patrons and associated glyphs, determined whether the day was lucky or unlucky. These various lords and patrons, with their accompanying birds, could bode good or ill or could stand as neutral for events or projects taking place on that day. Actually, with all of the accompanying divine attributes and patrons, each day had to be determined as good, bad or neutral on five separate levels, which made computations extensive and sophisticated. Certain rituals or practices could render bad days less ominous, and the priests knew the propitiatory customs involved.

The *Xihuitl*, the calendar called the Solar Year, was composed of 18 named months of 20 days each, with five epagomenal days provided in order to remain as true a calendar as possible. Each month had its own festival in

THE *TONALPOHUALLI*

Cipactli	1	8	2	9	3	10	4	11	5	12	6	13	7
Ehecatl	2	9	3	10	4	11	5	12	6	13	7	1	8
Calli	3	10	4	11	5	12	6	13	7	1	8	2	9
Cuetzpallin	4	11	5	12	6	13	7	1	8	2	9	3	10
Coatl	5	12	6	13	7	1	8	2	9	3	10	4	11
Miquiztli	6	13	7	1	8	2	9	3	10	4	11	5	12
Mazatl	7	1	8	2	9	3	10	4	11	5	12	6	13
Tochtli	8	2	9	3	10	4	11	5	12	6	13	7	1
Atl	9	3	10	4	11	5	12	6	13	7	1	8	2
Itzcuintli	10	4	11	5	12	6	13	7	1	8	2	9	3
Ozomatli	11	5	12	6	13	7	1	8	2	9	3	10	4
Malinalli	12	6	13	7	1	8	2	9	3	10	4	11	5
Acatl	13	7	1	8	2	9	3	10	4	11	5	12	6
Ocelotl	1	8	2	9	3	10	4	11	5	12	6	13	7
Cuauhtli	2	9	3	10	4	11	5	12	6	13	7	1	8
Cozcacuauhtli	3	10	4	11	5	12	6	13	7	1	8	2	9
Ollin	4	11	5	12	6	13	7	1	8	2	9	3	10
Tecpatl	5	12	6	13	7	1	8	2	9	3	10	4	11
Quiahuitl	6	13	7	1	8	2	9	3	10	4	11	5	12
Xochitl	7	1	8	2	9	3	10	4	11	5	12	6	13

Tenochtitlan, and the calendar was closely associated with the agricultural basis of Aztec life. In time, of course, this calendar, which did not allow for an extra quarter day each year, did not reflect the true solar year.

The months of 20 days in the *Xihuitl* calendar were called *meztli,* and the count of all of them was called the *meztlipohualli.* The *nemontemi,* the epagomenal five days at the end of the year, were deemed particularly perilous for all Aztec. The *Xiuhmolpilli,* the "century" or "calendar round," was also formed by meshing the Solar Calendar with the Ritual Calendar. A complete calendar round resulted from such a meshing and was important to the celebrations of certain events, such as the lighting of the New Fire. The term *Xiuhmolpilli* means the "tying of the years," and was thus designated because 52 reeds were literally bound up, symbolizing the end of the round. Such a cyclical approach was important to the Aztec and to other Mesoamerican cultures, as their cosmology was composed of cycles and ending of eras, even worlds. Other cycles, involving the movement of the heavenly bodies, such as Venus or Mars, were also incorporated into the calendars. When two calendar systems and the rotation of Venus coincided, the cycle was called the *Huehuetiliztli.*

AZTEC CALENDAR STONE   A magnificent sculptured work, also called the Sun Stone, discovered by workers laying the foundation of the Cathedral of Mexico in 1790 on the site of an earlier Roman-type Aztec shrine. Now in the *Mueseo Nacional de Antropologia* of Mexico City, the stone is a national treasure and provides information concerning not only the religious, astronomical and cosmological aspects of Aztec thought and life but evidence of Aztec achievement in artistic creativity and skill.

A circular monolith, the Calendar Stone is more than 10 feet in diameter. It graphically depicts the Aztec preoccupation with time and space, particularly in relation to human affairs and the continued strength of the Aztec Empire. The central figure of the stone is believed to be Tonatiuh, the deity of the sun during the day. Some have identified the central figure as Yohualtecuhtli, the Aztec god associated with the ending of the fifth world, or the Fifth Sun, according to Aztec calculations. This deity is surrounded by hieroglyphic symbols that represent the cosmic cycles, also called "suns," as well as days and months. This monumental work clearly reflects the Aztec knowledge of astronomy. (See AZTEC ASTROLOGY; AZTEC ASTRONOMY; AZTEC CALENDAR; AZTEC COSMOLOGY; AZTEC GODS; AZTEC PRIESTS AND RELIGION.)

Aztec jaguar vessel

AZTEC CARDINAL POINTS AND COLORS   The four corners of the earth, the directions, were vital to calendric computations and in the practice of religious tradition. The Aztec shared this concern with other Mesoamerican cultures, as almost all of them were aware of the directions and believed that they governed particular virtues, events and religious customs. The colors listed here were not used in every Aztec territory. Regional variations existed, particularly concerning the color designated for each point. The general color and patron scheme was:

South.   Represented by the color blue. The rabbit served as the animal insignia, corresponding to the year named Rabbit (Tochtli). The patron was the god Huitzilopochtli.

North.   Represented by the color red. The jaguar was the animal insignia, corresponding to the year Tecpatl, the Flint Knife. The patron was Tezcatlipoca.

East.   Represented by the color yellow. The eagle was the animal insignia, corresponding to the year Acatl, the Reed. The patron deity was Tonatiuh.

West.   Represented by the color white. The serpent was the animal insignia, corresponding to the year Calli, the House. The patron deity was Quetzalcoatl.

AZTEC CERAMICS   The products of various Aztec periods reflecting Aztec heritage and traditions of past civilizations in the region. Other cultures had excelled in ceramics, and the Aztec, controlling vast regions during their eras of political expansion, employed many earlier shapes and patterns in making their pieces. The ceramics recovered from Aztec sites have been assigned to four specific historic periods.

Aztec I is the ceramic period that predates the settlement in Tenochtitlan, also called Culhuacan and dating from A.D. 900 to 1200. Traditional black-on-orange ceramics were made at Culhuacan (hence the name), but it has links to the domestic pottery that evolved in the region of Puebla. Aztec I ceramics usually include tripod bowls with feet of stylized serpent heads. Designs were stamped into the clay while it was still wet. Decoration in paint, which could be simple or complex, was provided by using black on the orange base.

Aztec II is the ceramic period dating from A.D. 1200 to 1350. Again largely pre-Tenochtitlan, called Tenayuca, this was another black-on-orange style. Aztec II probably was a development of Aztec I, which had become popular. The decorations employed were irregular marks on plates and other objects, stamped on the inside or exteriors. Exterior decorations were formed by the use of parallel lines with circular motifs.

During the Aztec III period, called Tenochtitlan (A.D. 1350 to 1450), a black-on-orange ware that is distinctly Aztec in origin was produced, although Mixteca-Puebla influences still are evident. Open bowls, plates, tripod vessels and flat objects on tripods were well designed, with elaborate painted surfaces. Lines, circles, depictions of animals and mystic symbols were used. Some temple models were made, as well as pipes, seals, spindle whorls and a pantheon of small deities. The Aztec polychrome developed in this period as well, based probably on Texcoco black on red and using orange clay. These wares were highly polished and were sometimes painted red or brown inside.

Aztec IV, called Tlatelolco (A.D. 1450 to 1521), another black-on-orange ware that is distinctly Aztec. At this point artisans from other cultures were brought to Tenochtitlan-Tlateloloco, and thus many influences are evident. Tripod slab supports and ladles were made as well as the usual plates, open bowls and tripod vessels. Lines, circles, pictures of animals, mystic symbols and other designs were used, and these wares were sometimes painted red or brown on the inside and highly polished. The Aztec polychrome was also in use during this era. Naturalism was a hallmark of this period of ceramic development, and birds, plants and fish themes predominated. There was also a high standard of design.

As elsewhere in Mesoamerica, ceramic wares, whether used for functional or decorative purposes, were important. In many instances, recovered ceramics have provided information on the various Aztec eras. The Aztec do not appear to have used the potter's wheel but made vessels by building up strips of clay by hand, formed individually. They do not appear to have used molds either, although molds appear elsewhere in Mesoamerica, as in the late periods of Teotihuacan.

Textured clay, orange in color after firing, a product originally from Culhuacan, was the basic material. There are some indications that the Aztec also used a dark gray ware for a thicker pottery that was covered by red slip. This was a later style, used in spherical or conical vessels and plates. Designs on these wares were in black or white, or in both. The newer styles and the improvement on the original orange ware may have been brought to Tenochtitlan in the late empire, as workers from Mixteca Puebla were imported to work on these ceramics.

Polychromes, made of orange clay with sand tempering, are typical Aztec pottery. They were made locally in rather coarse fashion. The interiors were painted red or brown and highly polished. Decorations were achieved using black paint on red or black and white on red. Motifs on the vessels were parallel black bands with circles and wavy lines. Dots and vertical stripes also appear. The Aztec polychrome wares have been found throughout the Aztec domain. (See MESOAMERICAN CERAMICS AND CULTURAL DEVELOPMENTS.)

AZTEC CODICES The books composed by Aztec scribes, covering an extensive variety of subjects, including religion, government, history, geography, tributes and calendrics. They are some of the most important documents available to the modern world for information on Aztec life and civilization. While the Spaniards systematically destroyed the codices that came into their hands after the conquest, some survived. Others, such as the *Codex Mendoza*, were copies of pre-conquest codices or compiled especially in order to provide the Spanish, particularly the emperor Charles V of Spain, with detailed information concerning Aztec holdings. Aztec customs, rites, traditions and other extensive data thus gave the conquerors insight into the people of the New World. Spanish priests who studied the Nahuatl language added marginal notes.

Aztec *Codex Mendoza* painting

Because some of the codices were produced in regions other than those of the Aztec, identification of the individual codices has been complex. Mixtec histories include the *Codex Nuttall, Codex Bodley, Codex Selden, Codex Colombino, Codices Becker I* and *II, Codex Sanchez Solio* and the reverse of the *Codex Vienna* (or *Vindebonensis*). The Borgia Group consists of codices that are similar to the Mixtec genealogical and historical manuscripts but are not part of that group, named after the *Codex Borgia*. Others were the *Codex Laud, Codex Fejervary-Mayer, Codex Cospi, Codex Vaticanus B* and the *Mexican Manuscript 20,* in the Bibliotheque Nationale in Paris.

The Aztec codices were painted or written on fig-bark paper or deerskin. They were manufactured by Aztec scribes called *tlacuiloanime,* who were fluent in the use of pictograms or symbols. Their work, generally meticulous, can be seen in the *Codex Mendoza;* a Spanish priest trying to record Aztec history after the conquest complained that they took so long to read that he was allowed only a few days in which to make his editorial changes and notations. Scribes did not always agree on certain facts or figures from the past, especially the meanings of certain symbols. The following is a list of the most important or interesting Aztec codices:

Codex Azcatitlan. A document concerning Aztec historical events.

Codex Bodianus. A document providing information on herbs and medicinal plants. It is now in the *Museo Nacional de Antropologia* in Mexico City.

Codex Borbonicus. A document considered pre-conquest by some scholars and a history of the Spanish occupation by others. Tenochtitlan was its place of origin, and the codex provides details on the Aztec ritual calendar. Primarily concerned with the subjects of religion and divination, the codex contains two main sections: the ritual calendar and the *Tonalmatl,* the *Book of Days,* a manual on divination that preserves the activities, songs, rituals and customs of the Aztec priestly schools.

Codex Boturini.   A document from Tenochtitlan also called *Tira del Museo* and *Tira de la Peregrination,* a peregrination painting depicting the great Aztec trek toward Tenochtitlan.

Codex Chimalpopoca.   A document also called *Anales de Cuauhtitlan,* a historical account.

Codex Florentine/Primeros Memoriales.   A Nahuatl document with pictorial adjuncts, also called the *Medico-Palatino* and the "General History of the Things of New Spain." It was written by Fray Bernardino de Sahagun and influenced by parts of the *Codex Borbonicus.*

Codex Magliabecchiano.   A document of importance in depicting the various aspects of Aztec life. It is a useful source in explaining the game *patolli,* elements of Aztec dress and various deities.

Codex Mendoza.   A document very likely prepared at the order of Don Antonio de Mendoza, the viceroy of New Spain for Emperor Charles V in early 1504. It provided information on a pre-conquest history of the region as well as information concerning tribute demands by Aztec rulers and the daily life of the Aztec. The codex is now in the Bodleian Library at Oxford.

Codex Moctezuma.   A document also known as the *Matricula de Tributos,* an account of tribute collection and the assessment of tributes brought to Aztec emperors in Tenochtitlan from their conquered provinces.

Codex Ramirez.   A document also known as the *Historia de la Mexicanos Por Sus Pinturas,* a "History of the Mexicans Through Their Paintings."

Codex Telleriano-Remensis.   A document concerning the history and ritual of Aztec life.

Codex Vaticanus A.   A document compared to the Borgia Group.

Vaticanus B.   A historical account with a corresponding text written by Ferdando de Alva Ixtliochtl.

AZTEC COSMOLOGY   The views adopted by the Aztec that have been described by scholars as death-based, a system dominated by the concept of death and endings. The Aztec believed in "worlds," or "suns," and they anticipated the end of the one in which they existed, a belief that provoked certain ritualistic responses and demanded religious practices such as human sacrifice on the altars of their temples.

The cosmology of the Aztec, the system by which they sought to explain their origins, their relationship to the universe and their ultimate destiny, was sophisticated. It evolved into a formidable and complex view of human endeavor and divine intervention, based on ancient Mesoamerican themes. To the Aztec no human activity was independent or isolated. No era or aspect of life was unrelated to the universal scheme. Their concept of worlds in flux and their divisions of heaven and the underworld

were based on ancient tradition concerning creation and the elements of time and space as they related to human affairs.

The Aztec had a tradition of creation that included a primeval couple, called the Old Sorcerers. There were similar figures in earlier cultures of Mesoamerica. The female mother of the world was Oxomoco, and the male was Cipactonal. Depictions of these ancient beings have been discovered in ruins that predate the Aztec by centuries, indicating a possible link in tradition. Also part of the creation process were Tlaloc, the rain deity, and Chalchiuhtlicue, the goddess of water. The eons of the world were categorized, too, into certain periods, which were destroyed due to human frailties and were thus dependent upon the nurturing aspects of the gods. This concept of worlds, or suns, became an impetus for Aztec activities and in time assumed a vital importance in the practice of the all-encompassing Aztec religion.

The first cosmologic sun of the Aztec was called Four-Ocelotl, the Jaguar, and was assigned to the earth. The god Tezcatlipoca presided over this world, in which giants flourished, surviving by eating acorns. Traditionally when these giants were no longer worthy of existence, they were eaten by jaguars, thus bringing the first sun to an end.

The second sun was Four-Ehecatl, the Wind, and was assigned to the air or the wind. Quetzalcoatl presided over this world, in which human beings, when unworthy, became monkeys. This sun was destroyed by hurricanes.

The third sun, called Four-Quiahuitl, the Rain, was assigned to fire. The god Tlaloc presided over this sun, in which humans, when unworthy, were transformed into turkeys, butterflies and dogs. This sun was destroyed by a fiery rain. It was followed by the fourth world, Four-Atl, Water, and was presided over by the deity Chalchiuhtlicue. Humans, failing once more, were transformed into fish as floodwaters ended the world. The fifth sun, Four-Ollin, Movement or Earthquake, was the one in which the Aztec

Aztec brazier

THE AZTEC UNIVERSE

The ancient Aztec, who arose in Aztlan, "the place of the Herons" or the "White Place," had a specific view of the universe in which they lived. They believed that the surface of the earth was a flat disk, located in the center of the universe and extending in both horizontal and vertical directions. Surrounding the earth was water, extending as a vibrant ring.

The universe itself was believed to be divided into four quadrants, beginning at the center of the earth and extending to the celestial water rings. The Aztec were "in front of the west, contemplating the progress of the sun," which was to be found in the "country of the red color." Above and below the earth were 13 heavens and nine levels of the underworld. The heavens lay beneath a blue vault, formed by the celestial waters, crossed by celestial crossbeams at certain intervals. The moon, stars, Venus and the comets were contained in the first five levels.

In the very center of the universe, and at the core of Aztec religious belief, was Omeyocan, the place of duality, where the principle of the universe existed in dual form. The Aztec were spectators on the universe and also at the root of its salvation, exemplified by a complex system of beliefs.

---

existed. It was presided over by the god Tonatiuh and, when humans failed to provide human hearts as sacrifices, would be ended in earthquakes. Many legends and tales were associated with this fifth world, which was rebuilt for human beings by the gods Quetzalcoatl and Tezcatlipoca. In one version, the waters were dispersed by the gods and then four roads were constructed by Tonacatecuhtli's four sons and their aides, who raised up the collapsed sky and then held it firmly in place.

Quetzalcoatl and Tezcatlipoca transformed themselves into trees, and their divine father made them the lords of the sky and the stars, with a throne in the Milky Way. Legends describing how they entered the earth to rebuild it depict Tezcatlipoca going in through the mouth and Quetzalcoatl through the earth's navel. They met in the center to raise the sky. Another legend depicts them as swimming as great serpents in the flood, grappling with the earth, which had become a ferocious monster, and then splitting the earth into two to form the heavens and the land.

Accounts concerning the descent of the gods depict the earth and the fifth sun in vivid terms. In order to bring fire to humans, the gods transformed themselves and produced fire. Other divine beings aided the pair by making the stars, night, water, rain and the underworld. The creation of human beings by Quetzalcoatl was also part of the cosmogonic accounts. He descended into the underworld, Mictlan, in order to retrieve the ashes and bones of previous generations. Mictlantecuhtli, the lord of the underworld, tried to prevent this, causing Quetzalcoatl to drop some of the bones, which accounts for the variety of sizes and shapes among men and women. Quetzalcoatl took the bones to the gods at Tamoanchan, where they were ground up in vessels and sprinkled with blood. The male was created after four days, followed by the female. Other legends concerning this creation include one about the 1,600 gods of Chicomoztoc, the Seven Caves (the Nahua birthplace). Man arose from the stone knife of one of these gods. Another myth recommits a cleft made in the earth by an arrow aimed at the sun from which human beings emerged. Other traditions involve a primordial couple, Iztac Mixcoatl and his wife, Ilantecuetli.

The Aztec were precise about the various tiers of heaven, earth and the underworld. These levels, presented in the following table, represented various aspects of Aztec cosmology and religious belief.

The fifth sun, the world of the Aztec, was thus deemed both finite and ultimately doomed by earthquakes. The Aztec were compelled by their own beliefs to resort to sacrifices, rituals and magic in order to stave off the disaster that had been bred into their conscious minds. The magical essence of human hearts was believed to be the elixir that would keep the gods content with human beings, thus providing reparations and a placating grace that would save the world. (See AZTEC ASTROLOGY; AZTEC GODS; AZTEC PRIESTS AND RELIGION.)

AZTEC DEATH TRADITIONS A vital aspect of Aztec culture, reflected in the people's religious tenets and therefore the essence of their cosmological view of the world and of human beings. Following the traditions of earlier Mesoamerican cultures, the Aztec associated or personified

LEVEL	NAME
I	*Tlalticpac*—the Earth
II	*Ithuicatl Tlalacan Ipan Metztli*—the heaven of the paradise of rain, or the Milky Way
III	*Ilhuicatl Citlalicue*—the heaven of the star-skirted goddess—with female sky monsters present
IV	*Ilhuicatl Tonatiuh*—the heaven of the sun
V	*Ilhuicatl Huixtotlan*—the heaven of the salt-fertility goddess—associated with birds
VI	*Ilhuicatl Mamalhuazocan*—the heaven of the fire drill, with fire serpents and comets
VII	*Ilhuicatl Yayauhcan*—the black heaven, associated with wind
VIII	*Ilhuicatl Xoxouhcan*—the blue heaven, associated with dust
IX	*Itztapal Nanatzcayan*—"Where the Stone Slabs Crash Together"—the abode of the gods
X	*Teotl Iztacan*—the White God Place
XI	*Teotl Cozauhcan*—the Yellow God's Place
XII	*Teotl Tlatlauhcan*—the Red God's Place
XIII	*Omeyocan*—the Place of Destiny

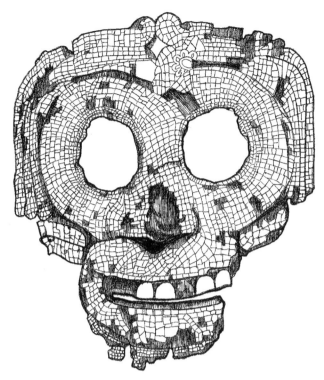

Aztec death mask

death in many ways with the agricultural product maize. This grain was sown, nurtured and harvested and thus in their view slain. Its cycle therefore represented human existence. Death haunted the Aztec, as their sculpture and ceramics reflect. Several extant pieces depict the head of a living being side by side with a skull. This is their proclamation that life is always accompanied by death. Death, however, held no meaning without new life; thus humans were promised that death was not a lasting, eternal state. The Aztec created highly complex doctrines regarding the subject of death, involving a world beyond the grave that would be well ordered and could provide a place for each individual.

As in other aspects of Aztec life, death and burial were accompanied by considerable ceremony. The manner of one's death, rather than his or her life, determined the individual's ultimate destination. The signs indicated at one's birth, as calculated in the calendar system, also had severe repercussions on the ultimate place of abode beyond the grave. To celebrate the death of an individual, then, was to reaffirm the importance of death, and the Aztec maintained elaborate funerary rites.

When an Aztec ruler died, the entire civilization was affected. Word was sent to neighboring communities, and dignitaries from vassal and allied states arrived with funerary offerings, including cloaks, green feathers and slaves for sacrifice. The ruler's body was wrapped in rich cloaks covered with semiprecious stones and golden ornaments. A piece of jade representing the heart was placed in the deceased's mouth, and locks of his hair were cut off and placed in a box along with the hair that had been taken from his head at birth and saved for the occasion. A slave was killed to act as a companion, and the ruler was then

covered in the chief symbol of the local deity. A procession carried the body to the temple, where it was met by priests who entombed it at the foot of a stairway. Sprinkled with incense, the remains were sometimes cremated. Many slaves, both male and female, were then executed to serve as the ruler's retinue beyond the grave. The slaves' hearts were removed from their bodies and burned. In some instances wives and court jesters, possibly dwarves, were also executed.

Following rites of cremation, the ruler's ashes and bones were placed in the box containing his hair, as was the jade piece that was symbolic of the heart. The box was then sealed and a wooden statue dressed in the robes of the dead ruler surmounted it. Offerings were made during a ceremony called the *Quitonaltia,* translated as "They give him good fortune." These rituals continued for four days, and 20 days after the cremation more slaves were sacrificed. Such 20-day ceremonies were repeated for some time, with slaves offered up on each anniversary. On the 80-day commemoration of the ruler's death, more slaves were sacrificed. After these initial rituals, observances accompanied by ritual drunkenness were practiced at the gravesite each year; rabbits, butterflies, wine, birds, flowers and tobacco were offered to the dead. These practices were generally continued for four years.

Very grand ceremonies were provided for Aztec nobles not of a royal caste; Aztec commoners were cremated with the few goods that they had accumulated in their lifetime. Anyone judged eligible to attain the paradise of the god Tlaloc, however, was not cremated. Death by drowning was one way to merit admission to the rain god's paradise; in such cases victims were believed to have been slain by a water creature called the *ahuitzotl,* who supposedly ate the corpse's eyes, nails and teeth. Only priests were permitted to touch such a corpse, and burials were conducted in specially built temples on the lakeshores. Those who died by being struck by lightning were also considered specially called by Tlaloc and were eligible for eternal bliss. Women who died in childbirth were uniquely blessed as well. The act of childbirth was equated with the taking of an enemy, and a woman who died in such circumstances was given the rank of warrior, belonging to the House of the Sun. Such a woman was believed to accompany the sun from its zenith to its setting. These women were also feared, as it was thought that they could return in a special form in order to interfere in the lives of their relatives still living.

The Aztec clearly believed in an underworld, which was part of their universe. There were nine levels in this underworld and three abodes:

First Abode, the House of the Sun.   The most pleasant and beautiful of the afterworlds, where warriors, victims of sacrifice and women who died in childbirth spent eternity. In time the warriors were transformed into hummingbirds.

Second Abode, the Home of the Tlaloc (Tlalocan).   A happy place with bountiful fields and beautiful plants. Only those who drowned, were struck by lightning or afflicted by certain mortal diseases were welcome here.

Third Abode, *Mictlan.*   The site to which all who suffered natural deaths were sent, both commoners and nobles.

The region was ruled by the god Mictlantecuhtli and his spouse, Mictlanchuatl. A dark and cheerless place, Mictlan was reached only after four years of dangerous travel through the underworld.

In order to attain these abodes, the dead must have moved through the levels listed in the ritual records, such as the *Codex Vaticanus:*

Level 1: the earth, called *Tlalticpac.*

Level 2: *Apanohuayan,* the passage over the water.

Level 3: *Tepetl Imonamiquiyan,* called Where the Hills Collide.

Level 4: *Itztepetl,* a region called Obsidian Knife Hill.

Level 5: *Itzehecayan,* the Place of the Obsidian Sharp Wind.

Level 6: *Pancuecuetlayan,* Where the Banners Flourish.

Level 7: *Temiminaloyan,* Where People Are Shot with Arrows.

Level 8: *Teyollocualoyan,* Where Someone's Heart Is Eaten.

Level 9: *Iz Miotlan Opochcalocan,* The Place of the Dead.

Another list, compiled by Sahagun, the Spanish historian, suggests the existence of other levels as well. Both lists provided a similar description of the Aztec after-death journey. The dead passed between two hills or mountains, which crashed together. The next two dangers brought conflict between a giant snake and a great lizard or crocodile. There were then eight deserts on plateaus that must be crossed, followed by a mountainous region called the Eight Hills. Here the dead confronted a cruel wind, a deep stretch of water and a final river on the border of Mictlan.

The ceremonies involving burial and its rites were designed to succor the deceased on this dreadful journey. Arms and protective clothing were provided for them, and the heat of the cremation itself served as a defense against the sharp winds. In some funerary rituals a vermilion-colored dog was provided for crossing the deep waters, as the animal was believed to be capable of supporting its owner, who clung to it by holding on to a cord. Other ceremonies offered solutions to other perils the dead would face.

For burial, Aztec corpses normally were placed in the fetal position, reflecting the connection between birth and death. The bodies were sprinkled with water, and the legs drawn up toward the torso. If cremation was the form of funerary ritual, as in some cases, the ashes were placed in a jar or box, sometimes containing locks of the deceased's hair. Such rituals attest to the Aztec view that death was the great leveler, shared by men and women of all ranks.

AZTEC DRESS The attire that not only provided protection against the natural elements but also clearly reflects the rank and status of individuals within Aztec society. The social structure of the Aztec communities was clearly visible in the sort of clothing worn, with various adornments further indicating privilege. Commoners wore few ornaments, while the nobles' clothing reflected changes in fashion and new styles. The priests and Aztec warriors also wore distinctive garb representing their ranks and roles in the community. The Aztec possessed considerable textile resources, especially during the period of empire. Various forms of cotton, flax, feathers and wool were provided. They often received special fabric as tribute from vassal or allied states. Such fabrics included embroideries from the Totonac region, Huaxtec fabrics and shirts, cloaks, mantles and loincloths, especially from the eastern and southern provinces.

As textiles are fragile, none have survived to document the rich variety of materials available to the Aztec. Much about what they wore has been deduced, therefore, from written accounts of tribute and from the attire seen in extant statuettes and paintings. Textiles are a definitive art form in many cultures, and the Aztec believed that the patron goddess of textile workers, Xochiquetzal, was creator of spinning and weaving.

Some basic fabrics were produced in each Aztec household, and the young women were trained in textile making at an early age. Noble women were trained in the making of textiles in special schools associated with temples. White and brown cotton and yucca and agave fibers were used. Dyed furs, such as rabbit skins, were incorporated into clothing styles, as were feathers, raw silk and bark cloth. Aztec dyes (see table) included substances made from certain shellfish, brought as tribute from the Mixtec and Zapotec regions. Alum and ferrous sulfates were also employed, as well as vegetable dyes, taken from wood, roots, leaves, flowers and fruits.

Spinning and weaving produced beautiful, high-quality materials, although the Aztec lacked complex equipment. They used the backdrop loom and the spindle whorl. Spinning was accomplished by the draught-and-twist method, taught by one generation to the next. Decorations were woven, painted or embroidered. Little documentation concerning such decorations is available. Pattern weaving was clearly known at the time, but its use is difficult to trace historically. Brocading dates to the Post-Classic Period in Mesoamerica, and embroidery was also used. Artisans employed bone and, later, copper needles. These tools were pictured in various codices, which also mention embroideries. Painted designs often were used for religious or ceremonial purposes, and priests were clothed in textiles bearing appropriate symbols. Warriors also wore feathered and painted attire. Such feather works, called *amanteca,* were highly prized.

The general costume for all of the Aztec social classes

AZTEC DYES

Black *(Ocotlilli),* made from pine soot.

Indigo *(Xuihquilatl pitzahoac),* made from *Indigifera anil* (L.)

Orange, made from achiote seeds, *Bixa orellana* (L.)

Red *(Tlauitl),* made from mineral oxides.

White (1) *Tizatl,* made from chalk.

White (2) *Chimaltizatl,* made from gypsum.

Yellow *(Tecozahuitl),* made from yellow ocher.

Yellow gold *(Zacatlaxcalli),* made from *Cuscuta americana* (L.)

was more or less the same, consisting of a loincloth (*maxtlatl*) for men, with a cloak (*tilmatli*) and sandals, called *cactli*. Women wore a skirt (*cueitl*), with a belt (*nelpiloni*) and a long, sleeveless tunic called a *huipilli*. Clothing also distinguished the classes, as the *tilmatli* when worn by a noble was richly embroidered or painted with designs. Commoners' cloaks were normally fashioned out of maguey fibers, and nobles wore maguey or cotton, sometimes with rabbit hair woven into the fabric for warmth.

The Aztec priests usually wore black or dark-green cloaks, embroidered with the design of skulls and human bones. Most priests had dried blood on their cloaks, mementos of sacrifices. Emperors wore a turquoise *tilmatli* called a *xiuhtilmatli*.

Cotton was highly prized and in time was made a mandatory tribute from some of the Aztec's conquered provinces. It was especially valued by the nobles. Sandals, made of stronger fibers, had straps, heels and hide soles. Soldiers and nobles laced their sandals almost to the knees. At times sandals were decorated with gold, jewels, feathers or animal skins.

The Aztec also appreciated jewelry and body ornaments. Women wore necklaces, earrings and bracelets, and men pierced the septum of their noses to hold gems and metal pieces. Aztec men also wore ear plugs designating rank. Shells were placed in lip holes, as were bits of gold, amber, crystal and other semiprecious stones. The sort of ornamentation worn by an Aztec depended very much on his or her rank in society.

Only the emperor could wear a turquoise nose plug, and the insertion of that ornament was part of the coronation ceremony. Other headdresses, plumes, banners and displays were reserved for Aztec of certain rank or for specific occasions. Anyone who disobeyed the rigid code for adornment was sentenced to death.

AZTEC EMPIRE The domain extending at one time from the Gulf of Mexico to the Pacific Ocean, from the Valley of Mexico to the Guatemalan border, including the Isthmus of Tehuantepec. Such lands were not occupied by Aztec (Mexica) forces but were probably governed by Aztec officials as vassal states or allied to the empire. As such, these cities and regions were subject to the tribute system instituted by the Aztec to provide the capital of Tenochtitlan and the state government with valuable resources and products. Acamapichtli (ruling from A.D. c. 1376 to c. 1391/96) began the strengthening of the Aztec holdings. Huitzilihuitl (c. A.D. 1391/96–1415/17) led campaigns also, including one to the region of Cuernavaca. During this period and in the reign of his successor, Chimalpopoca, the Aztec were vassals to the Tepanec and received some territories from King Tezozomoc. When a feud erupted in the Tepanec kingdom following Tezozomoc's death, Chimalpopoca was killed. His successor, Itzcoatl (A.D. 1427–1440), rebelled, thereby initiating the TRIPLE ALLIANCE of Tenochtitlan, Texcoco and Tlacopan (Tacuba). The combined forces of the Triple Alliance, joined in time by other cultures, enabled the Aztec to launch their imperial campaigns in earnest.

Motecuhzoma I (A.D. 1440–1469) attacked north-central Veracruz, the land of the Huaxtec, which already had been invaded by the Texcoco ruler, Nezahualcoyotl, and his army. He then attacked Coixtlahuaca and the territories of

Mask of Motecuhzoma II

the Mixtec. By the end of his reign, Motecuhzoma I had received tribute from Oaxaca, from the Totonac, and from Tuxpan in the Huaxteca region. The northeastern highlands also sent tribute to Tenochtitlan. Motecuhzoma's heir, Axayacatl (A.D. 1469–1481) took Tlaltelolco, the sister city of Tenochtitlan. He then attacked Toluca and tried unsuccessfully to conquer the Tarascan. His successor, Tizoc (A.D. 1481–1486), was forced to deal with regional rebellions and tried unsuccessfully to attack Metztitlan. He was probably murdered. His successor was Ahuitzotl (A.D. 1496–1502), a veteran warrior, whose campaigns were swift and ruthless. Facing a rebellion in the region of Toluca, he put it down rapidly, going then to the gulf coast to demand tribute from the groups and cities there. Sacrifices in the capital of Tenochtitlan became another weapon in Ahuitzotl's campaigns, as any group fighting against his armies faced the terror of serving as human sacrifice in the temples of the capital. He conquered Guerrero, Oaxaca and the lands down to the Isthmus of Tehuantepec. Again, such lands were seldom occupied, although they remained within the empire and provided tribute. In the tradition of earlier emperors, Ahuitzotl encouraged Aztec to settle in the frontiers. He also erected fortresses, thus stabilizing and strengthening the empire. Malinalco became a warrior-based shrine during his reign.

His heir, Motecuhzoma II (A.D. 1502–1520), continued the military campaigns and put down rebellions. Only the Tarascan and the Tlaxcalan defied Motecuhzoma successfully. He fought four separate times in the Tarascan region, suffering defeats at the hands of the warriors there. The tribute system, taxation and the imperial administration probably added to the success of the Spanish conquest, as the groups remaining free of the Aztec yoke were happy to see the Spaniards defeat them. Other groups, anxious to overthrow the Aztec domination of their lands, also allied themselves with the Spanish. No one recognized the ramifications of such alliances, which would include the fall of Tenochtitlan and total domination by the Spanish invaders.

Motecuhzoma II was murdered by his Spanish captors, and was succeeded by a prince of the royal line, Cuitlahuac, who remained in power for less than a year. The Aztec were not ready to surrender their lives or their empire, however, and Cuauhtemoc, an Aztec general, took up the standard and led a rebellion against the Spanish. He and his army were besieged a few years later by a relentless combination of the Spanish and their allies. After withstanding this onslaught for more than 90 days, Cuauhtemoc was captured. It is reported that Cortez, so impressed by the Aztec general's bravery and military brilliance, received him and his family courteously and with honor. Cuauhtemoc, however, was hanged three years later. Thus the empire waned, and Tenochtitlan was razed by the Spanish, as the new Mexico City with its European architecture rose up in the Valley of Mexico.

AZTEC GAMES Recreational and religiously significant exhibitions throughout Aztec history, corresponding to the traditions of the Mesoamerican region. Games were part of the shared Mesoamerican culture, dating from early times. With regional variations, they were played almost universally in the area. Three important types of game include the ball game, the *patolli*, and the *volador*.

The Ball Game. The paramount sport of the Aztec, played in courts constructed in occupied cities as well as in Tenochtitlan. The patron deity of Aztec ball games was Macuilxochtli. Thousands attended the games, and Aztec gambled heavily on the outcome. As a result of such betting, some Aztec lost their worldly goods and had to sell themselves into slavery.

The Aztec ball game was called the *tlachtli*, and it can be traced to the culture of the Maya and others. The Aztec were both participants and spectators in the *tlachtli*. Some sources state that only the nobility could take part in these games, but it is probable that commoners took part as well, given the historical precedence of the game and its popularity. *Tlachtli* held both mythological and religious significance. The ball courts represented the world, and the ball was symbolic of the sun and the moon. The rules were precise, and the ball courts were constructed according to historical tradition. Most Aztec cities possessed a court, and reportedly during the Aztec's long journey toward Tenochtitlan they erected courts at intervals along the way. Such courts were normally I-shaped, where two teams faced one another on either side of a center line. The object of the game was to move a large ball into the court of the opposing team or through one of the two rings carved into the sides of the court. Players could not touch the ball with their hands or feet; only knee or hip contact was allowed. Because of these regulations and the hardness and speed of the ball in use, the players wore protective clothing, such as padded coverings, a waist yoke and other gear. Reportedly, any player who managed to put the ball through one of the

rings was entitled to snatch clothes or ornaments from the spectators, aided by team members. Ball players who scored consistently won lasting fame and rich rewards.

The *Patolli*. Another religiously significant game, in which all classes might participate. Described in the *Codex Magliabecchiano, patolli* was presided over by the god Macuilxochtli and was played on a mat, with a cross-shaped design, marking off separate zones, probably 52 in number in order to equal the solar and divinatory cycles. Beans (dice) were thrown, and the players advanced colored stones as tokens from square to square. Victory was achieved when one player returned to the original square, as in the Indian game Parcheesi.

Games of chance and riddles were also part of Aztec recreation. One such game involved tossing reeds that had been cut down the center. The object was to score points by making the cut portions fall facing upward on a mat. This game, still popular in some regions of Mexico, required the blessing of the mat with prayers and incense. Riddles and puzzles were also a form of entertainment, with participants being required to come up with the proper responses.

The *Volador*. A Mesoamerican ritual associated with the calendar and with the celebration of the New Year having deep religious significance for the Aztec and other groups. Tenochtitlan and other Aztec cities had special sites for the observance of this daring event. Four Aztec warriors, dressed as birdlike creatures, hung from ropes attached to the top of a pole and to belts around their waists. They jumped from a high platform and swung around the pole, as the ropes slowly unwound. Another performer was on a platform at the top of the pole. After 13 or more revolutions, the dancers reached the ground. In some instances the ropes were tied to the performers' feet.

AZTEC GODS Divinities associated with traditional Mesoamerican religious concepts or worshiped solely by the Aztec throughout their history. Such beings assumed different roles and natures, with some representing rather complex spiritual ideals. The more esoteric concepts, actually cosmological in nature, involved the beings associated with the layers of the universe, the vital principles and the cardinal points of the earth.

Omeyocan, in the center of the universe, was considered the place of duality, the realm where the battle between good and evil was waged. Ometeotl, the creator of the

Aztec fire god painting

world, called the navel of the universe, resided within this realm. He was believed to be a combination of Ometecuhtli and Omecihuatl, the masculine and feminine forms of the generative force. Their divine presence was manifested in the blue color of the waters and the heavens. Ometeotl's four divine sons were the four elements of the world: earth, air, fire and water.

Ipalnemohuani, the Giver of Life, also called Tloque-Nahuaque, the God of the Near and the Immediate, was another deity worshipped by the Aztec, following the Nahual tradition. Another divinity, Moyocoyatzin, called the Lord Who Invented Himself or He Who Fashions Himself by His Own Thoughts, was included in this specialized pantheon, whose members occupied the cardinal points. North was the dwelling place of Tezcatlipoca. South was the dwelling place of Huitzilopochtli. East was the dwelling place of Tonatiuh. And West was the dwelling place of Quetzalcoatl.

The major deities of the Aztec include one god who is unique to them and one who was worshipped throughout centuries of Mesoamerican tradition. Huitzilopochtli, called the Hummingbird of the South, was the guardian of the Aztec from the beginning of their recorded history. Quetzalcoatl, the Feather Serpent, was a deity popular throughout Mesoamerica in all eras. Huitzilopochtli appears in the earliest histories of the Aztec, as patron and protector on the long journey out of Aztlan to Tenochtitlan. In times of good fortune and in strife this god was with the Aztec people, speaking through the mouths of four priest-kings who ruled for a time and then through Tenoch, who led his people to greatness. The god was faithful to the Aztec, providing miraculous powers to thwart their enemies, such as the Tepanec; he safeguarded the people, announcing times of suffering and encouraging the Aztec to heights of civilization. Quetzalcoatl appears early in Mesoamerica, undergoing severe trials; always appealing to the gentle side of his worshippers, rituals in his name exuded peace and beauty. Taking the form of Venus or of the wind, as Ehecatl, Quetzalcoatl was associated with the creative force in fertility and the wind. He was the Feathered Serpent, the sacred representative of life and abundance, superceding the more bellicose of the Aztec gods.

With their rise to power, the Aztec began to organize their pantheons and to develop a system of complexes that included certain rites, each with its role and purpose. These complexes included:

Ometeotl Complex. The "creator," associated with other deities involved in caring for the Aztec. Ometeotl was believed to be bisexual and paternal, associated with fire and maize and called the Old Sorcerer. As a female he was maternal, the earth, associated with maize and fertility. The god of prayers and offerings, he fashioned the souls of newborn infants.

Tezcatlipoca Complex. The company of sorcerers, the seer of all things, and patron of young warriors; omnipotent and omnipresent. The universal power, sometimes malevolent, Tezcatlipoca was associated with the earth and, in some instances, with the moon. Other deities with the same roles were included in this complex.

Xiuhtecuhtli Complex. The cult of the Aztec fire god having a role in the New Fire rituals and the various calendrical cycles. Xiuhtecuhtli was called the Turquoise Year Lord according to some lists, thus associating him with the sacred calendars. Other deities were included in this complex.

Tlaloc Complex. The agricultural deities who were associated with farming and the cardinal points of the earth. Tlaloc, the god of rain, was vital to agriculture, as was his wife, Chalchiuhtlicue, the goddess of water, called the Lady of the Jade Skirt. Also important to this complex are the Tlaloques, the dwarfish minions of the god Tlaloc: Opochtli, Nappatecuhtli, Yauhqueme and Tomiyauhecuhtli. They were brewers of rain, living in the mountain ranges of the Aztec domain. Other deities associated with farming and crops were in this grouping.

Centeotl-Xochipilli Complex. The cultivation cult group, associated mainly with the growing of maize, dominated by the traditional goddesses of the region. Centeotl, however, was the son of the earth mother and could be male or female in nature. Xochipilli, the other patron of this complex, was called the Flower Prince. The deities of this group were chiefly sun deities, associated with maize, flowers, feasting and pleasure. The patron of featherworkers was in this group.

Huitzilopochtli Complex. The group to which the patron deity of the Aztec belonged by tradition since the time of the first journey from Aztlan. This complex included fire worship. The messengers of Huitzilopochtli were the traditional priest-kings of the Aztec, normally four in number, the last of whom was Tenoch, who led the people to the site of Tenochtitlan and ordered the building of the capital. In time this complex guided the military in Aztec life, its gods requiring human sacrifice.

Quetzalcoatl Complex. The group incorporating the Feather Serpent cult, ancient and widespread in Mesoamerica, and the Morning Star. The complex was associated with astronomy, astrology and the art of divination. Quetzalcoatl at times took the forms of Ce Acatl and Ehecatl (the wind god), both of whom were included in this group.

Ometochtli Complex. A group of divine beings associated with agriculture and fertility rites, especially in the cultivation of the maguey plant, which was an important Aztec crop, most notably before the introduction of cotton. A particularly popular deity of this complex was Centeotl, also called 400 Rabbits.

Teteoinnan Complex. A group associated with the worship of the earth mother, with fertility, birth, medicine and flowers. It was popular everywhere because it concerned fundamental aspects of Aztec existence. The patroness of flowers, Coatlicue, was among the deities honored in this complex.

Tonatiuh Complex. The deities worshipped as the primordial creative forces, the sustenance of the worlds and the sun. In time, Tonatiuh was merged with the sun, and he became the recipient of the blood sacrifices conducted to prevent earthquakes, which were the destructive forces that had been foretold as destroying the Fifth Sun, the era in which the Aztecs lived. Warriors had a special affinity for this complex, and sacrificial victims were called the "chil-

AZTEC DEITIES

Ahuiateotl	Mixitli
Atlahua	Moyocoyatzin
Atlatonan	Nahui Ehecatl
Chalchiuhtlatonac	Omacatl
Chalchiuhtlicue	Omecihuatl
Chalchiuhtotolin	Ometecuhtli
Chantico	Ometeotl
Chicomecoatl	Ome Tochtli
Cihuacoatl	Oxomoco
Cihuateteo	Painal
Cinteotl	Piltzintecuhtli
Cipactli	Quetzalcoatl
Cipactonal	Teicauhtzin
Citlalinicue	Telpochtli
Citlacue	Tepeyollotl
Citlaltonac	Tepoztecatl
Coatlicue	Teteoinnan
Copil	Tetzahuitl
Coyolxauhqui	Titlacahuan
Ehecatl	Tlacahuepan
Fire Serpent	Tlahuizcalpantecuhtli (Venus)
Huehueteotl	Tlaloques
Huitzilopochtli	Tlalteuchtli
Huixtocihuatl	Tezcacoac
Ikil	Teuhcatl
Ipalnemoani	Tlazolteotl
Itzpapaleotl	Tonacatecuhtli
Itztli	Tonatiuh
Ixcozauhqui	Tzitzimitl
Ixlilton	Xilonen
Ixnextli	Xipe Totec
Ixtlilton	Xiuhtecuhtli
Macuiltonaleque	Xochipilli
Macuilxochitl	Xolotl
Malinalxoch	Yoalli Ehecatl
Mayahuel	Yaotl
Mictlantecuhtli	Zapotlantenan
Mixcoatl	

dren of the sun" or the "messengers to the sun." Tonatiuh at times assumed another form, that of Nahui Ollin, included in this group.

Mixcoatl-Tlahuizcalpantecuhtli Complex. The group belonging to the star cults and the deities deemed military in nature. At one time, Mixcoatl, called Cloud Serpent, was worshipped by older Mesoamerican groups, including the Chichimec. He was adopted by the Aztec and became the patron of some of their cities. Venus was part of this complex's domain, as were the gods of fishing and aquatic hunting.

Mictlantecuhtli Complex. The Lord of Mictlan, the abode of the dead, reached after four years of dangerous travel across the various levels of the underworld, was chief of this group of deities associated with death. Ancestors, heroes of the past, and those who died natural deaths were associated as well. All Aztec, whether noble or commoner, journeyed in Mictlan if they died naturally. In this respect the complex appears to have exercised a certain democratic or equalizing effect among Aztec.

The following list cites deities associated with the complexes.

Other prominent deities in Aztec life include Yacateuchtli, the guardian of Aztec merchants and traders, called *pochteca*, who conducted vital economic activities and at times served as intelligence agents throughout Mesoamerica. Xipe Totec, called the Flayed God, was a fertility deity whose sacrificial ritual required the victim to be flayed. He could also take the form of a sacrificial knife, and at these times he was called Red Tezcatlipoca. Xipe Totec was widely worshipped in other Mesoamerican cultures as well.

Gods mentioned in the accounts of the Aztec journey from Aztlan to Tenochtitlan include Malinalochitl, the sister of Huitzilopochtli. She was a sorceress who gathered a small contingent of supporters and hindered her brother god and the people. She was abandoned by the Aztec upon Huitzilopochtli's advice and swore vengeance. In time she sent her son, Copil, to the place where the Aztec had settled. He caused trouble there and was killed. When the Aztec reached Tenochtitlan, Huitzilopochtli pointed to the place where Copil's heart was buried, and the first temple was erected on the spot. In some legends Copil's heart became the cactus plant, the traditional emblem of Tenochtitlan. (See AZTEC COSMOLOGY; AZTEC PRIESTS AND RELIGION.)

AZTEC GOVERNMENT   The administration and rule of the first territories and then the expanded empire, based on the traditions of other Mesoamerican nations and on the concept of the city-state. Coming into the Valley of Mexico, the Aztec quickly absorbed the processes of government, especially those of the former Toltec rulers. Some scholars have proposed that the Toltec were instrumental in providing a direct model for the Aztec government as well as having inspired their art and religious practices.

Aztec life was entirely concerned with the basic social unit, the *calpulli*, the clanlike organization whose members lived within separate compounds and wards in Tenochtitlan. The *calpulli* was the heart of Aztec life, each group having its own noble caste, gods, temples and schools. At the inception of Tenochtitlan there were supposedly seven such units; by the time the Spanish arrived they numbered 20 or more. The young men of the *calpulli* were trained by their own elders, and each group had its own government building, or *ateocalli*.

Within the *calpulli* system, the Aztec social structure was divided into two basic groups: the *pipiltin* and the *macehualtin*. The *pipiltin* were the hereditary nobility who controlled Aztec affairs, including maintenance of production, art, warfare, political and religious events. The *macehualtin* were the laboring classes: the farmers, workers, artisans and soldiers.

The chief of the Aztec state was the *tlatoani*, always drawn from the *pipiltin*, and carefully guarded against intrusion by commoners. All of the economic and political dignitaries were nobles. A privileged rank just below that of the blood nobles was composed of warriors who had distinguished themselves in battle and in military campaigns. The *pipiltin* and the warrior and priest segments of society served the *tlatoani* (pl. *tlatoque*), who was chosen by a council to act as king or emperor. Such rulers claimed descent from Quetzalcoatl and from the Toltec. They held religious as well as administrative positions in the Aztec domain, and normally the throne was inherited by brothers or sons, or by a chosen neighboring noble. These rulers were:

Tenoch. The last of the priest-kings during the journey of the Aztec. He was depicted in the *Codex Mendoza* and apparently guided the Aztec to the island where Huitzilopochtli, the patron deity of the nation, provided him with the proper signs for the establishment of the final home of the people. Tenoch was a priest of Huitzilopochtli's cult, serving as a sage for the people and as the voice of the god.

Acamapichtli. Called Handful of Reeds, ruling from A.D. 1376 to c. 1391/96. He was a prince of the Toltec, or possibly came from Azcapotzalco or was raised in Culhuacan. The Aztec asked that he be given to them as their ruler, as a similar king with Toltec background had been found for Tenochtitlan's sister city, Tlatelolco. One record, however, indicates that Acamapichtli was the son of an Aztec nobleman and a Culhuacan princess. After accepting the throne, Acamapichtli married a royal Culhuacan woman named Ilacueitl and said by some to be the true political power. He also wed as many as 20 princesses of other groups in order to consolidate his claim to the throne. He launched building projects in the capital and designed canals and *chinampas,* floating gardens. Acamapichtli led the Aztec in battle against Xochimilco and other sites and died in c. A.D. 1391/96 after a 19-year reign. His son was Huitzilihuitl II.

Huitzilihuitl II. Called Humming-Bird Feather, ruling from c. A.D. 1391/96 to 1415/17. He was elected to the throne upon the death of his father. Married to a princess from Tlacopan, who died, he then wed the granddaughter of the Tepanec king Tezozomoc. Huitzilihuitl regulated the religious customs of the Aztec, welcomed immigrants to Tenochtitlan and led military campaigns to expand his domain. He reportedly brought cotton to the Aztec after visiting the region of Cuernava. A legend concerning a princess of the region and her wizard father is told about him. He discovered a beautiful princess in a magical garden and overcame dangerous creatures in order to win her hand and take her to Tenochtitlan. This princess was the mother of Motecuhzoma I.

Chimalpopoca. Called Smoking Shield, ruling from c. A.D. 1415/17 to 1427. He was the son of Huitzilihuitl and the grandson of Tezozomoc of Tepanec, whom the Aztec served as vassals. Becoming involved in the Tepanec feud after the death of Tezozomoc, Chimalpopoca was put to death by Maxtla.

Itzcoatl. Called Obsidian Serpent, ruling from A.D. 1427 to 1440. He began a slow revolt against Maxtla and the Tepanec, eventually establishing the Triple Alliance of states in 1430 and overthrowing Maxtla. The Aztec became independent as a result, and the beginnings of the empire through conquest came about during his reign.

Motecuhzoma Ilhuicamina. Called Heaven Shooter, the Archer that Shoots the Sky or the Angry Lord Who Shoots at the Sky, ruling from A.D. 1440 to 1469. A battle-hardened warrior, Motecuhzoma conducted many campaigns and began construction of the Great Temple in Tenochtitlan. Many disasters took place during his reign, and he launched the "Wars of the Flowers" in order to obtain sacrificial victims.

Axayacatl. Called Water Face, ruling from A.D. 1469 to 1481. He became emperor at age 19 and was responsible for much regional expansion. Eventually he attacked Tlatelolco, the sister city of Tenochtitlan, annexing it to the capital.

Tizoc. Called Leg of Chalk, ruling from A.D. 1481 to 1486. A religious man who often sought seclusion, he enlarged the Great Temple of Tenochtitlan and added the Stone of Tizoc. He took part in some imperial campaigns. It is possible that Tizoc was murdered because of his ineffective administration.

Ahuitzotl. Called Water Creature, ruling from A.D. 1486 to 1502. One of the great Aztec rulers and a vital member of the Triple Alliance, he led campaigns and brought the Aztec army as far as the border of Guatemala. He is remembered for the dedication ceremonies of the Great Temple in the capital, an event in which thousands of victims were reported to have been sacrificed.

Motecuhzoma (Moctezuma) Xocoyotzin. Called Angry Lord, the Youngest, ruling from 1502 to 1520. This renowned Aztec ruler met his death at the hands of the Spanish after a long period of successful but harsh rule. He was interested in mysticism and became deeply religious after relinquishing his prestigious military career.

The Aztec government, which dominated many cultures and vast territories during the period of empire, was based on earlier state models, such as Teotihuacan and the Toltec cities. The king, or *tlatoani,* was not only the military chief but the religious leader as well. He was also responsible for fiscal affairs, civil administration and maintenance of agricultural production. His royal fields, called the *tlatocamilli,* were hereditary lands that served as the economic base for agricultural programs. Aiding him in all of these responsibilities was the *Uey calpixqui,* called the majordomo or the caretaker of the palace, a vice-ruler. They relied on other notables as well, such as Tlacaelel, who advised both Itzcoatl and Motecuhzoma I.

Officials assisting the vice-rulers included the chiefs of 20, 40 or 100 families. Such officers collected taxes, organized collective labor units, kept accounts and rolls of personnel, tribute, vassals and all palace and state resources. Directly below this bureau were the *calpullecs,* the leaders of the *calpullis,* the wards of the city. Military leaders also worked side by side with their civil counterparts to ensure administrative stability. Governors, normally two in number, regulated the affairs of conquered regions, with garrisons established to keep the peace.

On all levels there were *calpixques,* the tribute collectors, who handled the details of taxes, crops, tribute and public works, reporting to the *tecuhtli,* the noble in charge. Such nobles lived well and received tribute and services from the local farmers and artisans as well as lands set aside for their sole use. They represented their districts before the emperor, led military campaigns, prepared defenses, directed the cultivation of crops, collected tribute and appointed local officials. The *tecuhtli* was elected to his position for life, and he was normally advised by a council and conferred with the local priests.

Another prestigious governmental group was judges of the Aztec courts. Sometimes half their number were commoners, to ensure equal justice and because they were aware of local customs, traditions and mores. Aztec judges were known for their strict adherence to the law and for their dedication to the emperor.

AZTEC LANGUAGE   Called Nahuatl, belonging to the Uto-Aztecan language family, linking the Aztec to the other tribes that originally came from Chicomoztoc, the region of the Seven Caves. Nahuatl still is spoken in many Mexican highland regions and is a beautiful and melodious tongue with many intricacies and polite terms. The Aztec brought Nahuatl into many regions of Mesoamerica, where it is believed to have influenced other languages.

In the written form, called hieroglyphs, the Aztec language was not as complex as that of other lands, such as Egyptian. Maya hieroglyphs, for example, are older and more complex. Some scholars, however, believe that when the Aztec written language is studied in depth, it will prove to have great sophistication and a wide range of nuances. The written language was the result of the traditional Mesoamerican forms, remnants of older cultures.

As is clear from the codices, such as the *Codex Mendoza*, the Aztec written language was sufficient to maintain records in government accounting, calendars, myths and historical facts. Aztec writing relied on pictographs, or images of actual people or activities. Flora and fauna were inscribed as well as dances, processions, sacrifices, gods and rulers. Each one was distinguished by clothes, forms, activities or postures, all known to the people as a result of the oral tradition. Aztec writing is also ideographic in nature, in that symbols were used to convey meanings and events. A flower, for example, denoted sacrificial blood in religious ceremonies, hence the name "Flower Wars" to specify the warfare in taking victims for sacrifice and in conquest. A bundle of reeds, which clearly depicted the result of harvests, was used in the Aztec hieroglyphs to symbolize the 52-year cycle of the calendar system. The literate, aware of the significance of this particular image, could comprehend its hieroglyphic form instantly.

Actually, the two forms of Aztec hieroglyphs, pictographic and ideographic (with phonetic elements), were used together in some instances. The ritual codices use both, stressing one over the other in depicting events or ceremonies, leading some scholars to consider the combination as "picto-ideographic" writing. Place-names or personal names appear in other codices, beside the "picto-ideographic" forms. It is believed that there was an aspect of phonetic development in the language, an evolution of sound as the language was introduced to larger populations. The Aztec form, however, cannot be characterized simply or in standard forms. It was a system in transition, cut off while in an evolutionary state, showing both phonetic tendency and syllabic forms. The Aztec had moved from mere pictographs and ideographs to the use of syllables in only half a century. The surviving codices portray this leap quite clearly. The stage was thus set for the move into an alphabetic form, a move that was quickly halted by the Spanish Conquest. (See AZTEC LITERATURE.)

AZTEC LAW   The court system of the Aztec, dependent on the king or emperor. Aztec law is a remarkable achieve-

Aztec carved head

ment in its abiding concern for the rights of people and for property. From the beginning judicial tribunals were in effect, in the individual *calpullis* and their holdings as well as in the major divisions of Tenochtitlan. Several kings were noted for the laws they enacted, most notably Motecuhzoma (Moctezuma) I. The system evolved slowly until the period of empire, when the government needed to devise ways in which to maintain order and civil liberties within vast regions. In this period principal cities of the vassal states were provided with judges appointed by the crown; these officials had jurisdiction in both civil and criminal cases. Judges appointed as superior magistrates normally served for life; they were considered capable and were trained to remove themselves from any scandal or wrongdoing. Anyone who assaulted or usurped the power of such a judge was sentenced to death.

These magistrates presided over a series of courts, with three judges sitting during civil cases. The lower courts conducted civil and some criminal cases, but the defendants could appeal to higher judicial levels as well. Local magistrates handled minor infractions in their communities, aided by officials. Appeals indicate a highly developed sense of justice among the Aztec. The penal code, however, was extremely severe, thus the need for prudence in the judiciary. Even the superior judges, appointed by the king, were independent of him in their final decisions and sentencing, which safeguarded the courts from outside interference. If convicted of accepting bribes, the judges themselves faced the death penalty.

The Aztec code of law was sweeping and severe, dealing mostly with persons rather than with property and imposing the death penalty for almost all crimes against society.

Adulterers were stoned to death, and thieves faced death or slavery. Altering boundaries, squandering wealth, drunkenness (outside of religious festivals) and other acts were dealt with harshly, depending on the age, standing and past record of the accused. Slaves fared uniquely under the Aztec system. Many taken prisoner were sacrificed on the altars, a fate that promised them eternal bliss. Others, including those who were reduced to slavery because of poverty, could have substitutes from their own family brought in to take their place after a period of service. In the era of the great famine in Tenochtitlan, children were sold into slavery with the agreement that they could be bought out again after the famine for the same price. Some slaves were even allowed to own other slaves as well as property, and they were permitted to have families.

AZTEC LITERATURE A compilation of the written philosophical, mythical and romantic works surviving the ruthless destruction of the Spanish, who set about erasing all such treasures after conquering Tenochtitlan. Considered to be pagan and thus unworthy, most such documents were put to the torch. The few literary works that remain, usually called codices, provide data on historical, religious, artistic and social development in the Aztec world. The Aztec accumulated texts and used them in their various educational facilities, normally accompanied as well by an oral tradition, including religious tales, myths and legends.

The Aztec manuscripts were made of various materials. Skins, cotton cloth and bark paper fabrics were used, as well as pages made from the maguey plant. Most were beautifully illustrated with bright colors, and they were rolled or folded accordion style into books with leaf or wood covers.

The surviving works include maps, historical accounts, tax records, religious documents, songs, hymns, myths and stories. The eloquent fluidity of these works attests to the growing complexity of the Aztec language. Rhetoric and poetic style was dominant, and the chroniclers of past events could develop vivid images of the facts that they commemorated. The annals of history did not always contain such imagery, but other literary works employed marvelous images and symbols that brought the past to life for each succeeding generation. They wrote as they spoke, in fluent measures, with eloquence and drama.

The poetic style is evident in the *teocuicatl*, the hymns handed down from one age to another. These are filled with mystical names and titles. War songs, love songs, odes to the changing seasons and praises of the gods were also intoned on various occasions. Religious ceremonies included such recitations, performed by choirs, priests and narrators and accompanied by music and dancing. (See AZTEC LANGUAGE.)

AZTEC MAGIC Practices by magicians in honor of Tezcatlipoca, Ehecatl-Quetzalcoatl, Teteoinnan-Toci and the goddess Tlazolteotl. The magicians of the Aztec were called *nahualli*, and it was believed that they could shape-change or shape-shift into animals or inanimate objects. There were white magicians *(cualli-nahualli)* and black magicians *(tlahueliloc nahualli)*. Astrologers, prophets and sages composed the white magicians, who were under the protection of the deities associated with rain and water. Diviners among these magicians called *tlapouhque*, the "counters," were versed in the use of the calendar. The *tlaolchayauhqui*, the scatterers of the maize seeds, were used to determine supernatural causes of any crop problems. The *atlanteittani*, or the *amanani*, used mirrors or water surfaces for divination. Some white magicians used peyote and other hallucinogens to call up visions. Curers, called *ticitl*, healed certain physical ailments, and the *teixcuepani* were the illusionists who conjured up spectacles for the edification and delight of their audiences.

Among the black magicians were the *tlacatecolatl*, the "human owls." They were noted for transforming themselves into birds or demons. They bled victims of disease, and the historical annals ascribe assorted powers to them.

AZTEC MARRIAGE The union of two Aztec for the purpose of raising a family. From the earliest times Aztec laws defended the marriage bond. There was divorce, and polygamy was practiced by the upper classes, but the Aztec family was held in respect. The king or emperor, because he was involved in political alliances and statecraft, married many women in order to maintain alliances with other groups and the security of imperial borders.

Marriage for the commoner was understood and valued as an aid to the state and critical for population growth. Each family was part of the *calpulli* and thus was integrated into the framework of society as a whole. Women maintained the households, and men were the heads of the families, with the eldest son inheriting the rank and the property. Land normally remained intact as a single inheritance. The marriage age varied according to the Aztec historical period. Families used mediators who negotiated for the bride and groom and drew up the final contracts. The actual ceremony was a solemn occasion, accompanied by serious admonitions, especially in the upper classes where hereditary rank and power were involved. These nobles seldom married outside their class, as a safeguard to ensure that offspring inherited fairly the rank and prestige as well as the holdings of the line.

Marriage celebrations, whether noble or common, were always elaborate occasions, festive and involving banquets and prolonged galas (depending on financial resources), and were times of reunion. The brides were often attired in costly robes and jewels, and male and female friends joined the newlyweds in a hall or home to celebrate the occasion. Dancing, drinking and sermons on the obligations of the bride and groom were followed by the bridal couple's bestowing gifts upon the guests.

When the ceremony was over, the bride normally took up residence in her husband's home. If the marriage did not survive, the courts provided for divorce.

AZTEC MATHEMATICS The system of notations employed for architectural, calendrical and divination activities. In the Aztec numerical system, the first 20 numbers were expressed by dots. The first five numbers had specific names, and these were combined with dots to provide the sums required. Ten, 15, and the other numbers also were named. The number 20, important because the system was vigesimal, was represented by a flag, and it was the basis for the designation of all of the larger totals, which were multiples of 20. When delineating fractions, the Aztec simply drew a portion of a particular number. When dealing with the calendar of the two types of years, the Aztec could mark time with their sophisticated system. They did not employ the bar-dot system of the Maya, as their numbers, names and glyphs were sufficiently precise to enable calendrical evaluations.

AZTEC MEDICINE   The healing arts based on scientific as well as religious or magical foundations. Both men and women performed the various functions of healing, relying to a great extent upon their religious beliefs. They held the Mesoamerican view that illness was part of the natural woes visited upon human beings by the gods. If a deity was not proven to be the source of the problem, the victim was considered imbalanced internally and spiritually, perhaps as the result of black magic. The Aztec believed that evil acts could result in evil visiting the perpetrators of such activities.

Aztec medicine, however, was not dependent solely upon a religious base, as the medical people of Tenochtitlan and its domain understood the properties of plants and herbs. They used steam-bath treatments to alleviate certain conditions and practiced bleeding techniques with success. The male or female doctor was called a *ticitl*. Most were revered as sorcerers as well, the practitioners of white or benevolent magic, capable of undoing the evil spells cast by their black counterparts.

The Aztec also understood contagion in sickness, using the term "airs of sickness" to explain such a phenomenon. They understood, too, the insects, unhealthy winds or cold spells of some regions that produced diseases. The night air, for example, was considered bad for some patients. Because Tlaloc, the god of rain, mists, lightning, thunder and storms, was involved in weather conditions that caused or promoted illness, this god was thought to be particularly potent in causing suffering. His assistants, the *Tlaloques*, dwarfs who aided him, were also held responsible for illness. Certain goddesses were believed to go about afflicting children with convulsions and a form of paralysis. As a result, Tlaloc was placated, so that skin diseases, gout, palsy and other ills could be eased.

While purification ceremonies and religious rites were enlisted as an aid to healing, Aztec physicians also employed products made from herbs and plants. They used lances to bleed patients, provided purges and dressed wounds. Illnesses of the chest, for example, were treated with maize porridge, which contained drugs known to alleviate conditions of that nature. These medical procedures were considerably advanced. The Aztec treated wounds efficiently and immobilized fractures and breaks. They had also amassed a diverse pharmacopoeia of herbs and plants known in the region for centuries, which were used as emetics, sedatives, fever reducers and diuretics. Spanish chroniclers were impressed by the resources utilized by the medical practitioners.

AZTEC PRIESTS AND RELIGION   Ceremonies and traditions and their practitioners who maintained the cosmological view of the Aztec world and served the ranking

Aztec tiger knight emblem

deities of the nation. The history of human sacrifice and cannibalism has created a biased view of the Aztec religion and its priests, but such practices must be understood in relation to other Mesoamerican cultures and to the cosmology of the Aztec themselves.

Throughout the Aztec world, three basic religious themes engendered religious ceremonies. The first was that of celestial creativity. This concept of divine paternalism, symbolized by flowers and the butterfly, involved to some extent the practice of monotheism. Nezahualcoyotl, the ruler of Texcoco, maintained a temple to the creator god, a shrine in which no blood could be shed. Another aspect of divine paternalism was the cult of Tezcatlipoca, the Smoking Mirror, who was prominent in the Toltec legends. This deity was the supernatural magician, the symbol of darkness and night, engendering the pessimistic fatalism evident in Aztec art.

The second basic theme in Aztec religion was that of Tlaloc and the *Tlaloques*, the god's assistants. The worship of these divine beings had evolved from the early fertility rites invoking rain and abundance in an Aztec agricultural setting. Tlaloc and his dwarfish aides were the keepers of the bounty of the Aztec, the insurers of rain and harvests. Alongside Tlaloc were Xipe Totec and Coatlicue, the other fertility symbols of agricultural bounty. Xipe Totec was spring, death, and rebirth, the activity of maize seeds in the fields. Coatlicue, the mother of the gods, was emblematic of all growing and prospering things.

The third Aztec religious theme involved the ending of worlds, a state-organized form of spiritual awareness that called for war and blood to sustain the sun. Human sacrifice was the essential element in the state religion, which some scholars say was encouraged by Tlacaelel, the adviser to some Aztec emperors. War meant fresh sacrificial victims for Tezcatlipoca and Tonatiuh, and the altars of these gods regularly ran with blood.

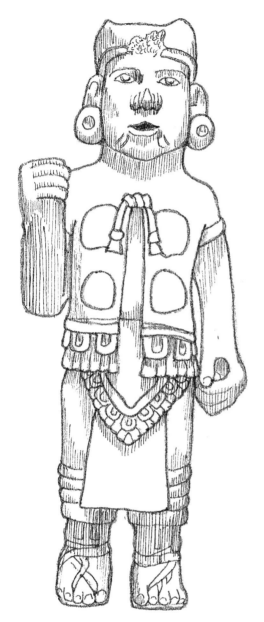

Aztec Tezcatlipoca statue

The need for these human sacrifices evolved from the Aztec view of worlds in flux, by the collapse of the various suns or worlds as decreed and the impending doom of the fifth sun, the one in which the Aztec found themselves. All rituals involved the general populace, and the spacious ceremonial sites provided room for many people. Individual involvement was also possible, as some festivals demanded certain purifications and preparations. Periods of fasting were associated with some feasts, called *nezahualiztli*. High-ranking priests fasted for a year, taking only one meal a day. They abstained from sex and bathing, appearing in bloodstained robes. The offerings provided in the temples were called *tlamanaliztli* and consisted of food, flowers, blood-splattered papers—the blood provided by self-immolation—as well as clothing and incense.

Musicians and singers accompanied the important ceremonies, and great processions wound through the ceremonial centers, with the priests representing the gods being

honored. Dancers performed on raised platforms, and tableaux depicted the deities. In some ceremonies animals were killed on the altars of the pyramids and birds were beheaded. Toward the end of the Aztec Empire, however, human sacrifice became more and more prevalent and its victims were generally prisoners of war. These victims, especially captured enemy warriors, were feted and honored before the rituals. On the altars their chests were cut open with obsidian knives and their hearts were ripped out. Women were sometimes decapitated. Some sacrificial victims were shot with arrows; others faced death in a gladiatorial bout of ritualistic battle. During the New Fire ceremonies, a fire was ignited in a victim's chest after his heart was removed. Others, especially children, were drowned or smashed to death. Strangulation was used in some rites, and on rare occasions victims were walled up and starved to death.

The hearts of victims were placed in sacred vessels, designed to provide a proper resting place for a "messenger to the sun," as they were called. Heads were placed on a skull rack, called a *tzompantli*, which was part of the architectural design of some sites. Some cannibalism was also practiced in conjunction with certain feasts or as part of the rituals of certain gods. Priests, and on some occasions the population at large, conducted bouts of autosacrifice. They put reed straws into holes cut into their own flesh in order to draw out blood, then splattered the blood on sacred papers or sprinkled it on altars.

Agricultural gods were important to the Aztec and given great state ceremonies, particularly at sowing and harvest times. Divination was practiced throughout the year and on feast days, and propitiatory solemnities were arranged for individuals as well as for the Aztec state as a whole.

The priests involved in such sacrificial rites held various titles and roles. Included were *tlamacazton*, the little or lesser-ranked priests; *tlamacazqui*, the more advanced priests; *tlenamacac*, the "fire-giver" priests taking part in calendric feasts; *quequetzalcoa*, the high priests or "feathered serpents," and *chalcuihquacuilli*, the slayers or priests of "the precious stone."

Such priests were trained for specific roles from an early age and were well versed in astrology and divination. There were many priests in Aztec society, with as many as 5,000 attached to the major temples of the various cities. Their rank depended on their designated duties, knowledge of the calendric arts, music, sacrifices, divination or the education of young nobles. Hieroglyphic painting and oral tradition were encouraged in the priestly schools, which were open to noble and common candidates alike.

Some priests resided on temple grounds but were allowed to marry. Others lived in the *calpullis*, the wards of the city; and they heard confessions and generally influenced the attitudes of those in their care. They also educated the young men in the *calmecac*, the noble school, where students learned about the gods, tended the various temple precincts and performed as singers or dancers. These priests taught writing, astronomy, history, government, calendrics and the natural sciences. All priestly duties were supported by income from landholdings and by portions of the tributes.

Unlike the older civilizations in Mesoamerica, the ceremonies conducted by these Aztec priests were held in public. The military orders were somewhat secretive about their rites, but the priests went about the city and conducted rituals for the general populace. The massive pyramidal temples were designed to make such rituals visible and accessible to all. Each month was dedicated to a particular deity, and traditional ceremonies were held on set dates. (See also AZTEC ASTRONOMY; AZTEC CALENDAR; AZTEC COSMOLOGY; AZTEC TEMPLES.)

AZTEC SOCIETY   The structure of Aztec groups revolving from the primary unit, the *calpulli*, from their earliest times. Tenochtitlan, Tlatelolco and neighboring cities had *calpullis*. There were originally seven; by the time the Spanish arrived in the region, there were as many as 15 or 20. Each *calpulli* had its own district or ward in the city, and each held land available only to its members. Directed by a *capulec*, who served as the custodian of land maps and general administration, the *calpulli* also had a council drawn from the participating families. All land was held in common, with each family alloted its portion according to need and rank. There were *capulli* nobles. Group projects, such as farming, irrigation and public works, were performed by the *capulli* members, and they were responsible for the functioning of schools and temples as well. The taxes raised by the *capulli* were paid in services, labor or produce. The *calpulli* was also responsible for a levy of soldiers for all military campaigns. In times of war they entered service as a single unit, led by their own commander, and they generally numbered from 200 to 400 men.

The *capulli* school, the *telpochcalli*, concentrated largely on the martial arts and military training and also served as a residence for the local unmarried men. Priests were available, and they conducted services in honor of the district patron and assisted in state ceremonies.

The *capulli* was based largely on lineage. The nobles from the high-ranking *capullis* were chosen for the upper echelons of government. Yet upward mobility within the *capulli* and the state was possible. Special achievements, including those in religious practices and especially in military affairs, governed individual advancement. Such honors endured only while the individual lived and were not hereditary.

The highest-ranking members of Aztec society were called the *pilpiltin* (sing. *pilli*) and were of the highest *calpulli*. From their ranks came the rulers of the city-states, and their rights and privileges were inherited by members of their families. Their descendants held the same rank at birth. Such male nobles attended a separate school, called the *calmecac*, and were trained to perform the duties of their caste. These nobles owned private land, worked by tenants, and they had access to temple and governmental inner circles. Military castes were separate, and esteemed warriors were granted their own honors and privileges.

The royal house of Tenochtitlan included Aztec and foreign high-ranking groups. The kings and emperors married heirs to other states for the purpose of alliance, which did not stigmatize their heirs. It was the custom of Post-Classic civilizations to bind themselves to older cultures in claiming descent, especially from the Toltec. When the Aztec were vassals of the Tepanec in their early stage, marriage into the Tepanec royal line was politically shrewd and enhanced the royal line.

The commoners who made up the bulk of Aztec society were divided into their own categories. The free men, called the *machualtin*, were members of the *capullis* of their districts and were basically well cared for by the state. They could enter temple service or become warriors in order to achieve social advancement. Commoners paid taxes, supported temples and schools and served in military campaigns conducted by the state. Free men held land in common, normally holdings that were passed on to the eldest son, who was responsible for the care of his brothers and nephews. If a free man died without an heir, his holdings reverted to the *calpulli*.

The next rank included the *mayeque* or the *tlalmaitl*, the tenant farmers, who worked the lands of the nobles. As part of the Aztec feudal system, they paid tribute to their noble lord rather than to the state, and lived on the more extensive holdings of the upper classes. They were not part of the *calpulli* system and were thus bound to the land and to service in the fields.

Slaves, called *tlatlacotin* (sing. *tlacotli*), were the lowest-ranked members of society. Most were taken in battle and divided into categories when brought to Tenochtitlan. The majority were killed as sacrificial victims, but some were given to the temples or to the noble castes. Slavery could also be the result of personal bankruptcy, in which an individual gambled away an inheritance or met with some other financial disaster. Some Aztec families sold their children to stave off financial setbacks. During the reign of Motecuhzoma (Moctezuma) I, when Tenochtitlan was struck by terrible famine, families sold their children to the eastern peoples for cobs of maize, with the proviso that after the famine they could be purchased back for an equal number of cobs. Some children sold into slavery were replaced in service by younger brothers or sisters after a certain length of time. Slaves could also buy their freedom, marry, amass wealth and own other slaves. All children born to slaves were granted the rights and privileges of free people.

AZTEC TEMPLES   The religious structures of the Aztec were the heart of each Aztec city. Most state ceremonies were conducted in these buildings, which were designed to project a sense of power and religious fervor, thereby enhancing the role of the emperors and their gods. In order to provide for the maintenance of these institutions, temples were given their own priests, residences, schools and public works, as well as landholdings. The temple was considered the household of the god, called *teocalli*, the "god's house." The priests assigned to this temple performed the prescribed rituals and maintenance tasks; it has been reported that one temple employed as many as 400 such priests during the course of a year. They conducted the affairs of the deity and the accompanying religious rites. Each rank in the priesthood had its own title, down to the novitiate who gathered wood or water for the services. Women held distinctive roles in some temples and were called *ciatlama-cazqui*. They usually remained celibate during their term of service.

Aztec temples were the stages upon which the cosmological and religious ideals of the nation were played out according to the seasonal or festival calendars. The divine

Aztec *pochteca* deity

mandate to provide nourishment for the gods in order to prevent disaster and the end of the world transformed some of these sites into grisly charnel houses. This was especially true during the later periods of the empire. The temple, however, was also the place of renewal for the nation, the altar of rebirth and hope. Not all Aztec ceremonies involved human sacrifice or death. The agricultural foundation of the nation's prosperity and the Aztec delight in flowers, colors and music provided, from the earliest times, ceremonies invoking regeneration and seasonal splendor. (See AZTEC COSMOLOGY; AZTEC GODS; AZTEC PRIESTS AND RELIGION.)

AZTEC TRADE   The system developed by the Aztec for the exchange of goods throughout Mesoamerica that employed a series of networks. Both the Aztec and the Maya, grasped the importance of gathering the natural resources of the various geographical regions available in order to create a vast system of exchange that could span the geographic and climatic diversities of Mesoamerica and still serve a secondary purpose. The Maya utilized extensive trade to further Maya culture. The Aztec performed the same task, extending their own imperial mastery. In some cases, in fact, the Aztec merchants, the *pochteca*, served as intelligence agents for the state.

Trade was always a vital aspect of the Mesoamerican communities, a system that the Aztec adopted in Tlatelolco and then in the capital, Tenochtitlan. Aztec trade followed the ancient patterns well established in the region, and was dependent on the products of the various ecological zones. Some of these regions were remote, wild lands that were daunting to the human beings who took them as trading routes. For this reason the Maya and the Totonac had developed a maritime trade that provided more direct routes to consumers in thriving centers of trade. Rafts and boats ventured onto rivers or sailed along coastal regions for generations.

Early traders plied the Gulf of Mexico and Pacific coastal waters to extend commercial enterprise. An established route was laid down between Veracruz on the Gulf of Mexico to the mouth of the San Juan River, which marks the boundaries between modern Nicaragua and Costa Rica. Some regions of Panama lured traders into the interior there as well. The southern gold fields of this part of Mesoamerica were essential to the Aztec economy.

Trade did not evolve in the future Aztec domain but in the coastal, and highland regions that sheltered the emerging cultures earlier. By the second millennium B.C., obsidian, for example, was being traded over long distances as a resource for hunting tools. As agriculture and ceramic industries developed, the new wares followed obsidian over the well-worn obsidian trade routes.

Aztec trade included a number of wares, and agricultural goods were highly prized. The original trade network was limited, confined to the Valley of Mexico, Morelos, Puebla, Toluca and the Mezquital. As the Aztec gained power, they began to explore the long-distance systems that had lain dormant since the fall of Teotihuacan and the collapse of the Toltec. Agricultural products traded in Aztec commerce included amaranth, beans, cacao, chia, chilies, cotton, fruits, maize, peppers and tomatoes.

As in the earlier historical eras, the networks of trade relied upon commercial centers which arose in the religious and social complexes of these cultures. Tlatelolco's market was well known throughout Mesoamerica and admired for its spaciousness and for the diversity of products which it handled on a day-to-day basis. Tlatelolco's dealers conducted their affairs in stalls or cubicles in the marketplace. On an average day these dealers offered gold, silver, semiprecious stones, feathers, slaves, cloth, cotton, thread, elaborate items of attire, some woven with decorations and embroidery, cacao, sandals, ropes, herbs, skins, animals and prepared foods. Other parts of the vast marketplace were set aside for the selling of pottery, salt, mats, dogs, tobacco, honey and medicinal products, each placed according to type.

The vastness of the markets demanded a set of regulations for all trading practices, and officers were constantly on the scene on market days to observe the method by which merchants weighed products, distributed goods, traded and served customers. Severe penalties were imposed on those who knowingly cheated buyers or other merchants. A special court was set up to settle disputes, charges and suspected cases of fraud. Punishments could be handed down by the magistrates of this court, and continued observation and regulation were enforced.

The Aztec merchants themselves, having acquired the knowledge of their predecessors as to routes, available products, hostile elements among the various regional populations, special industries and artistic centers, held a unique place in Aztec society. They had their own guild, with members from the noble and common ranks working together to accomplish the spread of trade and the continued protection of individual traders and their wares. Called *pochteca*, the traders held ranks and were responsible for carrying out certain obligations. The *pochteca tlaloque* was the trader chief for a given region. The *pochteca huehuetque* was a merchant elder, a veteran leader who served as a guide for the younger generation. The *pochteca* were part of a semielite class in Aztec society. They were usually directed by the nobles within the group, but they could attain political and social standing after years of loyal and valiant service. The *pochteca* was not only a merchant and a trader of goods, but in some cases an intelligence agent as well—then called an *oztomeca,* trained to spy or to intervene in the affairs of other nations.

The Aztec *pochteca* was carefully trained to maintain standardization of trade and to establish levels of workmanship in the regions they visited. At the same time, they served as pioneers or explorers to distant regions, visiting new markets, bearing gifts for the local aristocracy and asking permission to conduct trade in the region on behalf of the Aztec emperor. They did not venture out into the wilderness alone but provided their own large and well-armed caravans, which included military or paramilitary units. If attacked, such caravans could exact terrible losses among the enemy. One such caravan was put under siege near modern Acapulco and withstood repeated assaults. The ultimate result of attacks or interference with the Aztec trade system, however, was an invasion by Aztec or Triple Alliance armies. The empire responded quickly to such incidents, using them as provocations for domination of outlying areas.

As an *oztomeca,* or spy, the *pochteca* traveled in disguise, dressed as a simple traveler or as a survivor of some fallen city or state. Never admitting to being an Aztec, such a person set about learning the local language, customs, religious beliefs and military defenses or capabilities of a particular region. All information gathered on such reconnaissance trips was faithfully reported to the Aztec officials, who then decided on the potential of the region and the probability of its successful invasion. (See MESOAMERICAN TRADE.)

AZTEC TRIBUTE   The system by which vassal and conquered lands provided the products of their region, in finished form or as raw materials to the Aztec state. These tributes were divided at times between Texcoco and Tlacopan (Tacuba), members of the Triple Alliance. Such tributes often included raw materials that were processed in a manner that allowed them to be transported and sold elsewhere. The payment of tribute was a well-established Mesoamerican custom and was a reward of conquest. Such a system allowed the Aztec and their allies to amass the natural resources and the local wares of the various regions. Knowledge of local products based on *oztomeca* (spy) reports often determined the particular tribute exacted from a region, especially one rich in mineral deposits. Special ceramic wares, feather works, intricate carvings and metallic products were especially prized. Some tributes were stored against the threat of famine, distributed among acclaimed warriors, or used to finance further conquests or to enhance the emperor's way of life.

The tribute system began with the basic social unit, the *calpulli,* in Aztec lands. Such units were required to provide wood, water, agricultural goods, clothing or personal services to their leaders. The *calpulli,* as a whole, owed tribute to the state. Tribute also had to be paid to the temples. A portion of such tribute was distributed to the needy, at least during the reign of Motecuhzoma (Moctezuma) I when famine struck. The division among the Triple Alliance nations followed a pattern of two-fifths paid each to the Aztec and Texcoco, and one-fifth to Tlacopan (Tacuba).

A special administrative unit, the *calpixque,* handled tribute in each region, governing the region's natural resources and dictating the production industries of the local population.

AZTEC WARFARE   The system that became a consuming passion among the Aztec and the principal activity during much of their history. War was signified by the cry *atl-tlachinalli,* "water and fire, flood and flames," and in each generation warfare was a way of life for Aztec young men. Essentially a military society from its early beginnings, the Aztec originated from the Chichimec tradition and invaded the region of the Valley of Mexico. They had to defend themselves from attacks by their less-amicable neighbors and as vassals of the Tepanec had to participate as mercenary units in the military adventures of the Tepanec kings. They proved ferocious in battle, especially when such campaigns provided them with additional landholdings.

The Toltec, the models for the Aztec, had left a powerful military legacy, engaging in activities that had not been entirely popular in earlier eras. The Aztec thus inherited not only the traditions of war from the Toltec but the mystique of battle and the glamorization of the warrior life. War was not limited to the nobility, because Aztec survival depended on the valor of their troops and because the art of war was consistent with Aztec ideals of bravery and service. The empire was won by wars in a system that introduced spies, called *oztomeca,* who were actually traders involved in intelligence work. The Aztec expansion period was dominated by war and by the advance of intelligence agents into new territory. Garrisons and military units were employed to maintain peace in territories.

In the beginning, the Aztec marched to war as part of the *calpulli* system, with members of each *calpulli* following their own leaders and advancing their own assault techniques. When war became more vital to the nation, the *calpulli* levies were absorbed into major forces and controlled by the military structure of the empire. For both nobles and commoners, training for war began early. Most noblemen were dedicated to war at birth. They were given tiny shields and arrows in their first infant ceremonies and were under the patronage of Tezcatlipoca in the form of the warrior. Educated in schools according to their rank, young Aztec men wore a lock of hair called the *piochtli,* signifying youth. This lock remained on their heads until they took one prisoner of war. Upon taking four prisoners, a young Aztec was called a *tequiua,* which translates as "he who has a share of the tribute." Advancement in the military was then automatic. In time the man could aspire to the rank of *quauhchichimecatl,* a Chichimec eagle, or an *otomitl,* a warrior with elite corps and insignias and ranks. The *otomitl* were not chosen for government office, as they were believed to be too unrestrained for such responsible positions.

All of the Aztec military ranks shared a common belief concerning their ultimate destiny. They hoped to die in battle or as sacrificial victims on the altars of the gods. Such deaths assured them of eternal bliss. Some would become the companions of the sun and then hummingbirds. The Old Eagles, the *quauhuehuetque,* the veteran commanders of past victories, were always buried in keeping with the eternal happiness awaiting them. Military leaders could also enter the ranks of nobles, and their sons inherited the newly granted titles. Besides providing incentive for military leaders, this process widened the gene pool of the aristocracy.

The emperor was the *tlacatecuhtli*, the "Lord of Men." He commanded the Aztec forces, assisted by four other officials, one of whom maintained the nation's arsenals. The Aztec maintained garrisons in some conquered territories and devised a series of post houses for couriers so that daily intelligence reports could be made. The colors the couriers wore reflected the news they were carrying, either victory or defeat.

Military clothing consisted of quilted cotton "armor," heavily padded and adopted by the Spanish after their arrival. Some warriors wore wooden helmets, and all wore elaborate headdresses or emblems signifying their rank and distinctions. Those belonging to the Knights of the Eagle or the Jaguar wore clothing with the feathers of the bird or painted jaguar-skin designs. Warriors also wore mantles and shields of feathers and hides, and carried arrows, spears, javelins and the *atlatl*, the spear-thrower.

The city of Tenochtitlan could field as many as 8,000 warriors for campaigns, divided into units of 300 to 400. The warriors sought to take live prisoners, and strict regulations maintained standards of conduct, nonadherence to which was punishable by death. Two regulations were never to attack until so ordered and never to plunder another warrior's booty or prisoners. Campaign veterans were given medical care and housed in special hospitals designed for their comfort.

Besides actual campaigns in the field, Aztec warriors had other state duties. They participated in festivals honoring the nation's martial gods. Wearing special clothing with marks of rank and honors received, these warriors attended the festivals and contributed to the celebrations. The higher-ranking warriors lived in fashionable homes and palaces and served as administrators of entire territories or as the emperor's councilors. Councils of war preceded each major military campaign, as the Aztec did not rush into battle. Usually they alerted the enemy as to their intent and requested submission and tribute. If the enemy persisted in refusal, the Aztec and their allies requisitioned the necessary equipment and gave the order to fight.

The Flower Wars of the Aztec and the Triple Alliance were named because of the symbol for bloodied sacrifice, using the red color of blood evident in many local blossoms. Designed to support conquest of other regions, these Flower Wars, called *xochiyaoyotl*, were also fought to provide the temples of the land with sacrificial victims. Dating to around A.D. 1450, although such types of campaigns had been conducted before, the Flower Wars allowed the Triple Alliance to battle enemies with a dual purpose. The Flower Wars and the entire Aztec military system were believed to be protected by the deity Tezcatlipoca, the Smoking Mirror, a ferocious Toltec god of war. Tepeolotl, an Aztec god, called the Heart of the Mountains, also cared for the Aztec military forces.

AZTLAN A site thought to have been surrounded by lagoon waters and purportedly the home of the Aztec (Mexica) until around A.D. 1111. Some scholars equate Aztlan

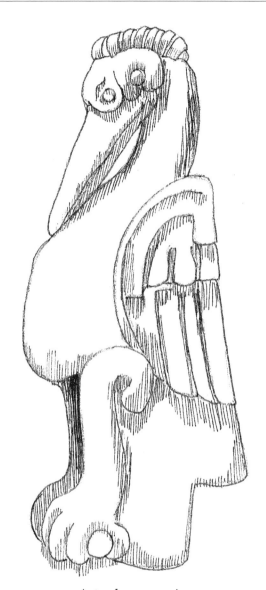

Aztec heron carving

with Cuitlahuac (modern Tlahuac), called the White Island. Others point to Mexcaltitlan, a lagoon on the coast of the present-day region of Nayarit. Another view is that Aztlan is Culhuacan, now San Isidro Culiacan, more than 150 miles northwest of modern Mexico City, the site of the Aztec capital, Tenochtitlan. It is also possible that Aztlan exists only in legend.

During his reign, Motecuhzoma I began a quest to find the original Aztlan. An expedition of 60 priests and aides set out for the region beyond Tula. They claimed that there they met a divine being who transformed them into birds and winged creatures that could fly to Aztlan. A group of Nahuatl-speaking people welcomed them there. On their adventures, the priests met other magical beings and had dangerous encounters. In their accounts, the priests claimed that they met the divine mother of Huitzilopoctli, the Aztec deity, who predicted eventual doom for Tenochtitlan. The expedition returned to the capital and made its report to the emperor in person.

B

BABY FORMS Large carved boulders found in Maya ceremonial complexes along the Pacific coast as far south as El Salvador. The city of Kaminaljuyu boasts several examples of this particular monument. Tall carved forms with heavyset limbs, baby faces and no apparent gender, they lack detailed planes and were seldom carved at the back. The volcanic basalt stone of the region was the resource for these forms. Another baby form was associated with the Maya jaguar cult. This indicates a lasting Olmec influence, reminiscent of the Olmec were-jaguars.

BACAB A son of the Maya god Itzamna or a manifestation of that deity, usually grouped in fours. They were the Atlantean supporters of the 13 levels of the Maya heavens. The *Bacabes* (or *Bacabs*) took on their role when the *Oxlahuntiku* (the 13 Lords of the Day, the patrons of the heavenly levels) were defeated by the *Bolontiku* (the Nine Lords of the Night), who ruled Xibalba, the Maya underworld. The *Bacabes* also served as the cardinal points of the earth; in this capacity they were associated with the *Acantun,* the spirits of the cardinal points. The *Ritual of the Bacabes,* a surviving Maya codex, provided information about their role. When functioning as the cardinal points, the *Bacabes* consisted of Hobnil, god of the east, whose color was red; Zac Cimi, god of the west, whose color was black; Can Tzional, god of the north, whose color was white; and Hozanek, god of the south, whose color was yellow. In some Maya regions, the *Bacabes* also served as the patrons of bees and apiaries.

BACALAR LAKE A natural water reserve in the Yucatan, near the Caribbean Sea, associated with Maya trade routes.

BAJAS Fields built up by layers of earth from the normally flat, level ground by Maya agriculturalists. The Maya used *bajas* in their garden plots and orchards to provide plants with protection and achieve greater harvests.

BAJIO PHASE A cultural development in the Olmec territory on the gulf coast, dating to c. 1350/1250 B.C. The sites associated with the Bajio Phase reflect Olmec influence as well as the advancing techniques of other regions and groups. The Olmec site of San Lorenzo incorporated the Bajio Phase in its own ceramic development. During this period the inhabitants erected sand platforms for religious settings, a forerunner of those used during the Olmec For-

mative Period (2000 B.C.–A.D. 250/290). (See SAN LORENZO for details of this phase.)

BAJIO PLATEAU A site in the Olmec territory on the gulf coast. Settlements there date to the Paleo-Indian Period (11,000 B.C.–7000 B.C.).

BAKHALAL A Maya site on the eastern coast of the Yucatan Peninsula, a Xiu territory during the Late Post-Classic Period (A.D. 1200/1250–1521). Bakhalal was deserted by the Xiu, who went to Chichen Itza and then to Chakanputun on the coast of Campeche. The full extent of this site is unknown.

BALAMKU Maya site in southeastern Campeche, dating to the Late Classic Period (A.D. 600–900). Balamku was called the Jaguar Temple and was dominated by a pyramidal shrine 130 feet long and almost 50 feet high. The facade of this temple had bas-reliefs in painted stucco. The jaguar form was depicted with circle designs and a border. Frontal masks were placed on either side, with serpent heads completing the design. A seated jaguar figure from Balamku is an unusual one.

BALANKANCHE A Maya cave in the central part of the Yucatan Peninsula, called the Throne of the Jaguar Priest or the Hidden Treasure of the Jaguar. This underground cavern, situated four miles east of the city of Chichen Itza, had a natural throne formation and a vast domed chamber. Colored clay incense burners, carved stone cylinders depicting dancers, warriors and women, and a considerable amount of pottery were discovered on the site and have been left in situ. Three chambers behind the main hall contained other artifacts. The cave is believed to have served as a ceremonial site for the cult of Maya god Chac, a rain deity similar to Tlaloc of other cultures. Many artifacts were Toltec in origin, reflecting that group's dominance in the area after the collapse of the Maya domain.

BALL GAMES Forms of athletic competition with great religious significance, played by most Mesoamerican cultures. Ball courts of various kinds were constructed in cities and at ceremonial sites throughout the Mesoamerican region to provide stages for the games, which were called *tlachtili* by the Aztec and *pok-ta-pok* by the Maya. In Monte Alban, an independent city-state, the ball games were called *lachi.* Every ball game was linked to cosmological tradition.

The Maya maintained a tradition that the Hero Twins played a ritual game for their lives. The Twins defeated the evil team from Xibalba, the Maya underworld, and became the sun and the moon. In later eras, the ball game symbolized a cosmic duel between good and evil deities.

Players of the games used rubber balls, some weighing as much as seven pounds. This made it necessary to wear protective covering. Players were also outfitted with yokes, U-shaped belts with carved designs. Other padded protections included the *palma*, a ball-throwing aid adorned with images of human heads and other symbols. Players could not use their hands during the games. The ball, bounced from the knee, elbow or hip, was propelled through stone rings (*mercadores*), fastened to the sides of courts, which were painted or represented by stone disks. In some games the *hacha*, carved stone heads, had a specific role.

Courts used for the ball game varied in size. Some were rectangular, with raised sides and spectator areas. It is believed that the games originated in Veracruz, the source of rubber for Mesoamericans. (See ball games in individual cultures for details.)

BALSAS RIVER The second-longest river system in Mesoamerica, originating in Tlaxcala and Puebla and fed by many tributaries. This river surged through a hilly terrain to form the Pacific coastal delta. The Balsas drained the region at Cholula, accounting for the name of the site, the Place Where the Waters Spring. In Guerrero, where the river formed a natural port, the Balsas was called the Mezcala. The tributaries of the Balsas include the Atoyac, Poblano, Nexapa, Amacuzac, Zitacuaro and the Tepalcatepec. (See BALSAS-TEPALCATEPEC DEPRESSION.)

BALSAS-TEPALCATEPEC DEPRESSION The largest natural basin in southern Mexico, separating the Mexican Plateau from the Oaxacan and Guererro highlands. The Tepalcatepec River was a tributary of the mighty Balsas River, and in southern Michoacan formed another natural basin, called the Apatzingan Plain.

BARRA See ALTAMIRA-BARRA CULTURE.

BARRA DE NAVIDAD PHASE A cultural development of the Colima region, dating to the Formative Period (2000 B.C.–c. 250/290 A.D.) on the coast of western Mexico. Colima art is treasured for its highly developed skill and sensitivity. Colima wares include large hollow figurines, with dog forms especially popular.

BARRANCA A deep, steep-sided gorge, usually caused by rivers, especially those moving headward from mountain slopes. *Barrancas* are the result of centuries of hydroerosion.

BASIN OF MEXICO See MEXICO, VALLEY OF.

BAT A Zapotec form worshipped as a deity, representing fertility and depicted in ceramic figurines discovered in Zapotec ruins. Bat forms were also used as *accompañantes*, architectural decorations, in Zapotec buildings. The bat appears to be a truly ancient Zapotec god, whose name has

Zapotec bat god

been lost. Other cultures probably had forms of bat deities, as the creature flourished throughout Mesoamerica.

BAT CAVE A site associated with the Flacco Phase of the Tamaulipas Sequence on the gulf coast. An early form of maize was discovered in Bat Cave. Habitations there date to 2200 to 1800 B.C.

BEAN A plant (*Phaseolus vulgaris*) that served as a staple of Mesoamericans during the earliest times, joined in later eras by other varieties. The protein content of beans complements those found in maize, hence enhancing the nutritional benefits of both foods. Beans are believed to have been one of the first plants domesticated in the region.

BECAN A southeastern Guatemalan Maya site, called the Ditch Filled with Water, a reference to the fact that Becan was encircled by a wide moat, roughly 40 feet deep. This moat spans the narrow causeway that was held by a small number of warriors against enemies when the city was originally constructed. The moat is kidney-shaped and encloses 46 acres of the site. It was crossed by seven causeways. Becan dates to the Middle Formative Period (900–300 B.C.) and was built defensively on a limestone rise that towers at least 30 feet above the surrounding area. The city's various edifices date mostly to A.D. 150–250, and they demonstrate a definite Quintana Roo influence, with some

Rio Bec styles evident. Becan may have been within the Teotihuacan sphere when that vast city was in power, as a two-piece statuette, 10 solid figures and a cylindrical tripod vessel of Teotihuacan style have been found there.

Becan, surrounded by the moat that was dug more than a mile long to enclose 46 acres, has a plaza in the southeastern section. This plaza opens onto two tiered towers that have rounded corners. The undecorated towers were at one time linked by a solid piece of masonry. To the north of the plaza is a monumental stairway, leading to a structure with sculpted reliefs. A central plaza opens onto another twin-towered building with a stairway. On the top is a structure with several chambers. To the west of the central plaza is an edifice some 100 feet high. Beyond that is a mound with a stairway and another chambered shrine, which was covered with sculptured reliefs, painted red. Other ruins were also found on the site. No inscribed stelae have been found in Becan, which appears to have been occupied from c. 550 B.C. until around A.D. 1400.

BELIZE   A nation formerly called British Honduras, on the coast of the Yucatan on the Gulf of Honduras. A Maya stronghold, the name is from the Maya, meaning "muddy waters." A mountainous region with granite deposits, Belize has tropical jungles and swamps. The Maya and Cockscomb Mountain chains dominate, and Victoria Peak rises 3,681 feet there. The Belize River drains the northern lowlands with the Nuevo and Hondo rivers. The southern region of Belize is composed of coastal plains and highlands. Just off the coast is the second-largest barrier reef in the world. The climate of Belize is subtropical, with rains from June to November. Belize contains a vast variety of wood species and abundant animal life, including jaguars, pumas, tapirs and crocodiles.

Belize was occupied early on with coastal settlements that used marine products, cacao and wild grains, as many of the interior plains are not fertile or cultivatable. The sites conform to the agricultural patterns and to soil distribution. The site called Cuello dates to around 2500 B.C., with stratification evident, in some places as deep as 10 feet. The Swasey Culture originated there. Trade items found in Cuello indicate that Belize was part of the extensive Maya trade system. Altun Ha, another ceremonial center, was occupied as early as 100 B.C. in Belize. Cerros, yet another Maya site, dates to around A.D. 100, and later settlements date to around A.D. 200. There is evidence that, in time, the non-Maya inhabitants of the Belize region were incorporated into the Maya realm. Belize sites are under separate entries and include: ALTUN HA; BLACKMAN EDDY, CAYO; BLUE CREEK; CAHAL PECH; CARACOL; CERROS; CHAN CHICH; CHAU HIIX; CUELLO; EL PILAR; LAMANAI; LA MILPA; LUBAANTUN; NIM LI PUNIT; NOHMUL; RICHMOND HILL; SANTA RITA; TZIMIN KAX; UXBENKA; XUNANTUNICH.

BELIZE RIVER   A natural waterway in Belize, serving the local Maya centers.

BERNAL DE HORCASITAS   A needlelike peak situated in the gulf coastal lowlands northwest of Tampico.

BILBAO   A site discovered on the Guatemala coast near Santa Luisa Cotzumalhuapa, which is near El Baul (Finca El Baul). Bilbao was possibly a colony of the great city of Teotihuacan at one time. Stone sculptures discovered there correspond to the Late Formative (300 B.C.–c. A.D. 250/290) and Early Classic (c. A.D. 1/250–600) periods. The entire region is noted for exquisitely carved monuments.

BIRD JAGUAR   An eighth-century ruler of the Maya city of Yaxchilan, whose birth date is recorded as A.D. 709 in Maya glyphs on lintel carvings. He ruled the city from A.D. 752 until his death. Bird Jaguar is celebrated for capturing a rival Maya ruler, Jeweled Skull, and is reported to have attended the funeral of a noblewoman in the company of other Maya aristocrats. He succeeded Shield Jaguar in Yaxchilan.

BLACKMAN EDDY, CAYO   A Maya site in Belize, near the capital, occupied from around 900 B.C. to A.D. 1000. Now under extensive study, this site is composed of two plaza complexes, temple mounds and a ball court. One decorated temple dates to c. 300 B.C.–A.D. 250, and a stela recovered from there is from the same era. The original Maya name is not known.

BLANCO RIVER   A natural waterway on the gulf coast of Mexico, draining the region. Cerro de las Mesas was established near the Blanco.

BLUE CREEK   A Maya ceremonial site located at Orange Walk near Belize City. Occupied from 300 B.C. to A.D. 900, it became well known when over 900 pieces of jade were recovered there. A tomb has been found on the site, as well as a building with a pair of finely carved stucco masks. Excavations are currently under way in Blue Creek.

BOLANOS RIVER   A natural waterway in southern Zacatecas and in Jalisco on the Mesoamerican northern frontier. With the Juchipila River, the Bolanos joined the Lerma-Santiago River system in the Sierra Occidental region.

BOLANOS-JUCHIPILA   An archaeological zone of southern Zacatecas and Jalisco, which formed the northern Mesoamerican frontier at the time of the Spanish conquest, A.D. 1521. The Bolanos and Juchipila rivers are part of the Lerma-Santiago River system, joining the main waterway in the Sierra Madre Occidental region. Sites dating to the Paleo-Indian Period (11,000–7000 B.C.) have been uncovered in this zone. The ceramic wares found include white on red, red on buff, painted cloisonné, negative painted, brown, and red and white. Sites in this region include Rio Bolanos Barranca, Totoate, Banco de las Casas, Teul and Las Ventanas.

BOLOM DZ'ACAB   The God K of the Maya codices, called the Long-Nosed God, the Serpent Food deity. He was patron of the lists of aristocratic lineage and ancestry among the Maya elite, holding information considered vital to the standing of each individual and especially important for the arranging of marriages. The god's name means "Nine Generations," revealing how far back the Maya went in order to trace the lineage of each member of the noble clans. Bolom Dz'acab was also called the God of the Kan and was invoked in the rituals celebrating the cardinal points of the earth.

BOLONTIKU The Maya Nine Lords of the Night, the rulers of Xibalba, the Maya underworld, who defeated the *Oxlahuntiku,* the 13 Lords of the Day, in a cosmic battle. The *Bolontiku* glyphs were included in the Maya Long Count inscriptions. Their numbers—nine—correspond to the levels of Xibalba, called Mitnal in the Yucatan region.

BONAMPAK One of the most distinctive of the Maya sites, located in Chiapas near the Guatemalan border. The name, meaning "Painted Walls," was bestowed upon the site in modern times because of the murals discovered there. The original Maya designation of the city is unknown. Bonampak is located deep in the jungle on the Usumacinta River in a region still inhabited by the Lacandon Maya. Small, with temples built on terraced hillsides, the city was designed with a main plaza. Bonampak was a vassal city of Yaxchilan, and some of the murals that have made the site famous have to do with its political situation. A causeway built in Bonampak is believed to have led toward Yaxchilan.

A stela discovered in the city is called the Warrior. The stela dates to around A.D. 780, stands 16 feet tall and depicts a man with a large mask at his feet. Two other stelae depict

Bonampak lintel scene

women in garments, flanking men. The images of the god Tlaloc and the Mexican year sign suggest Mexican influence or occupation. A bound captive is on one of the stelae, all of which were originally situated on the stairs of a mound, leading to an upper terrace. Altars with carved panels were part of the overall design. The Temple of the Paintings has three chambers, each with its own entrance. These rooms are not connected interiorly. The doorways were designed with niches and were part of a frieze. A carved and painted stone lintel depicting warriors and prisoners was incorporated into the entrance design. The walls of the temple are now world-famous because of their murals, which depict a gathering or procession of Bonampak's elite. One scene portrays musicians playing for a festival, each figure bearing a separate instrument in a display of pomp and ritual. The musicians are elaborately attired and are shown moving toward the site of the celebrations. Another mural depicts a battle in progress. One illustrious leader of Bonampak was the Maya lord Chaanmuan.

BOOK OF DREAMS A spiritual work described in the Teotihuacan legends as the product of the "Lords of Wisdom," the *Tlamatinime,* the great sages of that city. In some traditions these wise ones abandoned Teotihuacan in order to discover a more enlightened place. In another tradition the Lords of Wisdom remained in the city to complete the *Book of Dreams* when everyone else had abandoned the site. While the work is not described in records, the legends concerning the document give evidence of Teotihuacan's collapse.

BORGIA GROUP A set of codices named after the *Codex Borgia,* now in the Bibliothèque Nationale in Paris. (See CODICES.)

BREADFRUIT A tree that provides highly nutritious nuts that can be stored for long periods. Breadfruit trees are visible around many Maya ruins.

BUNDLES A unique Mesoamerican religious symbol found among many cultures of the region. The Aztec (Mexica) designated priests as bundle-bearers during their historic journey from Aztlan to Tenochtitlan. These bundles were dedicated to or contained, according to tradition, the remains of deities, such as Huitzilopochtli. The Maya bundle tradition concerns the deities associated with the worlds of the Maya cosmological myths, a tradition practiced in Teotihuacan. Masked deity bundles are often shown in the hands of Maya rulers. The Mixtec and other cultures observed the same tradition.

In the funerary rituals of the various Mesoamerican groups, bundles were part of the mortuary traditions. Rulers in some cultures were not buried but kept in bundles with masks. In some instances the remains were cremated. The heads of warriors slain in battle were also carried in sacred bundles.

BUTTERFLY A symbol used in Teotihuacan and in other cities and temples of Mesoamerica, depicted with wings and often other accurately portrayed human limbs. In some instances, as among the Maya and Zapotec, the butterfly shown in the mouth of a jaguar symbolized war or suffering. In the Valley of Mexico, the butterfly was the soul of a dead warrior. It might also represent fire or war.

BUTTERFLY CLUSTER   A religious theme associated with the god Quetzalcoatl and reflected in the decorations and style of the deity's shrine in the city of Teotihuacan. Quetzalcoatl, the popular Mesoamerican god, promised eter-nal bliss, and the butterfly was an emblem of his cult. In Teotihuacan women who died in childbirth (an event of religious significance in most Mesoamerican cultures) were believed to be destined for Quetzalcoatl's paradise.

BUTZ CHAN   The eleventh ruler of the city of Copan. This Maya noble died in A.D. 628, and his death was com-memorated by a monument in his city.

C

CABO ROJO A major lagoon in the gulf coastal lowlands in Mexico, important to local populations during the Paleo-Indian Period (11,000–7000 B.C.), supporting later historical developments as well. The Pacific coastal regions typically featured lagoons, barrier beaches, salt formations, estuaries and marshlands, including the Madre and Tamiahua lagoons.

CABULCO A basin in the Chiapas region, located north of the Chuaca Mountains, in the Sierra de Omoa of Guatemala. With the Rabinal, Chicaj and Salama basins, Cabulco was important to emerging cultural groups there and probably was a source of jade in later historical periods.

CACAMA A nephew of the Texcoco ruler Nezahualpilli, chosen by the Aztec ruler Motecuhzoma II to succeed Nezahualpilli to the throne. Commencing his reign in A.D. 1515, Cacama confronted the campaigns of the Spanish in the region.

CACAO *(Theobroma cacao)* A widespread Mesoamerican crop, used by many groups as currency for the integrated trade systems in historical times and prized as chocolate. Cacao beans were grown in the rich soils of the coastal region and the Isthmus of Tehuantepec as well as on the Guatemalan Pacific plain. Cotzumalhuapa was a vital source. Cacao trees produce pods containing seeds or beans. It is believed that the Maya produced the first cacao in the form of the tree that (uncultivated at first) grows in the lowland Maya domain.

Cacao served a monetary function because unpicked beans rotted and became food for rodents. This vulnerability forced circulation of the beans and tended to discourage hoarding. In time, however, the beans were counterfeited. The insides were removed and replaced with wax or dirt to add weight. Avocado rinds inserted inside the beans also added weight and bulk. Some groups, especially aristocratic castes, drank cacao in liquid form.

CACAXTLA A city in Puebla, in the Tlaxcala region, northeast of Cholula, associated with the Olmeca-Xicallanca people but displaying Maya influences. The Olmeca-Xicallanca were not true Olmec but resided there during the Classic Period (c. A.D. 1/250–900). In one structure that was designed with patios and plazas, extraordinary murals have been discovered. The architectural style is similar to that of Xochicalco and Tula. The paintings are Maya polychrome murals with Peten symbols, similar to those found in Seibal.

It is believed that the Olmeca-Xicallanca were related to the Peten Maya, hence the influence evident there. Unfired clay masks were also uncovered in Cacaxtla, shaped as figures or as monster masks. One, a jaguar man, holds a Maya ceremonial bar and is called Nine Wind, the Maya calendric title of the god Quetzalcoatl. Another figure wears an eagle costume and carries a small conch shell from which a deity is seen emerging. Wars between Realistic-looking jaguars and eagles are also depicted in the Cacaxtla murals, possibly recording events of historical conflict between rival warrior groups. (See EAGLE; JAGUAR.)

Maya style painting from Cacaxtla

CAHAL PICH   A maya site in Belize, called the Place of the Ticks. It is extensive, with 34 separate structures within a three-acre area. Exploration of Cahal Pich is not documented.

CAKCHIQUEL MAYA   See MAYA GROUPS, CAKCHIQUEL.

CALAKMUL   A vast Maya center in southern Campeche, Mexico, called the Place of the Two Mounds. Some of the ruins in Calakmul date to around A.D. 500, a period of intense trade and expansion in the Maya domain. A pyramidal mound discovered on the site contains a vault in which 2,000 pieces of jade were recovered. A jade mosaic mask was also found there. The central plaza of Calakmul had a stela depicting a royal couple, dating to A.D. 623. Another Calakmul pyramid contains a dozen separate chambers. Also on the site are the remains of a rather vast system of canals that provided water for the entire urban district. Calakmul is over 25 square miles in diameter and was once a powerful Maya city on the eastern fringe of the lowlands region, near the stronghold of Tikal. The site has over 6,500 structures and 100 stelae, 70 of which are inscribed. An estimated population of 60,000 Maya lived in the city in the period of its dominance.

CALENDAR   The chronological computations unique to Mesoamerica and comparable to ancient systems in other parts of the world. These calendars, evolving over the centuries in the region and produced by various civilizations, were used for both religious and secular purposes, providing a basis for the cosmological rituals and setting the annual schedules for agricultural activities. The Mesoamericans computed time, cycles and the movement of celestial bodies. A Mesoamerican tradition states that the Maya, Zapotec and other cultures met in Xochicalco in A.D. 650 to synchronize the calendars in use. A Xochicalco panel depicts this gathering. Several types of calendars remained in use afterward, reaching a high degree of sophistication in the Classic Period (c. A.D. 1/250–900) under the auspices of the Lowland Maya. When the Toltec and the Aztec came to power and ruled their vast domains, calendars were adapted and employed extensively in a complex religious system. Four calendars were in use in Mesoamerica.

Ritual Calendar.   Called *tzolkin* by the Maya and *tonalpohualli* by the Aztec. This computation system was also the Divinatory Calendar or the Name-Day Calendar. Twenty gods were assigned for the days, united to a system of numbers from one to 13. The Maya divided the calendar into four segments of 65 days each or five segments of 52 days each. These were again divided into a series of irregular intervals, in Maya records accompanied by hieroglyphs and illustrations. The *tonalpohualli* of the Aztec (Mexica) was also divided and the designated segments were assigned cardinal points and colors. Divided into five separate segments, the fifth part becomes the center of the world, according to Aztec tradition. They added 13-day periods, defined by day numerals. Twenty such periods were placed under the patronage of a particular deity. Such patronage was listed in the *tonalmatl*, the *Book of Days*. Twenty gods

were used; 13 as Day Lords and nine Gods of the Night. This calendar was in the care of the *tonalpouhque*, the divinatory priests.

Almanac or Solar Calendar.   A 365-day calendar divided into 18 named months of 20 days each. Five epagomenal days, called *vazeh* (or *uayeh*) by the Maya and *nemontemi* by the Aztec, were viewed as unlucky. The year and the number of months were divisible by five. Four names, accompanied by 13 numbers, began the year and were called the Year Bearers, associated with the cardinal points of the earth. The years in the Maya lands were not always synchronized; their start was celebrated at different times in the various regions. The Aztec adopted this calendar almost entirely. They also used 52-year cycles of the Calendar Round that involved the lighting of the New Fire.

The Calendar Round.   A Maya system of calendrics that included the Almanac, also called the Vague Year, and the 52-year cycle, adopted by the Aztec. This calendar involved "seating" the month to follow, designated by a particular sign used to reflect the character of the month. Also, a day was designated by its name, number and the name of the current month, plus the number of days that had elapsed. A date in the Calendar Round thus occurs once every 52 years. The Aztec called the system the Year Bundle *(Xihuitl)*.

The Long Count.   Once believed to be Maya in origin and now associated with the Olmec, this computation system started dating at 4 Ahau 8 Cumku. This date has been correlated with 13 August 3114 B.C., according to the Gregorian Calendar. A Long Count was discovered in Tres Zapotes, which dates to around 1000 B.C. The last Maya Long Count date was recorded in Tonina, in the central Chiapas region, dating to A.D. 900. The Long Count fell out of favor in the Classic Period and was replaced by the Short Count, a cycle of 13 katuns (7,200 days or 256 1¼ years. A stela bearing the Long Count was also found in El Baul (Finca El Baul), a Formative Period site on the Pacific Coast. According to the Long Count cycles, 20 kins equal 1 uinal, or 20 days; 18 unials equal 1 tun, or 365 days; 20 tuns equal 1 katun, or 7,200 days; and 20 katuns equal 1 baktun, or 144,000 days.

CALERA PHASE   A cultural development of the Chalchihuite people in the Sierra Madre Occidental region in northern Mexico. Dating to the Early Post-Classic Period, the Calera Phase was prominent in the region from A.D. 1150 to 1350 and was influenced by the Toltec, who were dominant at the time. (See CHALCHIHUITE.)

CALICHEL PHASE   A cultural development of the Chalchihuite people of northern Mexico in the Sierra Madre Occidental region during the Classic Period (c. A.D. 1/250–900). This Calera Phase dates to around A.D. 500–650.

CALIXTLAHUACA   A Matlatzinca site in the Valley of Toluca, southwest of modern Mexico City, and dating to the Early Post-Classic Period (A.D. 900–1250). Called the Place Where There Are Houses on the Plain, this city evinces definite Toltec influences, as well as Aztec (Mexica) styles. Calixtlahuaca occupied a vulnerable position between the

Aztec Empire being formed in the Valley of Mexico and the Tarascan domain in the west. The city, on the Tejalpa River, had terraced hills, fortifications and granaries placed in protected areas to withstand a siege. The hill terraces had stone retaining walls, ramps and staircases.

Among the major monuments of the site, the Temple of Quetzalcoatl stands on a fortified hill. Another temple, honoring the god Ehecatl, has four consecutive layers of structures evident. Rounded to depict the sweeping powers of Ehecatl—a form of Quetzalcoatl as the wind—the temple was damaged by the regional earthquake of 1475. A finely wrought statue of Ehecatl was recovered from this shrine.

The Aztec conquered Calixtlahuaca in the reign of Axayacatl (A.D. 1469–1481). An estimated 11,000 prisoners were taken from the city to Tenochtitlan, the Aztec capital, for sacrifice in temple rituals there. Aztec families were then moved into the region to serve as a buffer against the Tarascan. An Aztec military garrison was set up at the site. The people of the city rebelled after Axayacatl's death, and Emperor Tizoc marched into the region to quell riots. Motechuzoma II returned with military forces again in A.D. 1510.

During their occupation of Calixtlahuaca, the Aztec added major temples to the city's ceremonial complex. Seventeen mounds are now visible, including the Temple of Tlaloc, the Aztec rain deity, which has an altar of skulls in a cruciform design, with rows of stone skulls. Matlatzinca pottery was also recovered from the site, mostly geometric in design, including open bowls with tripod legs.

CALLI   The Aztec word for house, used as a day sign for the *tonalpohualli*, the calendric system. (See CALENDAR.)

CALMECAC (1)   An architectural complex used in Mesoamerica that incorporated pyramidal platforms for ceremonial purposes. (See CALIXTLAHUACA.)

CALMECAC (2)   A school for young Aztec (Mexica) noblemen, designed to train them for the duties befitting their rank and social caste.

CALPULLI (1)   A social designation among the Aztec for a kinship group inhabiting the urban and rural districts defined by the same term.

CALPULLI (2)   The urban districts of the Aztec capital, Tenochtitlan, the basic units of residence within the city, also called *chinacalli*. The Aztec groups founded their own districts, with seven recorded at the founding of Tenochtitlan and 20 by the time the Spanish arrived on the scene. Each *calpulli* had its own temple, ceremonial center, school for young men and a government building called the *ateocalli*. Individual residences in the *calpulli* were laid out in precise, geometric designs, normally single-storied and rectangular, with flat roofs. Windowless, these residences were nevertheless airy because of the attached patios.

CALPULLI (3)   A division of land ownership among the Aztec, partially worked in common by members of a particular group. Most groups held *capulli* lands in a single or adjoining district. Temple tributes came from the *calpulli*

fields. Other plots were divided among the families of the group, passing from father to son and reverting to the group if a family line ended. Any assigned plots not worked for two years were also reclaimed by the group. The *calpulli* acreages were not privately owned by individuals within the group, but all crops grown on such plots were privately claimed.

CAMAZOTZ   A Maya deity, depicted as a vampire bat, having large teeth and claws and a flint-knife-shaped nose. The god could sever the heads of its human victims. Camazotz plays a role in the adventures of the HERO TWINS in Xibalba, the Maya underworld, as recorded in the *Popol Vuh*.

CAMPECHE   A region in the northern part of the Yucatan Peninsula, a rather arid area with swampy plains in the south. The Peten Maya controlled the region, calling it Ah-Kin-Pech, using Xicallanca and other centers in their vast trading system. A mural discovered in Cacaxtla, a Maya site in Puebla, gives evidence of the Olmeca-Xicallanca influences there. This site on the Tlaxcala border is believed to depict a battle that took place in Campeche. The Maya city of Chicanna was in the southern part of the region and more than 100 other cities were established there. The Chenes, Peten and Rio Bec Maya art forms were in use here. (See CACAXTLA; CHENES; and OLMECA-XICALLANCA.)

CANADA   A flat-topped mesa that dominated the terraced hills of the Mesa Central and elsewhere.

CANDELARIA RIVER   A vast waterway in the gulf coastal lowlands of Mesoamerica, a region of low mountains, hills and flood and delta plains. The Candelaria River is one of five major systems in the region, also serving Acalan, in the Chontal Maya domain. (See MAYA GROUPS, CHONTAL.)

CANITAS   The oldest type of small figurines found in Mesoamerica. Associated with the Ticoman Phase and the Pre-Olmec Period, the figurines were discovered in the city of Cuicuilco, which flourished from 900 B.C. to c. A.D. 300/400. The statues depicted nude females with long hair. The eyes of the figures were holes, surrounded by circles or tiny piercings.

CANTERA PHASE   A cultural development in the Formative Period, dated to 700 to 500 B.C. in the city of Chalcatzinco. This site was an Olmec frontier post. A *talud-tablero* (a slope-and-slab style) altar was found in levels of this phase. Farmers were active, and terraces are also evident.

CANUTILLO PHASE   A cultural development of the Chalchihuite people in northern Mexico in the region of the Sierra Madre Occidental. This phase is dated to A.D. 200 to 500 and is evident in remains on the Suchil River in the area. (See CHALCHIHUITE.)

CAPOCHA PHASE   A cultural development of the Colima people during the Formative Period (c. 2000/1600 B.C.–A.D. 250). The Colima lived on the coast of western Mexico, and their ceramics are well known. (See COLIMA.)

CARACOL A Maya site near the great center of Tikal in the interior of Belize, in the region known as the Maya Lowlands. The site was occupied from 300 B.C. to A.D. 1000 and at its height had a population of 115,000. The major feature of the city is the *canaa*, or "Sky Palace," the highest man-made structure in the region. An altar discovered on the site has the Ahau glyph incorporated into its design, a rarity in Belize. A stela found there contains two glyphs and two figures and is believed to date to A.D. 593. Agricultural terraces and extensive water reservoirs are also evident. Caracol was begun around A.D. 300 to 600, part of Tikal's political sphere. The ball court of Caracol dates to A.D. 633. Notable rulers of Caracol include Kan II (born A.D. 588) and his father, Lord Water, who conquered Tikal and other regions in A.D. 562. Excavations are taking place at Caracol, covering over 70 square miles.

CARACOL, TUMBA DE A Maya site on the southern part of the island of Cozumel in Quintana Roo, containing one small structure. Dating to the Late Post-Classic Period (A.D. 1200/1250–1521), the building was erected in two stages and contains chambers and a gallery, as well as medial and cornice moldings, once painted red. A dome in the shape of a conch shell topped the structure. Natural conch shells were also used in the architectural decorations, possibly honoring the Maya deity Kukulcan, a Yucatan version of Quetzalcoatl.

CARDINAL POINTS Representing the four corners of the earth, a religious concept fundamental to many Mesoamerican cultures and a method by which all earthly creatures were grouped. Consequently the numbers four and five had religious significance for most cultures of the region. The cardinal points, assigned divine patrons, colors, days and year signs, were deemed favorable or unfavorable in divination. The calendar systems of regional civilizations also utilized the cardinal points. The Maya and the Aztec both looked upon the quadrants of the earth as religious entities. Death, for example, ruled from the north among the Aztec and from the south among the Maya. According to a Chac legend, the cardinal points were formed by Chac, the Maya rain deity. The Maya used them in their early tomb decorations and in their codices. The points were also associated with the *Acantun* and with the *Ritual of the Bacabs*. They were applied by the Olmec during their ascendancy. The remains of the Olmec city of La Venta clearly demonstrate the significance of the four directions in religious rites. Codices and other monumental remains of the Valley of Mexico cultures depict the cardinal points as well, complete with colors, deities, temples and trees associated with the M. The table below left depicts the Maya and Aztec designations for the cardinal points.

CASTILLO DE TEAYO A site in northern Veracruz, founded in c. A.D. 815, with a well-preserved pyramid in the Post-Classic style. Probably influenced by the Toltec, Castillo de Teayo's pyramid is similar in design to pyramids found in the cities of Tula and Calixthuaca. Some sculptures in the round were used as decorations, depicting Nahual and Huaxtec deities. A good many cultures inhabited the site, each one leaving evidence of developments.

CATACAMAS See CAVE OF GLOWING SKULLS.

CATEMACO A volcanic lake in the Tuxtla Mountains of southern Veracruz, near the San Martin and Santa Marta volcanoes. There are two small islands in the lake, Agaltepec and Tenaspi. Terraces discovered in the region formed natural levees, where early Mesoamerican groups used the floodplains for agriculture.

CAUAC SKY A ruler of the Maya city of Quirigua, commemorated on stelae there. Of unknown origin, he came to power in c. A.D. 724. After defeating the forces of the city of Copan in A.D. 737, Cauac Sky turned Quirigua into a magnificent ceremonial center, laying out a plaza as well as seven monuments. Five stelae in Quirigua were erected to commemorate him and his reign. He died in A.D. 784.

CAUSEWAY A road used to connect various sites or to span waterways, as at Tenochtitlan. Called a *sacheob* by some groups. Maya causeways were normally two to four feet above ground level, but were elevated to eight feet over water or swampy terrain. One causeway discovered between Coba in Quintana Roo and Yaxuna is 62 miles long. The *sacheob* was made of large stones, overlaid with rubble and then surfaced with cement. The Aztec incorporated many of the traditional aspects of earlier causeways but raised them higher and designed them to span vast areas.

CAVE OF THE GLOWING SKULLS A recently discovered site in the Catacamas region of Honduras, near the Mosquitia rain forest. The cave contains stacked bones and skulls of approximately 200 bodies, all glistening because of calcium crystals that have been deposited on them over the centuries. The culture represented by the cave lived in c. 1000 B.C., predating the Maya in the region. The practice of disarticulating the dead and dyeing the bones are evidence of an organized society. Architectural styles and the remains of residences support this evidence. Manioc eaters, the group did not leave remains of maize.

CAVES See the table for a list of Mesoamerican caves.

MAYA AND AZTEC CARDINAL POINTS

MAYA	AZTEC
North: the color white, presided over by a *Bacab* or Chac (Death).	North: the color red, presided over by Tezcatlipoca.
South: the color yellow, presided over by a *Bacab* or Chac.	South: the color blue, presided over by Huitzilopochtli.
East: the color red, presided over by Chac.	East: the color yellow, presided over by Tonatiuh.
West: the color black, presided over by Chac or a *Bacab*.	West: the color white, presided over by Quetzalcoatl.

MESOAMERICAN CAVES

NAME	LOCATION	PURPOSE
Actun Balam	southern Belize	Site of Maya religious ceremonies
Balankanche	central Yucatan	Site of Maya rituals
Bat	gulf coast	Flacco Phase habitat
Cave of the Glowing Skulls	Honduras	Burial site of Mayan
Chalcatongo	Oaxaca	Mixtec burial site
Chama	Guatemala	Maya ritual site
Coxcatlan	southeastern Puebla	Tehuacan Sequence site
Juxtlahuaca	Guerrero	Jaguar ritual site
Loltun	Yucatan	Puuc Maya ritual site
Naj Tunich	Peten (Putun)	Peten Maya ritual site
Ocampo	northern Mexico	Prehistoric site
Oxtotitlan	Guerrero	Olmec ritual site
Oxtoyahualco	Teotihuacan	Religious site
Santa Marta	Chiapas	Paleo habitation site
Sistema Huautla	Oaxaca	cavern system

CAYNAC PHASE A cultural development in the city of Chalchuapa, a Maya frontier site near the border with El Salvador. The phase, noted by ceramics, is dated to sometime between 400 B.C. and A.D. 200 and is associated with the manufacture of Usulatan wares.

CE ACATL An Aztec deity, actually a form of Quetzalcoatl. The god was associated with astrology, astronomy and divination and was listed in the Quetzalcoatl complex of deities.

CE ACATL TOPILTZIN A prince of the Toltec, son of the renowned Mixcoatl, who was educated in a shrine school of the god Quetzalcoatl. After his father was murdered, Ce Acatl had to reclaim his throne. He defeated the usurper and declared himself an incarnation of Quetzalcoatl. The adherents of the deity Tezcatlipoca managed to have Ce Acatl exiled from Tula. He is listed as having died on a pyre, and as having sailed to the Yucatan, where he landed around A.D. 987 and became Kukulcan—the Maya Quetzalcoatl. (For details see QUETZALCOATL.)

CEIBA A tree of the breadfruit variety, also listed as a type of wild cotton, that was honored in some Mesoamerican cultures. The ceiba was called the Tree of Life. The Tarascan used the fiber of the tree to make a type of highly prized down, combining it with maguey, rabbit fur and feathers for elaborate garments.

CELESTIAL BIRD A Maya religious image, also called the Serpent Bird. This creature has a pectoral around its neck and sometimes carries an amulet in its beak. The Celestial Bird appears at the center of many Maya depictions of the World Tree. (See TREE OF THE WORLD.)

CELESTIAL MONSTER A Maya religious symbol resembling a dragon but having the hooves of a deer or crocodile parts. The mythological being is sometimes called the Cosmic Monster. In some renderings, the Celestial Monster is portrayed by a sky-band decoration. Its two heads, positioned at opposite ends, are believed to represent astronomical orbits, linking the material and the spiritual tiers of existence.

CELTS Olmec ritual objects, carved out of serpentine and other stones, and probably associated with the were-jaguar cult. A great number of celts were found in the city of La Venta, the mother culture of the Olmec. At times celts were used in conjunction with humanoid statues and many bear the were-jaguar design. Normally small and easily carried, celts were found throughout the Olmec territories. In La

Quetzalcoatl figure

Venta a cache of jade celts was discovered. They were also manufactured in Mezcala in the Late Formative Period (300 B.C.–A.D. 250/290). In some instances, celts were listed in Maya records as ceremonial axes. The Maya and Zapotec used celts as part of the noble costume. (See OLMEC ART.)

CENOTE   An underwater river system, taken from the Maya *dz'onot,* which was exposed when the limestone coverings collapsed into them. *Cenotes* became Maya water reservoirs. Highly prized, in some cases they became sacred sites. Maya ceremonial centers were erected beside *cenotes.* When a *cenote* was designated as a religious site, temples were built beside it and objects of worship were thrown into its depths. Sacrifices were also conducted on its shores, as the water served a spiritual purpose. The most famous *cenote* was at Chichen Itza, the site of Maya pilgrimages in honor of the god Chao. A Maya lord, Ah Dzun Titul Xiu, was murdered with his son while on a pilgrimage to the Chichen Itza *cenote.*

CENOTE XLACAH   A notable *cenote,* one of several located beside the city of Dzibilchaltun. This *cenote* is 140 feet deep and was a site for sacrificial ceremonies.

CENTEOTL   The Aztec god depicted as the son of the earth mother, who headed, as did Xochipilli, an Aztec religious division called a complex. A solar deity, Centeotl was associated with flowers, magic, feasting, pleasure and feather workers. He is also called Centeote and 400 Rabbits (denoting forms of intoxication) and the Magic Cob Lord, and was Xochimilco's patron deity of corn.

CERAMICS   See MESOAMERICAN CERAMICS.

CERRITOS   An island off the northwestern coast of the Yucatan Peninsula, near Chichen Itza. The island probably served as a garrison or as a storage depot for traders while Chichen Itza was in power in the region, sometime around A.D. 1000.

CERRO CHALCATZINCO   A site in eastern Morelos, on the Amatzinac River, the location of the ancient Olmec city of Chalcatzinco. The rocky wall of the cerro, a type of hill or ravine, contains a carving of a king seated on a throne fashioned out of a serpent's mouth. (See CHALCATZINCO.)

CERRO CHAVIN   A Maya site in Chiapas, near modern Las Rosas, dating to the Late Classic Period, around A.D. 900. The Cerro Chavin site reflects the upheaval in the Maya domain of the period. It was militarily fortified, constructed on a high hill and isolated by the surrounding cliffs of the region. Little is known of the city, although some mounds remain at the site.

CERRO CINTEPEC   A site in the Tuxtla Mountains, about 50 miles from the great Olmec ceremonial center of San Lorenzo. Volcanic in origin, this cerro had considerable significance in Olmec art. It is believed that the Olmec quarried the stone there for their colossal heads. They were probably taken in rough form, each one weighing several tons. These stones were hauled to the nearby Coatzacalcos

River, placed on balsa rafts, then floated to San Lorenzo and once again hauled over rough terrain to the finishing workshops within the ceremonial center. The Olmec apparently did not use rollers, which made their hauling process unique, dependent upon human endurance alone.

CERRO DE LA ESTRELLA   A well-known hill, called the Hill of the Star, situated above the modern village of Ixtapalapa, south of Lake Texcoco in the Valley of Mexico. The site was probably used before the Aztec (Mexica) as a religious center, as the records indicate that it was venerated, as was the Hill of the Sun in Pueblo. Such elevations offered settings for religious ceremonies of the various cultures. When the Aztec entered the Valley of Mexico, they used the Cerro de la Estrella for their New Fire ceremonies. The New Fire was a constant and highly regarded religious aspect of Aztec life; they even stopped on their journey into the Valley of Mexico at appropriate intervals to conduct the ceremonies. When the New Fire was ignited on the Cerro de la Estrella, the priests could announce to the people that the world, or the sun, would remain in operation for another designated cycle. At the end of the Aztec Empire, when the sacrifices were conducted to protect against the collapse of the sun, the Cerro de la Estrella held even more significance. (See AZTEC COSOMOLOGY; AZTEC PRIESTS AND RELIGION; and NEW FIRE for further details.)

CERRO DE LAS MESAS   A site located on a broad stretch of land near the Tuxtla Mountains in the Olmec territory near the ceremonial center of Tres Zapotes. Founded 600 B.C., Cerros de las Mesas contains evidence of both Olmec and Izapa influence. In time, Teotihuacan was also associated with the site. Stelae recovered there contain

Cerro de las Mesas fire god

low reliefs, portraying personages of high rank, elaborately adorned and shown in profile. Face masks produced in Cerro de las Mesas incorporate the Olmec were-jaguar theme. One stela recovered also employs the Maya Long Count, which makes the piece a significant discovery. A ceremonial deposit in Cerro de las Mesas yielded 782 pieces of jade and a depiction of a deity. These pieces are believed to have been artifacts from the founding era, buried at a later date. Another mound contained a beautifully carved turtle shell with an Izapa-deity motif. The buildings in Cerro de las Mesas were made of stucco, with lime from crushed seashells and sand.

CERRO DEL GALLO   A site in Tabasco, near Cerro de las Mesas, where a pyramidal base and a mound were discovered. A single stela was recovered here. The site dates to the Early Formative Period (2000–900 B.C.) or perhaps earlier.

CERRO DE TEPALCATE   A site west of modern Mexico City, occupied in the Late Formative Period (300 B.C.–c. A.D. 250/290). It is believed that Cerro de Tepalcate was erected soon after the region of Tlatilco was abandoned. Evidence indicates that a ceramic industry was in place here as early as 2000 B.C.

CERRO ENCANTADO   A site in western Mexico associated with the Jalisco-Chupicuaro culture. This arid region has shaft-style tombs containing grave offerings. Male-female pairs of horned figures, dated to c. A.D. 100–250, were found on this site.

CERRO MONTASO PHASE   A Totonac cultural development in Veracruz and in the coastal regions. Wares from this phase, which is associated with the Isla de Sacrificios Phases I, II, III, and with the Tres Picos Phases I, II, III, include black or red-on-orange ceramics. One bowl discovered from this ceramic period is decorated with a centipede.

CERRO PINACATA   A volcanic site in the Pacific coastal lowlands, bordering on the Altar Desert.

CERROS   A site in northern Belize on the Nuevo River, Maya in association, serving as an important trading center by A.D. 100. The settlement, dating to around 50 B.C., was situated on a small, narrow peninsula on the southern edge of Chetumal Bay. Cerros was surrounded by a moatlike canal that was probably part of the irrigation system for nearby Maya agricultural plots. Four pyramids were built in Cerros, forming a ceremonial complex with other structures. One pyramid has a two-tiered platform with a central stairway flanked by four sculptured masks, depicting jaguar deities. Jade carvings were also recovered there. Cerros is believed to have been abandoned abruptly, probably caught in the shifting political and trade contests in the Maya domain. An early Maya king ruled there at one time. The morning and evening stars were honored there, depicted on temple masks.

CHAACAL III   A Maya ruler of Palenque, the son of Kan Xul. Chaacal II assumed power in A.D. 721. During his reign he erected two temples in Palenque's ceremonial complex.

CHAANMUAN   A Maya heir of Bonampak, listed in that city's records as the son of the king and a princess of the city of Yaxchilan. His wife was Lady Yax Rabbit. Chaanmuan ruled in A.D. 783, as a stela depicts his reign in that year.

CHAC   The Maya rain god, listed as Chaac, Chac Ib Chac in some records, comparable to the Aztec Tlaloc. The Chac deity was sometimes listed as four separate beings, considered in some traditions to be the manifestation of the god Itzamna. They represented thunder and lightning and were associated with the Tree of Life, called the Evening Star. The multiple Chacs were also related to the cardinal points of the earth, in association with the *Bacabes*. In the Yucatan, Chac was depicted as an old man, and in the codices of the Maya he is shown as a long-nosed god. He was sometimes shown with whiskers. An early Izapa stela indicates the god's long-lived popularity. The deity, associated with thunder, was honored in a summer ceremony in ceremonial centers such as Balankanche. Chac masks were incorporated into the designs of the structures on many sites. Chac was believed to have sent white maize from the mountains for human beings. In hurling thunderbolts to carry the maize, Chac singed the grain, which resulted in the colors of the earth designated in the cardinal points. (See BALANKANCHE; CHAC MASKS.)

CHAC (2)   A Maya ruler of Uxmal, commemorated on a capstone in the monument called the Nunnery. The capstone is dated at A.D. 907. Chac is listed on it with his parents, Uinal Kan and Lady Bone.

CHACHAPA   A cultural group associated with the regions of Cholula and Puebla in the Middle Formative Period (900–300 B.C.). The Chachapa and others were part of Cholula's development, at least in the earlier stages.

CHACHOAPAN   A site in western Oaxaca, called Cloud Mountain, one of the traditional homelands of the Mixtec. It is associated with Yucunudahai in some records.

CHAC MASKS   Maya decorations and architectural designs used in the building of certain ceremonial centers, such as Balankanche. Some Chac masks, which were fashioned to honor the rain god Chac, were six and one-half feet high and eight feet wide. Most were used to decorate the pyramids erected in the name of Chac. The *Codz Pop* in the city of Kabah, in the Yucatan, displays as many as 250 Chac masks.

CHAC MOOL   Also called Chac Mul, a reclining stone figure associated with the Maya and the Toltec. The first Chac Mool form was discovered in the city of Chichen Itza. Probably representing the deity Chac, the Maya rain god, the Chac Mool figures were once prominent in the Toltec city of Tula. These figures are geometrically stark, as they repose amid temples and columns. Researchers once believed they were used during ceremonial sacrifices, as they

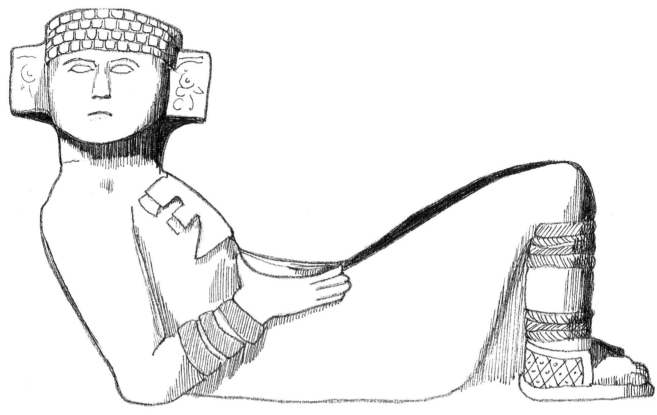

Chac Mool

hold round dishes that could serve as receptacles for human hearts. This connection is now under debate. (See CHAC; MAYA ART.)

CHACMULTUN   A Maya site in the south-central part of the Yucatan Peninsula, called the Mounds Made of Red Stone. A spectacular site, Chacmultun has three groups of structures, predominately Puuc in style, indicating that the city was active in the Late Classic Period (c. A.D. 1200/1250–1521). The first group, called Chacmultun, contains three separate monuments. Building One is large and has a central stairway, decorated with banded columns and columned doorways. Phallic structures were discovered in this building as well as a niche. The rooms are large and contain foot-shaped stones. Three-dimensional sculptures were incorporated into the design of this structure. Building Two in the Chacmultun group has a central stairway, flanked by two vaulted chambers. The only opening to this building is on the west, where there is a narrow gallery. Building Three is an elaborately painted structure with many chambers. The painted figures are moving in a procession and are elegantly costumed. Vaults and carved moldings complete the design.

The second group, called Cabalpak ("Lower Terrace"), is a single multistory building with 12 separate chambers on the lower level. Banded columns and a central stairway were part of the original design. The first three levels are on terraces, and the fourth was constructed on the top of a natural hill.

The last group is called Xetpol, and it is dominated by a long building with five separate doorways. An altar or possibly a bench was located inside, and there are remains of a mural on the walls. Another structure is set on a terrace and has vaulted chambers and stone lintels.

CHAC ZUTZ   A Maya lord, the ruler of Palenque as successor to Chaacal III. Chac Zutz came to the throne in A.D. 722, ruling for eight years. His 50th birthday was commemorated by the Tablet of the Slaves, which dates to A.D. 729.

CHAKALAL   A Maya site on the Yucatan Peninsula in Quintana Roo. A beautiful two-chambered structure, called the Caleta Temple, dominates the site. This temple has a vaulted roof and exterior molding. A jaguar-serpent motif was incorporated into the design of the structure, as were hand symbols, painted both positively and negatively.

CHAKAN MAYA   See MAYA DYNASTIES.

CHAKANPUTUN (Champotun)   An Itza-Maya site on the western coast of the Yucatan Peninsula. The Itza came to this region from Chichen Itza around A.D. 1145, when they were driven from that city by the Xiu family of the Maya. This site is undocumented, but it appears to have been occupied by the Itza for more than two centuries. The Itza then returned to Chichen Itza, driven finally into the area of Lake Peten, where they founded their capital of Tayasal.

CHALCATONGO   A cave site near Tilantongo, in the region called Mixteca Alta in Oaxaca. The cave was used as a repository for the remains of local Mixtec rulers. Such remains were placed in masked funerary bundles.

CHALCATZINCO Also called Chacalzingo, an Olmec frontier site in eastern Morelos, south of Popocatepetl Volcano on the Amatzinac River. The site was designed to blend into the natural amphitheater formed by paired hills rising from the valley floor. It was built at the base of one of these hills around 700 B.C. Named the Revered Place of the Sacred Water, Chalcatzinco was probably inhabited as early as 1500 B.C. Local farmers no doubt used the natural terraces of the region before the Olmec built the city as part of their trade system. Commanding three directions, Chalcatzinco was able to regulate travel in the region. The city was probably garrisoned by the Olmec and involved in the jade trade. It became one of the most important metropolises between 700 and 500 B.C.

The public section of Chalcatzinco was incorporated into the terraces of the hills, and many monuments on these levels exist to this day. Rectangular stone-faced platform mounds were constructed, with at least one stela erected in association with religious ceremonies. Some stelae found at the site depict individuals of rank; one is portrayed with a scepter, something not seen elsewhere. Another portrays a woman, unusual in the region. It is believed that this woman married into the royal family of the city to make an alliance or to honor a treaty.

Altars, both round and rectangular, were erected on the site. The most spectacular discovery, however, is a carving found on the rock wall, the Cerro of Chalcatzinco. Called El Rey, or the King, the carving depicts an elaborately attired figure on a throne, accompanied by a large cartouche or name design. The motif is thought to represent a cave, but fangs are evident, which indicates that the outline represents the mouth of a supernatural being. Many Mesoamerican caves were associated with deities or earth creatures. Other monuments include a jaguar relief on a boulder, with the feline combating a human form. A feathered serpent relief, possibly an early Quetzalcoatl image, was found, as were reliefs depicting humans and ceremonial rituals. Elaborate crypt burials are evident on the site, and remains of the Cantera Phase of ceramic development have been found. A *talud-tablero*, a tabletop altar, was discovered in Chalcatzinco, with the remains of a child, possibly a sacrificial victim, found inside. When the Olmec culture collapsed, Chalcatzinco was abandoned.

CHALCHIHUITE (1) A cultural group of Mesoamerica that entered the region of the Sierra Madre Occidental in northern Mexico during the Toltec era, in the Early Classic Period (A.D. 900–c. 1200/1250). They came into prominence soon afterward, and their domain, which included Zacatecas and Durango, was the last truly Mesoamerican culture in the northern regions. Their original sites, including Alta Vista, were constructed on hills, containing walls, chambers, and platforms. The Arizona cultures arose beyond their borders.

The Chalchihuite were dominated by the Toltec, who entered their lands with merchants and religious leaders. The Chalchihuite had alum, incense, salt and raw copper to trade at the time. They underwent definite cultural phases

over the centuries, before their collapse in A.D. 1400. These phases include:

Canutillo Phase: A.D. 200–500 (on the Suchil River)
Ayala Phase: A.D. 450–700
Calichel Phase: A.D. 500–600
Las Joyas Phase: A.D. 700–950
Rio Tunel Phase: A.D. 950–115
Calera Phase: A.D. 1150–1350

In these phases, the Chalchihuite developed a unified ceramic ware, including red-on-buff tripods, plain bowls and cloisonne decorations. They also made copper bells.

The Toltec collapse harmed the Chalchihuite, who did not fare well under Aztec domination.

CHALCHIHUITE (2) A site in the region of La Quemada in central Zacatecas that is believed to have served as a link between the Toltec, Chalchihuite and the American Hohokam cultures. It is called Precious Stones and is actually a chain of hilltop settlements that marked the northern frontier of Mexico. The site has central courts, platforms and structures with columns and chambers. There is some evidence of Tarascan pottery, including black polished ware.

CHALCHIUHTLICUE (1) The Olmec water goddess, consort of the rain god.

CHALCHIUHTLICUE (2) The Teotihuacan water goddess.

CHALCHIUHTLICUE (3) She of the Jade Skirt, an Aztec (Mexica) goddess. In the Aztec creation traditions, Chalchiuhtlicue presided over the fourth sun, or world, which was destroyed by flooding. She was also honored as a patroness of birth and baptismal ceremonies.

CHALCHIUHMOMOZCO See TAMOANCHAN.

CHALCHIUHTLANETZIN A Toltec ruler, listed in the *Historia Tolteca-Chichimeca*, recorded as ruling from A.D. 510 to 562.

CHALCHUAPA A frontier Pokom Maya site near the border of El Salvador, possibly started by the Olmec culture. The site is believed to have been a manufacturing center for Usulatan wares, part of the vast Maya trade system. Three ceramic phases have been uncovered in Chalchuapa, dating from 400 B.C. to A.D. 200: the Kal, Chul and Caynac. Early paintings in the Olmec style were also discovered in Chalchuapa, as well as a trapezoid pyramid with stoneworks and mounds. A large population is believed to have inhabited the site, where ceramic production took place. After the region was ravaged by Ilopango Volcano, the Chalchuapa fled into the Maya lowlands, taking their ceramic skills and their Usulatan wares with them.

CHALCO (1) The region in the southern part of the Valley of Mexico, extending from the eastern shores of Lake

Chalco to the volcanoes Iztaccihuatl and Popocatepetl. It was home to a group of Paleo-Indian cultures (11,000–7000 B.C.) and to later emerging groups, which appear to have formed a confederation that included the Axcotec, Colcolca, Contec, Miahuaque, Quiyahuitzteca, Tlailotlaque, Tlaltecahuaque, and Xochtec peoples.

This confederation, called the Chalco-Amecameca, is reported to have had 13 rulers and a vast standing army.

CHALCO (2) is an important site in the region, as is Xicco, on an island in Lake Chalco. The people of the region were reputedly expert sorcerers and rainmakers. Chalco was engaged in war with the Mexica forces, composed of Aztec and Tepanec, from A.D. 1376 until around 1458. The Chalco-Amecameca federation maintained a military force ready to defend its confederates. By 1408, however, the Aztec dominated the region. Chalco flourished and sought independence, probably during the reign of Itzcoatl. In 1428, while on a campaign in Huexotzingo, Motecuhzoma I was taken prisoner by Chalco forces and put into a cage. He managed to escape, and when he came to the throne he began a campaign of vengeance. He attacked Chalco in 1446 but was forced to withdraw. When Motecuhzoma I demanded stone for the Great Temple of Tenochtitlan a series of battles followed, and during one particular assault the brother of Motecuhzoma was taken prisoner. He was honored by the Chalco-Amecamecan and offered a chiefdom, but he committed suicide, an act that incited the Aztec to attack. Chalco was defeated and became part of the Aztec domain.

CHALCO (3) A site in the region of Chalco near the Hondo River, linked to the Tamaulipas Sequence. Early habitation is evident on the site, and there is evidence of seed grinding and the use of knives and other tools.

CHALCO-AMECAMECA See CHALCO (1).

CHALCO ATEMPAN A lakeside site in the region of Chalco, venerated in Toltec records as the "mother" of numerous peoples.

CHALCO CHICHIMEC A group associated with the Chichimec confederation. They are listed in some histories as invading the Valley of Mexico after the fall of Tula, the Toltec capital, in c. A.D. 1156/1168, when Huemac, the ruler there, abandoned the site for Chapultepec.

CHALCO LAKE A site in the region of Chalco, in the southern part of the Valley of Mexico, including Xicco, an island associated with the Chalco-Amecameca development. The Tepanec claimed the region in later eras. Lake Chalco is connected with Lake Xochimilco and then to Lake Texcoco and Lake Xaltocan.

CHAMA A cave in the Maya Verapaz region, south of Peten, in modern Guatemala. Chama was revered by the local Maya as the entrance to the Place of Fright, Xibalba, the Maya underworld. As such it served as a ceremonial site for rites concerning death.

CHAMELECON RIVER A waterway that flows into the Gulf of Honduras, draining the Sula Plain. Mexica and Maya merchants kept storage facilities on the banks of this river over the centuries.

CHAPALA, LAKE A natural water reserve in the region of Jalisco, Mexico, and an important archaeological site. The Colima culture was present to the south, and El Openo and inhabitants of other sites made use of Lake Chapala.

CHAN BAHLUM A Maya ruler, also called Serpent, Jaguar, of the city of Palenque. The son of Lord Pacal, Chan Bahlum dedicated the Temple of the Inscriptions to his father and provided him with a vaulted tomb within the temple. Chan Bahlum died in A.D. 702.

CHAN CHICH A Maya site in northern Belize, near the border of modern Guatemala. This ceremonial center has two levels of plazas preserved there. Each has its own temples and platforms, and the largest temple has painted friezes.

CHANEQUE Ancient dwarfs, revered by the Olmec and depicted on figurines. The Popoloca, a mysterious culture associated with Teotihuacan, believed in the *Chaneque*, as did the Mixtec. (See DWARFS; see also TLALOQUES.)

CHANTUTO A Maya-related culture on the Pacific coast of Chiapas, dated to 3000–2000 B.C. The mangrove swamps of the region provided shellfish as well as small mammals, reptiles and an occasional deer. The Chantuto area contained *metates* and *manos*, suggesting plant use, but no agricultural industry is evident here. There were residences with clay floors, and basic tools and obsidian remains have been found. The Chantuto took part in regional trade, offering products from their estuary-lagoon environment.

CHAPULTEPEC A site in the western part of modern Mexico City, the Toltec capital in the reign of King Huemac (c. A.D. 1156/1168). It was called the Hill of the Locust. Huemac killed himself in the city. A spring in Chapultepec provided water for the Aztec capital of Tenochtitlan. The Aztec ruler Chimalpopoca (c. A.D. 1415/17 to 1427) brought fresh water by canals from the spring for the use of his capital's inhabitants. Some traditions hold that the Aztec attempted to acquire Chapultepec early in their history but failed. At one time the site was in Culhua hands. (See CINCALCO.)

CHAU HIIX A Maya city, possibly a vassal of Altun Ha, located in the Crooked Tree Audubon Sanctuary in Belize. The site was occupied as early as 1200 B.C., rising to prominence in the Late Classic Period (A.D. 600 to 900). It is believed that the local inhabitants produced cotton and stone tools for the Altun Ha trade. Chau Hiix remained an active Maya site until A.D. 1600. A 70-foot temple and a large platform supporting five structures are being excavated. An agricultural site just outside of Chau Hiix has canals, water reservoirs and dams.

CHENES A heavily populated zone of northern Campeche, between the Rio Bec–dominated Maya domain and the Yucatan Puuc (hill) territory. A specific Maya art style emerged from this region, similar to Rio Bec but distinguished by its own architectural components. Chenes architecture is rather heavily ornamental, as evidenced by the buildings of the Late Classic Period (A.D. 1200/1250–1521) at Chichen Itza and Uxmal. Hochob was another site having Chenes designs. The Chenes did not employ the Rio Bec false towers but incorporated open-mouth serpent styles. Chicanna is another Chenes site.

CHETUMAL A bay in northern Belize where the Maya city of Cerros was located. Chetumal Bay was part of the vast trade network of the Maya in that region. (See BELIZE; MAYA TRADE.)

CHIA A flax seed that could be ground to make a beverage or an edible oil. The Tarascan in the area of Michoacan cultivated *chia* plants along lakeshores.

CHIAPAS A highland region of Mesoamerica, formed by the Sierra Madre de Oriental and including the Pacific coastal region, down to the Bay of Honduras. These highlands are also part of the Sierra San Cristobal, leading into Guatemalan territories, from Peten and the Maya Mountains in modern Belize (British Honduras). The Sierra Madre de Chiapas range has steep crests that tower above the ocean and extend in a northeasterly direction to the central Chiapas Valley. Geological activities formed V-shape basins and valleys throughout the region, and a feature of the area is the *llano*, a grass-covered area with streams that eventually opens onto alluvial lands. The Sierra de Omoa chain in Guatemala continues these highland characteristics, as do the Chuacas, Minas and Montana del Mico ranges in the east. North of the Chuacan Mountains are the Cabulco, Rabinal, Chicaj and Salama basins. This region may have been a source for jade, especially near Manzanai, in the Motagua Valley, at the base of the Minas Mountains.

The Chiapas highlands are steep and narrow, with some stretches reaching 5,000 feet. Pine forests and belts of live oak predominate. The Meseta Central, on the San Cristobal plateau overlooking the central Chiapas Valley, contains terrain sinkholes, hills and canyons. Streams provide natural irrigation. The Guatemalan extension of these highlands are the *Altos Cuchumatanes*.

The central valley of Chiapas is a wide region of hills, terraces, slopes and mesas drained by the Upper Grijalva River, called the Rio Grande de Chiapas by the local inhabitants, and rises near the Mexican-Guatemalan border. Also here is the *Sumidero*, a canyon formed by waters entering the Sierra San Cristobal. To the west is the Rio de la Venta, a tributary of the Grijalva, which forms another gorge. The Motagua River sweeps through sloping hills and valleys, joining the Grijalva near Huehuetenango. The divide there between plains and rises provides drainage. The Motagua Valley widens and extends into the Maya Quirigua in the east.

Additional features of Chiapas include rain forests on both the gulf and Pacific coasts, offering a variety of vegeta-

tion. Two types of mountain forests exist in Chiapas: the lower mountain (*selva de cajpoqui*), in the Mesa Central, and the higher mountain (*selva baja siempre verde*), found in the Sierra Madre de Chiapas and on the Mesa Central.

Seasonal forests are located in the interior basins of Chiapas and on the Pacific slopes. Lowlands cover the region as well, with thorny woods and vast pine stands that give way to savannas or smaller woodlands.

CHIAPAS DE CORZO A site founded around 1400 B.C. in the central part of the Chiapas region, in the Grijalva River Basin. Occupied almost continually from 1400 B.C. to the present, Chiapas de Corzo is considered one of the earliest sites of human habitation in Mesoamerica, influenced originally by the Olmec and noted for its public architecture. The public structures of Chiapas de Corzo date to around 550 B.C. Pyramids and other civic buildings were fashioned with stucco exteriors and thatched roofs. There were also elaborate residences on the site, surrounded by complexes designed for families of lesser rank. The culture was stratified, and the city's burial grounds give evidence of a clear denotation of rank, at least in the funerary rites. The grave offerings of important individuals of Chiapas de Corzo were elaborate and included obsidian lances, pottery, jade and carved human bones.

The city did not develop in isolation but was influenced by surrounding city-states and nations. Izapa styles are evident, as well as ceramics from Kaminaljuyu and Monte Alban. Chiapas de Corzo was part of the changing cycles in the Grijalva River area. It was invaded by the Zoque but then abandoned. Evidence of deliberate destruction has been discovered in one mound excavated on the site, probably an act of ritual abandonment, believed to be Maya in tradition. Some researchers consider the CHIAPAS STELA 2 found there to be one of the most ancient dated monuments in Mesoamerica. Palaces of cut stone appeared in the city as early as 150 B.C., with polished stucco finishes and roofs of beams and mortar. The site was reoccupied after the Zoque departed. Ceramics recovered in Chiapas de Corzo include globular jars, *tecomates* (neckless jars), clay figurines, rocker stamps and other pieces of Olmec influence. The region went through several ceramic phases and was noted for a variety of well-developed wares and techniques.

CHIAPAS STELA 2 A stone monument found in the city of Chiapas de Corzo, a site founded in c. 1400 B.C. in the Grijalva River Basin in Chiapas. This is one of the oldest dated monuments in Mesoamerica, dating to 36 B.C.

CHICAJ A river basin in the Chiapas highlands, north of the Chuacan Mountains.

CHICANEL PHASE A Maya cultural development associated with the city of Uaxactun and with the great ceremonial center of Tikal. Chicanel nobles were buried in elaborate tombs in Tikal. One such tomb contained a greenstone mask with shell inlaid teeth and eyes. The Chicanel Phase dates from 100 B.C. to A.D. 130/150. Usulatan wares were manufactured in this era, and ceramic pieces reflect Olmec tradition. The ceramics include legless pots, black or red monochromes and glossy slips. The Maya used moldings and geometric designs on their pottery as well as negative painting. Elaborate architecture also dates to the Chicanel Phase, as the Maya used plaster made out of water and limestone fragments, with limestone and marl fill. A platform and ball courts reflect this era's achievements. The first anthropomorphic figures in the region date to the Chicanel Phase as well.

CHICANNA   A site in the southeastern part of Campeche, near Becan, Maya in origin and called Serpent Mouth House. Small, Chicanna is noted for its monumental architecture and for the design of the buildings as sculpture, a facet of the Chenes style, found from Uxmal to Rio Bec. A main plaza in Chicanna is surrounded by low structures, one with a twin-tower building. These towers are joined by a single-story structure with 10 chambers and a stairway. Monster masks decorate the building in four panels. The towers are rounded and once held false temples. The second structure has a highly ornamented Chenes-style facade that profiles monster masks flanking the entrance. Actually, the door serves as the open mouth of the serpent depicted, probably Itzamna, the Maya creator deity. This second building has eight chambers and the remains of a roof comb. The walls were painted red originally, with lateral wings extending outward. Other buildings on the site use shell designs and stucco figures. Some of these contain as many as 12 chambers. The best preserved of these additional structures is called Building XX, the last one constructed in Chicanna. Two-tiered, it is decorated with Chac masks, depicting the Maya rain god.

Chicanna dates from A.D. 150 to 250, at which time it appears to have been abandoned. The construction evident today was begun between A.D. 550 and 830, although inhabitants returned around A.D. 400.

CHICARRA PHASE   An Olmec cultural development taking place in the gulf coastal region and associated with the ceremonial center of San Lorenzo in southern Veracruz. The phase dates from 1200 to 1100 B.C. During this time ceramics were produced and stone monuments were introduced in the region. (See MESOAMERICAN ART.)

CHICHEN ITZA   A Maya-Itza-Toltec site in the central part of the Yucatan Peninsula, called the Mouth of the Well of the Itza by the Maya, but also bearing an earlier name, *Uucil-abnal*, or the Seven Bushes. One of the most frequently visited sites in Mesoamerica, the city reflects both Maya and Toltec influences, a blend resulting in a harmony of line and style, while mirroring the development of the region. Historical accounts credit the Itza with founding the site around A.D. 435/455. They abandoned Chichen Itza and then returned, only to be routed again. The Itza were Mexicanized members of the greater Maya family, involved in the legendary adventures of Kukulcan, the Maya Quetzalcoatl. Kukulcan introduced the worship of the Feathered Serpent into the region and made Chichen Itza a favored pilgrimage site, a status maintained even after the city was abandoned in the 13th century A.D. The last dated monument in the site was erected in A.D. 889.

The modern ruins are divided into three groups: the northern structures, the southern ones (sometimes called Old Chichen), and the outlying southern buildings (called Old, Old Chichen). One major monument of the site is the Temple of Kukulcan, called El Castillo by the Spanish. This is a pyramid approximately 75 feet high, opening onto what is called the central plaza or the north terrace. The pyramid, stretching some 180 feet along a side, has nine levels and at one time had four stairways. The original design also included an interior staircase, part of the first temple constructed at the site, which was somewhat smaller in size and buried under the new pyramid. This inner shrine can be reached through an entrance in the north base of the pyramid, and contains a throne and a Chac Mool monument. The throne reflects the jaguar theme and was originally painted red with jade decorations. A disk made of turquoise completes the design.

Another monument is the Temple of the Warriors, which also contains an interior structure. A Chac Mool and serpent columns adorn this inner temple, which was originally built for rituals. The Temple of the Warriors is noted for its serpent columns, warrior columns, Chac Mool, carved reliefs and Atlantean altar. The style is basically Toltec, except for the Maya Chac masks.

A third structure is the Group of a Thousand Columns, which was erected as support for a roofed area. A marketplace is located to one side, and there is an altar and a square patio with more columns. Two ball courts and an area for sweat baths was constructed beside the columns. The Venus Platform, designed as a square platform with four stairways, is north of this plaza. The platform is decorated with bas-reliefs and serpent heads. Quetzalcoatl or Kukulcan was honored as the evening star, hence the name.

The Sacred *Cenote* was part of Chichen Itza's ceremonial complex. A natural depression used by the Maya throughout the region for water storage, this particular *cenote* was probably enlarged and formed into its present circular shape. It is approximately 180 feet in diameter. The Sacred *Cenote* was a site for rituals and human sacrifice in honor of Chac, the rain god, and human remains have been found there. The Platform of the Tigers and the Eagles is west of the Sacred *Cenote*. It has reliefs of tigers and jaguars holding human hearts in their claws. A skull rack, or *tzompantli*, is located nearby, covered in bas-reliefs. Individual skulls are depicted on the structure, as well as warrior figures. Chac Mools were also found there.

The ball court of Chichen Itza, the largest in Mesoamerica, is to the west. Its walls are 272 feet long, and the playing area extends beyond that. Bas-reliefs are on the walls, depicting both the game and human sacrifices. The court has temples at either end and is said to have acoustic peculiarities that allow a voice to be carried some 150 feet. Beyond the court is the vaulted Temple of the Bearded Man, which has two columns at its entrance and interior walls and columns carved in bas-relief. Another monument, the Temple of the Jaguar, is also located near the ball court. Its shrine has serpent columns and the remains of murals. A chamber below the temple was also painted.

To the south, the grave of a high priest was discovered, called the Ossuary. This grave is Toltec in design. In its serpent columns, human figures and reliefs on the walls of the grave, its design is the same as that in El Castillo. The Red House, or the Chichen-Chob, is to the west. This is a platform with slightly rounded corners and a single stairway. The temple on its summit has a simple roof comb and Chac masks. This structure is purely Maya in design. The House of the Deer, just beyond, is so named because of a mural. This is also a Maya structure.

El Caracol, to the east, is one of the most impressive monuments on the site. The Spanish called it the "snail" or the "spiral" because of the circular staircase in its interior. Caracol was probably an astronomical observatory, both Maya and Toltec in style, with three-dimensional heads depicted on the upper level. South of this observatory is the Temple of the Sculptured Panels, with carved reliefs and connection to the Nunnery, or *Las Monjas,* as the Spanish called it. The Nunnery is 210 feet long, 150 feet wide and more than 50 feet high. It is a typically Classic Maya building, complete with Chac masks. The doorway in the annex forms the mouth of a serpent. The Spanish called the structure the Nunnery because it reminded them of convent buildings in Spain. It is accompanied by a smaller structure called *La Iglesia,* or the Church. This small building is covered with Chac masks and has a roof comb.

Beyond these two buildings is the Akab Dzib, the building called Obscure Writing. It was built in two stages and has wings. The name was derived from the discovery of hieroglyphs on a lintel of the shrine. Near Akab Dzib is the *Cenote Xtloc,* which once had a small temple on its rim. The last group of monuments on the site, called Old Chichen, date to A.D. 879. Among the monuments here is the Temple of the Phalli, which contains Toltec phallic structures. The nearby Temple of the Four Lintels and the Temple of the Three Lintels contain interesting examples of older Maya construction techniques. The use of Chac masks denotes Maya origin. Other buildings include the Temple of the Lintel, the Temple of the Sculptured Jambs and the Temple of Hieroglyphic Jambs. There is also another building similar to *El Castillo* in this area. (For traditions concerning Chichen Itza, see AH DZUN TITUL XIU.)

CHICHIMEC (1)   A term used by Mesoamerican cultures to denote the tribes that invaded from the north. The name means "lineage of the dog," derived from *chichi* (dog) and *mecatl* (rope). It was applied to all hunters and gatherers who entered the Valley of Mexico, and after the fall of Tula it became the name of a powerful group who entered the region. (See Chichimec [2]). The Chichimec can be divided into two major categories: the Teo-Chichimec and the Tamime.

The Teo-Chichimec were the "true" Chichimec, the original hunters and gatherers who wore animal skins, produced stone and feather products and used peyote. Cave dwellers, these were the more nomadic members of the group. They ate rabbits, roots, seeds and fruits and used yucca-plant fiber for sandals.

The Tamime, called the "shooters of arrows," were a cave-dwelling offshoot of the Teo Chichimec. They made homes in gorges or on rocky slopes, eventually constructing grass huts and engaging in agricultural activities. They understood both the Nahual and Otomi languages and are

listed as Uto-Aztecan by some, related to other groups in origin.

Other groups with whom the Chichimec had relations include the Chalco Chichimec, Chichimec Totolimpanec, Choltec, Cuauhtitlan, Cuitlahuac Chichimec, Matlatzinca, Otomi, Tecuanipantlac, and Toltec-Chichimec.

CHICHIMEC (2)   A group entering the Valley of Mexico, originally part of the original Chichimec confederation. Xolotl, called the Monster, was the warlord of this group, and he and his forces routed the remaining Toltec with bows and arrows around A.D. 1200. Xolotl married a princess of the region and went to Tula and other places, settling finally in Tenayuca, which he made his capital. His son, Nopaltzin, assisted him in founding the city. Nopaltzin was called the Revered Fruit of the Cactus. Xolotl offered shelter and welcome to other groups coming into the region. He is credited with the first census in Mesoamerica, commemorated in Nepohualco, the Place of the Count. By A.D. 1246 Xolotl had extended Chichimec rule over the northern part of the Valley of Mexico, defeating a Culhua-Toltec alliance. He then married a Culhua princess. In Puebla these Chichimec lived in Tlaxcala, Huexotzinco, Totomihuacan and Cuauhtinchan. The groups there were related to Xolotl's people but apparently were autonomous. All shared artistic and religious ideals, worshipping the god Itzpapalotl, the Obsidian Butterfly, as well as Mixcoatl, Cloud Snake, who was called Camaxtli in Puebla. The *Codex Xolotl* and the *Codex Ixtlilxochtli* are sources of information on the Chichimec.

Xolotl's wife, Tomiyah, wielded authority in some areas of the Huaxtec. Their son, Nopaltzin, inherited the throne of Tenayuca and built a great pyramid there in A.D. 1304. He introduced Toltec ideals and agriculture to the region, as the Chichimec took on the illustrious Toltec mantle. Walled buildings were constructed, and the people moved out of their cave dwellings. Nopaltzin's son, Tlohtzin, called Hawk, established Nahuatl as the basic language of the Chichimec; his son, Quinatzin, occupied Texcoco and started the Chichimec phase of that city, ruling until A.D. 1337. His son, Techotlalatzin, in turn, welcomed new groups arriving after the collapse of Culhuacan, including the Colhua, Mexiti, Huitzahua and Tepanec. In time the Chichimec married into the royal houses of Coatlinchan, Acolhuacan, Tenochtitlan and Huexotla. The rise of the Aztec Empire, however, forced their ultimate decline, and they were absorbed by the imperial realm.

CHICHINAUHYA MOUNTAIN   A peak in Tamoanchan, situated between the Valleys of Mexico and Morelos. The Huaxtec are recorded as arriving on this mountain to meet with other regional groups to celebrate the adoption of a ritual calendar. On the mountain the Huaxtec chief drank too much *pulque* and exposed himself to the assembly. This was considered a shameful act, and the Huaxtec had to move to the wilderness to escape recriminations from the other groups.

CHICLE   The raw product that is the ingredient for chewing gum. Chicle is bled from the sapodilla tree, a plant that grows in Peten and other Mesoamerican regions.

CHICOMICOATL (Chantico) A goddess worshipped in Xochimilco as patroness of the hearth. The Aztec considered her to be an earth goddess, and she also was revered by the Chichimec in Tenayuca. She was called the Mother of Corn.

CHICOMOZTOC (1) The legendary Nahua homeland, the region of the Seven Caves, from which the major Mesoamerican groups of the Classic and Post-Classic periods (c. A.D. 1/250–900; 900–1521) migrated into the Valley of Mexico. The groups recording their Chicomoztoc beginnings include the Chichimec, who arrived in the Valley of Mexico in A.D. 1244; the Alcohua, who arrived in 1260; the Otomi, who arrived in 1250; and the Tepanec, who arrived in 1230. The Aztec (Mexica) were by their own account the last to leave the Land of the Seven Caves. Debate continues as to the actual location of Chicomoztoc, although some scholars list Mount Culhuacan, the Curved Mountain, northeast of the Valley of Mexico, as a possible site. This mountain has caves.

CHICOMOZTOC (2) See LA QUEMADA.

CHICOMULCELTEC MAYA See MAYA GROUPS, CHICOMULCELTEC.

CHICONAHUIZCUINTL A god worshipped in the city of Xochimilco, honored as the patron of the aged.

CHILAM BALAM OF CHUMAYEL Sacred Maya books, native chronicles known as the *Katun Prophecies of Yucatan*. They are named for a Maya seer who foretold the coming of the European conquerors. They date to the period immediately following the Spanish conquest of Mesoamerica, originally composed by the Maya in 10 or 12 books, which were later translated into Spanish. The *Chilam Balam* (*chilam* meaning "sage" or "soothsayer" and *balam* meaning "jaguar") have also been called the *Books of Occult Matters*. Fragments of this work were discovered at Maya ceremonial sites. The documents explain the Maya and Nahuatl religious traditions, particularly the cosmological aspects of creation. "The Book of the Spirits," and "The Book of the Tiger," parts of the collection, concern the "first time" of the world. The books also explore the procession of eternal heavens, with cycles marking progress toward fulfillment and peace.

CHILI (*Capsicum frutescens C. annum*) Pepper plants cultivated by the early Mesoamericans, which remained a basic element of their diet. Both wild and domestic chili peppers are an important source of vitamins and add considerable taste to food.

CHIMALPANEC A group related to the Toltec who joined the Chichimec when they invaded Texcoco. They were either invited into the city by the relatives of Xolotl or claimed descent from this Chichimec leader.

CHIMALPOPOCA Called Smoking Shield, an Aztec ruler from c. A.D. 1415/17 to 1427. He was the son of the Aztec emperor Huitzilihuitl and a Texcoco princess, making him a grandson of the illustrious Texoco king Tezozomoc. Elected by the Aztec council to succeed his father, he took the throne at the age of 18. One of his major accomplishments was the introduction of stone into the residential sections of Tenochtitlan, the Aztec capital. The ceremonial centers had been built in stone from the earliest times, but residences did not become elaborate until his reign. Facing a serious water-pollution problem and a problem with the maintenance of the *chinampas* (the floating agricultural gardens), Chimalpopoca brought fresh water to Tenochtitlan from the spring at Chapultepec by means of canals and ditches. His reign also spurred trade and the increase of markets. Long a favorite of his grandfather Tezozomoc, Chimalpopoca became involved in the brutal struggle for the throne when the old king died. Chimalpopoca opposed the rise of Maxtla, one of the heirs, and he advised Maxtla's rival to murder him at a banquet. When Maxtla heard the story, he sent an army to Tenochtitlan to kill the young king. Records state that Chimalpopoca dressed himself in his royal robes and went to his death calmly. His murder motivated the Aztec to rise against Maxtla and the Tepanec. The Triple Alliance thus arose and Maxtla was killed. (See TRIPLE ALLIANCE.)

CHINAMPA A "floating island," a manufactured bed on which crops were grown in water, and one of the most successful and extensively used agricultural methods in Aztec (Mexica) life. Researchers believe there were as many as 25,000 acres of *chinampas* in Chalco alone by A.D. 1519. Originating during the Formative Period (2000/1600 B.C.–A.D. 250/290), use of the *chinampas* was spurred by a drop in the level of Lake Texcoco around A.D. 1200. By A.D. 1400, the increased population in the region encouraged increased use of the *chinampas* in marshy places, a process so successful that the program may have been promoted by the Aztec state. A vast labor force was required to introduce the *chinampas* on such a scale. The *chinampas* are believed to have been in use in the Chalco Lake region first, as it was warmer there and less susceptible to frosts. There was more fresh water in Chalco Lake as well, which cut down the chances of crops being spoiled by saltwater infiltration.

Most *chinampas* were used to grow corn (maize), the major staple. Smaller sections were set aside for use as seedbeds. Once the seeds had germinated, the healthy seedlings were transported for planting on larger *chinampas*. Another seedbed, made of reeds, cattails and other water plants, was then used as a floating nursery surrounding the germinated plants. As the crop matured, the entire bed was floated to the main *chinampas* for transplanting. The mud used to create them was fortified by the addition of night soil, collected from the latrines in Tenochtitlan and other cities.

When the *chinampas* of Tenochtitlan were threatened by the infiltration of salt water, an aqueduct was erected, sometime around A.D. 1416. King Nezahualcoyotl of the city of Texcoco had erected a vast dike to close off the western bay, where there was a supply of salt water. To provide for freshwater supplies, an aqueduct was constructed to bring water from the Chapultepec springs during Chimalpopoca's reign. More water was brought from Cayocan at a later date. The Texcoco ruler considered this source inadequate and advised that such a waterway could not be controlled. Later floods in Tenochtitlan proved him correct.

Chinampas could be owned by groups or by families, and considerable wealth could be amassed by such ownership. *Chinampas* proved advantageous because of the number of plantings and the variety of crops that a single floating bed could produce. During a single year as many as seven different crops could be produced on one *chinampa*. Each crop grew at a different time of the year, with no slack time in productivity because the soil was constantly replenished. It has been calculated that 25,000 acres of *chinampas* could support as many as 180,000 people. Not all of the *chinampas* were used for food, however, as the Aztec grew flowers for their fragrance and for decoration. Flower production was a vital part of the *chinampas* agricultural programs. (See AZTEC AGRICULTURE; MESOAMERICAN AGRICULTURE.)

CHINKULTIC A Maya site in the highlands of eastern Chiapas, on the Naranjo River near the Guatemalan border. The city was built on a rise overlooking a series of lakes that extend into Guatemala. This is a Late Classic Period (A.D. 600–900) site, associated with the Maya trade system. The monuments date from A.D. 590 to 897. El Mirador, the main complex of Chinkultic, is composed of approximately 200 ruins, clustered in the fashion of the Maya ceremonial center. Carved stelae were also found there, as well as a ball court decorated with stelae.

CHITAM A Maya ruler of the city of Tikal, the son of Yan Kin Caan Chac. Chitam was depicted on a lintel, approximately 14 feet square, with other court figures. Chitam is dressed in jaguar skins and a jaguar headdress with quetzal feathers and jade and shell decorations.

CHIXOY RIVER A Guatemalan highland waterway that flows from the interior peaks, northwest to the Gulf of Campeche.

CHOCHO-POPOLOCA A culture composed of Nahuatl-speaking people who entered the Mixtec domain in Puebla around A.D. 800. The great city of Cholula was a creation of the Chocho-Popoloca and the other groups. (See POPOLOCA.)

CHOL MAYA See MAYA GROUPS, CHOL.

CHOLOLLAN A region in the highlands of the Mesa Central, near the volcano Malinche (Matlalcueye). The Olmeca-Xicallanca were probably the oldest inhabitants of the region. Other groups joining them took the name Chololtec. In time they and the region came under the domination of the Chichimec.

CHOLOLTEC See CHOLOLLAN.

CHOLTEC One of the groups associated with the Chichimec. They arrived in the Valley of Mexico in c. A.D. 1200 and took part in establishing the Chichimec city of Tenayuca.

CHOLULA An independent city-state arising in the Middle Formative Period (900–300 B.C.) in the region of Puebla.

Mexico's great volcanoes, Iztaccihuatl and Popocatepetl, loomed above the plains there, and the Sierra Madre Oriental was nearby. The Balsas River drained much of the land around Cholula, perhaps accounting for the city's name, meaning "the Place Where the Waters Spring." Cholula is believed to have been the home of the Olmeca-Xicallanca, taken by the Toltec and then the Chichimec in later eras. Cholula controlled much of the high-plateau regions of Puebla and Tlaxcala. In turn, the city was heavily influenced by the great center of Teotihuacan. The population of the city was a confederation of smaller cultures, including the Manzanilla, Chachapa, San Mateo and Flor de Bosque. One of the holiest sites in Mesoamerica in all historical periods, Cholula emerged as an outstanding ceremonial center. Pilgrims from surrounding districts worshipped Quetzalcoatl there, as the center always welcomed groups to its festivals.

The focal point of the religious ceremonies in Cholula was the Great Pyramid, believed to be one of the largest pyramids ever constructed in the Americas. The original foundation of the shrine dates to the Middle Formative Period, but it was continually enlarged over the years. Its final massive form was completed during the Classic Period (c. A.D. 1/250–900). Then the pyramid measured approximately 1,400 feet on its sides and covered 42 acres. Mud and brick were used as fill. The first version of the pyramid appears to have been Teotihuacan in design, with the *talud-tablero* motif (an Olmec art form), and insect symbols incorporated into the decorations.

Historical references to the circular style of the Great Pyramid of Cholula abound. Quetzalcoatl took the form of Ehecatl, the wind god, at times, and he was usually provided with round shrines reflecting incorporeality and movement. The circular pattern was thus a recognizable image for the people, exemplifying the god's nature. At one time the entrance to the pyramid was fashioned in the form of a stone serpent, having fangs at the sides of the doorway. The pyramid also had stairs, labyrinths and beautiful frescoes depicting butterflies and insects, which were associated with Quetzalcoatl. Beneath the west face of the pyramid was a stone temple with mosaic textile motifs. At the south was a patio with four stone altars and two stelae, reflecting the Classic Veracruz artistic influence. A long polychrome mural was discovered, depicting life-size figures called the Drunkards. These are males involved in some sort of ritual, possibly using hallucinogenic drugs rather than alcohol. The temple on the summit of the pyramid was said to have contained a statue of the deity being honored. The entire structure is made of adobe bricks covered with stucco. According to traditional sources, these bricks were not made on the site but in Amecameca, some 30 miles distant. Reportedly, some 20,000 prisoners of Cholula were used to transport them. The prisoners lined the road between the cities and handed on the bricks, one at a time, to their ultimate destination.

The Patio of the Altars, to the south, was flanked by two separate plazas and surrounded by *talud-tablero* architecture on three sides. Fretwork designs were incorporated into the panels, and two of the four altars are thought to have Tajin influence; one has carved edges. There is also a wide staircase there, and on the floor are three-dimensional sculptures, one a crude head and the other a fragment of an ancient figure. The western altar has carvings of a serpent. The southeastern plaza associated with the Patio of the Altars contains an Aztec shrine, which was placed there long after Cholula's original inhabitants had moved on. This shrine contains grave offerings and two human skulls. The southwestern plaza associated with the Patio of the Altars contains many structures representing the various phases of construction. To the north is the Stone Building, composed of three sloped tiers with a central staircase. This structure was formed out of large cut and fitted blocks. The inset panels incorporated into the Stone Building are in the *talud-tablero* style and are decorated with a braid symbol. This building may once have formed a projecting platform from the Great Pyramid.

Cholula was an important ceremonial center with ties to Monte Alban and Teotihuacan, whose influence it came under in A.D. 200–300. Another Olmec group invaded the city around A.D. 700–800, reducing the local population. The Toltec won control of the city in the Post-Classic Period, around A.D. 1168. The Aztec also made it part of their imperial domain. It remained a holy site, visited by worshippers until the Spanish conquest. The last reported ruler of Cholula, Quetzalcoatzin, was killed by the Spanish along with thousands of other inhabitants, a feat that enhanced Cortez's reputation for having supernatural powers.

CHONTAL (1) An art form developed in the Guerrero region that was once linked to the Mezcala style but is now viewed as a separate cultural development. Chontal art was rounded and gentle in appearance but at the same time highly realistic.

CHONTAL (2) (Tequistlateco) A group living on the Oaxacan coast in the Late Post-Classic Period (A.D. 1200–1521), having ties to Guerrero and possibly to the Chontal Maya in Peten (Putun) and to other cultures in the preceding historical periods. The Chontal fought against Aztec imperial expansion, refusing to surrender their city of Alahuitzlan to Ahuitzotl's Aztec armies. Reportedly as many as 44,000 Chontal inhabitants were killed or taken prisoner as a result of their defiance of the Aztec forces. Alahuitzlan was a site near the border of the Tarascan domain, considered an important buffer zone for the Aztec. Another Chontal city, Teloloapan, was also attacked by Ahuitzotl and his army, and the local inhabitants fled to nearby settlements. In time the Chontal settlements of Oztoma and Ichcateopan were also placed under siege.

Speaking a form of the Tuztec language, the Chontal were an agricultural people, producing cacao, honey, cotton, chili and fruits. Their houses were constructed of adobe or stone, with cane roofs and cane fences. They used some fortifications and fought well with bows, arrows and spears. The Chontal also carried shields into battle and wore waist-length padded armor. They had a stratified social structure like that consisted of noble castes as well as commoners. Their temples were administered by priestly elders.

CHONTAL MAYA (Chontalan) See MAYA GROUPS, CHONTAL.

CHORTI MAYA See MAYA GROUPS, CHORTI.

CHUACAN MOUNTAINS Also called Chuacas, a highland chain of Guatemala's Salama Basin, formed by the Salama River. The Chuacan Range continues the highlands of Chiapas.

CH'UL BALAMIL The earth as envisioned by the Maya. It was deemed a sacred and nurturing source of life. (See MAYA RELIGION.)

CHUL PHASE A ceramic development in Chalchuapa, a Maya frontier site near the borders of El Salvador. The city of Chalchuapa was believed to be a manufacturing center for Usulatan wares, dating from c. 400 B.C. to A.D. 200.

CHULTUN A Mayan architectural innovation that served as a chamber tomb or storage area in pyramids and temples. The *chultunes* were bottle-shaped pits or buried chambers. The city of Ake and other Maya centers incorporated the *chultun* into their religious structures. It appears to have developed in the Formative Period (c. 2000/1600 B.C.–A.D. 250/290) among the Mamon Maya of Belize, although possibly in Altun Ha in particular. *Chultunes* were also used to store *sascab* lime, a Maya building material.

CHUMBICUARO PHASE A cultural development in the Tepalcatepec Basin in Michoacan, dating to the Late Formative Period (300 B.C.–A.D. 250/290) or the Early Classic Period (c. A.D. 1/250–600). In this phase, red-and-gray ceramics with incised decorations were manufactured. Bowls and *ollas* were recovered from the sites of the Chumbicuaro era. The phase is not well documented but is evident on the Apatzingan Plain.

CHUNHUHUB A Maya site known as the Place of the Huhub Tree in the northeastern area of Campeche whose remains exhibit remarkable architectural innovations. The largest palace structure at the site has four rooms with four other chambers on the north and a central room with an annex. Stepped-fret decorations are visible, as well as cornice moldings. The doorway in the palace is imposing, with a three-member rectangular molding. A vault, a pyramid and other residences are on the site, which is near the great ceremonial center of UXMAL.

CHUNYAXCHE a Maya site on the Caribbean coast of the Yucatan Peninsula, located on an inland lagoon. More than 100 surviving structures, including palaces, mark Chunyaxche as an important site in the region. The main palace is larger than the one at the Maya center of Tulum.

CHUPICUARO (Guanajuato) A site on the Lerma River in western Mexico, in a region called Guanajuato, which was important in the Formative Period (c. 2000/1600 B.C.–A.D. 250/290). Now covered by an artificial lake, Chupicuaro has provided vast amounts of Formative Period material. No massive monuments or religious complexes were erected by the people of Chupicuaro, who appear to have followed the general artistic traditions of the region. The settlement, as the rest of Guanajuato, was based on agricultural and agrarian lifestyles, with little outside influence evident. A cemetery discovered near Chupicuaro contained nearly 400 graves, giving evidence of burial rituals

Chupicuaro figure

and religious life. The grave offerings were elaborate, and the cemetery also contained rectangular ash-filled pits. It is assumed that these pits were set on fire as corpses were deposited in nearby graves, as part of a funerary rite.

Chupicuaro pottery has been recovered in Guanajuato and other sites, including Cholula. It was composed of two basic types: Black-brown, unpainted wares usually fashioned into silhouette forms or tripods, and elaborate polychromes, usually in red and black, red on buff or brown on buff.

Geometric scrolls were popular, and triangles, crosses and other symbols were also employed as decorations. Many Chupicuaro vessels were incised, and negative painting was a Chupicuaran hallmark. The forms include shallow bowls with spider legs, stirrup-spout vessels and kidney-shaped or elongated wares. The figurines found in large numbers in Chupicuaro include both large and small forms, hollow and solid. The solid figures have flat bodies, shortened arms and undefined hands and feet. They are often painted.

By the end of the Formative Period, the people of Chupicuaro had ceased their ceramic production, having moved elsewhere or become integrated into nearby groups.

CHUTIXTIOX A Quiche Maya site in the Yucatan Peninsula in the Post-Classic Period (A.D. 900–1521). Built on a 300-foot ridge, surrounded on three sides by the Rio Negro, Chutixtiox was fortified. A removable bridge spanned a moatlike gap as a defensive measure. The site has an enclosed ball court and an acropolis with a pyramidal colonnaded building along a plaza.

CIHUACOATL (1) A goddess popular in the Valley of Mexico, the patroness of midwifery and sweatbaths. She

was often depicted with a warlike appearance. In some instances, Cihuacoatl was shown as a hag; in others she was a beautiful woman. When exhorted during the act of childbirth, the goddess was associated with the god Quetzalcoatl. Her name means "woman snake."

CIHUACOATL (2) A title given to an Aztec administrator, usually in charge of internal affairs in the capital. One of the most celebrated of these was Tlacaelel, who directed the day-to-day administration of the empire. He was also the director of ritual sacrifices and a counselor to four emperors.

CIHUATETEO A term used by the Aztec to distinguish women who died in childbirth. They were honored as valiant souls who perished in battle, and were thus considered to be female warriors. A tradition arose suggesting that these departed women haunted crossroads after sunset, seeking children and other victims.

CINCOC A hill north of the Toltec city of Tula. The hill was the site of commemorative ceremonies, possibly of a religious or state nature.

CINCALCO An Aztec (Mexica) paradise believed to be situated on the promontory of Chapultepec. The entrance to Cincalco was believed to lie there, and it was called the House of the Maize. Water was thought to pour from the rock of this paradise. The legendary Toltec ruler Huemac was believed to be in command of Cincalco, taking the form of the rain deity, Tlaloc.

CINNABAR A reddened form of mercuric sulfide that was mined in Alta Vista and prized throughout the Chalchihuite region and elsewhere in Mesoamerica. The substance was traded in the system that flourished on the Turquoise Road around A.D. 350 and was used in Maya burials and for decorations.

CIPACHTLI (1) An alligator symbolizing a day sign in the Aztec *tonalpohualli*, their calendar system.

CIPACHTLI (2) An Aztec goddess believed to represent the unformed earth, chaos and the matter of creation. Quetzalcoatl and Tezcatlipoca coiled themselves around her in the act of creating the world and divided her into two parts, the earth and the sky.

CIPACTONAL A deity popular in Morelos and in other Nahua cultures, including the Aztec (Mexica), who resided in a sacred cave with his consort, Oxomoco. These were the Divine Ancestors, the grandparents of Quetzalcoatl and all humans.

CITLALATONAC An Aztec (Mexica) deity associated with the Milky Way. His consort was Citlalinicue. The god was called Starshine.

CITLALINICUE See CITLALATONAC.

CITLATEPETL The volcano now called Orizaba. It is included in the Transverse Volcanic Axis in the Mesa Cen-

Aztec *Cipachtli* glyph

tral of Mexico. (See MESOAMERICAN GEOGRAPHIC DIMENSIONS; VOLCANOES.)

CIUDAD GUZMAN   A site in the region of Jalisco, also called Zapatlan el Grande. It is noted for rock paintings, most of which date to the Early Formative Period (c. 2000/1600–900 B.C.) or perhaps earlier.

CIZIN   Also called Kisin, a Maya god of death, revered in the Yucatan and Chiapas regions as an earth deity. (See MAYA GODS.)

CLOUD PEOPLE   The *Ben Zaa* or the *Binii Gula'sa*, the name given to the Zapotec nation by its contemporaries and also found in its own records.

COA   A digging stick essential to the sowing processes of Mesoamerican farming. The *coa*, one of the tools developed in the region in the early historical eras, was used throughout Mesoamerica.

COAHUILA   Modern Mexico's third-largest state, bordering the United States, Chihuahua, Durango and Nuevo Leon. A desert region, untamed and arid, Coahuila was the habitation for the early nomadic groups that lived in caves, and founded the Desert Culture.

COAPEXCO PHASE   A cultural development of the Ixtapaluca culture in the Valley of Mexico. This phase dates to the Formative Period (c. 2000/1600 B.C.–A.D. 250/290) and is associated with the Ayotla and the Mamantial cultural developments in the region.

COASTAL LOWLANDS   See MESOAMERICAN GEOGRAPHICAL DIMENSIONS.

COATEPANTLI   A wall of stone serpents at the Great Pyramid of Tenayuca, the Chichimec city. The wall was designed to surround the temple on three sides. Built of mortar and stone, the *coatepantli* was originally painted and plastered. The wall was accompanied by individual stone serpents with crests. They are identified in some records as Xiuhcoatl, the fire serpent. The wall's symbols were also in honor of the sun cult.

COATEPEC   A Toltec site near Tula, visited by the Aztec (Mexica) during their imperial eras and called the sacred mountain. The site was renowned for a turquoise-covered column. Considered by many modern researchers to be a reflection of Toltec arts and crafts, Coatepec may have inspired the later Mesoamerican name for the Toltec, the Lords of Turquoise. A quetzal feather-work industry was also located in Coatepec, providing the Toltec with ornaments and other elaborate wares. In other records Coatepec is listed as the Hill of the Serpent, visited by the Aztec in A.D. 1163, during the early stages of their activities in the Valley of Mexico. The Aztec New Fire ritual was reportedly celebrated there, and the site was revered as the birthplace of the god Huitzilopochtli. Coatepec was reproduced in a ceremonial center in the city of Tenochtitlan.

COATEPETL   A site listed in Aztec (Mexica) records, now believed to have been situated near Tula. The name means "Serpent Mountain." The summit of Coatepetl held an earth shrine that served as the home of a priestess, an embodiment of Coatlicue, the earth goddess. The site was also associated with traditions concerning the deity Huitzilopochtli.

COATL   The snake or serpent representing a day sign in the Aztec *tonalpohualli*, the calender system.

COATLICUE   The Aztec goddess described as the consort of the sun, one of the five moon deities. The patroness of flowers, Coatlicue was a member of the Teoteoinnan Complex, an Aztec religious division. Because she also represented the earth and the mother of the god Quetzalcoatl, Coatlicue was greatly revered.

COATLINCHAN (1)   An Acolhua capital on the eastern shore of Lake Texcoco, meaning "In the House of the Serpent." The city was celebrated for a statue of the god Tlaloc, standing 23 feet high, 15 feet wide and weighing 180 tons. Unfinished, the statue was discovered in a gully in Coatlinchan and is now in Mexico City.

COATLINCHAN (2)   A group who joined the Acolhua in establishing Tlaxcala. In some records this culture also is associated with the Culhua.

COATZACOALCOS   A site in the region of Tabasco, listed in Toltec records as one of their settlements. It is possible that it had another original culture and was taken over by the Toltec.

COATZALCOALCOS RIVER   A waterway in the gulf coastal lowlands, joining the Uspana River in some regions. Important to Olmec life, the river made possible the transport of stones for the colossal Olmec heads in San Lorenzo.

Coatlinchan

The stones, quarried in the Cerro Cintepec of the Tuxtla Mountains, were floated on the river on balsa rafts.

COBA A Maya site called Ruffled Waters by its original inhabitants, erected among a group of shallow, reedy lakes in northern Quintana Roo. A complex of various structures was discovered there, connected by 16 straight masonry causeways, with 30 more in the city. Coba was the largest and most powerful ceremonial center in eastern Yucatan in the Classic Period (c. A.D. 1/250–900). The site contains the remains of vast residential quarters as well as the usual temple structures. Coba was associated with the Peten (Putun) region in its ceramic phases and probably was included in the Maya trade system there.

The major portion of the site is located between Lakes Coba and Macanxoc. Two other sections contain monuments typical of ceremonial center clusters. A seven-level pyramid with rounded corners and a single stairway supported a temple. This monument is joined by a section having a platform and a stela. Beyond is a ball court. A nearby pyramid, called the *Conjunto las Pinturas* by the Spanish, was built with a single chamber temple, two doorways and a column. The temple was painted, and the remains of these murals prompted the Spanish name. Another pyramid, called *Nohoch Mul*, is 120 feet high and seven-tiered. A temple was erected on the summit of this platform with paintings of a deity in the niches. A plaza and another pyramidal platform accompany the *Nohoch Mul*. A stela was also discovered in this temple complex.

A cache of stelae was found in Coba. Considerable Maya ceramic evidence exists, and inscriptions date to A.D. 613 to 682. Some structures were erected at a later time. Coba is mentioned in Maya writings after the Spanish conquest.

COBA LAKE A water resource located in northern Quintana Roo in eastern Yucatan. A shallow, reedy lake, Coba is near Lake Macanxoc and is the site of the Maya city of Coba.

COCIJO A Zapotec rain deity, highly stylized on urns and other ceramics of the culture of Monte Alban. In four separate forms Cocijo also represented the CARDINAL POINTS. Figures of the deity wear headdressses having the water glyph on the crown, and they bear a resemblance to the Maya rain deity Chac.

COCI'JOEZA See COSIHUESA.

COCIJOPII The son of the Zapotec ruler Cosihuesa and the Aztec-born queen Pelaxilla (called Coyolicatzin by the Aztec). He was born in 1502. His name means "Lightning Wind," and a seer predicted that he would become powerful and then face humiliation. Ruling Tehuantepec at the age of 16, Cocijopii became a Spanish vassal after the conquest. In time he had to defend himself in a court of the Spanish Inquisition, where he was tried for adhering to the old ways of his people. He was freed but died soon afterward as the result of mistreatment by the Spanish.

COCOM MAYA See MAYA DYNASTIES, COCOM.

CODICES Books or documents, folded screens of animal skins or bark paper, covered with a thin coat of lime plaster and then decorated with images in color, sometimes encased in black outlines. Prepared by the scribes and sages of Mesoamerica, these books cover an extensive variety of subject matters. The surviving codices provide a glimpse into the government, history, calendrics, religious beliefs and cosmological views of Mesoamerican peoples. They are important documents because of the information they contain and because of their scarcity. The Spanish destroyed most of the codices they found on the grounds that retaining them would impede the dissemination of Christianity in the region. Some documents and books, however, were gathered by Spanish decree to provide Emperor Charles V of Spain with details and historical accounts of his lands in the New World. The codices are discussed in entries on each culture, but the following are important among those still extant.

Codex Azcatitlan. An Aztec history, in Mexico.

Codices Becker I, II. Mixtec histories, in the Museum für Volkerkunde in Vienna.

Codex Bodianus. An Aztec botanical and medical account, now in the Museo Nacional de Antropologia in Mexico City.

Codex Bodley. A Mixtec history in the Bodleian Library, Oxford.

Codex Borbonicus. An Aztec document from the Spanish era concerning calendrics and divination.

Codex Boturni. Also called the Peregrination Painting or the *Tira del Museo*, depicting Aztec travels.

Borgia Group. Six painted, pre-Columbian codices, ritual works detailing practices based on the *tonalpohualli*, the ritual calendar. The origin of these codices is under debate, as some may have come from Puebla, Tlaxcala or from another Mixtec region. The Borgia Group includes the *Codex Borgia* (the work for which the group is named), which is in the Vatican Library in Rome; *Codex Laud,* in the Bodleian Library, Oxford; *Codex Fejervary-Mayer,* in the Liverpool Free Public Museum; *Codex Cospi,* in the University Library of Bologna; the *Vaticanus B Codex,* in the Vatican Library, Rome; and the *Mexican Mss. No. 20,* in the Bibliothèque Nationale, Paris.

Codex Chimalpopoca. See ANALES DE CUAUHTITLAN.

Codex Colombino. A Mixtec history, in the Museo Nacional de Antropologia, Mexico City, in the care of the Tototepec until 1717.

Codex Dresden. A Maya astral treatise with calendric dates, now in Dresden but originally discovered in a museum in Vienna.

Codex Florentius. An Aztec document also called "The General History of the Things of New Spain," compiled by Fray Bernardino de Sahagun. This codex is also called the *Medico-Palatino.*

Codex Grolier. A document found in fragments in a Maya cave, now in the Grolier Club in New York.

Codex Magliabecchiano. An Aztec history concerning life in the empire, including descriptions of Aztec dress and games.

Codex Moctezuma. An Aztec list of tax collections and tribute assessments, also called the *Matricula de Tributos.*

Codex Mendoza. A document written for Don Antonio de Mendoza, a Spanish official, with marginal notes by Spanish priests. The document, now in the Bodleian Library, Oxford, depicts the founding of Tenochtitlan.

Codex Nuttall. A Mixtec history, also called the *Codex Zouche-Nuttall,* now in the Museum of Mankind, London.

Codex Peresianus. A document concerning Mesoamerican calendric celebrations, now in Paris, also called the *Codex Paris.*

Mixtec Codex *Zouche Nuttall*

Codex Ramirez. An Aztec history called "A History of the Mexicans Through Their Paintings."

Codex Sanchez Solio. A Mixtec history (Egerton 2895), now in the British Museum.

Codex Selden. A Mixtec history, now in the Bodleian Library, Oxford.

Codex Telleriano-Remensis. An Aztec history that also gives information on traditions.

Codex Tre-Cortesianus. A document concerning temple ritual. Also called the *Codex Madrid,* and now in that city. This codex is noted for its formal style.

Codex Vatican A. An Aztec treatise concerning the concept of the universe in that nation. It is in the Vatican Library in Rome.

Codex Xolotl. A Chichimec history with a corresponding text written in Spanish by Fernando de Alva Ixtli. (For other codices, see under individual cultures.)

CODZ-POP The palace of the god Chac, a Maya structure erected in the city of Kabah in west-central Yucatan. Puuc in style, the *Codz-Pop* is more than 150 feet long and has 10 chambers. The presence of 250 Chac decorative masks makes this place unique.

COFRE DE PERATE (Naucampatepetl) One of the major volcanic peaks in the Transverse Volcanic Axis on the Mesa Central of Mexico. (See MESOAMERICAN GEOGRAPHICAL DIMENSIONS.)

COIXTLAHUACA (1) A Mixtec site that served as one of the four capitals of that nation, located in the Mixteca Baja region. Actually a residential suburb of a ceremonial center, Coixtlahuaca became dominant in c. A.D. 1350, although ceramic phases are evident in much earlier eras. These ceramic phases include:

Cruz: 1300–200 B.C.

Ramos: 200 B.C.–A.D. 500

Las Flores: A.D. 500–1000

Natividad: A.D. 1000–c. 1520/1535

Convento: A.D. 1520–1535

COIXTLAHUACA (2) A Mixtec group, part of the general confederation composing that nation. The Coixtlahuaca were located in the Mixteca Baja, probably in the region of the same name.

COLCOLCA A group inhabiting Chalco, in the southern part of the Valley of Mexico. There the Colcolca belonged to the confederation called the Chalco-Amecameca. They were associated with several other small cultures that united to form a standing army and were reported to have had 13 rulers.

COLIMA A region on the coast of western Mexico, now a modern state, and the home of a remarkable culture whose ceramics are treasured and well known in the modern world. The people of Colima pursued their own artistic goals with highly developed skill and sensitivity. New exca-

Colima ceramic dog

vation conducted in the region has determined that several phases can be attributed to Colima during the Formative Period (2000/1600 B.C.–A.D. 250/290): Ortices, Capocha, Periquillo, Colima and Armeria.

The Colima culture developed large, hollow figurines at an early stage. These figures included warriors, dwarfs and hunchbacks as well as effigies of birds, turtles, snails, fish and dogs. Some of their work also incorporated Atlantean-style figures. Many Colima figures were fashioned out of red slip. The statues, especially the dogs, may have had a mortuary function, as they were found in the shaft tomb complexes of the region. Red pottery flutes were also used as grave offerings, as well as long-necked, flaring-rimmed jars. The Colima decorations included negative and polychrome paintings. Other wares included red on orange, red, creams and red on creams.

COLORS The Mesoamerican cultures ascribed certain religious or spiritual values to specific colors. The cardinal points were assigned colors by the various groups, and the deities associated with certain aspects of temple ceremonies also were accorded colors, denoting their purpose.

Colors known throughout Mesoamerica include:

Black—the color of the west, signifying war (because of obsidian), fasting, the unmarried state

Blue—the color of sacrifice and the priestly role

Green—the color of royalty, from the feathers of the Quetzal bird

Red—denoting the eastern direction, signifying blood, the married state, death and mourning

White—the color of the north, purity

Yellow—the color of the south, signifying maize. (See individual cultures for details.)

COLOSSAL HEADS A feature of the Olmec civilization, recovered from such sites as San Lorenzo, La Venta and Tres Zapotes. These heads range in size from just under five feet to nine feet six inches. They are all fashioned of basalt and appear to depict men rather than deities. The features are usually similar, having wide faces, thick lips and flat, broad noses. Distinctive features stylize the heads and seem to portray individuals. Some are stern, while others have pleasant expressions. Teeth are evident in two smiling faces. The iris of the eye in each head is indicated in a low relief circle in the eyeball. All of the colossal heads wear a close-fitting, helmetlike headdress adorned with designs or are plain. The rounded edges of the helmets

Colossal head, Villahermosa

would appear to prevent easy damage by projectiles. Most have ear ornaments. Since the heads have a smooth portion extending up their backs, presumably the statues were fashioned to be set against walls. The heads at Tres Zapotes and La Venta were found upright. At San Lorenzo they had been dropped or rolled into ravines.

COLUMBIA RIVER A natural waterway in Belize, draining the region and providing water and transport to cities such as Lubaantum, the Maya ceremonial site.

COMALCALCO A Maya site in the northern part of Tabasco, on the western edge of the Maya domain near the Gulf Coast, constructed entirely from clay brick. The use of clay in this city is unique, and the structures are even more distinctive in that they are built of brick thin enough to be termed clay slabs. Dominating Comalcalco is a building called the Acropolis, where a large pyramidal platform serves as the base of two small shrines. A large palace was constructed on the platform, which contains tombs as well. The tomb was provided with nine bas-relief figures, three to a wall and originally painted red. These are probably portraits of the Nine Lords of the Maya underworld. On a lower level of the pyramid two other temples stand side by side. One contains a stucco mask, incorporated into the southern staircase. Seated figures and religious themes are displayed in the second shrine. A plaza faces the Acropolis, surrounded by mounds. A large pyramid with a central staircase is on the plaza, with a temple on its summit. Stucco figures also adorn this shrine. A third temple was discovered on a nearby mound. Dating to the Classic Period (c. A.D. 1/250–900), Comalcalco reflects a blend of cultures, including that of the Mexicanized groups. It had a ceramic industry that produced paste vessels.

COMALTEPEC A site in Guerrero, dating to the Late Formative Period (300 B.C.–c. A.D. 250/290) or Early Classic Period (c. A.D. 1/250–600) and located near the Oaxaca border. Plain and carved stelae were found in the city, along with sculptures in the round. These were obviously monumental works for mounds or pyramids. The surviving pieces reflect the skill of the Guerrero groups who worked in ceramics or metal and whose wares were in demand in the extensive trade systems of the period. Comaltepec reflects the influence of both Monte Alban and Teotihuacan, which flourished at the time.

COMETS   The orbiting celestial travelers noted by the ancient Maya astronomers. It is believed by some scholars that God L, shown smoking a cigar in a Palenque relief honoring Pacal and Chan Bahlam, two rulers of the city, is Halley's Comet. The date on the relief is January 17, 684, some six months before the comet was visible in Maya lands. The Maya astronomers used the 76-year interval of the comet's appearance for calculating a multiple for setting the date of divine or royal births in chronicles.

COMITAN   A site in Chiapas, near the Guatemalan border, dated to the Paleo-Indian Period (11,000–7000 B.C.). Comitan holds evidence of human habitation and development in the region during that historical era.

COMPLEXES   Divisions of Aztec deities including particular groups of gods with specific traditions and particular religious spheres and functions. The Aztec (Mexica) used the following complexes in their ceremonial and religious activities: Centeotl-Xochipilla, Huitzilopochtli, Mictlantecuhtli, Mixcoatl-Tlahuizcalpantecuhtli, Ometeotl, Ometochtli, Quetzalcoatl, Teteoinnan, Tezcatlipoca, Tlaloc, Tonatiuh and Xiuhtecuhtli. (See AZTEC GODS.)

CONCHAS PHASES I AND II   Large cultural developments on the Pacific coast dated to 800 to 600 B.C. and reflected in village clusters. A pyramidal mound and clay platforms were constructed by the Conchas Phase groups. Ceramics from their period include composite silhouette

Aztec Tonatiuh statue

forms and natural figurines. (See MESOAMERICA, FORMATIVE PERIOD, for details of this era.)

CONSOLATION PYRAMID   A Huaxtec site located in the central region of San Luis Potosi. A Maya-style pyramid, the Consolation Pyramid is surrounded by a group of smaller platforms, called the Birds of Stone by the local inhabitants of the region. (See HUAXTEC.)

CONTEC   A group involved in the development of the region of Chalco in the Valley of Mexico. The Contec were part of the Chalco-Amecameca confederation and took part in the activities of confederation in the region.

CONVENTO PHASE   A developmental period associated with the Mixtec group in the city of Coixtlahuaca, one of the Mixtec capitals. This phase dates from A.D. 1520 to 1535. (See MIXTEC.)

COPAL   A resin plant (*Protium copal*), used as incense in Mesoamerican religious ceremonies and highly valued. The substance was widely traded during various eras.

COPAN   A Maya site in the western part of Copan on the Chamelecon River in Honduras, made world famous in 1980 when it was designated a world heritage site by UNESCO. The city was already well known because of its impressive ruins and a tomb found in a pyramidal mound called 10-L-26. Copan is believed to have been more than a Maya ceremonial center, probably having been an artistic and scientific site for the entire Maya realm. Located about 2,000 feet above sea level, Copan has a commanding view of a valley that is roughly eight miles long. It is surrounded by small hills. The earliest emblem glyph dates the city to A.D. 554 or earlier.

The city has a ceremonial complex and 16 adjacent groups of structures built in conjunction with the ceremonial role of Copan and its learned Maya inhabitants. Several theories concern the name of the site. It was possibly named for Copan Calel, who was the ruler during the time of the Spanish conquest, or it could have been derived from references to local sites. The name could represent the capital of the region or could have been derived from *copantl*, meaning "bridge." Inscriptions on the stelae recovered at the site date to A.D. 465, with the last hieroglyphic monument erected in A.D. 800. This places Copan in the Classic Period. Ceramic phases associated with the site, however, come from an earlier period.

The Ceremonial Plaza or Grand Court of Copan, contains stelae from various eras of development. Some are a mixture of the Olmec and Maya styles. One altar on the site depicts a serpent. This was the last monument erected in Copan, with the A.D. 800 dating. Some stelae also depict women, and some have a unique basketweave style of glyphs.

The Copan ball court is the third version of the structure, with the present one covering older versions. Stelae associated with this court were recovered, as was a marker and a circular altar. The Court of the Inscribed Stairway is near this ball court and includes stelae and a temple. Many researchers believe the hieroglyphs found on the stairway to be the longest inscription in the Maya domain. Another

Copan Maya stela

staircase, dedicated to Chac, the god of rain, is nearby and has an accompanying altar.

Several pyramids and temples stand in the complex now called the Acropolis. The Temple of the Inscriptions and an altar contain glyphs, and a stone head was discovered there. The Temple of Meditation opens onto another court, which has an open serpent's mouth design. Chac masks are incorporated into the design of this shrine. The nearby jaguar stairs are three levels high and contain glyphs and representations of the jaguar. There is also a Venus altar in the complex, associated with the worship of Quetzalcoatl, called Kukulcan by the Maya. Another jaguar altar and two other sacrificial tables are nearby, all having carved hieroglyphs.

Copan is renowned for its stelae, which were fashioned of andesite. They include monuments carved on one, two, three and four sides. Stelae having human figures on two sides were also found. Other stelae, usually cruciform in design and hollow, appear to have served as repositories for pilgrim offerings.

Copan overlooked the Rio Copan, which extended north into Motagua. The Sky dynasty was in control of the region, and it is believed that other cities, such as Quirigua, received their rulers from Copan. The valley of Copan sheltered the city's suburban population, and rather imposing structures in the valley served as residential sites and administrative offices. A causeway connected the suburban quarters with the main city and its ceremonial complex. One large structure in the valley served a politically and religiously powerful family and reached the causeway via a special branch. More than 50 tombs in Copan have been excavated recently, attesting to the large population and the richness of life among the noble class of the city. Copan served as a regional capital and had considerable influence throughout the entire area. Dates important to Copan include the capture of 18-Rabbit, a ruler, by Cauac Sky of Quiriqua in A.D. 731, and the accession of Sun-at-Horizon in A.D. 751. Another ruler, Yax Sky, took the throne in A.D. 771.

COPAN RIVER A waterway in the western part of Copan, Honduras, extending into Motagua and serving as a resource and possible travel route for the great Maya city of Copan and its surrounding territories.

COPIL A divine being, the son of the Aztec sorceress goddess Malinalxoch and the sister of the patron deity, Huitzilopochtli. After his mother was abandoned by the Aztec (Mexica) for her evil deeds, she raised Copil to be vengeful. At Malinalco, Copil attacked Huitzilopochtli and was slain after attempting to foment trouble among the people. His heart was thrown "over the water," apparently falling on the future site of Tenochtitlan. Tenoch, the Aztec leader, predicted that the great capital would be built on the spot where Copil's heart rested.

COPILCO A site just outside of modern Mexico City, which contained a cemetery dating to the Early Classic Period (c. A.D. 1/250–600) or to the Formative Period (2000/1600 B.C.–c. A.D. 250–90). Those remains, now called El Pedregal, were discovered under a thick lava flow from Xitle Volcano, which erupted in c. A.D. 400. Copilco was probably uninhabited at the time, as the people are believed to have abandoned the area about a century and a half earlier, moving to the great city of Teotihuacan with their skills. Copilco was a trade and ceremonial center for the region. The pyramid and burial sites found there are being studied. The city was called the Place of the Diadem.

COPPER BELLS Wares from the Mexica regions of Mesoamerica, molded in special forms made of charcoal and clay. These forms were then cut open. Pebbles serve as clappers. The bells themselves are pear-shaped, about one to two inches long. Some were button-shaped, others bore designs, but all have small top loops. The highly prized copper bells were worn on ankles and wrists. A cache of

800 were found in a cave in Honduras. Presumably they were stored there by a trader who never returned.

CORALILLO PHASE   A cultural development in the southern Jalisco archaeological zone of Tuxcacuesco-Zapolitan, associated with Autlan wares. The phase dates to the Formative Period (2000 B.C.–c. A.D. 250/90). Coralillo wares include red on buff and red on brown. Mazapa ceramics are also associated with the products of this cultural development, as were clay whistles.

CORRAL PHASE   A cultural development associated with the Toltec city of Tula, dating to A.D. 800 and associated with Mazapa-style ceramics. Monochromes, dichromes and other styles were found in the region, as well as water jars and legged vessels. The monochromes and dichromes were shaped into bowls. (See MAZAPA PHASE.)

COSIHUESA (Cocijoeza)   The most illustrious Zapotec ruler, son of the "Deceiver." His name means "Lightning Creator," and he lived sometime in the Late Post-Classic Period (A.D. 1200–1521). Cosihuesa defended Zapotec lands against Aztec assaults, allying himself with the Mixtec, who were also defying Aztec imperial expansion. A battle at Guiengola ended in a truce between the Aztec and the Zapotec, and Cosihuesa, admired by his enemies, was given an Aztec princess, Coyolicatzin, as his bride. She became Queen Pelaxilla and gave birth to Cocijopii, who eventually ruled Tehuantepec. The Aztec, attacking Zaachila, Cosihuesa's capital, expected the queen to open the gates for them, but she took the part of her husband and his people. Cosihuesa had five children, including Princess Donaji, who married a Mixtec noble and died after having accepted Christianity. Cosihuesa is recorded as having reclaimed the city of Zaachila, which the Zapotec had lost during prolonged Aztec imperial assaults. An alliance eventually restored his throne to him.

COSMOLOGY   The system through which Mesoamerican civilizations explained relationships between the material and spiritual world. These cultures asked the primordial questions concerning life and death. Most of the major groups in the region throughout the centuries viewed the material world as a single layer in a complex, tiered universe that included levels of punishment for misdeeds and realms of bliss for service, sacrifice and faith. Such a view presupposes a sophistication concerning the relationship of human beings to the universe and was based on an intricate system of moral values. The creation myths that evolved in the various cultures were elaborate and enduring, in many cases stamping the individual civilizations with recognizable practices and outlooks. The cosmology of each major culture is included in the entries concerning that culture.

COSTA GRANDE   A site on the Pacific coast of Guerrero, just north of modern Acapulco. The people here had contact with several major Mesoamerican cultures and were influenced especially by the city of Teotihuacan and by the Maya. They were responsible for the artistic and cultural development of Guerrero.

COTORRA PHASE   A cultural development in the region of Chiapas de Corzo. An obsidian industry flourished in the region during the Cotorra Phase, which is dated from 1500 to 1100 B.C. Weaving is also evident in this era.

COTTON   The plant (*Gossypium hirsutum, L.*), grown in Mexico, with a Peruvian variety and associated with *G. arboreum* and *G. herbaceum;* hybrids were used in Mesoamerica from the earliest periods. Mexica cotton dates to around 1700 B.C., but its use was not widespread and it was not available to all cultures. The way in which cotton plants were hybridized is unknown. During the Aztec period, the Late Post-Classic (A.D. 1200–1521), cotton was grown in Cuernavaca and other regions. Emperor Huitzilihuitzl is reported to have brought the cotton to Tenochtitlan for use by the Aztec.

COTZUMALHUAPA (Santa Lucia)   A unique site on the Pacific plain of Guatemala, one of the richest cacao-producing regions in Mesoamerica. Dating to the Classic Period (c. A.D. 1/250–900), Cotzumalhuapa, as it was known before the arrival of the Spanish, was characterized by cobble-covered structures and stone monuments. The style of architecture at the site is a combination of Mexica and Maya designs. The local culture used the 260-day calendar and worshipped Mexica gods. Ball games were also conducted in Cotzumalhuapa, and large courts were erected there. At the time of the Spanish conquest (A.D. 1521), the region was populated by a non-Maya group called the Pipil, related to the Aztec and other Nahuatl speakers. Cotzumalhuapa's people may have immigrated from the Valley of Mexico sometime during the sixth century A.D. A very graceful, fluid sculptural style is associated with the city, clearly evident from the more than 200 carved monuments discovered at the site. The Cotzumalhuapa style includes speech scrolls, non-Maya glyphs and beautiful monumental sculptures, including the heads of wrinkled old men, bearded men and stelae. The death theme predominates, as do representations of the ball game. El Baul and other sites, especially along the Pacific slopes of Guatemala, provide examples of this style. (See PIPIL.)

COUIXCA   One of the myriad small cultures that settled south of the Valley of Mexico during the Classic Period (c. A.D. 1/250–900). The Couixca are believed to have had ties with the great Toltec nation.

COXCATLAN CAVE   A site in southeastern Puebla, where Paleo-Indian Period (11,000–7000 B.C.) groups ranged through the arid, mountainous terrain. The cave served as a seasonal habitation for these nomads. Choppers, *manos,* scrapers, stone bowls and jars were found at the cave site, with seeds and maize cobs. It is believed that this was an original region for the domestic production of maize. Some 26,000 corncobs were discovered. Cotton was in use here in c. 2000 B.C. In later periods the people here gathered other plants and began using *metates* and nets. They settled into communities as early as 4800 to 3500 B.C., perhaps continuing their seasonal rounds. The Coxcatlan Cave is also associated with the Tehuacan Sequence, and gives evidence of cremation rituals and possible cannibalism.

COXCATLAN PHASE A cultural development dated to c. 5000 to 3400 B.C., demonstrating the first appearance of the use of wild and domestic maize in the Coxcatlan Cave region, associated with the Tehuacan Sequence. The maize used was of the corn-pod type.

COXCATLAN VIEJO A site in the Tehuacan Valley of southern Puebla. Built on a series of ridges, the site has plazas situated on crests. Another large plaza is visible at the foot of the ridges. The urban plan appears to be related to fortifications that are no longer extant. The hillsides surrounding Coxcatlan Viejo were also terraced. A ceramic workshop was discovered on the site, which is believed to date to the Late Formative Period (A.D. 600–900).

COYOACAN A site in the Valley of Mexico, near modern Mexico City, which dates to the Late Post-Classic Period (c. A.D. 1200/1250–1521), the time of the Aztec dominance. Coyoacan was an ally of the Tepanec, who were the most powerful people during the reign of Tezozomoc. When the Aztec attacked the Tepanec after Tezozomoc's death, the Coyoacan went to the assistance of their allies. Itzcoatl and his Aztec armies assaulted them in return. When Tlacaelel, the high-ranking councilor of the Aztec, went to offer terms to the Coyoacan, he and his aides were forced to wear women's clothes and dance for the citizens of that city. As a result, the Aztec increased their hostilities, and Tzutzumatzin, the last ruler of Coyoacan, was slain by Aztec emperor Ahuitzotl. The city became a vassal of the Aztec Empire. Later, when the Aztec diverted fresh spring water from Coyoacan to their capital, Tenochtitlan, the ruler of Texcoco, Nezahualcoyotl, advised them that their efforts would result in floods. The Aztec persisted, and Tenochtitlan was inundated. Dikes, levees and canals had to be built as a result.

COYOLXAUHQUI An Aztec (Mexica) goddess, the sister of Huitzilopochtli, who slew their mother, Coatlicue, with the aid of her 400 brothers. When Coatlicue gave birth to Huitzilopochtli just before dying, he took his revenge on his siblings. On the sacred mountain of Coatepec, Coyolxauhqui was cut to pieces. A magnificently carved circular commemorative stela depicting the dismembered form of the goddess was discovered in the Great Temple of Tenochtitlan. The possible source of Coyolxauhqui's cult among the Aztec may have been the goddess Chantico of Xochimilco.

COYOTLATELCO PHASE A cultural development following the fall of the great city of Teotihuacan, associated with Tula and with the Corral Phase and its Mazapa wares. The Coyotlatelco Phase ended with the fall of Tula, the Toltec capital, in c. A.D. 1156/1168. It was characterized as a phase by the discovery of bowls decorated with spiral or wavy motifs, drawn between fine parallel lines, painted in red or in the natural clay color. Tripod vases of polished brown clay with large hollow legs were also produced in this era. These were decorated with wide bands and incised designs. Bottles and flat figurines were also created.

COYOLATE RIVER A waterway in the Guatemalan highlands, flowing from the interior peaks to the Pacific Ocean.

COYUCA A site in the middle Balsas regions in Guerrero, where an Olmec stela was discovered. Coyuca dates to the Formative Period (2000 B.C.–c. A.D. 250/290).

COZUMEL A Maya site on an island off the eastern coast of Quintana Roo, which served as a pilgrimage center. The site was occupied from the Late Formative Period (300 B.C.–A.D. 250/290) and reached a position of dominance in c. A.D. 1400. The shrine of Ix Chel, a Maya goddess of medicine, childbirth and floods, was located on Cozumel. The island was visited by Maya who wanted special intercessions. Rituals concerning the calendric system were also conducted on the island. Beyond its religious importance, Cozumel served as a "free port" for traders and merchant groups. The Peten (Putun) Maya maintained storage platforms there. In later eras Cozumel became a center of the Toltec-Itza administration. There are several ruins in Cozumel, including shrines overlooking the sea. Its major surviving temple is at El Cedral, in the southern part of the island. This temple is two-chambered.

CRUZ PHASE A cultural development associated with the Mixtec city of Coixtlahuaca, serving as one of the capitals of that group. The phase, one of several discovered in the city, dates from 1300 to 200 B.C.

CUACUAPITZHUAC "Pointed Arch," the founder of the Aztec (Mexica) city of Tlatelolco, the sister city of Tenochtitlan on Lake Texcoco. He was a son of Tezozomoc, the celebrated Tepanec ruler. The Tepanec were considered the regional heirs to the Toltec, thus Cuacuapitzhuac legitimatized the rule of the Aztec in that city. He collected tributes but gave them to his father. In turn, Tezozomoc built a royal residence for him in Tlatelolco.

CUADROS A Pacific coast (Suconusco) culture, dating from 1000 to 840 B.C., probably related to the Ocos people, using estuaries, beaches and forests as habitats. Salinas La Blanca, a site in that region, gives evidence of only seasonal occupation, but other settlements were soon developed and occupied year-round. The remains of *tecomates* (neckless jars) and flat-bottom bowls with slanted sides and rocker-stamp designs indicate the relationship between the Ocos and the Cuadros. Shells and the remains of corn were also discovered there. (See also JOCOTAL.)

CUANALAN A site in the Valley of Mexico, dating to c. 1300 B.C., with houses constructed in clusters. Compounds were erected there for entire families. The people of Cuanalan were part of the surge in cultural development in the region that took place in the Formative Period.

CUAUHTEMOC An Aztec commander, also called Descending Eagle. Listed in some accounts as the "last Aztec emperor," who led the Aztec forces from A.D. 1520 to 1525 in a rebellion against the Spanish occupation of the city of Tenochtitlan. A prince of the royal line, Cuauhtemoc confronted the Europeans and their Mesoamerican allies, and was eventually isolated with his troops in the northern section of the city of Tlatelolco, then part of Tenochtitlan. There they withstood a siege of 93 days before he and his family were taken prisoner. Cortez is reported to have received him graciously because of his brave stand, but eventually he was hanged by the Spaniards.

CUAUHTINCHAN   A site in the Valley of Puebla, possibly founded by the Cuauhtinchan, a group associated with the Chichimec who entered the Valley of Mexico in c. A.D. 1200. Led by Xolotl, known as the Monster, the Chichimec confederation made their home in the region. The city of Cuauhtinchan was attacked in c. A.D. 1396 by a combined force of Tepanec and Aztec. During the reign of Huitzilihuitl, the Aztec were vassals of the Tepanec. They attacked Cuauhtinchan and defeated the people there. The city and its inhabitants became part of the Tepanec domain. When the Aztec and the Triple Alliance forces crushed the Tepanec, Cuauhtinchan became part of the new empire. (See TRIPLE ALLIANCE.)

CUAUHTITLAN   A site in the Valley of Mexico dating to the Late Post-Classic Period (A.D. 1200/1250–1521), considered part of the active trade system of the region. The people of Cuauhtitlan, believed to be related to the Chichimec who had entered the Valley of Mexico in A.D. 1200, used bows and arrows in their battles with local populations. They worshipped the Chichimec gods and pursued the agricultural customs of the region. The Cuahtitlan fought the Tepanec and with the fall of Culhuacan welcomed the immigrants from that city into their community. The information about this site and people is largely drawn from the *Codex Chimalpopoca.* (See ANALES CUAUHTITLAN.)

CUAUHTLA RIVER   A waterway in the regions of Morelos and Guerrero, joining the Amacuzac River and becoming part of the great Balsas system. The Cuauhtla River was used by the Olmec. The site of San Pablo Pantheon is on its banks.

CUAUHTLI   The eagle, day sign in the Aztec version of the *tonalpohualli,* the calendar system.

CUAUHXILOTITLAN   See HUITZO.

CUELLO   A Maya site in northern Belize, dating to c. 2500–2000 B.C. and the heart of the Swasey culture there. The site has been investigated in modern times and contains the remains of one of the oldest Maya unearthed. Stratified building and debris remains, some as deep as 10 feet, have been studied. The burials unearthed include a female with the cranial deformity of the Maya (the custom of shaping infant skulls), believed to date to 1500 B.C. The graves contained jade beads, some of the earliest known in the Maya domain, but since the graves are uniform no aristocratic ranks are evident. The presence of jade indicates trade, because the source of such beads was 250 miles away. Limestone tools, from the Maya Mountains, were also found in Cuello, which is named for its current owners.

By 400 B.C., Cuello had become a ceremonial center for the surrounding region, with a cluster of pyramidal temple platforms constructed from lime and plaster. Wooden shrines were built on the summits of these platforms. The pyramids here show evidence of the earliest known use of

plaster on a Maya public monument. One pyramid, standing 12 feet high and spread over an acre, was completed in c. A.D. 200/300. Taller pyramids followed, and plazas and stelae were incorporated into the design. An unusual urn was used to cover the heads of corpses. A cache of remains of human sacrificial victims was found on the site. It is believed that 1,000 Maya lived in the city at the start of the Classic Period (c. A.D. 1/250).

CUEPOPON   A district in the northern part of the Aztec capital city of Tenochtitlan. *Cuepopon* means "the place of the blossoming of the flowers."

CUERAVAPERI   A goddess worshipped by the Tarascan people. She was believed to be the mother of all other Tarascan deities.

CUERNAVACA (1)   Called Cuauhnahuac or Quauhnahuac by the Mesoamericans, a site south of modern Mexico City in the Valley of Mexico. The ruler of Cuernavaca was noted as a powerful sorcerer. Huitzilihuitl, the Aztec king, dreamed of this king's fabulously beautiful daughter, Miahuaxihuitl. Supposedly spiders, bats and other creatures surrounded her palace courtyard so that no man could witness her beauty. Huitzilihuitl wooed Miahuaxihuitl, who became the mother of Motecuhzoma (Moctezuma) I. The region of Cuernava was also known for cotton crops. Huitzilihuitl is reported to have brought the cotton to Tenochtitlan, offering it as a finer material than the usual Aztec fiber cloths.

CUERNAVACA (2)   A site in Morelos, at an altitude of 4,500 feet. This settlement and the surrounding region were involved in the agricultural development of the Formative Period (c. 2000/1600 B.C.–A.D. 250/290 evident here. Gualupita, now destroyed, was another nearby site. Olmec ceramic wares were recovered there.

CUETZAPALIN   The lizard, a day sign in the Aztec version of the *tonalpohualli,* the calendar system.

CUEXTECATLICHOCAYAN   A fabled site whose name means "the Place Where the Huaxtec Weep," near modern Panuco. The Toltec, invading the Huaxtec realm, punished the local inhabitants at Cuextecatlichocayan. It became a sacrificial site mentioned in Huaxtec records but not identified geographically.

CUICUILCO   Called the Place of Singing in Nahuatl, a site in the southern part of modern Mexico City, in the present university quarter. Cuicuilco flourished from 900 B.C. to A.D. 300/400 and was one of the major linking cultures between the Formative Period and the Classic Period in Mesoamerica. Presumably an independent city-state, Cuicuilco contains evidence of several separate phases of historical development. The first settlement took place 900 B.C., and by 600 B.C. the site had become a major population center. This prestige lasted until c. 150 B.C., when the city was eclipsed by the great city of Teotihuacan. Sometime between A.D. 300 and 400, Cuicuilco was covered by lava from the erupting Xitle Volcano. The lava flowed directly

Cuicuilco Ticoman statue

through the city, rising in time to the third level of the buildings and monuments there. For this reason Cuicuilco has been called the Mexican Pompeii, although there are no remains comparable to those of those of the ancient Roman city.

The first settlers of Cuicuilco farmed, fished and raised dogs, perhaps as food. They used quartz and obsidian arrowheads and received jade and shell ornaments in trade. The pyramid erected there in c. 400 B.C. was constructed of adobe, standing 65 feet high and approximately 400 feet in diameter. The pyramid did not adhere to the usual Mesoamerican pattern but was a rounded cone with four rows of steps and a platform. A temple on the top level was probably dedicated to the wind god, Ehecatl, a form of Quetzalcoatl. Stairs on the east and west sides led to this temple.

The population of Cuicuilco, estimated as reaching 10,000, required an extensive agricultural system, and a ditch irrigation system was also used. Cuicuilco appears to have served as the capital of a confederation of groups in the area. The first population increase dates to around 600 B.C. By 150 B.C., the population is believed to have risen to 20,000, giving further evidence of Cuicuilco's status as a local capital. A massive ceremonial complex was erected; a grid pattern is evident in the layout of streets and housing areas. Cuicuilco may have dominated the entire southern region of the Valley of Mexico, as other centers suffered declines in this era. Outlying areas served as expanded agricultural and industrial bases. A cemetery was also located near the city.

Ceramics recovered in Cuicuilco include *canitas*, the oldest type of small figurines found in the Valley of Mexico. These are associated with a ceramic phase called Ticoman, probably dating to the pre-Olmec period and the Tlalpan phase. The statues are naked females with long hair. Their eyes were fashioned out of large holes, surrounded by

circles or tiny indentations. The potters of Cuicuilco also used banded geometric designs, as well as composite silhouette forms and tripod bowls.

Because of the dominance of the city of Teotihuacan, researchers believe that most of the people abandoned the site of Cuicuilco before the volcano erupted. Tremors and other natural warnings may have caused such a migration. Cuicuilco is important because it controlled some of the finest agricultural land in the Valley of Mexico. The local population of Cuicuilco also employed innovative techniques in farming, including crop rotation and irrigation. In its own era, the city was the largest in the Valley of Mexico and perhaps the first city-state in the region. Scholars believe that the city of Teotihuacan was laid out according to the patterns evident in Cuicuilco to this day.

CUITLAHUAC (1)   An area in the southern part of the Valley of Mexico that was noted for its Chichimec kings, called sorcerer chiefs (*tzompanteuctin nahualteleuctin*). These Chichimec rulers claimed the god Mixcoatl as their ancestor and were celebrated for their cultic lore.

CUITLAHUAC (2)   A prince of the Aztec (Mexica) royal line who succeeded Motecuhzoma (Moctezuma) II after his murder by the Spaniards in 1520. Cuitlahuac, however, was unable to rally his people, and the Spaniards quickly dealt with him. He was succeeded by a general named Cuauhtemoc, who started a massive rebellion.

CUITLAXOCHITZIN   The daughter of King Xolotl, "the Monster," of the Chichimec. She was given in marriage to Acolnahuacatl of the Tepanec and became the mother of the illustrious Tepanec ruler Tezozomoc.

CUITZEO   A lake in the region of Michoacan, associated in historical records with the development of the Tarascan civilization.

CULHUA   A group related to the Chichimec who entered the Valley of Mexico in the 12th century A.D., settling in the southern part of that region. Their origin is traditionally believed to be Teoculhuacan, a region beyond Tula, and they appear to have journeyed to the Toltec capital, taking part in affairs of that city. When Tula collapsed, the Culhua were forced to seek new lands and a new beginning. Artistic and educated, they entered the Valley of Mexico and soon transmitted Toltec civilization to new generations. Settling in a place they called Culhuacan, meaning "the Place of the Turning" or "the Place of the Twisted" in Nahuatl, the Culhua achieved prominence and power. Culhuacan was located near the *Cerro de la Estrella*, "the Hill of the Star," south of Lake Texcoco. Because of the political conditions in the Valley of Mexico at the time, the Culhua are believed to have made alliances with the Tepanec and the Acolhua. When the Tepanec confronted the Triple Alliance and the Aztec forces, the Culhua became part of the emerging empire, as the Tepanec were destroyed.

Culhuacan was an independent city-state for many centuries, but it collapsed when a civil war ravaged the region. Achitometl, the ruler who welcomed the Aztec (Mexica) into the Valley of Mexico, was forced in time to exile the

Aztec, chasing them into Lake Texcoco, where they founded Tenochtitlan. In time, because the Culhua retained the legitimizing mantle of the Toltec and because the Aztec needed to be allied with stable forces in the region, a prince of the Culhua line became the Aztec ruler.

Another Culhua site was Chapultepec, which was the setting for the suicide of the last Toltec king, Huemac. Called the Hill of the Grasshopper, Chapultepec lay east of Mexico City. Aqueducts were erected there to provide fresh water for the Aztec capital from Lake Texcoco. The Culhua worshipped Centeotl, the god of maize, and other Nahuatl deities. They were influential in cultural developments during their era, carrying on the great Toltec traditions.

CULHUACAN (1)   See CULHUA.

CULHUACAN (2)   A site believed to be in the northeastern part of the Valley of Mexico, called Curved Mountain. It was recorded as a resting place of the Aztec. Some scholars believe that Culhuacan, a mountain with caves, was the fabled Chicomoztoc, the Place of the Seven Caves of Nahuatl tradition.

CULHUACAN PHASE   A cultural development also called Aztec I (A.D. 900–1200) and associated with Culhuacan and Puebla. Tripod bowls with serpent feet in black-on-orange ware were manufactured, sometimes with stamped designs. (See AZTEC CERAMICS.)

CULIACAN RIVER   A waterway in the Pacific coastal lowlands, forming flood and delta plains.

CUPUL MAYA   See MAYA DYNASTIES, CUPUL.

CURATAME   The son of the Tarascan national hero Tariacuari, who completed the conquest of Lake Patzcuaro and divided the Tarascan kingdom into three parts.

CURIACAVERI   A Tarascan deity, patron of fire and part of the solar worship.

CURL HEAD   A ruler of the Maya dynasty of the city of Tikal, listed in some records as the 19th such lord of the great ceremonial complex. Commemorated on a stela found in Tikal, he is depicted wearing ceremonial robes with a captive at his feet. The stela dates to A.D. 527.

CURL SNOUT (Curl Nose)   A Maya ruler of the city of Tikal, c. A.D. 379. He is depicted on a monument at that site wearing the robes of a Teotihuacan noble, and his tomb contained Teotihuacan artifacts. It is believed that Curl Snout ruled for about 26 years and was the father of Stormy Sky. He was entombed in the Acropolis of Tikal.

CURRENCY   See MESOAMERICAN TRADE; see also under CURRENCY in the entries on the major cultures; see also CACAO.

DAINZU A vast Zapotec city of central Oaxaca, in the Tlacolula arm of the valley, dated to the Classic Period (c. A.D. 1/250–900). Probably founded by a local group, the site became part of the Monte Alban realm during the Zapotec era. Some Olmec influence is evident in Dainzu, which was partially fortified, erected on the arm of a chain of hills and backed by the outcropping of a large butte. The remains of the city lie in two separate sections: a pyramidal structure that dominates the eastern part and an elaborate ball court with other buildings in the west. The pyramidal mound is 150 feet along its north-south axis and originally stood approximately 25 feet high, three-tiered with a central stairway. The temple on the summit is built of stone. The pyramidal platform is adorned with inlaid, carved stones having bas-reliefs, similar to the *danzantes* of Monte Alban, a style familiar in Oaxaca. These figures, once 50 in number, wear ballplayer costumes, each having a face mask and

protective gear. They hold balls, perhaps denoting their ranks in the ball games. The pyramid also contains a tomb, constructed with a staircase and bas-reliefs of masonry. The western complex of Dainzu dates to the period called Monte Alban I (c. 500–22 B.C.) and now contains only walls and a single stairway. A tomb was also constructed in the complex, fashioned of carved stones depicting a crouching jaguar. Another nearby chamber holds carved slabs and a stairway for effect. A sunken patio lies beyond the tomb, and there is a second chamber with a drain. The ball court of Dainzu, dating to c. A.D. 1000, has been partially restored. A reservoir, 14 feet deep, had clay pipes that carried water into the city.

DANZANTES Unusual figures discovered in the city of Monte Alban in the Valley of Oaxaca, associated with the Temple of the *Danzantes*, dating to Monte Alban I (c. 900–

Dainzu pyramid relief

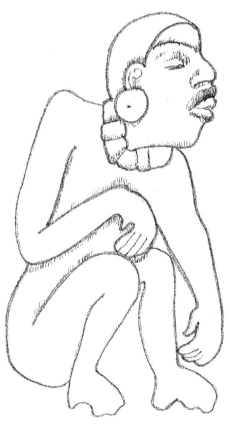

Danzante figure

200 B.C.). The *danzantes* date to the Rosario Phase, or perhaps earlier, in the region (c. 700/600–c. 500/450 B.C.). The name was given to these fluid reliefs by the Spanish, who saw them as dancers. They are nude males, slightly Olmecoid in style, either bearded or shaved, with or without teeth. More than 150 *danzantes* were discovered in Monte Alban. Their original purpose remains open to debate. Some scholars believe that they represent corpses, as their eyes are closed. Others view them as priests in rituals or as prisoners of war. The *danzantes* exemplify sacrificial mutilations, as some portray physical damage. Glyphs accompany each figure.

DATED MONUMENTS   In the Maya territories, such monuments exemplified calendar systems and religious concepts. The dating of monuments was an innovation used by some groups, especially the Maya, to provide historical continuity and to propagate the king-myths of power. By A.D. 450, more than half a dozen sites in northern Peten (Putun) had dated monuments. By the end of that century, the custom was in use throughout the peninsula and in the region now called Honduras as well. The cult of dated monuments spread to the Usumacinta Valley and to southern Campeche by A.D. 550. Dated monuments were in Chiapas and Belize by the end of the century. Not appearing for a time, probably as the result of Mexican invasions, the dated monuments reappear in Maya cities in the Classic Period (c. A.D. 1/250–900) and then vanish. The last dated monument in Palenque was erected in A.D. 784. Oxkintok raised its last in A.D. 849, and Seibal and Chichen Itza erected theirs in A.D. 889. (See EMBLEM GLYPHS.)

DELICIAS PHASE   A ceramic and cultural development associated with the Tepalcatepec Basin in Michoacan, dating to the Late Formative Period (300 B.C.–c. A.D. 250/290) or to the Early Classic Period (c. A.D. 1/250–900). Four types of ceramics are associated with this phase: red on brown, red on buff, polished and plain. Cream to dark-gray wares with a dull polish and *ollas* were recovered at sites associated with this phase, as were shell and pyrite ornaments and mirrors. Two figurines also were found.

DESERT CULTURE   Those nomadic groups inhabiting regions north of the semiarid regions of Mexico, Belize and as far south as the Guatemalan border. As far back as the Incipient Agriculture Period (7000–c. 2000/2500 B.C.) in the Tamaulipas region and elsewhere, bands of hunters and gatherers lived in caves and rock shelters. Some sites date from 6500 B.C. to 2000 B.C. These Desert Culture groups used a variety of tools, nets and baskets. The yucca and agave plants provided cordage materials, and *petates*, twilled mats, date to this period. (See ZACATECA (1); ZACATECA-DURANGO.)

DIABLO COMPLEX (or Focus)   A canyon site in the Sierra Madre de Tamaulipas, associated with the sequence recorded there and dated to the Paleo-Indian Period (11,000–7000 B.C.). Located near the site of Repelo, the Diablo Complex contained hammerstones, crushers, choppers and scrapers, some of which have been dated to 9000 B.C. (See TAMAULIPAS SEQUENCE.)

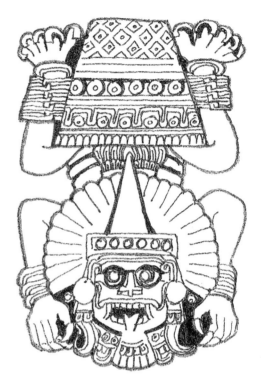

Diving God

DIVING GOD (1)   A Huaxtec depiction of a monster-faced deity appearing to descend headfirst. Formed out of stone and part of a temple design in Tepetzintla, the Diving God was probably a Huaxtec version of the deity Quetzalcoatl, manifested as Venus.

DIVING GOD (2)   A Maya deity depicted in Yucatan motifs, called the Bee God in some records. The Diving God was usually portrayed as a young man diving from the sky. Such a portrait is extant in Tulum, in Quintana Roo. Another one was discovered in Mayapan. The Diving God has also been equated with God E.

DOGS   Animals popular in almost all Mesoamerican cultures as pets and as a food source, even as a religious symbol. The hairless Mesoamerican dog was associated with Xolotl by the Aztec (Mexica) and with Pek, or lightning, by the Maya. The Aztec revered dogs as guides for the soul after death. In the Colima culture, the dog assumes a charming, lovable image. Pottery dogs appear in the Abejas Phase (c. 7000–2500 B.C.). (See XOLOITZCUINTLI.)

DONAJI   A Zapotec princess, the daughter of King Cosihuesa, who regained the city of Zaachila through a treaty with the Spanish and the Mixtec. The king died in A.D. 1529. Donaji, who probably became a Christian, was buried in a Zaachila church. Her tombstone calls her Maiona Cortez.

DOS PILAS   A Maya site on the Laguna Petexbatun in southwestern Peten in Guatemala. The name is Spanish for "Two Poles" or "Two Mounds." Subject to Tikal for much of its history, Dos Pilas is noted for its carved monuments

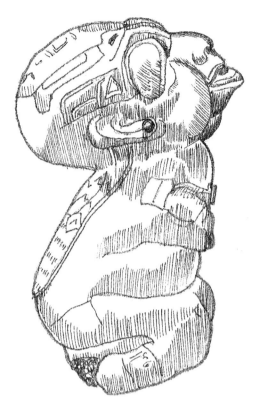

Olmec dwarf figure

and stelae. One, now fragmented, depicts a Maya noble in an elaborate costume. A glyph-carved staircase is an important element in the architectural design of the city. The kings of Dos Pilas took part in military actions that took many lives in Maya lands in the seventh century A.D. The wars, conducted by Jaguar Paw and other Maya rulers, hastened the collapse of the Maya cities. A stela found on the site depicts the Seibal ruler, Yich'ak Balam, as a prisoner of war brought to Dos Pilas for ritual sacrifice.

DOUBLE BIRD   A ruler of the great Maya city of Tikal, commemorated on a stela discovered there. The stela is dated to A.D. 557 and is believed to be the last one erected in Tikal before a long unrecorded period of local wars. Double Bird is listed in some records as the twenty-first ruler of Tikal. He was slain by Lord Water of Caracol in 562, and the dynasty came to an end.

DOUBLE-HEADED MONSTER   A Maya religious emblem, also called the Cosmic Monster. The creature's body may assume a reptilian or other form. Its second head is usually portrayed with a skeletal design. This being was

associated with the ascendancy of Maya rulers in their roles as Venus and as the sun.

"DRUNKARDS, THE"   Life-size figures in a long polychrome mural discovered in the great pyramid in the city of Cholula, a Puebla site dating to the Middle Formative Period (900–300 B.C.). The figures probably represent men involved in an intoxicating religious ceremony, probably using hallucinogenic drugs rather than alcohol.

DWARFS   Beings revered in several Mesoamerican cultures as semidivine. In the Olmec tradition, dwarfs were called *chaneque* and were the brewers of rain, depicted in Atlantean altars. In the Aztec tradition, dwarfs were also revered as rain brewers and associated with the rain god Tlaloc, hence their name: *tlaloques.* Aztec rain brewers were also believed to inhabit several mountain ranges. Aztec emperors employed dwarfs as counselors and entertainers. In the Maya, dwarfs were called *ch'at*, revered as Chac's offspring. The Zapotec honored them as aides of the mountain gods.

DZIBILCHALTUN   A Maya site near Merida in the northwestern part of the Yucatan. The name of the site is Maya for "the Place of Writing on Flat Stones." It is a mix of both Maya and Mexica styles of architecture and was occupied from around 500 B.C. until the present time. The Temple of the Seven Dolls, the major monument in Dzibilchaltun, was erected during the Late Classic Period (A.D. 600–900) and then covered by a second structure. Abandoned for a time and accessible only by a tunnel, the shrine contained seven figures, hence its name. The temple has a truncated tower and stucco decorations. The main plaza of Dzibilchaltun contains a Spanish chapel, with a patio and plain stelae preserved nearby. A short distance away is the *Cenote* Xlacah, one of several *cenotes* in the region. This one is 140 feet deep and possibly served as a place of human sacrifice and religious ceremonies. The city of Dzibilchaltun once covered more than seven square miles and is believed to have contained more than 8,000 separate structures and to have had an estimated population of 20,000 people.

DZIBILNOCAC   A Maya site in east-central Campeche displaying the Chenes form of architectural design and dating to c. 500 B.C.–A.D. 950/1000. The temple-palace, the best-preserved structure on the site, rests on a 250-foot platform and is noted for its three towers. Double rows of vaulted rooms complete the basic elements. Three other pyramidal bases on the site have temples with two rooms. The monster-mouth Chenes design is evident on the facades. There are seven large pyramids in Dzibilnocac and many smaller pyramids. It is believed that the site was abruptly abandoned.

E

EAGLE   A bird of the raptor category sometimes used with the jaguar as a totem in Mesoamerican cultures. Both animals were associated with the divine and represented strength and valor. The Olmec employed the fierce harpy eagle in their religious art, adorning the bird with flaming eyebrows. In Caxcaxtla, a Classic Period site (A.D. 1/250–900), murals depict wars between eagles and jaguars.

The Maya made the bird a calendrical symbol representing the sky. Eagles thus depicted have feathered crests. The Aztec (Mexica), inheriting the Toltec reverence for eagles, called the bird the *cuauhtli* and associated it with the sun. Tenoch, their priest-king, received a message from Huitzilopochtli that an eagle on a cactus would be the omen for the founding of their capital, Tenochtitlan. The Aztec city of Malinalco served as a warrior shrine and had an "Eagle's Nest," dedicated to the military groups associated with the bird. Human hearts offered up in sacrifice were called *cuauhnochtli,* or "eagle cactus fruit." (See KNIGHTS and MILITARY SOCIETIES.)

EARTH MOON GODDESS   A Huaxtec deity, depicted as a young woman. The cult of this goddess was widespread in the Huaxtec realm and dated to the earliest periods.

ECLIPSES   Celestial events that had profound religious significance for Mesoamerican cultures. The Maya, especially in the Yucatan, viewed eclipses as the "biting of the sun" or the "biting of the moon," usually by celestial ants. Maya astrologers were able to predict such events. The local populace took protective measures to avoid what were believed to be related catastrophes, such as birth defects. In the Aztec tradition, eclipses were terrifying events during which demons might roam the earth. During such times the Aztec created noise to banish the demons and to bring back the sun.

EDZNA   See ETZNA.

EHECATL   A form of the deity Quetzalcoatl, with the god of winds, usually honored with temples with round corners representing his sweeping, limitless powers. Figures of Ehecatl usually depict him as black, wearing a beaked mask. Sometimes he was portrayed with long canine fangs, and was often adorned with shell ornaments.

Maya figures include a form of Ehecatl at Seibal, dating to the late ninth century. Among the Aztec and other Valley of Mexico cultures, the deity was the patron of wind and a creative force benefiting humans. Popular throughout the region of Mexico, Ehecatl was worshipped by the Mixtec as well, appearing in the codices as the ancestor of the ruling noble clans.

One tradition credits Ehecatl for having brought love into the world, through his desire for the goddess Mayahuel. Their passion bore fruit in a beautiful tree that took root on the ground where Ehecatl and Mayahuel had descended from the sky.

EIGHT DEATH   A Toltec high priest, recorded as having taken part in the honors bestowed upon the Mixtec ruler Eight Deer during his visit to the capital of Tula in A.D. 1045. This ceremony provided Eight Deer with legitimate claims to his throne. (See EIGHT DEER.)

EIGHT DEER   Also called Jaguar or Tiger Claw, a Mixtec king born in A.D. 1011, the son of Five Alligator, also called Rain Sun. He was the ruler of the city of Tilantongo in the northern regions of Mixteca Alta. One of the illustrious

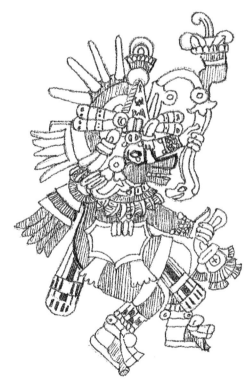

Ehecatl

Eight Deer

Second Dynasty in this region, he assumed the throne in A.D. 1030 and forged a political alliance. Eight Deer also inherited the throne of Tututepec and through marriages and campaigns added to his holdings. In A.D. 1045 he supported the Toltec in their expansion efforts; as a reward, during a ceremony in Tula he received a jade nose plug. This represented his elevation to the rank of lord in the Toltec domain. Eight Deer's career ended abruptly in A.D. 1063 when he attacked the native city of his latest wife and was taken prisoner in battle and then sacrificed. Eight Deer is also recorded as having visited the Hill of the Sun in Puebla, a journey lavishly documented because of its religious importance. The Hill of the Sun was the site of important ceremonies and rituals. Eight Deer is mentioned in seven surviving Mixtec codices.

EIGHTEEN RABBIT   The thirteenth ruler of the Maya city of Copan. He was captured during a battle with the forces of the city of Quirigua and decapitated.

EK BALAM   A Maya site in the northern Yucatan region, near modern Valladolid. The city dates to the Late Pre-Classic or the Early Classic Period in some sections, and to the Late Classic in others. It was not occupied over a long period. Covering some four square miles, the site has an oval outer wall and *sacheobs*. Platforms and buildings were discovered there as well as a headless statue and stelae. A temple dedicated to "The Twins," and a *chultun* having a carved stone relief and an altar were also discovered. Ek Balam was originally named the Black Tiger.

EK CHUAH   The patron deity of the Maya trader, the *ppolom*, usually depicted with a long nose and a black face.

Ek Chuah was also associated with war and was the patron of cacao plantations. As a war god he took on the role of a death deity. Itzamkanac, the capital of the Acalan region of the Chontal Maya, contained a temple honoring Ek Chuah.

EKIXIL   A lake in the Yucatan Peninsula, home of the city of Tayasal, the Itza capital. The city occupied five small islands in Lakes Ekixil and Peten.

EL ARENAL PHASE   A cultural development in the Jalisco region of western Mexico, dating to the Paleo-Indian Period (11,000–7000 B.C.). Tombs uncovered in El Arenal contained skeletons and grave offerings.

EL BAUL (Finca San Francisco)   A site on the Pacific coast near modern Guatemala City in Guatemala, reflecting Izapan and Pipil influences. The site dates to the Formative Period (2000 B.C. to A.D. 250/290) and is considered an important developmental stage. Three-dimensional monuments found here reflect Izapan styles, with some Teotihuacan influences. Other monuments in the Cotzumalhuapa are associated with the Pipil culture in the Late Classic Period (A.D. 600 to 900. Seventeen mounds are visible on the site, and more than thirty stone pieces have been recovered, including eight Pipil stelae. Sculpture includes the head of a bearded man, mythical beings, animals and deities. One head depicts a wrinkled, very aged man. El Baul was probably a ceremonial site, and some of the larger carved figures

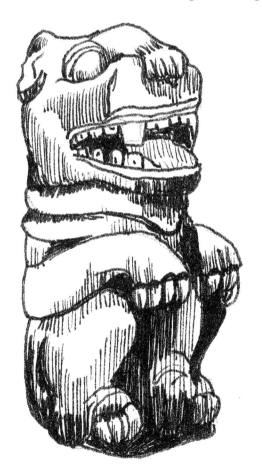

El Baul jaguar figurine

have shanks, indicating that they once adorned temple or shrine walls. The well-known Herrera Stela, with the Maya Long Count and an Olmec jaguar form as part of its design, was also recovered at El Baul.

EL CEDRAL   A small Maya site in the southern part of Cozumel on the eastern coast of the Yucatan Peninsula. A two-chambered temple was erected there, but little else is known of El Cedral's role. Vaults were discovered in the temple. The site is named for a nearby cedar grove.

EL CHAYAL   A Maya site southeast of modern Guatemala City in Guatemala, located in an area of obsidian deposits. In the Early Formative Period (2000–900 B.C.), flints and other obsidian ware were manufactured there. El Chayal remained a source of obsidian until the Spanish conquered the region, and thousands of blades were found there.

EL MECO   A Maya site in northeastern Quintana Roo, established sometime during the Early Classic Period (A.D. 250 to 600). The major structure, called El Castillo, is a five-tiered pyramid temple, having a stairway on the east side. The temple has a triple doorway with rounded columns. An older temple was discovered beneath it. Other temples in El Meco have columns, doorways and serpent-head designs. The city reached its peak between A.D. 1200 and 1500.

EL OPENO   A site south of Guadalajara on the eastern end of Lake Chapala in the Jalisco, a Colima culture region. Dating to around 400 B.C., El Openo is noted for shaft tombs and for a stone plaque recovered there. The shafts contained multiple burials. (See EL OPENO PHASE.)

EL OPENO PHASE   A cultural development, part of the Zacatenco-Arbolillo era in Michoacan. Graves and funerary passageways with stairs were uncovered in the sites of this phase, dating to the Middle Formative Period (900–300 B.C.) or earlier. Funerary offerings recovered include an Olmecoid statuette carved of green stone. Another figure, in the jaguar motif, was carved of jade. The clay statuettes manufactured in El Openo reflect local themes. Skulls buried without bodies were used for religious purposes. In full skeletal burials, the bones were painted red. In these graves, jade ear plugs and jade beads, obsidian points and serpent-motif adornments were also recovered. Jaquilipas is one site of the El Openo Phase.

EL PILAR   A Maya site on the border of northern Belize and Mexico, occupied from c. 300 B.C. to A.D. 1000. The city is located in the center of a tropical rain-forest preserve of Belize and is now being excavated.

EL PITAL   A newly discovered site on the Gulf of Mexico, north of Veracruz. The site includes the ruins of over 100 structures, clear evidence of urban development. Plazas, adjacent communities, ball courts and irrigation canals are laid out in a 40-square-mile area. El Pital dates to the Late Formative (c. 300 B.C.) Period, and contains Classic Period (A.D. 100 to 600) structures as well. Taking part in trade and agricultural ventures, El Pital is near Tajin, a former major power in the region. A number of neighboring sites on the Nautha River are also being excavated.

EL RIEGO PHASE   A cultural development dated to c. 7200–5200 B.C. in the Tehuacan region, indicating the beginnings of agriculture in their area. Nomadic groups gathered chili, squash, avocados, wild maize and cotton. Tools were used, including scrapers and choppers, mortars, pestles and *metates* and *manos*. The people wove materials and fashioned blankets out of the local fiber plants. Elaborate burial rituals took place in this phase, some multiple, and skulls were buried without bodies in cultic rituals during this era.

EL REY   A Maya site on Cancun island in Quintana Roo. It was named after a stone head depicting Kinich Ahau found there. The site includes two plazas, L-shaped structures and a three-level pyramid.

EL TAJIN   A Totonac site in the region of Veracruz on the gulf coast. The city was called the Place of Much Smoke, Incense, Thunder and Lightning or simply Lightning in the Totonac language. The Totonac culture was associated with the site, but it is believed that El Tajin was an independent city-state; Totonac records indicate that El Tajin was inhabited by the minions of the rain god, Tlaloc, who brewed thunder and lightning. The site covers 1.9 square miles and contains over 200 separate mounds. Two distinct phases can be documented for the city's development. In phase 1, dated from A.D. 100 to 500, El Tajin was a minor center with relatively small pyramidal platforms and some temples, associated with the developments in Teotihuacan. Trade wares have also been uncovered from this phase, probably some of the goods produced for the vast trade system in place then, including cacao, the local crop. In phase 2, dated from A.D. 550 to 1000, El Tajin was prominent, profiting from the decline of Teotihuacan. Historians believe that the city influenced a large region culturally, perhaps extending to Guatemala. All the major monuments on this site date to phase 2.

The dominant structure in El Tajin, the hallmark of the city, is the Pyramid of the Niches. This and the other structures are presented in a natural setting, as the site is surrounded on three sides by hills. The present form of the pyramid is believed to date to A.D. 300. This monument stands 60 feet high and is composed of six terraces and a central staircase. A temple once graced the summit, and a thick coat of stucco had covered the entire structure. The unique aspect of the pyramid is the 365 niches carved on six levels, probably mirroring the calendar system that provided 365 days for each year. The exact purpose of the niches, other than this calendric association, has not been determined. It is possible that effigies of local deities, perhaps those associated with Tlaloc, were in the spaces originally. Because of this pyramid and other structures, El Tajin is a major Veracruz archaeological site. An earlier pyramidal monument, dating to A.D. 100 and associated with the founding of the site, was discovered under the surviving one.

The great stairway that ascends the six levels of the Pyramid of the Niches has ramps decorated with stepped-fret designs and stone mosaics. Some scholars believe they reflect the artistic styles of Mitla, the Mixtec-Zapotec city in Oaxaca. The Pyramid of the Niches in its current state is believed to have been completed in c. A.D. 600/900. The great ceremonies of the city attracted pilgrims and devotees, and the city served as a regional trade center and cultural core. The Totonac appear to have occupied the site at a later date. The main sections of El Tajin were abandoned in A.D. 1200, possibly because of the continued military activity in the region and also as the result of a fire on the site. The Otomi and Teo-Chichimec groups probably entered the city at the time. Some records list the destruction of the site as dating to c. A.D. 1180/1230.

The ceremonial center that served El Tajin and the surrounding countryside was divided into two sections, one called El Tajin, a portion of which lies between two streams, and the other called El Tajin Chico (Little Tajin), on a level elevation. The Pyramid of the Niches dominated the first section. To the southeast of the pyramid is another platform with two temples. A stela was recovered there, reflecting the El Tajin style. A ball court lies to the south, a pyramid wall being one of its retaining elements. Intricate bas-reliefs adorn the other walls of this court. These carvings date to the Late Post-Classic Period (c. A.D. 1200), and they depict priests with sacrificial victims, *palmas*, the palm insignia used in the games, and the god of death. These particular decorations are Totonac and probably were added later. Another stepped pyramid, with niches and painted stucco designs, is on the same plaza, alongside a low, rectangular platform.

Four separate structures are still visible in the district called El Tajin Chico. The first was designed with a corbeled vault and an elaborate staircase. The second and fourth buildings were joined and a third structure was niched and terraced, with a western staircase still intact. A nearby ball court was constructed of large stone blocks, with bas-reliefs dating to A.D. 800. Other ball courts, a dozen in all, were constructed throughout the city, reflecting the Mesomerican preoccupation with the game and with the secular and religious implications of its performance. A third complex of structures, including a 36-foot-long tunnel house, were also found. These were decorated in similar fashion and appear to have been built during a later period of occupation. The roofs in this section are composed of lime and finely ground shells or sand.

EL ZAPOTAL

A Veracruz site of unknown origin but serving as a trading center for the region. It linked Teotihuacan, Kaminaljuyu and the Guatemalan highlands during the Late Formative Period (300 B.C.–c. A.D. 250/290) or perhaps in the Early Classic Period (c. A.D. 1/250–600).

"EMBLEM GLYPHS"

Hieroglyphic symbols employed by the Maya to denote certain noble rank in cities or kingdoms. Those having *ch'ul ahau* in their names were known as holy lords. Those having *ahau* were lords, and those having *na ahau* were noble ladies. These nobles held various ranks within their own cities and sometimes ruled vassal states or territories on behalf of the *ch'ul ahau*, the king. The symbol of *ahau* denoted the highest rank of nobility.

A lesser rank was *cahal*, of the nobility but in service to the *ahau*. The *cahalob* (members of the *cahal*) were provincial governors or capital administrators. Women of the *cahal* often married the *ch'ul ahau* for political reasons.

ESPERANZA PHASE

A Maya cultural development, actually a hybrid Maya-Mexica form evolving from the fall of Teotihuacan and the absorption of Mexica from that city into Kaminaljuyu. The Mexica-Maya of the Esperanza Phase controlled Kaminaljuyu by A.D. 400. Esperanza architecture in Kaminaljuyu is evident, including the *talud-tablero* form. The Esperanza nobles held ceremonies with music and processions. Esperanza corpses were buried with jade, mica, pearls, knives and mirrors. No sculpture on a large scale is evident in this cultural development. This phase represents change and upheaval in the Maya territories.

ESPIRIDION PHASE

A cultural development emerging in Oaxaca in c. 1400 B.C., in the Early Formative Period, evolving largely around San Jose Mogote. The people inhabiting this region manufactured ceramics and resided in wattle-and-daub houses. The ceramics produced were unpainted and did not have slip or plastic decorations, and usually took the form of hemispheric bowls. A figurine discovered on a site of this phase was in the form of a cat. (See SAN JOSE MOGOTE for details.)

ETLA RIVER

A waterway in the Valley of Oaxaca, upon which the important San Jose Mogote culture emerged c. 1150 to 850 B.C.

ETZALQUALIZTLI

An Aztec festival honoring maize and a ritual dedicated to the god Tlaloc, the dispenser of rain, associated with agricultural practices. Dancing and feasting were included in the rituals. The sacrifice of children in honor of the god was also conducted at this festival.

ETZATLAN

A site in western Mexico associated with the Jalisco culture, dating to the Late Formative Period (300 B.C.–c. A.D. 250/290) or perhaps earlier. Jalisco ceramic wares are highly prized.

ETZNA (Edzna)

A Maya site, thought to be the southernmost Puuc complex in the region, located in the north-central part of Campeche. The city was constructed with a sophisticated system of canals and reservoirs. The shallow canals went on for miles, retaining reserves of water in the dry seasons. The site is also noted for its combined styles of architecture and covered approximately 2.3. square miles. Some canals at Etzna date to the Formative Period (2000 B.C.–c. A.D. 250/290), and the architectural styles conform to this same era. Etzna (or Edzna) is a modern name given to the site, and the original Maya name was House of Visage. A noted structure there is a five-tiered edifice combining a temple and a palatial residence in one massive monument. This pyramid is more than 120 feet in height. Another pyramid was discovered within the present one. A main plaza is surrounded by monuments, and carved stelae were recovered as well. The ceramic history of Etzna also dates to the Middle Formative Period (900–300 B.C.). The last dated monument, among 32 recovered from the site, is from A.D. 810.

EVENING STAR, LADY   A Maya noblewoman who became the wife of Shield Jaguar, the ruler of Yaxchilan. She was depicted in monuments as taking part in religious and civic ceremonies with her husband, who was on the throne in A.D. 742.

FAT GOD   A deity worshipped in the city of Teotihuacan and by the Maya. A patron of *pulque,* the liquor made from maguey or agave plants, this god was associated with ceremonies and festivals and perhaps with gluttony. He was portrayed as a corpse with a swollen belly and a deformed head. Maya ceramics from A.D. 600 to 900 depict this deity.

FEATHERED SERPENT   A Mesoamerican image associated with cosmological and religious tradition, especially those pertaining to the god Quetzalcoatl. The Feathered Serpent theme was also an Olmec artistic device at Chalcatzinco and other sites. In some depictions a serpent with feathers is shown swallowing a man or serving as a throne. In Juxtlahuaca Cave in Guerrero, the deity wears green plumes on its head. Throughout the various historical eras, the Maya worshipped the Feathered Serpent, and images of the god were incorporated into ceremonial centers. The Feathered Serpent was also thought to be a manifestation of Quetzalcoatl, the ranking deity of Teotihuacan, depicted there in elaborate carvings. By the Classic Period (c. A.D. 1/ 250–900), the rising Mexica groups had adopted the Feathered Serpent as a cultural icon, revering the creature as Quatzalcoatl, who was honored for introducing arts and learning to the region. As the Feathered Serpent, Quetzalcoatl represented the essence of life and civilization. (See GUCUMATZ; KUKULCAN [1].)

FEATHER MURALS   The beautiful decorations made by laying feathers on a woven base of fibers and then tying or pasting each stem to form a design. Once in place, the feathers were carefully trimmed to conform to the chosen pattern. The Maya used the colorful feathers of the quetzal bird to make their murals and designs. The Toltec and the Aztec continued the practice, making feathers part of the tribute required of vassal states. The Toltec city of Coatepec, near Tula, was noted for featherwork, and entire workshops were constructed there to support this industry. Bird plumage was also woven into materials to form distinctive and colorful mantles for the noble castes. Other feathers were applied to fans and standards. The celebrated quetzal headdress sent by Emperor Motecuhzoma (Moctezuma) II to Cortez demonstrates the artistic skills of the feather workers. Another gift to Cortez, the well-known shield depicting a coyote, is another fine example of the artisans' skill.

FINE ORANGE   A variety of Mesoamerican ceramic wares, used in Totonac regions and by the Toltec and others.

Mazapa wares popular in the Yucatan are also Fine Orange. These wares include tripod bowls and cups, effigy vessels and figurines.

FIRE GOD   An ancient deity of Mesoamerica, depicted usually as an old man and called the patron of volcanoes. The Olmec worshipped a fire god, as did the people of the city of Cuicuilco. The Maya, Aztec and others continued the tradition.

FIRE SERPENT   A creature associated with the cosmological and religious traditions of various Mesoamerican cultures. The Fire Serpent carried the sun on its back daily through the heavens and was usually depicted with an upturned snout. In the Temple of Quetzalcoatl in Teotihuacan, the Fire Serpent is carved of stone, alternating with the Feathered Serpent, a form of Quetzalcoatl.

FIVE ALLIGATOR   Also called Five Crocodile, Rain Sun or Tlaloc Sun-Dead. He was the father of Eight Deer and the founder of the Second Dynasty of the Mixtec city of Tilantongo. Five Alligator made calendric reforms and possibly invaded Maya lands. He is listed on pottery recovered in Altar de Sacrificios, located south of Tikal, although this could be a reference to another historical figure of the same name. Five Alligator died in A.D. 1030, leaving the throne to Eight Deer.

FIVE DEATH   A Mixtec god whose form was recovered in the city of Tilantongo. Little is known of the deity's role in Mixtec society.

FLACCO PHASE   A cultural development associated with the Almagre Phase in the Tamaulipas Sequence, dated from 2200 to 1800 B.C. Agriculture increased in the region by 20 percent during this phase, and an early form of maize was recovered near the site of Bat Cave, associated with the Flacco era.

FLOWER WARS   Ritualized campaigns employed by the Aztec and members of the TRIPLE ALLIANCE around A.D. 1450 to increase the number of human sacrifices available for religious ceremonies and for imperial expansion. Historians believe that Tlacaelel, the Aztec councilor, suggested the system during the reign of Motecuhzoma I. The Aztec, in control of many regions, did not have the normal battle-won prisoners because few such battles took place. Thus a method had to be found to provide adequate numbers of sacrificial victims. The Flower Wars, ritualized campaigns called *Xochiyaoyotl*, were begun by Emperor Motecuhzoma I and conducted by Tenochtitlan, Tlacopan (Tacuba) and Texcoco against Tlaxcala, Cholula and Huexotzingo. It is believed that some 20,000 captives from these wars died in the ceremonies of dedication in the Great Temple of Tenochtitlan. Thousands of severed heads were exhibited on the *tzompantli,* the skull rack used in some Mesoamerican cultures. While actual combat did take place during the Flower Wars, warriors' goals were not to slay victims but to capture them alive for sacrifices.

FOLIATED CROSS   A Maya religious symbol representing a maize tree, which serves, according to tradition, as the central axis of the world. The Kan-cross Water Lily Monster forms its base. Human heads represent maize grains, a traditional cosmological image, and a bird wears the Celestial Bird mask.

FOUR HUNDRED RABBITS (1)   Also called Centzon Tolochtin, the patron deity of Tepoztlan. The name refers to the many forms of intoxication possible as a result of drinking *pulque,* the liquor processed from maguey or agave plants.

FOUR HUNDRED RABBITS (2)   See CENTEOTL.

FROGS   Called *uo* by the Maya, the heralds and attendants of the divine Chacs, the rain bringers. The Maya revered the croaking of frogs as a signal announcing the arrival of rain, vital for agricultural regions.

FUERTE RIVER   A waterway in the Pacific coastal lowlands that joined other streams in forming floodplains and deltas. In some regions the Fuerte River drainage area marks the boundary between Mesoamerica and the American Southwest.

GOD A   See AH PUCH.

GRAN DESIERTO   See ALTAR DESERT.

GREAT ARTIFICERS   The name given to the Toltec, the *toltecoyotl*, by their contemporaries. The Toltec were revered as masters of architecture and the civilizing arts, especially by the Nahua groups following them. The name "Great Artificers" paid tribute to Toltec accomplishments and demonstrates the awe inspired by this nation.

GREAT TURTLE ALTAR   Found in Quirigua, one of the most magnificent stone works of the Maya, called Monument 16. Decorated in high relief, it bears intricate designs of human and animal forms. A ruler holding the MANIKIN SCEPTER is in the center. The Great Turtle Altar is over nine feet long and seven feet high. A large mask forms the top.

GRIJALVA RIVER   A highland Guatemalan waterway that flows to the Gulf of Campeche from the interior mountain and volcanic peaks. The Grijalva drains the central valley of Chiapas and is called the Rio Grande de Chiapas there, a region near the border of modern Guatemala. A tributary is the La Venta River. The Grijalva is also joined by the Motagua River near Huehuetenango, serving as one of the major waterways in the gulf coastal lowlands. A volcanic axis dominates the Grijalva region.

GRIJALVA RIVER BASIN   Also called a depression, the region of development in Chiapas during the Early Formative Period (200–900 B.C.). Chiapas de Corzo is a major site associated with this region.

GUADALUPE PHASE   A cultural development on the site of Huitzo, northwest of San Jose Mogote in Oaxaca. This phase is dated from 850 to 700 B.C. Agricultural remains reveal its existence.

GUALUPITA   A site in Morelos, west of Puebla, where peaks and plains offer a temperate climate. The area was influenced by the Olmec culture. Open forests of pine and oak and abundant rivers provided habitats for various groups entering the region. Gualupita and other Morelos sites date to c. 1300 B.C.

GUANAJUATO   A region on the Lerma River in western Mexico. Chupicuaro, with its cultural and artistic phases, was an influence here.

GUATEMALA   Called the Land of Eternal Spring, the nation bordering Mexico; in Mesoamerican eras a Maya domain. One of the world's most beautiful countries, Guatemala consists of approximately 42,000 square miles, noted for its geographic and geologic variety. Chains of towering mountains, some almost 14,000 feet high, cross the country, which is cut by ravines called "barrancas" and by more than 30 valleys. Jungles, deserts, swamps and cool highlands exist with savannas and hardwood forests. Volcanic lakes, streams and rivers flow toward the Atlantic Coast's white sands or the Pacific Coast's volcanic black sands. Geysers and mountain springs also can be found in the region.

The Sierra Madres form the *cordillera,* or mountain ridge, that extends to the Mexican ranges and toward the Andes. The Cuchumatanes Mountains are also visible, these having steep slopes and plateaus. The region is called the Maya Highlands. The western and central parts of these highlands parallel the Pacific coastal plain. In the south, a line of active volcanoes rim the region. Inland, in *Tierra Fria* or *Los Altos,* high valleys and pine- and oak-lined plateaus are ringed by mountains. The *Tierra Templada,* the subtropical foothills, are drained by rivers. The land is fertile, with volcanic deposits. Due to plentiful rainfall, two planting seasons are available in some farming regions. Cool, temperate climates in the highlands offer other agricultural advantages. Guatemala abounds in volcanic stone, lime, obsidian, clay, iron pyrite, hematite, cinnabar, copper, gold, jade and salt.

Although dominated by the Maya through many historical periods, Guatemala was also subject to Olmec influence, especially in the Pacific coastal plains. Teotihuacan-style ceramics were recovered in the region, associated with a ware called *tiquisate,* which was probably traded with vari-

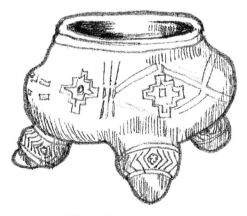

Guanajuato ceramic

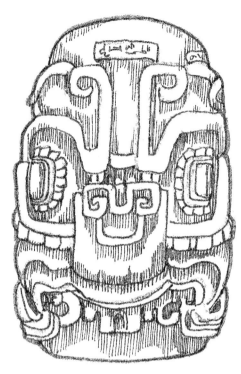

Guatemalan sandstone head

ous cultures. Kaminaljuyu, a Maya stronghold, controlled the plain and the Maya trade routes. El Baul (Finca El Baul) was another trade center, associated with Izapa and with the groups called Epi-Olmec. In time, El Tajin exerted a powerful influence over the Guatemalan groups. The central highlands remained home to the Quiche Maya, and the eastern and northern lowlands served other Maya groups. Cities influenced by Maya dominance of Guatemala include Tikal, Yaxchilan, Seibal, Dos Pilas and Uaxactun.

Guatemala has some of Mesoamerica's tallest volcanoes, 33 in number. Several, including Fuego, Pacaya and Santiaquito, are active. The volcanoes run along the major fault line, parallel to the Pacific coast. Volcanic ash made certain sections of the land extremely fertile.

GUAYALEJO RIVER A waterway in the Sierra Madre Oriental, a region of pine ranges, grasslands and arid wastes.

GUAYAMAS RIVER A major northwestern Mexican waterway, part of the frontier zone of Mesoamerica, bordering on the American Southwest.

GUCUMATZ A Guatemalan Maya deity, called the feathered serpent, the patron of culture and the arts. With the god Hurakan, the patron of storms, Gucumatz created human beings. (See FEATHERED SERPENT.)

GUERRERO A wild and desolate region of Mesoamerica, located in western Mexico. The territory, still undeveloped, is crossed by the Balsas and Cuauhtla-Amacuzac rivers and is rich in ores and semiprecious stones. The

Balsas forms a natural port in Guerrero and provides the coastal portions of the gulf with water. Evidence of human habitation confirms the presence of early hunter-gatherers here. At Puerto Marquez, near modern Acapulco, a type of Early Formative Period (2000–900 B.C.) ceramic ware was recovered, as well as Olmec pottery. The regions of Iguala and Chilpancinco offer evidence of similar ceramic ware. The entire region also contains Olmec artifacts, and the caves at Juxtlahuaca and Oxtotitlan are noted for some of the oldest known paintings in the Americas. An Olmec stela was discovered near Coyuca in the middle Balsas region.

As untracked and desolate as Guerrero is, the region has provided the modern world with a number of distinct art styles, each one reflecting the traditions and influences of the civilizations in the area. The Olmec were present in Guerrero, but they appear to have accomplished little there beyond lending artistic motifs and styles to the local emerging groups. These groups maintained a certain artistic independence despite the presence of more powerful cultures.

The archaeological sites located in the region vary, marking the location of extinct or vanished villages to ceremonial centers and large settlements. These ceremonial centers have truncated pyramids and residential quarters. Ball courts and cemeteries were found. The grave complexes uncovered were mostly in caves, pit clusters or stone tomb sites. The people of Guerrero also practiced urn burial and cremation. Recovered grave offerings provide historical information on the development of the various local groups.

The people of Guerrero produced three distinct art forms: MEZCALA, CHONTAL and XOCHIPALA. The Guerrero groups used stelae and other artistic commemorative monuments, both plain and carved. Sculpture in the round was also used in Ometepec and Comaltepec, near the Oaxacan border. The stelae and statues were used as accompanying pieces for the mounds and pyramidal platforms. These reflect Monte Alban and Teotihuacan influence as well as Maya art styles. The Guerrero craftsmen used copper and gold, beads, shells and bone in their manufactured products. The usual variety of ceramics is also evident in the region, indicating that Guerrero participated in the trade system of Mesoamerica in various historical periods.

GUIENGOLA A Zapotec site in southern Oaxaca, called the Great Rock. An important hilltop fortification, complete with mounds and a rectangular four-tiered pyramid with a main staircase on the east side. The pyramid also has two lateral staircases. Slabs placed one on top of another were finished with plaster and used throughout the structure. Platform terraces are decorated at intervals and projecting stones are evident—actually mortar covered with stucco and painted red, prefiguring a style used by the Aztec (Mexica) in their imperial era. Guiengola was occupied from A.D. 1000 to 1300, but there are indications of earlier, perhaps seasonal populations. The Aztec and the Zapotec fought a battle on this site, with the Zapotec being led by Cosihuesa (A.D. 1200–1251). As a result of the continued Zapotec victory a truce was arranged, and the Aztec awarded honors to Cosihuesa.

GULF COAST A lowland region extending from the Rio Grande to the Yucatan Peninsula, varying in width throughout, from a few miles to 50 miles. These lowlands taper to a narrow strip in Veracruz. The gulf coastal region is one of low mountains and hills with flood and delta plains. Five major rivers serve the region: Candelaria, Coatzalcoalcos-Uspana, Grijalva, Tonala and Usumacinta.

Low-relief sierras or mountain chains exist in other parts of the coastal region. These sierras include the Cruillas, San Carlos and Tamaulipas.

In northern Veracruz, hills dominate the landscape, offering slopes of vegetation and sites for farming. Low coastal plains lie in the more southerly region of Tabasco. Volcanic remains are present throughout. A lava dome is located near Aldama, and basaltic necks and needle peaks are abundant, including the Bernal de Horcasistas, northwest of Tampico. In southern Veracruz the volcanic Tuxtla Mountains dominate a plain between two rivers, creating the hub of Olmec civilization. Nearby are the San Martin and Santa Marta volcanoes and the volcanic lake, Catemaco.

Natural terraces form levees, and river and floodplains provide adequate agricultural regions. Many archaeological sites have revealed evidence of habitation, from the Rio Tamesi to the Yucatan Peninsula. Smaller rivers include the Atoyac, Nautla, Panuco and Tecolutla. Other distinctive features of the coastal region include salt formations, natural islands, barrier beaches, lagoons, estuaries and marshlands. All of these provide food and other resources for local inhabitants. The three major lagoons in the region are the Cabo Rojo, Madre and Tamiahua.

H

HACHA **(1)** A stone marker, also called a *mercadore,* used in the ball courts of Mesoamerica. *Hachas* were carved with stone heads and are associated with ceremonial axes. The *hacha* had ritual value, possibly used in decapitation rites.

HACHA **(2)** A ceremonial battle ax, often in the form of human profiles, some with geometric motifs intertwined with the features. The axes had sharp edges and were skillfully made. One, of Totonac origin, depicts an elegant human profile. These axes were probably used in the ball games of Mesoamerica. (See HACHA [1].)

HACHOB A Maya site dating to the Late Classic Period in east-central Campeche, having elaborately designed structures incorporating Chac masks. Also revealing Chenes influences, Hachob was called the Place Where Ears of Maize Are Stored. A plaza and a large palace form one compound. The palace includes a central section having two lateral arms with vaulted rooms. A monster-mouth motif covers the entire central facade of the palace, which also has a roof comb. Chac masks adorn the corners.

HAPAY CAN A Maya deity, called the Sucking Snake, worshipped among the various Maya groups. This god required human sacrifices and was associated with the city of Izamal.

HAYA A pocket of soil found in the Yucatan region, usually in depressions or in rocky areas of the peninsula. *Hayas* were particularly prominent in the region of Sierra de Ticul and in the northeastern hill region of Campeche. The Maya utilized such pockets of soil for farming.

HERO TWINS Also known as the Ancestral Twins or the Headband Twins, these are Maya cosmological figures mentioned in the great epic *Popol Vuh.* The Hero Twins represent change, courage, resolve and sacrifice in challenging evil. One Hero Twin was Hunahpu (Hun-Ahau) and was associated with Venus in some versions. The second was Xbalanque (Ixbalanque—"Little Jaguar") and was associated with the sun as Yax Balam.

The Hero Twins were born to Lady Blood of Xibalba, a princess of the underworld. They arose to serve the deities of Creation when Vucub-Caquix interrupted the cosmological processes. Vucub-Caquix had to be destroyed before humans could be created. The Hero Twins engaged Vucub-Caquix and his offspring in mortal combat, which in some instances was included within the framework of a ritual ball game. They battled the Lords of Xibalba, a team from the Place of Fright, and then they were transformed into the sun and the moon, to be followed by any innocent creature slain by evil doers while defending them. Such martyrs became eternal stars. All the virtues of Maya spirituality were embodied in the Hero Twins.

HERRERA STELA A monument found in El Baul (Finca El Baul) on the Pacific coast. On the right side of the stela is a profiled figure with a spear, below a cloud scroll. The lower part of the figure's face is covered, and he wears a chin strap and a headdress. Beside the warrior are vertical columns of glyphs. On the left of the monument is a Maya date, with the Mexica *Ek* day sign and Long Count numerations. The date is believed to correspond to A.D. 36.

HIEROGLYPHS An artistic and elaborate method of inscribing information onto monuments, considered a hallmark of ancient civilizations. The term hieroglyphs means "sacred writings," and those employed by Mesoamerican groups were no exception, as the state, rulers and cities were part of the overall religious practices. Four major hieroglyphic systems were extant in Mesoamerica: the Maya, in southern Mexico, Belize, Guatemala, and Honduras; the Aztec, in central Mexico and then in their imperial domain; the Mixtec, in Oaxaca; and the Zapotec, in Oaxaca as early as 600 B.C.

Hieroglyphs, or "glyphs" as the individual units of the system are called, are associated with the major Mesoamerican cultures. Monte Alban had glyphs as early as 500 B.C. The Olmec used them, as did the Izapa, the linking culture between the Olmec period and that of the Maya. The Zapotec are believed to have spread the use of the system through Chiapas and the Pacific coastal region. The first carved glyph is believed to have originated in Cerro de la Malinche. It was associated with the god Quetzalcoatl and was a Toltec insignia. The Isthmus of Tehuantepec had early forms, and the Toltec used them. The Maya used hieroglyphs extensively, employing them in the dated monument tradition that now provides so much information on the rise and fall of the vast network of Maya ceremonial centers. Glyphs transcended the linguistic barriers of Mesoamerica, and they were adapted by many groups at different times and with varying effectiveness. The entries on the individual cultures detail the use of such a linguistic system in the historical periods. (See LANGUAGE in the various cultural entries.)

HISTORIA DE LOS MEXICANOS POR SUS PINTURAS A Spanish text derived from studies of Aztec art. The 13 levels of the Aztec heaven are reported in this document, as they were depicted in Aztec paintings.

HISTORIA TOLTECA-CHICHIMECA A historical document listing reigns of nine Toltec rulers, one of a number of lists of kings available from Toltec records. Six of these rulers reigned for periods of 52 years, the sacred cycle in the Mesoamerican calendar. The author of the *Historia* is listed as Ixtlilxochtli.

HONDO RIVER A waterway in Belize that joins the Belize and Nuevo rivers to drain the region. The Hondo forms the modern frontier between Belize and Mexico and empties into the Caribbean Sea.

HONDURAS A Central American nation of 42,000 square miles, occupying a pivotal position between Guatemala and Nicaragua. A territory with many natural resources, Honduras is, however, mountainous, with few Pacific ports. In Mesoamerican historical eras, the land was associated with the Maya of Guatemala and the Yucatan, linked to them by the vast Motagua River. Copan, one of the great Maya cities and centers of astronomy, lies in Honduras. Some Toltec, including the Chorotega and the Cholulteca, entered Honduras. The Pipil also established settlements there.

HORMIGUERO A Maya site in southestern Campeche, part of the Rio Bec area. There are several groups of structures in Hormiguero, and one building is believed to be the largest such monument in the region. Decorations employed in these structures include Chenes monster masks, visible today on the main level of Structure II. Rio Bec false towers are evident. In the various buildings there are also inset panel masks, columns and stairways. The site was occupied as early as A.D. 50/250, and was abandoned around A.D. 1450.

HORNO A tube fashioned out of burned clay, discovered in the Olmec city of San Lorenzo, associated with mounds and grave sites. *Hornos* could have served as passageways for spirits or perhaps as simple ventilation tubes used during tomb construction or burial rituals.

HUAMELULPAN, SAN MARTIN A Mixtec site with historical significance, located in the central part of the region of Oaxaca, Mexico. This site dates to 400 B.C. to A.D. 600. Three distinct cultural phases are evident there. It was founded as a city in Mixteca Alta and flourished from 100 B.C. to A.D. 200. An elite caste developed in Huamelulpan during the last phase, from A.D. 200 to 600. Tombs, walls and the remains of a pyramidal platform are visible on the site, as well as a carved arch. The relief of a jaguar, dating to the original site, has been incorporated into the wall of a Spanish church erected on the ruins. Huamelulpan was connected with the city of Monte Alban, corresponding to Monte Alban I and II historically. It was also associated with the Nochixtlan Valley in trade and cultural development. The cultural periods of the site are Huamelulpan I:

400–100 B.C.; Huamelulpan II: 100 B.C.–A.D. 200; and Huamelulpan III: A.D. 200–600.

The city's pyramidal platform was fashioned from stone blocks weighing from three to four tons apiece. Calendric glyphs as well as a serpent carving were discovered on this platform.

HUAPALCALLI A site near the city of Tula in Hidalgo, Mexico, settled by the Toltec. It was called the House of Beams.

HUAXTEC A civilization called the *Cuextactl* originating in a region of northern Veracruz and southern Tamaulipas. It is recorded that the Huaxtec were originally part of the Maya protocommunity called the Mam. They left that group in c. 1800 B.C., settling in Veracruz and establishing a domain called Huaxteca or Huasteca. Actually, the Huaxtec were a confederation of several groups, linked by a common language and by shared cultural traditions. Some of these groups broke away from the main body in Veracruz and entered a region called Panusco. Others went on to the Tuxpan Basin. The region was controlled by the Totonac at the time, and Panusco itself was called the Place of the Crossings because various cultures migrated there. The Huaxtec name for their homeland translates to a place "across the sea," but their Mam connections are documented.

As early as 1500 B.C., the Huaxtec established cave settlements and villages in the Tamaulipas region and embarked on expansion. There were three specific periods of development. The Mesa de Guaje Phase lasted from 1000 to 900 B.C. and witnessed a great agricultural expansion. Domesticated crops accounted for as much as 40 percent of the Huaxtec diet. The Palmillas Phase, which opened in c. 200 B.C., gives evidence of a vast increase in Huaxtec population and agricultural endeavors. Water-storage facilities and ball courts were constructed in this period. During the La Florida Phase, which dates to c. 100 B.C., in the last stages of the Formative Period, temples and ceremonial complexes arose. Huaxtec settlements had increased, and the agricultural skills of the people had improved.

The Huaxtec were advanced, especially in agricultural efforts, but they never assumed the sophistication of their neighboring cultures. While they influenced many groups and their songs, dances and artistic customs were models

Huaxtec rocker stamp

for other cultures, the Huaxtec remained rural and pastoral in their way of life. The great capital of Tamuin reached artistic heights, but it was a singular achievement that was not duplicated in other Huaxtec regions. Teotihuacan and other neighboring cultures perhaps had something to do with the static condition of the Huaxtec. Teotihuacan dominated the regions surrounding it from the start. Other groups also joined the Huaxtec and took on their customs as their own. A tradition holds that a place called Tamoanchan, originally inhabited by the Huaxtec, was the first place where *pulque*, the fiery liquor made from the maguey or agave plant, originated. At Tamoanchan, lying between the Mexican and the Morelos valleys, the Huaxtec gathered to celebrate with other cultures. A festival was held on Mount Chichinauyha, a ritual calendar feast, during which time the participants drank *pulque*. Each group chief was allowed to take four cups. The Huaxtec ruler, intoxicated, allowed his loincloth to fall, an enormously shameful act. The response from the other groups was so intense that the Huaxtec were exiled from the region, going into the Panusco River Basin and then along the Tamesi, Moctezuma and Tuncuilin rivers, reaching the Tampoalan Valley and the region that was to become Huaxteca Potosina.

The Huaxtec were confronted by invasions throughout their history, including the armies of the Toltec, Chichimec, Otomi, Acolhua and Aztec. The Toltec were reported to be harsh with the Huaxtec, naming one sacrificial site Cuextecatlichocayan, "the Place Where the Huaxtec Weep." The Chichimec made an alliance with the Huaxtec to acquire lands, and a queen was reported to have had dominion over some Huaxtec settlements. The Otomi invaded Huaxteca Potosina, followed by the Acolhuan and the Aztec.

HUAXTEC AGRICULTURE The systems by which the Huaxtec nation provided the local communities with food supplies in Veracruz and Tamaulipas. From the earliest eras the Huaxtec employed rather sophisticated methods and reaped good crops. The Aztec called the Huaxtec region *Tonacatlapan*, "the land of food." Tropical and forested, Huaxteca abounded in a variety of useful plants, and the soil was rich. The Huaxtec employed the *milpas*, or slash-and-burn agricultural practices. Forested regions were cut down and then burned, and some larger trees were felled by hand. Cleared and then irrigated, the land did not undergo much erosion. The Huaxtec were careful to set aside certain fields each year as reserves, allowing them to lie fallow and thus recover. The crops grown by the Huaxtec include beans, cacao (in the south), chilies, cotton, gourds, maize, manioc, peppers, sisal, squashes and sweet potatoes. Other products gathered or hunted for food included arum, birds, dogs, fruits, honey, insects, salt, shellfish and turkeys.

HUAXTEC ARCHAEOLOGICAL SITES The areas known for Huaxtec habitation, containing examples of Huaxtec art and architectural achievement. (See LAS FLORES, SAN LUIS POTOSI, and TAMUIN.)

HUAXTEC ARCHITECTURE The style and building techniques that distinguished the settlements and structures of this nation, reflecting evolutionary development. The original Huaxtec settlements were composed of wooden houses having wattle-and-daub walls. These houses were oval in form or sometimes rectangular or round, with the latter style being most prevalent in many regions. The houses had burned-clay floors or plastered floors with painted decorations. Some remains of Huaxtec houses show evidence of asphalt-surfaced floors as well. Few furnishings have been recovered, indicating either that few items of furniture were used or that the furnishings were made of highly perishable materials.

Huaxtec temples and ceremonial centers had rounded corners following the circular form that dominates in the region in honor of the wind god. Such ceremonial centers followed the traditional Mesoamerican patterns, with platforms, plazas and structures lined up on an east-west or north-south axis. Sites in the Tuxpan portion of Huaxteca appear to have held true pyramids. These were probably fortified, as the Huaxtec have a history of military activities and were confronted by many invading cultures. The platforms discovered in Huaxteca were tiered, with stairways and accompanying buildings. There were also palaces and residential quarters for the Huaxtec elite, usually found outside of the ceremonial complex, as at Tamuin. The small villages were established on riverbanks, usually on elevated tracts, to avoid floods. The Huaxtec constructed reservoirs in most of their settlements, man-made depressions designed to retain floodwaters and rain.

HUAXTEC ART The creativity distinguishing this nation's efforts in building and manufacture. The Huaxtec were noted for their sculpted pieces, especially the statues portraying their gods and priests. Sculpture appeared early in Huaxtec historical development. The figures, fashioned in the round, were life size and carved of stone. Large, flat statues depicted men and women, either nude or simply attired. The figures were formal, upright and in a frontal position. The skirts of the statues were trapezoidal, and the bodies were rectangular. Round faces were frequently depicted, with the Huaxtec headdress, conical in form. Some headdresses depict the sun, using feathers or folded materials. The arms of the figures are crossed or positioned at their sides. Men sometimes have pierced hands, a technique obviously designed to allow the statues to hold objects. The Huaxtec often tattooed the body of the statue or the clothing.

The celebrated "Adolescent" of Tamuin, a Huaxtec depiction of the god Quetzalcoatl as the evening star, is one of the most vibrant examples of Huaxtec art. Quetzalcoatl is shown carrying his son on his back, entering the Kingdom of the Dead. His body is tattooed and covered with carved flowers and profiles of mythical creatures. Other statues include heads, phallic male statues, and phallic symbols. Reliefs, panels and stelae made by the Huaxtec are always religious in nature, and the geometric elements make them unique and remarkably appealing to contemporary viewers. The wall paintings discovered in Tamuin combine several cultural styles, indicating invasion by other groups there. These paintings depict a procession of gods and aristocrats, and the design is in monochrome red. Warriors with lances, priests wearing skull headdresses and nobles wearing crowns are portrayed on their way to a religious ceremony. Other frescoes discovered in Huaxtec sites suggest a definite Maya influence, both in style and design. The panels of these frescoes were carved to depict local deities. The minor

Huaxtec "Adolescent" statue

teapots with spouts and flat, ribbonlike handles. The black-and-white ceramics do not appear to reflect the true Huaxtec traditions and possibly reflected another culture's influence.

HUAXTEC CLOTHING   Attire worn by the people of this culture throughout their history, despite their well-known tradition of practicing nudity, especially on Mount Chichinauhya. A legend concerning this practice tells of a princess of Tula, a woman of the Toltec line. She saw a nude Huaxtec man and was overcome with desire for him. After marrying him, the princess was confronted by Toltec opposition. The Huaxtec, however, was the god Titlacauan, and the Toltec were forced to pay for their efforts to undermine his marriage. (See HUAXTEC GODS; TITLACUAN.)

Huaxtec clothes consisted of loincloths, capes and sandals, with breast coverings and skirts for women. Dyed hair was considered attractive, with reds and yellow favored. Women wore their hair in braids, gathered into crowns. The men wore various styles of head coverings, including the typical conical form. Bands of leather were tied to their arms and legs, with plumes and beads attached. Feather plumes adorned the women's crowns of braids.

HUAXTEC DEATH RITUALS   The traditions practiced in burying the dead in Huaxteca. Grave sites uncovered in the region indicate that most Huaxtec were buried directly in the ground, as few stone or brick tombs are evident. The corpse was placed in the grave in a crouching position, a widespread Mesoamerican custom. The Huaxtec, however, buried their dead facedown. Some corpses were provided with masks and tools; weapons and pottery comprised the usual grave offerings. No documents exist regarding Huaxtec burial tradition or graveside rituals.

HUAXTEC GODS   The cosmological and religious figures dominating the Huaxtec ceremonies and aspirations. Statues made by the Huaxtec are the major source of information concerning these deities, although some legends have been preserved. These gods include:

Tlazolteotl.   Called Our Grandmother, a fertility goddess who was the patron of divination, childbirth, sexual love and ritual medicine. Under the title of *Tlaelquani*, the Eater of Dirt, this goddess presided over ritual confessions. She was also honored by the Aztec and was portrayed by them in a Huaxtec conical headdress. The ceremonies of Tlazolteotl were conducted throughout Huaxteca.

Titlacauan.   A Huaxtec god of magic, who was personified in a legend concerning the downfall of the great Toltec city of Tula. Seen nude by a Toltec princess, the god was mistaken for a mortal and was desirable to her. So enamored was the Toltec princess, in fact, that she married him. The Toltec thought that he was a Huaxtec commoner and attacked him. In retaliation, Titlacauan invited his Toltec relatives by marriage to a banquet. After serving a fine meal, he began to play beautiful flute music that drove the Toltec nobles mad. They leaped to their deaths as a result of his enchantment, thus depopulating the city of Tula. This was an act of vengeance by the god Titlacauan, not only for the insults to his divine person but for past Toltec outrages against the Huaxtec.

arts of the Huaxtec include a variety of jewelry and other ornaments, such as bracelets, breastplates, earrings, lip plugs, necklaces, rings and pendants.

In time the Huaxtec were praised for their colored cloth, probably made of brown and white cotton, both locally grown. Brocading added decorative patterns that were prized later by the Aztec.

HUAXTEC CERAMICS   Clay products of the Huaxteca region that were skillfully manufactured, most with pink or cream hues. In later eras the distinctive black-on-white ceramics were developed as well. Huaxtec ceramics include

Huaxtec painted frieze

Quetzalcoatl. A Huaxtec version of the popular Mesoamerican deity, called the Evening Star (Venus) in this region. The Huaxtec had always revered the god.

Mam. Called Our Grandfather, the patron of *pulque* (the liquor distilled from the maguey or agave plant). Mam is also a reference to the protocommunity of the Maya, from which the Huaxtec emerged. He was also the patron deity of the earth, thunder and the lord of the year.

Tlaloc. The rain god worshipped by several Mesoamerican groups for his association with the agricultural seasons. Tlaloc was considered vital to Huaxtec farming and was revered by other cultures in the same role. The rituals of Tlaloc normally included human sacrifices, especially the prolonged and agonizing deaths of children.

Earth-Moon Goddess. A deity usually depicted as a young woman. The cult of this deity dates to earliest times in Huaxtec lands.

Huehueteotl. The fire god, adapted by the Huaxtec from other Mesoamerican cultures. This deity was usually portrayed as an old man but could also take the form of a serpent. Huaxtec artists fashioned heads in his honor.

Diving God. A vividly portrayed monster-faced deity depicted in stone in a position of descent. The Diving God is believed to be a form of Quetzalcoatl, as the planet Venus.

The Huaxtec also celebrated solar myths and performed rituals in honor of the sun. Women who died in childbirth were granted semidivine status. The rituals performed in honor of the gods in Huaxtec temples included human sacrifice, with the hearts torn from the breasts of victims. The rite of flaying victims was also recorded in the region, and some ceremonies involved the use of arrows as sacrificial weapons. In one Huaxtec district, children were beheaded in services honoring Tlaloc, the rain god.

The people of the Huaxtec culture practiced cannibalism and displayed human skulls. Other religious observances in honor of the gods involved priests who served in the temples for a period of one year. Stringent regulations governed their sexual activities and bathing. Some priests painted themselves black for the rituals. Religious customs obliged the Huaxtec people to fast, and various forms of self-mutilation in atonement were provided. There were also ceremonies of ritual drunkenness and nudity. The Hu-

axtec were well known by other cultures for their involved ceremonies and their tendency to imbibe at such rituals.

Music, songs and dances were incorporated into most of the religious rites of Huaxteca. The music of the Huaxtec was so celebrated that other cultures adopted the songs for their own ceremonies, even dressing like the Huaxtec as they chanted their own liturgies. The instruments used in religious observances in the Huaxtec region (as in many Mesoamerican regions) included skin drums, bones, whistles, bells, conch shells, flutes and rattles. Dances were performed for all major festivals, especially those honoring the jaguar cult. The *Voladores*, the dance performed by four men swinging from a gigantic pole, honored the cardinal points of the earth and the calendar systems. Fertility cults were honored as well with special ceremonies, and on these occasions slaves carried phallic symbols. The phallus was also carved in detail and placed in various locations in the ceremonial centers or at temple sites.

HUAXTEC GOVERNMENT The form of rule and administration adopted by the Huaxtec people, involving the *pipihuan,* the hereditary noble caste. The Huaxtec adopted the word *pipihuan* from Nahuatl. The noble caste probably won power and prominence originally through agricultural holdings (the usual Mesoamerican means of attaining aristocratic dominance). This would have been especially true among the Huaxtec, as they were a predominantly agricultural society.

The Huaxtec *pipihuan* lived in elite compounds and palaces, such as those found in the city of Tamuin. All of their agricultural holdings would have been tenanted by commoners, who worked the land. There is some evidence that the farms were held in trust by the families, although some nobles did sell portions of their estates to the Spanish after the conquest.

Below the noble caste was the line of chiefs, called the *tlahuani,* who ruled the various villages and settlements. These were also part of a hereditary caste. Their duties included the collection of tribute for the aristocracy, the raising of forced-labor levies for public works, the settlement of disputes and judicial matters on the local level and the declaration of war in times of peril for the local district. The priests had their own caste, as the higher-ranking members of the temple hierarchy made temple service a full-time career, wanting to maintain continuity and exercising their hereditary rights and obligations to the state. The Huaxtec also had a warrior class called *tiacham,* or "the valiant." These warriors were nobles, trained in the martial arts as befit their hereditary ranks.

Huaxtec commoners worked the land or traded with other regions and were in all ways subject to the local chiefs. Below the commoners were the slaves, usually prisoners of war who were forced to work on agricultural estates. A unique group among the Huaxtec were the magicians, who were esteemed by their countrymen. Illusionists and gifted as diviners, these magicians practiced curative magic and fortune-telling. The chiefs, magicians and commoners lived together in the villages of the Huaxtec, sometimes joining with other villages in a confederation surrounded by farms. Such villages or confederations were independent where defense, war, management of lands and social affairs were concerned. They were obliged to pay tribute, form labor levees and perform other services for the elite, but in every other way they functioned independently. Some villages waged war regularly to add lands and slaves.

In time, all of these social castes and the localized governments came under the jurisdiction of more powerful civilizations that invaded and absorbed the Huaxtec people and the confederacies into their own empires.

HUAXTEC TRADE The system by which the Huaxtec moved wares through the great markets of the Mesoamerican cultures, especially within the region of the central plateau of Mexico. The Huaxtec held local markets every 20 days at least, in keeping with their calendars. Tribute was then sent on to the dominant groups or cultures of the region. Huaxtec trade goods included bark paper; cotton; dried peppers; feathers; gourds; honey; jadeite; live eagles, deer and parakeets; mats; skins; and turquoise.

When the Aztec acquired the region during the empire period, human beings were included in the trade systems. The Aztec took the Huaxtec people as slaves or as prisoners for their temple sacrifices.

HUAXTEC WARFARE The military system of the region, born of centuries of invasion and harassment. The Huaxtec armies had full-time commanders, drawn from the caste of warriors (the *tiacham*), the hereditary group trained in martial arts. The Huaxtec were noted as ferocious warriors who sang as they approached the battlefield. The Huaxtec military used the following weapons: bows and arrows, bronze axes, curved clubs, flint blades, obsidian blades, throwing sticks *(atlatls),* and wooden swords with obsidian blades.

The commanders depicted in Huaxtec art wore sophisticated armor, with suits of quilted cotton and conical hats. Some were dressed as jaguar or eagle warriors, indicating separate caste groups, and most wore animal skins. The commanders and soldiers used round shields made of split and braided reeds. Some had belts to which rattles and bells were attached so that their movements enhanced music or made sounds designed to unnerve enemies.

HUEHUECOYOTL An Aztec deity, "Old Coyote," patron of the dance, music and feather workers. Appearing as a coyote-headed man, the god presided over part of the calendar year.

HUEHUETENANGO A region of Guatemala, listed in some records as the domain of the Mam Maya, the mother culture of that nation. The Mam are reported to have been in the Huehuetenango region in c. 2600 B.C.

HUEHUETEOTL (Xiuhtecuhtli) A fire deity worshipped in the city of Cuicuilco and other cultures in central Mexico as the patron of volcanoes. The god was venerated by the Huaxtec also, and was depicted as an old man or as a serpent. Huaxtec artists fashioned heads in his honor. The Aztec called him the Old God. A statue of the deity was found in Kaminaljuyu wearing a brazier on his head. This portrayed him as a patron of the hearth.

HUEMAC A Toltec ruler listed in the *Historia Tolteca Chichimeca* and in the *Anales de Cuauhtitlan.* He abandoned the capital of Tula in c. A.D. 1156/68 and went to the city of Chapultepec, where he killed himself. The records in the *Historia* and the *Anales* concerning his rule do not coincide.

HUETZIN A Toltec ruler listed in the *Historia Tolteca Chichimeca* as reigning from A.D. 614 to 666. He is also listed in the *Anales de Cuauhtitlan.*

HUEXOTLA A city founded by the Acholhua in A.D. 1409, called the Place of the Willows. Located in the western part of Mexico, Huexotla had a large defensive wall, measuring 15 feet high, with wedge-shaped structures on the top. Mounds found at the site were connected to a pyramid and stone platforms. Toltec influence is evident in Huexotla. Nezahualcoyotl took Huexotla as part of his domain.

HUEXOTZINCO A Chichimec-related city-state that was the most important site in Puebla during the Classic Period (A.D. 1/250–900). Originally of Olmeca-Xicallanca stock, the people of Huexotzinco also were related to the Acolhua of Coatlinchan, at least according to their own records. They were also associated with the Chichimec. Huexotzinco, influenced by the city of Teotihuacan and by older cultures, also developed its own architectural and artistic styles. It had a circular temple dedicated to Ehecatl, the wind god, a manifestation of Quetzalcoatl. The patron of Huexotzinco, however, was the hunting god, Mixcoatl Camaxtli. The city claimed to have relics of this deity and maintained a temple in his honor.

When Nezahualcoyotl of Texcoco attacked the Tepanec, the people of Huexotzinco went to his assistance, assaulting Tenayuca led by Xayacamachos, the ruler. They also participated in the Flower Wars, allied with Cholula and Tlaxcala against the Triple Alliance of Tenochtitlan, Texcoco and Tlacopan (Tacuba). The city-state was mentioned in the *Codex Chimalpopoca.* A respected sage, Ayocuan, resided in Huexotzinco.

HUEYAPAN RIVER A waterway on the gulf coast, a region inhabited by the Olmec. The city of Tres Zapotes was built there.

HUEYTECUILHUITL Called the "feast of the lords," an Aztec festival. Celebrated as part of the agricultural cycle, the feast was a time of dancing. During it a woman, personifying the goddess Xiloman, the Aztec patroness of maize, was ritually slain.

HUEYTOZOZTLI A major Aztec festival honoring the male and female deities of maize during the agricultural celebrations in the capital of Tenochtitlan and throughout the region. Centeotl and Chicomecoatl were the deities venerated. Elaborate displays of flowers and food were offered to them, as the people gathered for rejoicing. The temples were decorated with flowers; dances and parades of young women moved through the streets of the city performing traditional hymns. The women carried maize through the streets and into the temple courtyards. This and other festivals were staged throughout the empire in the great ceremonial centers. The city of Tenochtitlan was designed to accommodate vast crowds where the ceremonies took place, and the streets were laid down to receive the throngs attending the celebrations.

HUITZILIHUITL   An Aztec ruler called Hummingbird Feather, on the throne of Tenochtitlan from A.D. 1391/96 to 1415/17. He was the son of Acamapichtli and was elected by the Aztec council to succeed his father. Claiming the throne, he married a princess from Tlacopan (Tacuba) but when she died within a short time, he married a Tepanec princess who bore him a son, Chimalpopoca. Huitzilihuitl was also the father of Motecuhzoma I, whose mother, Miahuaxilhuitl, was an exotic princess of Cuernavaca. This princess, a ravishing beauty according to tradition, was guarded by serpents and strange creatures in a garden of Cuernavaca. Her father, a noted sorcerer, kept her safe from prying eyes. Huitzilihuitl, however, lured her out of the garden and married her. In addition to his new wife, the king is reported to have brought cotton from Cuernavaca.

A military leader and an organizer, Huitzilihuitl organized and streamlined the many religious ceremonies and the temples in Tenochtitlan. He passed civil laws and ordinances in the growing capital. Son-in-law and a vassal of the Tepanec king Tezozomoc, Huitzilihuitl served the ruler. Chimalpopoca, Tezozomoc's grandson, won the favor of the Tepanec king but became embroiled in Tepanec affairs after the old king died and was himself killed.

HUITZILIHUITL THE ELDER   Aztec chief who led his people to Chapultepec at the time of their great trek into the Valley of Mexico. He was slain in an ambush by local warriors of the region.

HUITZILOPOCHTLI   The ancient Aztec god who was called the savior of the nation and the patron of military campaigns. Called Hummingbird on the Left, Huitzilopochtli also represented the sun. Worshipped by the Aztec from earliest times, the deity was honored by fire ceremonies. The first priest-kings of the nation were believed to be the messengers of the god, and Tenoch, who led the Aztec to Tenochtitlan, made precise prophecies regarding the founding of the great capital near Lake Texcoco. Huitzilopochtli had a tradition of his own in which his exploits were related and his victories over his fellow gods were revealed. He was a personal god of the Aztec, providing them with weapons in times of need, as during the campaign demanded by Achitometl, king of Culhuacan. He led his people to Tenochtitlan and provided miraculous signs and objects to assist them. Huitzilopochtli announced times of suffering and encouraged the Aztec to attain the height of civilization. He was also the chief deity in one of the complexes, which were the religious divisions of the Aztec religion.

Huitzilopochtli was also called the Blue Tezcatlipoca of the south. He was born miraculously from Coatlicue, a female form of the god Ometeotl, and he had to slay enemies and put down revolts by his own family. As the warrior

Huitzilopochtli

god of the sun, Huitzilopochtli needed human hearts and blood in order to rise from the east each morning. Hymns of praise were sung to the god, extolling battle, blood and honor in the field.

The god was depicted as a man wearing a hummingbird-feather headdress and a golden crownlet, and his face bore blue and yellow stripes. Huitzilopochtli was born in Coatepec. There his mother was slain by his sister, Coyolxauhqui, and their 400 brothers, called the *Centzon Huitznahua*. Huitzilopochtli rose fully armed from the body of Coatlicue, his mother, and slew his sister and brothers.

HUITZNAHUA   A Toltec-related group that joined the Chichimec after the fall of the city of Culhuacan. The original deity of the Huitznahua was Tezcatlipoca.

HUITZO   Also called Cuauhxilotitlan, a site in central Oaxaca, occupied by the Zapotec. The site has a long history, dating to the Guadalupe Phase, a cultural development of the region that includes the advancements made at San Jose Mogote and dates to c. 850–700 B.C. A small village was started at Huitzo, and agricultural endeavors began with maize, squashes, chili peppers, avocados, cactus fruits, hackberries, acorns and prickly pears. Huitzo's people erected a pyramidal platform with sloping walls and three tiers. Earth-filled, the platform was faced with boulders. The Zapotec entered in c. A.D. 100–700 and developed the site. The city was large during their occupation, and two suburban districts were added, Suchilquitongo and Telixtlahuaca. The Mixtec arrived and occupied Huitzo just before the Spanish conquest.

A Huitzo tomb is noted for its stone slabs. Above the entrance a sculpted coyote head is visible, and there are panels with abstract and geometric designs in the doorway. Huitzo boasted a vast ceremonial complex at one time.

Foundation walls are evident in some places, as is the setting for an elaborate plaza. The ceramic remains uncovered in Huitzo are largely Mixtec in design, including the Huitzo polished wares and Huitzo cream pottery.

HUNAB KU   A Maya deity addressed as "the only living and true god," worshipped in the Yucatan. He was never depicted in statuary because of his spiritual nature. Hunab Ku was believed to have created the elements: *chac,* lightning; *kak,* fire; *kin,* the sun; and *U,* the moon. The actual beginning of this deity's cult is debatable. It is possible that this deity began after the arrival of the Spanish, in order to rival worship of their Christian god. (See MAYA GODS.)

HUNAC CEEL CANUCH   Also called Cauich-ment in the *Books of Chilam Balam of Chumayel,* a man who appeared at a sacrifice at the sacred *cenote* of Chichen Itza. He announced a prophecy there and was named king. Hunac Ceel Canuch then dove into the *cenote* to retrieve a sacred object. He is listed historically as the ruler of Mayapan who drove the Itza people from Chichen Itza. He also directed a league formed by Mayapan, Chichen Itza and Uxmal in A.D. 1200.

HUNCHABIN   A Maya site in Chiapas, just north of Comitan. Dating to the Late Classic Period (A.D. 1200 to 1521), Hunchabin has a fair amount of ruins, including tiered structures grouped around a plaza. The city was essential to Maya trade, bordering on Peten and the great Maya trading centers there. Burials of Hunchabin nobles took place in nearby caves.

HUNHAU   A Maya death god, associated with Ah Puch. Dogs and lightning were believed to be manifestations of Hunhau. The deity was also popular in the Chiapas region.

HUN HUNAHPU   See HERO TWINS.

HURAKAN   A deity of the Guatemalan and Honduras Maya, also called Tohil. This was the god of storms, whirlwinds and thunder, who maintained three kinds of prisons. One was filled with serpents, one with flying arrows and the last with jaguars. Called the Heart of Heaven in the *Popol Vuh,* Hurakan was the unharnessed forces of nature in creation myths.

I

ICHEATEOPAN A Chontal Maya site in Oaxaca destroyed by an Aztec assault, led by Emperor Ahuitzotl, who ruled from A.D. 1486 to 1502. The Aztec were attacking the Chontal capital of Alahuiztlan and involved Icheateopan during their campaign. The Maya there fled to interior strongholds.

ICHPAATUN A Maya site on the coast of the Yucatan, of Chontal design and dating to c. A.D. 900.

IGUALA A region in Guerrero that was a Paleo-Indian Period (11,000–7000 B.C.) habitation. Ceramics from the Formative Period (2000 B.C.–A.D. 250/290) were also found in Iguala, as well as Olmec goods. The region was included in the trade systems during various historical periods.

IHUATZIO (1) A Tarascan site in central Michoacan, on the southeastern arm of Lake Patzcuaro near the island of Janitzio. The capital of the Tarascan at one time, Ihuatzio dominated the region. The site was chosen for its strategic location, and the Tarascan fortified the city. Ihuatzio contains two pyramids, stepped and sharing a common rectangular base constructed within an enclosed rectangular plaza. The pyramids were built of rubbish cores and stone slabs, with cut facings. Other mounds formed the plaza.

IHUATZIO (2) A division of the Tarascan Empire during the reign of Curatame, the son of Tariacuri, the Tarascan national hero. The other divisions of the Tarascan were Patzcuaro and Tzintzuntzan. (See IHUATZIO [1]; TARASCAN.)

IHUITIMAL A Toltec ruler recorded in the *Anales de Cuauhtitlan* as ruling from A.D. 887 to 923.

IKIL A Maya site in northern Yucatan, near Chichen Itza, originally called Place of the Wind. Low platforms and a pyramid have been discovered there, one of the largest temple monuments in the northern Maya territory. A three-tiered platform supported the temple originally, with six tiers and rooms later added on either side. Staircases and passageways are part of the pyramid, whose original structure is believed to date to the Classic Period. Carved stone lintels and niches adorn the highest chambers. The unusual feature of the shrine is the use of giant stones, some estimated at 3,000 lbs., forming walls called megaliths.

ILAMATECUHTLI A deity whose battle with the god Cichuacoatl is reflected in the ball games of some Meso-american cultures. A goddess of earth, death and the Milky Way in Aztec traditions, Ilamatecuhtli wore a star skirt and carried a shield and a wand. Cosmic and religious themes were woven into the traditions of these games, which demonstrated the creation and the salvation of the various Mesoamerican groups. (See BALL GAMES.)

ILANCUEITL A Culhuacan princess who was given to Acamapichtli, the Aztec who ruled from A.D. 1376 to 1391/96. She is reported as having assumed considerable political power during her husband's reign. Ilancueitl, as a princess of Culhuacan, would have given Acamapichtli considerable prestige.

ILOPANGO VOLCANO A peak located in the southeastern lowlands; its eruption in A.D. 260 is recorded as having destroyed the site of Chalchuapa, near the border of modern El Salvador. The volcano spewed ash and pumice throughout the region, and the Maya fled, transporting their skills and their cultural advances into other regions.

INCENSE Used in ceremonial rituals throughout the Mesoamerican region, the most popular and the most readily available incense was copal, a resin from trees of the Bursera genus. The Nahuatl-speaking people called this *copalli*. The Maya called it *pom*. Copal provides a considerable amount of aromatic smoke, believed to have been visible to the divinities during ceremonies. Braziers were in frequent use in many cultures, and copal or other resin or gum substances were burned to create smoke. The Aztec (Mexica) also used rattle ladles in order to direct the smoke. In some cultures the incense was placed in pots, dishes or on boards.

INFIERNILLO PHASE A cultural development associated with the Tamaulipas Sequence in the Tamaulipas region, dated to c. B.C. 9000 to 7000. During this phase, people here subsisted by gathering plants, which accounted for as much as 50 to 70 percent of their food supply. Seasonal habitation is in evidence, and groups gathered at certain times of the year. Projectile points, some attached to spear shafts or dart foreshafts, were discovered at sites of this phase. Planes, choppers, nets, scrapers, mats and baskets were also recovered.

IPALNEMOHUANI An Aztec creator deity, also called Tloque Nahuaque. (See under TLOQUE NAHUAQUE.)

IQUEHUACATZIN   An Aztec prince, son of Motecuhzoma I, passed over as heir to the throne according to some records. He was reported as angry and eager to kill the chosen heir, Axayacatl.

IRA THICATAME   A Tarascan ruler who is recorded as having led that nation into the Michoacan region in c. A.D. 1000.

IRON PYRITE   An iron ore, yellow to brown in color, called fool's gold, and mined in Huaxteca, in the Guatemalan highlands and in other Mesoamerican regions. Mirrors were produced from the ore, and the pyrite was cut into hexagonal and pentagonal pieces, attached to slate or sandstone. These were probably ornaments worn on belts. The mirrors were popular and were traded extensively throughout Mesoamerica. Pyrite was also made into beads and used as fillings for teeth. As with jade and obsidian, the ore was used in the manufacture of jewelry. (See MIRRORS.)

ISLA DE SACRIFICIOS   An island off the coast of Veracruz, where Totonac pyramids and tombs were discovered. The site also has provided evidence of regional ceramic phases. (See ISLA DE SACRIFICIOS PHASES I, II, III.)

ISLA DE SACRIFICIOS PHASES I, II, III   Three cultural developments that are evidence of a Totonac renaissance in art. Possibly the result of the establishment of Totonac coastal communities, the Isla de Sacrificios Phases provide an elegant display of ceramic wares. Hard, half-clay pieces, with red, white or black designs, the ceramics were manufactured in deep red and in black. The Totonac are considered one of the most refined and elegant groups of Mesoamerica, and their cultural phases provide evidence of their skills. (See TOTONAC for details.)

ISLA MUJERES   A Maya site in the northern Yucatan Peninsula, an island that served as a shrine and pilgrimage place for the goddess Ixchel, the consort of Itzamna. The ruins of a lighthouse and an observatory are on the site. There are some Toltec-Chichen influences evident on the island. The Spanish named the site Island of the Women because of the large number of female figurines recovered there.

ISLONA DE CHANTUTO   A Paleo-Indian Period (11,000–7000 B.C.) site on the Pacific coast. Evidence of early habitations have been discovered there. The preceramic levels uncovered there give some indications of an "Incipient Agricultural" way of life emerging in the region.

ISTHMUS OF TEHUANTEPEC   A region of eastern Mesoamerica linking the gulf coast and the Pacific slopes of Guatemala. The cultures within its borders evolved within their own perimeters, responding to their natural resources and to the varying pressures of neighboring groups. Trade was conducted within the isthmus also, providing intercultural exchanges. As a result, various groups emerged in the Early Formative Period (2000–900 B.C.), with more than 35 sites already uncovered. The cultural developments associated with the Isthmus of Tehuantepec include Arevalo and Las Charcas.

Arevalo.   A culture with a ceramic heritage, as burned adobe fragments have been recovered on sites associated with this phase. The Arevalo camped in the open air, in undefended sites, attesting to the peaceful conditions of the period. The ceramics of the Arevalo were of a high quality, reflecting advanced skills and techniques. Monochromes— red wares, buff, black and gray-brown—and bichromes—a combination of red or white on buff—have been found at sites used by the Arevalo.

Las Charcas.   A cultural development that brought about the formation of bottle-shaped pits and the rise of kaolin pottery. The ceramics fashioned in this period were usually in the shape of monkeys or dragon masks. Some had abstract designs. Pyramidal platforms, made of clay, were also erected on the Las Charcas sites.

In the Middle Formative Period (900–300 B.C.), the groups in the Isthmus of Tehuantepec experienced religious revivals leading to the establishment of ceremonial centers. These complexes also served as burial sites for royal personages. Several cultural developments date to this era, which was a time of comparative calm in the region, the Miraflores, Las Charcas B, and the Providencia Majada Phases among them.

ITZA   A cultural group called the *Ah-Tza* or the *Ah-Xulpiti* in some records. The Itza have been associated with the Chontal Maya of Tabasco and are considered Mexica because of their relationship with the Toltec. They were always despised by their contemporaries, considered lewd, tricky

Itza chieftain

and foreign. Their original home was Chakanputun on the west coast of the Yucatan Peninsula. They stayed there for more than 250 years. The Itza appear to have entered the region with the Toltec. In c. A.D. 1200 they were driven from the coast, fleeing to Lake Peten Itza and to the eastern shore of Belize. By c. A.D. 1224/44, they were in the city of Chichen Itza, led by a man called Kulkulcan II. The city flourished as a pilgrimage site during this period.

The Itza founded the city of Mayapan in A.D. 1263/83 but were driven from there. Attacked by Mexica groups, the Itza returned to Lake Peten, where they built the capital of Tayasal (modern Flores) on islands in the lake. King Canek of Tayasal allowed the Spanish to rest there during their conquests. They are also associated with the founding of Mayapan.

The Itza had a stratified society with separate temples or shrines, with the commoners using caves. They wore cotton mantles, woven with stripes or insignias, of an almost linenlike weave. They also wore breechcloths and capes, and admired jewelry. Ear plugs, nose rods and beads were made of silver, gold, crystal or shells. Men wore tattoos and painted their faces. Some used red paint, reserving black for war. They consumed the usual Mesoamerican foods, as well as bananas and pineapples, and used vanilla and indigo. Fish and prawns supplemented their diet. A seafaring people, the Itza made dugout canoes that had no sails but carried as many as 40 individuals.

The Itza utilized the Maya Katun Count and the Maya-style codices. They built homes of stone and wood, or of wood entirely, with thatched roofs. They also had wooden bed frames.

A definite pantheon of deities was honored in their religious ceremonials. The major gods were Iztamna Kauil, Ah Cocahmut, Kinchilcoba, Hobo, Pakoc and Hexchuncham. Stone columns, called *Yaxcheelcab,* were revered as the "first tree in the world." The statues in their temples were made of wood, alabaster, stucco or stone. The Itza also believed in *naguals,* spirits that took the form of jaguars or other animals. They conducted human sacrifices, taking the hearts of victims who died on X-shaped crosses. Skulls were collected and placed on racks, and cannibalism was practiced. Some traditions state that the priests of the Itza were slain at the age of 50, before they became powerful sorcerers.

At Chichen Itza the Itza extended or established the cult of the rain god at the sacred *cenote,* by the Well of Sacrifices. Mayapan appears to have served the Itza for some time, and they erected 2,000 structures within its walls. Tayasal remained the Itza capital until the Spanish conquest.

Reported as being tall, well built and fair-skinned, the Itza were normally ruled by a hereditary chief, who either shared power with a high priest or held a dual role by serving in both capacities. They wore feather crowns and carried fans as symbols of rank. Trumpets, flutes and drums were among the religious and state musical instruments in use. Four lesser chiefs, each called *Batab,* governed specific districts, which, in turn, were divided into smaller districts ruled by assistants. The military leader was called the *Nacon.*

ITZAMKANAC The Chontal Maya capital in the Candelaria River basin in the northeastern Yucatan Peninsula.

Large and prosperous, the city was divided into four quarters having several hundred splendid residences, some with masonry walls. Several temples were constructed in Itzamkanac, the primary one dedicated to Kukulcan, the Maya Quetzalcoatl. Other deities honored in the city were Ix Chel and Ek Chuah, the patron of traders and cacao producers.

ITZAMNA A Maya deity called Lizard's House, the Lord of the Heavens, and revered as the creator of all things and the patron of learning. He was also the model priest-ruler. Itzamna accomplished this creation through a power granted also to the divine Hunab Ku in some Maya traditions. Rain was one of Itzamna's elements, as *Itz* means "raindrops" or "teardrops." The Itzam, an iguanalike lizard, was the god's symbol. His consort was Ix Chel. Itzamna could appear as a crocodile or as the antlers or hooves of a deer. He was the patron of the cardinal points of the earth and as such was associated with the *Bacabes.* As the earth itself, the deity was addressed as Itzam Cab Ain. (See also *ACANTUN; AH PUCH.*)

ITZCOATL Called Obsidian Serpent, the ruler of the Aztec from A.D. 1427 to 1440. He succeeded Chimalpopoca, who was slain by the Tepanec after conflict erupted over Tezozomoc's throne, a feud perhaps started by Itzcoatl. Itzcoatl began a pattern of revolt against Maxtla, the successful claimant for the Tepanec throne, encouraging rebellion in other regional vassal states. Coming to the support of Nezahualcoyotl in Texcoco, Itzcoatl found his own capital, Tenochtitlan, blockaded by the Tepanec. He was counseled by Motecuhzoma, his younger brother, and by the esteemed court adviser Tlacaelel. With their support he founded the Triple Alliance, the union with Texcoco and Tlacopan (Tacuba). Eventually other vassal states joined as well, including Tlaxcala and Huexotzinco. The united forces waged war against the Tepanec, and Maxtla was slain in c. A.D. 1428. The victors divided the Tepanec holdings. Itzcoatl added to the great ceremonial center of Tenochtitlan until his death. He also attacked Coyocan and is noted as having burned the Toltec records in his possession. During his assault on the Cuitlahuac region, the Aztec used a fleet of canoes, a rare example of naval warfare in Mesoamerica. Itzcoatl aided his nephew, Nezahualcoyotl, in gaining the Texcoco throne. He was succeeded by Motecuhzoma (Moctezuma) I, Ilhuicamina.

ITZCUINTLI A god, a day sign in the Aztec version of the *tonalpohualli,* the calendar system. The Aztec used older calendars but updated and streamlined them for more accurate calculations whenever possible.

ITZTLACOYOLIUHQUI-IXQUIMILLI A god worshipped in the Valley of Mexico, representing stones and the cold. He is depicted in full armor with a stone face, sightless or blinded. Once called Tlahuizcalpantecuhtli, he is associated with traditions concerning creation.

ITZPAPALEOTL A goddess of the Toltec, Zapotec and Aztec (Mexica), as well as other cultures. She was usually depicted as a skeleton having jaguar talons and blade-tipped wings. The name of the goddess can be translated as "taloned butterfly" or "obsidian butterfly." She also appears in some reliefs as having bat wings. Itzpapaleotl represents demonic forces associated with death in childhood and during eclipses.

ITZPAPALOTL   See OBSIDIAN BUTTERFLY.

IX CHEL   The Maya goddess of medicine, floods and childbirth. A shrine to the goddess was erected at Cozumel, an island off the eastern coast of Quintana Roo. Her name meant "Lady Rainbow." When called by the name Chac Chel, the goddess protected weavers, midwives and those skilled in divination.

IXIMICHE   The capital of the Cakchiquel (Cakchikel) Maya, at Lake Atitlan in northwestern Chimaltenango, in Guatemala. The Quiche Maya once dominated the region, but the city remained independent until the Toltec occupied it in c. A.D. 800. The Aztec claimed Iximiche when the Toltec collapsed, but the Cakchiquel Maya returned in the mid-15th century A.D. The city was surrounded by a defensive ravine and erected on a hill. Pyramids and small platforms were built around four large courts and on natural terraces, and there were two ball courts. The murals remaining in Iximiche reflect Mixtec influence. A tomb discovered there contained a cache of gold, including 10 jaguar masks and a crownlike headdress. The corpse of a noble buried in the site was accompanied by three other bodies, presumably victims sacrificed to escort him into the underworld.

IXIPTLA   An Aztec mask of a god, deemed magical. The Ixiptla represented the appearance of the deity, including robes and symbols. When worn, the "mask" was believed to be the god in person.

IXLILTON   A deity listed in the traditions associated with the playing of the ball game, the various forms of athletic contests in the Mesoamerican region. These ball games had religious significance, having cosmological connotations among the many cultural groups. Some traditions record the god Ixlilton as supporting the god Quetzalcoatl in his battle against the gods Xochipilli and Centeotl. (See also HERO TWINS.)

IXTAB   A Maya goddess, the patroness of suicides, depicted in the *Codex Dresden* as hanging from the sky by a rope. The Maya revered suicides as individuals performing a great sacrifice. They were blessed by priests and considered worthy of immediate reward in the afterlife.

IXTEPETE   A Teotihuacan/Tarascan site near Guadalajara in Jalisco, begun around A.D. 100. Six pyramids were discovered on the site, one showing Teotihuacan influence, as Teotihuacan figurines were discovered there. The people of Ixtepete cremated their dead and placed the ashes in urns. It is believed that Ixtepete became part of the Tarascan sphere of influence around A.D. 1000.

IXTILCUECHAHUAUAC   A Toltec ruler, listed in the *Historia Tolteca-Chichimeca* as having ruled that nation from A.D. 562 to 614.

IXTLILXOCHITL   A ruler of Texcoco, he was a son of Quinatzin and the father of Nezahualcoyotl. He declared himself the Texcoco emperor, the Lord of the Chichimecs, challenging the power of Tezozomoc, a leader in the region around 1418 and the ruler of the Tepanecs. The Tepanecs declared war on Texcoco as a result of the announcement, and Ixtlilxochitl was defeated in battle and forced to flee Texcoco. He took Nezahualcoyotl into the mountains but was tracked there by the Tepanecs. Placing Nezahualcoyotl in the high branches of a tree, Ixtlilxochitl turned to face his pursuers. The Tepanecs slew the king as Nezahualcoyotl witnessed the scene. When the slayers left, Nezahualcoyotl climbed down and stayed beside his father's corpse until other Texcoco aides arrived. He then swore vengeance on Maxtla, the heir of Tezozomoc, and thus began his remarkable career, becoming one of Mesoamerica's outstanding leaders.

IXTLAN DEL RIO   A site in southern Nayarit, called Of the River by the Spanish and Where There is Obsidian in Nahuatl. A circular structure having stairways dominates Ixtlan del Rio. Two rectangular platforms made of stone slabs were constructed within its walls. To the northeast is a rectangular building with a platform and rectangular columns. Other columns and platforms can be seen on the site, as well as an L-shaped building on a platform. The site is noted for unique shaft tombs, which came into use in the

Ixtab, Maya goddess

Formative Period (before A.D. 290) or perhaps later. No documented culture has been associated with Ixtlan del Rio.

IZABAL A lake in the southeastern Maya region at the Gulf of Honduras. The lake was productive for local fisherman and for transport of local trade.

IZAMAL A Maya site located in the central part of the Yucatan Peninsula and also believed to have been a shrine to the god Itzamna. The city was named for the god Itzamal and was called the Dew of Heaven. The site contains one of the largest pyramids ever built in the Yucatan, called Kinich-Kakmo and dating to c. A.D. 900. The pyramid rises in terraces, and the base is 640 by 570 feet. A second pyramid stands 59 feet high and has rounded corners. Izamal covered two square miles and was associated with the renaissance in the region prompted by the great city of Mayapan at the end of the Post-Classic Period (A.D. 1200/1250–1521). Izamal prospered until it was drawn into the territorial expansion of Mayapan, which was supposedly triggered by the kidnapping of the bride of Izamal's ruler, Ah Ulil. In time, because of the resultant war Mayapan attacked Izamal, and its status was reduced.

IZAPA A site in Chiapas, near the Pacific coast, rooted in the Miraflores culture of eastern Mesoamerica, part of the cultural development of the Isthmus of Tehuantepec. The city is believed to be the major tie between the civilizations of the Olmec and the Maya. Located on the banks of a tributary of the Suchiate River, which divides modern Mexico from Guatemala, Izapa was founded in the Early Formative Period (c. 2000/1600–900 B.C.) and reached the height of its dominance in the Late Formative Period (300 B.C.–c. A.D. 250/290).

The original source of Izapa's power was its agricultural prosperity in general, but the city also possessed a virtual monopoly on cacao products during some periods. Its domination of the cacao-growing region provided Izapa not only with a highly stable economic base but with far-reaching influence. Cacao itself was an actual monetary symbol in the vast trading systems of Mesoamerica. Cacao beans are perishable and could not be stored or hoarded successfully for long periods, as they rotted and were subject to damaging insect infestation. Traders used fresh beans for their transactions and turned surplus reserves into the liquid so prized by the elite of the various Mesoamerican cultures. The people of Izapa, in control of this vital resource, even deposited some cacao beans into the foundations of their monuments, as offerings to the gods or as thanksgiving for their bounty.

Izapa was very large, with as many as 80 temple pyramids, surrounded by courts and plazas. Little remains evident today on the site, but stelae, altars and elaborately carved stones exemplify the artistic skills of the inhabitants. One figure, a long-lipped deity, resembles the Olmec were-jaguar. In time the Maya would used a similar motif. Over 200 such pieces of sculpture have been recovered on the site of the city.

Izapa used many Olmec artistic elements, including the St. Andrew's cross device and the Olmec U-shaped design. The jaguar motif was incorporated into many pieces, including the combined jaguar mouths and cloud-scroll patterns. Izapa scenes, however, are cluttered when compared to the Olmec art, and baroque effects are integral to the style. The narrative form dominates Izapa reliefs, which are lively and filled with competing design elements. Humans, animals and gods interact and war with one another in stone. Birds soar, and gods call down storms or descend mightily to the earth. Fish swim in water, and humans fight wars or tend elaborate incense burners in acts of worship. Such scenes grace the stelae recovered from Izapa, which also bear the sky-band insignia of the region.

An original cultural and artistic innovation of Izapa was the Tree of Life, which was possibly an early depiction of the great Maya *ceiba* tree, believed to support the heavens. The tree was depicted in a great plaza scene.

Izapa was built in two sections, north and south, in keeping with the usual axis adopted by early Mesoamerican city planners. All that remains of the monumental structures that once made Izapa a splendid metropolis are crumbling earthen mounds surrounded by stelae, altars and other stone artifacts. Plazas having stelae and carved altars also contain pillars that have small balls at the top. Beyond the pillars is a monument depicting a figure seated in the jaws of a jaguar.

The northern section of Izapa has similar mounds, platforms and a ball court. Altars there are carved with frog symbols. The ball court houses a rectangular throne with an animal head on its western end. Beyond the court is a tall pillar with the remains of a kneeling figure at its top. Beyond the pillar is a stone basin, set into a plaza. Long-lipped deity motifs were also employed.

During the period of its dominance, Izapa influenced eastern Mesoamerica. During that time other settlements, such as La Victoria and Salinas la Blanca, which had been occupied during the Early Formative Period, were abandoned as the local populace moved into Izapa and related sites.

IZTACCALTZIN A Toltec ruler listed in the *Historia Tolteca-Chichimeca*. He is recorded as being in power from A.D. 833 to 885.

JADE A variety of stone, properly termed jadeite, varying in color and prized by Mesoamericans in all historical eras. As many as 782 pieces of jade were discovered in Cerro de las Mesas, which dates to c. 600 B.C. Evidence of jade use in celts, beads and ornaments date to even earlier periods in some cultures. In Altun Ha, in the Temple of the Green Stone, more than 300 pieces of jade were found in a tomb. Cabulco, a Chiapas basin, is thought to be a possible source of the stone. Quirigua, on the Motagua River, was a trade center for jade, which was also mined in the Motagua Valley. The Olmec mined a blue-green jade in Guerrero. In the central highlands, Tlatilco corpses were buried with jade grave offerings, and Chichen Itza, Teotihuacan and other cities displayed jade masks, statues and ornaments.

JADE SHRINE A sacred mountain, also called Chalchi-uhmomozco, near the city of Chalco. This mountain was revered during the various historical periods. It is associated with the site called Tamoachan.

JADE SKY A ruler of the Maya city of Quirigua. He is recorded as coming to the throne in c. A.D. 805.

JAGUAR A large feline mammal *(Panthera onca)*, a tropical predator with a tawny coat and black spots. The jaguar was the focus of religious traditions in many cultures, and the Olmec, in the La Venta culture (Middle Formative Period, 900–300 B.C.) developed a unique were-jaguar theme. This religious image incorporates babies and jaguars in celts and statues. Round infant forms bear fangs and are shown snarling, signifying jaguar origins. In the Juxtlahuaca Cave in Guerrero, a jaguar warrior relief dates to the Olmec era of occupation. The fascination with the animal spanned centuries. Its appearance and its hunting skills made it an impressive religious symbol. In some cultures jaguars were beheaded and sacrificed. The hides, teeth and claws were prized.

In the city of Teotihuacan (300 B.C.–c. A.D. 250/290), processions of jaguars adorn palaces and shrines. These animals are depicted as blowing trumpets amid dazzling lightning images. In this portrayal they are guarding the Rain Paradise of Tlaloc. In Monte Alban jaguars were depicted on urns. As the Maya built their great ceremonial centers, they honored the jaguar as the sun or as an underworld deity. The god Ah Kinchil (called Kinich Ahau in the Yucatan)

Jaguar relief from Teotihuacan

took the form of the jaguar in Maya traditions. The Balankanche Cave was called the Throne of the Jaguar Priest or the Hidden Treasure of the Jaguar Priest. The jaguar was also a symbol in use in the military warrior societies of later civilizations. The Toltec used the jaguar, eagle and coyote as totems. Zapotec priests wore jaguar skins. The Mixtec carved jaguars with mythological scenes into bones, and their codices display priests and warriors with jaguar heads and skins. In the Aztec Empire the jaguar remained dominant, as the warriors honored the deity Huitzilopochtli, the god of war, who led his valiant young men to the battlefield, "where the jaguars howled." The Aztec jaguar god was Tepeyollatl.

JAGUAR, BABY A Maya divine being, possibly associated with the Olmec were-jaguar cult. The dancing Baby Jaguar is depicted on Maya monuments. He can also take on human physical attributes. This deity was possibly the patron of the city of Tikal, and is mentioned in Caracol.

JAGUAR PAW Called the Great, a Maya ruler of the city of Tikal. He was a military leader of note and the tenth ruler of Tikal in a single dynasty. Jaguar Paw took the throne of Tikal sometime before A.D. 376. He attacked the city of Uaxactun, employing new techniques in battle and retaining the services of a military leader called Smoking Frog. His daughter married Curl Snout (Curl Nose), making him an eligible successor to the throne of Tikal.

JAINA A limestone island off the coast of Campeche, chosen by the Puuc Maya as a cemetery for the burial of aristocrats. A temple probably dedicated to funerary functions was built on the island. The elite of the Puuc were interred with vast grave offerings, including sophisticated handmade or molded figurines reflecting the Maya skills of the Classic and Post-Classic periods (c. A.D. 1/250–900; A.D. 900–1521) in the region. These handsome pieces portray warriors, young women, matrons and deities. The popular

Jaina vase

Fat God is also among the figures. The statues made in Jaina were hollow, with whistles attached to their backs. Now celebrated for their workmanship, these figurines were painted and elaborate, both in style and detail.

JALIEZA A site in the Valley of Oaxaca, perhaps a vassal of the city of Monte Alban, reaching its own height of power in c. A.D. 250 to 450. Jalieza is reported to have had more than 10,000 inhabitants, and 700 residential terraces were uncovered there. An important religious center with economic ties to Monte Alban, few monuments survive on the site, and the architecture is massive in style.

JALISCO A region in western Mexico, now a modern state, which dates to the Early Formative Period (2000–900 B.C.) or perhaps earlier in Mesoamerican history. Rock paintings have been discovered on various cliffs and walls in the region, at such sites as Ciudad Guzman (Zapatlan El Grande). Ahualaco is also associated with this cultural development. Shaft tombs and a ceramic industry existed in Ahualaco. Tomb sites in San Sebastian, northeast of Etzatlan in Jalisco, contained skeletons and the remains of headless bodies. Hollow figurines, rectangular ceramic boxes with lids, polychrome bowls and dishes were recovered there, as well as conch-shell trumpets and shell and obsidian ornaments. In the El Arenal tomb site, more skeletons and grave offerings were found. Another site, Cerro Encantando, yielded a shaft tomb complex with horned figurines as grave offerings.

The people of Jalisco produced ceramics and incense burners made of stone. Figurines, usually hollow, depict warriors, chieftains, females (alone or with children) and people wearing conical headdresses. Statuettes, chunky and having stubbed arms and legs, were also produced, some with shoulder pellets (symbolic designs). Their faces are elongated, with a headband design and appliqued eyes and mouths. They wear earrings and nose rings and were fashioned out of red slip. The Jalisco ceramics included burnished buff, gray or brown clay. The ceramic industry in Jalisco probably dates to the Late Formative Period (300 B.C.–c. A.D. 250/290).

JANITZIO A Tarascan island domain in the southeastern part of Lake Patzcuaro in Michoacan. The city of Ihuatzio, a Tarascan capital, was built near this island.

JAQUILIPAS A site in Michoacan, dating to the Formative Period (2000 B.C.–c. A.D. 250/290) and associated with the various ceramic phases of the era. The El Openo Phase is evident in Jaquilipas.

JOCOTAL A development of the Cuadros culture, dated to c. 850 B.C. on the Pacific coast (Soconusco), with Ocos traditions. The people of this region inhabited the banks of estuaries and tropical forests. They produced ceramics of the Cuadros variety and a fired white-rimmed black ware.

JUCHIPILA RIVER A natural waterway in the Sierra Madre Oriental. The Juchipila joined the Bolanos River and became part of the Lerma-Santiago system, which is still used today. The river was part of the resources available to early Mesoamerican settlements.

JUSTO A cultural developmental period in the Valley of Mexico, associated with the Ayotla Phase, around 1100 B.C. The Ixtapaluca people also emerged here. Ceramics recovered from Justo give evidence of Olmec influence there. Ceramics include white-rimmed black ware and large, hollow doll figurines.

JUXTLAHUACA CAVE A site in Guerrero, located above the Balsas River near the Oxtotitlan Cave. The Juxtlahuaca Cave contains paintings believed to be some of the oldest in the Americas, reportedly 3,000 years old. Found deep within a mountain, the paintings are in black, green, red and yellow. A great bearded figure wears a quetzal-plumed headdress, tunic, cape and jaguar-skin leggings. He holds a type of rope and is accompanied by a smaller, crouching figure. In another chamber of Juxtlahuaca Cave, a red serpent and a small feline face one another. The paintings are believed to be Olmecoid, as the Olmec were once active in this region.

K

KABAH A Maya site in north-central Yucatan, built on a series of hills, noted for its Puuc architecture and for a stylish structure called the *Codz-Pop*, or the "coiled mat." This ceremonial center was built c. A.D. 900/1200, when Maya decline was evident in the southern part of their realm. Kabah apparently attracted Maya immigrants from that region and is believed to have been associated with the ceremonial center of Uxmal. The *Codz-Pop*, also called the Palace of the Chac, is more than 150 feet long and is supported by an elaborate terrace. A two-story structure, the palace contains 10 chambers and is covered with 250 masks honoring Chac, the Maya rain god. The masks appear to have been made locally, as was the roof comb, which has a stepped fret design.

A second palace in Kabah also has two stories and a columned temple. This shrine is over 100 feet long and has five doorways. Columns were placed in the doorways and on the exterior. The corbeled arch, a Maya architectural innovation, was incorporated into the design. Another high pyramid was also uncovered on the site. A causeway leads from Kabah to the city of Labna.

KAL PHASE A cultural development in Chalchuapa, near the border of El Salvador, a Maya frontier territory. Usulatan wares were manufactured in Chalchuapa. The Kal Phase is dated to c. 400 B.C.

KAMINALJUYU A site on the edge of modern Guatemala City in Guatemala, named the Hills of the Dead by the Quiche Maya. It is believed to have been built during the Arevalo Phase, c. 850 B.C., although there is some evidence that the foundations of Kaminaljuyu date to as early as 1000 to 1500 B.C. The Mexica invading the region added to the construction c. A.D. 400. Kaminaljuyu was a large and prosperous city that influenced many smaller cultures, and in its turn was included as part of the great Miraflores Phase of the Late Formative Period development (300 B.C.– c. A.D. 250/290).

The city was designed with several districts or precincts, all evolving in different historical eras to accommodate the city's changing population and role. Each precinct had its own ceremonial platforms, made of earth and clay, and there were high, terraced platforms as well, containing elaborate tombs with rich offerings. Kaminaljuyu became economically strong and an important district in the Las Charcas Period, in the Middle Formative era (900–300 B.C.). The site was known at that time for the high quality of its sculpture and its network of pyramids. Remains of more

than 200 pyramids on the site can be seen. During the Late Formative Period, in the Miraflores Phase (300 B.C. to A.D. 200), Kaminaljuyu constructed the last of the pyramids and is believed to have supported a population of between 25,000 and 50,000. Some pyramidal mounds from this era indicate that they were constructed over as many as seven earlier structures, demonstrating the constant rebuilding that took place.

The districts of Kaminaljuyu may have been ruled by different clans, a system repeated in the later major Post-Classic cities. The precincts' nobles appear to have lived on three-tiered platforms, which supported double-chambered wooden-frame, thatched houses that were rather elegant for the period. The precincts, with their individual aristocratic castes, were joined by a loose political confederacy, which predates the Maya unity.

In time the city of Teotihuacan influenced Kaminaljuyu, although Izapan influence as well as Maya styles are reflected in the remains of the site. The beginnings of Maya hieroglyphs were uncovered there. The structures were built of painted adobe, with plain basalt columns forming accompanying monuments for the various pyramidal platforms. Also present in Kaminaljuyu is the *talud-tablero* style of architecture.

A remarkable aspect of Kaminaljuyu art that has survived over the centuries is the presence of natural boulders shaped like potbellied men. Mushroom stones and depictions of

Kaminaljuyu vase

frogs are also evident, probably a reference to the use of hallucinogenic drugs in the religious rituals conducted at the ceremonial sites. The city was also noted for its remarkably carved stelae. One stela depicts a beautifully attired individual between two incense burners. A black basalt sculpture found nearby depicts three human figures in relief. This detailed portrait included the intricate lines of feathers. Another stela bears hieroglyphs believed to be accounts of rulers and are clearly Maya in style.

In the Late Formative Period, Kaminaljuyu had assumed the role of a regional ceremonial center, attracting pilgrims from the surrounding districts. The individual precincts and their aristocrats were now involved in regional affairs, maintaining the confederation that allowed the city to function as a single entity in trade, social and religious matters. At the close of the Formative Period, however, Kaminaljuyu declined. It is believed that the city was abandoned or at least lost most of its population at that time, c. A.D. 290, until the Esperanza Phase, c. A.D. 400, whereupon the people returned to Kaminaljuyu and the city came to life again, following the invasions of the Mexica. The *talud-tablero* architecture of the city probably dates from this period.

Historians believe that both Maya and Mexica groups inhabited Kaminaljuyu at this time. Tombs were placed in front of the public buildings, although prior custom had dictated interior burial. Grave offerings recovered from these sites include jade, obsidian and iron-ore mirrors. Pieces from Teotihuacan have been found among the grave offerings as well. Kaminaljuyu was a shrine city for the deity Tlaloc, the god of rain, and for Xipe Totec, the flayed god of spring. The city was occupied well into the Late Classic Period (A.D. 600–900) but no longer dominated the region.

KAN BOAR A Maya ruler of the city of Tikal, the son of Stormy Sky and the father of the Woman of Tikal, a local figure. He is depicted on a stela in the city, dated to A.D. 475. There he is portrayed in ceremonial dress. He is believed to be the 12th ruler in the Tikal dynasty.

KAN-CROSS WATER LILY MONSTER A Maya religious symbol, representing the canals and irrigation levels of Maya agriculture. The symbol apears in the Foliated Cross, a celebrated religious symbol.

KANHOBALAN MAYA see MAYA GROUPS, KANHOBALAN.

KAN The Maya ruler of the city of Caracol, the son and heir of Lord Water. Taking the throne in 599, he ruled for 19 years, and Caracol prospered. He was succeeded by his brother, Kan II.

KAN II A Maya ruler of the city of Caracol, the son of Lord Water and the heir to his brother, Lord Kan. In 618 he became king and set out to conquer the area around Caracol. His goal was the city of Naranjo, a major Maya site to the east of Tikal. He made an alliance with Calakmul and its ruler and then, in 627, after a preliminary assault, began the war in earnest, defeating Naranjo by 631. Kan II em-

ployed the planet Venus in making his military plans, calculating the position of the feared celestial object.

KAN XUL (Hok) The younger brother of Chan Bahlum and his successor as the ruler of the Maya city of Palenque. He assumed power in the city in A.D. 703. Kan Xul is reported to have enclosed the palace of Palenque during his reign.

KATUN See MAYA CALENDAR.

KEKCHIAN MAYA (Kekchi) See MAYA GROUPS, KEKCHIAN.

KIN CANEK An Itza-Maya noble, the high priest of the temple of Tayasal. The cousin of Ahau Canek, the ruler of that city, Kin Canek was a trusted adviser in the affairs of the court and the region, as well as the chief participant in religious ceremonies.

KINICH (Kinic) A Maya site in the west-central part of the Yucatan, demonstrating Classic Puuc architecture, dating to A.D. 700 to 830. Derived from the Maya word for market or plaza, the city includes a pyramid temple and three groups of structures. One building has a banded-column design that is unusual and striking. The city probably lay within the Uxmal sphere of influence.

KINICH AHAU See AH KINCHIL.

KNIGHTS Aztec (Mexica) warriors who belonged to that nation's military religious orders, such as the Knights of the Eagle and the Knights of the Jaguars. These military groups were headquartered in "the house of the eagle," the *cuauhcalli,* the primary shrine in the city of Malinalco, in east-central Mexico, south of Toluca. Other shrines were used as headquarters also. The military castes of knights followed earlier cultural models, especially those of the Toltec. The use of the eagle and the jaguar totems dates to earliest times in Mesoamerica. (See AZTEC WARFARE.)

KOHUNLICH A Maya site in Quintana Roo, in the Rio Bec style, dating to c. A.D. 900, or perhaps later. The city has an acropolis, with large structures surrounding a sunken plaza. There is a Pyramid of the Masks set on a hill. The pyramid is 50 feet high and has rounded base corners and carved stucco masks portraying the sun. The present pyramid was once surrounded by a larger structure that has since collapsed. Kohunlich also includes a ball court.

KUK A son of Chaacal III, who became the ruler of the Maya city of Palenque in A.D. 764. The Maya decline became evident in Palenque during Kuk's reign.

KUKULCAN (1) The "Feathered Serpent" (*Kukul,* feathered; *can,* serpent) among the Maya groups of the Yucatan, worshipped as a god, associated with Quetzalcoatl. Kukulcan arrived in the Yucatan in c. A.D. 987, after miraculous journeys. He originated in the Toltec city of Tula, where he was called Ce Acatl Topiltzin. Kukulcan was the patron of the Maya elite and in some records is associated with the Peten Maya group. He controlled the region and established his cult in the city of Chichen Itza. He was thought to be a reincarnation of Quetzalcoatl. (See MAYA GODS; KUKULCAN [2].)

KUKULCAN (2)   A ruler of the Itza people, who led them to the city of Chichen Itza in c. A.D. 1224/44. He took the name Kukulcan II in honor of the former ruler. (See Kukulcan [1].) The city flourished as a place of pilgrimage during this period.

LABNA A Maya site in west-central Yucatan, dating to A.D. 900. One of the largest ceremonial centers, Labna was called the Old Ruined Buildings, built by Maya migrating from the south. The center was located on a site occupied since the Formative Period (2000 B.C.–c. A.D. 250/290). A palace found in Labna was supported by a terrace over 500 feet long. Chac masks, columns and Puuc mosaics decorate the structure, as well as an open-mouthed serpent figure. A *chultun* was incorporated into the palace, and there is another smaller structure nearby. South of the palace is a second group of buildings, including a pyramidal temple called El Mirador by the Spaniards. Once quite large, El Mirador supports a shrine with a stone roof comb. Nearby is the notable corbeled arch of Labna, having doorways and stone models of the original huts used in the region. The use of latticework and a roof comb makes the arch unique. This entire structure was set on a stepped platform with two courtyards serving as part of the complex.

LACANDON MAYA See MAYA GROUPS, LACANDON.

LACANHA RIVER A tributary of the Peten Usumacinta River system in Guatemala. The city of Bonampak, a Maya center, lies near the Lacanha.

LACANHAI A Maya site in the Chiapas forest region, south of the Usumacinta River. Little is known of this ceremonial center.

LACHIZAA A Mixtec capital called the Place of the Oldest Things, flourishing in c. A.D. 1200. A tomb uncovered in Lachizaa contained an antechamber and a room covered with slabs. Stuccos and vases with animal and human faces were also found there. The sepulcher in the tomb has six lateral niches, and jaguar forms were discovered on the walls and on small bowls. Tripod decanters, funerary urns and other grave offerings were also recovered. A second tomb opened on the site contained the bodies of seven males, with eight others in the antechamber and three more in a central corridor. Grave offerings in this tomb include clay *apoztles* (sieves used to wash impurities from corn before grinding), images of the caracol snail carved in jade and stone turquoise disks and six-legged vessels.

LADY BLOOD A Maya deity, one of the cosmological traditions as the mother of the Hero Twins. Lady Blood was a princess of Xibalba, the Maya underworld. She discovered a body hanging from a tree and became pregnant upon touching the head of the corpse. Banished from Xibalba, she left the underworld for earth to give birth to her sons, Hunaphu and Ixbalanque, the heroes of Maya tradition. (See HERO, TWINS.)

LA FLORIDA PHASE A cultural development in the Sierra Madre region, associated with the Huaxtec and dated to c. 100 B.C. The phase is marked by the presence of temples in village complexes. Huaxtec settlements increased in this era, and agricultural activities expanded.

LAGUNA DE LOS CERROS An Olmec site built south of the Tuxtla Mountains, at one time containing 95 mounds and covering 94 acres of land. Laguna de los Cerros was a ceremonial center, powerful in the region and located midway between San Lorenzo and Tres Zapotes. Twenty-eight stone monuments were found on the site, mutilated by vandals. They are pure Olmec in style. The St. Andrew's cross and the jaguar motifs are evident. An altar found on the site was designed with a projecting top and a figure seated within a side niche. Another statue, decapitated, depicts a man wearing a breechcloth and a cape with aristocratic devices. Llano de Jicaro, another site, lies a few miles from Laguna de los Cerros and is believed to have been a workshop area for Laguna de los Cerros artisans.

LAGUNA DE TERMINOS A site in northern Yucatan, where traders and Aztec merchants established the trading center of Xicalango, deep in Chontal Maya territory. In the Chontal Acalan region, these traders maintained ties with the local groups while servicing the long-distance trade systems of Tenochtitlan.

LAGUNA PETEXBATUN A district in the Peten (Putun) region of Guatemala, the site of the Maya city of Dos Pilos. The entire site of Laguna Petexbatun appears to have been dominated by the Maya ceremonial center of Tikal.

LAGUNA PHASE A cultural development dating to c. 500 B.C.–A.D. 500. It is associated with the Tamaulipas Sequence.

LA JUANA A site in Morelos, the highland region of Puebla, where settlements of early eras have been uncovered. Part of the San Pablo Pantheon, La Juana dates to c.

LAKES OF MESOAMERICA

NAME	LOCATION	ROLE
Amatitlan	near Guatemala City	served Kaminaljuyu
Atitlan	northwest Chimaltenango, Guatemala	site of Iximiche
Bacalar	Yucatan	Maya trade site
Catemaco	southern Veracruz	agricultural resource
Chalco	Chalco	local site resource
Chapala	Jalisco	Colima site
Coba	northern Quintana Roo	site of Coba
Cuitzeo	Michoacan	site of Tarascan realm
Ekixil	Yucatan Peninsula	site of Tayasal
Etla	Oaxaca	San Jose Mogote site
Fuerte	Pacific coast	Northern boundary
Izabal	Honduras gulf	Maya trade site
Macaxoc	northern Quintana Roo	Coba resource
Patzcuaro	Michoacan	site of Ihuatzio
Peten-Itza	Peten (Putun)	Maya resource
Texcoco	Valley of Mexico	site of Tenochtitlan
Xaltocan-Zumpango	Valley of Mexico	site of Xaltocan
Xochimilco	Valley of Mexico	site of Xochimilco
Yurira	Michoacan	Tarascan domain
Zirahuen	Michoacan	site of Patzcuaro

1300–1100/900 B.C. At that time Olmec influence was powerful there. La Juana participated in the vast trade system.

LAKES OF MESOAMERICA   See table.

LAMANAI   A Maya site in Belize, south of Cerros on the Nuevo River, once called the Indian Church on local maps. Lamanai was constructed beside a lake formed by the river and participated in the vast Maya trade system. Because of its geographical position on the edge of the Maya domain, Lamanai escaped much of the damage inflicted by the continued warfare and ecological collapse of the region. The city continued to remain vital, with more than 700 structures designed to serve the needs of those around it. One of these buildings, a beautifully executed vast pyramid, was constructed sometime between 150 B.C. and A.D. 200. This Maya Classic pyramid stood more than 100 feet high and had multiple tiers and three stairways. Lamanai remained active until the Spanish arrived there. Lamanai was involved in trade as a producer of cacao and cotton. Stelae and large masks were part of the design. It is possible that the site was occupied from 1500 B.C., continuing until the Spanish conquest.

LAMBITYECO   A site located in the central part of Oaxaca, near Tlacolula, dating to the era called Monte Alban III (c. A.D. 100–700), the period of Zapotec domination. The city is situated on a plain in the Tlacolula valley region. Lambityeco is highly regarded because of the valuable sculpted decorations that are still visible, set into patios that originally formed part of a vast building-complex series. Carved friezes depicting an aged couple, possibly the Mesoamerican creation pair, called the Divine Ancestors, were found on the tomb entrance. Some historians describe them as the possible owners of the tomb. The couple's heads

were covered in red paint originally, and were accompanied by stone glyphs.

A stucco head of the Zapotec rain god, Cocijo, was also uncovered at Lambityeco. There was a plaza as well, with a pyramidal base and an altar, undoubtedly serving as the ceremonial site for the city and the surrounding region. The people of Lambityeco used both stone and adobe in its construction and more than 35 mounds are evident. The site also contained fine orange ceramics, imported into the region probably in the trade system that crisscrossed Oaxaca, leading north and south and linking the Zapotec to other cultures and products. Lambityeco was abandoned after a short period, probably having served the Zapotec when they were in a period of decline or migration.

LAMENTATIONS   A philosophical treatise concerning life written by King Nezahualcoyotl of Texcoco around A.D. 1400. He was called the Sage of Anahuac by his contemporaries, and his views were revered by the various cultures in the Valley of Mexico.

LA MILPA   A Maya ceremonial site located in the Rio Bravo Conservation and Management Area of Belize, part of the Orange Walk district. It was occupied from c. 300 B.C. until the 16th century A.D. During the period of A.D. 400 to 800, La Milpa flourished. Now being excavated, the site includes large pyramids, temples and a ball court. Inscribed stelae were discovered there as well.

LANGUAGE   See MESOAMERICAN LANGUAGES.

LA PERRA PHASE   A cultural development associated with the Tamaulipas Sequence, dating from 3000 to 2000 B.C. During this phase, the people appear to have hunted for only 15 percent of their dietary needs, with 10 to 15 percent of their food domestically grown and the rest consisting of wild plants. There is an indication that early *Nal-Tel* corn was in use. Dart points, gouges, choppers, *manos*, scrapers, mats, baskets, nets and blankets were all recovered from the region involved in this phase.

LA QUEMADA (Chicomoztoc)   A site named for the region of the Seven Caves in Nahual traditions, called The Burned One (La Quemada) by the Spaniards. La Quemada is a hilltop fortress fashioned out of tabular stones at an elevation of 6,500 feet in the center of the modern state of Zacatecas in central Mexico. Stone walls surround the northwestern side of the hill. The palace complex uncovered there has a large platform with seven columns and a stone structure. A corbeled vault and a passageway complete the complex, which faces a plaza. North of the palace is a small platform with a southern stairway and a ball court, rare in northern Mesoamerican complexes. A votive pyramid located at the northern end of the court is called the Temple of the Sun in some records. The Citadel, or Acropolis of La Quemada, is a courtyard surrounded by platforms and by a maze of interconnecting chambers. The Temple of Sacrifices is on a higher level nearby, with a two-tiered altar and stairs. Another section, called La Terraza, at the top of the hill, has steep stairs and balustrades. The site of La Quemada was abandoned by A.D. 1350/1400 after 1,000 years. Some records indicate that the city may have originated with the Malpaso. It was burned in some civil or religious strife, hence the Spanish name.

LAS BOCAS   An Olmec site in the Morelos Valley, serving as a gateway to a plain. The site is associated in artistic style with the earlier phases evident in Tlatilco (around 1500 B.C.). Graves in Las Bocas contained Olmec offerings, dolls and jaguar-motif vessels.

LAS CHARCAS PHASE   A cultural development associated with the Isthmus of Tehuantepec, dating to the Early Formative Period (c. 2000/1600–900 B.C.). In this phase the *chultun*, the bottle-shaped pit, was developed, and kaolin pottery was manufactured. Ceramics from the phase were usually in the form of monkeys or dragon masks, some having abstract designs. Pyramidal platforms were also erected, fashioned of clay. Another phase, Las Charcas B, appeared in the Late Formative Period (300 B.C.–c. A.D. 250/290), followed by the Miraflores Phase.

LAS CHARCAS B   See LAS CHARCAS PHASE.

LAS FLORES (1)   A Huaxtec site in Veracruz noted for a round pyramid, having stairs and a round temple on its summit. This pyramid was built of stone covered with stucco. The temple on the top had a thatched roof. Similar pyramids from the Huaxtec period were discovered at Pavon, Tancal and Buenavista Huaxcama.

LAS FLORES (2)   A beautifully carved petroglyph found in the cemetery of Xochimilco, in the Valley of Mexico. The petroglyph depicts the goddess of the cardinal points, the four corners of the earth.

LAS FLORES PHASE   A ceramic development associated with the Mixtec city of Coixtlahuaca and dated to A.D. 500–1000.

LAS HIGUERAS   A small Totonac ceremonial center, located near the gulf. Totonac paintings portraying rituals were found on the site as well as images of priestly processions. Also depicted were the gods, fishing and the Totonac version of the Mesoamerican ball game.

LAS JOYAS PHASE   A cultural development dating from A.D. 700 to 950, associated with the Chalchihuite. The decorations of pottery from this phase indicate Toltec influence. Colonnaded masonry was also manifested in this development.

LA VENTA   One of the finest Olmec sites, built on the northern part of an island approximately 18 miles from the gulf coast in the region of Tabasco. The Olmec city was built in the middle of the Tonala River and was approximately two square miles in diameter at the height of its power. The modern name, La Venta, is Spanish for "roadside inn"; and the original Olmec designation for the site remains unknown. La Venta was founded sometime c. 1000 B.C. during the La Venta Phase, which is also called Olmec II. The city endured as an Olmec stronghold until c. 400 B.C. Considerable historical knowledge has been acquired from La Venta, which represents entire stages of development among the Olmec in the region. La Venta was designed with a north-south axis. The dominant structure is a volcano-shaped pyramid made of clay and originally over 100 feet high. Fluted, the structure is believed to have been begun c. 800–700 B.C. Records indicate that the pyramid took generations to complete, with the Olmec bringing in more than 18,000 laborers.

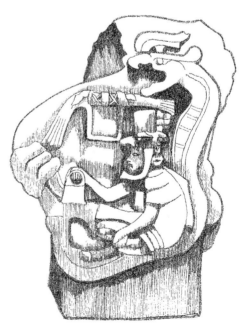

La Venta monument

La Venta was an Olmec ceremonial site, serving the religious life of the culture with its pyramid and other shrines. From 25 to 30 priest-caste families maintained permanent residence there. Originally the site was composed of wooden buildings, the usual pole structures with thatched roofs and platforms. Stone was used to build the ceremonial structures, as the population's demands for the center warranted this.

To the north of the fluted pyramid are two long, low mounds that extend from each side of a center line. Another low mound lies between them. A rectangular, broad court or plaza contained hand-carved basalt columns, set side by side on a low adobe brick wall. A large, terraced clay mound was also incorporated into the design. The columns weighed from 1,500 to 2,300 pounds, and they stood probably in sunken courts having mosaic floors depicting jaguar faces. These floors were laid out in colored clays, and the walls were painted. A large number of basalt carvings, including four colossal heads, were part of the design, as were large stelae. One such commemorative slab, labeled Number Three, has been called Uncle Sam by excavators, because of its resemblance to the American patriotic figure.

The altars at La Venta reflect the jaguar theme, and some have figures emerging from side niches. Of particular importance was a cache of 16 jade and serpentine figures discovered on the site. Beside the figurines were six celts, all arranged in a circular group. The figures stand in consultation, surrounded by the celts. Jade was common in the grave offerings recovered in La Venta.

Three rectangular pavements uncovered in the center have unique historical and cultural value. Each of these pavements, which are designated as "massive offerings," and was composed of 485 blocks of serpentine, fashioning a jaguar mask. These pavements were probably part of the grave goods of a tomb. They were laid out and then covered with clay and adobe. It is possible that the pavements also honor some deity of the city.

Few human remains are evident at La Venta. One tomb, the most elaborate at the site, was surrounded and roofed with basalt columns. Two juvenile corpses were discovered on the floor of the tomb, each wrapped and covered with vermilion. Offerings were provided for the bodies, and a sarcophagus was positioned outside the tomb. Vermilion was used in other tombs found in La Venta as well.

The ceremonial center was deliberately destroyed sometime in c. 400–300 B.C. It was probably abandoned, but late period ceramics indicate that some people continued to live on the site. (See "MASSIVE OFFERING.")

LA VENTA PHASE A cultural development also called Olmec II, dating from 1200–c. 600/400 B.C. The La Venta Phase followed the San Lorenzo Phase in this period; this gave rise to an alternative name for the Olmec as the La Venta People. In this period of development, the Olmec participated in complex trade and manufacturing endeavors, creating a market for jade (jadeite) in the region. The Oxtotitlan murals discovered in a cave in Guerrero are believed to have been painted during this phase.

LA VENTA RIVER A tributary of the Grijalva River forming a gorge in the Chiapas Valley.

LA VICTORIA A site on the Pacific coastal plain (Soconusco) and part of the Ocos culture, thought by some scholars to be one of the oldest settlements in the New World. Pole houses were constructed at La Victoria c. 1500 to 1150 B.C. These were covered with mud and placed on mound platforms as a defense against tidal floods. The lagoons, estuaries and alluvial fields provided by the local rivers also posed threats to habitation in certain seasons of the year. Maize was grown in La Victoria, and the people hunted in the mangrove swamps and in the forests. Of particular importance to the site and to the development there was the presence of salt beaches and the *madresal* tree, called the mother of salt. La Victoria ceramics include globular jars and *tecomates* (neckless jars). Rocker stamping with the sharp edges of shells was used on flat bowls and vessels. The people of La Victoria also produced figurines.

LA VILLITA A region in Michoacan, in western Mexico, active in the Formative Period (c. 2000/1600 B.C.–c. A.D. 250/290). More than 60 separate sites have been uncovered there. House clusters, patios and stratified burial complexes mark it as a place of early habitation. Ceramics from La Villita include hemispherical bowls, bottlelike jars and *ollas* decorated with incising and rocker stamping. One grave site of an aristocratic woman contained elaborate funerary offerings of shells, turquoise and jade.

LAXEE A Zapotec deity, honored in Zapotec ceremonies as the patron of sorcery and magic.

LEIDEN PLAQUE Also called a plate, a royal ornament found in the Maya city of Tikal. The jade plaque, believed to have been a belt adornment, depicts the Maya ruler Zero Moon Bird, who ruled in that city from A.D. 320. Possibly designed to commemorate the king's accession to the throne, the Leiden Plaque depicts Zero Moon Bird with royal insignias and glyphs. (See ZERO MOON BIRD.)

LERA ACUECE A Zapotec deity. In Zapotec ceremonies, Lera Acuece was honored as the patron of medicine and the healing arts.

LERMA PHASE A cultural development associated with the Tamaulipas Sequence, believed to have lasted until around 6300 B.C. In this phase the people made hunting weapons, including laurel–leaf projectile points. The remains of deer and other animals, their prey, were found beside the weapons. These weapons are similar to those found in other Tamaulipas Sequence sites of the same era. Such similarity suggests cultural contacts and perhaps trade.

LERMA RIVER A waterway joining the Santiago River in the Toluca Valley in central Mexico to form a plain. The Lerma is in the coastal region of the Sierra Madre Occidental.

LILANO A grassy terrain, such as those found in Chiapas. *Llanos* usually contain streams opening onto alluvial plains. (See also ALTOS CUCHUMATANES.)

LLANO DE JICARO See LAGUNA DE LOS CERROS.

Loltun cave relief

LOLTUN CAVE A Maya site in the Puuc region of the Yucatan Peninsula, actually a massive group of caves containing remains and artifacts from c. 2500 B.C. Ceramics uncovered there predate that era, indicating habitation in the region from an earlier date. A bas-relief at the entrance of Loltun Cave depicts a large man dressed in an elaborate costume and is dated to the Formative Period. Probably a deity or a warrior, the figure carries a lance. The glyphs in the sculpture are the earliest evidence of such symbols in the Yucatan region. The interior caverns of the Loltun Cave group are vast and contain the remains of other murals. The Loltun Head found deep within the cave is two feet tall and Olmec in design. Some remains discovered there date to 2200 B.C. Ceramic wares were in use in 700 B.C., perhaps earlier.

LOMA DE AYUXI The Mixtec capital of Yanhuitlan, dominating the Mixteca-Puebla region in A.D. 1200 and later. A ceremonial site as well as the seat of government, Loma de Ayuxi was a large complex having palaces and compounds to house the elite.

LOMA SAN GABRIEL A group of settlements, including Hervideroas and Zape, on the Durango border in southern Durango and northwestern Zacatencas. These settlements were usually established on the tops of rocky mesas or on hills beside water reserves. The people of Loma San Gabriel erected residential compounds and individual houses having hearths and circular platforms. The sites bear evidence of the Desert Culture, which dates to the Incipient Agriculture Period (7000–c. 2000/2500 B.C.). Ceramics from the settlements include plain brown and red on brown in bowls, jars and other vessels. (See ZACATENCO-ARBORILLO.)

LORD OF THE FOREST A title bestowed by the Maya on the deity Ah Mun, the patron of maize. As the Lord of the Forest, Ah Mun battled Ah Puch, the god of death, thus acting out the traditional rebirth cycles associated with agriculture.

LORDS OF THE DAY Symbols in the Aztec calendar system, as well as in that of the Maya, who called them the *Oxlahuntiku*. Various deities assumed roles in this system, accompanying the numbers of the days. The Volatiles, glyph signs in the form of birds, accompanied the Lords of the Days.

LORDS OF THE HOUSE OF TURQUOISE A name given to the Toltec by their contemporaries. (See COATEPEC.)

LORDS OF THE NIGHT The Maya and Aztec symbols for their calendar systems. The Maya called their Lords of the Night the *Bolontiku*. The Aztec symbolized these lords with the numbers of the days. In the Maya traditions, the Lords of the Night were also the rulers of the levels of Xibalba, the Maya underworld.

LORDS OF WISDOM A name given to the founders of the city of Teotihuacan. (See also *TLAMATINIME*.)

LORD WATER A Maya ruler of the city of Caracol in Belize who ascended the throne in A.D. 553. He defeated the city of Tikal in 562, after an initial battle in 556, slaying Double Bird, Tikal's ruler, as noted in a Caracol shell-star glyph. Lord Waters ruled for 46 years.

LOS TAPIALES A Maya territorial site in the western highlands of Guatemala, occupied as early as 11,000 years ago. This dates Los Tapiales to the Paleo-Indian Period. Some remains recovered there date to c. 8760 B.C. Recent excavations at Los Tapiales, which lies on the Continental Divide, indicate its having been perhaps a temporary or seasonal habitation. Basalt quarried in nearby ravines was a common stone used in the manufacture of points, bifaces, gravers, scrapers and blades.

LOST WAX PROCESS Also called *cire perdue*, a casting method used by the Maya, Tarascan and others to manufacture metallic items. It is also associated with several types of ceramics, including Usulatan wares. In this method, wax is used as a mold, melting and running off in the process of firing. The Tarascan employed the lost wax method c. A.D. 1000. (See MESOAMERICAN CERAMICS AND CULTURAL DEVELOPMENTS.)

LUBAANTUN A Maya site near the Columbia River in Belize, called the Place of the Fallen Stones. A Late Classic Period ceremonial center, Lubaantun has 11 major structures, each grouped around 18 plazas. Three ball courts are also at the site. Pyramidal temples in Lubaantun are rounded, making them unique. Clay whistle figures found there are Jaina in style; a carved glass skull, turquoise, pottery and other items were also recovered.

M

MACAXOC A lake in northern Quintana Roo, in the eastern part of the Yucatan Peninsula. Lake Macaxoc was a resource for the nearby ceremonial center of Coba, the largest Maya city in the region.

MACUILCALLI A Xochimilco deity, believed to protect virgins.

MACUILXOCHITL An Aztec deity and the patron of courtiers, gambling and games. The god was associated in some rituals with the deity Xochipilli.

MADRE LAGOON An inlet on the gulf coast, part of a system of beaches and estuaries associated with developments in the Paleo-Indian Period (11,000–7000 B.C.). The lagoon also served emerging groups in later eras.

MAGUEY A plant cultivated in Mesoamerica, prized for a variety of products that could be fashioned from its fibers and distilled from its juices. The plant fibers were similar to twine or jute and were used for mats. The juice strained from the maguey was fermented and turned into *pulque* or *actli,* intoxicating liquors used in ceremonial and civil rituals.

MAIZE One of the staple crops of Mesoamerica, once believed to have been developed from a grass called *teosinte* (*Zea mexicana*). It is now documented that the maize (*Zea mays*) grown in Mesoamerica was a hybrid of a domestic form with tripsacum (*Zea tripsacum*). The wild maize plants altered by mutation were collected by early inhabitants of Mesoamerica and slowly domesticated. The wild form appears to have become extinct, possibly through backcrossing with domesticated forms. In the same way, the maize in the fields were crossbred with teosinte. The Mesoamerican region responsible for this development of maize may be in or near Jalisco. A perennial form of teosinte (*Zea diploperennis*) has been found there, having the same chromosomal make-up as maize and freely crossing with that species. Modern forms of the annual teosintes are not hybrids of maize and tripsacum. They stem from perennial teosinte and a primitive domestic maize. Backcrossing annual teosinte with maize allowed it to influence the future forms of this staple. Maize appears in the Coxcatlan Phase in the Tehuacan Valley (c. 5000 to 3800 B.C.). Actually, the first forms of maize in the New World were wild, with one domesticated form that can be found at levels of this historic development. Other forms appear in the Abejas Phase (c. 3400 to 2300 B.C.) and in subsequent cultural phases, as the early Mesoamericans became more settled and interested in agriculture.

Tradition holds that the widely worshipped Mesoamerican deity Quetzalcoatl was believed to have transformed himself into an ant in order to bring a grain of maize from the interior of a sacred mountain to humans.

Types of maize include:

pod corn maize—a hybrid form, possibly from South America. Domestic maize may have been backcrossed with wild forms, making hybrids and eliminating the previous wild strains

teosinte (*Zea mexicana*)—a wild form

(*Zea mays*)—a wild form no longer available

tripsacum (*Zea tripsacum*)—a hybrid, both wild and domestic, thought to be a possible ancestral form of maize

Zea diploperennis a species of maize having the same chromosomal makeup as maize, and which can be crossed with maize

MAJADES A development period of the Miraflores Phase, occurring in the Middle Formative Period (900–300 B.C.), with special emphasis in the period of 300 B.C. to A.D. 200 as well. The Miraflores Phase is associated with Usulatan wares in El Salvador, the Isthmus of Tehuantepec and other regions.

MALACHITE A natural copper carbonate ranging in color from green to nearly black. Malachite was mined in Alta Vista in the region of the Chalchihuite, included in the Turquoise Road trade route, c. A.D. 350.

MALINALCO A city in the central eastern part of Mexico on the crest of Montes de Mixtongo, taken by the Aztec in c. A.D. 1469/1476, in the reign of King Axayacatl. The name is Nahuatl for grass, *malinalli.* It is believed that the city was established by the Matlazinca. Located south of Toluca, Malinalco was widely known for its rock-cut temples, structures similar to those found in India. A fortress, the city was called the Eagle's Nest by the Aztec, with the major shrine called the House of the Eagle (*cuauhcalli*). As such, the site served the Aztec military religious society and was headquarters for the Aztec military castes or warrior groups, the Knights of the Eagle and the Knights of the Jaguar.

The circular *cuauhcalli,* which was accompanied by other stone monuments, had a pyramidal base and a staircase, carved from a mountainside. The interior chamber of the temple is approximately 19 feet in diameter and painted. A conical thatched roof covered the chamber originally. Three stone animals and a semicircular bench were part of the structural design when it was built. A circular hole in the floor, about 12 inches wide and 13 inches deep, probably served as a repository for the hearts of warriors sacrificed during the military religious ceremonies. A mural in the chamber depicts captive warriors, perhaps as the chosen messengers from the Aztec to the sun. Other paintings depict sacrifices and religious rituals. Five other shrines erected on the site of Malinalco follow the same basic design as the *cuauhcalli*. Altar carvings and platforms were incorporated into these buildings. Malinalco is important to the religious history of the Aztec as well. Copil, a nephew of the god Huitzilopochtli, the son of Malinalxoch, fought Huitzilopochtli on the site. He was slain there, and his heart was thrown "over the water," coming to rest on the island site destined to become Tenochtitlan, the Aztec capital.

MALINALLI   The grass symbolizing a day sign in the Aztec version of the *tonalpohualli*, the calendar system.

MALINALXOCH   An Aztec legendary being, sister of the god Huitzilopochtli and mother of Copil. She is associated with the journey of the Aztec toward Tenochtitlan. An ambitious sorceress, Malinalxoch gathered a small group of devotees to oppose her brother as he led the nation to its destiny. Recognized as evil, Malinalxoch was abandoned by the people at one stage of the journey. In revenge, she sent her son, Copil, to cause difficulties for the Aztec on the site of Malinalco. His plots were detected and he was slain there, with his heart thrown to the site that would become Tenochtitlan. The first temple in the Aztec capital was erected on the spot where Copil's heart rested. In variations on this theme, Copil's heart became the cactus upon which the eagle landed, thus fulfilling the prophecy given by Huitzilopochtli about Tenochtitlan. In some records Copil's mother is called Malinalxochtli.

MALINCHE   Also called Matlalcueyetl and Matlalcueye, a volcano on the Mesa Central in the Mexican highlands. Malinche was part of the Transverse Volcanic Axis.

MALPASO   A culture arising near the Chalchihuite site of La Quemada (Chicomoztoc) in Zacatenco. The group dates to the Early Classic Period (c. A.D. 1/250–600). It is believed that the Malpaso were the original builders of La Quemada. They had brown, polished red, black, red-on-brown, gray and black engraved ceramics. They also manufactured grooved polished axes, stone scrapers, flints and pieces made of obsidian and bone.

MAM (1)   The Maya protocommunity, the mother group. (See MAYA.)

MAM (2)   A deity of the Huaxtec, called Our Grandfather, the patron of *pulque*, the fiery liquor distilled from the maguey plant. Mam was also revered as an earth god, the bearer of thunder and the lord of the year. This deity may have served as a link to the Huaxtec ancestry as part of the Maya protocommunity, the Mam (1).

MAMANTIAL PHASE   A cultural development of the Ixtapaluca people of the Valley of Mexico, accompanied by the Ayotla and Coapeco phases. The Ixtapaluca are noted for having maintained their independence from 1250 to 900 B.C., at a time when group rivalries and migrations threatened the region. Figurine cults were part of the Mamantial Phase.

MAMON PHASE   A cultural development of the Formative Period (2000 B.C.–A.D. 1/290) in the Maya realm, having the first widespread ceramic style. The Mamon culture was also associated with the Las Charcas Phase. Dating in some Maya regions from 800 to 300 B.C., the Mamon culture included *tecomates*, cylindrical vases, bowls, flat-bottom plates, effigy vessels, tripod jars and incense burners as well as red and orange-red monochromes. Figures were made with applied strips of clay. The eastern lowlands had a particular Mamon style, and Mamon influence is evident in Belize. The Mamon was not a cohesive generalized style but a development of regional forms based on older patterns. Chicanel, another phase, appears to have evolved from the Mamon. The *chultun*, the bottle-shaped pits of the Maya, date to the Mamon Phase and were discovered in Tikal. (See MAYA ARCHITECTURE; MAYA ART.)

MANIKIN SCEPTER   A Maya religious symbol, and a manifestation of BOLOM DZ'ACAB, also called Kauil (possibly Tohil). The scepter, depicting the deity with a tube in his forehead and one leg in the form of a serpent, was carried in the hands of Maya rulers.

MANIOC   A root crop (*Manihat esculenta* and *Manihat dulcis*), used as early as the Altamira-Barra Phase (c. 1600/1400–1400/1200 B.C.) in Chiapas. The source of the original forms of manioc is undocumented, and its antiquity in the Mesoamerican region is unknown.

MANOS   Stones or pebbles used to grind maize and other plant substances against flat stones, called *metates*. Both the *manos* and *metates* appear in Mesoamerica during the Paleo-Indian Period (11,000–7000 B.C.).

MANZANAI   A region in the Motagua Valley that extends from Chiapas to the base of the Maya Mountains in Guatemala. It is listed in some records as a continuing source of jade.

MANZANILLA   A group associated with the city of Cholula in the Middle Formative Period (900–300 B.C.) in the Puebla region. With other small cultures, the Manzanilla took part in the development of Cholula, joining a confederation of groups there.

MAPA QUINATZIN   A document of the late imperial Aztec era in which Nezahualcoyotl's districts and administrative quarters in Texcoco are illustrated. It probably dates to around the 1460s, as Nezahualpilli is mentioned. Acolhuan council deliberations are also portrayed. The document also refers to local political alliances and the TRIPLE ALLIANCE. The *Mapa Quinatzin* suggests the rather sophisticated and complex legal system laid down by Nezahualcoyotl. Punishment and trial systems are clearly delineated. There were some 80 laws laid down in the Texcoco legal system.

MARIA LINDA   A river in Guatemala, flowing from the volcanic peaks of the interior to the Pacific Ocean.

"MASSIVE OFFERING"   A unique Olmec religious art form, uncovered in the ruins of the ceremonial sites of that culture. The "Massive Offerings" were serpentine mosaic pavements, designed as symbols. Each mosaic was composed of dozens of pieces of stone, filled in with colored clay. When completed, the "Massive Offerings" were covered with adobe and more clay and then buried. They thus became hidden offerings honoring deities or perhaps notable individuals in Olmec communities.

MATACHAN   A site in the region of Nayarit, in western Mexico, dating to the Early Formative Period, c. 2000 B.C. A shell-shaped mound was discovered in Matachan as well as ceramics. Shaft tombs were also uncovered on the site. San Blas, another site nearby, dates to 500 B.C. Figures found in Matachan reflect a sophistication and elegance of style.

MATAPACAN   A site located in the Tuxtla Mountain region on the southern gulf coast, an independent city-state arising in the Early Formative Period (2000–900 B.C.). Matapacan was possibly part of the Teotihuacan sphere and achieved considerable prestige during the Classic Period (c. A.D. 1/250–900) as well. The site may have been a garrison of the Teotihuacan trade system, serving as a gateway to Kaminaljuyu and the coastal plain of Guatemala. The city was noted for its production of obsidian tools and weapons. Some 70 separate mounds were discovered in Matapacan, and there is evidence of both ceramic and obsidian workshops. Teotihuacan ceramics and a *talud-tablero* platform were discovered on the site, which is believed to have had a population of 3,000 to 7,000 people.

MATEO SALDAMA   A Toltec site located west of Tula, near the Diablo Canyon. Toltec petroglyphs and paintings depict deities and sacrificial rituals there.

MATHEMATICS   See MESOAMERICAN MATHEMATICS.

MATLACCOATL   A legendary Tepanec king regarded as the grandfather of King Acolnahuacatl, who led the Tepanec into the Valley of Mexico in the Late Classic Period (c. 1200/1250–1521 B.C.). Matlaccoatl is reported to have ruled in Tamoachan, the site of religious ceremonies. The lineage of this ruler became a point of honor and royal legitimacy among the Tepanec.

MATLACCOATZIN   A Toltec ruler listed in the *Anales de Cuauhtitlan* as ruling from A.D. 997 to 1025.

MATLACXOCHTLI   A Toltec ruler listed in the *Anales de Cuauhtitlan* as being on the throne from A.D. 947 to 983.

MATLATZINCA   A Nahual culture related to the Aztec (Mexica) and emerging in c. A.D. 1200/1474. Matlatzinca

Matlatzinca urn

people founded the city of Calixtlahuaca some 40 miles from modern Mexico City, south of the Toluca Valley, to serve as their capital. Calixtlahuaca was noted for its temple of Quetzalcoatl in the form of Ehecatl, the wind deity; hence the temple was a circular structure with a staircase. Matlatzinca people were called those Who Have Little Nets by their contemporaries. They are recorded as coming from Chicomoztoc, the legendary Seven Caves, and had association with the Otomi people. The Aztec attacked Calixtlahuaca, which was called the House on the Plain in Nahuatl. When the Matlatzinca retaliated, in or around A.D. 1510, or possibly when they rebelled against Aztec influences, the armies of Motecuhzoma II burned the city to the ground and then rebuilt it.

Peoples of this culture also occupied Malinalco and are given credit for its founding in some records. They remained there until A.D. 1469, when the Aztec, during the reign of Axayacatl, conquered the site. Some accounts place the Matlatzinca in Tula before the arrival of the Toltec. After the fall of Calixtlahuaca, the group went to the Valley of Toluca, settling at Tecaxic, near their fallen capital. Traces of the culture's ceramics and art forms remain in Morelos and in Tlapacoya in the Valley of Mexico. A fiercely independent people, they could not ward off the emerging imperial forces.

MAXTLA   Also called Maxtlatzin, a Tepanec ruler involved in a series of rivalries following the death of his father, the illustrious King Tezozomoc. Maxtla argued with his brother Tayauh (also called Quetzalayotzin) in a conflict for the throne, as Tayauh had been designated as the heir. Hearing that Tayauh planned to strangle him at a banquet (the suggestion reportedly of the Aztec king Chimalpopoca), Maxtla gathered noble allies and took the throne, probably murdering Tayauh. He hunted down Chimalpopoca in Tenochtitlan, slaying him and the Aztec ruler of Tlatelolco, a man called Tlacateotl. Maxtla also continued to pursue Nezahualcoyotl, the respected heir to the throne of Texcoco, whose father had been slain by Tezozomoc. Placing Texcoco under siege, Maxtla found himself confronted by the newly formed Triple Alliance, the union of Tenochtitlan, Texcoco and Tlapacoya (Tacuba). He blockaded Tenochtitlan, an act that ignited the spirit of Aztec independence. When other city-states joined the Triple Alliance, Maxtla found his own capital, Azcapotzalco, under siege in retaliation. Despite a valiant effort by a Tepanec general, probably Mozatl, to avert disaster, Maxtla's defenses collapsed. He was discovered in his steam baths in his palace and slain by the Aztec and Nezahualcoyotl. The Tepanec empire thus ended.

MAYA One of the major Mesoamerican cultures, dating to the protocommunity of the Mam, c. 2500 B.C., and still vibrant. It is estimated that over 2 million descendants of the historic Maya live today in the Yucatan Peninsula; Guatemala; Belize; Tabasco and Chiapas, Mexico; as well as El Salvador and Honduras. In the past the Maya were described by their contemporaries as sturdily built, with black hair, dark brown eyes and muscular legs. They still have aquiline profiles and at one time reportedly encouraged flat heads and crossed eyes in some regions. In the pre-Colombian eras the Maya were called the Sorcerers and the People of the Jaguar.

The realm of the Maya once covered 125,000 square miles: 550 square miles from north to south and 350 square miles from east to west. The vast Maya holdings included highlands and lowlands; the different climates and terrains shaped their way of life. The domain held by this culture is usually divided into northern lowlands, southern lowlands, southern highlands and northern, central and southern regions.

The northern lowlands encompassed the upper part of the Yucatan Peninsula, including Campeche and Quintana Roo. This is a flat, tropical plain broken by a series of hills, called *puuc* by the Maya, which form an inverted V design. The soil here is thin and rocky, and only scrub palms, pines, oaks and palmettos grow. As little surface water is available, the Maya used *cenotes*, the underground river systems that were exposed when their limestone crusts collapsed. The Yucatec Maya lived in this region.

The southern lowlands in the lower Yucatan Peninsula are drained by the Usumacinta, the Pasion and other rivers and receive more rain than their northern counterpart. The Maya Mountains also break the pattern of the terrain, which is marked by tropical rain forests. Ridges and depressions create microenvironments here, and swamps form in the rainy season. This region includes the Pacific littoral of Guatemala and El Salvador, and has lagoons, tidal estuaries and alluvial plains. The Chontal, Chol, Chorti and Lacandon Maya established their realms here, and in time it was considered the cultural heart of the entire Maya world. In later eras the southern lowlands became a frontier zone where the Maya came into contact with the Nahuatl Mexicans.

The southern highlands are marked by the great volcanic cordillero that rises out of Chiapas, stretching southward. The land rises to a height of 13,000 feet in some places, usually leveling off to 1,000 feet. Extinct and active volcanoes stand at a line at its very heart. The southern highlands is a region of steep valleys, gorges and alpine meadows. There are pine and oak forests, with cloud forests on the upper levels of the mountains. Streams and lakes provide

Maya stela

water resources there. Farther south the terrain alters abruptly into what is now called the Pacific coast and slope region. There lagoons, estuaries and mangrove swamps offer marine products and habitations. In the west the highlands were the home of the Tzeltatlan Maya. The central and eastern portions of this region contain Olmec remains as well. Here the Maya also came into contact with the great city of Teotihuacan. The Quiche Maya dominated the region in some eras, side by side with smaller groups. The Quiche were clustered around Lake Atitlan.

The origins of the Maya are still somewhat obscure, as there is little documentation available concerning their beginnings. Scant evidence concerning their presence is available from the Pleistocene Period. The earliest prehistoric site in the Maya realm was discovered at Los Tapiales in the western highlands of Guatemala, which was probably occupied as early as 11,000 years ago. In the Quiche-dominated portion north of Los Tapiales, more than 100 sites have been found, dating from 8000 to 1000 B.C. A second series of prehistoric settlements on the coastal region of Belize date to before 2000 B.C., with some perhaps being occupied as early as 9000 B.C. In the Puuc hill country, sites with deep ceramic levels are believed to have begun in 2000 B.C. Evidence has been uncovered in Cuello, in Belize, that makes this region important in tracing Maya ancestry. The stratified building and debris sites here, some as deep as 10 feet, indicate their use from c. 2500 B.C. Nearby burials include the grave of a female with the typical cranial deformation of the Maya. Graves of a later period (c. 1500 B.C.) here contained jade beads, the earliest such beads found in Maya territories. The presence of the jade gives evidence of the trade system already in place because the beads originated some 250 miles away. Such trade, in which the Maya would excel during the Classic Period, brought wares from the Rio Hondo or along the Caribbean coast. The *manos* and *metates* discovered at Cuello were fashioned out of limestone from the Maya Mountains, almost 100 miles distant. Some scholars believe the Swasey culture evident here is the source of the true Maya ancestors.

The Maya protocommunity, called the Mam, is known to have been in the region, expanding the group's territory around 2600 B.C. into what today is called Huehuetenango, Guatemala. Other groups belonging to the Mam community left the region and established their own realms at later dates. The Mam, in the region of Uaxactun in the Peten forests of Guatemala never migrated, but the other groups within the protocommunity went elsewhere. These groups include the Huaxtec, Yucatec, Chontalan, Tzeltatlan, Tojolabal, and Quiche.

The Huaxtec migrated to the northeast about 1800 B.C. They became a large and vital culture in Mesoamerica. (See HUAXTEC.) In 1200 B.C. they moved to the northwest to begin their own traditions. They were followed from the Mam region by the Chicomulceltec, who went to Chiapas in c. A.D. 1000.

The Yucatec migrated out of Mam lands in about 1600 B.C., settling in the peninsula now bearing their name and in regions to the south. The Lacandon, originally part of the Yucatec migration, separated from them around 1400 B.C.

The Chontalan left the Mam c. 900 B.C., going to the Usumacinta River area. In turn, the Chol and the Chorti, who had left with the Chontalan, broke away to inhabit their own lands.

The Tzeltatlan left the Mam protocommunity around 750 B.C., moving into the Chiapas highlands. There the Tzeltatlan splintered into the Tzeltal or Tzotal and the Tzotzil, c. A.D. 1200.

The Tojolabal left the Mam in 400 B.C., followed by the Kekchian in A.D. 900 and then by the Pokoman and the Pokonchi.

The massive Quiche group left the Mam around 200 B.C. They were joined by the Kanhobalan in A.D. 100 and then by the Motozintlecan in A.D. 1000. (For details about these Maya, see MAYA GROUPS and under Quiche Maya.)

In their various regions, the Maya embarked on growth and expansion running parallel with that of other Meso-american groups. This growth pattern was once called the Maya Old and New empires, but that distinction is no longer used. Instead, the Maya development is placed within the general context of Mesoamerican evolution.

Having reached their particular domains after leaving the Mam, the Maya groups began with the usual Neolithic techniques. The early Maya used scrapers, dart points, drills, *metates, manos*, choppers, knives and other tools. They made ceramic wares and went through the ceramic phases similar to those that were widespread in the region. Similarities existed, but the geographic locales did not match others in development or that display a uniformity of evolution. Much depended on the terrain and climate, and on the people's ability to adapt to the demands of the growing trade and to the community life and achievements awaiting them. Maya craftsmen emerged, artisans and women working in their homes who used awls, needles, looms, cotton and sisal fibers. The Barra, Ocos, and the Xe ceramic complexes took place within the borders of the Maya realm, and in 800 B.C. the Mamon Phase was widespread.

Other cultures, such as the Izapa, had an influence on the Maya. The Izapa, considered by many to be the linking culture between the Olmec and the Classic Maya, offered cultural developments to the emerging groups. One of the gods worshipped at Izapa, for example, was the long-lipped deity who was a forerunner of Chac, the Maya god of lightning. The Izapa also worshipped Vucub Caquix, the vulture of the heroic traditions of the Hero Twins in the Maya *Popol Vuh*. Kaminaljuyu, another Pacific coastal independent site, was a ceremonial center and a rival of Izapa. Kaminaljuyu flourished in the Miraflores Period (300 B.C.–A.D. 200), and the sculpture recovered in that city is Izapa in style but is a precursor of the Classic Maya designs. The entire Miraflores Phase, in fact, is related to the Classic Maya in architectural and artistic techniques and vision. The Maya around Tikal and Uaxactun began their own artistic development in earnest, and between A.D. 220 and 633, these great ceremonial centers were erected, as well as other Maya cities.

In the central and northern regions that would become a vital part of the Maya territories, the Chicanel culture was present. Usulatan wares were available, and trade systems were put into place, with the Maya elite acquiring power and prestige. In Belize, in the city of Lamanai and in Cerros, sophisticated cultural forms were evident. Ceremonial centers vied with one another in art and architecture as well as in land and maritime markets. By A.D. 250, in fact, the Maya had reached artistic and intellectual heights unmatched by any other Mesoamerican culture of the time. The Long Count was used effectively, as the stelae from Tikal demonstrate. Some of these date to A.D. 292. After A.D. 400, the Esperanza culture replaced the Miraflores Phase, and with that change came new political and military realities, borne out by data from archaeological studies of the region. Kaminaljuyu fell to an army of central Mexica, which ruled the remaining Maya in the city.

The social ranks developed during the Formative Period (which ended c. A.D. 250/290) as populations increased and cities emerged with definite trade systems and industries. A true aristocracy arose having hereditary rights, wealth and dominance. A powerful priesthood, drawing candidates

Maya relief, La Amelia

temples were created. Trade with the Mexica, newly arrived in the Valley of Mexico, was strong, and the Maya ceremonial centers seemed secure. The Classic Period was dynamic in Mesoamerica, especially in Maya lands. The arts and sciences were reaching new heights, and the lowland Maya centers were expanding, using the Long Count on their stelae and monuments. The great city of Teotihuacan, not a Maya stronghold but an independent city-state in the central region, was part of this flowering, and it linked the various cultures, drawing others into the realm of its cultural influence. Teotihuacan possibly had military dominance over some lowland Maya regions, but the city had no need to mount military campaigns to draw the Maya into its circle of allies and confederates.

By A.D. 700, however, Teotihuacan was witnessing the disintegration of its empire. In that year, or soon after, the city was deliberately burned by unknown invaders. The ceremonial complex was rendered useless, and the entire region suffered a catastrophic blow that set in motion other disintegrating forces. The loss of Teotihuacan was immeasurable. Within a single century the collapse of the Classic Maya was inevitable. The end of the stela cult was evident in the ceremonial complexes. Every Maya complex in the southern lowlands suddenly stopped erecting stelae. In many cities public building came to a halt; others slackened in their own building. There were exceptions, of course. Seibal, for example, reached its peak while other ceremonial complexes were collapsing around it, but within another 100 years that city was also abandoned. By the mid-10th century A.D., every Maya southern ceremonial complex was a discarded ruin. The local Maya farmers continued in their ways, but the elite of the Maya moved on.

The process was actually less sudden than it appears. Between A.D. 672 and 751, while the arts flourished, the Maya halted their territorial expansion. Alliances between

from the noble castes, was also in place. The arch and corbeled vault became a hallmark of Maya architecture in some places, and use of the calendar and writing had been incorporated into all aspects of Maya life. The cities of the Maya, all serving as regional ceremonial centers or as pilgrimage sites for various deities, were widespread and powerful, each dominating a particular region but linked by trade, traditions and similar artistic visions. From A.D. 633 to 790, in fact, new Maya ceremonial centers were added to the region, including Jaina, Bonampak, Etzna, Quirigua, Seibal and Chinkultic.

The Maya, however, were not insulated against the rapid changes taking place in Mesoamerica, which stemmed from the rise of other groups and the natural conditions of weather and terrain. The virtue of the Maya system proved its undoing in time, especially when external pressures began to take their toll. An early example of the sort of disaster that would bring harm to the entire Maya domain was evident c. A.D. 200–250. The volcano Ilopango, located in central El Salvador, erupted. As a result, a 60-mile radius of land instantly became uninhabitable, a condition lasting for more than two centuries. Trade between that region and the great ceremonial centers linked to it broke down, and newer lowland centers rose as competitors, no doubt revitalized by the vast numbers of Ilopango survivors who flocked to them.

In the central Maya region the Tzokal culture arose, experiencing a flowering of the arts. This was a period when murals, sculptures, reliefs and elaborate tombs and

Maya noble, Palenque

the ceremonial complexes collapsed, and wars increased between competing locales. From A.D. 790 to 830, Maya cities were visibly dying, with few new settlements being erected as replacements. At Palenque, the last Long Count date, a vital point of reference for its collapse was A.D. 799. The elite Maya soon abandoned the city, with Bonampak and Piedras Negras following soon after. Some scholars believe the last Long Count in southern Quintana Roo, inscribed in A.D. 909, marks the end of the stela cult and the last stages of Maya expansion and prosperity. This Maya decline, of course, was directly related to contacts with foreign groups in the north and the west. When Palenque's elite ceased their public activities, Mexica wares began to appear there. Seibal, having survived the changes in the region, began to display variations in architectural designs in monuments and stelae, reflecting the Yucatan situation. Seibal dated its last stela in A.D. 889 and then collapsed. It is believed that the Peten (Putun) Maya moved into Seibal and other ceremonial complexes in the region. These Mexicanized Maya had begun a network of cities on the eastern gulf coast, eventually working their way to the Usumacinta River. In turn, the Maya began aggressive campaigns against one another. Quarrels damaged entire regions, and the ceremonial cities were devastated and left empty.

There are many reasons for the decline of the Maya in this era. Some scholars have indicated that the local geological conditions—drought, storms, volcanoes, depletion of arable land—alarmed the Maya populations. Others consider Mexica inroads as the sole reason. Civil wars are cited, as well as the presence of malaria and yellow fever. Two other major causes have been cited over the years, and their combination probably brought down the ceremonial complexes, prompted by the Mexica presence and by feuds among the nobles. The first reason, and probably the most far-reaching one, is the exhaustion of the Maya soil. Local farming techniques destroyed vast tracts of land and allowed for no natural replacement. The vast ceremonial complexes were dependent on the surrounding farmlands for food. When such lands failed, as they appear to have done in many places, the resulting devastation was inevitable. There are historical references to famines in the Maya regions. The cities might have survived such disasters if the aristocrats had remained active and viable. The elite of each Maya city stood isolated and autonomous in many ways, guiding the destiny of their regions and administering the resources and labors of the surrounding areas toward public projects and the maintenance of the standards of construction and religious ceremonies. Each elite core understood its own rank and obligations, serving the ruler in designated offices and raising new generations to inherit the same tasks. These elites were also associated with the aristocrats of other ceremonial complexes by marriage and social customs. Alliances and visits, traditions and festivals linked these groups, and they were bound by interlinking trade systems and religious rites. These sophisticated, internationally minded individuals collaborated on new methods in the face of change and shared in the administration of all facets of the Maya domain.

When the first ceremonial complexes began to deteriorate, the close ties of the various aristocratic groups were threatened. The collapse of other such complexes appears to have

immobilized the remaining nobles. At the same time, these aristocrats became vulnerable to the commoners in their midst. Many nobles fled because of warring neighbors, while others simply retired to distant places to salvage their memories of the past. The nobles' exit from the ceremonial complexes sealed the sites' doom.

In the Yucatan, however, as the Post Classic Period dawned in Mesoamerica, the situation was not as dramatic or as perilous. The Puuc culture flourished there between A.D. 987 and 1194, apparently isolated enough to remain secure during the periods of crisis. The vast trade systems were certainly damaged, but the Maya devised their own methods of stabilizing the region and of remaining in control of the resources. In the Yucatan, the Kulkulcan cult, partly Itza and partly Mexica, made itself known through rituals and missionaries, and added another dimension to the peninsula. The great ceremonial complex of Mayapan erected in this era was linked to Kulkulcan. The Cocom dynasty was its elite. Uxmal was begun by the Xius, and other regional aristocrats took defensive measures to avoid suffering the fate of their southern neighbors. The Mayapan League, an alliance between Mayapan, Uxmal and Chichen Itza, allowed these complexes to flourish in comparative safety. New ceremonial complexes, such as Kabah, Sayil and Izamal, emerged, and other cities prospered because of the joint defense measures. Then a war between Chichen Itza and Mayapan broke the peace sometime in the 14th century as the Cocom won political ascendancy. They were not destined to rule for long, however. In A.D. 1441 a revolt took place, and the Cocom ruler was slain. Small groups set up their own defenses and avenged insults with military campaigns. A hurricane struck the peninsula in A.D. 1464, followed by a series of epidemics brought on by the Spanish invasion. When the Spanish began their assaults on the Maya lands, little unity was available and little opposition possible.

MAYA AGRICULTURE The farming methods employed by the Maya, traditional in some respects but also indicating adaptations to regional conditions. Slash-and-burn farming was employed in the Maya realm. The erosive nature of this technique damaged the land, despite efforts at soil preparation, field rotation and fertilizer use. The Maya employed intercropping and multicropping along with terracing and canal irrigation. Orchards were developed to protect soil and natural vegetation in some locales. The orchards also offered space for individual family garden plots. The Maya used raised plots for certain crops. They grew the Mesoamerican staple crops of beans, maize and squash. They also planted corn, papaya, peppers, chayote, cotton, cacao, amaranth, henequen, breadnuts, gourds, avocados, jacama and sapote. The game and other nonagricultural items available to them included turkeys (wild and domestic), bees, ducks, dogs, tapir, agouti, rabbits, monkeys, snakes, quail, peccaries, coatimundi, foxes, lizards, toucans and jaguars. (For more agricultural details, see AGUADA; CENOTE; and MESOAMERICAN AGRICULTURE.)

MAYA ARCHAEOLOGICAL SITES The cities and ceremonial centers of the Maya domain that have been recorded in the various historical eras. These sites, with the exception of those in Belize, which are lesser known, are covered in separate entries and include:

Acanceh	El Rey
Actun Balam Cave	Etzna
Aguateca	Hachob
Ake	Hormiquero
Akumal	Hun Chabin
Alahuitzlan	Icheateopan
Altar de Sacrificios	Ikil
Altun Ha	Isla Mujeres
Bakhalal	Itzamkanac
Balamku	Iximiche
Balankanche	Izamal
Becan	Izapa
Blackman Eddy, Cayo	Jaina
Blue Creek	Kabah
Bonampak	Kaminaljuyu
Cahal Pich	Kinich
Calakmul	Kohunlich
Caracol	Labna
Caracol de Tumba	Lacanhai
Cerro de Chavin	Lamanai
Cerros	La Milpa
Cerritos	Loltun Cave
Chacmultun	Los Tapiales
Chakalal	Lubaantum
Chakanputun	Mayapan
Chalchuapa	Mirador
Chama Cave	Monte Alto
Chan Chich	Motul de San Jose
Chau Hiix	Mul Chic
Chicanna	Muyil
Chichen Itza	Naco
Chinkultic	Naj Tunich Cave
Chunhuhub	Nim Li Punit
Chunyaxche	Nohmul
Chutixtiox	Nohpat
Coba	Oxkintok
Comalcalco	Oztuma
Copin	Palenque
Cozumel	Piedras Negras
Cuello	Quirigua
Dos Pilas	Richmond Hill
Dzibilchaltun	Rio Bec B
Dzibilnocqc	San Gervasio
Ek Balam	San Jose
El Cedral	Santa Rita
El Chayal	Santa Rosa Xtampak
El Meco	Sayil
El Pilar	Seibal
Tancah	Uxmal
Tapachula	Xkichmook
Tayasal	Xlapak
Teloloapan	Xicallanco
Tihoo	Xpuhil
Tikal	Xunantunich
Tonina	Yaxchilan
Topoxte	Yaxha
Tulum	Yaxuna
Uaxactun	Zaculeu
Utatlan	Zincantun
Uxbenka	

MAYA ARCHITECTURE   As Maya cities were all ceremonial centers to some degree, they followed a general, religiously oriented and spiritually motivated plan. Each city, however, also reflected the geographic and climatic conditions of its setting while mirroring regional cultural influences. Thus a hallmark of Maya architecture became diversity in unity, a remarkable display of individual achievements within cohesive patterns and artistic ideals.

The geographic conditions of the Maya realm imposed certain adaptive measures in their cities. A lack of water resources was a major problem; the Maya compensated by including aqueducts, cisterns and *cenotes* in their urban designs. For defense, the Maya favored hilltop sites and built moats, earthworks and causeways. These causeways, called *sacheobs*, also linked sites in certain regions, as the Maya often duplicated entire ceremonial complexes, moving the newer ones a short distance from the original and then using causeways as direct routes to accommodate growing populations.

In the Formative Period (c. 2000/1600 B.C.–c. A.D. 250/ 290) the Maya builders used only flat stones, joined by mortar or pebbles, to create simple structures. By the Classic Period (A.D. 1/250–900), the Maya had a larger assortment of materials available and the skills to use them effectively. In the Peten (Putun) region, for example, limestone was used extensively; in the Usumacinta Valley the main building material was dolomite. Copan structures were made of trachyte; Quirigua's, of sandstone; Belize's, of slate; and Chiapa's, of fired bricks. The Maya also learned that if limestone was burned, the resulting powder could be mixed with water to form a white, highly durable plaster. They also used a concretelike fill, composed of marl and limestone rubble. Smaller dressed stones were set into foundation walls of temples. In some cities, such as Copan, stones weighing several tons each were used as blocks for the temple bases. A type of lime was also used and stored in *chultunes*, bottle-shaped pits discovered in Maya shrines. This lime was called *sascab*. Because the religious ceremonies were somewhat uniform throughout the Maya realm, the ceremonial complexes were similar, at least in their general format. The principal architectural elements of these complexes are as follows.

Pyramids.   These were designed on a vaster scale in the Maya domains than anywhere else in Mesoamerica. Tikal's pyramids, for example, are higher than the Pyramid of the

Sun at Teotihuacan, although not as broad. Tikal and other Maya sites had narrow, tall pyramids; their architectural style was accented by the steepness of the stairways incorporated into the design. Maya pyramids, whether as high as those at Tikal or rounded and shorter, are always imposing and inspiring. The eye is drawn upward by the pyramidal design, without many diversions. The pyramids were decorated with masks or motifs of Maya culture, fashioned from stucco, but the imposing lines of the structures remain dominant, so that the eye is always ascending the monuments.

Terraces. The Maya used terraces as foundations for structures in their ceremonial complexes, especially in Chiapas in the Peten (Putun) regions. Such terraces were constructed as high as 10 feet in some sites, serving usually as the base for a single building, although more were included in Uxmal and other Yucatan sites. The exact purpose of the terrace is not known, but even Maya pyramids were constructed on these dramatic stone stages.

Temples. Temples served as shrines or houses of worship placed on the summits of the pyramidal bases in Maya sites. Such temples were constructed to endure climatic conditions and the passage of time. Earlier temples, enclosed within later constructions, were able to better withstand the centuries. It is believed that the Maya insured the enduring quality of their temples by choosing particular building materials. The classic lime-and-sand mortar, Maya thick walls and corbeled vaults insured structural longevity. The chambers of these shrines usually were not large, even though they stood on massive bases. Religious ceremonies were obviously conducted in plazas associated with the temples, or in antechambers, courts and on the platform exteriors. Most temples had roof combs and coping formed by one or two walls, usually twice as high as the actual building. The combs were sometimes latticed, or decorated with reliefs and openwork designs. Some shrines were covered in hieroglyphs or with stucco panels depicting personages and religious motifs. Some used columns to advantage. Murals and bas-reliefs were also placed on the walls of the temples, which had benches along the sides. These murals were usually religious in theme, but secular scenes are present as well. Symbols used in decorations related the Maya to the cosmic forces, which were viewed as ruling the destinies of men and women. These cosmic forces were intrinsic to the Maya calendar system, used for divination and calculations and vital to astronomical observations, which were conducted throughout the Maya world.

Vaults. Called false vaults or corbeled vaults, the Maya vaults were a distinct architectural innovation in Mesoamerica. They were first used in the Maya domain during the Classic Period, and the designs remained somewhat uniform after their introduction, with some variations in the different regions. Walls of buildings were thicker at a designated height, usually no more than 10 feet, thus bringing the walls closer. The thickness increased toward the top until the walls were approximately one foot apart. The remaining space was then covered with a flat capstone, or the stones used in the walls were increased and angled. The vault was thus formed interiorly. The exterior roof was usually flat or else displayed the angles of the vault. No buttresses or groins were used. The vaults were solid masonry. The flat ceilings over the vaults and in other chambers were composed of beams and lathwork. A foot of lime was then placed over the construction.

Arches. Maya used arches either in conjunction with vaults or freestanding. The arches were varied both in design and in material, depending on the locally available resources. In the Usumacinta region, for example, thin slabs of stone were placed in the arches. In Comalcalco simple bricks were used, and in the Yucatan it was thought necessary to combine lime cement and stone.

The arch was probably inspired by the *choza*, the simple Indian huts of early development eras. As in the construction of vaults, the walls were sloped inward until a single stone joined them. The walls were then filled with concrete to strengthen them. The angle and style of the arches could vary considerably. All of them, however, probably were fashioned over wooden forms, which were removed when the stonework was completed and dried in place. The internal sections of arches were completed first and then the exterior parts, which leaned against the central core.

Palaces. Palaces were usually massive structures with heavy exterior decorations that served as residential quarters for nobles or priests of the ceremonial complexes. Sculptures and bas-reliefs adorned the building faces, and murals, reliefs and carved inscriptions were used on the interior walls. The inner chambers were quite narrow, with few windows and little light. There were no chimneys in the rooms, but some were equipped with ventilation tubes.

The larger palaces were multileveled, usually from three to five tiers. One, at Labna, had an interior cistern. Some palaces were also built as adjuncts of the temples, in combination with the religious structure. It is possible that such residences were not inhabited but were simply used for storage or as audience sites. The buildings might have served as workshops.

Before the Classic Period, the nobles of each ceremonial complex performed the religious rituals and the cultic observances. Such nobles and their families would have expected an elite residence. The palaces constructed as part of the ceremonial complexes would have served as convenient residences for them. At a later date the palaces could have housed the resident priests or served as dormitories for the young candidates for the priesthood, usually hereditary positions available only to the elite classes.

Ball Courts. Ball courts were constructed by the Maya for playing and for religious and secular observances. Ball games were a universal Mesoamerican religious and recreational activity. Most Maya courts were single, but some cities had triple courts. Maya ball courts are rectangular in shape, with parallel walls. These walls were sometimes decorated, and markers were used. Terraces were provided for spectators. In time the ends of the courts were also enclosed by walls.

Plazas. Plazas were the large open-air courts provided for the ceremonial complex's populace. Many religious celebrations were held on the higher levels of the pyramids or in plazas in front of the temples. For this reason each rectangular area designated as a plaza was elaborate and of massive proportions. Surrounding buildings had religious significance.

Each city usually had one immense plaza, designated as the primary gathering place. Other plazas, scattered in the groups of buildings or in the acropolises, served the same purpose or were used for audiences, smaller religious events or even as marketplaces. Most courtyards were faced with white stucco and sometimes covered with bas-reliefs. Many levels of floors have been discovered, indicating numerous repairs. The plazas could be level with the ground or sunken.

Causeways. Called *sacheob* (white roads), causeways served as thoroughfares connecting various temples at a single site or in the cities of a region. The causeways were usually two to four feet above ground level but could be up to eight feet high to span swampy terrain. *Sacheobs* were made with large stones overlaid with rubble and then surfaced with a smooth layer of cement.

While the various structures of the cities and ceremonial complexes in the Maya realm resembled one another, the styles of architecture varied according to region and historical era. Two of the more notable architectural patterns used by the Maya were Puuc and Rio Bec.

Puuc. This style was utilized by the Maya living in the Yucatan, a region dominated by low hills, called *puuc*. Some scholars associate this style with the migration of the Maya from the south in c. A.D. 900 to 1200. The Puuc style began in the Late Classic Period and is evident in Etzna, in north-central Campeche, in the noble's cemetery in Jaina, and in Labna and other sites. The characteristics of the style are facades of thin squares of limestone placed over cement-rubble cores, boot-shaped vaults, decorated cornices, round columns in doorways, stone mosaics and latticework. The Puuc style also employed balustrades and cylindrical stones set close together. Architects designed smooth walls with ornate friezes at the top and provided buildings with *moldura de atadura* (broad moldings). These were derived from the rope bindings used in earlier settlements to secure the wooden structure of a straw-thatched hut. In the Puuc region there was little surface water. The Maya called this area *Zahcah*, meaning "the white earth," because it was rich in limestone, a material used in Puuc architecture.

Rio Bec. The style of architecture found in Campeche and in Quintana Maya sites is called Rio Bec. Here building design relied on detailed facades that were more decorative than functional. The use of false towers and narrow, steep stairs provided an unusual appearance for the Maya pyramids and temples. In some instances the towers were actually solid, not meant for habitation, as they had no interior chambers. The people of the Chenes region used the same elaborate decorations for their structures, although they did not employ false towers in their complexes and used the open-mouthed serpent designs. (For additional information, see MAYA CEREMONIAL COMPLEXES.)

MAYA ART   It was once believed that all Maya art was religious iconography, but evidence of secular themes has

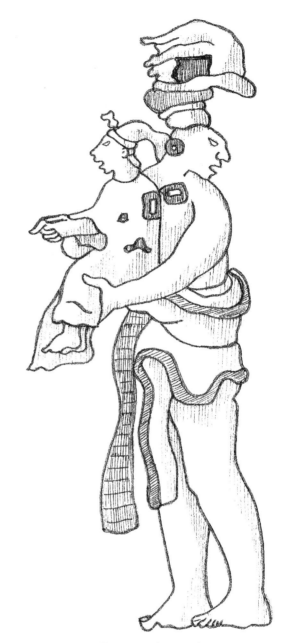

Bonampak mural

been found. Within the religious and secular motifs, the Maya were able to develop perspective, movement, startling realism and a conventional formality that lent an impersonal aura to many works. The Maya worked in a number of artistic mediums, bringing their own views of the cosmos and humankind to bear.

The Maya used a variety of forms of sculpture decorations for ceremonial complexes. They used freestanding sculpture, such as stelae or altars, decorative masks and designs that were incorporated into the design of temples and pyramids, and carved panels. Like the Greeks, the Maya painted most of these pieces, usually using dark red pigment, probably iron peroxide or hematite. Blue was popular, as were black, yellow and white. The paints were powdered and probably combined with copal resin for durability.

The oldest Maya sculptures are the monoliths discovered at Uaxactun, depicting the elite of that city. The Leiden Plate (or Plaque), which dates to A.D. 320, duplicates the same sort of figures. By A.D. 445, the Maya were producing full-face figures, a style that was incorporated into stelae from Seibal, Palenque, Copan, Quirigua and other sites. Maya stelae were carved of stone slabs, some reaching over 30 feet in height. Some stelae were plain, but more often they were carved in intricate detail. Religious and secular themes provide the iconography for the stelae and altars. Represented are deities, mythical beings, animals and persons of elevated rank. Shown in elaborate costume, accompanied by glyphs and appropriate symbols, these imposing forms have a distinct perspective and feeling of movement. While poses are formal, there is a startling realism in the figures.

Early stelae were carved only on one side, but in later eras all four sides were worked. A decline in style and technique is observable after A.D. 830. The stelae found at Copan and Quirigua are in such high relief that they are practically statues in the round. Human forms occupy the entire stela, and the costumes and the headdresses are elaborately detailed. At other sites the stelae are carved in low relief or are plain. At Copan a stela taking a female form, an unusual representation for that era, is known.

Zoomorphic figures were popular in many regions, depicting the forces of nature, animals and divine beings. A stela recovered in Quirigua depicts serpents, covering the entire length of the monument slab, with a human head appearing in a creature's open mouth. Scrolls and hieroglyphs were incorporated into that design, so as to heighten the effect. Thrones and altars in the shapes of jaguars and serpents were another Maya sculptural form. The jaguar-shaped thrones imitated the dimensions of the cat, with the back of the animal serving as the royal seat. The head was turned either to the right or to the left, and the entire throne was painted red. A version of a jaguar throne was also recovered from Uxmal.

Carved panels were another Maya art form. These were usually used in conjunction with door lintels or ramps, particularly as commemoratives. The panel discovered at Piedras Negras, for example, depicts a lord on a throne or altar. He is addressing a council of nobles, all elaborately costumed. Hieroglyphic panels, incorporating inscriptions and dates, were used as well as temple panels, which reflected the basic themes of the local shrines and their religious traditions. Wood sculpture is rare in Maya sites, probably because such material does not preserve well. Tikal, however, had magnificent lintels with portraits. The finest recovered wooden sculpture was found in Tabasco, depicting a nobleman with a realistic mustache, kneeling with arms folded. The figure was originally painted. Another artistic innovation of the Maya was the Tree of Life, symbolized in a crypt in Palenque. The tree represents life and death, and stars accompany the image, signifying the cosmic nature of human existence.

The Maya used painting on shrine walls and in ceramics and codices. While codices have been known for a long time, wall paintings were unfamiliar until they were uncovered in Uaxactun. These date to before A.D. 633. Bonampak holds the most extraordinary frescoes, although similar works of varying quality were found in Chichen Itza, Chacmultun and Tulum. Bonampak's murals are among the most valued historical documents left by the Maya. Beautifully rendered, and both narrative and cyclical in style, these paintings depict men, women and children in scenes reflecting their daily activities. These murals include the ritual robing ceremony, the enthronement of a lord, warfare, the taking of prisoners, even a celebration complete with a musical band. Wives, counselors, dancers and nobles mingle in elaborate, detailed processions. The paintings were executed on a layer of lime, between one-half and two inches thick. They are painted in yellow, white, black, ocher, red, blue, green and orange. The walls on which they were painted are vertical to a height of almost six feet, at which point they slope upward in a vault, reaching 16 feet or more. The building containing these murals is 44 feet long and more than 13 feet wide.

Minor arts were manufactured by the Maya as part of their religious traditions and for trade. Carvings were a significant minor art in the Maya territories. Images of plants, insects, humans and animals were carved on bones, shells and wood. The engraved inscriptions on wood, especially at such sites as Tikal, were religious in nature and part of the overall architectural design. The doors of the temples there depict the quetzal bird, the jaguar and the local ruler, accompanied by hieroglyphs. Other carved lintels were recovered at Uxmal and Chichen Itza. The design and manufacture of textiles was another Maya art form, but the total amount of information about such fabrics comes from the paintings and bas-reliefs discovered at the Maya site. Cotton was a popular material, and sisal was used as well. Spindle whorls in baked clay have been found, and backstrap looms and needles of wood or bone have also been recovered. Some Maya statuary depict women weaving such textiles. The patroness of the weaving arts was Ixchebel Yax, the daughter of Itzamna and Ixchel. The colors used in manufacturing such textiles were symbolic and had religious connotations. Mantles, panaches, capes (some made of feathers), banners, shields, textiles of all qualities and styles, and embroidered and dyed materials were manufactured throughout the Maya domain.

Mosaics appear to have been rare among the Maya, but a few have been recovered. A turquoise mosaic was found at Chichen Itza, although it does not seem to have originated there. Masks were an art form, and these involved mosaics in some cases. Feather mosaics were also a Maya trade item. The Maya also used copper and gold, materials imported from other regions. They delighted in filigree work and used the lost wax (cire perdue) casting technique for such metal objects. Tin and bronze appear to have been unknown in the Maya regions. Maya gold pieces are exceptional, and the more elaborate ones, such as those discovered in the Sacred Cenote of Chichen Itza, were probably created elsewhere and brought to the site as an offering. The Maya also made thin disks of gold, and they used silver sparingly. (See also MAYA CERAMICS.)

MAYA ASTROLOGY The art of divination and prophecy in association with celestial movements. Maya astrology and divination were related to this culture's concept of time as an element carried on the backs of divine beings, related as well to its calendars. Some of the gods who bore the days in calendrical cycles were benevolent to human beings, while some were hostile. Projects undertaken or events occurring on the days controlled by the malevolent gods were deemed unlucky. Conversely, projects and events taking place on the days carried by the kindly deities were considered lucky.

Astrologers used particular astronomical studies concerning the heliacal rising of Venus, called the Wasp Star by the Maya, to ascertain the future. Venus was very much feared by the Maya as harboring evil and ill will toward humankind.

Birth dates were of vital importance in divination and prophecy, because they linked the individual to astronomical cycles and to the gods endowed with the keeping of time. Maya astrologers and diviners consulted the calendrical materials to learn the name and the number of the date of an individual's birth. The fact that such detailed information was available is a testimony to the research and scientific correlations conducted by the astronomers and sages of the Maya world.

Because the Maya feared Venus, its aspects in the heavens were considered when they planned military campaigns or raids on enemy territories. Extant records indicate that several cities undertook wars with their neighbors based on the various aspects of Venus. The planet was deemed malevolent to humans and could exert evil influences, especially in battles.

Before the Classic Period, divination was part of the religious role of nobles. After the emergence of the various priesthoods, the priests took over the divination aspect of the temple rites. Traveling diviners existed among the Maya, but their specific roles and importance are unknown.

MAYA ASTRONOMY The science of sighting and computing the changes and movements of celestial bodies in the night sky. Some scholars believe the Maya were as sophisticated as the Han Chinese in astrology, as they appear to have used similar formulas and calculations for predicting eclipses. The Maya mathematical and calendrical advances were part of their astronomical knowledge, enriched by a recognition of celestial beings and, in turn, forming the basis for further calculations and predictions. The sun, revered by the Maya and other Mesoamerican cultures, was charted precisely; temples were erected to catch the rays of the sun on certain days or at certain hours. The sun, moon, and Venus were incorporated into the Maya pantheon of gods, and Maya texts also mention the Pleiades, Gemini and the phenomenon of solstices. Venus, called the Wasp Star, was never viewed as benevolent, and the Maya maintained accurate accounts of its movement for astrological and divinatory purposes. Apparently Venus held a role similar to that of Mars in the later Mesoamerican civilizations and was viewed as a cosmic force that affected the outcome of military campaigns and the decision to wage war. In later cultures, Venus was associated with the cult of the god Quetzalcoatl.

Maya lunar calculations are evident in the glyphs connected with the "Initial Series" of the Long Count on monuments in the various regional ceremonial complexes. Such inscriptions contained details about the moon in relation to

Maya Chiapas relief

lunar semesters. These lunar calculations remain the subject of much modern speculation because of their calendrical implications. As astronomy evolved into a true science among the Maya elite, buildings were erected in the various ceremonial centers to serve as observatories. The great Palenque observatory and the Caracol at Chichen Itza served such a purpose and were so designated by glyphs and by design.

Maya religious beliefs mirrored their astronomical concerns. Part of their creation legends included a conflict between the Jaguar God of the dark sky, assisted by the sun, moon and stars, as well as by the dry season, versus the Serpent of the Storms, who was helped by rain, lightning and the rainy season. The planet Venus was allied with the serpent. Maya astronomers followed definite procedures in making their nightly calculations of the stars and the other visible heavenly bodies, and they had a wealth of written computations upon which to rely. They established fixed lines of sight, aligning buildings or landmarks as observation points. Some held crossed sticks to obtain sightings, and evidence of other devices exists as well. The Group E buildings at Uaxactun, for example, are believed to have served as sight guides for astronomical observations concerning the solstices. The northern temples in that ceremonial complex were used for the summer solstice and the southern buildings for the winter solstice.

With these methods, and with their mathematical and calendrical skills, the Maya studied the night skies of Mesoamerica. Some scholars believe that these early astronomers had identified Mars, Jupiter, Mercury and Saturn. They made only slight errors in calculating the orbits, rotations and eclipses of the celestial bodies they recognized.

MAYA CALENDARS The systems by which these people calculated time and the seasons. The Maya calendar began in the era of the Olmec and further, perhaps to c. 500 B.C. The Maya calendar was a complicated synthesis of prior systems, with innovations and cosmological nuances. Maya sages could measure and determine the quarters of the universe and the revolving cycles of time. They not only recorded the past and the present but were able to make specific prophecies concerning future happenings because of their knowledge. The Maya did not rely on one single

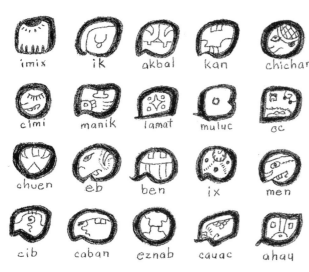

Maya day glyphs

calendar system. They employed the Ritual Almanac, the Solar Year, the Calendar Round, the Long Count and the Short Count.

The Ritual Almanac

The Ritual Almanac was a system of determining the year as 260 days, as a religious and divinatory device. It was called the *tzolkin*, the count of the days. The 260 days, called *kin*, were divided into 20 periods of 13 days, which were called by the names of the days used in the Solar Year:

Imix	Chuen
Ik	Eb
Akbal	Ben
Kan	Ix
Chicchan	Men
Cimi	Cib
Manik	Caban
Lamat	Eknab
Muluc	Canac
Oc	Ahau

These day names were preceded by a number indicating their position from one to 13, with the day *Ik* marking the beginning of the first period. The calendar would thus read 1 *Ik*, 2 *Akbal*, 3 *Kan*, and so on. The first day of the second period was 1 *Men*. The day designated as 1 *Ik* could not take place until the first day of the second *tzolkin*, after the passage of 260 days.

The origin of this Ritual Almanac is unknown, although it has been equated with the term of human pregnancy, the period of time between the zenith passages of the sun and the length of the rainy season in the Maya territories. Its exact significance or derivation remains unknown. The numbers 13 and 20 were thought to be beneficial or fortunate for human beings. The same calendrical system can be seen throughout Mesoamerica in various forms. It was first recorded in the Valley of Oaxaca as early as 500 B.C.

The Solar Year

The Solar Year calendar system, also called the Vague Year, was called *haab* by the Maya and corresponded to the actual year as determined by the solar manifestations. It is composed of 20 days (with the same names as in the Ritual Almanac) composing 18 months, with five epagomenal days. The months, known as *uinal*, were called:

Pop	Yax
Uo	Zac
Zip	Ceh
Zotz	Mac
Tzec	Kankin
Yul	Muan
Yaxkin	Pax
Mol	Kayab
Chen	Cumhu

The days within each *uinal* were written with the numbers from 0 to 19: 0 *Pop*, 1 *Pop*, 2 *Pop*, and so on.

In the Solar Year or Vague Year, the Maya also used the following designations:

Tun = 18 *uinal*, or 360 days (with epagomenal days)

Katun = 20 *tun*, or 7200 days

Baktun = 20 *katun*, or 144,000 days

Piktun = 20 *baktun*, or 2,880,000 days

Kalabtun = 20 *piktun*, or 57,600,000 days

Kinchiltun = 20 *kalabtun*, or 1,52,000,000 days

Alautun = 20 *kinchiltun*, or 25,040,000,000 days

The Solar Year had no provisions for leap years and was actually longer than 365 days. The months had patron deities, either amicable or hostile to humankind, who bore the allotted amount of time on their backs. This calendar was used in conjunction with the Ritual Almanac, which allowed the Maya to mark a date in relation to its position in the religious year and the Solar Year. The calendars were like two wheels that could turn on their own but that could also be interlocked, with one piece fitting into the pattern of the other to form a whole.

The Calendar Round

The Calendar Round is the computation system resulting from the repeating cycles of the 13 numbers and the 20 names of the Ritual Almanac when correlated with the Solar Year. The Calendar Round was thus 18,980 days, or 52 Solar Years. The earliest Calendar Round date is also the first evidence available for the Solar Year. The Maya calendar system did not rely solely on this computation for establishing specific dates, employing instead the Long Count, a unique series.

The Long Count

The Long Count is a system that kept account of the Great Cycle and used 13 August 3114 B.C. (according to the

Gregorian calendar) as a starting point for computing dates. (The derivation of this starting date is unknown. Some Maya inscriptions note that this date commemorated the birth of the gods, but this is not entirely documented.) The system used various time specifications as listed in the Solar Year and allowed the Maya to assign a specific date to all happenings, real or mythical, by relating them backward or forward from the starting point in 3114 B.C. The Long Count also allowed the Maya to compute a particular position in the Calendar Round by indicating the number of elapsed days.

Called the Initial Series, the Long Count always opened the inscriptions made during the Classic Period. This dating marker provided the Ritual Almanac position, the Solar Year position, the attendant deity, as well as information about the moon and the lunar year. Inscriptions in the Long Count were portraits, abstract forms and in some instances figures of the gods. The deity portraits repeated the Maya concept of time being carried on the backs of the various gods.

Short Count

The Short Count is an abbreviated form of the Long Count that was used in the Maya lands after the decline. Called *u kahlay katunob* ("the count of the katuns"), the Short Count measures time in a 7,200-day period of the original Long Count. A *katun* is named after the Ritual Almanac position of the day on which it ends. The final day is always *Ahau*, with one of the 13 numbers used as coefficient. Such a reckoning creates a cycle of 13 *katuns*, which add up to 256 years. The Short Count is thus more precise than the Calendar Round.

MAYA CERAMICS   The wares that resulted from evolving techniques and skills in providing pottery for the various regions and for trade. Ceramics were important to the trade developed by the Maya; they moved along the trade routes with salt and obsidian. Marketplaces in the various regions received the wares of others, and in time entire communities for the production of ceramics sprang up. Some of the Maya cities and ceremonial complexes also provided workshops for the growing ceramic industries. Historically, several cultural developments are associated with the Maya regions. These include:

Swasey.   A cultural phase dating to the beginning of the Formative Period, c. 2000 B.C., discovered in the city of Cuello, in Belize. The site, believed by many to be the oldest in Maya lands, provides examples of Swasey wares produced by the local inhabitants.

Barra.   A ceramic production complex in southern Guatemala and in Chiapas. The Barra cultural development dates to sometime between 1700 and 1500 B.C.

Ocos.   A cultural development on the Pacific coast of Guatemala. The Ocos products date to 1500 B.C.

Xe.   A cultural development discovered in the city of Altar de Sacrificios and also in Seibal on the Pasion River. Such developments date to 900 B.C.

Mamon.   A widespread ceramic production complex existing in the Maya lowlands, dating from 800 to 300 B.C. The Mamon people used *tecomates* (cylindrical vases), bowls, effigy vessels, tripod jars and incense burners. (See separate entries for these phases.)

The ceramics of various phases recovered in Maya sites were usually incised with geometric designs, with appliques or painted motifs. They range from white-cream or gray to red, orange, buff, brown and black wares. Other ceramic influences among the Maya include the Chicancel, Tzakol and Tepen, both early and late. In these periods Maya manufactured jars, bowls, plates, vases and diverse objects, and were considered highly skilled. Such wares have been found in tombs of the Maya aristocrats. Some depicted animals, nobles, mythological or daily human activities, reflecting Maya life at various stages of development.

MAYA CEREMONIAL COMPLEXES   The urbanized settlements designed to provide the proper settings for the religious ceremonies so vital to Maya culture. These complexes were also vital to trade and economic efforts in some regions. Religious ceremonies permeated Maya life and were inspirational to every facet of Maya development. Trade was a major aspect of their existence, and thus ceremonial complexes often were linked to the operation of the vast trade systems. It was once believed that the Maya ceremonial complexes, like those of the Olmec, contained only religious structures that were purely functional and designed exclusively for ceremonial activities. It is now known that secular and residential buildings were incorporated into the larger complexes, probably providing an economic base for the site and enabling the religious and secular personnel to handle the influx of pilgrims, trade and other economic and administrative aspects. Smaller ceremonial complexes lacked such additions, and industries and residential districts were located in nearby suburbs. Such smaller sites probably served the far-flung agricultural communities in their regions.

The Maya ceremonial complexes included the basic structures discussed under Maya Architecture, the complexes and buildings designed to accommodate the varied needs of the metropolises. Marketplaces were also provided within the complexes, where surpluses of maize, beans and other local products could be exchanged for other necessities, such as salt. Elite traders and merchants furnished goods for such markets, importing speciality items and staples of other regions for trade. Markets in various centers attracted local populations and provided these cities with prestige and prosperity. Tikal was probably the greatest ceremonial complex in its day, and its market was located in the heart of the ceremonial complex. Chichen Itza, created by a merchant people, boasted a similar market structure. The ceremonial complexes thus provided a stage for religious events and encouraged local craftsmanship and manufacture, as well as contacts with other cultures. When a region outgrew its ceremonial complex, the Maya cleared new fields and erected a second, similar pattern of structures, joining the old and the new with causeways. Adept at massive construction, the Maya provided grand structures for the ceremonial aspects of their lives, incorporating their dominant religious motifs and the regional art forms into their designs.

The basic elements of the Maya ceremonial complexes appeared in the Early Classic Period (c. A.D. 1/250–600) and included buildings with large tenoned stones set deep in mortar. By the Late Classic Period (A.D. 600–900), the Maya were using veneer masonry with shallow facing stones over mortar and limestone. The slopes of the vaults erected as part of the design originally began at floor level but were later positioned higher. The Classic Maya ceremonial complexes were noted for corbeled arches and vaults. In time these cities followed established architectural plans and local styles in order to achieve a certain richness and splendor. The basic structures are discussed under Maya Architecture, including pyramids, terraces, temples, vaults, arches, palaces, ball courts, plazas and causeways. (See MAYA ARCHITECTURE.)

Ceremonial complexes also included the following structures:

Sweat Baths. Sweat baths were provided for nobles and priests, who were obliged to undergo ritual cleansing in preparation for religious ceremonies. In some regions they were open to the general population. Some baths had hearths and stones, and all provided steam and heat.

Chultunes. Bottle-shaped storage pits, or *chultunes*, were incorporated into the ceremonial complex buildings. These pits may have served as grave sites but are believed to have been used as storage reserves for limestone and other construction materials.

Astronomical Observatories. These structures, incorporated into several of the ceremonial complexes, served as centers for the study of the night sky. Calendrical and astronomical lore was part of the religious tradition of the Maya, and scholars watched the night skies and computed changes and patterns there for dating and to calculate time and spatial alterations. They studied the sun, the moon and Venus, the Wasp Star.

Cenotes. In the Yucatan these underwater river systems, exposed when the limestone coverings collapsed into them, were used as reservoirs. It is believed that the sites of some ceremonial complexes were chosen because of the presence of such *cenotes*. Temples were constructed on the banks of some *cenotes,* and objects of worship or sacrifice, including human beings, were thrown into the waters.

Defense Works. In the early stages of Maya development, bridges, moats and earthworks were built for protection. These defenses were deliberate and effective, and in the period of turmoil and decline, such measures were revived and reincorporated into the Maya ceremonial complexes. With their usual skill, the Maya provided handsome fortifications, adapted to the theme and the general architectural design of the various ceremonial complexes.

The overall architectural beauty of the various ceremonial complexes depended very much on their geographic locations and on the local artistic traditions. Some incorporated stone latticework, serpent themes and roof combs, adding height to the temples and providing distinctive appearances. The temples found at Palenque and Tikal were high and

Maya Chan Bahlum

steep, rising above the surrounding vegetation, while others were wide and elaborately decorated with stucco masks, serpent designs and murals. Some even had false towers, placed beside the temple complex for purely decorative purposes. The ceremonial complexes in the Rio Bec area are examples of this style. Palaces and shrines were provided for the elite, and there were seasonal residences for the royal families. Other structures served as audience chambers or as ceremonial stages.

MAYA CODICES   The manuscripts or documents written by the Maya sages, stylistically formalized and containing hieroglyphic accounts of knowledge. The surviving Maya codices deal mostly with deities and religious concepts; they probably have survived extant because they were hidden in temple vaults. Codices, called *huun*, were written on treebark paper taken from the *Ficus coltinifola*. The fibers of the tree were impregnated with gum and then covered with a layer of a starchy substance, giving them body and durability. The codices were formed of pages connected in a long band, folded like a fan, and then stored and used as reference material by Maya priests and scholars. The destruction of many Maya codices by Bishop Landa and other Spanish deprived the world of a great deal of historical information. Codices dealing with trade or other secular matters fared little better; probably they were not stored safely and were subject to the ravages of time, weather and insects.

Three codices discovered in the Maya domain have been authenticated: the Dresden, the Tro-Cortesianus and the Peresianus. They are believed to have been produced in the Yucatan region sometime between A.D. 1200 and 1450.

The *Dresden Codex* was discovered in Vienna in 1739, having been brought there after its recovery from Maya territory. It is now in the *Sachsische Landesbibliothek* in Dresden, hence its name. The codex is an astral treatise, based on accurate observances of the sun and Venus. The text also contains the revolutions of the moon, information about eclipses and calendrical records. The Long Count was also used in the codex, thus providing tables for predicting eclipses and offering divinatory almanac information.

The *Codex Tro-Cortesianus*, also called the *Madrid Codex*, was originally discovered in two separate pieces. The text is now in the *Museo de America* in Madrid. It is formal and conventional in style and offers information concerning rituals conducted in various temples and divination material in the Maya tradition.

The *Codex Peresianus* is also called the *Paris Codex* because it was discovered in Paris after having been brought there from its original Maya location. The codex is now in the *Bibliotheque Nationale* of Paris. It contains material pertinent to calendrical ceremonies of the Maya and other religious traditions and customs.

Another codex, called the *Grolier*, was found in fragmented condition in a Maya cave. It is now at the Grolier Club in New York and is under study. Some researchers believe further authentication is needed.

The hieroglyphic writing in the codices consists of painted or engraved glyphs and demonstrates considerable mathematical skill as well as a remarkable facility for language. The actual hieroglyphs used are different in style from those employed in sculpted inscriptions in the Maya ceremonial complexes. Other damaged documents have been discovered at Uaxactun, Altun Ha and at Mirador in Chiapas.

MAYA COSMOLOGY   The system of looking at the universe, especially as it related to the role of human beings on earth and their eventual destiny beyond the grave, varying from region to region within the realm of the Maya. Certain basic elements, however, were common in the cosmological (or cosmogonic) outlook for the entire Maya populace. To begin with, all Maya viewed the universe as a single entity, with the physical or material world composing only a part of the whole. Second, the Maya envisioned a duality in all existence, the constant war between good and evil, with the outcome of these cosmic duels affecting humankind and its eventual destiny. Thus the Maya viewed the supernatural and spiritual activities to which they were called in their ceremonial centers as part of daily life for mortals abiding upon the earth.

The world in which each generation found itself was not a single phenomenon. Various worlds had been created and destroyed in the past. According to some researchers, the Maya tradition lists as many as four such worlds as having existed and then being devastated by divine forces. The *Dresden Codex* refers to a deluge ending the world in which the Maya of the Classic Period existed.

Humankind also underwent successive changes, according to Maya legends. The first human beings who walked upon the earth were created out of the earth itself. They were considered mindless by the gods, however, and thus destroyed. The second group of human beings were fashioned from wood and were judged soulless and ungrateful. The gods had demons set upon these humans, although some regional traditions among the Maya had this group drowned in a flood. Then the ancestors of the Maya were formed from maize gruel.

This act of creation was viewed as a dawning, taking place just after the gods created the sun and the moon to end the eternal blackness of the abyss. Thirteen separate levels of the heavens resulted in this dawning, and then the earth was formed, followed by Xibalba, the underworld. The earth, inhabited by humankind, was believed to be flat. The cardinal points, or major directions, of this earth were vital to calendrical and religious practices. In some regions during the Classic Period, the earth was envisioned as resting on the back of a gigantic crocodile that, in turn, floated in a lily pond.

The cardinal points of the earth were held up by four divine beings, the *Bacabs*, who were represented in inscriptions by celestial monsters or by two-headed lizards or serpents. Each of the cardinal points was related to a *Bacab* and to a sacred *ceiba* tree (the wild cotton). Each point of the earth was represented by a patron bird and color. These were:

East: color red, Kan years symbol, the god Hobnil
West: color black, Ix years symbol, the god Zac Cimi

Maya relief

South: color yellow, Cauac years symbol, the god Hozanek
North: color white, Muluc years symbol, the god Can Tzional

Green was the color of the center of the earth. According to one Maya tradition concerning the colors of the earth, the thunder deity, Chac, sent white maize from the mountains for humankind. In the process of hurling a thunderbolt, however, Chac burned the maize, resulting in the various colors that became the hues attributed to the cardinal points.

Thirteen heavens existed in Maya lore. Thirteen gods, called the *Oxlahuntiku*, presided over these heavens. These deities were overcome by the Nine Lords of the Night, the *Bolontiku*, who ruled the underworld. This underworld, called Xibalba, the Place of Fright, consisted of nine layers and was depicted as a cold, cheerless place where the souls of humans went for a time. One Lacandon legend held that the sun rested in the underworld at night. The underworld was called Mitnal in some places in the Yucatan.

The *Popol Vuh* contains an important myth concerning Xibalba. Two young Maya lords were supposedly chosen by the *Bolontiku* to suffer and then to die at their hands. The head of one Lord, named Hun Hunahpu, was hung on a tree, where Lady Blood, a Xibalba princess, found it. She touched the head and was immediately impregnated by it. Banished from Xibalba in disgrace, Lady Blood fled the underworld for the earth and gave birth to the supernatural Hero Twins, Hunahpu and Xbalanque. These heroes had many adventures and defeated mythical enemies, including their own evil half brothers. The Hero Twins transformed these brothers into monkey men.

The lords of Xibalba, however, demanded that the Twins play a ritual ball game, the price of which was their lives. The Twins defeated the team from the underworld and became the sun and the moon. This theme of suffering and resurrection was vital to Maya religion because it offered a similar hope for human beings as well.

The present world of the Maya was believed destined to end in one of the same disasters that befell the previous ones. The priests taught that time evolved back upon itself in cycles. The *Chilam Balam* predicted that such disasters would bring the world to a sudden end. A new world, however, would be created instantly, so that the eternal cycles could resume.

The cycles of time were an important cosmological and religious element in Maya belief. The Maya viewed time as a measurable entity having direction. Time could be calculated and pinpointed as to past or future. As in most Mesoamerican cultures, the Maya viewed time as cyclical, bound to repeat itself in the affairs of humanity. The various components of time thus were incorporated into human affairs and were subject to the whims of divine beings. The calendar studies of the Maya had cosmic significance because they were imbued with this unique view of time and with events that were believed capable of repeating themselves as part of the great cycles of development, with crises, disasters and good fortune. This philosophical view of time was reflected in the calendar systems, which depicted time as a burden borne on the backs of gods, who were both hostile and benevolent. The Long Count, the system connected to the Solar Year, was a product of this awareness.

The Maya also saw themselves as inhabitants of all of the various levels of the universe at one time or another. On earth the Maya still believed themselves to be governed by forces in unseen domains. Time, space and the physical world served as links to the other levels of the universe, which would open to them in an appointed sequence. Nobles and priests were unique mediators between the people and the unseen forces of good or ill. In the early periods, the rulers of the various cities served in a priestly capacity. Then genuine priestly orders were initiated for ritual purposes. These priests, students of calendrics and astronomy, had a sophisticated awareness of time and played a vital role in bringing this awareness to the people.

MAYA CURRENCY   The medium of exchange used by the Maya in their extensive trade networks during all stages of development. As in other Mesoamerican cultures, the primary Maya currency was the CACAO bean. The beans were used in local and far-flung markets. Cacao was an ideal medium of exchange because it was prized by all peoples. No hoarding was possible because the beans decayed and insects destroyed those kept in storage. Unused cacao beans were taken out of circulation to be turned into the chocolate drink favored by the elite of many regions. In time, the people learned how to counterfeit the beans' weight by inserting other materials into them, thus rendering their use ineffective. Cacao was grown primarily in the region of Tabasco, along the Belize River and in parts of El Salvador, as well as on the coasts.

Other currencies in use in addition to beans were copper axes and maize, as well as jade, obsidian, salt, shells and cloth. The value of the currency varied from region to region, and the distribution of such a medium of exchange depended on the sources and availability of the items. (See MAYA TRADE.)

MAYA DEATH RITUALS   The traditional burial practices and the rites of passage that evolved in the Maya culture. The Maya greatly feared death, and it evoked sincere religious fervor among the survivors. By contrast, however, the Maya also looked upon death as something that did not prevent their ancestors from returning to play an active role in human affairs. Suicide was viewed as a pious act, and women who died in childbirth, as well as warriors who perished in battle, were believed to ascend directly to heaven. Evildoers endured eternity in Xibalba, the Maya underworld. Those unfortunates who were given up in human sacrifices in the temples were also believed to be worthy of eternal bliss.

The concept of death was a vital part of the Maya religious traditions, and early on the Maya provided mortuary symbols and customs for honoring both the process of dying and the dead. Only the highest-ranking member of each city's aristocracy was honored with burial within the ceremonial complex. Reflecting the ancestor worship that permeated the death traditions, these noble dead were placed in vaults and temples erected above them. Such an attitude toward the ancestral dead may have been an indication of the influence of the great city of Teotihuacan, which was called the Place Where Men Become Divine. Maya elite burials mirrored those in Teotihuacan. Maya commoners were deposited beneath or beside their original residences. All of the dead, however, commoner or aristocrat, were wrapped in cotton mantles and placed in an extended position or in a flexed one. Maize was placed in the mouth of the deceased, with jade or stone beads to serve as currency on the journey into the afterlife. The dead of more lowly Maya were placed on wooden litters. The bodies of those of higher rank were placed inside sarcophagi. When commoners were buried beneath or near their homes, their families usually abandoned the site.

In later eras, the bodies of the Maya elite castes were often cremated, and their ashes were buried in vaults in the temples. In certain instances, as among the Cocom, parts of the face of the deceased were removed and preserved. The skull was then provided with mortar or resin features designed to resemble the original ones. Elaborate grave offerings were also placed in the tombs, including ceramics, effigy figurines, jade, marble pieces, mosaic masks, mushroom figures, obsidian, pyrite plaques, shells, soapstone bottles, and stones.

The mushroom figures undoubtedly were related to the custom of taking hallucinogenic drugs before ceremonies in order to enhance spiritual receptivity.

Certain ceremonial complexes contained tombs that were distinctive for their contents or their artistic style. Four such complexes are those at Altun Ha, Palenque, Tikal and Uaxactun.

Altun Ha. In a building called B-4 of this Belize site was found the tomb of an important Maya aristocrat, either a noble or a priest, or both. Ceramics, ointments, ceremonial flints, pendants, jade pieces and other offerings were provided for the deceased. Another remarkable offering was a carved life-size head depicting the god Ah Kin (called Kinich Ahau in the Yucatan), who represented the sun. Weighing over nine pounds, the head is the largest portrait found in the Maya territory.

Palenque. The tomb discovered in the Temple of the Inscriptions in this ceremonial center was a crypt located some 73 feet below the temple. The walls were 12 feet thick, and the tomb was reached by descending stone steps. The actual tomb was sealed by a triangular stone door. The crypt, which bears stucco reliefs, is a cave of stalactites that has a 12- by 7-foot sculptured stone floor. Lord Pacal is depicted in the center, jeweled and wearing a headdress. He is up on a monster, above an ornate cross, with a two-headed serpent and a mythical bird on top. Six skeletons were also found here, youths sacrificed to accompany the noble.

The walls of the tomb depict figures of the Nine Lords of the Night. An immense block, 7 feet by 13 inches, with round holes, had a slab resting on it that weighed five tons. This block contained green jade ornaments, red-painted teeth and bones, as well as parts of a mask. A man believed to have been 40 years old and approximately five feet eight inches tall was found there.

Grave offerings provided for this corpse included a diadem of tiny disks, headdress decorations, ear plugs, collars of beads, a breastplate and a pectoral. The corpse had rings

Pacal's sarcophagus lid

on its fingers, bracelets, ornaments designed as human effigies and a batlike plaque. A single jade bead was found in the corpse's mouth, probably for food in the afterlife or as an offering.

The Lord's body was wrapped in a cotton shroud and sprinkled with cinnabar. The face was covered with a mosaic jade mask, with shell and obsidian eyes. Other offerings were also discovered on the floor beside the burial block.

Tikal. This site contains tombs beneath the floors of plazas and temple platforms. Rectangular crypts made from cut stone, roofed and corbeled, were provided with vaulted ceilings. Jade and shell ornaments, figurines, ceramics, masks, obsidian blades, gourds, polychrome murals and inscriptions were provided for the deceased as offerings and as mortuary decorations.

The great Maya lord Ah Cacau's tomb was built in Tikal. The lord was buried in a cotton mantle, laid upon a bench, with a woven mat and mortuary offerings of polychrome wares, pearls, oyster-shell ornaments and jade. A bundle of finely carved and incised bones was also discovered in the tomb. The body was clothed in strands of massive jade beads and tubes. A jade cylindrical base, probably containing a portrait of Ah Cacau, was covered with glyph inscriptions.

Uaxactun. This site in the Peten district of Guatemala had 12 separate mounds in the group of structures termed E by modern scholars working there. The seventh structure of this group, a pyramid called E-VII-sub because it was discovered beneath another building, was 27 feet high. It was fashioned from earth and rubble and covered with white stucco. Terraced sides, and stairways decorated with large and elaborate masks, representing jaguars and serpents, gave this tomb of the local lord an elegant appearance. The grave site was filled with offerings, including Chicanel pottery.

MAYA DRESS AND APPEARANCE The styles and physiological traits that distinguished the ancient Maya, as depicted in their artistic renditions or described by their contemporaries. The millions of Maya still inhabiting many of their original territories have maintained the same appearance over the centuries. The Maya men, as described by the Spanish chroniclers, were small, the average height being five feet. The women were smaller. Both sexes had prominent noses, which were sometimes aquiline or Roman. Their faces were broad and flat, with prominent cheekbones. The Maya eyes appeared Asian, with a fold at the inner corner. Their skin was brownish or copperish, and their hair was either dark brown or black. Maya men wore no beards, and their dark hair was soft, worn long and often cut in a tonsure. Long braids were fashioned and then worn around the head, with a pigtail hanging in back. Bangs were considered fashionable in some regions and were held in place by an elaborate headband.

The Maya admired cranial deformations, brought about deliberately in the crib by the use of bands. Because they also regarded crossed eyes as a mark of beauty, small beads were dangled before the eyes of Maya babies as they matured, forcing the eyes to turn inward. Teeth were filed down to points, and the upper classes inlaid jade, obsidian, shells and iron pyrite in their front teeth.

All the Maya people admired color, designs and clean apparels. There were elaborate costumes for religious functions, and the everyday wear of the Maya took into consideration the tropical climate and the necessity of dressing sensibly. Cotton was the primary material chosen for clothes, as the crop was raised early in Maya history. Commoners wore short lengths of cotton, unadorned, but the cloth could be transformed into elaborate mantles and gowns for the nobility, with geometric designs and other embroidery. Commoners wore loincloths, *maxtlatl* (a Nahuatl term), that were plain and bound with the ends hanging in the front and back. Nobles wore a similar loincloth, decorated on the ends. A mantle *(pati)* was draped about the shoulders of the upper classes, who wore deerskin sandals with cords woven of fibers. They also wore headdresses fashioned from feathers, jewels and small carvings. They had jeweled rings and bracelets, sandals, armlets and leg guards, covered with appliqués and ribbons or feathers. Ornaments were considered fashionable when worn in the

nose, ear or lower lip. The images of the various rulers depict elaborate costumes, with feather headdresses, skins, golden ornaments, jade, ribbons and other fashionable touches that indicated the individual's rank and power. Priests, who belonged to the upper ranks of society, wore white cloaks made of cotton or material from tree bark that covered them to their ankles.

The Maya women wore a long skirt and a *huipil* (Nahuatl term), a loose cotton tunic. Some wore a simple *pati*, a mantle that covered just their breasts. Some commoner women wore just the long skirt. Mantles covered the Maya women's heads, and they wore bangs and dressed their hair in two or sometimes four heavy plaits. Ear ornaments were popular, and women of the nobility wore elaborate headdresses. All Maya, both men and women, painted their bodies, using stamps of engraved clay as applicators. Warriors used red and black designs, and slaves were painted with black and white stripes. The priests of the various temples usually covered their bodies with blue paint. Tattoos were also in fashion, and many Maya had elaborate designs tattooed into their skins.

MAYA DYNASTIES The families or royal lines who ruled or influenced the various Maya regions throughout the history of the civilization. There were 16 such regions in the northern Yucatan in the sixteenth century, when the Spanish arrived. Before that era, the families of cities and ceremonial complexes rose to power and then fell victim to other, more aggressive families or watched their power disintegrate as their regions confronted hostile Mexican invaders or met with natural disasters. There were as many dynasties as there were Maya cities and ceremonial complexes, but the following lines are the most accurately documented:

Bonampak ruler

Canul.   A Yucatan family that controlled the western portion of the peninsula, ruling various regional cities but always working in concert for the family's betterment. The original Ah Canul were Mexicanized mercenaries who had served the Cocom family until the fall of that royal house. The Ah Canul were not driven from the Yucatan but granted lands there. This royal house may have descended from the mercenaries.

Chakan.   A Maya clan of nobles who ruled the northwestern portion of the Yucatan. Members living in several places seem to have maintained only a casual dynastic alliance.

Chikinchal.   A Maya dynasty ruling in the northern coastal portion of the Yucatan Peninsula in the Post-Classic Period (A.D. 900–1521) and evident in several sites. These Maya aristocrats maintained a casual alliance throughout their realm.

Cocom.   One of the major Maya dynasties, at least as far as documentation is concerned, ruling in the northern Yucatan region from their capital of Mayapan. They brought in the Ah Canul (the "guardians") to cement their domination and to protect their vast trade system. One Cocom, Hunac Ceel, ruling in Mayapan from 1441 to 1461, offered himself as a sacrificial victim at the Sacred *Cenote* of Chichen Itza. He survived the sacrifice and announced a prophecy from the rain god, Chac, thus winning the respect and following of the local populace. Hunac Ceel also encouraged the ruler of Chichen Itza, Chac Xib Chac, to abduct the bride of the ruler of Izamal. The result was the overthrow of Chac Xib Chac's rule in Chichen Itza. Hunac Ceel then turned on Izamal as well. The Cocom intermarried with other noble families and forged upper-class alliances. When burying their dead, the Cocom removed the facial bones and replaced them with other durable materials or with

Usumacinta ball player

feathers molded in bitumen. The name of the family was derived from a flowering plant in the region.

When the ruling family of Xiu, near Uxmal (some records list their home as Mani), began their rise to power in the Yucatan, the Cocom retaliated. In c. A.D. 1450, however, a Xiu noble, Ah Xupan, led a revolt against them. Neighboring aristocrats accused the Cocom of abusing their power and of selling Maya into slavery. Mayapan was sacked by an allied force, and the Cocom were slain, with only one prince of the royal line escaping, as he was on a trading expedition at the time. The Cocom survivors went to Sotuta, near the Xiu stronghold, where they lived in retirement for a time and then attempted to reestablish their power on a lesser scale. Another Cocom noted in historical records was Nachi Cocom, who gave permission to Ah Dzun Titul Xiu (Napot Xiu) to take part in rituals at the Sacred *Cenote* in Chichen Itza. When the Xiu lord arrived with his son and servants, they were feted for five days and nights and then murdered. This was supposedly an act of vengeance upon the Xius for the death of previous Cocom victims.

Cupul.   A Maya noble family that ruled cities in the east-central plains of the Yucatan Peninsula. Little is known about their activities.

Jaguar.   A Maya noble family ruling in the city of Yaxchilan. The ruler Shield Jaguar was well known in his time. His son, Bird Jaguar, took the throne of Yaxchilan in A.D. 752. Bird Jaguar attended the funeral of a noblewoman in the city of Altar de Sacrificios. That event appears to have been the reason for a gathering of many noble clans.

Sky.   A Maya noble family ruling in Quirigua as early as A.D. 724. The most notable rulers of this line were Sky Xul and Cauac Sky, who ruled around A.D. 724.

Xiu.   (Tutul Xiu) A Maya noble family claiming to be the lords of Uxmal, although their origins appear to have been at nearby Mani. Late arrivals in the region, the Xiu apparently revived the abandoned city of Uxmal and consolidated their position. Some scholars believe they were Mexican in origin, or at least Mexicanized. Ah Dzun Titul Xiu, one of their rulers, was murdered with his son in Chichen Itza by Nachi Cocom. Another member of the family, Ah Xupan, led the revolt against the Cocom line in A.D. 1450, destroying the Cocom capital of Mayapan.

According to the *Popul Vuh*, the dynasties continued to wage war upon one another over the centuries. Their competitions and ambitions may have led to the decline of the Maya cities in the south, weakening them so that they were unable to stand against the political and military changes taking place in the regions. Other dynasties, such as the line in Tikal that produced Ah Cacau, or the dynasty at Palenque, exemplified by Lord Pacal, added greatly to Maya cultural development, at least in their own territories. These great houses worked together at times, and they intermarried and formed alliances with one another in some eras.

MAYA GAMES   The sports activities that provided recreation for the Maya while at the same time symbolizing the religious and cosmological aspects of their culture's beliefs. The Maya, like the people of other Mesoamerican groups, played a ritual ball game that had both religious and secular significance. All of the Maya ceremonial complexes and cities had at least one ball court, and some had as many as 15. These courts were usually from 75 to 150 feet long, 25 to 50 feet wide, with low masonry walls or benches, some sloping and covered with reliefs. Stone markers were on the walls or floors. Formative Period (2000 B.C.–A.D. 250/290) figurines depict the ball players, but the earliest known court was built in Copan, dating to the Early Classic Period (A.D. 1/250–600). Highland courts had walls, but lowland courts were generally in the open.

Called *pok-ta-pok*, the ball courts were often in the shape of capital I's. Rituals were associated with the games. Nobles and priests watched all of the games, along with commoners, who stood on the walls or in the nearby open areas. The ball games were usually played with solid rubber balls, but on occasions human heads or skulls were used. The ball courts also served as arenas for divination ceremonies, and some were equipped with altars for that purpose. Despite the religious implications, the ball courts staged secular games as well, and then there was heavy betting on the outcome. In some instances during ritual games, the losing team members forfeited their lives.

The aim of the game was to score by propelling the balls through rings installed on the side walls. The players could toss the balls using the head, chest, foot, knee or thigh, but they could never use their hands. Points also could be made by hitting the side markers.

Two teams competed. The solid-rubber balls measured two to 10 inches in diameter and weighed approximately five pounds. The players wore elaborate uniforms made of leather or wicker. Belts, hips and knee pads protected them, and they wore gloves and helmets. The protective gear also included U-shaped pads that shielded the players against the impact of the balls.

MAYA GODS A diverse and vast pantheon of deities worshipped by the Maya throughout their history. Many of these gods appear to have evolved out of fertility or agricultural rituals. They were invoked for blessings of the various elements and spirits embodied in the natural forces of the Maya region. Early on the Maya recognized the natural forces as playing vital roles in the climatic and geographic environments; thus the Maya deified them, viewing them as both feminine and masculine, and revering or fearing them depending on their impact on human affairs. In the Yucatan region, behind the pantheon of gods, playing a distinct cosmological role in Maya mythology, was Hunab Ku, whom the priests considered to be "the only living and true god." The deity was all spirit, all-powerful and an unlimited force. He was never represented by temple images and was deemed a true spirit that had created *chac*, lightning; *kak*, fire; *kin*, the sun; and *U*, the moon. Hunab Ku may have been revered early in Maya history or may have been introduced after the Spanish conquest as a rival to the god worshipped by the invaders. While there is some question as to when this creator deity arrived on the scene, in many ways Hunab Ku represented a centuries' old Maya concept about matter. The Maya considered all living things as possessing elements of vitality and power, through a substance called *ik*. Because of the presence of *ik*, all living

Maya Ah Mun

things must be revered and placated if used in any fashion by human beings. The earth itself, the nurturing source of all life, was equally sacred and was called *ch'ul balamil*.

While the Maya held these general cosmological views, the deities they worshipped in their temples had the greatest impact on the culture's religious traditions. These gods combined mythological animal and human characteristics in beings that ruled the earth and the forces of nature. The gods also represented vividly and beautifully the duality of existence as the Maya understood it. Good and evil were in constant conflict in the Maya religious concept about existence and human goals. The deities could be either benevolent or malevolent toward human beings, depending on their nature or their role in the drama of duality. The deities could also multiply themselves for their own purposes and assume disguises and various forms. Because of these mysterious and potent abilities, and because of the gods' association with the natural forces that posed constant threats, the gods were adored and offered sacrifices and great ceremonies. Human sacrifices and self-mutilation by priests, nobles and commoners were pious demonstrations of faith. Such spilling of blood was not localized or constant in a single Maya region but was a general tradition.

The ranking god of the Maya was Itzamna, called the Lord of the Heavens, or the Lizard's House. Itzamna, beloved by the people, was considered an incorporeal being as well as the creator of all things. Rain was one of his elements, as *Itz* also meant "raindrops" or "teardrops." The Itzam, an iguana type of lizard, was the god's symbol, but he was also believed to manifest himself in the crocodile or in the antlers and hooves of deer. As the patron of the cardinal points of the earth, Itzamna assumed various colors and roles. As the earth itself he was called Itzam Cab Ain. He assumed many roles and forms over the ages, all pivotal in protecting the people from natural forces. Other members of the Maya pantheon included the following:

Acantun. The Maya demons, four in number, associated with the colors of the cardinal points. They were prominent in the Maya New Year celebrations and were called the patrons of carvings and idols. The *Acantun* were referred to in the Ritual of the *Bacabes* or *Bacabs* and were associated in some ways with Itzamna.

Acat. The Maya god of life. This deity was believed to shape babies in their mothers' wombs.

Ah Chac Mitan Ch'oc. Translated as "He of the great stench," the Maya name for Venus, linked to 1 Ahau in the calendars. As Itzamna's brother, he was called Xux Ek or Xamam Ek in some regions.

Ah Kin. Called Kinich Ahau in the Yucatan, the god of the sun. Ah Kin was a powerful deity, and he played a role in the agricultural life of the Maya, the foundation for their economic prosperity in the early years. His name was translated as the "Day Lord." In the codices he is depicted as being somewhat malevolent toward human beings, probably a reference to the relentless sun in the tropical climes. In some communities Ah Kin was believed to revert to the form of the jaguar at night, thus becoming a mysterious and mystical being. In other regions he was believed to descend each night into Xibalba, the underworld, where his brother, Usukunkyum, protected him from the evil spells of the earth god, Kisin (Cizin).

Ah Mun. Also called Yum Kaax, the Maya corn god, usually depicted as a handsome young man with maize sprouting from his elegant head. He was symbolized by the Kan day glyph in inscriptions and was associated with God E of the codices. As the Lord of the Forests, Ah Mun was depicted in combat with the god of death, Ah Puch.

Ah Puch. The god of death, called also God A in the Maya codices. Ah Puch was depicted with a death's head, bony ribs and a spinal cord made visible by starvation and suffering. If he was garbed he was given black spots, symbolizing the rot of corpses. Ah Puch presided over the lowest level of Xibalba, the underworld. He fought both Itzamna and Ah Mun, in the continuance of the duality of good and evil in Maya religion. Ah Puch was associated with gods and with the owl, a bird that Maya believed called their names before summoning them to the grave.

Bacab. A son of Itzamna, or a manifestation of that god; four in number, they are Atlantean supporters of the 13 levels of heaven. The *Bacabs* took over their task when the *Oxlahuntiku,* the Thirteen Lords of the Day and the patrons of the levels of heaven, were defeated by the *Bolontiku,* the Nine Lords of the Night who ruled the levels of Xibalba. The *Bacabs* served as the patrons of the cardinal points of the earth:

East, color red, the god Hobnil
West, color black, the god Zac Cimi
North, color white, the god Can Tzional
South, color yellow, the god Hozanek

In some regions they were patrons of bees and apiaries, in conjunction with a lesser deity, Ah Mucen Cab.

Bolom Dz'acab. The god K of the Maya codices, the so-called Long Nosed-God. This was the Serpent Food deity, the patron of the lineage and descent among the elite Maya. Such information was vital to arranged marriages and standing in the community. His name meant the "nine generation," referring to the lengths to which the Maya elite went in order to trace the geneology of each member of the aristocratic society. He was also called the god of the Kan and was associated with the cardinal points of the earth in some Maya regions.

Bolontiku. The Nine Lords of the Night, the rulers of the nine levels of the underworld, Xibalba or Mitnal (in the Yucatan). These lords defeated the *Oxlahuntiku* of the 13 levels of the heavens in the enduring duality that permeated Maya religion. Their glyphs were included in the Maya Long Count inscriptions.

Chac. Called Chac Xib Chac in some regions, or Chaac, the rain god of the Maya, sometimes appearing four in number. They are considered the manifestations of Itzamna in some mythologies, and each was assigned to a corner of the earth, as were the *Bacabs.* In the Yucatan, Chac was depicted as an old man, and in the codices he was a long-nosed deity. The god of thunder, Chac was summoned in a late-summer ceremony. At that ritual four young boys were tied to the corners of an altar, where they made croaking noises, imitating the sounds of frogs, which were the harbingers of the rainy season in Mesoamerica. The boys were probably sacrificed at the close of the ceremony, as human sacrifice was part of the usual rites in worshipping Chac. Chac supposedly determined the colors of the cardinal points of the earth. He sent white maize down from heaven to humankind, but the maize came in a thunderbolt, which scorched it, turning it the various colors considered sacred to each point.

Cizin. Also called Kisin, who was worshipped as a god of death in the Yucatan and in Chiapas and as an earth deity. His name meant "stench" or "foul odor," and he was usually depicted as a walking skeleton. In the Lacandon legends Cizin attacked Ah Kin, the sun, each night in Xibalba but was defeated by Usukunkyum, the sun's brother.

Ek Chuah. The patron deity of the merchants of the Maya realm, generally depicted with a black face and a long nose. Ek Chuah was also worshipped as a god of war and as the patron of cacao and the cacao plantations in certain regions. As war god he assumed the role of a death deity.

Hero Twins.   The mythological young Maya lords who were selected by the *Bolontiku*, the Nine Lords of the Night, who rule the nine layers of the underworld, to suffer and then to die at their hands. The head of one of them, called Hun Hunahpu, was hung on a tree, and LADY BLOOD, a Xibalban princess, discovered it there. She touched the head and was instantly impregnated by it. Banished from Xibalba in disgrace, Lady Blood went to earth to give birth to twins. They were supernatural beings, called the Hero Twins, Hunahpu and Xbalanque. The heroes had many adventures and defeated mythical enemies, including their own half brothers, who were evil. The Hero Twins transformed these half brothers into the Monkey Men.

The lords of Xibalba, however, demanded that the Twins play a ritual ball game, the price of losing being their lives. The Twins defeated the team from the underworld and became the sun and the moon. These themes of duality in the world and of suffering and resurrection were vital in Maya religion.

Hunhau.   A death god associated with Ah Puch. Dogs were considered to be manifestations of this deity, as was lightning. The god was popular in Chiapas.

Ixchel.   The moon goddess, the consort of Ah Kin, the sun. She was celebrated in Maya erotic legends as wayward by nature. One such tale relates that she eloped with the king of the vultures. Using deception, Ah Kin, her husband, made his way to the king's palace and reclaimed her. Also called the Lady of the Rainbow, Ixchel was sometimes depicted as an evil old woman. She was patroness of childbirth, divination, medicine and weaving. Ixchel was associated with regional lakes and at one time held rank as an earth deity.

Ixtab.   The goddess of suicide, depicted in the *Dresden Codex* as hanging from the sky by a rope. The Maya revered suicides as humans performing great sacrifices.

Kulkulcan.   The Feathered Serpent (*Kulkul*, feathered; *can*, serpent) among the Maya groups in the Yucatan, associated with Quetzalcoatl. Kulkulcan arrived in the region sometime around A.D. 987, having experienced a miraculous journey from the Toltec city of Tula. There he had been called Ce Acatl Topiltzin. Kulkulcan was the patron of the Maya elite and in some records connected to the Peten (Putun) Maya. He took over the region soon after his arrival and established his cult in the city of Chichen Itza, and was thought to be a reincarnation of Quetzalcoatl. The Quiche and Cakchiquel Maya called him Gucumatz, which means "Quetzal bird-snake." A ruler called Nacxit is also associated with the god in some records, having the power to invest Maya rulers of other sites with legitimacy. The *Popul Vuh* mentions Kulkulcan as Nacxit. The cult of Kulkulcan appears to have practiced traditions arising with the arrival of Mexicanized groups into the Maya realm. (See CE ACATL TOPILTZIN; QUETZALCOATL.)

Oxlahuntiku.   The 13 Lords of the Day, the rulers of the 13 layers of heaven. These gods were defeated by the Nine Lords of the Night, the *Bolontiku*, who ruled of Xibalba, the underworld.

Usukunkyum.   The brother of Ah Kin, the sun, who protected him each night in the underworld against the evils of Cizin.

Vucub Caquix.   A vulture god slain by the Hero Twins in the Maya cosmological legends. (See also MAYA PRIESTS; MAYA RELIGION.)

MAYA GOVERNMENT   The system by which the individual Maya territories administered the lands and peoples. Divergent groups and geographic variations generally allowed the Maya groups to exist within their own environments on an autonomous basis, linked by alliances, shared customs and intermarriages but ruling independently in their own domains. Independent families had capitals in their regions, usually ceremonial complexes. The head of each ceremonial complex was called a *halach uinic*, a "true man." Other names for such lords were *Ahpo* and *Makina*. These rulers carried scepters and round shields as symbols of their authority. In some places the "true man" was held to be so sacrosanct that an attendant held a cloth before him so that no one would dare to speak to him face-to-face.

The centers of Maya population were also involved in trade, military campaigns and defensive projects, supported and administered by a Maya elite class that served their rulers as judges, counselors, bureaucrats or as governors of important cities. The elite nobles implemented directives, counseled the ruler and allocated labor and resources for public works. They also employed scribes to maintain accounts and make reports on activities. Many nobles lived with their ruler or at their own posts. The nobles also maintained the military forces, although the actual administration of the various units probably came under a branch of the aristocratic family trained solely for that purpose. The nobles also formed a council that convened at the death of a ruler to verify the claims of the deceased's younger brother or firstborn son as heir. If the ruler died without an obvious heir, the noble council reviewed the qualifications of candidates from noble families, thoroughly investigating their lineage and political and familial relationships. All candidates had to be members of the *almehen* or the *ch'obal* classes within the ranks of the elite.

Under the first-ranked nobles were the *batoles*, the ax-bearers. These members of lesser aristocratic families governed the smaller communities. They had duties of a mayoral type, keeping the peace, gathering tributes, judging local cases and maintaining order. Nobles of this rank could also serve in the various units of the palace guard. Each Maya town also had the *ah kulelob*, the administrative group, and a council, the *ah cuch cabobn*. Constables, or *tupiles*, served as police, and the *ah hopopoh* led the various religious rites. The *ah hopopoh* also chaired public meetings and was responsible for the musical instruments used in rituals and in religious ceremonies in the temples. Men called *ppolom* formed a special group in charge of trade. Priests, who were also of the noble class, were responsible for various temple duties, and there was a distinct caste system evident within the temple hierarchies.

Some scholars believe that the Maya used a system referred to as "cargo," still evident in some Maya lands today.

This was a method by which men of all ranks could hold offices, each one more elevated, for one year. Fulfilling the duties of each office assured the man a promotion, thus opening the door for talented individuals who were not born with the rank necessary for public service. Some Maya offices, however, were open only to the nobllty, thus limiting the ambitions of lesser-ranked individuals.

MAYA GROUPS The various cultures evolving from the Mam, the protocommunity of the Maya, called the Grandmother Stage. Arriving in Guatemala, or known there by the third millennium B.C., these Maya eventually broke away from the Mam and migrated to the territories that would become their homelands. The groups were unified by tradition and religious concepts but competed for lands or dominance in some eras. These Maya also witnessed the collapse of the southern domains and invasions by the Mexicanized groups, but they remained largely in their original territories and are very much in evidence today. The major reported Maya groups include the following.

Cakchiquel. One of the Maya groups that left the Mam and settled around Lake Atitlan in northern Chimaltenango, Guatemala. Their capital was at Iximche, but they are also recorded as occupying the area around Mixco Viejo. Their history is recounted in the *Annals of the Cakchiquels* (also called the *Memorial de Solala*, the *Memorial de Tecpan Atitlan* or the *Anales de los Xahil*). The Cakchiquel were closely linked to the Quiche Maya, joining that group in the mid-fifteenth century A.D. Lord Quikab, the Cakchiquel ruler, led his people to the Quiche. He was then slain during internal revolt. The Cakchiquel left the Quiche at that point. They were good at trade and continued to work with the Quiche but maintained independence. The *Annals of the Cakchiquels* was written by a member of this group and entrusted to the keeping of the Franciscan friars in the village of Solala, near Lake Atitlan.

Chicomulceltec. A Maya group that left the Mam protocommunity around 1800 B.C. but remained close to the original lands of the Mam. Little is known of this group.

Chol. The Maya group belonging to the Mam until around 900 B.C., when they accompanied the Chontal Maya to the area of Usumacinta River. Later the Chol migrated to Lake Izabal in Guatemala. The Chol belong to the Cholan linguistic branch of the Maya, spoken in southern Yucatan regions. They dominated the Sula plain, which was a rich source of cacao, and they were also on the Motagua River and in the Gulf of Honduras in the sixteenth century A.D. Some references also associate the Chol with Palenque.

Cholan. This group is listed in some records as breaking away from the Mam protocommunity c. 800/750 B.C., going to the central part of the Maya realm. Cholan is listed as one of the branches speaking the Maya language, but little information is available about their past history.

Chontal. A group that left the Mam protocommunity around 900 B.C., accompanied by the Chol and the Chorti Maya. The Chontal went to the Usumacinta River and then settled in the Acalan region. A Chontal group also is listed in Michoacan, on the Apatzingan Plain. The Acalan Chontal in the Yucatan Peninsula had their capital at Itzamkanac,

and from there they conducted vast trade networks. Noble families ruled the area, which was a source of cacao for the Maya. This group was associated with the cult of Kukulcan. They traded with groups on the gulf coast and were associated with northern Yucatan traders. The notable Peten (Putun) spoke Chontal. (See ACALAN; APOXPALON.)

Chorti. A group that left the Mam protocommunity in c. 900 B.C., accompanying the Chontal and Chol Maya to the Usumacinta River area. Soon thereafter the Chorti migrated to the region around Copan in southern Yucatan.

Eznab. A Maya group that entered the ruins of Tikal after that great city was abandoned and remained there for over a century. They attempted to share in the faded glories of Tikal but were unable to restore it. The Eznab disappeared after a time.

Kanhobalan. A Maya group that left the Mam protocommunity around A.D. 100, when they migrated to the Guatemalan coastal region. They are recorded as joining the Quiche Maya in later eras.

Kekchian. A Maya group, also called Kekchi, that left the Mam protocommunity around 900 B.C. They went to Alta Verapaz and then to Belize. The descendants of the Kekchian Maya now live in the highlands of their original holdings.

Lacandon. A group, related linguistically to the Yucatec, that left the Mam protocommunity around 1600 B.C. They migrated to the region west of the Usumacinta River and settled there in c. 1400 B.C. Farmers and hunters, the Lacandon remain in the remote forest regions and maintain their own ways even today.

Mam. The protocommunity, the mother civilization, arising in the region around Huehuetenango in the third millennium B.C. By 2600 B.C., the Mam had extended their territories and had begun developing a unique culture. Certain groups within the Mam confederation broke away and migrated to other regions, but the Mam remained static from 1500 to 1000 B.C. A record indicates that the Mam had a capital at Zaculeu in the eastern highlands.

Motozintlecan. A Maya group departing from the Mam protocommunity around A.D. 1000, when they moved to the Guatemalan coastal region. They are reported as joining the Quiche in a later era.

Peten (Putun). A vigorous group that spoke the Chontal language but who appear to have been Mexicanized. The Peten maintained a storage platform at Cozumel, off the coast of Quintana Roo. They are recorded as dominating the region of Campeche, using the city of Xicallanco and nearby sites for trading purposes. The site of Acanceh is stylistically associated with Peten art.

Pokoman. A Maya group departing from the Mam protocommunity around A.D. 900. They migrated to the region around Mixco Viejo in Guatemala, maintaining spheres of influence but having no no major settlements. In time the Pokoman joined the Chontal and other groups.

Pokomchi. A Maya group belonging to the Mam protocommunity until A.D. 900, at which time they migrated to the eastern highlands.

Quiche. A large Maya group leaving the Mam proto-community in 1500 B.C., migrating to the Pacific coast and to Lake Atitlan. The Quiche were associated with several other Maya groups but in time claimed to be the true heirs of the Toltec. A capital of the Quiche was Utatlan, built on a series of plateaus. Nobles lived in palaces, and the cult of Kukulcan was imposed upon the region during the Classic Period. The Quiche controlled the cacao trade and vast markets. When the Cocom dynasty's great capital of Mayapan fell, the Quiche suffered. The *Popol Vuh* is a Quiche epic.

Tojolabal. A Maya group that left the Mam proto-community in 400 B.C. They migrated to the central and eastern highlands and settled there.

Tzeltal. A Maya group, part of the original Tzeltalans, that, with the Tzotzil, left the Mam proto-community around 750 B.C. The Tzeltal Mayans went into the Chiapas highlands, leaving that region in A.D. 1200. They went into the western highlands, where they remained.

Tzotzil. A Maya group, part of the Tzeltalan, who left the Mam proto-community around 750 B.C. with the Tzeltal Maya. They settled in the Chiapas highlands until around A.D. 1200, when they moved back to the west, near the Mam region. Zincantan became their trade center, so prosperous that it attracted Aztec merchants, who came in disguise because they viewed the Tzotzil and the region as being dangerous.

Tzutuhil. A Maya group living near the Quiche Maya around Lake Atitlan. They served some Quiche rulers but remained independent.

Yucatec. A Maya group that left the Mam proto-community in 1600 B.C., migrating to the Yucatan peninsula. The Lacandon Maya went with the Yucatecs, remaining for two centuries. The Yucatec Mayan are numerous and widespread in the peninsula, speaking their own dialect, which was distinct by 1000 B.C. During the Classic Period (c. A.D. 1/250–900), they served as a cultural link between the highland and lowland Maya groups, establishing the Cocom dynasty. Yucatec trade used waterways extensively.

Zoque. A group associated with the Maya in language and in original settlements, but called non-Maya in some records. They entered the Chiapas de Corzo region during the Early Classic Period (c. A.D. 1/250–500). Their homeland, the western Pacific coastlands, was a Maya domain. There are debates concerning the Zoquean language and affiliation.

MAYA HIEROGLYPHS The system of writing in the Maya domain; an artistic and elaborate method of inscribing names, dates, events and historical information onto stone or tree-bark paper. Hieroglyphs flourished within the Maya realm between A.D. 300 and 900. They have been recovered in ruins from Honduras in the east to Tabasco in the west, and from northern Yucatan to southern Chiapas. The principal sources of Maya hieroglyphs are codices, inscriptions on stelae, lintels and wall panels. Some were used as decorations for murals, pottery, and incised on jade, bones and shells.

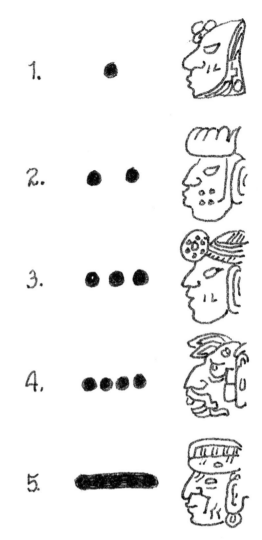

Maya number glyphs

Scholars have had difficulty deciphering such glyphs because the glyphs had standard meanings but different sound values among the different Maya dialects. The six major branches of the Maya language divided into more than 30 such distinct dialects.

To date, the glyphs associated with calendars and astronomical matters have been the most easily translated. In general, Maya texts were divided into square glyph blocks, with grooves carved into the stones as borders. The glyph blocks were generally arranged in vertical columns. In earlier eras one vertical column was used, and later a double-column format evolved. The glyphs are read in pairs, starting with column 1 at the top, on the left, and then column 2. The reader moves to the second glyph block in column 1, and to the second glyph block in column 2 and so on. If the glyph blocks are positioned in a single horizontal line, they are read from left to right. Some texts, particularly those concerning divination, are divided into four units of four glyphs per block, also read in pairs, from the top to the bottom. In large inscriptions, the glyph blocks are halved or quartered to allow more information in a limited space.

Such glyphs demonstrate the fact that the Maya hieroglyphic system is a true writing form, providing an unlimited range of information, with nuances and shades of emotional coloring. Whereas scholars once interpreted glyphs only phonetically, now they are understood in relation to other principles, especially as utilized in calendars, astronomical studies and mathematics. The Maya used phonetic and nonphonetic signs to make available information and record events. In some instances, a glyph represents a word or an idea in one context while providing a sound in another. Scholars interpreted this as a writing system combining linguistic and phonetic characteristics. Some Maya glyphs appear to represent a consonant-plus-vowel combination, which is interpreted as syllabic rather than alphabetic/phonetic. In the early colonial days, Bishop Landa compiled a phonetic alphabet for the Maya. According to his alphabet, the Maya glyphs indicated phonemes (smallest distinguishable units of speech) rather than syllables (the units of a spoken word). The syllabic writing of the Maya, however, maintains a phonetic principle but is far more complex than the system Landa envisioned.

The glyphs found on stelae and elsewhere in the Maya ceremonial complexes indicate the fullness of the Maya language. Some newly discovered elements have allowed for a truer appreciation of the Maya writing styles, providing vast amounts of information concerning individuals, dynasties, events and basic facts. Maya glyphs represent nouns, adjectives, verbal stems, prepositions and speech particles, mostly monosyllabic. Compound glyphs, formed by joining two nouns or an adjective or speech particle to a noun or verbal stem, form compound words. Other compound glyphs have been discovered that demonstrate that a glyphic element representing a definite sound or object or idea did not change when joined to others. The Maya also used homonyms, employing the rebus technique. They also incorporated ideograms, glyphs that represent an object but not its sound value. At times these ideograms were pictograms; for example, the heart was the symbol for sacrifice, especially when accompanied by the head of a bat (a reference to vampire bats in the region). Attributive glyphs, normally identifying a deity, were in use in the Maya realm, as were portraits and symbolic forms. Emblem glyphs, designating a special ceremonial complex, were placed beside other glyphs to represent rulers or events taking place within the site. An internal pattern seems repeated again and again to recount eras or events concerning rulers. Their births or ritual baptisms are marked by the glyph of an upended frog, while the accession glyph is that of the ruler in a niche. Thus deciphered, the glyphs give information on Maya dynastic lineages and histories.

Yet many Maya glyphs remain undeciphered because they cannot be fully excavated or uncovered and because of the varying ways in which a translation might be made. (See also DATED MONUMENTS.)

MAYAHUEL A Toltec/Aztec goddess of milk, having 100 breasts. She was patroness of *pulque*. The Quetzalcoatl legend concerns *pulque* and Mayahuel. Fertility is the symbol. Since *maguey* was a source of *pulque*, the goddess was depicted amid maguey fronds. She was also invoked in fertility rites.

MAYA LANGUAGE A diverse and fluid means of communication among the Maya, directly related to the movement of the Maya groups from the Mam, the Maya protocommunity, at different times. The groups evolved their own languages, within distinct Maya family language branches, probably before they left the Mam. Each maintained its language in the new homeland and during periods of migration. Most Maya, however, were sufficiently familiar with the nearby languages for trade and other transactions to be possible. These languages were related, as was that of the Huaxtec, who went far afield of the Maya territories in time. The other languages in use in the Maya realm are generally placed in relationship to the original Mam or protocommunity division, which was their source. The major languages of the Maya include Aztecoidan Family, Lencan Family, Mixe-Zoquean Family, Quichoid Family, Totonacan Family and Xincan Family.

The separate languages spoken throughout the Maya realm include Yucatec Maya, Col, Tzeltal, Mamean and Quiche. They are listed here in descending order of population.

Yucatec Maya. A language still in use in the Yucatan Peninsula and in Campeche. The people living here at the present call themselves the Masewal. The Itza were once part of the original cultures that brought this tongue into the region. Other similar languages in the region include Lacandon, maintained by a group in Chiapas, and Mopan, in use in the Peten frontier and in Belize.

Col. A Maya language related to the Tzeltal and Yucatecan Maya, once spoken from Tabasco to Honduras. The people who speak this language today suffered greatly during the Spanish colonial period. The Col-Lacandon were sent to Chiapas, and their descendants still occupy the region around the ceremonial complex of Palenque. The Chontal, once part of the Col family, speak their own language in the regions of the Usumacinta and Grijalva rivers. Several languages came into use in this district and then disappeared as the various groups integrated into larger units or were absorbed. Peten (Putun) was one language that apparently vanished.

Tzeltal (or Cholan). The language that has connections to both the Mam and the Col. It is used in Chiapas and southward today. Tzotzil, a variation, and Canabal and Cuxe are part of this family. Canabal is spoken around Comitan and Cuxe is used in western Guatemala.

Mamean. A Maya language that includes several separate branches and is spoken today on the Mexican-Guatemalan frontier. The branches of this family include:

Agwakatek	Takana
Ixil	Takaneko
Kanxobal	Takyal
Kayotin	Tlatiman
Motosintlak	Tutuapa
Salomek	Xakaltek
Subinho (now extinct)	

Quiche. A language still spoken in Guatemala in the region of Lake Atitlan and the Motagua River. It is also spoken in some places south of Chiapas. Branches of this language include Kakcikel, Kekchi, Pokomam, Pokomchi, Tsutuhil and Usumacinta. (See MAYA GROUPS for details about the movements of the various Maya as they broke from the Mam protocommunity.)

MAYA LITERATURE Manuscripts reflecting artistic and intellectual traditions that have their origins in the Maya region. The literature of the Maya relies basically on an enduring oral tradition, which was vital in many communities. Literacy, at least among the elite of the various cities and regions, was present in the Maya territories, dating to the Classic Period (c. A.D. 1/250–900). The Maya language provided a fluid, colorful and dramatic tool for its peoples who wished to transmit their knowledge of historical events, the sciences and Maya culture into vibrant texts that would inspire later generations. The documents available today provide a glimpse of an innate intellectual curiosity, accompanied by genuine literary ability.

Maya codices have added to the appreciation of the literary achievements of this civilization. Bishop Diego de Landa, who supported the Spanish destruction of written Maya materials, nonetheless recognized Maya literary skill. Studying materials before they were destroyed as heretical testimonies, Bishop Landa acknowledged that the Maya nobles were skilled in writing, intellectually curious and well acquainted with things of artistic and scientific value. Landa even admitted that the Maya elite were esteemed by their fellows for their knowledge, which they took pains not to display in public. The prelate wrote the *Relacion de las Cosas de Yucatan,* an extensive ethnographic account of the Maya of the region. A copy of the original was found in the Academia de Historia in Madrid, Spain.

The documents that have been preserved offer not only historical and religious information but reflect Maya cultural and intellectual interests as well. These books, for the works are large enough to merit that designation, are both historically and linguistically valuable. They are listed here in descending order of importance.

The Books of Chilam Balam

These documents, written by the sages of the Yucatan region, were originally composed in ten or 12 separate volumes. *Chilam (Chilan)* translates from the Maya as "sage" or "soothsayer," and *Balam* means "Jaguar," the symbol of mysterious and hidden domains. The works could thus be translated as "The Books of Occult Matters." Fragments of the *Chilam Balam* were discovered in the ceremonial complexes of Mani, Tizimin, Chumayel, Kaua, Ixil and Tusik. One of the most important parts of the documents is the compilation of the *u kahlay katunob,* which chronicles events in the various Maya historical eras.

One unnamed book in *Chilam Balam* volumes was discovered in Chumayel in the Yucatan, and is the only one to make use of the Long Count. This book also details Maya history and elaborates on the Maya philosophy concerning time as a dimension. The book was written during the Spanish occupation period, perhaps as an apologia of sorts, an explanation of what the Maya held sacred. Certainly the

book demonstrates that the Maya viewed Christians with the same distaste they reserved for the Itza and others. Foreign elements were not readily accepted by the Maya, who considered their own religion and philosophy worthwhile and not to be abandoned for the hasty embrace of another way of life.

The Maya viewed Itza eroticism as lewd. Nor did the Maya care for the Spanish, and they flatly refused to accept the Christian tenets the occupying forces tried to press upon them.

In their documents the Maya explained their own historical presence from the point of view not of the individual but as part of a cosmic whole. The Maya survivors of cataclysmic forces that had brought down their civilization, rendering it vulnerable to the rapacious Spanish, looked to their own golden age, dreaming of the time to come. The books contain exquisite laments about a lost world, eras of study, worship and praise to the gods. This nostalgic view summons up the wider circle of Maya knowledge of history, medicine, astrology, folklore, calendrics and the dignity of the human intellect when it is bent on the study of the composition and the destiny of humankind.

In the story of the creation of the *uinal,* the 20-day period, the author personifies the divisions of time, depicting them as a great procession that moves out of human dimensions into eternal realms. In Maya religious tradition the world was in darkness until the sun was born. The days, however, predated the sun.

From a literary point of view, the *Books of Chilam Balam* reflect oral traditions of great beauty and repeat lovely Maya ancient songs. They are antiphonal in style, something fostered by the richness of the Maya hieroglyphic expression.

Popol Vuh

This Quiche document, also called *The Book of Counsel,* is a long Maya epic poem of considerable literary merit. The poem was probably written in the sixteenth century in Utatlan. The work survived in translation from the mid-1800s. The *Popol Vuh* concerns the creation myths of the Maya, recording three of them. The original was no doubt written as one or more hieroglyphic codices. The mythology and traditional history of the Quiche were generally presented in oral form, recited during festivals and on important ceremonial occasions. How accurate the version in the *Popol Vuh* is in recounting the oral tradition is not known.

The *Popol Vuh* has been translated from the Quiche Maya as often as 11 times. The fundamental poetic form of the work is evident in these translations, evoking the rich Quiche religious and mystical symbolism. The work is an example of heroic literature, an account of the cosmological origins of people.

The story of creation as related by the Maya concerns the remarkable quest of the gods to create some sort of intelligent being capable of acknowledging them and of granting them due respect and praise. The *Popol Vuh* recounts the efforts of the gods to create beings capable of recognizing their great gifts to humanity.

After two attempts at fashioning men from clay and then wood, the gods discover that an imposter has risen up, claiming to be both the sun and the moon. The imposter is the vulture, Vucub Caquix, who must be destroyed if man is to be created anew. The Hero Twins, Hunahpu and Ixbalanque, destroy the vulture and then have other adventures. They even fight XIBALBA, the underworld, defeating the team from that Place of Fright in a ritual ball game. In time the Hero Twins are transformed into the sun and the moon, followed by those innocents who were slain by evildoers on their behalf, people granted eternal life in the sky as stars. As a result of the Hero Twins, the gods set about creating man again. The latest creation succeeds, but because of the pride that grows in man, the gods blur his senses.

The basic theme of the work is the greatness of the Maya people. Typical of the philosophical and cosmological concerns evident throughout the Maya world, the book takes a cyclical view of events and individuals. It reflects definite Christian influences but provides an accurate portrait of the truly ancient civilization that gave it birth. All the virtues of the Maya world are played out by the Hero Twins, who attain the heights of duty, loyalty and honor—virtues required of each generation of Maya when that civilization was expanding in the Mesoamerican region. The setting of the *Popol Vuh,* however, is a mystical landscape in which the primordial mysteries of the Mayans are played out with grace and elegance. The last section of the work concerns the lineage of the Maya from the first four created men and their wives. The essence of this and the other sections regards spiritual transformation as a necessary activity of humankind and regards compassion and loyalty as the outstanding virtues.

The Annals of the Cakchiquels

This work, a history of the Cakchiquel Maya of Guatemala, is also called the *Memorial de Solala,* the *Memorial de Tecpan-Atitlan* or the *Anales de los Xahil.* The Cakchiquels, closely linked historically to the Quiche Maya, lived in the mountainous regions of Guatemala.

Under the rule of Lord Quikab, the Cakchiquels were united to the Quiche Maya in the mid-fifteenth century. When an internal revolution caused Quikab's death, the Cakchiquel moved to Iximche and started life anew. The Spanish conquered them within a century.

The annals relate the life of these Maya under foreign domination. The completed documents were kept in the village of Solola near Lake Atitlan and later were given into the care of the Franciscan monks at a nearby monastery. *The Annals of the Cakchiquels* corresponds to the views of creation as presented in the *Popol Vuh* and relates some events from the Maya mythological treasury. It also details the sufferings of the Maya at the hands of the Spanish during the early colonial period.

The Title of the Lords of Totonicapan

This document was written sometime around A.D. 1554, in the Quiche language of Guatemala. It is a brief history of of the Quiche Maya from the beginning of their recorded time to the reign of the ruler called Quikab. The original was translated into Spanish in 1834 and then copied in 1860. This copy was given to the National Library of Paris.

The book corroborates the legends and cosmological details provided in the *Popol Vuh,* adding other information concerning Quiche Maya life. The document was signed by members of the Quiche court at the time.

MAYA MARRIAGE   The union between men and women that assumed political and religious importance when it involved members of the elite castes of the various ceremonial complexes throughout the region. These aristocrats made alliances, united royal families and abided always by the strict genealogical designations drawn up for their social group. Such records, which detailed the aristocratic lineage of the Maya on both sides of their families, were studied before each marriage in order to preserve the true standing of the families. It would have been unthinkable for an elite Maya to marry anyone of lesser standing. Any children resulting from such a union would have been deprived of rank and privileges. Definite taboos existed about intermarriages, which would have resulted in a lack of eligible candidates for the official duties allotted to the upper classes.

The union of less aristocratic Maya may or may not have depended on such details of lineage. Wealthier commoners may have been eager to maintain purity of their own lines, with advancement in mind. In the lower classes such distinctions would not have mattered.

In all categories, young Maya men and women were considered eligible for marriage at any time after puberty. Usually, however, the young men were allowed to marry at the age of 18. The young women might be 14 or 15. They were introduced, most likely, through the services of an official matchmaker or marriage broker hired by both families and who provided a series of consultations concerning the advantages of a union. Such an office was considered most respectable among the Maya and accepted as part of the marriage ritual.

Prior to marriage, young Maya girls were expected to remain extremely chaste. Social customs demanded that they refrain from any sort of display of interest in the opposite sex. If a young woman was discovered to have taken certain sexual liberties before marriage, she was whipped. Her wounds were rubbed with pepper, and she was paraded before the local populace, which expressed its own outrage at her behavior.

Prior to marriage, young Maya men appear to have been allowed more liberty. Prostitutes existed in Maya communities, and no stigma was apparently attached to them or to their profession. One Spanish observer commented that such young women were much overworked in the region that he visited.

Young Maya men, however, had certain restrictions placed upon them as well. They could not marry their maternal aunts, their brother's widow, a stepmother or the sister of a dead wife. If a Mayan was found guilty of commiting adultery with a woman, her husband could kill him with impunity. When adulterers were discovered in the Yucatan region, both were shot with arrows. Maya men who corrupted maidens or violated a woman faced the death penalty. This and other marriage details are drawn from colonial sources.

Single men and women painted their bodies with stamp decorations in black. After their marriage they painted themselves with red colors. This paint provided information as to their status, availability and required behavior. The change in color also signified a certain position for the young men. Those who desired to enter the "cargo" system of holding government offices had to be married to be eligible.

When two Maya decided to marry, after the conferences with the marriage broker and receiving parental permission from both sides, negotiations began in earnest. If the aristocracy was involved, priests would begin the long genealogical studies and diviners would be called in to decide if the marriage would prosper. These seers probably consulted the calendar material in order to decide upon a propitious date.

The families of the bride and groom then had to decide on the amount of the dowry, which generally consisted of clothing and would be provided by the father of the groom.

When the day of the marriage dawned, the families gathered in the presence of a priest, who lectured the assembly sternly about the goals of marriage. Sums were then pledged by families, the house was cleaned of insects, and prayers and blessings followed. The families and friends then feasted.

After marriage, a bride and groom lived with the bride's family for six or seven years. The groom had to attend to the tasks set for him by the bride's father, and he had to demonstrate his affection for his wife and his personal integrity. If he failed these demands, he was evicted from the house and the marriage ended. In some cases the bride and groom lived in a separate residence. If a marriage was ended because of the groom's failings, the daughter was provided with a new groom. Divorce in the Maya communities was granted at the request of either party. In some cases, men simply left their wives, taking up residence with another woman. Throughout the marriage the women maintained domestic routines and did not expect to conduct conversations with their husbands or even to eat with them. Most cooking and cleaning of utensils occurred outside the residence. In some communities the women used courts or plazas for the performance of domestic chores.

MAYA MATHEMATICS   A theoretical and utilitarian system devised over the centuries by the Maya. The advanced architecture and calendar developed by the Maya, especially in the Classic Period (c. A.D. 1/250–900), relied heavily on the mathematical skills of builders and sages. The architects designing new ceremonial complexes, the keepers of the vast calendric systems in use in the Maya realm and the diviners compiling mythical or true events for religious purposes had to have a system that far-off merchants and traders could share. Both groups, the religious and secular in Mayan society, needed a reliable system by which they could perform their tasks with speed and accuracy.

The Maya mathematical system evolved with two means of representing numbers, the bar and the dot, and the head variant symbols. These two modes of representing mathematical equivalents allowed the Maya to develop accurate computations. Their measurement of their tropical year, for example, was 365.2420 days. The modern computation for the year is 365.2422.

In the Maya bar-dot system, the bar had a value of five and the dot had the value of one. The symbol for zero was a stylized shell. The use of the zero clearly proves the Maya to be innovative and sophisticated. It demanded a certain advanced intellect not shared by all Mesoamerican groups.

In listing their numerals, the Maya employed a vigesimal system, increasing from the bottom to the top in vertical columns. One was the lowest, with the next number representing the sum of 20, then 400, then 800, then 160,000 and so on. A numeral placed in any one of these vertical positions was recognized as bearing the increased value determined by its corresponding multiple. The column could thus be added up for an accurate total. Such a vigesimal system could also allow the Maya to multiply, divide and solve other intricate mathematical problems. They did not use fractions, however, and they did not advance higher forms of mathematics.

MAYA MEDICINE   See MAYA PRIESTS.

MAYA MEXICA   The group that emerged from the association of the Maya of the southern lowlands and their tropical forests with the Mexica of the highlands in the north. These cultures developed separately, each having a unique vision and its own priorities, but living side by side in the frontier or intermediate zone. This zone extended from the gulf coastal plain to the Isthmus of Tehuantepec, then east along the Pacific coast. The Maya traded with the Mije-speaking groups on the Pacific coast and with the Olmec descendants on the gulf coast. They confronted the Zapotec and others in Oaxaca and felt the impact of the cities of Teotihuacan and Monte Alban long before the great Toltec and Aztec cultures arose.

In the Post-Classic Period the Maya cultures on or near the frontier zones were impacted by the Mexica. The Itza, for example, dominated part of the lowlands from Chichen Itza. When the city fell in 1200 A.D., the Itza moved further south. The Maya in Yaxchilan were Mexica-ized by A.D. 840.

The people of this region survived because they adapted to new ways. These new ways included imperialism, militarism and state control, aspects of life brought to Mayapan, the Maya center in the Yucatan, by the Cocom dynasty. Other Maya rulers followed this example. Also, the Mexica were serving as mercenary soldiers in some Maya cities. The Pipil and Toltec invasions of the Yucatan, in search of trade and resources, also had an effect on these people. Because of this intermingling, the Quiche Maya in the Yucatan began to claim descent from the Toltecs, and their rulers went to Tula to receive symbols of authority. The Mexica influence brought renewed wars to the Maya region, and those who could not adjust to the new ways were forced to abandon their settlements.

MAYA MOUNTAINS   A series of ridges on the northeastern side of the Yucatan Peninsula, the Maya domain. The mountain region offered seasonal habitation for humans as well as the natural products of marshlands. The mountains also held large quantities of limestone, used in Maya buildings.

MAYAPAN A Maya ceremonial complex in northern Yucatan, called Standard of the Maya, reported in Maya legends as having been built by KUKULCAN, the Yucatan Quetzalcoatl. The records of the Itza describe the site as the "tear-shaped city." It supposedly served as an Itza capital for a century before becoming a Maya stronghold. When the Maya took control of Mayapan, it was a minor center, associated with CHICHEN ITZA. In A.D. 1200, however, Mayapan began to assume importance when its ruler became a political leader in the area. Indigenous Yucatan nobles, the Cocom dynasty, ruled there and controlled Mayapan's trade and affiliations with other complexes. Located in a region that contains 20 CENOTES (Maya water reserves), the complex was surrounded by a wall more than five miles long and six feet high, enclosing one and a half square miles. Mayapan is believed to have had around 12,000 to 15,000 inhabitants and had over 3500 structures. The original architectural style of the city was PUUC.

The main plaza of Mayapan served as a stage for the stepped pyramid called *El Castillo* (the castle), by the Spanish. This platform had four stairways, but there is no evidence of an original temple on its summit. Another building to the east of the pyramid has Chac mask decorations, altars and columns. Beyond is another pyramid with carved serpent heads and columns. Stelae, altars and figures were recovered from Mayapan's monuments, which at one time numbered as many as 4,000. The city appears to have been congested, with none of the coordinated spaces of other Maya sites. Mayapan was burned and abandoned in A.D. 1450, when the XIU, a new dynastic line from Mani, near Uxmal, led a rebellion against the Cocoms, Mayapan's traditional dynasty. (See MAYA DYNASTIES for details.)

MAYA PERSONALITIES The rulers and outstanding individuals of the Maya (also discussed under separate entries) who added dimension to Maya development and cultural achievements. Most of these individuals are known through the hieroglyphic evidence recovered at various Maya sites. As more and more of these hieroglyphic inscriptions are deciphered, new evidence will be gathered about them and their contemporaries. The Maya personalities included in this book are:

Ahau Canek An Itzan Maya who was the ruler of the city of Tayasal.

Ah Dzun Titul Xiu A Xiu noble murdered by the Cocom.

Ahpo Hai The sister of Lord Pacal of Palenque. A stucco head of this noblewoman was found in Pacal's vaulted tomb in the Temple of the Inscriptions in Palenque. The head, beautifully formed, is approximately 11 inches high, depicting a handsome, strong-featured female aristocrat.

Ah Naum Pot. The ruler of Cozumel when the Spanish arrived there in 1527. He greeted them courteously and allowed them to linger in his territory before moving on to other regions.

Ah Ulil The ruler of Izamal in 1194, whose bride was abducted by Chac ib Chac, the ruler of Chichen Itza. Chac

Ib Chac, upon seeing the bride, was smitten with love and ran off with her. Hunac Ceel, the ruler of Mayapan, sought to avenge the deed, and it became a rallying cry for the destruction of Chac Ib Chac.

Ah Ziyah Xiu. See XIU.

Ah Zuitak Titul Xiu. See XIU.

Apoxpalon. Also called Paxbolonacha, an Acalan merchant who was elected chief of his own territory. The people of Acalan voted into office men such as Apoxpalon who demonstrated ability in trade and in amassing products and wealth.

Bat Jaguar. A ruler of Piedras Negras.

Bird Jaguar. An eighth-century ruler of Yaxchilan, who was commemorated on lintel carvings there. He ruled Yaxchilan from A.D. 752 until his death. Bird Jaguar is celebrated for his capture of a rival chieftain called Jeweled Skull. He was a successor to Yaxchilan's ruler, Shield Jaguar.

Butz Chan. The eleventh ruler of the city of Copan. His death was recorded as having taken place in A.D. 628.

Cauac Sky. A ruler of Quirigua, commemorated on Stela E there. Cauac Sky came to the throne in A.D. 724, from unknown origins. After defeating the ruler of Copan in A.D. 737, the ruler transformed Quirigua into a magnificent ceremonial complex. He laid out the plaza there as well as seven monuments. Five stelae in the city commemorated him and his reign. He died in A.D. 784.

Chaacal III. A ruler of Palenque, the son of Kan Xul. He took the throne in A.D. 721. During his reign he built two temples in the ceremonial complex of Palenque.

Chac Ib Chac. The ruler of Chichen Itza in 1194, who fell in love with the bride of AH ULIL, the ruler of Izamal. Chach Ib Chac kidnapped the bride, setting off a rebellion led by Hunac Ceel of Mayapan. The kidnapping was not the actual cause of the rebellion, and some Maya records attest that Chac Ib Chac was placed under a spell by Hunac Ceel, who was reputed to be a sorcerer. Hunac Ceel used the occasion, however, and put together a force large enough to storm Chichen Itza and to force Chac Ib Chac and his people into exile.

Chac Zutz. A ruler of Palenque, the successor to Chaacal III. He ascended the throne in A.D. 722 and reigned for eight years. Chac Zutz's 60th birthday was commemorated on the Tablet of the Slaves discovered in Palenque, dated A.D. 729.

Chan Bahlum. A ruler of Palenque, who is also called Serpent Jaguar. He was the son of Pacal, and he dedicated the Temple of the Inscriptions to his father, providing him with a vaulted tomb in the structure. Chan Bahlum died in A.D. 702.

Curl Nose. The ruler of Tikal from A.D. 378 to 426. He is believed to have been a member of the aristocracy of Teotihuacan or possibly Kaminaljuyu. Curl Nose married the daughter of Jaguar Paw and succeeded him.

Hunac Ceel. Also called Ah Naxcit Kulkulcan, the leader of the Cocom clan in Mayapan. Notable as a sorcerer,

Hunac Ceel dove into the sacred *cenote* of Chichen Itza, a revered place of pilgrimage and religious devotion. His survival in the waters of the *cenote* demonstrated his powers with the gods.

When Ah Ulil, the ruler of Izamal, was being married, both Hunac Ceel and Chac Ib Chac, the ruler of Chichen Itza, attended the ceremony. Hunac Ceel supposedly placed Chac Ib Chac under a spell that forced him to fall in love with Ah Ulil's bride. As a result, Chac Ib Chac kidnapped her. Hunac Ceel, using the occasion to rally his people, rose with an army and stormed Chichen Itza, driving Chac Ib Chac and his people into exile. Hunac Ceel employed Mexica mercenaries in his battles, which brought him victory in A.D. 1194.

Jade Sky. A ruler of the city of Quirigua, who came to the throne in A.D. 805.

Jaguar Paw. Called the Great, a ruler of Tikal, from c. A.D. 320/376. He married his daughter to Curl Snout. Tactics initiated by Jaguar Paw altered Maya warfare. He captured Uaxactun and conducted other campaigns of expansion.

Kan Boar. A ruler of Tikal, the son of Stormy Sky and the father of the "Woman of Tikal." He is depicted on Stela 23 there.

Kan Xul or Hok. The younger brother of Chan Bahlum and his successor as the ruler of Palenque, coming to the throne in A.D. 703. Kan Xul is reported to have enclosed the palace structure in that ceremonial complex during his reign.

Kin Canek. A high priest of the temple of Tayasal and the royal cousin of the ruler of the time, Ahau Canek.

Kuk. A son of Chaacal III, who became ruler of Palenque in A.D. 764. The Maya decline became evident in his city during his reign.

Nachi Cocom. A ruler of Sotita, who was approached by Ah Dzun Xiu, the king of Mani, for permission to enter his domain in order to make a pilgrimage to the sacred *cenote* of Chichen Itza. As the Xiu clan had long been an enemy of the Cocom, Ah Dzun Xiu felt it prudent to ask for Nachi Cocom's safe passage. Nachi Cocom granted permission to the Xiu party of about 40 pilgrims. He went out to meet them, feted them for five nights and days and then slew them all. His grandfather had been slain by the Xiu, and he was exacting revenge.

Pacal Also called Lord Shield Pacal, a ruler of Palenque. He was born on 24 March A.D. 603, and took the throne on 27 July 615. Pacal died on 29 September 684 and was buried in a magnificent vaulted tomb in the Temple of the Inscriptions. His tomb, discovered during excavations, provides evidence of the Maya artistic and architectural skills. There has been some debate over Pacal's age at the time of his death, as the skeleton recovered in the tomb is that of a man in his 40s.

Rabbit, 18. The thirteenth ruler of the ceremonial complex of Copan. He was captured during a war with Quirigua and was decapitated.

Shield Jaguar. The ruler of Yaxchilan, who was born in A.D. 647. He ascended the throne in 682 and lived to be 90 or more. Shield Jaguar was possibly a usurper of the throne of Yaxchilan. He purportedly won it in a battle fought on 23 February A.D. 681, although he may have been the rightful heir who had to fend off rival claimants. He is recorded as having died on 17 June A.D. 742.

Sky Xul. A ruler of Quirigua, the successor of Cauac Sky, probably his son as well. Sky Xul was middle-aged when he was crowned. He ruled 11 years.

Smoke Imix. Also called God E, the twelfth ruler of the city of Copan. He ascended the throne on 8 February A.D. 628 and ruled until his death on 18 June 695.

Smoke Money. The fourteenth ruler of the city of Copan, who appears to have been somewhat retiring and dependent on his nobles. He built a *popol na* (a community house) during his reign but left no other monuments.

Smoke Shell. The fifteenth ruler of Copan. His reign gives evidence of the decline of the Maya domain.

Stormy Sky. The son of Curl Nose and his successor to the throne of Tikal in A.D. 426. Stormy Sky adopted Mexica styles, indicating the increased presence of foreigners in the region.

"The Woman of Tikal" An unknown aristocrat, the daughter of Kan Boar. Her tomb is one of the few elaborate gravesites for women in the Maya realm. The site contained the remainder of a spider monkey, probably her pet.

Xiu, Ah Dzun. Also called Napot Xiu, the ruler of the Xiu clan at Mani. Ah Dzun made a pilgrimage with his son and 40 retainers, planning to worship at the sacred *cenote* shrine in the city of Chichen Itza. He asked for Nachi Cocom's permission to cross the Cocom domain and was welcomed by that ruler, feted for five days and nights and then slain. Ah Dzun's ancestor had slain an ancestor of Nachi Cocom. The slaughter was an act of vengeance.

Xiu, Ah Ziyah. The son of Ah Dzun Xiu, who accompanied him on a pilgrimage to the sacred *cenote* shrine of Chichen Itza and was slain at his father's side by Nachi Cocom.

Xiu, Ah Zuitak Titul. The founder of the ceremonial complex of Uxmal and a scion of the celebrated Xiu clan. Uxmal may have been in existence when the Xiu family arrived there.

Yax K'uk Mo. The founder of the city of Copan in the fifth century A.D.

Yax Pac. The sixteenth ruler of the city of Copan, coming to the throne on 2 July A.D. 763.

Xoc. A ruler of Palenque, the successor to his older brother, Kan Xul. During his reign Palenque became a prominent ceremonial complex.

Zac Kuk. Called the White Quetzal Bird, a woman listed as the mother of Lord Pacal. In some records she is given the rank of a ruler.

MAYA PRIESTS Holders of religious offices, usually members of the elite, who performed religious services as well as conducted secular affairs. It is believed that there were no official priests as a separate group during the Formative Period (c. 2000/1600 B.C.–c. A.D. 250/290). At that time the nobles ruling the various Maya cities were considered the true mediators between the gods and the people. Some evidence indicates that a true priesthood among the Maya may not have evolved until the Post-Classic Period (c. A.D. 900–1521). Certainly the noble families provided the only candidates for priesthood in the various ceremonial complexes, and in some regions aristocratic families specialized in priestly service, with the role becoming hereditary among family members. Some priests remained celibate, however, and they would have been drawn from other aristocratic ranks.

The high priests of each ceremonial center bore a distinct title. *Ah kin mai* or *ahau can mai*, translated as "he of the sun," was a common title for Maya high priests. The priests performing under the direction of *ah kin mai* were called simply *ah kin*. Other offices in the temple were: *ah nacom*, the sacrificer; *chilan*, the soothsayer or the "interpreter of god's message"; and *ahmen*, the diviner. All priests were bound by ceremonial routines, the time for which, in turn, was calculated by the calendar system.

The chief responsibility was the inculcation of knowledge and the preservation of the religious rituals according to the dogma of their particular temple or their local deity. The priests understood the computation systems and methods of divining. They were literate and skilled in mathematics. They also were versed in genealogy, the maintaining of records concerning the lineage of the elite families. They had to know the cosmological tenets of the Maya religion and the field of astronomy and to make astrological forecasts. Some were chosen as counselors for the *halach uinic*, the rulers of the various cities, who depended on such advisors and myriad assistants to administer the vast territories and populace under their control.

In personal matters, the priests were obliged to follow specific regulations before, during and after the major ceremonies of the Maya cultic religion. Prior to each feast dietary and sexual abstinence was required. During the ceremonial rites the priests were obliged to practice various forms of self-mutilation. Some jabbed needles into their tongues, earlobes, noses, foreheads, lower lips or genitals. The blood let as a result of these wounds was generally caught by treebark paper sheets, which were offered to the god as gifts of atonement. In some regions idols were splattered directly with the blood. The priests also underwent certain purification rites that required ritual baths and cleansing of clothes and utensils.

On most days in the temples, which were quite small and consisting of one or two chambers, positioned on the top of pyramidal platforms in most ceremonial complexes, the priests censed the idols of the gods with thick clouds of copal smoke. Some idols were ritually presented with food offerings as well. These temple rooms were private, reserved for the use of the priests alone. They kept utensils, sacramental items and other precious commodities within the temples. Some temples had benches along the walls and elaborate murals or inscriptions. Others were quite plain.

During the great religious festivals, the priests conducted the services on the platforms before the temples or in designated plazas. Before these rites most priests had abstained from meat, salt or chilis in their meals, and all sexual activity.

Offerings brought to the temples by people of various levels of society included:

animals, living or dead	incense
beads	jade
beans	maize
birds	pendants
crops of the first harvest	shells
feathers	skins
fruits	tobacco
honey	tortillas

Dancing was performed during the rituals, and each sex had its own particular dances to revere the gods. Sometimes the dancers were masked; sometimes they performed in groups or alone.

If the rituals involved human sacrifices, as decreed by the particular demands of the gods, the high priest was assisted by four men called *Chacs*. They held the arms and legs of the victim to position the body for the rite. The *nacom* priest opened the victim's chest cavity and pulled out the still-beating heart. The heart was offered to the god, and the body was thrown down the stairway of the pyramidal platform. In the case of warrior victims, the body was cannibalized in ritual meals, which the priests sometimes shared. Most victims of sacrifices were prisoners taken in battle. Children were also sacrificed, generally bastards or orphans.

The Maya priests also practiced medicine throughout the region. Some illnesses were thought to be the work of evil spirits or the disfavor of the various deities. In some regions the people left food out in the open to placate the dwarf demons who were thought to lurk nearby in order to inflict illness upon the unsuspecting. The custom of leaving food offerings is still practiced in modern Yucatan regions.

The priests were skilled at recognizing certain symptoms and signs of illnesses, despite the superstitious or magical connotations associated with the practice of medicine by the common people. Treatments included dosing with medicinal herbs, mineral spirits and potions that might contain worms, animal excrement, urine, blood, crocodile testicles, bird fat and other offal. The priests diagnosed the physical condition and then conducted elaborate ceremonies employing fetishes, divination and other magical incantations, probably because the people demanded a visible display of power and concern. The priest-physicians were highly skilled in their art, reported to having remedies for ailments ranging from toothache to insanity. As the various codices, historical documents and inscriptions attest, the Maya priests were not superstitious vagrants but an educated class of people with skills and resources derived from centuries of practice. They were of the aristocratic castes and thus shared in the educational requirement of that class. As a result, the priests had a wide and far-reaching knowledge of the human condition as well as the more specialized aspects of temple ritual for their role in day-to-day ceremonies and observances.

MAYA QUIRIGUA A region extending beyond the Motagua Valley in the highland regions of Chiapas.

MAYA RELIGION The theological and cosmological system by which the Maya celebrated the role of humankind and the transformations that could take place within individuals and an entire civilization. As the high degree of Maya artistry and government demonstrates, this culture was elevated beyond the level of most Mesoamerican cultures in the Formative and Classical Periods (2000 B.C.–c. 250/290 A.D.; c. A.D. 1/250–900). The religion of the Maya was also unique in its cosmological views and its administration through the many ceremonial complexes in the region. The Maya shared in many of the Mesoamerican religious observances, including human sacrifice, but they also brought their own cultural patterns to their performance of these rites.

The basis of the Maya religion was its view of the creation of the world and humankind, as related in the *Popul Vuh* and in other documents that the priests and the elite maintained in their city institutions. The Maya cosmological view was concerned with worlds and creation. Maya gods were eternally seeking to fashion beings who were capable of reason, gratitude and the act of giving praise in thanksgiving. This approach is singular in that historical period. The Maya feared the elements that raged in their part of Mesoamerica, and while they attempted to placate the forces and powers over which they had no control, they attempted to explain creation intellectually at the same time.

The gods destroyed whole worlds when they discovered that the human beings they had created were mindless, soulless and lacking gratitude. Finally, in the world the Maya believed they inhabited, the gods accepted the human beings that they had created but blinded them slightly when they saw pride there. The Maya believed their world would end eventually, but they lived each day fully and tried to combine material existence with what they believed to be the realities of spiritual realms. They knew the earth was one of several layers of existence, a realm of 13 heavenly tiers and nine underworlds.

The presence of these various unseen levels led to the inevitable concept of duality in the world. The Maya religion took into account the constant conflict between good and evil, not only in the hearts of people but in the cosmos. To safeguard against such duality in human beings, each child of the Maya community was baptized at the age of three to 12. Before the ceremony, the child's parents were required to fast and to practice sexual abstinence. Priests came to purify the young candidate with incense and then gave him or her tobacco and holy water.

An important aspect of Maya religious devotions concerned the calendar system. The *Bolontiku,* the Nine Lords of the Night, who had fought and defeated the 13 Lords of Heaven, were among the patrons of the days of the Maya calendar. There were also 13 patrons of the 13 different *Katuns,* the periods of 20 years. Nineteen patrons of the 18 months and the supplementary epagonemal days of the Maya year were also invoked. There were also divine patrons of the numbers from 0 to 15.

In rituals, the need to make propitiation, to prove themselves creations worthy of the gods dominated. In each ceremonial complex the priests conducted rituals at the appointed times, deemed propitious by divination or according to standard calendar dates. In the early years the religious functions belonged to the elite caste, but in the Classic Period or perhaps later, priests were trained to mediate between the people and the gods. Maya feasts were preceded by long periods of fasting, sexual abstinence and that of other pleasures. The actual ceremonies included purifications, prayers and sacrifices. Human sacrifice was not as widespread in the early years but became paramount to the religious customs in the Classic Period. This form of sacrifice may have been a Mexica influence in the Maya territories.

Human sacrifices were generally conducted with prisoners of war, although children and women were offered as well on the altars of the gods. Painted blue and stripped of clothing, the victims were adorned with headdresses and brought to the temple ceremonies. Most execution sites were at the summits of the pyramidal platforms or in temple sanctuaries. The altars of sacrifice were heavy stones, sometimes inscribed and sometimes zoomorphic in design.

Four men, each called a *Chac,* also painted blue, held the victims' arms and legs so they were forced onto their backs. The *nacom* (the sacrificer) used a flint dagger to open the left half of the victim's breast, so that he could tear out the still beating heart to place it on a plate held by the *chilan* (priest). The blood of the heart was smeared on the god's idol. The body was then thrown to the bottom of the pyramid where its skin was removed, except for the hands and the feet. The *chilan* then dressed himself in the bloodied skin. Sometimes ritual cannibalism followed the sacrifice, especially if the victim was a popular warrior. The priests received the hands and feet as their share of the body.

Some victims were pierced with arrows, others drowned in the sacred *cenote* in each ceremonial complex. The best known of these was the *cenote* at Chichen Itza. Women were thrown into the deep, dark waters of the *cenote* at dawn. At noon the priests and populace returned, and all survivors were rescued to deliver messages received from the gods. If no one survived, the ceremony was considered a calamity.

New Year's celebrations were particularly magnificent in most Maya cities. People remained in seclusion for the last five days of the old year, perhaps out of reverence for the worlds that had been destroyed in the past. A day such as the first one of a new year could have monumental importance. The idol representing the New Year was then taken to a local residence, which had been decorated for the occasion. Then offerings were made to the god, amid dancing and acts of self-mutilation among the priests and guests. The blood splattered on tree-bark paper as a result of wounds to various parts of face or on the genitals was offered to the gods as well. Then dancing and rejoicing began as the ceremony became one of thanksgiving and hope for the coming months. Similar celebrations, on a lesser scale, were held at the start of each month.

Other New Year's festivities recorded among the Maya suggest the same dread of the last five days of the year, called *Uayeb* and considered days of ill omen. Special roads were constructed for the New Year's celebrations, and idols of various gods were placed at the cardinal points around each settlement. A particular direction was chosen each

Shield Jaguar

Each Maya carried an ancestral name but also was given his or her own name, which was celebrated at a special ceremony. At the age of 12 the young Maya was greeted by friends, relatives and guardians, as four priests held a rope at the cardinal points of the earth. The rope was then wrapped around the child and the parents. Priests offered maize and copal on small braziers, allowing the child to participate in the ceremony. The rope and the brazier were then entrusted to an assistant, who walked from the scene without looking back. This ritual cleansed the young Maya from all demons. Name-day patrons were considered special guardians, and a name day was celebrated for all newborns after a priest had cast a horoscope to assess the future. Part of the name-day celebrations for young Maya always included ritual cleansings and the touching of ritual bones.

Thus the procession of festivals, some grim and rife with superstition, and others simple days of rejoicing, were celebrated eternally through the Maya lands. People had different levels of understanding of the ceremonies, and commoners may not have known the cosmological dogma or the tenets of the Maya religion. They might have come only to witness and participate, proving to the gods that their new creations were capable of giving praise and of showing gratitude. These people did not enter the great temple or talk with the learned sages who understood the stars and the revolutions of time. The *ahmen* (sorcerers) were enough for the commoners. These men handled the amulets and potions, prayers and legends.

During the great festivals the people walked into the magnificent plazas of the ceremonial complexes, where the pyramids rose heavenward and the priests called the faithful to prayer. Dancers wound through the streets, garlanded, and perfumes and incense wafted. Musicians brightened such festivals, playing wooden drums, shells (beaten with stag antlers), trumpets, wooden five-hole flutes, whistles, large wooden trumpets, cattle bells and the musical bow.

Such festivals honored the gods and those who died in battle. Women perishing in childbirth and warriors were granted similar acclaim, as all were believed to go directly to their eternal rewards. Common dreads rampant in the wilderness of the agricultural settlements included demons laughing behind the bushes and the *Xtabai* (the spirits of beautiful young women) attempting to lure men from their souls. In the great ceremonial complexes, however, the Maya sang united, and the gods heard them and sent the sun to dance on one pyramid and then another. The Maya world was not doomed for many generations because the gods had created an intelligent, gracious and reverent civilization.

year, and many divinatory activities occurred, seeking word of the coming months and their abundance. Expiatory rites, including self-mutilation and the walking on hot coals, were practiced. Similar rites on a lesser scale were held for agricultural events, with ceremonies also provided for hunters, fishermen, beekeepers and others.

Specific types of self-mutilation were found among the Maya, especially among the aristocracy. Penis perforators were available to men, and women mutilated various parts of their bodies. The Maya also used halluciogenic drugs to enhance spiritual inspiration. Some priests and others of rank drank a brew called *balche,* which was made with fermented honey and the bark of the *balche* tree *(Lonchocarpus longistylus),* although another record indicates the addition of the *Bufo marinus,* a toad whose skin secreted a powerful drug. Enemas containing *balche* or similar narcotics were also used.

Caves were essential to the performance of certain religious practices. The caves were used especially during the Formative Period in the region of the Maya Mountains. Thought to be entrances to the underworld, the caves were sacred places. Some cave sites in the Maya regions have yielded remarkable carvings and artifacts.

Ancestors were venerated in Maya religion, but it is not known if they believed that their ancestors became gods. Teotihuacan, which exerted considerable influence during the Maya period of dominance, has been called the place where men become gods. The Maya may have believed their dead ancestors had attained some sort of mystical power in a resurrected state. The aristocratic groups, especially the rulers of the various ceremonial complexes, were buried there, and temples were erected over their vaulted tombs.

MAYA SOCIETY The levels of Maya citizenry associated in their mutual ascent to civilization, achieving cultural goals and, in time, enduring with one another periods of decline and peril. The Maya lands, extensive in Mesoamerica, were not governed by a single dynasty but by aristocratic families who ruled the various ceremonial complexes. These complexes, prestigious because of their political power, were also pilgrimage sites for the surrounding regions and trade centers. The various aristocratic families amassed resources and labor forces and committed themselves and their people to magnificent public projects. The ceremonial complexes reflected not only the dominant theme of religion in the life of the various regions but the ambitions and visions of the ruling families as well. The Maya families engaged in such activities included ancient royal lines and newcomers to the region (such as the Xiu clan around Mani). (See also MAYA GROUPS.)

The ruler of each city or the head of each aristocratic clan was called the *halac uinic,* the "true man" representing all in the clan or city. In some regions similar titles were bestowed upon the rulers. He controlled entire districts or provinces, even those cities or villages that were autonomous. Control was not necessarily military. Many smaller communities became vassals or allies of the larger ceremonial complexes to benefit from trade and to have military protection. The ruler was not only head of the political and military arm of his region but, in the early days of Maya history, functioned as sole mediator between his people and the gods. The rank was entirely hereditary in each Maya region, passing to a younger brother or to a son when the ruler died. If a *halac uinic* died without an heir, a council of Maya met to select a new one from appropriate noble candidates.

The ruler came from the Maya aristocracy, and several titles and ranks appear in the Maya records, including: *Ah holpop,* the head of the most prominent regional family, who generally served as the *batab* (ruler of a particular city); *Ah pop,* a ranking ruler in the Quiche territories, assisted by an *ah pop q'am haa; Almehen,* male nobles with recognized aristocratic descent in both the male and female lines of their families; *Ch'ibal,* an aristocrat, usually belonging to the hereditary family that administered cities or served as commanders of the Maya armies. Members of the elite served the various rulers, who could not administer the vast territories and populations without their assistance. These nobles sometimes lived in the palaces of the ceremonial complexes or in large residences within certain districts. They wore elaborate garb, dined lavishly and were allowed to drink chocolate, made from cacao beans. They also visited other aristocratic families in other cities, celebrating feasts, birthdays, accessions to the throne or the burial of one of their own rank. In this manner, the aristocrats of the Maya realm were connected, linked often by marriages, alliances, trade agreements, pacts and the enjoyment of one another's company.

Most lands were owned in common by aristocrats. Women held property rights from their mothers and could pass on such estates. The bulk of the lands, however, were held by men. Each newborn in the elite caste was given the name of the mother, father and the *naal,* the house name. Noble young men lived in dormitories, where they were educated to hold the positions fitting their ranks. The elite young women were trained at home. Most young noblemen became officials in the local government or took up the family interest in trade. The lesser ranked might also turn their hand to farming their regional estates.

Ranked below the nobles and aristocrats in each ceremonial complex were the commoners, who made up the bulk of the population. The common class was rather sharply delineated, with craftsmen, small merchants or traders and artisans holding the highest rank and privilege. Many ceremonial complexes had workshops for the various craftsmen of the region, signs of the importance of such artisans. Trade often brought raw materials into these cities so that the small armies of craftsmen and artists could manufacture products that in time became renowned as hallmarks of the region or the particular Maya cultural tradition.

Traders who were commoners were answerable to their aristocratic administrators and led caravans into the far-flung regions in order to maintain the steady flow of wares. Distribution and quotas were generally in the hands of the elite, but the common merchants fared well under the system.

Below the rank of artisans and traders were the farmers, the true commoners of the Maya realm. Those who worked fields belonging to their particular clan or to an elite family who had used their services for generations were the highest-ranking farmers. Most of these families lived in small enclaves close to their fields. Such communities have been discovered, with rather prosperous clusters of homes around courtyards. The farmers did not take part in the political aspects of Maya life. They did, however, enter the ceremonial cities to participate in the feasts conducted there, and some made pilgrimages to shrines and complexes. While the elite practiced a more intellectual religion, the farmers believed more in magic and superstition and held to the custom of keeping evils at bay that still permeates much of the rural parts of the region.

These people usually conducted their lives in an orderly fashion, marrying and keeping their families together in good times and bad. They paid tribute to the local leaders, who in turn had to send a portion to the elite. They served in the military forces when needed, and they paid homage to the gods. Their lives, however, were bound to the fields and in the rotation of the seasons in the Maya world.

Common laborers lived in the cities or in the clusters of land around the ceremonial complexes, and they were on the same social level as the farmers. Many of these laborers worked on public projects, as the ceremonial complexes continued to expand their precincts and older structures had to be renovated constantly. The death of a ruler, for example, meant the construction of a vaulted tomb and then a pyramidal platform and temple to pay eternal homage to the deceased.

Below the laborers and the common farmers were the *uinicab,* the "lower men," the peasant farmers who worked on the vast estates of the elite. These were genuinely in the bonds of the feudal system that dominated in Maya lands, but they do not appear to have been exploited ruthlessly over long periods. They worked the lands, sent their harvests to their lords and lived as best they could. Some had small gardens beside their huts so that they could raise a few meager crops for themselves, and their women were industrious and frugal.

Below these peasants were the slaves, called the *ppentacoab.* Slaves were usually captured during wars or military raids on neighboring peoples. Some become temple servants, others went to the great aristocratic estates or served as domestics, and others were chosen as victims for the sacrificial rites in the ceremonial temples. Slaves were bound for life, and that condition was also a penalty for major crimes in the Maya judicial system.

MAYA TRADE The system of marketing and distribution of goods throughout the vast Maya realm. The respected Maya trader, called the *ah ppolom yac*, or simply a *ppolom*, was an integral force in the economic life of that civilization. A member of the elite castes in various Maya regions, these merchants, often accompanied by lesser-ranked commoners in their service, traveled across the vast Maya territories on foot, on litters or in sturdy canoes. Wearing elaborate headdresses that identified their rank, carrying the fan insignia common to the traders and accompanied by a small retinue, the traders went about with their staves of office. One such *ppolom* was immortalized on the Ratinlixul vase now in the Philadelphia Museum.

Maya traders provided the various regions with economic stability and power, utilizing the ceremonial complexes and the routes that had been explored by their ancestors in the dawn of Maya civilization. Their markets were both interior and exterior and were available for the distribution of raw products, domestic and from other regions' wares. Unlike the later Aztec *pochteca*, Maya traders were not concerned with intelligence reconnaissance or motivated by political aims. The goals of these traders were profit and the opening of new markets in far-flung lands.

Maya traders utilized the products of diverse geographic and climatic conditions in their territories and in the neighboring regions. These merchants also took advantage of the location of the various ceremonial complexes by cultivating the local artists, entering into alliances with the ruling families and providing the industry with raw products that could be transformed into trading items of worth.

The great cities, such as Tikal, Palenque, Mayapan and Cozumel, were linked by internal trade, and each sent its own caravans into the regions of other cities. These cities combined religious festivals with open markets, a custom still carried on today.

Changes eventually taking place in the Maya world altered trade, but the merchants shifted the emphasis and the flow of goods to accommodate the rise and fall of the various ceremonial complexes and regions. The rise of Putun and the organization of the trade in Cozumel, for example, put into place the mechanisms for seafaring expeditions, which revitalized trading ventures. Flexibility was the key to success, and as a group the Maya weathered political disasters, natural catastrophes and unrest to conduct business as usual.

The fact that these few elite traders could provide such an abundance of wares, some exotic and costly, others of a utilitarian nature, for so many people resulted in their acquisition of true power, a situation that remained stable as trade prospered. The caste of the *ppolom* gained ascendancy in the elite ranks over the years as the merchants acquired more and more raw resources and established connections with the markets of other cultures. Such foreign intervention held no peril for them as they absorbed the various traditions of other lands and imported their products freely.

Trade had another purpose as well. In the hands of the elite, the disbursement of goods and the subsequent wealth that resulted provided the various ceremonial complexes with necessary financial foundations to allow them to develop into the magnificent metropolises that arose throughout the Maya landscape. The vast bureaucracies of these ceremonial complexes and the military and religious units had to be endowed and supported by the noble castes. Kings and their counsels had to be able to avail themselves of laborers and resources for building temples, pyramidal platforms and public meeting places. The ceremonial complexes were actually the result of the flourishing trade conducted by the Maya, which, in turn, they helped maintain in a stable manner.

The diversity of the Maya territories offered a large variety of products and allowed each region a specific role in the manufacture of goods to be traded locally or internationally. The highland and lowland communities, for example, exchanged specific goods. From the highlands came albite, jade, obsidian, pottery, and Quetzal feathers. In return the lowlands supplied cacao, ceramics, cotton, flints, and obsidian.

Some products originated as raw material in one region and were manufactured into prized commodities in another. Jade, for example, was brought from the highlands to the lowlands, where it was carved and transformed into the exquisite items so cherished by the elite of other cultures. In some cases, cinnabar was added to the jade as ornamentation. Copper and gold did not originate in the Maya regions in the early periods, coming into use around A.D. 900, when the traders imported the metals from the central highlands and from Colombia, Panama and Costa Rica. Cotton was a major crop of the Peten (Putun) region, and the Yucatan specialized in manufacturing cotton cloth. Tobacco grew in the lowlands, as did vanilla, the rubber plant and honey. Lizards, used for food and medicine, were exported to the highlands as well.

The major items of trade were salt, obsidian, pottery and agricultural products. Salt was especially vital, and the Maya had access to it and the means of extracting it and delivering it to other regions. The largest beds were found in the coasts of northern Yucatan, and on the Pacific coast. Hundreds of laborers were required each day for the extraction and the processing of salt as a market commodity. Salt was not prized in the Maya but prized elsewhere. The Maya traders understood the basic need for salt and salt as a commodity provided a stable base for the expansion of trade. There is even some evidence that the collapse of the salt trade, when the southern ceremonial complexes were destroyed, brought about or contributed to the demise of the Classic Maya.

Obsidian (volcanic glass) was a highlands resource, although some was exported from the lowlands as well. There were major sources of the product in Maya lands. The merchants carried obsidian along the valleys of the Negro and Posides rivers. Still others followed the Motagua, Belize, Hondo and Sarstoon rivers with their obsidian wares. Seagoing vessels also traded in obsidian. The entire Maya region had an ample supply as a result, and the product became a stable source of wealth when offered to other cultures.

Plumbate pottery, the third vital trade item, moved on the exchange routes from the southern lowlands to the north along the Chiapas plateaus and then down the Grijalva River. Pottery also was distributed to regional ceremonial complexes. The city of Tikal was a major distributor of this and other ceramic wares.

Tikal warrior

The last major commodity in Maya trade was an agricultural product, maize. The grain was grown in the lowlands, traded locally and then moved to the highlands. Maize could not be grown well in the highlands. The lowlands also harvested maize earlier in the year than the highlands, and lowland farmers often planted and reaped two crops. Cacao was another agricultural crop of value to Maya traders. The beans of the cacao plant served as currency, and Maya trade devolved on cacao products and to the value associated with the beans throughout the Mesoamerican region. Cacao was cultivated in Tabasco, in the Belize River region and in parts of El Salvador.

The local trade and the regulated exchange systems developed over the decades provided a stable economic base for the early Maya, but it was the long-distance routes that ensured the Maya's real and enduring means to wealth and power. These long-distance trade routes came into play during the Classic Period (c. A.D. 1/250–900) when the ceremonial complexes located in the Maya lowlands and the elite traders dominated Maya affairs. By that time, the traders had become a highly respected hereditary class with specific duties and rights and with an active role in Maya government and economy.

Each *ppolom* was born into a family registered in the Maya noble class, and so supported continuance of the policies of this class. These policies have been listed as theocratic for much of the Classic Period and more secular-

ized in the Post Classic. The merchants conducted their affairs in line with the established procedures concerning local, regional and long-distance trade.

Local Trade. This included methods for the distribution of wares within a specific area, such as lowland cities or outlying agricultural settlements. The local ceremonial complexes provided the necessary products, and trade required little organization in terms of distribution. Some trade at this level may have utilized the tribute system among the small communities that were obliged to offer a percentage of their harvests and products to the local aristocracy. Simple market processes may have been the foundation for such local marketing, which, in turn, furthered the position of the ceremonial complexes in domestic economic affairs because of their geographic position and power.

Regional Trade. This included the cultivation of both highland and lowland markets, through which the trade goods could be funneled. The *ppolom* led a caravan along the many land and water routes; upon arriving at his destination, he exchanged his goods for those available there. No doubt the ceremonial complexes played important roles at each end of the trade routes. Canoes laden with granite, salt, flints, obsidian and other products plied the Belize River and other waterways. Throughout the Maya realm there were always willing customers to welcome the *ppolom* and his wares.

Long-Distance Trade. This was most vital to the broader economic development of the Maya. The early trader elite caste was associated with the Teotihuacan Empire and with Kaminaljuyu. Both cities offered unparalleled opportunities for growth because they had developed elaborate trading alliances and processes themselves. Obsidian, pottery, salt and a long list of basic items came by land and by sea into the great valleys of Mexico, allowing the Maya an economic base for their emerging civilization. This early trade was instrumental in elevating the lowland Classic Maya to the rank of the culturally developed Mesoamerican.

When Teotihuacan collapsed, however, the sudden vacuum affected Maya long-distance trading opportunities. Perhaps to limit their losses, the Maya tightened their control over trade. As a result, the ceremonial complexes began to compete with one another. The second result of the collapse of Teotihuacan was that the Maya no longer had to pay any tribute to participate in the trade of that empire. The Maya elite began to pocket the earnings instead, diverting them to more pressing causes.

Some scholars consider the eruption of the Ilopango volcano in El Salvador another peril to Maya trade, as the disaster rendered acres of land unhabitable for almost two centuries and sent hordes of survivors into distant places. Whether this had a direct impact or not, the Maya survived, just as they managed to adapt after the fall of Teotihuacan. New markets were cultivated to handle surpluses, and the Maya established firm trade relationships with El Tajin, Cholula and Xochicalco.

Overall, however, the fall of Teotihuacan brought about a certain period of indecision and inactivity. This hiatus ended with the rise of Tula (Tollan) and the Toltec. The very competition that flourished between the ceremonial complexes began to drain their resources. The great cities at the heart of distribution of trade wares found it increasingly difficult to support the local exchanges, and no bureaucracy existed to deal with the new problems, as those formerly in command were now isolated and diminished its ranks.

Regionally there was still vigorous trade with the highlands, but the long-standing trade routes began to break apart. As populations faced hardship in obtaining items, the routes became longer. Intensive agricultural efforts to provide exports had led to soil erosion and eventually to soil exhaustion.

Such a decline did not happen overnight in the Maya realm, and in some instances commoners in the cities attempted to rectify the situation, prolonging the existence of the various ceremonial complexes. The pattern of disaster was present, however, and the cultures surrounding the Maya were more than willing to advance their own causes at the expense of this once-proud civilization.

Non-Maya groups from the west entered the southwestern lowlands or brought pressure to bear there. Trade and the agricultural ventures were badly disrupted as a result. The loss of trade was one of the symptoms of the Maya collapse, and losses in both long-distance and local and regional trade hastened the decline. The shift in Maya power was then inevitable.

The Maya Post-Classic era was a time of remarkable change. The collapse left vacuums where power and social status had existed, but it also provided some within the Maya domain with tremendous opportunities for trade. New markets were available in the west as the city of Tula began its rise, and in the lowlands the once uniquely Maya culture lost much of its character when it confronted the Toltec-Mexica invasions.

The merchants of Tula began to imitate Teotihuacan and developed their own extensive trade. The Chichen Itza people were also in the region. The Chontal Maya in Chichen Itza at first, then grouped at Seibal and in the highlands. By A.D. 987, after a second migration, Chichen Itza assumed preeminence over all of the Yucatan.

The Chontal Maya of the Peten region (the area in Tabasco near the Usumacinta and Candelaria river systems) began to work in earnest in the region. As they had a water-based way of life and lived near most of the western trade routes, they used these routes to their own advantage. The Chontal avoided many of the tragic results of the general Maya collapse and brought a new energy to trade.

In time the Chontal became the finest merchants in the Maya world, single-handedly overseeing or personally conducting trade from Peten to the highlands, to Yucatan, around the peninsula to Quintana Roo, and by boat to Belize and Honduras. They were powerful traders and great seafarers, in time earning the respect of the Aztec. The Aztec called their region Acalan (or Acallan), the "land of the canoes."

The Chontal had the advantage of recognizing what products once considered necessary by the various regions of Mesoamerica were still in demand. Salt, obsidian, cotton and cacao were very much needed everywhere. The Putun people thus moved into the arena of trade, pushing their

canoes through the waters to deliver goods faster and more efficiently than anyone else. Also, the Chontal were the first to introduce true mass-produced pottery, which enabled them to broaden their market. They also supplied slaves to the newly created elite groups of the Yucatan regions, helping them to increase their own prestige, even as they remained vassals of a sort to Chichen Itza.

Cozumel became a valuable site for the Chontal, beginning as a necessary stopover point for traders going around the peninsula. The city offered the traders a protected site in which to store their goods. It was also ideally situated as a port of trade, and its rulers recognized the changes taking place in their world including the impact of the Mexica. In time Cozumel became the heart of the trading enclaves, offering assistance to all who worked to represent their own economic powers in a wider and more complex trade system.

The Chontal also controlled the limestone platforms that were as large as 17 acres at the site of Buena Vista. The site became a storage facility maintained to provide stability for the marketing of goods. Such a facility held prices firm and served as a basis for expansion and continuing growth. Inland platforms were also used, as evidenced by the remaining examples at the temple of the goddess Ixchel at Cozumel.

Chontal canoes, loaded with their wares, set sail up the coasts, stopping along the way to send off goods by land routes in the Yucatan to Chichen Itza and to Mayapan. Cozumel awaited these traders, holding seasonal supplies of salt and cacao that were then distributed. Merchants traveled down into Belize and the Gulf of Honduras, where the long-established Maya connections with the highlands and the cacao-rich region of Motagua were maintained.

Several factors are worth noting. The trade conducted in this period was much broader and far more complex than anything attempted by the Maya in previous eras. The Chontal, needing to travel farther, encouraged trade that was totally international. More important, and this is a reflection on what has been termed their "pragmatic mercantilism," the Chontal, unlike previous generations, were adjusting to changes and were flexible and more adaptive than anyone before them. Sea routes were added to their trade methods but the old land routes were not abandoned.

This flexibility can be seen in the long-distance trade the Chontal conducted with the Toltec and then with the Aztec of Tenochtitlan. As at Tikal, tremendous power was won through association, but the Chontal were capable of adapting to the inevitable decline of Tula's economic dominance in the 1200s. Such a collapse changed the political map of the region. The Chontal did not allow trade to be disrupted. Instead, they advanced simple solutions.

It is believed that the city of Mayapan was constructed to take the place of the fallen Tula and Chichen Itza. Mayapan is a smaller version of Chichen Itza. Its founders appear to have originated in Cozumel. Thus they would have been involved in the trade and would have been prompted to build a city capable of assuming the responsibilities for active trade.

Mayapan throve, and Chontal trade flourished. The trade networks remained in existence well into the Aztec era, when the new masters from Tenochtitlan arrived in the Valley of Mexico. It was actually through the *pochteca,* the unique Aztec traders, that the Chontal achieved even greater power. The largest city for trade became Xicalango, where the *pochtecas* dominated a large part of the city. Because of its size and location, Xicalango remained free of Aztec imperial ambitions.

The Aztec had little reason to conquer the Putun because the situation there allowed for mutual dependence and trust. Cozumel and Xicalango thus supported a blend of cultures in matters of trade. Alliances were forged between the remaining ceremonial sites and their elites, and religious pilgrimages to the temple of Ixchel at Cozumel helped to maintain a steady flow of buyers.

This pattern of Maya trade, the last of its kind, was well in place when the Spanish arrived, having proven itself crucial to the Aztec long-distance economic endeavors. The Chontal controlled vast, mutually supportive trading endeavors that were independent and yet participated in the wider economic world that existed at the time.

MAYA WARFARE   Tactics and campaigns devised in order to subjugate entire regions. It was once believed that the Maya were so highly developed culturally and intellectually that they existed in a peaceful world in which a military structure was not necessary. It was thought that the Maya used their cultural achievements as the bonds with which they united their vast territories to found a civilization rich in artistic ideals without the need for violence or war. It was also believed that during the Classic Period in Mesoamerica, there was only peace and a gentle flowering of the arts.

Yet nowadays some researchers claim that the Maya were obsessed with war throughout their history and well acquainted with the military arts. The walled cities and the defenses incorporated into the design of some ceremonial complexes are evidence of this militarism, as is the presence of the elite groups who served as war chiefs.

The Maya did understand military tactics and warfare throughout their long history, and many instances give evidence of the use of force in certain regions. The cities were built with defensives, especially during the Formative and Post-Classic periods. Such knowledge and such architectural and construction techniques would have been imperative for Mayan survival.

Whether they were obsessed with war, however, cannot be answered without understanding the role of the elite in each period. Certainly the elite of the Post-Classic Period, especially in the regions around Mayapan, Uxmal and Mani, cannot be tied to the elite groups that had built the Maya civilization. The groups differed in their purposes, their resources and in the criteria for which they functioned.

Maya warriors always accompanied exploratory treks into new regions. No group of people could march across vast regions without attracting some enemies or defenders of homelands. The pattern of migration from a proto-Maya community would make such encounters inevitable.

As the Maya moved into regions and began their transformation of settlements into vast ceremonial complexes of architectural and artistic achievement, a certain vigorous militarism would have been necessary to determine borders,

safeguard resources and develop and retain the trade routes vital to their economic stability. The elite groups that provided each ceremonial complex and those around it with military prowess began in these early Formative period.

The origins of Maya civilization began in a time when vast regions were the scene of restless migrations, encounters and trials with cultural development and evolution. Geographic and climatic diversities also had to be contended with, some of which brought about disasters and natural forces that challenged Maya sense of purpose and stamina. In such time, military units would have been required to maintain order and to discourage inroads made by survivors from other regions.

Once the Maya territories had been claimed and the vast public building projects were under way, the Maya would have been forced to protect their domains militarily. Defensive structures were incorporated into the designs of the ceremonial complexes erected during the Formative Period, and even in the Classic Period.

Some ceremonial complexes, for example, employed natural rock formations, ravines, hilltops and gorges as part of their defenses. In Becan and other sites, the ceremonial complexes were surrounded by actual moats, which a few warriors could defend easily. Others had palisades, gateways or earthworks guaranteed to slow an enemy advance. Even the Spanish, who arrived late in terms of Maya civilization, commented on the defenses they saw in Maya cities. These defenses were vital in Maya frontiers, exposed to the raids of the foreign groups beyond their sphere of influence. In some instances, such as at Palenque, signal systems were devised for the defenses. This would imply the presence of a highly developed militia, trained to come to the defense of a site immediately. Such a force would have to be mobilized quickly and capable of fending off attacks until reinforcements arrived.

The ceremonial complexes in the Maya realm were not only the heart of religious and secular affairs of the entire region but important to Maya trade as well. As such they had to be safeguarded, and the cities' aristocrats had to perform various duties concerning defense as well as administration. Rulers of the ceremonial complexes had their own palace guards, capable of protecting them in times of crisis.

During the Classic Period, the ceremonial complexes were erected in the open, without elaborate defenses, although a number of them were clearly built with the threat of potential hostilities in mind. Most cities had walls, however, if not on their perimeters then within the various districts, and most ceremonial complexes could be defended. Toward the end of the Classic Period, however, the complexes underwent notable design changes. Some scholars think these changes reflect the presence of the Mexica in Maya lands; others relate them to the fall of Teotihuacan and to the relentless abandonment of ceremonial sites. Practices of Maya elite caused the sites to decline even further. When aristocrats moved to safer areas, their original support suffered, for they had no administrators. (Nobles had functioned in that capacity for generations.) While the older aristocratic dynasties faded or fled, a new elite emerging in the Yucatan and elsewhere were a different breed entirely, arising from the needs of the Putun traders and pragmatic in their purposes and policies.

The Xiu and the Cocom clans are two examples of this new breed. These elite families feuded until the bloody deaths of their own rulers. Others in the region were involved in similar confrontations and wars and they began to abandon the old methods of creative unity in search of the only answer available, military aggressiveness. Disputes over boundaries took place because of the expansion policies of these new elite. The clans could merely have been ambitious for land and resources or could have adopted a militant stance merely to strengthen their hold on the local populace. Some may have looked to the city of Teotihuacan in its glory and wished to emulate that vast empire by attaching more and more communities to their own sphere of dominance.

Open competitions also arose between the ceremonial complexes for markets and for specific regional resources. The salt beds, for example, were constantly under dispute. The need for slaves also prompted raids and incursions into certain regions. The need for sacrificial victims was a traditional aspect of religion in the Maya domain, and it did not lessen in later eras. Victims had to be brought into the city in order for the priests to perform the rituals of expiation and reverence.

With the changes that took place in the Post-Classic Period, the Maya cities took up militarism with a fervor, relying on the customs of the past and implementing them with new vigor. The Mexica influences, especially in the Yucatan, brought about a need to improve Maya defenses. The new elite and the more experienced aristocrats who had survived recognized the perils. They not only enlarged their armies but in some cases, as with the Cocom, hired Mexica mercenaries as well. The effort was futile in some respects, as the ceremonial complexes were confronting forces that they could not defeat but only hold at bay for a time. By the mid-fifteenth century, the Yucatan was divided into separate provinces, with petty chiefs and armies at the ready for combat. Young men were conscripted into military service across the Maya territories. Raids were conducted as part of family rivalries, and settlements were torched to avenge ancient wrongs. The same disastrous events were repeated in the Guatemala highlands. The end result was the decline of the Maya, who could no longer stand against the invading Spanish and their allies. The visions of the past and the unity through alliances, intermarriages and visits had collapsed.

Maya military tactics, which served them well in their Formative periods and then evolved into fighting forces that tore the realm apart, were much like those of the modern Swiss. The ceremonial complexes and large cities had militias, men who came into action when an alarm was given. They fought and were paid for the duration of the battles, and then they returned to their fields or to their crafts. Such units were under the direction of an elite *nacom* (a war chief) or a series of *nacoms* if the region was large. This *nacom* served for three years. Most military leaders inherited their rank and the powers, and most were trained for military service from infancy.

Probably one or more core units stood guard in the ceremonial complexes and conducted raids as punishment or to take sacrificial victims. The Maya of each region needed skilled veterans to train militia recruits in times of peace and then lead small individual units in battles.

Such battles were spectacular events, preceded by vast parades. The *nacom*, attired in padded cotton armor, with leg and arm guards, an elaborate headdress, a mantle and appropriate insignias, led the troops to the battleground. The idols of the ceremonial complexes were also carried to the scene, flanked by special guard units. Behind them came musicians who played drums, shell trumpets and whistles and gave war cries to alarm the enemy before they ever laid eyes on them.

The *halcan*, the foot-soldiers, wore tight-fitting cuirasses of quilted cotton and carried spears, flint darts, bows and arrows and shields (round or square and covered with hide). They fought willingly and usually to the death, because in the Maya tradition being taken prisoner was worse than dying. The murals of Bonampak amply demonstrate the fate awaiting such prisoners. The Mexica brought newer tactics and ferocity. Battles raged between the ceremonial complexes, and then they were silent.

MAYO RIVER   A waterway in the Pacific coastal region. The river formed delta and flood plains.

MAZAHUA   A group domainted by the TEPANEC in the Late Classic Period (A.D. 600–900) and residing in northern Mexico near the Valley of Toluca. Called Those who Have Deer, the Mazahua were eventually assimilated by other surrounding cultures.

MAZAPA PHASE   Also called Mazapan, a cultural development that ran parallel to the Corral Phase in Tula and the Coyotelco Phase in other areas in the Late Classic Period,

Mayapan-Xolapan ceramic

A.D. 600–900. Bowls and dishes having straight and wavy lines were manufactured during this phase, as well as tripods with heavy legs, decorated with blotches of red. Molded spindle whorls emerged at this time, as well as flat figurines and large Tlaloc braziers.

MAZATL   The deer, a day sign used by the Aztec in the *tonalpohualli,* their calendrical system.

MEMORIA BREVE DE CHIMALPOHIN   A Toltec historical document recounting the first years of that civilization in the Valley of Mexico. In some accounts it is listed as the *Codex Chimalpopoca.*

MEMORIAL DE SOLALA   See *ANNALS OF THE CAKCHIQUELS.*

MEMORIAL DE TECPAN-ATITLAN   See *ANNALS OF THE CAKCHIQUELS.*

MERCADORES   The Spanish name for the markers used in Mesoamerican ball courts. These were either painted or represented by stone disks. In some ceremonial complexes and cities, the *mercadores* took the form of *hachas,* carved stone heads.

MERIDA (1)   A region in the Yucatan Peninsula that borders on Campeche, separated by the Sierra de Ticul.

MERIDA (2)   A capital city in the Yucatan Peninsula, erected by the Spanish on the ruins of a Maya ceremonial center called Tihoo. The remains of the original structures on the site include a palace that strongly resembles the Nunnery Quadrangle at Uxmal.

MESA CENTRAL   See MESOAMERICAN GEOGRAPHY.

MESA DE GUAJE PHASE   A cultural development associated with the southwestern Sierra Madre region, called the HUAXTECA area. At the time Huaxtec diets consisted of as much as 40 percent domesticated crops. The Mesa de Guaje Phase dates to the Early Formative Period, c. 2000/1600 to 900 B.C. In some records this phase is also associated with the Tamaulipas Sequence in the Incipient Agricultural Period (7000–c. 2000/2500 B.C.) and perhaps earlier.

Valley of Mexico stamp design

MESA DEL NORTE   See MESOAMERICAN GEOGRAPHY.

MESETA CENTRAL   See MESOAMERICAN GEOGRAPHY CHIAPAS HIGHLANDS.

MESOAMERICA   A term introduced a few decades ago to describe Mexican regions along with those of the neighboring states of Central America that had achieved distinctive heights of civilization by the time the Spanish arrived in the New World. This region has a history of advanced cities, cultures and artistic and architectural splendors as its unique civilizations brought their own religious and social aspirations to the geographically diverse landscape.

The region of Mesoamerica was formed by gradual and sometimes violent upheavals, mirroring the development of peoples over the centuries amid a changing geological scene. The borders between such groups were never static for long, as the cultures had impact upon one another and upon subsequent generations in the region. Mesoamerica thus remained a fluid, turbulent stage upon which remarkable human beings marched toward their own goals. The history of Mesoamerica has been documented and divided into the following periods.

Paleo-Indian Period: 11,000–7000 B.C.

Incipient Agriculture Period: 7000–c. 2000/2500 B.C.

Formative Period

    Early: c. 2000/1600–900 B.C.

    Middle: 900–300 B.C.

    Late: 300 B.C.–c. A.D. 250/290

Classic Period

    Early: c. A.D. 1/250–600

    Late: c. A.D. 600–900

Post-Classic Period

Early: A.D. 900–1200/1250

Late: A.D. 1200/1250–1521

Each historical period reflects specific developments, both culturally and socially among the groups. Documentation from the sites involved in these historical eras provide portraits of the people and the land at various times.

Paleo-Indian Period (11,000–7000 B.C.)

Some call the Paleo-Indian Period, the time of human beings' entrance into the Mesoamerican region. The Mesoamericans, like their northern and southern counterparts, no doubt entered the American continent from northeastern Asia, crossing at the Bering Strait, the modern accepted gateway into the New World. Finds in other parts of the continent give evidence of very early prehistoric habitation, but in Mesoamerica the first documented finds place human beings in the region by approximately 11,000 B.C. By 10,000 B.C., nomadic groups were technically advanced, particularly in the manufacture of weapons and tools. As in other territories of the Americas, these groups traveled the vast natural highways and probably were composed of two types of social units: microbands, or units composed of a single family or perhaps two related families; and macrobands, units composed of many families, united for seasonal hunting and gathering.

Macrobands grouped when prey animals herded together or when vegetation was concentrated enough to support large gatherings. Single families merged with neighbors to camp together, to conduct interfamily marriages, to exchange information about local resources and to learn new methods of securing a living. The people also exchanged techniques for making tools and weapons during these gatherings. The social aspects of such seasonal events provided confederations and strength. When the herds dispersed and the local resources dwindled, the macrobands broke apart, and the single families returned to their own lands to take up their hunting and gathering routines. These groups were coming under pressure cause of climatic changes and by the failing numbers of the megafauna—mastodons and mammoths. Much has been written about the mammoth-hunting processes, and there are many views concerning this activity. While the various groups probably hunted the megafauna in their region, but they did so infrequently. Gathering and the hunting of smaller game were surer methods of maintaining food supplies. The finds at Tepexpan, Iztapan and elsewhere indicate that some mammoth-hunting did occur there.

The first human beings entering Mesoamerica would have followed the north-south corridors of northern Mexico, coming upon vast tracts of untouched lands in their wanderings: valleys and basins, soaring crests that offered caves, lakes, rivers and plains filled with grasses, vegetation and game. Mammals, fruits, cacti, grains, wild fowl, fish, marine products and dogs served as food sources. Domesticated canines were probably used in hunting, but some varieties were raised for eating. Due to hunting and environmental changes, in time the mammoths, mastodons, camelids and horses and a special species of bison faded from the scene.

With the passing of such large game, the early Mesoamericans became more and more dependent on the vegetation in their areas. In the process, the people began to develop a genuine knowledge of such plants and grasses. This intimate knowledge led to the mastery over the patterns of vegetation growth and development. Thus the stage was set for the more permanent settlements that soon developed in the region. Evidence of nomadic migrations with temporary settlements and the slow but continuing focus on vegetation and small prey have been documented in the Tamaulipas Valley, the Tehuacan Valley, the northern frontier, the Sinaloa River in northwestern Mexico, the Sierra Madre Occidental, the Bajio plateau, the banks of the Tamuin River, the banks of the Tamesi River and the beaches and inlets of the Gulf coasts.

The Mesoamericans of the Paleolithic Period lived in various types of shelters, all seasonally and climatically oriented. Caves and grottoes were some of the earliest sites of human habitation in the region. These have yielded evidence of food preparation, fires and residential debris. Tehuacan and Tamaulipas were home to macrobands of Mesoamericans during this era. Elsewhere Mesoamericans erected shrub barriers or possibly used pelt tents.

The first settlers of the region practiced specific burial traditions that indicate a belief in an afterlife, coupled with some social stratification and honors paid to certain individuals. The bodies deposited in the grave sites of the Paleolithic Period were buried in a flexed position, possibly as a precautionary method of burial to insure that the body remained in the grave or to imitate pre-birth attitudes. Gifts for the deceased or for supernatural forces involved with death were provided. Painted symbols, magical spells and chants were undoubtedly intended to keep the body immobile and impotent. The grave offerings were scant, indicating the absence of elaborate specialized industries, but the mortuary traditions in all cultures including the chants and services, were very much evident in written materials and in reliefs.

At an early stage of their development, the early Mesoamericans also began to deify the forces of nature and the elements, probably because of the impact of geological and climatic forces on society. The complex religious and cosmological systems of the great Mesoamerican cultures can be traced to this historical period, although few archaeological discoveries have provided evidence for this.

Paleolithic tools and weapons, which were evolving in this period, demonstrate the early Mesoamericans' attempts to meet environmental challenges. Such tools and weapons allowed the macrobands and their growing populations to sustain themselves. These tools and weapons included: projectile points, spears and darts (both the Clovis and Folsom, with Lanceolate and Lerma flints), blades, stone scrapers, bones, awls and javelins.

The following sites are considered belonging to the Paleolithic Period. (See discussions under individual entries.)

Ajuereado Complex	Puerto Marquez
Chalco	Repelo
Comitan	Santa Marta Cave
Cotorra	San Vicente Chicoloapan
Coxcatlan Cave	Sierra de Tamaulipas
Diablo Complex	Tepexpan
Islona de Chantuto	Tequixquiac
Iztapan, Santa Isabel	Upper Becerra Formation
La Perra	Valsequillo
Lerma	Yanhuitlan
Nogales	

Incipient Agriculture Period (7000–c. 2000/2500 B.C.)

The title of this historical period refers to the fact that at this time domestic food plants played a minor but increasingly significant role in the diets of nomadic hunters and gatherers. Gradually, as the people learned to raise other plants and to select certain strains for mutation and hybrid forms of the crops, the proportion of domestic food plants as part of the diet increased. Such advances took place from 6000 to 1500 B.C. in various region of Mesoamerica; for which considerable documentation is available.

Before 7000 B.C., the megafauna—vast herds of mammoths, mastodons, camelids and a form of bison—roamed the territory. The warming trend took place when the glaciers in the north withdrew c. 7000 B.C., or earlier, altered the fauna available. As a result, humans began to emphasize the hunt for smaller game and wider gathering of plants.

Selected plants, discovered in their wild forms, were domesticated in various locations; in Mesoamerica there were many microenvironments with specialized vegetation adapted to specific geographic and climatic conditions. The first staples of the Incipient Agriculture Period were maize, beans, squashes and chilis, which were domesticated at different times. Squash and chili domestication took place early, then beans and then maize. These flourished in the semiarid highlands, which were generally free of insects and the fungal growth of the tropical lowlands. The earliest examples of highland plant domestication was found in Tamaulipas, on the northeastern margin of Mesoamerica, and Puebla, located near the center. The gradual domestication of crops depended on suitable climate and a stable environment. The nomadic Mesoamericans, following their hunting-gathering routines, discovered that the humid river bottoms that they came upon were places where plants flourished easily. They gathered the seeds of wild plants and began planting them, crossing with other types to achieve their desired form. Others used irrigation systems to divert water into fields for cultivation. The *chinampas*, the "floating" gardens so common in Aztec agriculture, may, perhaps date to this period, or soon after.

Archaeologists have divided this historical period into certain periods of development, each of which has separate phases. One, the Tehuacan Sequence, dates from 7000 to 1500 B.C. in the Tehuacan Valley. Several eras of development have been documented there. The Tamaulipas Sequence, which took place from 7000 B.C. to A.D. 500 in the Sierra de Tamaulipas, included several phases and developments. Throughout Mesoamerica, hunter-gatherers were refining their tool kits, learning new skills to adjust to the change in available game, altering their activities and settling in the locales where crops and small mammals were plentiful. During the Incipient Agriculture Period, farmland increased.

In the beginning of this period, domestic food plants composed a small percentage of the people's diet. Squash and chili were the first cultivated, but by 2200 B.C. cultivated crops had become 40 percent of the average diet, based on the Tehuacan data. By this time, as new hybrid plants were developed, especially maize, the people had become sedentary. Obsidian was in use, and weaving, basketry and pottery making were in an experimental stage. Village complexes arose in many areas, and in the Formative Period that followed, ceremonial complexes were begun. Agricultural products assumed more and more importance, as surpluses were gathered, freeing some people from farming duties and allowing them to engage in creative pursuits. Priests and religious ceremonies flourished, and ceramic industries opened. It is probable that the *milpa* (cultivated field) techniques were used in addition to more sophisticated irrigation projects.

New agricultural products emerging in this period include tomatoes, peanuts, guavas, turkeys, agave, prickly pear cactus, runner beans, gourds, chili peppers, summer squash, millet, new hybrid corns, manioc, tobacco, cotton and various forms of maize. The settlements, no longer so vulnerable to drought, became stable and adapted to regional changes, and were connected by a growing trade system and the exchange of ideas and techniques.

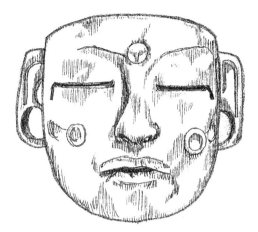

Guerrero Olmec mask

The Formative Period

The Early Formative Period (c. 2000/1600–900 B.C.) in Mesoamerica opened with the flowering of the prior historical advances, as the various cultures began to expand their horizons. The Mexican highlands apparently proved too arid during the warmer period that prevailed from 5000 to 1500 B.C., and agricultural gains did not support large populations there. For this and other reasons, the regional development of village life was not uniform. Many settlements from this era were established in the southern lowlands. The Pacific littoral of Chiapas in Mexico and Guatemala offered good habitats, as did the gulf coast. The Ocos and Cuadros Phases on the Pacific coast of Guatemala reveal the early village structures. Lagoons and estuaries there provided marine products and fields for cultivation. Eventually the highlands were also used for year-round habitation, these different environments in the regions demanded cooperation among the various settlements. The people in the highlands raised their own crops, all dependent on the changing seasons, gathered products and traded or shared with nearby groups, receiving additional food items or manufactured products in return. Diverse crops were grown consistently throughout the year in the lowlands, and the people were able to till large tracts. Thus the local villages began to consolidate into stable and rather large communities.

In the Middle Formative Period (900–300 B.C.), ceramic industries increased and included new techniques. The rocker stamping common in the Early Formative Period, and the *tecomates* (globular, neckless jars), gave way to the hard white pottery. These ceramics were decorated with incised lines. Solid pottery figurines also were made. Cultural regionalism and the changing of small settlements into urban areas are evident. The Olmec civilization, in its La Venta Phase, impacted on surrounding regions, and the Olmec colonized various areas. Sites of Olmec origin were erected on important highland trade routes, especially those leading to the west, and the Olmec trafficked in jade, serpentine and iron ore for mirror manufacturing. Most sites were constructed at the ends of valleys or on major passes, an indication that many of these sites began as trading posts that were later garrisoned.

Maya lowland sites began in this historical period as well, and Monte Alban, the prominent metropolis situated on interconnecting hills, served as the Zapotec capital. The celebrated *danzantes,* the sculptures and reliefs that decorated Monte Alban, were created at this time. The calendar and writing was also initiated by the elite of Monte Alban. In the Valley of Mexico, development moved at its own pace, although the Olmec-influenced territories indicate remarkable advances. The Maya highlands became a developed region at the same time, and Mamon, the Middle Formative Period culture, began to permeate from the PETEN (Putun) area north to the Yucatan.

In the Late Formative Period (300 B.C.–A.D. 250/290), Olmec civilization rose to cultural heights, and city-states such as Teotihuacan flourished in the Valley of Mexico. Most civilizations that were to reach pinnacles of success during the Classic Period arose in this era. In the Valley of Mexico, the Cuicuilco-Ticoman culture developed, as did the groups in the region of Oaxaca. Monte Alban remained a vital link to the past, and Tres Zapotes carried on the great Olmec tradition even as that civilization waned. The Izapan culture was the intermediate between the Olmec and the emerging Maya. The site of Kaminaljuyu in particular stood as the focal point of both civilizations, bridging the artistic traditions and carrying on the basic structures of culture as they were experienced in Mesoamerica. The Miraflores Phase in Kaminaljuyu gives evidences of this link.

The Formative Period featured stabilized groups, agricultural areas and local minerals and ores; the shared traditions of the people cut across regional boundaries as trade routes sliced the landscape and brought caravans of goods and

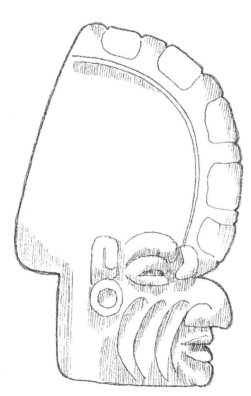

Tlaxcala hacha

news into far-flung regions. Agriculturally, isolated settlements near farmlands were undertaking the way of life and making the advances necessary for shouldering the burden of the new economy. Such settlements were generally composed of former macrobands, based on familial rather than cultural ties. In time, these villages welcomed outsiders into their lands and set about establishing agricultural complexes to provide the crops necessary to support the population. The Ocos, the primary culture on the Pacific coast of Guatemala in the Early Formative Period, raised maize, which they ground using *metates* and *manos.* The Ocos raised beans, chili peppers, type of squash and probably cotton. People of other settlements raised similar crops or traded for the products unavailable to them.

The *milpas* technique of farming was standardized, a technique called "slash-and-burn" or "swidden." Terracing, staggered planting times and rotation of field use allowed the farms to flourish, despite the ecological damage resulting the slash-and-burn technique. Coastal lagoons and estuaries provided irrigation and marine products to enhance the people's diets. In regions farther inland, other irrigation systems were begun, with rainwater and river systems diverted for farm use. The *cenotes,* sinkholes, common in the Yucatan, and the *aguadas,* small reservoirs used to hold rain water, were necessary to farm these regions. The major crops of the period were maize, beans, squash, chili peppers, pumpkins, avocados and cotton.

The art and architecture of the Formative Period demonstrate advances made during this historical era. The Ocos villages on the Guatemalan Pacific coasts and the Cuadros settlements typify the beginning stages. Ocos pottery was highly developed, and the Ocos people manufactured tiny female figures, probably designed for a fertility cult. The temple pyramid may have begun in this early period as well, as the Ocos built an earthen mound about 20 feet high. Such a building indicates a social structure capable of coordinating a large work force. Ceramic advances are evident in the figures found at Zacatenco and Ticoman, the two-headed figures from Tlatilco in the Valley of Mexico, and clay idols of the fire god. The pyramid at Cuicuilco, near modern Mexico City, was built during the Early Formative Period. This was a truncated cone with a stone core, faced with stone upon a sun-dried brick base.

The Olmec on the gulf coast opened the field of sculpture and monumental structures for Mesoamerica. They rank among the most advanced sculptors of the period. The Olmec also manufactured small jadeite figures. The extraordinary stone monuments at the site of San Lorenzo give evidence of a sureness in sculpture. These monuments were defaced or smashed and buried in long lines within the ridges of San Lorenzo. Each weighed as much as 40 tons and was carved from basalt from the Cerro Cintepec, a volcanic deposit in the Tuxtla Mountains, some 50 miles to the northwest.

The colossal heads of the Olmec are the most dramatic representatives of the artistry of the Early Formative Period. Some as tall as nine feet, they have flat faces, thick lips and staring eyes. Each head was sculpted with a helmetlike covering on the top, probably representing the protective coverings worn by ball players. The were-jaguar symbols and the infant-style figures also date to this period. The

Teotihuacan ceramic

were-jaguars were either feline in design or combined cat and human traits. They were carved skillfully in the round. Iron ore mirrors and other ornaments were also manufactured.

Plazas and mounds were constructed, and ceremonial enclosures were provided for the settlements with various levels and fences made of basalt. Jadeite grave offerings were placed in the tombs under the mounds, along with concave iron-ore mirrors. Jadeite, serpentine, cinnabar and other materials were transported from the outlying regions into the Olmec territory for manufacturing.

Cave paintings are also one of the hallmarks of the Middle Formative Period, as were carved reliefs on the first monumental religious structures. Such reliefs are unique at Monte Alban in the highlands, where the *danzantes* were recovered. Some of these reliefs are calendric, as Mesoamerican calendars date to this site and to this period.

The Late Formative Period witnessed the spread of the pre-Maya civilization and the appearance of the city-states that in time would produce the cultural and artistic splendors of Mesoamerica. The great temple pyramids emerged in this period, derived probably from the earlier custom of using house platforms as burial sites. These pyramids served as tombs for nobles and as the focal point of religious ceremonies, accompanied by plazas and open air spaces for the gathering of the populace. The Cuicuilco-Ticoman civilization with its round pyramids remained a heritage for successive generations. The Zapotec, likewise, initiated certain cultural techniques and processes in Monte Alban. Calendric studies, astronomical observatories and buildings designed with corridors and galleries appeared.

Stone stelae were made by the Izapan culture, which had a vast temple complex near Tapachula, Chiapas and pyramidal mounds. These stelae and monuments recording

the activities of the age and its powerful rulers, were carved in relief. The Miraflores Phase at Kaminaljuyu, with its log tombs and jadeite mosaic masks, stands as evidence of the artistic and architectural achievements of the period.

In the Peten (Putun), meanwhile, the Maya civilization was beginning, with temple platforms built with cement-rubble cores and thick layers of plaster. Uaxactun and El Mirador reflect this development. The temple platform style, termed "Chicanel," was four-sided in design, covered in stucco and decorated with stylized god masks on the stairways flanking the sides. Tikal rose as one of the great ceremonial complexes of the Maya, with platforms and stairways lending architectural grace to the temples. There the Maya builders also designed the corbeled vault and incorporated that principle into their structures.

Burial sites from the Early Formative Period indicate that the corpses were still placed in the flexed position. Grave offerings were evident, usually predicated on the deceased's rank. The burials reflect the social distinctions already in place. Many burials in the Early Formative Period probably took place in the individual house platforms in the villages. Massive platforms, tombs for rulers, emerged in the Middle Formative Period. At La Venta, a low, round mound was discovered on the north side of the ceremonial enclosure, containing several tombs. This Olmec tradition was repeated elsewhere.

By the Late Formative Period, the great temple pyramids were being established throughout many regions. The rulers' tombs became the "houses of the gods," as the deceased normally claimed to have descended from various deities. Sometimes the tombs were built into the pyramids and then larger structures were raised over the original ones, developing into the massive structures that still dominate the landscape in some regions. In the Izapan lands, where that culture linked the Olmec and the Maya civilizations, log tombs of incredible richness were discovered within the pyramidal mounds. The Maya temple form, emerging in the great ceremonial complexes, would usher in the Classic Period.

Clay figures placed in tombs or grave sites indicate the rise of religious traditions and practices during the Early Formative Period. Some of these figurines have been identified as fertility goddesses, probably associated with the agricultural trends being practiced. They were probably not deities; the two-headed figures of Tlatilco are believed to represent the emerging forms of deities. The statues of Zacatenco and El Arbolillo may have had some religious significance. The first truly religious monument in the era, however, was erected at Cuicuilco, in pyramidal form. This site indicates that the open-air ceremonies were now being centralized and regulated. The pyramidal form was highly significant to the religious beliefs of the Mesoamericans. Mountains always had particular religious significance, perhaps representing the sky. They served as elevated settings for great religious observances, such as the lighting of the New Fire. The sun climbed the mountains each morning and descended behind them at night. The pyramids may have represented mountains in the various cultures, manufactured images that provided elevated settings for services. Originally the pyramids were simple mounds of earth, built without the geometric configurations of true pyramids. On

La Venta were-jaguar

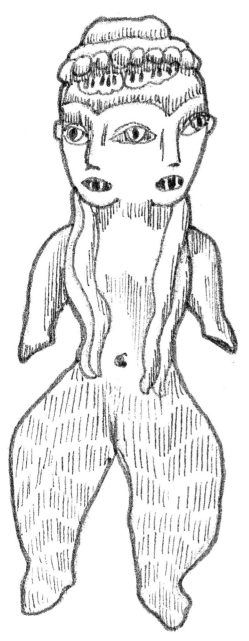

Tlatilco figure

the summit of the "mountain," however, a thatched-roof structure was placed for ceremonial use. In time, the Mesoamericans learned how to construct stone pyramids.

The Olmec developed the were-jaguar religious image in the early stages of the Formative Period. The jaguar was associated with rain. Altars appeared in this same era, and stelae were erected as part of the ceremonial complex designs. The *danzantes* and mushroom statues at Monte Alban probably were symbols of hallucinatory drugs designed to enhance spiritual experiences, and other religious images emerged. The beginnings of public gathering places for religious ceremonies and the use of plazas to accommodate the populace reflect religious concerns in this period. In time, a vast pantheon of gods and their accompanying rituals would be used by the various cultures to maintain a

balance of worlds and to fulfill religious obligations. The priestly castes would emerge, and ceremonies would become ritualized and constant through each succeeding generation. (See individual entries on the Mesoamerican cultural achievements [MESOAMERICAN ARCHITECTURE, MESOAMERICAN ARCHAEOLOGICAL SITES; MESOAMERICAN ARCHITECTURE; MESOAMERICAN ART; MESOAMERICAN CERAMICS AND CULTURAL DEVELOPMENTS; MESOAMERICAN CULTURAL EXCHANGE; MESOAMERICAN LANGUAGES; MESOAMERICAN MATHEMATICS; MESOAMERICAN TRADE]; see also entries on the individual cultures for details.)

Classic Period

The vast historical epoch called the Classic Period in Mesoamerica did not appear suddenly or with equal vigor throughout the region. This era was marked by specific stages of development, and the rise of major civilizations would affect regional affairs and dominate cultural horizons. During the opening decades of the Early Classic Period (A.D. 1/250–600), the various groups had evolved from the Formative Period and were each experiencing particular heights of cultural achievement. The Early Classic Period was also a time of comparative calm, despite wars between various cultures competing for the same natural resources or for overlapping territories. The Classic Period was an intellectual epoch in the Mesoamerican lands, with literacy common among the elite of many regions. Written documents were available, and the various civilizations had groups that were versed in their own literature and in historical and religious matters.

Mass production of various items, particularly wares for trade, was a definite aspect of the Classic Period. Various regions developed mass production to stimulate local manufacture and to encourage use of the trade routes established by such groups as the Maya. Teotihuacan, the great metropolis that influenced surrounding cultures and regions, offered a model for such industries. Archaeological remains include clay molds, incense burners, ceramics and fine statuary, all of which was produced on a rather large scale.

At the same time a definite pantheon of deities was manifested throughout Mesoamerica. Some were more popular and more revered than others, but the cultures appear to have recognized the gods of other groups.

Teotihuacan, Cholula and the Maya ceremonial complexes were not only models but their progress linked the Classic Period cultures to the Formative Period; they were the foundations for most of the advances made. Not every region in Mesoamerica experienced the Classic renaissance and impetus in the same fashion, and the achievements and the ensuing benefits were not uniform. The Classic Period is evident as early as A.D. 1 in some regions; it is dated from A.D. 250/290 in the Maya lowlands. The various cultures maintained the agricultural stability from the Formative Period, as an economic foundation and enhanced their standings through trade.

A hallmark of the Classic Period, begun in the Formative Period, was the shift to urbanization rather than agricultural villages. The Classic Period cities were large, incorporating sophisticated innovations and architectural splendors that reflected the individual cultures, traditions and religious ideals. Agricultural improvements allowed the cities to support burgeoning populations, sustaining their growth. Contact also allowed the groups to utilize the natural resources of various regions and to link their scattered population groups with those of other, perhaps more advanced peoples. Because of the Formative Period foundations and the changes taking place, the Classic Period became a time of remarkable development. Scholars have called it Mesoamerica's Golden Age. Achievements took place in art, astronomy, architecture, mathematics, calendrics, writing, ceramics and religious ceremonies. Monte Alban, Tikal, Teotihuacan and other cities were treasure houses for murals, mosaics, temples, statuary and religious symbolism, and they stood as magnificent urban masterpieces.

The Classic Period cities were also reflections of the growing complexity of religious institutions. Deities such as Quetzalcoatl, the rain gods (Chac and Tlaloc), and the gods of the sun and the moon were manifested in temples everywhere. In some cultures the priestly castes held power and prestige, and ceremonial complexes were erected to honor the deities and their earth-bound servants, providing at the same time space in which the general populace was able to worship the deities. These ceremonial complexes were stages for the religious rituals that had evolved out of cosmological traditions. The Maya complexes were pilgrimage shrines, welcoming those of distant cultures and offering ceremonies that involved the concepts of worlds in change, of creator gods and humankind's obligations. Teotihuacan was so revered that later generations referred to the city as the "meeting place" of the gods. Even after it was abandoned, Cholula remained one of the holiest sites in Mesoamerica. What had begun as simple burial structures in the Formative Period emerged as dynamic, visible symbols of faith attracting diverse populations. Such enlightened theocracies welcomed the migratory groups of

Colima figurine

Mesoamerica. Sacrificial victims were sought in military campaigns, and the rites of the various deity cults were preserved.

The Golden Age also had its problems, some of which became evident in the city of Teotihuacan. This metropolis, which had been the matrix for so many regional cultural beginnings and served as a unifying force for entire territories, witnessed changes and innovations. Metallurgy emerged as a craft, although the basic tool kits of the Mesoamericans remained Neolithic. Metals developed in Teotihuacan and elsewhere were for ornamental display, associated in part with religious fervor. Cast and beaten metal objects were used, usually fashioned out of copper, and smaller items were cast using lost wax process. Some Mexica cultures became highly skilled in the working of gold, which emerged as the prized metal of region. In the midst of such advances, however, there were strains and pressures and the first serious indications of decline. Teotihuacan, the great bridge between the Formative and the

Classic periods, collapsed in the seventh century A.D. While other cities rose to fill the political, economic and cultural vacuum, Teotihuacan's role could not be duplicated, particularly as a model of cohesiveness and as protector of small settlements. Few groups had the resources or the techniques of leadership on such a grand scale. The splintering of groups became evident, and the loss of Teotihuacan proved to be a profound and enduring crisis for Mesoamerica as a whole.

Many reasons have been put forth to explain the Classic Period decline in certain civilizations, ranging from agricultural crises—the loss of forested areas, the alteration of the landscape by damaging environmental practices, and infertility of the soil as a result of overwork or poor management—to pressure from the nomadic hunters and gatherers entering the northern territories.

The collapse of trade routes, stable markets and cultural advances, all a direct result of the loss of Teotihuacan, and the migrations of several groups who fled newcomers stunted economic and cultural developments and set the stage for revolutions, nomadic incursions and conquest.

Post-Classic Period

This Mesoamerican historical epoch has long been distinguished by the presence of change. At one time scholars believed that the era was marked by the total collapse of all of the great Classic Period civilizations that had thrived up to that point. However, some of these cultures, notably Monte Alban and El Tajin, survived the early years of the Post-Classic Period, while others simply disappeared. Some scholars equate the first stage (Early Post-Classic, A.D. 900–c. 1200/1250) with the rise and dominance of the Toltec and the second stage (Late Post-Classic), (A.D. 1200/1250–1521, the Spanish conquest), with the rise of the Aztec Empire.

Certainly the Post-Classic Period was a time of activity and the direction of cultural emphases in Mesoamerica. These activities included resettlement of diverse groups and the introduction of others to Mesoamerica, particularly the hardier, more experienced hunters and gatherers. The peoples of the northern regions of Mesoamerica were bent on continuing invasions expanding to regions of already established cultures. As a result, there was a diversity of peoples, languages and cultural goals throughout the region. The Totonac were carving out their territories on the Gulf Coast's central regions. The Mixtec and Zapotec were in Oaxaca, Puebla and Guerrero. The Tarascan kept their own cultural horizons in Michoacan, while the surviving Maya occupied Chiapas, Tabasco, the Yucatan Peninsula and Guatemala. The Huaxtec were in the northern gulf regions, and the Toltecs were in Cholula and other sites in central Mexico.

Smaller groups, dispersed as a result of the fall of Teotihuacan, withdrew to ancestral lands, where they farmed and maintained defenses. Most remained agriculturally productive throughout the eras of crisis and change, and they maintained association through trade and other contacts. The great Maya and Teotihuacan trading endeavors were no more, but the existing cultures maintained mercantile contacts and presided over the transfer of products from one locale to another. Ceramics, sculpture, featherworks,

metallurgy, basketry, woodworking and other crafts flourished, with the various peoples putting their own cultural stamp on their manufacture. Throughout northern Mesoamerica, art and literature flourished, but a new breed of Mesoamericans became evident. As the great ceremonial complexes of the Maya collapsed into ruin, the role of the Mesoamerican priesthood was altered.

Religion was to become paramount in the emerging empires, but the focal points of such beliefs were reemphasized and different from those of the Formative and Classic periods. The deities of the older civilizations appear far removed from the ferocious gods of the new Mesoamericans, with the exception of Quetzalcoatl, the rain god Tlaloc and a few others. The older deities were not abandoned but incorporated into new ceremonies, no longer giving impetus to development and change as they had in the past. The newer Mesoamerican cultures also introduced state religions, practices incorporating the goals of the empires into ceremonies and ideals among the people. During the Post-Classic Period, the role of the individual and the gods received different emphasis. Three major sites, probably begun in the Classic Period, clearly demonstrate this change of emphasis: Tula in Hidalgo, Cholula in Puebla and Xochicalco in Morelos. These cities benefited from the collapse of the city of Teotihuacan, gaining initiative and vitality. Their populations grew and adjusted to the changing times. People were migrating in this era, especially on the northern frontiers, and old sites were being abandoned. The surviving cities became a stage for public worship, but in time they too gave way as the influence of sages and priests declined. A new breed of Mesoamericans, the military professionals, rose up to serve the empires that had come to the region.

The nomadic invasions into the Valley of Mexico and the surrounding regions changed Mesoamerica forever. Battle-hardened groups, such as the Aztec (Mexica), had little use at first for the intellectual and artistic accomplishments of the Classic Period. Their emphasis was on survival at first, then on expansion and warfare. The populations of this period thus set themselves the tasks of conquest or defense, constructing fortified citadels that could withstand the assaults of their neighbors or invading forces. Such complexes took the place of the ancient ceremonial centers that had been erected in dense jungles in more peaceful times. Specialized military organizations, called totemic by some scholars, incorporated the Mesoamerican traditions concerning the mystical aspects of the eagle, jaguar and coyote, and they began to wield influence on the cultures of the time. God-kings and warrior-kings, intent on expansion and on subjugation of neighboring states, took the place of the former priest-kings. The Toltec, Tarascan and Aztec staked out their own horizons and fought for lands. Military alliances replaced old cultural ties, and various advances were achieved in agriculture and in trade as part of the imperial programs. Old trade routes were revived, and groups of merchants carried trade goods far and wide. The Aztec merchants, however, did not work as a simple mercantile structure but as an imperial force. Some formed the Aztec military spy system.

The professional warriors of the Post-Classic Period were the new bearers of cultural change in Mesoamerica, especially in the northern regions. Incursions of these warriors often caused migration and the abandonment of cherished homelands. War was glorified, and military orders were established to give battle and to honor bloodshed on the field as mystical experiences. The Toltec are usually credited with having introduced the concept of full-scale war in Mesoamerica. Their religious institutions demanded human sacrifices and thus a necessity for captives in military campaigns. Another aspect of militarism and the imperialism that followed was the tribute system. These empires demanded of conquered peoples levies of human beings as well as commodities. Such militarism even affected the Maya strongholds, especially in the Yucatan, where Mexicaized Maya dynasties waged war.

Actually, the militarism that characterizes the Post-Classic Period was rooted in the new religious traditions evident in the era and epitomized by Aztec cosmology. Mesoamerican gods were either replaced or transformed. The deities revered in Aztec strongholds and in the capital, Tenochtitlan, were stern and harsh, demanding human sacrifices and elaborate rituals to stave off the impending doom predicted in Aztec cosmological tradition. The theological tenets of this period, especially in the great empires, encompassed the ending of worlds or suns (the cycle of destruction and rebirth of humankind), with propitiations and sacrifices. The Aztec, obsessed with worlds or suns, eventually created one of the New World's largest metropolises. Their single chain of command ruled millions of acres of land and the destinies of millions of Mesoamerican human beings. This brilliantly conceived system, based on the older models of the Mesoamerican past, administered vast quantities of natural resources, labor and populations of allied or vassal cultures. The Aztec military efforts and the imperial campaigns provided them with territorial gains and tribute and taxes of other cultures. At the same time, however, it became a totalitarian regime. The Spanish, coming upon the Mesoamerican scene, recognized the inherent weaknesses of the Aztec Empire and played upon the hatred and the resentment of other cultures to forge alliances for their own purposes. When the Spanish took the capital of Tenochtitlan, the Post-Classic Period—and the splendor of Mesoamerica—came to an abrupt end.

MESOAMERICAN AGRICULTURE   The farming methods practiced by the peoples of the region to sustain themselves and to provide trade products. Agriculture was the economic base of these cultures, and in many groups deities and divine patrons were thought to protect seasons, crops and farmers. Linked also to the solar calendar, agricultural life, was the basis for festivals and rituals. The majority of Mesoamerican society was involved in farming in the early and late historical periods. The elite castes of the various civilizations probably earned their rank and power from amassing arable land. Agriculture was one of the first activities emphasized by the peoples coming into the Mesoamerican region in late Paleo-Indian epoch (11,000–7000 B.C.) On the northern frontier, in the Sinaloa River in northwest Mesico, in the Sierra Madre Occidental Mountains, in the Bajio Plateau, in the Tamuin and Tamesi River regions, in the Tehucacan Valley and on the beaches and inlets of the gulf coasts, seasonal settlements afforded the people the opportunity of observing and harvesting plants and grasses.

In the historical period called Incipient Agriculture (c. 7000– c. 2000/2500 B.C.), more definite agricultural strides were taken. The term Incipient Agriculture describes the process by which domesticated plants became a vital part of the lives of groups and prompted them to establish permanent habitation. Domestic food plants became more important among the nomadic groups, who were recognizing plant forms and experimenting with hybrids and other mutations. These Mesoamericans not only learned to grow domestic varieties of wild plants but began to select certain strains and hybrids for particular needs. This well-documented selection and breeding process took place from around 6000 to 1500 B.C. Agricultural settlements expanded as temperature warming trends developed in Mesoamerica.

The first staples were squash and chilis, followed by beans and maize. These staples flourished in the highlands, where the climate was moderate, semiarid and generally free of insects and fungal growths. Tamaulipas and Puebla were thought to be the earliest settlements where such farming took place. The processes involved in selecting hybrid strains and cultivating crops suited to the region's climatic and geographic realities included a constant agricultural awareness and increased farming activities. Rich soil was available in humid river basins, and the people diverted water from the rivers to irrigate other fields. At the same time, various settlements shared plant mutations and learned one another's farming techniques. The agricultural communities spread quickly, and by 2200 B.C. squash, chili and pumpkins were domesticated. During this time agricultural crops supplied as much as 40 percent of the people's dietary needs. The Tehuacan Sequence data gives evidence of this. Crop storage and seasonal labors allowed time for crafts, religious activities and the beginnings of architectural endeavors. The crops developed in the Mesoamerican region include:

agave	guava
amaranth	henequen
anona	indigo
avocado	maguey
beans, common	maize
beans, jack	manioc
beans, lima	millet
beans, runner	pacaya
beans, tepary	papaya
beans, yam	prickly pear
cacao	sapate
calabash	sapodilla
chacata	sisal
chili peppers	soursop
copal	squash (four varieties)
corn hybrids	sweetsop
cotton	tobacco
elderberry	tomatoes
gourds	vanilla
gourds, bottle	yucca

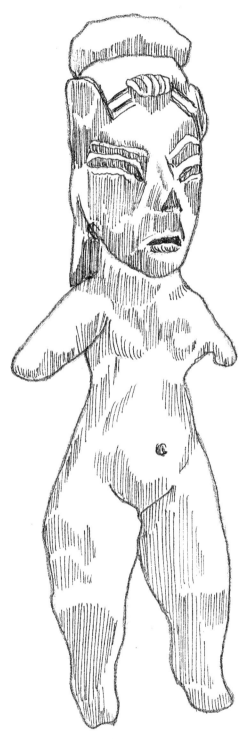

Morelos statue

The Maya, developing in the late eras of the Formative Period (300 B.C.–c. A.D. 250/290), along with other cultures, used the farming techniques called *milpas,* or swidden or slash-and-burn. This involved the yearly clearing of forested areas before the summer rains. Stone tools were used to destroy small shrubs and the trees that could be felled by hand. When the land was cleared of the smaller vegeta-

tion, the fields were set on fire, so that the underbrush would be destroyed and the large trees burned away. The fields were cleared again and small holes were made in rows of earth. Seeds were dropped into the holes, most coming from previous harvests or trade. The fields were guarded so that birds and animals did not root up the young sprouts.

The erosive quality of *milpas* agriculture forced Mesoamericans to seek new lands constantly, and the Maya and others terraced hills as a result. They farmed around the *aguadas* and *cenotes* available to them and also planted gardens and orchards. In time, the *milpas* technique damaged the general landscape, causing not only deforestation but a diminishing of swamplands and meadows as well. Especially damaging was the loss of savannas over the years. The Maya sought to correct some of the obvious damage by using fertilizers and field rotation. They allowed some plots to lie fallow for a certain number of seasons in order to replenish the soil. They also employed intercropping or multicropping in some fields, allowing one type of plant to nourish or to protect one another. Canals and the terraces alleviated the destructive nature of the farming techniques to some extent.

During the Classic Period the farming techniques continued much the same. When the Aztec came to power in the Post-Classic Period (A.D. 900–1421), they also employed the slash-and-burn farming methods, especially on the low-lying mountains slopes or in the lowlands. Among the Aztec, the work began in the dry season (in January), when the brush was burned off, thus adding nitrogen to the soil. Once the burned area was cleaned of debris, and once large trees had been removed, maize and other crops were planted in the fields, still called *milpas,* in holes that were approximately one yard apart. Three or four grains or seeds were dropped into each hole and then covered with soil mixed with ash. The Aztec also used irrigation techniques as well as *chinampas,* floating gardens. It is believed that the Aztecs relied so heavily upon the *chinampas* that by around A.D. 1519, there were as many as 25,000 acres of floating gardens in Chiapas alone. (For details about the various agricultural endeavors of the various cultures, see under individual entries; see also CENOTE; and CHINAMPA.)

MESOAMERICAN ARCHAEOLOGICAL SITES

Cities, shrines, Paleolithic settlements, caves and temple ruins discovered in the Mesoamerican region and now under study. Such sites, as diverse as the climate and regions of Mesoamerica, provide modern scholars with evidence of human habitation, architectural, artistic, ceramic and religious achievements of the cultures inhabiting these sites. Archaeologists and scholars from related academic fields study such sites and uncover remains of the recorded efforts of the various groups. These scientists always race against time, against the impact of human habitation and against the destructive forces of nature. The preservation of some sites has been endowed by international organizations, while others are preserved through the efforts of individually funded researchers.

The Mesoamerican sites of note are covered under separate entries. The table lists the sites of Mesoamerica.

MESOAMERICAN ARCHAEOLOGICAL SITES

NAME	LOCATION	CULTURAL AFFILIATION
Abaj Takalik	Pacific coast	Independent
Acanceh	western Yucatan	Maya
Acapulco	Guerrero	Independent
Achiotla	Oaxaca	Tototepec
Achuitla	Oaxaca	Mixtec
Acozac	Lake Teycoco	Independent/Aztec
Actun Balam	southern Belize	Maya
Aguateca	Peten	Maya
Ahualaco	western Mexico	Jalisco
Ajalpan	Tehuacan	Independent
Ake	north central Yucatan	Maya
Akumal	northern Yucatan	Maya
Alahuitzlan	southern Michoacan	Chontal
Altar de Sacrificios	southern Maya Lowlands	Maya
Alta Vista	Zacatecas	Chalchihuites
Altun Ha	north central Belize	Maya
Amapa	Pacific coast	Nayarit
Aparicio	Sierra de Puebla	Totonac
Arbolillo	Valley of Mexico	Independent
Arcelia	Guerrero	Independent
Atasta	Gulf Coast	Toltec
Atepehuacan, San Bartolo	Valley of Mexico	Indpendent
Atepehuacan	Valley of Mexico	Independent
Azcapotzalco	Lake Texcoco	Tepanec
Aztatlan	Sinaloa	Independent
Bakhalal	Yucatan	Maya
Balamku	Campeche	Maya
Balankanche	central Yucatan	Maya
Bat Cave	Gulf coast	Independent
Becan	southeastern Guatemala	Maya
Bilbao	Guatemalan coast	Independent
Blackman Eddy	Belize	Maya
Blue Creek	Belize	Maya
Bolanos-Juchipila	southern Zacatecas	Independent
Bonampak	Chiapas	Maya
Cacaxtla	Puebla	Olmeca-Xicallanca
Cahal Pich	Belize	Maya
Calakmul	southern Campeche	Maya
Calixtlahuaca	Valley of Mexico	Matlatzinca/Toltec/Aztec
Caracol	Belize	Maya
Caracol, Tumba de	Quintana Roo	Maya
Castillo de Teayo	northern Veracruz	Independent
Catacamas (cave)	Honduras	Independent
Cerritos	northwestern Yucatan	Itza/Maya
Cerro Chalcatzinco	Morelos	Olmec
Cerro Chavin	Chiapas	Maya
Cerro Cintepec	Tuxtla Mountains	Olmec
Cerro de la Estrella	Valley of Mexico	Aztec
Cerro de las Mesas	Tuxtla Mountains	Olmec
Cerro del Gallo	Tabasco	Independent
Cerro de Tepalcate	Valley of Mexico	Independent
Cerro Encantado	western Mexico	Jalisco-Chupicuaro
Cerros	northern Belize	Maya
Chacmultun	south-central Yucatan	Maya
Chacoapan	western Oaxaca	Mixtec
Chakalal	Quintana Roo	Maya
Chakan Putun	Yucatan	Itza/Maya
Chalcatongo	Oaxaca	Mixtec
Chalcatzinco	eastern Morelos	Olmec
Chalchihuites	Zacatecas	Independent
Chalchuapa	El Salvador border	Olmec
Chalco	Chalco	Independent

NAME	LOCATION	CULTURAL AFFILIATION
Chalco Atempan	Chalco	Toltec
Chama	Quatemala	Maya
Chan Chich	Belize	Maya
Chapultepec	Valley of Mexico	Toltec
Chau Hiix	Belize	Maya
Chiapas de Corzo	Chiapas	Independent
Chicanna	Campeche	Maya
Chichen Itza	central Yucatan	Itza/Maya/Toltec
Chinkultic	Chiapas	Maya
Chunhuhub	Campeche	Maya
Chunyaxche	Yucatan	Maya
Cholollan	Mesa Central	Olmeca-Xicallanca
Cholula	Puebla	Independent
Chupicuaro	western Mexico	Independent
Chutixtiox	Yucatan	Maya
Cincoc	Hidalgo, Mexico	Toltec
Ciudad Guzman	Jalisco	Independent
Coatepec	Hidalgo, Mexico	Toltec
Coatepetl	Hidalgo, Mexico	Aztec
Coatlinchan	Valley of Mexico	Acolhua
Coatzacoalcos	Tabasco	Toltec
Coba	Quintana Roo	Maya
Coixtlahuaca	Oaxaca	Mixtec
Comalcalco	northern Tabasco	Maya
Comaltepec	Guerrero	Toltec
Comitan	Chiapas	Independent
Copan	Copan, Honduras	Maya
Copilco	Valley of Mexico	Independent
Costa Grande	Guerrero	Independent
Cotzumalhuapa	Pacific coast	Maya/Mexica/Pipil
Coxcatlan Cave	Puebla	Independent
Coxcatlan Viejo	Puebla	Independent
Coyoacan	Valley of Mexico	Independent/Aztec
Coyuca	Guerrero	Independent/Olmec
Cozumel	Quintana Roo	Maya
Cuanalan	Valley of Mexico	Independent
Cuauhtinchan	Puebla	Chichimec
Cuauhtitlan	Valley of Mexico	Independent
Cuello	northern Belize	Maya
Cuernavaca (1)	Valley of Mexico	Independent
Cuernavaca (2)	Morelos	Independent
Cuicuilco	Valley of Mexico	Independent
Dainzu	Oaxaca	Zapotec
Dos Pilas	Peten (Putun)	Maya
Dzilbilchaltun	northwestern Yucatan	Maya
Dzibilnocac	Campeche	Maya
Ek Balam	Yucatan	Maya
El Baul (Finca El Baul)	Pacific coast	Izapa
El Cedral	eastern Yucatan	Maya
El Chayal	Guatemala	Maya
El Meco	Quintana Roo	Maya
El Opeño	Jalisco	Independent
El Pilar	Belize	Maya
El Pital	Veracruz	Independent
El Rey	Cancun Island	Maya
El Tajin	Veracruz	Totonac
El Zapotal	Veracruz	Totonac/Independent
Etzatlan	western Mexico	Jalisco
Etzna (Edzna)	north-central Campeche	Maya
Gualupita	Morelos	Independent
Guiengola	Campeche	Zapotec
Hachob	Campeche	Maya
Hormiguero	Campeche	Maya
Huamelulpan	Oaxaca	Mixtec
Huapalcalli	Hidalgo, Mexico	Toltec

MESOAMERICAN ARCHAEOLOGICAL SITES (*cont.*)

NAME	LOCATION	CULTURAL AFFILIATION
Huexotla	western Mexico	Acolhua
Huexotzinco	Puebla	Chichimec
Huitzo	Oaxaca	Zapotec
Hunchabin	Chiapas	Maya
Icheatopan	southern Michoacan	Chontal
Ihuatzio	central Michoacan	Tarascan
Ikil	Yucatan	Maya
Isla de Sacrificios	Veracruz	Totonac
Isla Mujeres	Yucatan	Maya
Islona de Chantuto	Pacific coast	Independent
Itzamkanac	Yucatan	Maya
Iximiche	Lake Atitlan	Maya
Ixtalapapa	Texcoco	Independent/Toltec
Ixtepete	Jalisco	Tarascan
Ixtlan del Rio	southern Nayarit	Independent/Nayarit
Izamal	Yucatan	Maya
Izapa	Chiapas	Izapa
Jade Shrine	Chalco	Independent
Jaina	Campeche	Maya
Jalieza	Oaxaca	Independent
Janitzio	Michoacan	Tarascan
Jaquilipas	Michoacan	Independent
Juxtlahuaca Cave	Guerrero	Independent
Kabah	central Yucatan	Maya
Kaminal juyu	Guatemala	Independent/Maya/Mexica
Kinich	Yucatan	Maya
Kohunlich	Quintana Roo	Maya
Labna	central Yucatan	Maya
Lacanhai	Chiapas	Maya
Lachizaa	Oaxaca	Mixtec
Laguna de los Cerros	Tuxtla Mountains	Olmec
Laguna de Terminos	northern Yucatan	Maya
La Juana	Morelos	Independent/Olmec
Lamanai	Belize	Maya
Lambityeco	Oaxaca	Zapotec
La Milda	Belize	Maya
La Quemada	Zacatecas	Chalchihuites
Las Bocas	Morelos	Olmec
Las Flores	Veracruz	Huaxtec
Las Higueras	Gulf coast	Totonac
La Venta	Tabasco	Olmec
La Victoria	Pacific coast	Ocos
Loltun Cave	Yucatan	Maya
Loma de Ayuxi	Puebla	Mixtec
Loma San Gabriel	southern Durango/Zacatenca	Independent
Los Topiales	Guatemalan highlands	Maya
Lubaantun	Belize	Maya
Malinalco	central Mexico	Independent/Aztec
Matachan	Nayarit	Independent
Matapacan	Tuxtla Mountains	Teotihuacan vassal
Mayapan	northern Yucatan	Maya
Mayotzinco	Puebla	Independent
Mirador	Chiapas	Maya
Mitla	Oaxaca	Zapotec
Mixco Viejo	Guatemala	Maya
Monte Alban	Oaxaca Valley	Independent/Zapotec/Mixtec
Monte Alto	Guatemala	Maya
Monte Negro	Oaxaca Valley	Zapotec/Mixtec
Motul de San Jose	southern lowlands	Maya
Mountain-That-Opens	Oaxaca	Mixtec
Mul Chic	Yucatan	Maya
Muyil	Yucatan	Maya

NAME	LOCATION	CULTURAL AFFILIATION
Naco	Honduras	Maya
Naj Tunich	Peten (Putun)	Maya
Nepohualco	Valley of Mexico	Chichimec
Nim Li Punit	Belize	Maya
Nohmul	Belize	Maya
Nohpat	Yucatan	Maya
Oaxtepec	Valley of Mexico	Aztec
Ocampo Cave	Northern Mexico	Independent
Oceloapan	Sierra de Puebla	Totonac
Ometepec	Guerrero	Independent
Oxkintok	western Yucatan	Maya
Oztuma	western Yucatan	Maya
Palenque	Chiapas	Maya
Paquime	northern Mexico	Independent
Patzcuaro	Lake Zirahuen	Tarascan
Penitas	Nayarit	Nayarit
Piedras Negras	northwestern Guatemala	Maya
Portrero Nuevo	southern Veracruz	Olmec
Puerto Marquez	Guerrero	Independent
Puertosuelo	Valley of Mexico	Independent
Quauhtocho	Sierra de Puebla	Totonac
Quiahuitzlan	central Veracruz	Totonac
Quiotepec	Oaxaca	Independent
Quirigua	Guatemala	Maya
Rabinal Basin	Sierra de Omoa	Maya
Remojada	central Veracruz	Independent
Remolino	Veracruz	Olmec
Repelo	Sierra de Tamaulipas	Independent
Richmond Hill	Belize	Maya
Rio Bec B	Yucatan	Maya
Salcaja	Guatemalan Highlands	Independent/Maya
Salinas La Blanca	Pacific coast	Independent
San Blas	Pacific coast	Nayarit
San Gervasio	Quintana Roo	Maya
San Jose	central Belize	Maya
San Jose Mogote	Oaxaca	Independent
San Lorenzo	Veracruz	Olmec
San Luis Potosi	northern Mexico	Huaxtec
San Martin Pajapan	Veracruz	Olmec
San Pablo Pantheon	Morelos	Independent
San Pedro de los Piños	Modern Mexico City	Toltec
San Pedro Zacachimalpa	Puebla	Independent
San Sebastian	Jalisco	Independent
Santa Cecilia	Valley of Mexico	Aztec
Santa Isabel Iztapan	Valley of Mexico	Independent
Santa Lucia	southern Veracruz	Independent
Santa Marta Cave	Chiapas	Independent
Santa Rita	Belize	Maya
Santa Rosa Xtampak	Campeche	Maya
San Vicente Chicoloapan	Valley of Mexico	Independent
Sayil	Yucatan	Maya
Seibal	central Peten	Maya
Solola	Guatemala	Maya
Tamuin	northern Veracruz	Huaxtec
Tancah	Yucatan	Maya
Tancol	northern Veracruz	Huaxtec
Tapochula	Chiapas	Maya
Taposcolula	Oaxaca	Mixtec
Tayasal	Yucatan	Itza/Maya
Teloloapan	Michoacan	Chontal
Tenayuca	Valley of Mexico	Chichimec
Tenochtitlan	Valley of Mexico	Aztec
Tenochtitlan Rio Chiquito	Veracruz	Olmec
Teopanzalco	Valley of Mexico	Tlahuican/Aztec
Teotihuacan	Valley of Mexico	Independent

MESOAMERICAN ARCHAEOLOGICAL SITES (*cont.*)

NAME	LOCATION	CULTURAL AFFILIATION
Teotitlan del Camino	Oaxaca	Independent
Tepexpan	Valley of Mexico	Independent
Tepoztlan (Tepozteco)	Valley of Mexico	Tepozteca/Tlahuica
Tequixquiac	Valley of Mexico	Independent
Texcoco (Tetzcoco)	Valley of Mexico	Acolhua/Chichimec
Texcotzinco	Valley of Mexico	Acolhua/Chichimec
Tihoo	Yucatan	Maya
Tikal	Peten (Putun)	Maya
Tilantongo	Oaxaca	Mixtec
Tizatlan	central Tlaxcala	Tlaxcala
Tlacopan (Tacuba)	Valley of Mexico	Independent
Tlalancaleca	Puebla	Independent
Tlapacoya	Valley of Mexico	Olmec/Independent
Tlatelolco	Valley of Mexico	Aztec
Tlatilco	Oaxaca	Independent
Tlaxcala	Puebla	Olmeca-Xicallanca/Chichimec
Tomaltepec	Oaxaca	Independent
Tonina	Chiapas	Maya
Topiales, Los	Guatemala	Maya
Topoxte	on Lake Yaxha	Maya
Totomihuacan	Puebla	Chichimec
Totonacopan	Gulf coast	Independent
Tototepec	Oaxaca	Independent/Mixtec
Tres Zapotes	Tabasco	Olmec
Tula	Hidalgo, Mexico	Toltec
Tulan Zuiva	Tabasco	Toltec
Tulixlahuaca	Coastal region	Toltec
Tulum	Quintana Roo	Maya
Tututepec	Oaxaca	Mixtec
Tuxcacuesco	Jalisco/Colima	Independent
Tuzapan	central Veracruz	Toltec
Tzintzuntzan	Michoacan	Tarascan
Uaxactun	Peten (Putun)	Maya
Utatlan	Pacific coast	Maya
Uxbenka	Belize	Maya
Uxmal	west central Yucatan	Maya
Valsequillo	Puebla	Independent
Xaltocan	Valley of Mexico	Independent
Xicallanco	southern Campeche	Maya
Xicco	Valley of Mexico	Toltec/Independent
Xicuco	Hidalgo, Mexico	Toltec
Xipe Bundle	Oaxaca	Mixtec
Xippacayan	Hidalgo, Mexico	Toltec
Xkichmook	Yucatan	Maya
Xlapak	Yucatan	Maya
Xochicalco	Morelos	Independent
Xochimilco	Valley of Mexico	Independent
Xochitlan	Hidalgo, Mexico	Toltec
Xpuhil	Quintana Roo	Maya
Xunantunich	Belize	Maya
Yagul (Tlacolula)	Oaxaca	Zapotec
Yanhuitlan	western Oaxaca	Mixtec
Yaxchilan	southern lowlands	Maya
Yaxha	Petēn	Maya
Yaxuna	eastern Yucatan	Maya
Yestla-Naranjo	Guerrero	Independent
Yucuita	Nochixtlan Valley	Mixtec
Yucundahai	Nochixtlan Valley	Mixtec
Zaachila	Oaxaca	Zapotec
Zaculeu	western Mexico	Maya
Zapotel, El	southern Mexico	Independent
Zempoala	Veracruz	Totonac
Zincantan	western highlands	Maya

MESOAMERICAN   ARCHITECTURE Buildings, monuments and vast gathering places that reflect the cultural and religious horizons of the regional cultures. Mesoamerican architecture, alongside the Inca achievements to the south, is the most elaborate and developed in the New World. Public architecture, designed to provide cities and regions with structures and spaces for festivals and ceremonies, evolved slowly. The historical dwelling places and shelters of the emerging groups are discussed under MESO-AMERICA. Architecture serving entire populaces evolved slowly and in divergent locales; most began in the Incipient Agricultural Period (7000–c. 2000/2500 B.C.). During this historical era the ceremonial complexes were taking form, having rudimentary ball courts and plazas. In the Formative Period (c. 2000/1500 B.C.–A.D. 250/290), the Mesoamerican architectural styles began to give life to cities and to reflect the vitality and the exuberance of the emerging cultures. The Olmec at La Venta, in the cities of Monte Alban, Teotihuacan and Cuicuilco, as well as the Ocos and others peoples were moving toward cities and ceremonial complexes of grand design. The linking culture between the Olmec and the Maya, the Izapa, were visible at Kaminaljuyu.

The colossal Olmec heads are the most dramatic representations of the Formative Period, but these were adjuncts to the mounds and plazas of the great sites. The Nochixtlan Valley in Mexico had pyramidal platforms by 1300 B.C., and the Miraflores Phase (300 B.C.–A.D. 200) is associated with mounds and plazas in Kaminaljuyu. The Cuicuilco-Ticoman culture, with its rounded pyramids, rivaled the temple platforms being constructed by the Maya in the Chicanel style. Tikal, the great ceremonial complex, was a large city during the Formative Period. There corbeled vaults were being incorporated into architectural design. Teotihuacan, dating to 200 B.C., was erected by "the Lords of Wisdom," and a true metropolis that stood as a model for other regions. The avenues of Teotihuacan are precisely laid out as a stage for the pyramids, surrounded by courts, plazas, palaces and platforms. The *talud-tablero* (slope and panel) was a prevalent architectural design. The multilayered pyramids evolved from this device and were raised by the various cultures, some with startling innovations, as at El Tajin. The steps or terraces were plain or intricately carved, with stairways.

The Olmec had pioneered architectural styles, and other cultures demonstrated similar abilities and visions. The Veracruz culture, for example, typified these advances, and in Oaxaca the plazas and mounds of earlier eras were incorporated into the vast city of Monte Alban. This city appears to have been an amalgam of the efforts of many cultures and was the setting for the architectural aspirations of each one. Again, the Teotihuacan *talud-tablero* style was instituted here. Paneled friezes were used in Monte Alban. Mitla, the Zapotec city, and other metropolises in the region reflect both Monte Alban and Teotihuacan styles.

The Maya, isolated in part for a time, raised magnificent ceremonial complexes throughout their territories. These are listed as Classic efforts, built before A.D. 1000 and pure Maya, and those combining Toltec-Maya or Mexica-Maya influence were made after A.D. 1000. The Peten (Putun) region in the Yucatan, Copan in Honduras, the Puuc site of Uxmal, the Rio Bec of Belize and other sites reflect the

Veracruz toy

dazzling Maya public architectural horizons. When Teotihuacan fell, the Toltec erected their great city of Tula, employing the *talud-tablero* style, with artistic innovations. Columns and other monuments were incorporated into the overall design for a stark effect. Such columns appeared on vestibules, erected at the feet of the pyramidal shrines.

The Aztec, successors to the Toltec in the Post-Classic Period (A.D. 900–1521), used the earlier architectural advances but added nuances of their own. The sacred ceremonial precincts of their capital, Tenochtitlan, were walled. Double shrines adorned their pyramidal platforms. Overall their monuments represented in many ways the culmination of Mesoamerican architecture, with massive lines and monuments used to reflect the power of the state. The Aztec were also adept at using the natural resources of their region, as at Malinalco, to set their temples and shrines into living rock.

All of the architectural advances of the various cultures are discussed in the entries concerning those cultures, but the basic elements of Mesoamerican architecture should be explained. The basic public architectural components employed in the various regions include pyramids, temples, plazas, and ball courts.

Pyramids.   Towering structures used as the bases for temples in Mesoamerica and in the ceremonial complexes of cities. These pyramids evolved from simple platforms in the Late Formative Period or perhaps earlier, 300 B.C.–c. A.D. 250/290. The city of Tlatilco had such platforms (c. 1200 B.C.), low structures with retaining walls added in time. They were faced with clay at first and then coated with thick layers of stucco. Some Mesoamerican cities maintained the platforms as stages for dances and festivals, probably for sacrifices as well. Most of these pyramids were fashioned of stone or masonry and rubble. Some were faced with limestone or other quality stone. The platforms and temples were sometimes newly constructed larger pyramids that enclosed earlier forms.

Such pyramids might have staircases on all sides, on two sides or on only one. There were tombs within the pyramids of Teotihuacan and in some Maya ceremonial complex temples. The walls might be ornate or plain, but most were carved and embellished. The pyramids dedicated to the god

Quetzalcoatl, in the form of Ehecatl, the wind, were rounded. The Maya built low elaborate pyramids and soaring narrow towers. In the Rio Bec region the towers were imitations, having no functional purpose. The Aztec incorporated two shrines on the summits of their pyramids, and built their platforms of solid rock if necessary.

Temples.   Chambers erected on the summit of the Mesoamerican pyramids and platforms. Usually one temple sufficed; double shrines were a later innovation. These structures contained one or several chambers. Many were roofed with thatch, as had been the early residences of the various regions. The Maya added roof combs of stone. Within these temples, which were generally not open to the entire population, were altars, benches, carved bas reliefs, murals, pits and hanging symbols. All public rituals were performed on the various pyramidal levels, outside the temples. The priests, nobles and the warrior societies conducted their rituals in secret within the temples, providing the more spectacular ceremonies for the populace outside.

The temples might stand as a single dominant monument in a region or be grouped within an acropolis or in a ceremonial complex. The major cities had groups of temples, all standing on pyramidal platforms, surrounded by other daises, plazas, palaces, columns, statues, patios and ball courts. The nature of the deity being honored often determined the architecture used in these cores.

Plazas.   Level, raised or sunken areas around which the religious and governmental structures of Mesoamerican cities were erected. Such plazas also served a stages for elaborate ceremonial events, such as those conducted in the Aztec capital of Tenochtitlan, where thousands of dancers performed on elevated plazas to the delight of throngs of worshippers. The plazas of many cities were architectural focal points, and they varied in size and in sophistication from region to region. Olmec stone mosaics, called MASSIVE OFFERINGS were found buried in the plazas.

Patios.   Level, raised or sunken areas that were incorporated into residential complexes in major Mesoamerican communities. These patios allowed small groups to gather to perform their tasks or ceremonies and also provided structural unity and harmonious design. Several individual residences shared a single patio, which served social or recreational function as well as a working area.

Ball Courts.   Sites designed for the playing of a game, sometimes shaped in the form of capital I's, found in cities and in ceremonial complexes throughout Mesoamerica. In some places several such ball courts have been uncovered. In the Classic Period (c. A.D. 1/250–900), the courts had raised platforms on the sides, and the lower walls were sloped toward the playing area. In the Post-Classic Period (A.D. 900–1521), the walls were vertical. Markers or (*mercadores*) were painted on the courts or represented by stone disks, or in the form of *hachas,* stone heads that were probably axes. The courts were usually divided into three sections. Citizens of the various cities and ceremonial complexes attended games in the ball courts, and there is evidence of heavy betting on the outcome of such games.

MESOAMERICAN ART   The expression of religious and social ideals in material form, including painting, sculpture, reliefs, mosaics, metalwork, weaving and featherworks. Mesoamerican cultures excelled in these endeavors, progressing from rudimentary levels to the splendors of the elaborate cities and ceremonial complexes incorporating art into all of their architectural designs. Mesoamerican art forms are detailed in the entries concerning individual cultures and sites, but a historical overview follows.

Painted symbols recovered from graves dating to the Paleo-Indian Period (11,000–7000 B.C.) give evidence of the ancient roots of Mesoamerican art form. During the Incipient Agricultural Period (also called the Archaic), 7000–c. 2000/2500 B.C., however, specific evidence of those art forms began to emerge. As villages were stabilized and expanded, the result of adaptation to an agricultural way of life, artists began their ascent toward excellence. Figurines discovered in Tlapacoya, in the southern portion of the Valley of Mexico, date to around 2300 B.C. In Belize, the Maya Swazey culture flourished, and throughout the various regions efforts were being made to translate the various cultural and religious ideals into objects of beauty. The "Mother Culture" of Mesoamerica, the Olmec, dominated the opening eras of the Formative Period (c. 2000/2500 B.C.), and the arts flourished in their domain and in other regions.

The Olmec, also called the La Venta People, are believed to have occupied the gulf coastal plains in southern Veracruz and Tabasco. The city of La Venta was built 1200/900 B.C., making it an Early Formative site. Olmec used artistic forms called iconographic, depicting the stages of their religious and social developments. Olmec bas reliefs are of exquisite composition, having skilled use of line and monumental unity.

During the Chicarra Phase (1200–1100 B.C.) or perhaps earlier, the Olmec displayed their mastery in stone. The colossal heads they produced are considered by many to be portraits of divine beings or nobles, and they set new standards for sculpture in the region. Other Olmec art forms include ornament of jade, basalt and other stones taken from their territories or imported for manufacture. Axes and celts produced demonstrated the art of Olmec composition, and their masks, some of wood, demonstrate a mastery with clear, flowing lines and geometric symmetry. The Olmec used mirror images in some sites, with duplicate figures facing one another. They also translated their cosmological views of life in the symbols of jaguars, were-jaguars and snarling infants. Their colossal heads, realistically sculpted, reflect Olmec skill in stone.

San Lorenzo, another Olmec site dating to the Early Formative Period, contains colossal heads as well as Atlantean altars. Niched altars were incorporated into the ceremonial complexes, with portraits of rulers and jaguars positioned in the niches. The altars may have been used as thrones. The Massive Offerings, the stone mosaics found buried in ceremonial compounds, were elaborately composed symbols relating to the gods or to particular eras. Figures also held religious significance in some Olmec sites. A cache of 16 such figures was discovered in La Venta. They, along with six celts, were made of jade and serpentine. Olmec artistic vitality declined during the Middle Formative Period, but other cultures in their region and elsewhere had begun their own artistic ascent.

The Zapotec in Oaxaca were evolving in their great city of Monte Alban, 200 miles southwest of La Venta. The city

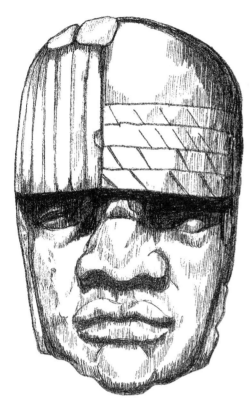

Colossal head, Olmec

maintained trade routes for the transport of goods across entire regions, thereby linking cultures. The cities of Teotihuacan and Cholula and those of the Maya were models for less advanced cultures, and linked them to the older art forms as well. These cities also represent the Classic Period shift to urbanization and to theocratic rule, two aspects that affected Mesoamerican art.

Teotihuacan, vast and powerful at the start of the Classic Period, incorporated the religious beliefs of its people into its architectural and artistic endeavors and dominated many other surrounding cultures. The god Quetzalcoatl, for example, was symbolized by the butterfly and the flying serpent, and these religious insignias were recognized by the people. In paintings, stone masks, moldings and stucco reliefs, the religious fervor of the people was clearly demonstrated. Teotihuacan was a designed city, and it became a major arbiter of artistic endeavors in the region. El Tajin and Cholula also emerged as new sanctuaries for the deities and for artistic vision. Maya paintings appeared in central Mexico at Cacaxtla and Xochicalco, while ceremonial complexes emerged. By the eighth century A.D., these were large and magnificent. While they lasted just a century in the lowlands, they were sustained and reintroduced in the highland Maya realms.

The Maya excelled in stone sculpture. On stelae divine beings and aristocrats are elaborately costumed, bearing symbols and set within a complex design reflecting religious ideology. Such stelae began to disappear around A.D. 800, as did the "dated monument" cult. Stucco work, reliefs and

of Monte Alban assumed the artistic mantle of the region. The site is renowned for the remains of many cultural phases, for its architecture and for the *danzantes*, figures carved into monuments. The Zapotec also specialized in beautifully carved and ornate braziers and funerary urns. Monte Alban was inhabited over several eras, and its remains reflect many artistic trends.

The Ocos, Cuadros and Chupicuaro cultures were developing their own artistic forms, and the cultures of Cuicuilco-Ticoman, Tlatilco and Zacatenco produced fine new wares. These groups manufactured hollow and later, solid figures, adding tempering materials to the basic clay. Such figures appeared in Chiapas, Guerrero and the Valley of Mexico. The geometrical Mezcala art of Guerrero contrasted with the fluid realism of western Mexico, where the Nayarit, Jalisco and Colima art included entire panoramas filled with recognizable citizens. The Izapa, however, were the people destined to carry on the great Olmec tradition, linking them to the Classical Maya.

The Izapa culture, located in the southeastern part of Chiapas, displayed skill and sophistication. The people were noted for fine bas reliefs, and the capital, Izapa, contained stone stelae, altars and artistic portraits that incorporate designs of clouds and sky bands. Glyphs flourished in Kaminaljuyu, and they show Izapa influences, heralding the Maya writing styles.

In the Classic Period (A.D. 1/250–900), the artistic traditions of the past were carried forward as new metropolises and great civilizations arose to seek new cultural horizons. Mass production of artistic wares was a hallmark of this historical period as the cities and ceremonial complexes

Classic Period stela

friezes also reflect the religious aspects of Maya art. Stucco became a valuable resource, as they paved with it, maked beautiful panels and used it for statuary portrait.

With the arrival of the Chichimec, the Toltec and then the Aztec, the Mexica influence in Mesoamerica brought a new vigor to local sculpture. Atlantean figures (introduced into the region on Olmec altars) appeared in the city of Tula in Hidalgo, Mexico. These figures, however, maintain the rigid, geometric severity of Toltec forms. Military motifs dominated art in this era, with space and lines composing monumental settings. Using porous materials, the art of the Toltec reflects rugged vitality. With the rise of the Toltec, the Maya faced Mexica influence and pressure. Mexica groups, such as those in Chichen Itza, brought new elements to Maya art, and Maya-Mexica forms were combined. The fall of the Toltec city of Tula in A.D. 1156 signaled the rise of the Mixteca-Puebla art form, but the Toltec vision remained.

The Aztec, heirs to the Toltec, having adopted their imperial ambitions, military activities and religious views, employed the military precision of the great civilization, and combined it with massive proportions to produce splendid settings. An undeniable exactitude in Aztec sculpture clearly stamps such works as state art. The fluid lines of their Quetzalcoatl statue, the intricate compactness of the statue of the goddess Coatlicue and their reliefs and ornaments reflect, too, a vitality that is the hallmark of this civilization. (For details on various art forms of the cultures, see entries for each Mesoamerican group.)

MESOAMERICAN CERAMICS AND CULTURAL DEVELOPMENTS Utensils and decorative wares, and the historical periods in which they were formed over the centuries in various Mesoamerican cultures. Each major civilization and the smaller, regional groups evolved during wide-ranging phases and produced unique ceramic wares, some indicating rapid advancements in skill and in design. Such wares were used locally and exported through the vast trade routes during various historical periods. Imports from other locales were not only prized but were an introduction new styles and new methods. The ceramic and cultural phases of Mesoamerica have been labeled in order to categorize the emergence of new methods and new approaches as they appeared. These phases are listed in an accompanying table and are also listed individually and in the general discussion of the cultures. The following general discussion provides details as to the development of ceramic wares.

The artisans of Mesoamerica did not mold their wares on a potter's wheel. They used coils of clay as a base, either fashioning each piece by hand or placing them in a mold. The anvil-and-paddle technique was a common method of shaping such wares. The anvil, or a simple stone, supported the inner surface of the pottery while a wooden paddle shaped the outer surfaces. As the coils were built up and shaped, various processes were used to give them a distinctive appearance. Scalloped effects could be achieved by punching the coils of clay as they were applied. Punctuation was the process by which small indentations were pierced into the wet clay surfaces. Incisions were made by using a sharp shell or bone fragment to scratch in a design. Stamp-

ing pressed designs into the surface with rockers or other tools created other designs.

After the vessel was prepared and the flaws corrected, the outer surfaces were burnished. Slip wares were given coats of water and colored clay. If the ceramics were not going to be painted, they were sometimes covered with layers of fat or resin and allowed to dry. To fire ceramic wares, they were covered with animal dung to provide a steady heat while protecting the work from flames. For a shiny black surface, the artisans made a smoky fire that allowed carbon particles to act as a coloring agent. Open fire processes created the usual reddish tones. Painted ceramics were colored with ground plant seeds, minerals or dye from plant juices. Negative painting effects were achieved by using black as a background, thus using the original color for a reverse design. A technique called resist painting required placing wax on the surface before applying color. As the paint did not adhere to the wax, the design emerged.

Ceramics are a hallmark of historical development in many regions of the world. With these products, however, other cultural developments, such as agricultural methods and tools, public architecture, artistic creations and clothing, weapons and other materials reflect definite stages and patterns of growth among a people. Cultural developments in Mesoamerica did not take place at the same time and are scattered among the various geographical regions. Such developments were dependent on regional conditions and available resources. They are diverse and are evidence of the cultural imperatives of the various groups at various times. The table lists the cultural developments and ceramic phases scholars have assembled to denote such advances. They are discussed under separate entries as well or are included in the entries on the various major groups of Mesoamerica.

The cultural developments and ceramic phases listed in the table represent the individual cultures and locations of Mesoamerican civilization. These are defined phases and developments, set to assist scholars in determining actual advances and changes. All were predicated upon intercultural exchange or upon adaptation to the wide variety of microenvironments provided by the geological development of Mesoamerica as a whole. Vast trade endeavors represented most efficiently historically by the Maya and the Aztec (Mexica), included whole territories and introduced products and techniques into broad regions. The Olmec, Toltec and other major groups also affected their neighbors culturally, as did cities such as Teotihuacan, Cholula and Cuicuilco. Some cultural developments and ceramic phases, such as the Ocos, San Jose Mogote, Tlatilco and the Miraflores, are historical watersheds in their own right. Others, such as the Colima phase, offer splendid glimpses of re-

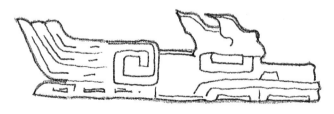

Jaguar symbol

CULTURAL DEVELOPMENTS AND CERAMIC PHASES

NAME	LOCATION	DATE
Abasalo	Sierra de Tamaulipas	2000/1600 B.C.–A.D. 250/290
Abejas	Tehuacan Valley	7000–2000/2500 B.C.
Ajalpan	Tehuacan Valley	1500–900 B.C.
Ajuereado Complex	Tehuacan Valley	6000 B.C.
Almagre	Sierra de Tamaulipas	2200–1800 B.C.
Altamira-Barra	Chiapas/Pacific coast	1700–1500 B.C.
Amacueca	southern Jalisco	1800/1400–1400/1300 B.C.
Apatzingan	Tepalcatepec Basin	A.D. 1/250–600
Arbolillo-Zacatenco	Lake Texcoco	2000/1600 B.C.–A.D. 250/290
Arenal	Guatemalan highlands	900–300 B.C.
Arevalo	Isthmus of Tehuantepec	2000/1600 B.C.–A.D. 250/290
Armeria	western Mexico	2000/1600 B.C.–A.D. 250/290
Ayala	northern Mexico	2000/1600 B.C.–A.D. 250/290
Ayotla	Valley of Mexico	c. 1100 B.C.
Aztec I, II, III	Tenochtitlan/Tlatelolco	A.D. 900–1521
Bajio	Gulf coast	1350–1250 B.C.
Barra de Navidad	Colima	2000/1600 B.C.–A.D. 250/290
Calera	northern Mexico	A.D. 1150–1350
Calichel	northern Mexico	A.D. 500–600
Cantera	Chalcatzinco	700–500 B.C.
Canutillo	northern Mexico	A.D. 200–500
Capocha	Colima/western Mexico	200 B.C.–A.D. 1/250
Caynac	Chalchuapa	400 B.C.–A.D. 200
Cerro Montaso	Veracruz	A.D. 900–1521
Chicanel	Tikal	100 B.C.–A.D. 130
Chicarra	Gulf coast	1200–1100 B.C.
Chul	Chalchuapa	400 B.C.–A.D. 200
Chumbicuaro	Michoacan	300 B.C.–A.D. 250/290
Chupicuaro	western Mexico	2000/1600 B.C.–A.D. 250/290
Coapexco	Valley of Mexico	2000/1600 B.C.–A.D. 250/290
Conchas I, II	Pacific coast	800–600 B.C.
Convento	Coixtlahuaca	A.D. 1520–1525
Coralillo	southern Jalisco	2000/1600 B.C.–A.D. 250/290
Corral	Tula	A.D. 800
Cotorra	Chiapas	1500–1100 B.C.
Coxcatlan	Tehuacan Valley	5000–3400 B.C.
Coyotlatelco	Tula	c. A.D. 1156/1168
Cruz	Coixtlahuaca	1300–200 B.C.
Cuadros	Pacific coast	1000–840 B.C.
Culhuacan	Culhuacan/Puebla	A.D. 900–1200
Delicias	Tepalcatepec Basin	300 B.C.–A.D. 600
Diablo Complex	Tamaulipas	c. 9000 B.C.
El Arenal	Jalisco	11,000–7000 B.C.
El Openo	Michoacan	900–300 B.C.
El Riego	Tehuacan	7200–5200 B.C.
Esperanza	Kaminaljuyu	A.D. 1/250–600
Espiridion	Oaxaca	1400 B.C.
Flacco	Tamaulipas	2200–1800 B.C.
Guadalupe	Oaxaca	850–700? B.C.
Huamelulpan I, II, III	Oaxaca	400 B.C.–A.D. 600
Infiernillo	Tamaulipas	7000–2000/2500 B.C.
Isla de Sacrificios I, II, III	Isla de Sacrificios	A.D. 800–1521
Jacotal	Pacific coast	850 B.C.
Justo	Valley of Mexico	1100 B.C.
Kal	Chalchuapa	400 B.C.
La Florida	Veracruz/Tabasco	100 B.C.
Laguna	Tamaulipas	500 B.C.–A.D. 500
La Perra	Tamaulipas	3000–2000 B.C.
Las Charcas	Isthmus of Tehuantepec	2000/2600–900 B.C.
Las Charcas B	Isthmus of Tehuantepec	300 B.C.–A.D. 250
Las Flores	Coixtlahuaca	A.D. 500–1000
Las Joyas	Sierra Madre Occidental	A.D. 700–950

CULTURAL DEVELOPMENTS AND CERAMIC PHASES

NAME	LOCATION	DATE
La Venta	La Venta	1200–600/400 B.C.
La Victoria	Pacific coast	1500–1150 B.C.
La Villita	Michoacan	2000/1600 B.C.–A.D. 250/290
Lerma	Tamaulipas	?–6300 B.C.
Loma San Gabriel	Durango/Zacatencas	7000–2000/2500 B.C.
Majades	Isthmus of Tehuantepec	900/300 B.C.–A.D. 200
Mamantial	Valley of Mexico	1250–900 B.C.
Mamon	Belize/Maya lowlands	800–300 B.C.
Mazapu	Tula	A.D. 600–900
Mesa de Guaja	Veracruz/Tamaulipas	1000–900 B.C.
Miccoatl	Teotihuacan	A.D. 150–250
Miraflores	Izapa/Kaminaljuyu	900–300 B.C. and 300 B.C.–A.D. 200
Nacaste	San Lorenzo	c. 700 B.C.
Natividad	Coixtlahuaca	A.D. 1000–1520/25
Nevada	Valley of Mexico	1400–1250 B.C.
Nogales	Tamaulipas	5000/4500–3000 B.C.
Ocampo	Tamaulipas	500 B.C.–A.D. 500
Ocos	Pacific coastal plain	1500–850 B.C.
Ojochi	San Lorenzo	1500–1350 B.C.
Palangana	San Lorenzo	600–400 B.C.
Palmillas	Tamaulipas	500 B.C.–A.D. 500
Palo Blanco	Tehuacan	200 B.C.–A.D. 700
Patlachique	Teotihuacan	100 B.C.–A.D. 1/250
Periquillo	western Mexico	2000/1600 B.C.–A.D. 1/250
Post La Venta	La Venta	600–400 B.C.
Providencia Majada	Kaminaljuyu	300 B.C.–A.D. 200
Purron	Puebla/Tehuacan	2300–1500 B.C.
Ramos	Coixtlahuaca	200 B.C.–A.D. 599
Remplos	San Lorenzo	100 B.C.
Rio Tunel	Chalchihuites	A.D. 950–1154
Rosario	Oaxaca	700/600–500/450 B.C.
San Jose Mogote	Oaxaca	2000/1600 B.C.–A.D. 250/290
San Lorenzo A, B	Veracruz	1100–1000/900 B.C.
Santa Clara	Izapa/Kaminaljuyu	900–300 B.C.
Santa Marta	Puebla/Oaxaca	7000–2000/2500 B.C.
Sayula	southern Jalisco	300 B.C.–A.D. 250/290
Swasey	Belize	2000–1000 B.C.
Tamaulipas Sequence	Gulf coast	11,000–7000 B.C.
Taposcolula	Oaxaca	A.D. 900–1521
Tehuacan Sequence	Puebla/Oaxaca	7000 B.C.–A.D. 1520
Tenayuca	Tenayuca	A.D. 1200–1355
Tenochtitlan (Aztec III)	Valley of Mexico	A.D. 1350–1450
Ticoman	Valley of Mexico	c. 500 B.C.
Tierras Largas	Oaxaca	1400–1150 B.C.
Tlamimilolpa	Teotihuacan	A.D. 300–500
Tlatelolco (Aztec IV)	Valley of Mexico	A.D. 1450–1521
Tlatilco	Oaxaca	1200–900? B.C.
Toliman	Jalisco/Colima	2000/1600 B.C.–A.D. 250/290
Tollan	Tula	A.D. 900–1150
Tres Picos, I, II, III	Veracruz	c. A.D. 1200
Tzacualli	Teotihuacan	A.D. 1–150
Tzakal	Peten (Putun)	A.D. 1/250–600
Venta Salada	Puebla/Oaxaca	A.D. 700/800–1520
Verdia	Jalisco	2000/1600 B.C.–A.D. 250/290
Villa Alta	San Lorenzo	A.D. 900
Xe	Altar de Sacrificios/Seibal	900 B.C.
Xochipilli	Guerrero	2000/1600 B.C.–A.D. 250/290
Xolalpan	Teotihuacan	A.D. 500–650
Zacapu	Michoacan	2000/1600 B.C.–A.D. 250/290

gional emergence and artistic endeavor among a single group or a small confederation.

MESOAMERICAN CLIMATE Conditions affecting the evolution and sustenance of human habitation. Mesoamerica is a region with remarkably diverse geographical configurations, and is subjected to extreme climatic variation. Such differences impacted upon the peoples of the region. Weather and climate altered the agricultural schedules in different regions. Seasonal crops depended on the condition of the soil and on rainfall and temperature. The region's microenvironments also predicated the types of grains and fruits that could be harvested.

In early periods, seasonal change promulgated migratory patterns among herds and game. The herds moved to heights to escape heat or cold and to graze upon vegetation available only during certain times of the year. The Paleo-Indian cultures followed these herds, entering new territories. During periods of settlement and later, the same climatic environments provided Mesoamericans with regional interdependence. The inhabitants of one region could not exist completely on the products available to them and migrated or traded for goods and products from other climate zones. It must be remembered that snow fell on the heights of Mesoamerica while volcanoe steamed and raged below. The highlands, usually temperate, were lushly forested and also contained desert regions where vegetation was scarce. In the torrid lowlands the soil was red and poor. Rain forests, savannas, grassland and plains lay in regions having coastal and barrier cliffs, and beaches, with their estuaries, encouraged settlements. All of these climatic conditions influenced Mesoamericans, altering the way they lived, the crops they raised and the religious and cosmological elements that inspired their cultures.

MESOAMERICAN CULTURAL EXCHANGE The artistic vision and adaptation to the diverse Mesoamerican geography and climate held in common among Mesoamericans or enjoyed on a mutual basis. The people of the region held certain beliefs in common and on many levels achieved cultural advances in a parallel fashion. Alert to one another's products, customs and beliefs, the people of the region were open to exchange. This sharing was not uniform throughout the region, however, and did not appear at the same time. Shared cultural attributes were dependent on the use of natural resources and political and social conditions. Distinct factors involved both in contact and in development, were very much tied to regional conditions and microenvironments. The following parallel cultural or artistic developments occurred in Mesoamerica.

Ball Courts. Arenas in the form of capital I's, found in ceremonial complexes and in cities throughout Mesoamerica. These courts were of different sizes and styles. There were ball courts in each ceremonial complex, except at Teotihuacan. Some sites contain many ball courts; excavations at El Tajin have uncovered 11. In the Classic Period (c. A.D. 1/250–900), ball courts had raised platforms along the sides, and the lower walls were sloped inward toward the playing area. In the Post-Classic Period (A.D. 900–1521), the walls of the ball courts were vertical. Markers, called

mercadores, were painted on the courts or represented by stone disks. In some centers the markers used were *hachas* a type of axe symbol. Citizens attended the games, and there is evidence of considerable betting on the outcome. The courts were also used for divination.

Ball Games. Forms of athletic competition probably held in imitation of the cosmic re-creations of the Mesoamerican deities, who were recorded as having played games with the sun, moon and other heavenly bodies. Such games were called *pok-ta-pok* by the Maya and *tlachli* by the Aztec. The players used hard rubber balls, some weighing as much as seven pounds. This required the use of play protective padding. The players were outfitted with yokes, U-shaped belts with carved designs, in the shape of the *hachas,* as well as other padded adornments, including a protective piece called a *palma* because it was carved with images of the human hand. The *palma* was helpful in ball throwing. Team members could not touch the rubber ball with their hands. It was bounced from the knee, elbow or hip, and the purpose of the game was to propel the ball through stone rings placed on the sides of the courts or probably to pass the ball into the opponent's end court. The use of rubber balls gives credence to the theory that the ball game originated in Veracruz, the origin of Mesoamerican rubber trees. The ball game is popular there still, and El Tajin, with 11 ball courts, is in Veracruz. Some games were envisioned as the battle between Quetzalcoatl and Ixlilton versus Xochipilli and Cinteotl, all divine beings. Still another form was a battle between Cihuacoatl and Ilamateuchtli.

Hieroglyphs. Writing in use in most Mesoamerican cultures, although not uniform as to sophistication, style or actual content. The hieroglyphs provided information, represented narratives and were incorporated into the artistic endeavors of most city-states and cultures. While phonetic elements were present to some degree in this writing form, hieroglyphic texts generally were mnemonic (memory-jogging) devices and required considerable memorization on the part of the writer and the reader. The presence of such writing puts to rest past claims that literacy and learning began in Mesoamerica with the arrival of the Spanish.

Numbers and Vigesimal (Base 20) Numerations. The mathematical systems employed by the various Mesoamerican cultures to determine their religious and secular calendars and to assist in architectural computations and agricultural planning. The number systems were valuable in census taking or recording tax and tributes. This form of mathematics was also used to maintain other religious and administrative records. Some civilizations of the Mesoamerican region employed the zero.

Valley of Mexico stamp

Public Architecture. See MESOAMERICAN ARCHITECTURE.

Religion. Acceptance of higher powers that governed the individual in daily existence and were believed to control human destiny, ethics and standards. Aspects held in common in the various Mesoamerican religion include pantheons of deities, human sacrifices, Flower Wars, and cannibalism.

The pantheons consisted of divine beings accepted as national or local patrons, generally associated with natural phenomena, agricultural needs, fertility or warfare. Most deities such as the sun, wind or rain, either humanized or presented as certain symbols, were revered by groups in various regions. A treasury of legends and mythical traditions arose concerning these pantheons, enriching the lives of the people with myths concerning creation of the sun, the origins of maize, death and other aspects of human existence.

Rituals of human sacrifices were conducted by most Mesoamerican religious priesthoods, associated with concepts of time and space, of dying worlds described in the calendars and the specific demands of the gods. The human sacrifices also represented the link between life and death. Through such sacrifices it was believed that the gods received nourishment, and were thus placated and willing to assure fertility and the sustaining worlds or suns.

Flower Wars were rituals conducted in Post-Classic Period (A.D. 900–1521) cultures to provide sacrificial victims. Called the *Xochiyaoyotl* in Nahuatl, the Flower Wars became more intense as time went on, culminating in large-scale human sacrifices by the Aztec. The victims, enemies captured in the Flower Wars, were slain. However, in some ceremonies specially selected persons, such as children, were sacrificed.

Cannibalism is recorded as occurring in the Post-Classic Period (A.D. 900–1521) but is not documented prior to that time. Cannibalism was related to the religious traditions of the era and was at times a part of the warrior group ceremonies.

Ritual Use of Rubber and Paper. Found in most Mesoamerican groups. Rubber balls were essential to the games conducted in the ceremonial complexes. Paper was manufactured by the Mesoamericans by beating the inner bark of the wild fig tree (*Ficus cotoni folia*), although some records list the maguey (*Agave americana*) as a source as well. Called *huun* in Mayan and *amatl* in Nahuatl, paper was used in the performance of Mesoamerican penitential rites. The priests drew blood from the fleshy parts of their bodies by piercing themselves with maguey spines. Nobles and others also took part in these mutilations during some festivals, allowing their blood to drip or splatter onto pieces of paper or on maguey leaves, which were then offered to the gods. Paper was also vital to the production of the various books or written materials of the various cultures.

Cardinal Points. See CARDINAL POINTS.

Cacao (Chocolate) Beans. See CACAO; MESOAMERICAN TRADE.

Warfare. See MESOAMERICAN WARFARE.

Step Pyramids. The towering, multi-tiered platforms that were used as foundations for temples. These pyramids were made of stone or masonry-rubble and varied in size and in purpose. The stone was generally sun-dried brick or local types of hewn stone. The structures were faced with limestone or with some other quality material from nearby quarries, and many were painted. Some pyramids held original, smaller platforms within; they were reconstructions, with the first temples simply enclosed within the larger edifice. Some had stairs on all sides, some on two sides and some were constructed with a single staircase. There were graves within some of the pyramids, as at Teotihuacan. The walls of the pyramids were ornate or plain, but most had carvings, balustrades, glyphs and idols incorporated into the design on the ascending levels. The bas reliefs in some pyramids were remarkable. In the Pyramid of the Niches at El Tajin, 365 niches were carved into the various tiers. By the Aztec era at least, the pyramids were sites for sacrifices, in many cases human, as part of religious or cosmological ceremonies. These sacrifices varied according to the cult of the god being revered and the traditions of the people.

Temples. Chambers that stood on the top of the pyramidal platforms throughout Mesoamerica. Normally one temple was built on each summit, but in some cases, as with the Aztec, two temples were built. These structures might contain one or more chambers. Many were thatch-roofed, but in some cultures, notably the Maya, the stone temples bore sculpted combs on the top. Within there were sometimes benches, carved bas reliefs, murals, idols or hanging symbols. The priests were usually the only individuals allowed within the temple sanctuaries. All rituals of a public or social nature were conducted outside, sometimes in enclosed courtyards, as at Monte Alban, or in open patios, as at Tenochtitlan. In some instances the various levels of the pyramid served as the ceremonial sites.

MESOAMERICAN FLORA Richly diverse vegetation available to the cultures of the region. Microenvironments were a particular aspect of the Mesoamerican region, engendered by vast geological and climatic extremes. These environments were dependent on varying rainfall, elevation, temperature and latitude, and in turn were vital to human existence. Erosion during the centuries and human habitation has altered the landscape of Mesoamerica to some degree, but here is a description of the flora present in the prehistoric and historical periods.

Tropical Rain Forests

In tropical rain forests, vegetation is dependent on hot, moist climates with continual and abundant rain. The soils of such forests are generally deep and well drained, often rising on slopes covered with rain-laden clouds or winds. The vegetation varies according to altitude. One feature of the rain forest is the profusion of growth under the canopy levels. These forests are typically multistory, with certain species climbing higher to seek nutriment and growth. Vegetation beneath the canopies often is on the banks of streams. Generally there is little seasonal variation in the growth of such rain forests. They contain a vast variety of plants, but any one species is sparsely distributed, so species are not grouped or clumped together. There are two types of Mesoamerican rain forests: Chiapas and Peten (Putun).

The Chiapas rain forests, located on both the gulf and the Pacific coasts, have tall trees and a great variety of floral species. Sapodillas, mahogany and other trees, including the *Castilla elastica* (latex), grow amid a tangle of orchids, bromeliads and wild yam vines, with ginger, laurel, sweet gum, oak and willows.

The Peten (Putun) rain forests are located south and east of Chiapas in present-day Guatemala, a region of high temperatures and only seasonal rainfall. They are broad and well drained, and mahogany, sapodilla, laurel, and hackberry trees, with orchids and Spanish moss, proliferates. The rain forests of the Peten usually had two to three stories of growth, with canopies.

Mountain Forests (cloud forests)

The mountain forests are formations found on higher elevations, with thinner canopies and generally only one story of trees. There are two types of mountain forests: Chiapas and Central Mexican. The Chiapas mountain forests reach the heights of the tropical rain forests and occur in two types: lower and higher mountain. The lower mountain forests *(selva de cajpoqui)* contain uniquely adapted vegetation found on the Mesa Central of Chiapas. The trees grow almost as tall as in the tropical rain forests of the region. The higher mountain forests *(selva baja siempre verde)* are found in the Sierra Madre de Chiapas and on the Mesa Central. These are dense forests with tree ferns, mosses, shrubs and evergreens. Another type of mountain forests, partially deciduous, grows in the same locale as the higher mountain forests. Pine forests are dominant in Chiapas as well, mixed with firs and junipers. The Central Mexican mountain forests are sparse in vegetation because of the lower rain levels there but have pine and juniper in certain regions. Oaks and dense forests are found at some elevations, with wild cherry trees and other varieties. Fir forests are also present at this altitude.

Seasonal Forests and Savannas

Seasonal forests and savannas vary considerably as a result of geological conditions, dependent always on water sources and the depth and quality of the soil. These include Chiapas seasonal forests and central Mexican seasonal region.

In Chiapas seasonal forests, stands of trees line the interior basins of the region and on the Pacific slopes. Deciduous forests are widely distributed throughout the region, especially on the Pacific Sierra Madre heights. Besides trees, shrubs and brush stands are present. The lowlands of the Chiapas region is covered with thorny woods.

Savannas are on the coasts and in the inland regions, with forests rising up as islands in the low vegetation. In its primeval state, the region of Chiapas had vast pine forests that gave way to woodlands and savannas.

The central Mexican seasonal regions originate in the Balsas and Papaloapan River basins. Low forests are also in the Pacific lowlands. In Oaxaca and in southern Puebla, seasonal vegetation is found in the basins. Tehuacan's rocky soil nurtures the yucca and other forms of cacti as well as grasses.

Dry Evergreen Forests

Dry evergreen forests are vast stands found in the eastern region of Mesoamerica, where pine woods and grassland merged, with sedge flourishing in areas that receive more rainfall. Rain continues through the year in these places, allowing for forest growth. Oaks, sand-paper trees and shrubs are also abundant.

MESOAMERICAN FAUNA   The remarkable variety of wildlife that teemed in the region, no longer extent in many regions because of the presence of human habitation. Location of species varied throughout Mesoamerica. Some species were indigenous to different altitudes, lake sites, rain forests or plains. The following extinct and continuing species were or are present in Mesoamerica during the prehistoric and/or historical periods.

Extinct Fauna.   Animals living in the prehistoric periods, including the Paleo-Indian (11,000–7000 B.C.), but now extinct. A combination of factors caused the decline and disappearance of such species, including changes in climate, excessive hunting and changes in the ecological balance of the various environments. Many species still present in Mesoamerica were in the region in the Paleo-Indian Period, but they adapted to alterations and flourished. The massive animals, called the Mesoamerican megafauna, available to the earliest peoples entering the region that have since become extinct include camelids, giant sloths, glyptodons, mammoths, mastodons, and wild horses.

Continuing Species.   The animals, reptiles and birds remaining in the Mesoamerican region after the arrival of humans. These are found in a dazzling variety and include mammals, birds and reptiles and amphibians.

More than 500 species of mammals have been noted in Mesoamerica, comprising up to 170 genera (including 60 genera of bats). The most common are:

agouti	mice
anteaters	moles
armadillos	monkeys
badgers	mountain lions
bats	ocelots
bears	oppossums
bobcats (lynx)	otters
chipmunks	paca
coyotes	porcupines
deer	prairie dogs
dogs	raccoons
foxes	rats
gophers	sheep
grison	shrews
jaguars	skunks
jaguarundis	squirrels—tree, flying and
kinkajous	ground
lagomorphs—hares, rabbits and cottontails	tapirs
	tayra
manatees	weasels
margays	

The birds of Mesoamerica include the beautiful tropical varieties with colorful and elaborate plumage and those found in other lands. The most common birds of the region include:

bitterns	ospreys
blackbirds	owls
bobwhites	parrots
cardinals	pigeons
cranes	pipits
cuckoos	plovers
doves	quails
ducks	quetzals
eagles	roadrunners
egrets	sandpipers
falcons	shrikes
finches	sparrows
flamingos	spoonbills
flycatchers	starlings
geese	swallows
grebes	swans
gulls	swifts
hawks	tanagers
herons	terns
hummingbirds (100 species)	tinamous
ibises	towhees
kingfishers	turkeys
larks	vultures
loons	wood warblers
macaws	woodcreepers
orioles	

The reptiles and amphibians are also well represented in Mesoamerica, with the following species most common:

amphibians	pythons
boa constrictors	racers
coral snakes	rattlesnakes
crocodiles	sea snakes
Fer-de-lance	skinks
fish (in great variety)	turtles (land and sea)
garter snakes	water moccasins
Gila monsters	water snakes
lizards	whip snakes
pit vipers	worm snakes

MESOAMERICAN GEOGRAPHY The pattern of lands that make up the region called Mesoamerica; from Mexico's Panuco River, along the River Lerma to the Sinaloa River, south to the mouth of the Motagua River in Guatemala, through Lake Nicaragua to Costa Rica, Guatemala, El Salvador, northwest Honduras and Nicaragua. Situated below the Tropic of Cancer, the mountain chains and high-lands altered the traditional climatic conditions of other realms in the same latitude. Mesoamerica includes diverse geological formations: elevations and depressions, tropical lowlands, mountain ranges, lakes, volcanic formations, rivers, coastal zones and climatic conditions among the most extreme found on earth. Such geographical variations nurtured the first human settlements in Mesoamerica and sustained the great civilizations that followed. The conditions also demanded a certain element of cooperation among groups facing seasonal and environmental challanges.

The usual geographic regions discussed in any study of Mesoamerica include highlands, lowlands, the Isthmus of Tehuantepec, and the Yucatan Peninsula. Further studies of Mesoamerica provide information on the geological and geographical diversity and include extratropical dry lands, cool tropical highlands and warm tropical lowlands.

While the northern Mexican drylands affected the Mesoamerican cultures, this territory is no longer included in usual definitions of Mesoamerica. Eleven regions are recognized today.

Mesa del Norte.   These arid and semiarid sections of the northern Mexican Plateau were once called *Atliplanicie Septentrional*. Deserts and vast interior drainage systems predominate, extending northward to San Luis Potosi, a land associated with the Huaxtec. The high elevation of the Mesa del Norte and the presence of winter polar air allows for freezing temperatures at night, contrasting with hot, sunny days. This combination makes the region one of the most inhospitable climates in Mesoamerica. The eastern two-thirds of the Mesa del Norte is composed of limestone rock formations, which receive little rainfall throughout the year. The region is also marked by extensive mountain ranges running parallel to one another, forming a funnel widest in the north. Plains and basins complete the topographical scene.

Mesa Central.   This region is adjacent to the Mesa del Norte. It exhibits all of the typical volcanic formations. Once called the *Altiplanicie Meridional*, the Mesa Central is noted for the Transverse Volcanic Axis (*Cordillera Neo-volcanico*) on its southern rim. This axis contains an east-west range containing the following major volcanoes: Citlaltepetl (Pico de Orizaba), Ixtaccihuatl, Matlalcueyetl (Malinche), Naucampatepetl (Cofre de Perate), Popocatepetl, Tancitaro, Volcan de Colima, and Xinantecatl (Nevado de Toluca).

The traditional volcanic formations in the Mesa Central are conical hills of cinder and explosion, with craters and vents formed during the original eruptions and thereafter. As many as 800 volcanoes have been recorded in the Tarascan region of the Mesa Central. This east-west range goes through the region and into the Sierra Madre Oriental on the eastern rim of Mesoamerica. Another volcanic axis extends from the Grijalva River almost to the southern borders of the region. Some volcanic peaks in this range reach 13,000 to 17,000 feet, and their activity shakes the surrounding lands, threatening whole populations.

The climate of the Mesa Central is cool, with tropical highland environments. There are some deserts, within the region, but there are also intermountain basins having rich forests of evergreens, pines and deciduous oaks. Fir and white pines grow on the higher slopes.

In the Valley of Mexico, as in the Puebla Basin, cinder cones (a type of volcano) and dry basins (*xalapazcos*, Nahuatl for "sand containers") appear beside cinder cones with small lakes (*axalapazos*, Nahuatl for "containers of sand with water"). Also present are gently sloping hills that were created by lava flows and erosions. Flat-topped mesas, or *canadas*, dominate the terraced hills. Such regions were well suited to the first efforts at plant and animal domestication and for incipient settlements. Geysers, lakes, springs and volcanoes also are present in the valley. The region from Lake Chapala across northern Michoacan currently exhibits these geological formations. The climate is relatively cool, with rainfall from June to November, allowing one good crop per year.

The Sierra Madre Oriental. This range of mountains and basins extends from north to south, forming the eastern flank of the Mexican Plateau. The Sierra Madre Oriental gives rise to the Oaxacan highlands and merges into the highlands of Chiapas, which have been altered from their original formation in northern Puebla and Veracruz by volcanic outpourings. Elongated valleys, called *potreros*, are a distinctive feature of the region, which has grassy plains with abundant game, at least in the older historical periods. *Resumideros*, or sinkholes, are present, as well as limestone caverns over underground streams, formed by the Guayalejo, Verde and Moctezuma rivers. Natural trails once spread all across the territory, enabling the Mesoamericans to move through the mountains to reach the coastal lowlands, which were seasonal habitats.

The Sierra Madre Occidental. This mountain range forms the western or Pacific flank of the region and reaches great heights. To the north is a narrow coastal plain, the terminal portion of the Lerma-Santiago river system that rises out of the Toluca Valley in central Mexico. Fertile plains narrow, and the coast becomes rugged and harsh. Within its towering chain, the Sierra Madre Occidental affords highland meadows, mesas and cliff habitations. Deep canyons, called *barrancas*, contained gold and other metals prized by Mesoamerican historical civilizations.

The Sierra Madre Del Sur. This mountain chain extends from the Sierra Madre Occidental on the Pacific coast of Mesoamerica to Oaxaca. Many rivers are found there, as well as a coastal plain with marshes, lagoons and mangrove swamps.

The Coastal Lowlands. The Coastal Lowlands are made of various regions having distinct microenvironments. These regions include the Pacific and the Gulf Coastal Lowlands. The Pacific Coastal Lowlands encompass a narrow strip of land that borders on volcanic masses and is characterized by definite periods of rainfall. The lowland topography includes the Altar Desert (the *Gran Desierto*), bordering on the barren volcanic Cerro Pinacate. There are also tropical deciduous or semideciduous forests and a plain almost 50 miles wide in some places. Hills and streams constitute much of the landscape, and there are a number of natural harbors. Mesoamericans used the river flood plains and the delta plains for transportation and trade or travel. The major rivers of Pacific Coastal Lowlands include the Culiacan, Fuerte, Mayo, San Pedro, Santiago, and Yaqui.

The northern coastal plains allow for flooding and irrigation projects, while the humid southern plains feature riverbanks from the waterways of the region and natural levees. Lagoons and beaches are also found here.

The Gulf Coastal Lowlands extend from the Rio Grande to the Yucatan Peninsula, varying throughout in width from a few miles up to 50 miles. The Gulf Coastal Lowlands contain low mountains and hills with flood and delta plains. Five major rivers supply the region: Candeleria, Coatzalcoalcos-Uspanapa, Grijalva, Tonala, and Usumacinta.

In other parts of the region there are low-relief sierras or mountain chains, including the Sierra Tamaulipas, Sierra Cruillas and Sierra San Carlos. In northern Veracruz, hills dominate the landscape, offering slopes of vegetation and sites for crops. There are also low coastal plains in more southerly portions, such as Tabasco. Volcanic remains are present throughout. A lava dome rises near Aldama, and basaltic necks and needle peaks are abundant, including Bernal de Horcasitas, northwest of Tampico. In southern Veracruz, the volcanic Las Tuxtla Mountains dominate a plain between two rivers, where the Olmec flourished. Nearby are the San Martin and the Santa Marta volcanoes, with the volcanic lake Catemaco.

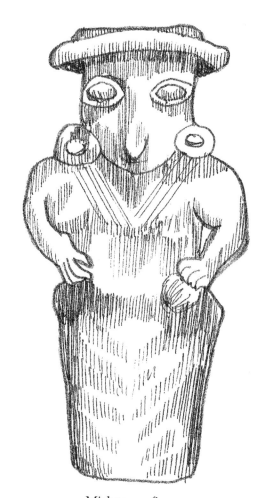

Michoacan figure

Natural terraces form levees, and river and flood plains provide agricultural lands. Much of this region, from the Rio Tamesi to the Yucatan Peninsula, holds evidence of human habitation through the historical period.

Other distinctive features include salt formations, natural islands, barrier beaches, lagoons, estuaries and marshlands. All of these offer diverse natural products for their inhabitants. The three major lagoons in here are the Madre, Tamiahua and Cabo Rojo.

Balsas-Tepalcatepec Depression. This is the largest basin or natural depression in southern Mexico, separating the Mexican Plateau from the Oaxaca and Guerrero highlands. Many tributaries meet the Balsas River, originating in Tlaxcala and Puebla, here. This waterway surges through hilly terrain to form the Pacific coastal delta. In southern Michoacan, the Tepalcatapec River forms another natural basin that, in turn, provides the region with the Plain of Apatzingan by draining the land. The Balsa River tributaries here include the Amacuzac, Atoyac, Nexapa, Poblano, Tepalcatepec, and Zitacuaro.

In Guerrero, where the Balsas River defines the boundary between Guerrero and Michoacan, the river is called the Mezcala.

Southern Mexican Highlands. The lands south of the Balsas River, where the Sierra Madre del Sur meets the Sierra de Coalcoman, a unique region. In the Oaxacan region, the Sierras rise to vast peaks, adjoining valleys and mesas. Volcanic evidence is present in the territory, with little level land available for agriculture. Streams carve V-shape valleys, but most of the land is steeply sloped. The Valley of Oaxaca, one of the largest basins, joins the Tlacolula in the east and Etla in the north, creating a varied landscape. This region is drained by the Atoyac River, a tributary of the Balsas. At one time the region was inhabited by the Mixtec and Zapotec. The great sites of Monte Alban and Mitla were erected in this hilly domain. To the northwest was Mixteca Alta, a region drained by the Balsas. To the east are the Mije Highlands. In the northeast, the Sierra Madre de Oaxaca is the barrier to the Oaxacan highlands and to the coastal lowlands of Veracruz.

The plains of Tehuacan, an arid depression that links Tehuacan and the Puebla Basin to the Valley of Oaxaca, is to the west. The nearby Papaloapan Basin is believed to have been the site of the gold mines worked during the Classic and Post-Classic Periods (c. A.D. 1/250–900; A.D. 900–1521). The Balsas and Papaloapan river basins are believed to have provided most of the gold the Aztec demanded during their period of domination (A.D. 1430–1519). The southern highlands also form a cliffed barrier on the Pacific coast. Lagoons, inlets and estuaries are present on the shoreline, and tropical and deciduous forests exist.

Chiapas and Guatemalan Highlands. The region formed by the Sierra Madre de Chiapas, which includes the Pacific coastal territory down to the Bay of Honduras. These highlands are part of the Sierra San Cristobal chain, leading into the territories of Guatemala from Chiapas, Peten (Putun) and the Maya Mountains in modern Belize. The Sierra Madre de Chiapas ranges in steep crests overlooking the ocean and extending in a northeasterly direction to the central Chiapas Valley. Geological activities formed V-shape basins and valleys in the region. A specific feature is the *llano*, a grass-covered territory with plentiful streams that open onto alluvial lands. The Sierra de Omoa chain in Guatemala continues the highland characteristics, as do the Chaucas, Minas and Montana del Mico ranges in the east. North of the Chaucas Mountains are other basins, including the Cabulco, Chicaj, Rabinal and Salama. This region may have been a source for jade (jadeite), especially near Manzanai, in the Motagua Valley, at the base of the Minas Mountains.

The highlands of Chiapas are steep and narrow. One region, called the *Meseta Central,* on the San Cristobal Plateau, overlooks the central Chiapas Valley. This region is filled with sinkholes, hills and canyons. Streams provide a natural irrigation. The Guatemalan extension of these highlands is in the *Altos Cuchumatanes.* The central Valley of Chiapas is a wide territory drained by the Upper Grijalva River, called Rio Grande de Chiapas by locals, rising near the Mexican-Guatemala border. It is a region of hills, terraced slopes and mesas. Also present is the *Sumidero,* a canyon formed by waters entering the Sierra San Cristobal. To the west is Rio de la Venta, a tributary of the Grijalva, which forms another gorge. The Motagua River wanders through sloping hills and valleys, joining the Grijalva near Huehuetenango. These plains and rises provide a drainage divide. The Motagua Valley widens and extends into the Maya Quirigua in the east.

The Isthmus of Tehuantepec. A lowland depression that lies between the southern highlands of Mexico and the Chiapas highlands. The isthmus was formed by a drainage divide, with crystalline hills that narrow at the Sierra Atravesada, another steep mountain chain.

The Yucatan Peninsula. A limestone platform, inhabited by the ancient Maya. Now called the *Antillean Foreland,* the peninsula is believed to be a recently emerged landmass, probably from the Pleistocene Period. The Sierra de Ticul, a ridge formed between Campeche and Merida, dominates the landscape and divides the Yucatan plain and the hills of Campeche, which lie to the north. The ridge continues in Guatemala as the Peten (Putun). Along the Yucatan Peninsula's eastern side, the limestone-ridged Maya Mountains are adjacent to swamps and marshlands. The peninsula is geologically designated as karstic, which indicates that a lack of surface water, because rain is absorbed by the porous rock and maintained in large underground channels. The famed *cenotes,* the Maya word for well, were formed when the surface rocks collapsed over a subterranean stream. Two types of *cenotes* were formed in the process: a true *cenote,* which is a round or oval-shape well with vertical walls; and the *resumidero,* which is a funnel-shape well.

Aguadas, shallow depressions of temporary water, are abundant in the Yucatan. Both *aguadas* and *cenotes* were vital to Maya agriculture. Caves were used as shelters and for defense purposes during Maya settlement times.

Although marked by depressions and rocky ridges, the Yucatan Pensinula provides *hayas,* pockets of soil that have been kept moist by abundant rainfall in the Sierra de Ticul and in the northeastern hills of Campeche. *Puuc,* a Maya word for hill, not only represented the region but came to signify cultural aspects as well. Such great *Puuc* ceremonial complexes as Labna and Uxmal were built there. The Peten (Putun) region of the peninsula covers most of northern Guatemala. It is an area of rolling hills, *aguadas* and conical volcanic features. Depressions in the southern region are generally filled with lakes or swamps, and tropical rain forests are present. The northern and northwestern areas form barrier beaches that enclose lagoons and tidal swamps, serving as salt formation sites. The eastern coast is a cliffed shoreline, with beaches and headlands. The northeastern region always has had faults, showing erosion and weather damage, and the island of Cozumel is a direct result of that geological phenomenon, having broken off from the mainland. A dense barrier coral reef extends from the northeastern corner of this part of the Yucatan Peninsula to the Gulf of Honduras.

MESOAMERICAN LANGUAGES
The vast variety of tongues spoken throughout the region in the past and the present. Some of these languages have similarities, and it is evident that some language families influenced others. As languages are fluid entities, subject to change and adaptation, documentation concerning their categories and basic elements has been difficult. In addition, recent studies have discovered previously unknown languages, particular among the Maya. This gives evidence once again of various adaptations of the languages in the region. Scholars have divided the Mesoamerican languages into the following families.

1. chinantecan
2. cuitlatec isolate
3. huave isolate
4. jicaque isolate
5. lencan
6. manguean
7. mayan
8. misulmalpan
9. mixe-zoque
10. mixtecan
11. oto-pamean
12. paya
13. popolocan
14. seri isolate
15. tarasco isolate
16. tequistlatec
17. tlapanec
18. totonacan
19. uto-aztecan
20. xinca
21. zapotecan

Chinantecan. Another family of Mesoamerican languages, called a group in some lists. Four separate languages, each called Chinantec, are included, all used in northern Oaxaca by approximately 25,000 people.

Cuitlatec (Teco) Isolate. An extinct family of Mesoamerican languages that was once used in Guerrero, Mexico.

Huave Isolate. A family of languages used in Oaxaca by approximately 6,000 people.

Jicaque Isolate. A language family with several dialects, spoken chiefly in Honduras.

Lencan. A family of Mesoamerican languages of Honduras and El Salvador. Languages in this family include Lenca and Chilanga, extinct in most regions and rare in others.

Manguean. A family of languages that includes Mangue (Dirian, Nagrandan), Chiapanec, Chorotega and Nicoya. This family ranges from Chiapas, Mexico to Nicaragua, Honduras, Costa Rica and southeastern Oaxaca. Only Nicoya, in Costa Rica, is spoken today. The rest are believed to be extinct.

Maya. One of the largest families of Mesoamerican languages, including many groups that are used by more than 3 million people today. A complex of one of the groups, Huaxtec, is spoken in northern Veracruz and in San Luis Potosi. Chicomuceltec is used in Chiapas.

In the Yucatec complex, the Yucatec language is spoken by over 350,000 individuals today in Yucatan, Campeche, Quintana Roo, northern Guatemala and Belize. Other languages in this complex include Lacandon (in Chiapas), Itza (in northern Guatemala) and Mopan (in northern Guatemala and in Belize).

In the Mayan western division, the Cholan branch includes Chontal, Chol and Chorti, which are used in Tabasco, Chiapas, northern Guatemala and Honduras. The Tzotzelan group of this division includes Tzotzil and Tzeltal, the languages of Chiapas, spoken by more than 200,000 people.

Another western division branch is the Kanjobalan. The Chujean group of this branch includes the Tojolabal and the Chul, spoken in Chiapas and Guatemala. A second group, called the Kanjobalan proper, includes Kanjobal (Solomec, Conob), Acatec, Jacaltec, Motozintlec and Tuzantec. The languages are spoken in Chiapas and in northwestern Guatemala by approximately 75,000 people.

The eastern division of the Mayan family includes the Greater Mamean branch. Mam, Teco, Aguacatec and Ixli are languages in this branch, spoken by approximately 400,000 individuals in Chiapas and Guatemala. A second branch is the Greater Quichean, which is spoken chiefly in Guatemala and includes Quiche, Uspantec, Achi, Sacapultec, Sipacapa, Cakchiquel, Tzutujil, Pocoman, Pocomchi and Kekchi, and the Quiche and Pocom complexes. More than 1 million people speak the languages of this branch.

Misulmalpan. A language family associated with the cultural groups now residing in Nicaragua, Honduras and El Salvador. This family contains three groups: Misquito, Matagalpa (complex) and Sumo (complex). The Misumalpan (Misuluan) family tongues are spoken by only a few groups today. The languages belonging to this family include Misquito; the Matagalpa complex, which includes Matagalpa and Cacacopera; and the Sumo complex, which includes the languages of Sumo, Ulua and Tahuajca.

Mixe-Zoque. A Mesoamerican language family in use by approximately 100,000 people in Tabasco, Chiapas, Oaxaca and Veracruz. The languages in this family include Zoque, Sierra Popoluca, Texistepec, Sayula, Oluta, Mixe and Tapachultec. The Mixecan group has the largest number of modern speakers. Tapachultec is believed to be extinct.

Mixtecan. A Mesoamerican language family that includes the Greater Mixtecan Branch, Amurgo, Mixtec 1, 2 and 3, Cuicatec and Trique. The Mixtecan family languages are spoken today by approximately 300,000 people in Guerrero, Puebla and Oaxaca, Mexico.

Oto-Pamean (Otomi-Pame). A family of languages that includes Chichimec, Matlatzincan, Otomi and Mazahua. These languages are spoken today in Guanajuato, Mexico, in San Luis Potosi, Hidalgo, and in the State of Mexico, as well as in Michoacan. As many as 300,000 people speak Otomi today, with 100,000 using Mazahuan.

Paya. A language complex of northern Honduras. Only a few groups use it.

Popolocan (Olmecan). A language family still in use in Oaxaca and in Puebla, Mexico. The Chocoan group in this family includes Ixcatec, and the Chacho complex includes Chocho and Poploc. The Mazatec complex of the Popolocan family includes Mazatec 1 and 2.

Seri Isolate. A family of Mesoamerican languages used on the Sonora coast of Mexico in modern times but rare.

Tarasco Insolate. A family of Mesoamerican languages in use by approximately 60,000 persons today in Michoacan in western Mexico.

Tequistlatec. A southeastern Oaxacan language family, used today in the mountains and coastal areas. This family includes Huamelultec and Tequistlatec, spoken by about 10,000 people.

Tlapanec. A language of several groups in use today in Guerrero, Mexico, in Nicaragua and in El Salvador. Tlapanec, the Guerrero language, is also called Yope and is spoken by around 25,000 people. The Tlapanec family languages of Nicaragua and El Salvador are rare.

Totonacan. A Mesoamerican language family that includes Totonac and Tepehua. Approximately 140,000 people in Veracruz and Puebla speak Totonac, and roughly 4,000 speak Tepehua in Veracruz and Hidalgo.

Uto-Aztecan. One of the major Mesoamerican language families, in use from Canada, down the California coast, to Panama. Several branches of Uto-Aztecan are in use in the regions of North America. The Pimon group is still spoken in Sonora and Jalisco, Mexico, and the Yaquian branch has some extinct tongues and others spoken in Sinaloa and in Chihuahua. Several thousand people use the Coran group spoken in the modern Mexican state of Nayarit.

The Nahua group of the Uto-Aztecan family is the largest, with Nahuatl tongues spoken in Nayarit, Puebla, Hidalgo, Michoacan and Veracruz. The Pipil in Mexico speak the Nahual language. Although Pochutec, one of the historical languages of this group, is extinct, as many as 1.5 a million people use Nahuatl root tongues in Mexico today. Toltec and Aztec impact on the Mesoamerican region may account for the dominance of Nahuatl even to this day.

Xinca. A complex, with types of languages, all called Xinca, spoken in Mexico, although most forms are considered extinct.

Zapotecan. A Mesoamerican language family that includes Zapotec, Papabuco and Chatino. The Zapotec group of this family includes Juarez Zapotec, Villalta Zapotec, Mountain Zapotec and Valley Zapotec. More than 300,000 people use the Zapotecan family tongues today.

The grammatical and written forms of some of these languages are included in the sections on the major cultures of Mesoamerica. See under separate entries, especially in the sections on the Maya, Aztec (Mexica) and others. The

divisions are not static but continue to evolve as more research uncovers their origins and as the modern descendants of the groups develop. Some of the languages no longer extant are being studied in order to translate and interpret the achievements of the cultures of ancient eras. The languages of Mesoamerica, fluid in their origins and in their use, remain a vital hallmark for study but at the same time present difficulties in ascertaining their development and where no longer extant tongues had been spoken.

MESOAMERICAN MATHEMATICS The system of vigesimal numerations used in Mesoamerica throughout the historical periods, called the base 20 system as opposed to the modern base 10. The Maya, and probably the Olmec before them, used three symbols as determinatives, allowing for the expression of values: the dot for one, the bar for five and a stylized shell for zero. The Maya system was vigesimal and increased from bottom to top in vertical columns. Thus the first and lowest place had a value of one, the next above it the value of 20, then 400 and so on. The sum of 20, written with a dot and a zero, also had its own symbol. Addition and subtraction could be accomplished speedily with such a system. Some scholars believe that multiplication and division are also possible, although such applications are not documented.

The Maya used mathematics for calendrical computation, with a modification introduced to signify certain sums as "many," which is believed to represent "millions." Mathematics was also necessary for Maya architectural purposes. It also was invaluable to accounting procedures, for computing taxes, tributes and in trade.

The Aztec, building their empire in the Post-Classic Period (A.D. 900–1521), inherited the Maya system and employed mathematics for architectural, calendrical and divination purposes. In the Aztec numerical system, the first 20 numbers were expressed in the Maya form, but the first five numbers were given specific names, as were 10 and 15. A flag represented the number 20 in this vigesimal system, and it was the basis for the designation of all larger totals, which were multiples of 20. When dealing with fractional amounts, the Aztec drew a portion of a particular number. When devising calendars, the Aztec calculated time by employing their sophisticated numerical system. Based on the Maya bar-dot system, the Aztec number-and-glyph system allowed them to calculate with an aptitude sufficient to handle the administrative and record-keeping offices of their vast empire. (See MATHEMATICS under individual cultures).

MESOAMERICAN TRADE The exchange of commodities throughout Mesoamerica during all its historical periods. From the Paleo-Indian Period (11,000–7000 B.C.), trade or barter brought the emerging cultures together. There is no documentation concerning trade in the Paleo-Indian Period, but the gathering of the macrobands (combined family groups) probably encouraged people to offer one another tools, weapons and plants in exchange for others recently manufactured or gathered. As the various civilizations arose, trade and agriculture became economic necessities for many of the cultures.

Miraflores ceramic

When the Olmec were in power (c. 1500 B.C.) in the Tuxtla Mountains and on the Rio Chiquito, their products began to influence other cultures. Trade was obviously a method of establishing the Olmec cultural and artistic influence, and their wares, particularly ceramics, began to appear in other regions. Olmec wares, including those having the jaguar motif, have been recovered from sites as far from the Olmec territories as Oaxaca and in the Valley of Mexico. The Olmec also established garrisoned trade outposts. These fortresses were built to safeguard the passage of raw materials into Olmec domains and the exportation of manufactured goods.

The cities of Teotihuacan and Monte Alban, following the Olmec, had vast trade enterprises, but the Maya started long-distance trade systems. Because the Maya were present in many locales, they adapted and realigned trade accordingly. The Maya traders, called *ah ppolom yac* or simply *ppolom*, were integral forces in Maya life. The great Maya cities and complexes were linked by trade, both internal and interregional, and most Maya cities combined religious festivals with open markets. As political changes took place in Mesoamerica, such as the disastrous collapse of Teotihuacan and the incursions of the Mexica, merchants shifted emphasis on goods to be traded and on its flow. The rise of the Peten (Putun) and the organization of Cozumel trade initiated the seafaring expeditions of Maya traders. Trade supported the administrative offices of entire cities and regions and provided Maya regions with specific roles in the manufacture of goods to be traded locally or internationally. Both the Maya highlands and the lowlands benefited.

With the rise of the Aztec (Mexica) in the Post-Classic Period (A.D. 900–1521), the emerging empire began to dominate other regions. The Aztec quickly grasped the importance of gathering the natural resources of vassal or conquered territories in order to pool them in an exchange enterprise that would span the geographic and climatic diversities of Mesoamerica. While the Maya had used trade to disseminate Maya culture, the Aztec merchants, called *pochteca*, reflected the militaristic and expansionist policies of city-state. Both Tenochtitlan and Tlatelolco had massive marketplaces, and *pochteca* began to enter into trade with other cultures, sometimes in disguise. Aztec trade was based primarily on agricultural products, but dealers could provide every known luxury or commodity in their vast warehouses and markets. So broad was the trade enterprise of the Aztec, in fact, that governmental regulations were established to maintain order, justice and service. In time, the Aztec *pochteca* held political and administrative power in their regions. (See TRADE under the individual cultural entries for details.)

MESOAMERICAN WARFARE Military activity and tactics practiced by the various historical groups of the region over the centuries, predicated upon political and social changes. Military activity of the Mesoamerican cultures was evolutionary in terms of defenses, forces and ferocity. The weapons remained paleolithic, but the extent and the level of force used by the various groups developed parallel to imperial and expansionist imperatives.

Even in the earliest historical periods in Mesoamerica, population pressure and the need for local resources prompted military action. The early nomadic groups competed in some regions for resources, and they confronted, the advance of other peoples who entered their region. Agricultural development in certain regions prompted the rise of aristocratic castes, with rank usually predicated upon land-holdings and upheld by the allegiance of those of lesser rank. Rivalries arose and territorial expansion was necessitated, as were confederations and alliances. Smaller cultures were absorbed or exiled from territories as the first dominant groups arose in the region.

The Olmec, considered the earliest major Mesoamerican culture, have left some military records in the form of reliefs depicting warriors using clubs. Trade outposts were fortified, perhaps even garrisoned by Olmec leaders. Such military actions may have been defensive in nature, perhaps associated with Olmec trade, vital to the economy of the culture. The extent and the level of military activity within the Olmec territorial limits is presently unknown. Olmec stone heads are adorned with helmets, which may or may not reflect a military stance. Certainly their rounded form was an artistic device designed to protect the sculptures by avoiding rough edges and the helmets may have been duplicates of those worn in Olmec ball games.

The rise of the city-states, such as Monte Alban, Teotihuacan and others, indicates that expansion and the establishment of small domains was very much part of the regional activities at the close of the Formative Period, c. A.D. 250/290. Such city-states may have evolved from confederations, alliances or military exploits. Certainly Teotihuacan used defensive methods to absorb its neighboring cultures, although vassal states may have come willingly in order to share in the cultural efforts being launched. Widespread trade, very much evident in this era, would have been a powerful inducement for small groups to ally themselves with Teotihuacan. No Mesoamerican group in this period maintained a standing army. Aristocrats played leading roles in military activities, as they did in trade and in the administrative aspects of Mesoamerican life, but the extent of their military actions remains obscure. Some wars or campaigns may have been conducted to provide the altars of the gods with victims for the death rituals of Mesoamerican tradition. Such victims, however, may have come as part of the tribute offered by smaller communities to the major city-states.

During their formative periods, the Maya do not appear to have been engaged in military activities. The Maya ceremonial complexes reflect an era of peace and nonaggression. These complexes stand in open places, with few visible defenses. Some, especially those near the borders of the northern Mexican regions, did have walls, and in later stages possible defensive measures may have been anticipated. This need for defensive architecture lasted until the close of the Classic Period, around A.D. 900. Then the Maya aristocrats began to abandon the cities, moving into more protected climates, and a new elite arose in the Yucatan, evidencing Mexica influences and a new outlook encouraging militarism and expansion.

Rivalries blossomed into military campaigns as various cities vied for power and began to extend their influence. The XIU and the COCOM, for example, were two noble families that conducted enduring and volatile feuds. Lords such as Great Jaguar Paw also conducted military campaigns with a new ferocity and a new cunning, bringing about a glorification of war in Maya realms. Such campaigns and continuing rivalries, abetted by the stress caused by Mexica influence and the arrival of Mexica groups into the region, splintered the Maya, bringing about a group of small, well-armed cities that vied with one another for power and for land.

The TOLTEC, arriving in the region around the same time, were a warlike people who honored warriors and battle. The military mystique was part of the Toltec tradition, evidenced by the *telemones*, the Atlantean warrior statues, and by the bas reliefs in Toltec cities. The CHICHIMEC and the ITZA, also warlike and aggressive, carried the military ideals into several regions of Mesoamerica, setting the stage for the final Mesoamerican dominant culture, the Aztec (Mexica).

Proving themselves ferocious in battle and quick to learn from the older traditions, the Aztec established the city of Tenochtitlan in Lake Texcoco and began to found their empire. Throwing off the confining yoke of the Tepanec, the Aztec succeeded in allying themselves with neighboring states and with militarily astute leaders, such as Nezahualcoyotl. The TRIPLE ALLIANCE, the league started by the Aztec, shared not only combative campaigns but the spoils of war including tribute, captives and land. Vassal states and allies were drawn into the Aztec Empire, and new military perimeters were established, allowing the Aztec and their confederates to plunder entire districts, as far as the border of Guatemala. Aztec emperors were warriors for the most part, impelled by the worship of Huitzilopochtli, their war god, and by the increasing demand for imperial domain.

The FLOWER WARS were begun for expansion and to gather human victims for the sacrificial rituals in Tenochtitlan. Knights, following the Toltec models, were grouped in military orders, establishing shrines, such as at Malinalco, as well as military training centers and the cults of the eagle, jaguar and coyote. A vast military system emerged in the Late Classic Period, although standing armies were not widespread or even permanently maintained. Smaller groups, such as the Tarascan, beyond the Aztec circle of power also maintained military readiness, and they withstood the onslaught of Aztec forces.

Throughout the Mesoamerican historical periods, the weapons used remained largely unchanged. The elite units and the various military orders were adorned with elaborate headdresses and with insignias of their particular affiliation. Other troops wore quilted cotton armor or no armor at all. The units marched under their own local leaders, joining the expeditionary forces summoned by the various aristocrats. When the campaign ended, most units returned to their own lands and to their agricultural activities. Shields, helmets, spears, bows and arrows, and obsidian clubs were part of the military weapon stores.

Another innovation of the Late Classic Period, perhaps based on earlier models, was the use of intelligence operatives, among the Aztec a function fulfilled by the *pochtecas*, the Aztec traders. Such Aztec spies were sometimes in disguise, especially when among the feared elements of the Maya in the Yucatan, playing the role of harmless merchants. They gathered information on defenses, alliances, morale, weapons, resources and readiness. These spies also assessed the value of the local commodities for trade, ascertaining the advantages to be gained by an Aztec assault on the region.

As among the Maya, most military units of the later periods went to war after careful consideration and after rituals and parades. The advances were colorful, with banners, totems and insignias shining in the field. (For details concerning warfare in the various eras, see the major culture entries.)

MESETA CENTRAL   A region in the Chiapas highlands, on the San Cristobal Plateau. (See MESOAMERICA GEOGRAPHY.)

MESOPOTAMIA OF THE AMERICAS   The name given to the region claimed by the Olmec. This domain encompassed from 6,200 to 7,200 square miles and included the swampy region of Veracruz and Tabasco, bordering on the gulf coast. The region is actually a coastal plain, bordering the Tuxtla Mountains.

METATES   The stones used with the *manos* for grinding maize. Large stones able to contain the maize or other grains, the *metates* were stationary, and the *manos* were moved back and forth over their surfaces in order to reduce the grains to a powder. Some *metates* were carved or decorated.

MEXICA (1)   The name adopted by the Aztec after they founded Tenochtitlan, (or according to some records before the founding of the capital). The Aztec were also called the Tenocha by their contemporaries.

MEXICA (2)   The groups entering Maya lands during the Post-Classic Period (A.D. 900–1521). Militaristic and vital, these Mexica exerted considerable pressure on the Maya, bringing about, in part, the collapse of some of their southern territories. In the Post-Classic Period, the Mexica and Mexica-influenced Maya moved from the gulf coast into the northern and eastern regions. After 1000 A.D., Mexica aristocrats and their western Maya allies, the Itza, dominated a large territory from Chichen Itza. Other Mexica served as mercenaries for the Maya ceremonial complexes.

So dominant was Mexica influence in Maya lands that the term Mexica came to represent any who were not Maya in the various territories.

MEXICO   The dominant nation in the region designated as Mesoamerica in modern times, linked to the Maya and others on their borders. Geographically, Mexico resembles a cornucopia, wide in the north and narrowing as it moves southeast toward the ancient Maya territories of the Yucatan. The entire region is one of the most geographically diverse regions in the world. All of the climatic extremes recorded on earth are evident there. Most of Mexico lies about 7800 feet above sea level, a land of volcanic peaks, rugged mountain chains and the lush Valley of Mexico (or basin). (See MESOAMERICA GEOGRAPHY for descriptive details; see also Mexico, Valley of; Mexico, Plateau of, Mexico, Southern Highlands of; Mexico, Western.)

MEXICO, VALLEY OF   Also termed the Basin of Mexico, the Mother of Mesoamerican Cultures, an ecologically and geologically diverse region of volcanic cones, dry basins, lakes and gently sloping hills evolving as the result of lava flows and centuries of erosion. Flat-topped mesas tower over terraced hills, with geysers, springs and mud volcanoes. The climate is relatively cool with a summer rainy period. Many cultures put down their roots in this region, from the Formative Period (c. A.D. 2000/1600) and on through the historical eras of Mesoamerica. Settlements in the region date to around 1300 B.C., with Tlaltilco and Tlapacoya playing roles in the development of the region, which also bears evidence of Olmec influence. The disappearance of the Olmec led to a decline, but the population increased, and by 600 B.C. the southern region of the Valley of Mexico had many settlements. Native ceramics flourished, manufacturing such wares as monochrome reds, blacks and browns; red and white ceramics with red and yellow decorations; bowls and water jars, and long-footed plates.

Clay platforms were erected at Tlatilco by 1300 B.C. and at Cuicuilco and Tlapacoya about the same time. The region continued to respond to outside influences, such as trade and artistic innovation from Teotihuacan. Cultural phases were evident in the Valley of Mexico as well, including the Nevada, Ixtapaluca, Cuicuilco and Zacatenco-Arbolillo. In the Classic Period the emergent cultures maintained their sites and industries in the valley, and in A.D. 1175 the Toltec arrived, followed by the Chichimec and other groups. In time the Aztec would dominate the entire valley, with the TRIPLE ALLIANCE, the Aztec league. (See entries on various cultures for details.)

MEXICO, PLATEAU OF   Also called Northern Mexican Drylands, the region composed of the Mesa del Norte and the Mesa Central, with the Sierra Madre de Occidental and the Sierra Madre de Oriental its mountainous flanks.

MEXICO, SOUTHERN HIGHLANDS OF   The region south of the Balsas River where the Sierra Madre del Sur and the Sierra de Coalcoman meet. Near Oaxaca, the sierra rose into vast peaks, with adjoining valleys and mesas. Volcanoes mark the territory, with little land available for agriculture. Streams carve V-shape valleys, but most of the region is steeply sloped. The Valley of Oaxaca, part of these highlands, is one of the large basins joining Tlacolula in the east and Etla in the north, forming a flat and hilly terrain drained by the Atoyac River, a tributary of the Balsas. At one time the Oaxacan Valley was culturally vital to all Mesoamerica, home of the Mixtec and the Zapotec. The great cities of the Monte Alban and Mitla were also established in this hilly domain.

To the northwest is the region once called Mixteca Alta, a region also drained by the Balsas, with the Mije highlands on the east. In the northeast the Sierra Madre de Oaxaca is the barrier to the Oaxacan highlands and to the coastal lowlands of Veracruz. The plain of Tehuacan and arid depression linking Tehuacan and the Puebla Basin to the Valley of Oaxaca, is to the west. The Papaloapan Basin was once the site of gold mines. It is believed that the Papaloapan and Balsas basins provided most of the gold demanded by the Aztec during their imperial period. The southern highlands of Mexico also form a cliffed barrier on the Pacific coast. The region offers lagoons, inlets and estuaries, with tropical and deciduous forests nearby.

MEXICO, WESTERN   A region of intense geological activity that that includes the modern states of Colima, Guanajuato, Jalisco, Michoacan, Nayarit and Sinaloa. Two major forces shaped this region, hydrography and volcanoes. Vast internal river basins extend between volcanic cones, and there are many waterways in the region. The basins served as human habitations from the earliest times. The San Pedro River is in the north and the Balsas in the south, with eight lesser streams covering the region. In the state of Jalisco there are lake-dotted plateaus. Colima is mountainous, while Nayarit is a vast plain bordering on the Sierra de Nayarit, part of the Sierra Madre Occidental. Michoacan is a complex of lakes and lowlands, with temperate zones and cool highlands. Guanajuato, the home of the Chupicuaro culture, is watered by the Lerma River and is the southern point of the northern sierras, a rugged, forested land. Sinaloa is the boundary zone between Mesoamerica and the American Desert Southwest, The drainage system of the Fuerte River marks this transition point.

Ceramics from Western Mexico during the Formative Period reflect individuality and skill. The region is believed to have as many as 15 separate archaeological zones. In time it gave way to Tarascan and other groups. (See ZACATENCO-ARBOLILLO culture for additional information.)

MEXITI   A small group associated with the Toltec that joined the Chichimec in the Valley of Mexico after the fall of Culhuacan in the Post-Classic Period (A.D. 900–1521).

MEXITLI   An Aztec deity worshiped originally in Tenochtitlan. The god was associated with the earth and protected agricultural workers.

MEZCALA   A basin area in the region of the Upper Balsas River (locally known as the Mezcala River), in Guerrero, home to a unique people with a renowned art style that reflects Olmec influence. Dated to the Late Formative Period (300 B.C.–c. A.D. 250/290), but possibly older, the

Mezcala people continued their ceramic industries through the Aztec eras in the Post-Classic Period (A.D. 900–1521). Vessels, masks, human and animal figures, tools and models of columned temples were typical of the Mezcala style. The starkness of these temple models, miniature structures, contrast with the human figures produced in the region, which was also notable for conch shell forms as well. Celts were another popular Mezcala art form, produced both grooved and flat. Artists of the region also produced masks and axes in geometric forms, with raised welts, sharp edges and trapezoidal or square designs. Many such objects were found in the Great Temple of Tenochtitlan, probably offerings to the gods. The Mezcala worked in diorite, calcite and porphyry, using these stones as the base for their wares.

MEZTITLAN   A region of Tlaxcala, where an independent city-state was founded during the Classic Period (c. A.D. 1/250–900). This city-state reportedly dominated parts of Puebla, Hidalgo, Veracruz and Tlaxcala, eventually falling to the Tepanec and their allies. The Otomi people are believed to have lived in Meztitlan for a time. Some records indicate that the Aztec never brought Meztitlan under their control.

MIAHUAXILHUITL   A princess of Cuernavaca, reportedly so beautiful that her royal father, a sorceror, kept her locked away from the eyes of men, guarded by spiders, scorpions and serpents. The Aztec emperor Huitzilihuitl, however, braved the reptile guardians in order to see the princess and to court her. She married him, returned with him to Tenochtitlan and became the mother of Motecuhzoma I.

MICCOAMAZATZIN   A Toltec king, listed in the *Anales de Cuauhtitlan.*

MICCOATL PHASE   A cultural development in the city of Teotihuacan, lasting from A.D. 150 to 250, the period of city's maximum expansion. There were an estimated 45,000 people living in that metropolis at the time.

MICHATAYA RIVER   A Guatemalan waterway that flows from the highland peaks of the interior to the Pacific Ocean.

MICHOACAN   A region of Western Mexico, named by the Aztec as "the Place of the Masters of Fish." It was home to Formative Period (c. 2000/1600 B.C.–c. A.D. 250/290) groups and in time became the territory of the Tarascan. A proud people, the groups of Michoacan were never subdued by Aztec armies. The *Relacion de Michoacan* provides details of the region and Tarascan life. The region has three separate geological and geographical zones: highlands, southern tropical lowlands and temperate zones. The Balsas River and its tributaries drain the region, offering plateaus and plains.

Ceramic phases are evident in Michoacan, and sites such as El Openo and Jaquilipas began early there. Zamora and Zacapu wares were also evident. Sites in Michoacan's Formative Period development include La Villita and El Openo.

La Villita is an area containing more than 60 separate sites, with house clusters, patios and stratified burial complexes. The La Villita ceramics were decorated, incised and rocker stamped. Hemispherical bowls, bottlelike jars and *ollas* were produced as well. One grave site, that of a high-ranking woman, contained elaborate offerings of jade, shell and turquoise.

El Openo is an area containing elaborate graves, with passageways and stairs. The offerings recovered there include an Olmecoid figure, a jaguar motif in jade and locally inspired clay figurines. Skulls without bodies were buried in El Openo. In full skeletal burials, the bones were painted red. Grave offerings were made of jade and obsidian.

MICTLANTECUHTLI (1).   The deity of death, worshipped by many cultures in the Valley of Mexico. He was depicted as a skeleton with red spots, wearing an elaborate headdress and a collar of human eyeballs. The god was believed to be the enemy of Quetzalcoatl's efforts to create humans.

MICTLANTECUHTLI (2)   The Teotihuacan lord of the underworld.

MICTLANTECUHTLI (3)   The Lord of Mictlan, the Aztec god of the dead. The deity was the patron of all Aztec ancestors who had died of natural causes. These ancestors were believed to have reached Mictlan after a four-year journey. Mictlantecuhtli was also chief of a complex of Aztec gods.

MIHUAQUE   One of the groups that took part in the Chalco region confederacy in the southern part of the Valley of Mexico. Living on the eastern shores of Lake Chalco, this confederation, called the Chalco-Amecameca, was reported to have had a standing army and 13 rulers.

MIJE   A highland region above Oaxaca, east of Mixteca Alta and part of the southern Mexican highlands. The Mije territory is drained by the Balsas River system and is considered geologically or volcanically active.

MILPA   A term used throughout the Mesoamerican region and historical eras. The word is derived from the Nahuatl language. The Maya equivalent is *chor.* A *milpa* is a field primarily for agricultural use, particularly for maize, and as such represents domestication imposed upon wild growth. In this context the *milpa* corresponds to religious aspects of Mesoamerican life as well. Humans were the crops of the *milpa,* the earth, tended by the gods.

MINAS MOUNTAINS   A chain of peaks in Guatemala, east of Chiapas. The Motagua Valley, believed to be an ancient source of jade, especially at Manzanai, opened at the base of these mountains.

MIRADOR   A Maya site on the Rio de la Venta, north of Tikal in the Peten, dating to c. 300 B.C. and abandoned by A.D. 3001. With pyramids larger than those at Tikal, Mirador was erected beside a well-used trade route and dominated the region. Mud structures were built using stucco masks, with the remains indicating Teotihuacan influence. Two major archaeological complexes are set in an east-west pattern there, with over 200 mounds and a dozen pyramids. The Dante Complex in the city has a pyramid that stands 230 feet tall. Mirador reflects Tikal influence and was possibly a vassal of that great ceremonial city.

MIRAFLORES   An important artistic and cultural phase in Mesoamerica, occurring during the Middle Formative Period, 900 B.C., to during A.D. 200. Separate phases indicate that this development was part of a cultural resurgence and ensuing construction of vast pyramids throughout the region. Such platforms were expanded frequently, with new structures built over the originals.

The great cities of Izapa and Kaminaljuyu participated in the Miraflores Phase, as did other civilizations. It was a time in which royal tombs were built in the pyramidal platforms, having wooden braces, sacrificial victims and elaborate grave offerings. The phase is also evident in remains on the Isthmus of Tehuantepec.

The Miraflores Phase lasted for a long time. Not only was public architecture constructed during this time, but aristocracy rose in various cultures and rituals and ceremonies revering the deities and the dead were established. Ornaments recovered from tombs of this period include hundreds of pots, jade pieces, marble, bone, shells, mica, necklaces made of stingray tails, obsidian blades, pyrite mirrors, mushroom-shape stones (probably copies of the hallucinogenic mushrooms taken for religious purposes), jade flasks and mosaics and clay figurines.

The Miraflores consisted of four subphases, the Providencia, Miraflores proper, Arenal and Santa Clara. The Miraflores Phase in El Salvador produced wares that are labeled Usulatan. This phase is also associated with Majada and Las Charcas B.

MIRRORS   Reflecting objects made of iron pyrite or obsidian, materials that can take high polishes. Many Mesoamerican cultures manufactured these mirrors, and they began in the region during the Formative Period (c. 2000/1600 B.C.–c. A.D. 250/290) or perhaps earlier, as the Olmec fashioned them. Mirrors were popular as trade items in the various regions of Mesoamerica. They were believed to open on other worlds of the spirit and were dedicated to the sun because of reflected light.

MITLA   A Zapotec city, called Lyobaa originally, which means the "Place of Rest" or possibly "the Tomb." It was called Mictlan in Nahuatl, translated as "the Place of the Dead." Located in the central part of Oaxaca, Mitla was a Zapotec ceremonial complex, administered by a high priest and temple personnel. The Zapotec elite of that era also used the site as burial grounds. When the Mixtec entered the region, in the fourteenth century A.D., the Zapotec lost control there.

Mitla always had an important role in the affairs of the region of Oaxaca, from the preceramic periods onward, achieving considerable prestige and power during the period called Monte Alban I, from c. 500 to 200 B.C. The site remained an active ceremonial complex until the Spanish conquest. It is one of the most enduring Mesoamerican sites,

Mixcoatl at Mitla

merging the Formative Period with the Post-Classic Period. Its artistic and architectural horizons, influenced other groups, thus transmitting the culture and traditions of the past to the burgeoning generations of the region. Throughout its history Mitla benefited from Zapotec royal patronage. Prominent priests were also associated with its various phases of growth and activity.

One priest, named Pezeloa, is credited with the founding of Mitla in some accounts. A tomb for another high priest, Huijatan, called "the One Who Sees All," was also constructed there. Zapotecan kings, too, were interred in Mitla, especially those from the city of Zaachila. A cave nearby was used to house the remains of victims sacrificed in rituals. Fallen warriors, always considered entitled to a special form of eternal paradise for their service to the nation, were also buried in the caves, to help them reach their unique final place beyond the grave.

Mitla was fashioned into five separate areas, with pyramids serving ceremonial purposes and palaces the residential requirements. These groups were:

Adobe Groups, Arroyo Group, Church Group, Group of the Columns, South Group.

Within these groups there were other structures, patios and central plazas. Passages made connected some of the buildings within the groups as well.

Group of the Columns.   An impressive complex dating to the Late Formative Period, within which is the Hall of the Columns, for which the entire precinct was named. The hall's massive facade is broken by three entrances, decorated with stepped-fret designs and geometric patterns, similar to those uncovered in the nearby city of Yagul. This hall was designed as a long and low structure, resting on a platform that had a central, interior stairway. The hall was a single chamber, 120 feet by 21 feet, dominated by large, monolithic columns, originally supporting a roof. The interior does not appear to have contained special decorations.

At the eastern end of the hall is a low doorway that opens onto a patio. This court is surrounded by four highly decorated chambers, all having panels of stepped-fret design. The panels incorporated there have inlaid cut stones that were painted and set in an intricate design, almost Grecian, with geometric themes. Probably fashioned to honor Quetzalcoatl, the chambers were no doubt used as individual shrines in which the priests conducted ceremonies open only to initiates or to highly ranked Zapotec.

Another patio incorporated into the structural design was decorated similarly. The walls of both sets of chambers and courts are of mud and stone, covered with plaster or trachite. The walls were filled with rubble in their initial stages of construction. Cruciform-pattern tombs were placed in the patio in the southwestern part of the complex.

In another tomb site in the northern building, a large monolithic column was discovered. It is called both the Column of Life and the Column of Death by modern local inhabitants. Popular tradition states that a person may foretell how many years are left to him or her by grasping the column as if in an embrace. The space remaining between the hands when the arms are wrapped firmly around the stone slab indicates how long he or she will live. Another tradition of measurement involves the distance between the person's head and the top of the column. Measuring the height between them will provide another answer as to the remaining years, as each finger represents a single year of life.

South Group.   The structures that probably served as the ceremonial complex of the city. These constructions date to Monte Alban III and IV–A.D. 100 to 700 and A.D. 900. They were erected slightly to the south of the Column Group. The center was probably the one erected by Pezeloa, the famous priest of the city, honoring Yozaltepetl, the patron deity of the city. The South Group buildings are the only known constructions on the left bank of the Rio Grande de Mitla, the river that was incorporated into the urban design. Tombs and other structures built later there appear to indicate that the city had declined somewhat. The artistic standards are lower in these areas.

Adobe Group.   A complex dating to Monte Alban V, after A.D. 900, a period in which Mitla experienced a renaissance of building and influence in the Oaxaca region. The structures in this group were built on the bedrock of the slopes of the river's right bank. In this era vast residential tracts adjoined the city, which had a stable and relatively high population. The Adobe Group may have been constructed to provide a symmetrical balance for the original ceremonial complex. Some pyramidal platforms were raised here, probably to complete the harmonious effect.

Arroyo Group.   Another section built on the river's right bank. These buildings and served as the residential palaces of the local Zapotec royalty or as residences for visiting prelates and nobles. These palatial residences were reportedly covered with beams and flat stone slabs. An administrative building was discovered here, with a patio that housed tombs for the nobility. These tombs were cruciform in design also. The structures in this district date to Monte Alban V (after A.D. 900).

Church Group.   The last complex at Mitla and the one in the best state of preservation. Three patios compose this district, which was constructed on a north-south axis. Originally it contained more residences for the prelates and nobles of both the Zapotec and Mixtec periods of occupation. Now only the patios are clearly visible, and the southernmost court now holds a Christian church. The remains evident in the central and northern patio, however, indicate that they may have resembled the Hall of the Columns originally. The panels and paintings in the north patio are clearly Mixtec in origin. Mitla is a combination of Zapotec

and Mixtec styles, representing the various eras in which these groups dominated the ceremonial complex. The city probably continued to serve as a regional religious site and was vital to trade under the influence of both cultures. In both cases, Mitla was probably ruled by a governor for kings who resided elsewhere.

MITL TLAOMIHUA   A Toltec king listed in the *Historia Tolteca-Chichimeca* as ruling from A.D. 770 to 829. He may have been the husband of Queen Xihuiquinitzin. Mitl Tlaomihua is associated in some records with the finer temples and platforms in the capital city of Tula.

MIXCOATL (1)   An Aztec deity called Cloud Serpent, an ancient god in the region. He was called Camaxtli in Puebla. Mixcoatl was the patron deity of cities and a stellar being, associated with the cult of Venus. Fishing and aquatic hunting were under his patronage as well. The god was honored by Tlaycala and Hueyotzingo, having been introduced by the Chichimec and Otomi. He was also associated with the stars and was depicted with red and white stripes painted on his body. Called the Red Tezcatlipoca, Mixcoatl was revered for bringing fire to humans and for introducing the flint.

MIXCOATL (2)   A Toltec war chief credited with leading his nation into the Valley of Mexico c. A.D. 900. Called Ce Tecpatl Mixcoatl, translated as "Cloud Smoke," he may have taken part in the destruction of the city of Teotihuacan. He led the Toltec from region beyond Jalisco and Zacatenco, going to Culhuacan. Mixcoatl married a Nahual woman and was the father of Ce Acatl Topiltzin (Quetzalcoatl or Kukulcan). He then civilized the Toltec and began the agricultural and social traditions for which they were celebrated. He was murdered in A.D. 935 or 947, by a relative, probably a brother called Ihuitimal, who took the throne. Ce Acatl Topiltzin avenged Mixcoatl's death and slew Ihuitimal. Some records indicate that Mixcoatl sacrificed on the sacred mountain, Cerro de la Estrella.

MIXCO VIEJO   A capital of the Pokoma Maya, located in the northeastern part of the modern Chimaltenango district of Guatemala. A fortified city on a hill, surrounded by deep gorges, Mixco Viejo was called the Place of the Clouds by the Maya. The Spanish added the word "viejo," or old, when they conquered the site in 1525. Well preserved, Mixco Viejo contains over 120 separate structures, built in defensive clusters. A Cakchiquel Maya garrison indicates that this group also occupied the site at one time. Mixco Viejo was started in the Late Classic Period (A.D. 600–900) and was designed with temples, a twin pyramid and ball courts. The city also had drainage systems, plazas, ceremonial centers and over 100 separate buildings.

MIXTAN   Territory on the border between Oaxaca and Veracruz, believed by some to be the original home of the Mixtec. Records indicate that the Mixtec also claimed to come from Yucunudahui in the Oaxaca Mountain range.

MIXTEC   Called the *Nusabi*, or the People of the Rain, a group who added artistic dimensions to Mesoamerican

Mixtec monolith

cultural development during their own era. Well established by the tenth century A.D. (thus contemporaries of the city of Tula), the Mixtec dominated a region they called the Land in the Clouds. This lay in the Sierras of Oaxaca. Their own legends recount their having come from a place called Apoala, where the first of their kind were born from trees. Other legends refer to Achuitla, a site in the Mixtec domain, as their homeland, and some scholars also cite Mixtan. The Mixtec had four groups that worked as a confederation, moving about in the territory but usually settled in certain areas. The Tilantongo were located in the Mixteca Alta region. The Tlaxiaco were located in the Sierras area. The Coixtlahuaca were located in the Mixteca Baja. And the Tututepec were located on the coast.

The entire Oaxaca region had Formative Period (c. 2000/1600 B.C.–c. A.D. 250/290) cultures, some of which may have been the direct ancestors of the Mixtec. Human beings evolved from a sacred tree trunk according to Mixtec legends, and the land was given to the chief of the group. After he shot an arrow at the sun, he saw the sun turn red and sink into the west, thus providing him with all of that heavenly body's earthly possessions as an inheritance. The Mixtec spread as a result of this encounter with divine forces, overthrowing the Zapotec and other groups to claim the region. A Mixtec Golden Age lasted from c. A.D. 1000 to 1521.

The Mixtec territories were a mountainous series of terrains in western and northern Oaxaca, where settlements were surrounded by arid and semiarid lands. Three separate regions composed the Mixtec realm: the Mixteca Alta, the eastern and southern parts of Oaxaca; the Mixteca Baja, the northern and northwestern sections of Oaxaca; and the Mixteca de la Costa, the southwestern part of the Oaxacan lowlands to the coast.

Generally the region was humid, with a mixture of highlands and lowlands that provided a vast diversity of soils and terrain. The region contains evidence of Paleo-Indian Period (11,000–7000 B.C.) habitation.

Mixtec codices that survived the Spanish conquest document considerable historical and sociological events. The Mixtec claimed descent from the Feathered Serpent, a name for Quetzalcoatl in his many forms, and they started their rise in the Post-Classic Period, around 1000 B.C., in a town called the Mountain that Opens, an unidentified location. The first Mixtec dynasty was established at Tilantongo, which ruled much of the territory, including a site called Xipe Bundle, also unidentified. The second dynasty at Tilantongo is recorded in the codices, recounting the reign of Eight Deer, a war leader who had Toltec patronage. He was killed in a war at the age of 52.

By A.D. 1350, the Mixtec were in the Valley of Oaxaca, where they intermarried with the Zapotec and buried their kings in the city of Monte Alban. When Monte Alban fell, Zaachila became the Zapotec capital, but the Mixtec were also there. As their fame as artists and metalworkers spread, the Mixtec influenced surrounding regions. Their role in Oaxaca was enduring and critical to the upgrading of the arts, especially the metal workers of the region. Several Formative Period phases attest to their habitation and their abilities. The Cruz Phase (1300–1200 B.C.) in the Nochixtlan Valley evidences the growth of the Mixtec villages. Pottery unearthed from this phase indicates that Mixtec ceramics predate the first phase at Monte Alban. The transition in the Mixtec territories corresponds to the Monte Alban II Phase and is represented by pottery found at Tiltepec. The Early Classic era was noted by the Mixtec Ramos Phase, when Yucuita was founded, around 200 B.C. Population growth, industries and the emergence of skilled craftsmen began cultural traditions that spanned centuries. It is believed that the population of Yucuita numbered around 7,000, with additional related communities nearby. The Las Flores Phase, A.D. 500 to 1000, witnessed a sharp population rise, probably to around 30,000 with continued development of the land. The Mixtec ruling classes had marked out their territories and were in command. In the Natividad Phase, A.D. 1000 to 1520/1535, the population is believed to have reached 50,000. This period of Mixtec history is called the Tilantongo-Coixtlahuaca Phase.

In the final period, the Mixtec were politically divided into small kingdoms throughout their territory. The dynasties fostered a martial approach to life, perhaps influenced by the Toltec. When the Aztec threatened the region, the Mixtec joined with the Zapotec to defend their lands. The battle at Giengola, c. A.D. 1494, pitted the Zapotec against the Aztec. The Aztec forces prevailed, and the Mixtec became a vassal group, with their artisans moving to Tenochtitlan to provide the empire with their skills. The Mixtec, however, survived as an independent culture, very much visible today.

MIXTEC AGRICULTURE The basis for the Mixtec economy, practiced intensively in the generally temperate valleys and on the humid coastal plains. The Mixtec supplemented their harvests with hunting and gathering, but they sowed diverse crops and various reaping seasons, in accordance with their geographical locations and varied topography. Growing the staple Mesoamerican crops, the Mixtec also raised dogs and turkeys, and it is believed that they tamed other fowl, prizing their plumage for their crafts. In the highlands, the Mixtec also used the dye-producing cochineal insects that lived on the prickly pear plant. Their salt resources were primarily in the highlands as well.

MIXTEC ARCHAEOLOGICAL SITES Known from contemporary and later sources, the cities inhabited by this culture, including Achuitla, Chacoapan-Yucunudahui, Chalcatongo, Coixtlahuaca, Huamelulpan, Lachizaa, Monte Negro, Mountain That Opens, Taposcolula, Tilantongo, Tototepec, Tututepec, Xipe Bundle, Yanhuitlan, and Yacuita.

MIXTEC ARCHITECTURE A true art form of the Mixtec that has not been fully explored. No typical Mixtec sites have been uncovered enough to evaluate their architecture in the Oaxaca region. Mitla, which was a Zapotec city occupied by the Mixtec, contains some examples of Mixtec architecture. They appear to have used long, horizontal masses, with elaborate cornices and panels. Exterior decorations as well as interior courtyards and chambers were covered with bas reliefs and repeated patterns, especially the stepped meander fashioned of fitted mosaics. Under Zapotec influence, at Mitla, Monte Alban and elsewhere, the Mixtec designed architecture incorporating themes drawn from the Zapotec cult of the dead.

MIXTEC ART The field in which this culture gained a considerable repute among their contemporaries, especially in the ceramic and gold ornamentation industries. Mixtec art influenced the cultures of other Mesoamerican groups, setting standards for production and skills. Objects made by the Mixtec have been recovered in most of the major cultural sites of Mesoamerica, including those of the Toltec. Mixtec art was fundamentally a pictorial, graphic display, highly decorative and dependent on a high level of skill. The craftsmen were masters in metallurgy, lapidary work, in decorative ceramics and carving wood and bone. Pictorial codices were also a Mixtec specialty.

Mixtec artisans employed ideographic painting as a principal art form. These artists were able to narrate highly complex sagas by stylizing, with a certain uniformity, characterizations of nature and of human beings. Standardized postures and conventions, such as scrolls to depict speech, allowed the stories to emerge, and each image contained its own meaning and purpose, well understood by the readers. The codices were prized by other cultures, who imitated their standards and style.

Mixtec sculpture is rare, and what has been recovered to date demonstrates a rather stylized geometric form, quite rigid in appearance. Carved slabs taken from the site of Tilantongo and a monolith from Tututepec demonstrate this. The Mixtec did not use large stones well, but they excelled in carving small, semiprecious gemstones. Mixtec artists carved figurines, pendants and other elaborately fashioned ornaments of jade, crystal, amethyst, opal, obsidian, agate and other gems. The typical Mixtec figure depicted was a personage of some note, either standing or seated. Images of the Mixtec deities were also produced. The Mixtec were masters of the art of creating images of animals in the various gems, using flint knives, tubular drills and other tools.

They also made fine alabaster vessels and mosaics of shells and turquoise, as well as wooden shields, masks, scepters, helmets and other ornamental wares. Alabaster (pots or bowls), and onyx, vessels are noted for their refinement and beauty. Most were shaped as animals. Unfinished stone vessels have provided insight into how Mixtec artists a fashioned objects with thin walls. A block of stone was cut from a larger piece, then hollowed out and smoothed. The heads, legs and tails of the animals depicted were then sculpted and polished.

Mixtec musical instruments were also popular among other Mesoamerican cultures. The Mixtec made fine drums and gongs of wood and bone. Wooden *atlatls* (spear throwers) were widely distributed, carved with mythological themes and sometimes covered with gold leaf. Mixtec metallurgy surpassed that of other Mesoamerican cultures. Metallurgy was introduced into the region around A.D. 900. Mesoamericans used metals for ornamentation; their tools and weaponry remained Neolithic. Mixtec metal wares set the standard for Mesoamerican cultures. The Oaxaca master silversmiths also used copper and gold to make pendants, masks, beads, buckles, bells and other display items. Thin gold sheets were hammered into the silhouettes desired and then decorated. The "lost wax" process was also used for gold objects. Wax, hardened with resin, was used to make the original form, which was covered with clay. When the clay hardened, the wax disappeared. Molten metal was then poured into the mold, which was broken to release the finished product.

MIXTEC CALENDAR A means of defining time borrowed from other cultures and following the general Mesoamerican system for calculation. The Mixtec used the *tonalpohualli,* the 260-day religious calendar, and the 365-day calendar, with the 52-year cycle employed elsewhere. Their day signs were obviously Zapotec-inspired.

MIXTEC CERAMICS One of the art forms in which the Mixtec excelled, and a major creative contribution to Mesoamerica. Of particular value were their lacquered polychromes, which other cultures adapted. The Mixtec made ceramic plates, cups, jars and vases. They used genuine lacquer, covering polished brown wares with a second firing and decorations of various motifs. These ceramics reflect the narrative and thematic skills of the Mixtec. Vessels became miniature codices in their hands, and seals, painted on the bottom, were carefully colored in various shades. Mixtec ceramics were produced for a time in Cholula, then exported throughout Mesoamerica through the trade routes of the period. The ceramics were polychromes decorated with stepped-fret designs and with depictions of gods, birds and serpents. Domestic pottery had birds or butterfly designs, referring to Quetzalcoatl's cult. Peruvian and other South American cultures appear to have been influenced Mixtec ceramics. One of the favorite shapes used by Mixtec artists was the spherical bowl, topped with a cylindrical neck, resting on three feet, at one time fashioned in the form of serpents. Other forms included cylindrical cups and cups on pedestals.

MIXTEC CEREMONIAL COMPLEXES

Communities generally constructed near residential districts and situated on a hill or mountaintop, with a river or a cave close by. Some of these sites, specifically shrines dedicated to the various gods, were built into the residences of the aristocrats and rulers. Natural sites were preferred, because of their affinity to the earth and to the Mixtec cosmological traditions. Mountains were considered close to heaven, and rivers were visible symbols of rejuvenation and fertility. Sites were also chosen if they displayed a particular aspect of a deity. Few details have survived as to the ceremonies conducted in such Mixtec complexes, but human and animal sacrifices were part of the rituals. It is not known what hymns, processions, and dances accompanied these sacrifices. Ceremonial complexes in the Mixtec lands varied in size and in purpose, with larger ones serving entire communities and those built within the aristocratic compounds designed for household or familial rites. The major surviving Mixtec sites were probably ceremonial complexes to some degree or another.

MIXTEC CODICES

Written documents of the Mixtec, eight of which survive today. These beautiful codices are useful in preserving details about Mixtec culture and legends. They are made of strips of leather or hide, cotton or bark, placed between wooden covers and folded like a screen. Pictographic and largely narrative, the codices use poses and well-known symbols to convey a story. Divinatory codices portray the gods and the heavens. Like the Mixtec historical works, they are meant to be read zigzag, from top to bottom. In time the Nahua groups in the Valley of Mexico adopted the Mixtec writing style as used in the codices. The codices created for the Mixtec nobles dealt with several aspects of Mixtec life, recounting history and the genealogy of the major Mixtec aristocratic families. They also contain information concerning the divine origins of Mixtec rulers and an introduction to divine ancestor worship, which permeated Mixtec society and was part of their religious concepts. The surviving Mixtec codices include:

Codex Nuttal, in the British Museum, also known as *Codex Zouche* or *Zouche-Nuttal,*

Codex Bodley, in the Bodleian Library, Oxford

Codex Selden, in the Bodleian Library, Oxford

Codex Vindobonensis, in the *Nationalbibliothek,* Vienna

Codex Colombino, in the *Museo Nacional de Antropologia,* Mexico City

Codices Becker I and II, in the *Museum fur Volkerkunde,* Vienna.

An additional set of codices, called the Borgia Group, are also associated with the Mixtec, although their origin is debatable. These codices have a different purpose than the Mixtec documents just described. (See CODICES for details.)

MIXTEC CURRENCY

The materials used by the Mixtec to conduct trade, consisting largely of cacao beans, the traditional Mesoamerican currency. The Mixtec, however, also used T-shaped copper blades, which they produced in large quantities. The use of these blades began after the introduction of metallurgy in the Mixtec region, c. A.D. 900.

MIXTEC DEATH RITES

A ceremonial aspect of Mixtec life, in most cases dependent on the rank and status of the deceased. Like other Mesoamerican cultures, the Mixtec had distinct concepts about the afterlife. For aristocrats, rituals were conducted at the onset of an illness, with appropriate prayers and sacrifices for a swift recovery. A cure was celebrated with a festival. If the noble died, however, offerings were made to the deceased on his or her deathbed. Four priests then buried the corpse at midnight on the side of a mountain or in a field. A slave who had impersonated the noble just before burial was also slain and interred, as well as women and other slaves. These victims were intoxicated and then strangled. The noble's corpse was wrapped in cotton mantles, with a mask placed over the face. Rings were placed in the ears and on the fingers, and jewels were wrapped around the neck. The corpse also wore a mitrelike hat. If of royal rank, the body was then wrapped in a mantle and placed in a sepulcher. Honors were paid once a year to the dead on the birthday celebration, not on the anniversary of the death. Commoners received a burial ritual equal to their station in life, interred in fields or on mountainsides as well.

MIXTEC DRESS

The attire that was quite similar to that of other Mesoamerican cultures, with the usual differentiation according to rank. The basic dress for men included the breechclout and shoulder cape or mantle. The cloak was fastened by a brooch. Women wore a sleeveless blouse and a wraparound skirt. The upper classes and priests wore more colorful, finer attire, with embroidery, featherwork and specific ceremonial costuming. The nobles also wore knee bands and wrist bands made of gold, jade, turquoise and other precious stones. They adorned themselves with other ornamentations, for which the Mixtec artists were celebrated throughout Mesoamerica. Rings, earrings, and lip and nose ornaments were considered appealing and were made of precious metals and semiprecious stones. Cotton was used governally for cloaks and mantles throughout the Mixtec region. The nobles wore finer materials, sometimes embroidered cotton or else skillfully fashioned skins, with bells. A headdress, using the feathers of the quetzal bird, was worn on certain occasions.

MIXTEC GOVERNMENT   A hereditary and aristocratically controlled form of rule practiced in the Mixtec confederation. There were actually four principal Mixtec kingdoms, working in unity: Tilantongo in Mixteca Alta, Tlaxiaco in the Sierra region, Coixtlahuaca in Mixteca Baja and Tututepec on the coast. The basic political unit, however, was the community, and the Mixtec did not evince any great desire for conquest. Beyond the need to enforce alliances within their domain or to settle disputes over territory, the Mixtec did not resort to warfare often. They held considerable prestige within their own region and dominated it politically without need for military measures.

At the head of each kingdom's government was the ruler and his family. The Spanish used an Arawakan term, *cacique*, to describe such chiefs: The rulers were from a hereditary caste that jealously guarded its lineage. The rights and privileges of this caste were virtually absolute, based on divine origin. Certain lines thus had the right to rule certain regions with the blessings not only of their ancestors but of the gods.

The rulers were also adept at political maneuverings to insure their bases of power. Intermarriage with local lines was one method, and the threat of war assured other gains or alliances. A series of dynasties appeared in the Mixtec territory, the second of great note being that of Tilantongo. This line extended its power over the villages of the region, including a site called Xipe Bundle, which had been coruler of the region but collapsed. The second dynasty at Tilantongo included Eight-Deer and his father, Five-Alligator, before the Toltec placed the region on a vassal status. The Tilantongo dynasty was deemed the most noble of the Mixtec, and it could regulate the ruling clans of other areas and received tribute. In the Mixteca Baja, the most important royal line was in Tututepec, where the rulers held sway over vast regions and conducted raids and assaults. In all of the outlying regions, nobles served as administrators and as advisors to the king. Priests were also of the noble clans, and they too served as counselors.

MIXTEC LANGUAGE   Speech and writing that the Mixtec shared with the Zapotec and others, belonging to the Oto-Manguean language family. In the written form, communication was expressed in pictographic symbols or in signs that conveyed essential information or narrative. Such languages no doubt were linked to the phonetic principles of the spoken language and remained quite basic. The historical codices were written in this fashion, reflecting vitality and enthusiasm in portraying events and people. The pictographs presented images of historical events, ideas, concepts and spiritual sentiments. The calendar names and Mixtec second names were represented by iconographs. The celebrated ruler, Eight-Deer, for example, was represented by the head of a deer and eight dots. The phonetic values of the written form of the Mixtec language have not been determined. When writing numbers, the Mixtec utilized the cumulative dot system.

The spoken form of the Mixtec language was very much dependent on emphasis and pronunciation to express meaning. Pitch determined the precise meaning of many Mixtec words, and the various regions spoke separate dialects. Two sources from the sixteenth century assist scholars in

Mixtec lip plug

attempting to determine the origin of the Mixtec language and the relationship between these dialects. These are the *Reyes Grammar*, first published in Mexico City in 1593, dealing with the Mixtec language spoken around Teposcolula but containing notes on other dialects and kinship terms used. The second is the *Alvarado Dictionary*, published in 1593, which was compiled at Tamazulapan, with an extensive word list.

MIXTEC MARRIAGE   An institution that varied according to the Mixtec social caste system, each regulated as to duties and obligations. Nobles and the ruling classes maintained strict control over marriages. Commoners practiced various modes of marriage, including those between many types of relatives. Most marriages were conducted within a single community, and marriages between close relatives were not proscribed. The taboo set on marriages between those having a similar calendrical number at birth appears to have been the only major restriction.

Mixtec conquerors wed members of the vanquished dynastic lines in order to consolidate their rule and to gain acceptance. Commoners remained within their own communal relationships, again to strengthen the local structures and to insure continuity in inheritances and customs.

The actual Mixtec marriage rites are not well known, but in typical Mesoamerican fashion they were generally arranged by a third party and included negotiations between the families concerning gifts and dowries. Priests were also consulted for divinations and the prospects of the new couple. When all of the negotiations were completed, a procession went to the girl's home with gifts of gold and jewelry. A mock battle was then staged in which a group of armed men intercepted the gifts temporarily. Willow branches and mats were used as decorations for the occasion, at which time the bride was asked to give her consent to the union. The actual marriage rite appears to have consisted of a simple tying of the mantles of the couple, with a symbolic cutting of hair and the sharing of tortillas. Feasts and celebrations followed the ceremony, and guests ate and drank liquor. The event appears to have been similar for both nobles and commoners, with those of the aristocrats conducted in a lavish style.

MIXTEC PERSONALITIES OF NOTE Outstanding individuals, largely from the ruling clans, who were distinguished in the Mixtec codices. These included:

Five-Alligator (or Five-Crocodile). Also called Rain Sun or Tlaloc-Sun Dead, the father of Eight-Deer and the founder of the second dynasty of Tilantongo, called *tlachito-natiuh*. He innovated calendric reforms and was possibly the invader of the Maya territories. He is listed on pottery recovered at Altar de Sacrificios, although this pottery may refer to another non-Mixtec ruler. He died in A.D. 1030, leaving Eight-Deer the throne.

Eight-Deer. Also called Tiger Claw, born in A.D. 1011 to Five-Alligator, the ruler of Tilantongo in the northern region of Mixteca Alta. Assuming the throne in A.D. 1030, Eight-Deer began to forge a political-tribute alliance and also inheriting the throne of Tututepec, through military force and marriages, Eight-Deer increased in power, including unions with Thirteen-Serpent (Serpent of Flowers) in 1051, with Six-Eagle in 1053 and with Eleven-Serpent in 1060. In 1045 he support the Toltec and was rewarded at Tula by having his nose pierced and a jade plug inserted, elevating him to the rank of a Toltec *tecuhtli,* (lord). The Toltec king Four-Jaguar, or his priest Eight-Death, performed the ceremony. Eight-Deer's wars and marriages continued until 1063, when he was attacked by the forces of the native city of his most recent wife. Taken prisoner in a battle there, he was sacrificed and buried with honor.

One-Death. The Mixtec ancestral female depicted in the *Codex Bodley.*

MIXTEC RELIGION AND PRIESTS The faith and its practitioners that provided the Mixtec with a lasting and pervasive spiritual awareness, and had an abiding influence on both nobles and commoners. The Mixtec pantheon of deities appears to be largely the same as that of other Nahual groups, including the Aztec (Mexica), with similar rituals and adapted names. Tlaloc, Quetzalcoatl, Xipe Totec and other gods worshipped throughout Mesoamerica, having survived from the earliest periods, evolved into deities that offered comfort and ideals. The Mixtec honored these deities and also had gods of particular sites and natural settings. Mountaintops, caves and other places were sacred to them.

Mixtec religion, mirroring other Mesoamerican beliefs, maintained the stability of the nation by appeasing the gods while offering the people lasting spiritual enlightenment through spectacular ceremonial events. Religious ceremonies were elaborate, having sacrifices, songs, dances and other activities, including the use of alcohol and hallucinogens. A calendar marked the celebrations of the feasts and the accompanying ceremonies. Priests who presided over such demonstrations also played a leading role in the social life of the people. The actual duties of these priests in the Mixtec regions are not well known. Contrary to the rigid social regulations in other Mixtec activities, the priests could come from the noble or the common classes.

As in other Mesoamerican cultures, birth had great significance and was regarded as a religious event. If the newborn was female it was given a spindle, if a boy, a dart.

Mixtec design

After the birth the mother bathed 20 days in a row and participated in the rituals of the deity of cleanliness. After a year another festival was held. The birth was celebrated, and the child's future was probably determined by divination. The major deities of the Mixtec were;

9-Wind, a Mixtec version of Ehecatl;

1-Death, a Mixtec version of Tonatiuh;

7-Flower, a Mixtec version of Yochipilli;

7-Rain, a Mixtec version of Xipe Totec

MIXTEC SOCIETY The organization of the Mixtec rank and obligations, an aspect of Mixtec life not well documented but probably imitating the other Mesoamerican groups of the time. The essential element of Mixtec society was its isolation and its concern with local communities. Two major groups existed in Mixtec society, nobles and commoners. These, in turn, can be divided into ruler-nobility and commoners-tenant farmers.

Mixtec Zaachila bowl

The Mixtec nobility were secondary to the ruling family of each separate kingdom, subject to the ruler and his immediate relatives. They governed territories for the ruler and guarded their own ranks and privileges. This hereditary class was an important part of the Mixtec structure of authority. They also held lands, were granted honors and received a portion of the tribute gathered.

Mixtec commoners were called *macehuales* and constituted the bulk of the agricultural force. They included artisans and traders. Below them were the various classes of tenant farmers, servants and slaves. These constituted the forces used for public works, such as irrigation projects. Priests had their own rank among the Mixtec, coming generally from the ranks of the nobles, but qualified commoners might enlist as well.

MIXTEC TRADE   Methods of exchange and barter practiced throughout the Mixtec domain and beyond, with merchants and traders having a unique role in local communities. They were responsible not only for maintaining relations within the local Mixtec regions but for negotiating trade with other Mesoamerican cultures. The basis of the Mixtec economy was agriculture, but products imported from other regions were sought after as well. The lowlands and coastal regions provided salt, fish as well as bird feathers, and they probably exported precious metals. The highlands provided maize, beans, chili, maguey fibers and precious metals. Of particular note was the cochineal insect that produced dyes, those used in manufacturing clothing in the lowlands and traded throughout the highlands. Outside contacts were regulated by the various trade routes taken over the decades. Available products and their popularity also governed the importation of the agricultural products and fabrics. Little is known about how extensive the contacts were between the Mixtec and others, but Mixtec metal wares and ceramics were popular and found in many Mesoamerican cultural sites, some far removed from the Mixtec homelands.

MIXTEC WARFARE   Military practices that were not actually institutionalized in the region but were employed only in cases of necessity or in times of threat. Wars were conducted both locally and regionally when the Mixtec were embroiled over land disputes or political ambitions. On these occasions they proved themselves competent warriors, especially when the Mixtec confronted a common enemy. Their stands against the Aztec displayed their ferocity, especially at Giengola and Tehuantepec. When Mixtec rulers and nobles went to war, they wore the lavish costumes of other cultures, in elegant cotton armor and elaborate headdresses, carrying finely decorated shields. The commoners were largely unadorned. The regular foot soldiers wore breechclouts or fought unclothed. Their weapons included bows, arrows, darts, spears, *atlatls* and shields.

MIXTECA ALTA   The region in the Sierras of Oaxaca inhabited by the Mixtec in the Post-Classic Period (A.D. 900–1521.)

MIXTECA BAJA   The region south of Mixteca Alta.

MIXTEQUILLA   A region in Veracruz-Tabasco, consisting of sandy plateaus or land-filled islands rising out of flat pasture and swamps that are flooded seasonally. Early habitation sites were discovered in Mixtequilla. Los Cerros, Cerros de los Mesas and Tres Zapotes, are found here.

MOCTEZUMA I   See MOTECUHZOMA I.

MOCTEZUMA II   See MOTECUHZOMA II.

MOCTEZUMA RIVER   A waterway in the region of the Sierra Madre Oriental, given this name by local inhabitants.

MOHO RIVER   A waterway in Belize, serving to drain the area. The Maya city of Pusilha is located on its banks.

MOLCAJETES   A Toltec ceramic taking the form of a medium-size hemispherical bowl having tripod supports. (See TOLTEC CERAMICS.)

MONKEY   Two types, howlers and spiders, are represented at Tikal. Common in Mesoamerica, monkeys were associated with promiscuity in Maya legends, and they are mentioned in the HERO TWINS tale. Designs including monkeys were at times symbols of fertility, often having phallic meaning.

MONKEY MEN   The evil half brothers of the Hero Twins of Maya legend. Hunahpu and Ixbalanque fought against these brothers and, defeating them, saw them transformed into monkeys. (See TWINS, HERO.)

MONTANA DEL MICO   A chain of peaks in Guatemala, associated with Maya historical eras. The Montana del Mico is located east of Chiapas.

MONTE ALBAN   One of the major distinguished cities of Mesoamerica, begun in the Formative Period (around 500 B.C.) and enduring until the Early Classic Period (until A.D. 900). The city was located in the Valley of Oaxaca and was influential in many Mesoamerican cultures, both because of its size and its artistic horizons. Originally named *Danipaan* or *Daniboan* by the Zapotec, meaning "Sacred Mountain," Monte Alban (White Mountain) is the Spanish name for the site. The Zapotec occupied Monte Alban during the third period of the city's history, and they designated the site as one of the holy places. Others would follow them to Monte Alban, which linked historical eras and cultures.

The original builders of this great ceremonial city are unknown, and the cultural origins of its vast residential districts are also unknown. It is known that the city's founders were part of the Oaxaca developmental process that was evident in the Middle and Late Formative Periods, carrying over into the Classic and Post-Classic historical eras. The *danzantes* figures, for example, have historical precedents in the region. These forms appear in a prior Oxaca cultural phase called the Rosario. The ceramic styles of Monte Alban indicate a steady development of the Oaxaca style. In time, Monte Alban, which was contemporary with the city of

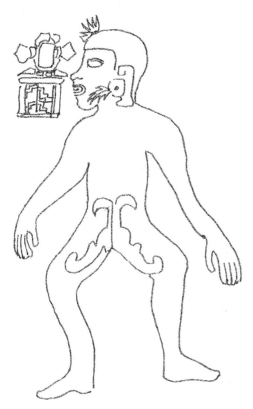

Monte Alban relief

Teotihuacan, influenced the Oaxaca and other cultures. Both cities conducted vast trading endeavors, and the artistic styles and standards adopted by both Monte Alban and Teotihuacan were reflected by other cultures and were highly prized in the markets of other regions.

As a ceremonial city, Monte Alban was a masterpiece of planning from its very beginning. It was situated in a strategically defensive position, on a series of ridges. These ridges were some six miles from modern Oaxaca City. The major section of the original settlement of Monte Alban lay on an artificially flattened hill that rose some 1,200 feet above the surrounding valley. This original foundation was begun c. 500 B.C., although some evidence indicates that the site may have been occupied as early as 900 B.C. Monte Alban I, the period of basic development there, endured until around 200 B.C.

Although Monte Alban was in existence during the Classic and the Post-Classic periods (c. A.D. 1/250–900; A.D. 900–1521), its roots were in the Late Formative (300 B.C.–A.D. 250). The most striking aspect of the site is its hilltop location. Ceremonial structures were erected there in the early stages of development, around which a series of plazas was constructed. The first such building was massive. In time, the hills of Chico, El Gallo and Atzompa were joined to Monte Alban by bridges for the continued construction of the ceremonial complex and the residential districts.

Monte Alban's architectural design is somewhat distinctive. The interior of the *danzantes* building, which was constructed during the Monte Alban I period, is a striking example. It and the adjoining gallery incorporated stone slabs carved with figures in fluid poses that resemble those

assumed by dancers, hence the Spanish names. The *danzantes* were not actual dancers but probably prisoners of war who had died or possibly priests involved in some sort of ritual. Male figures are mutilated, and hieroglyphs were assigned to each one. The eyes of the *danzantes* were usually closed. The *danzantes* complex was remodeled in the Monte Alban III period and was then provided with a tunnel. The original structure had a small platform that probably served as the foundation for a small wooden shrine.

In time the sacred precincts built in Monte Alban were surrounded by three core areas of residences that served a growing population. Other residential complexes were placed beside administrative buildings, which came into being as Monte Alban began to dominate the surrounding territories. From the earliest period the city controlled an area of approximately six to 10 miles, including the settlements at San Agustin de las Juntas, Zaachila and Ocotlan. A probable market center, designed to take advantage of the trade routes, was established in the south, near the Atoyac River at Zimitlan.

During Monte Alban I, the city constructed megalithic architecture and employed hieroglyphic writing, the earliest known writing system in Mesoamerica. The people of Monte Alban also used the dot and bar numeration system and had knowledge of calendrics.

The Monte Alban inhabitants knew how to erect stone buildings with stucco floors. They employed vertical walls instead of the sloped variety, which indicates progress in architectural skill. Their tombs were rectangular, having flat roofs, lined with stones. The ceramics of the early period were gray wares with linear incisions or religious motifs. The figurines of this period depicted men or animals as well as Olmecoid jaguar masks.

At the end of Monte Alban I and the beginning of Monte Alban II (200 B.C.–A.D. 100), the city appears to have suffered a decline in power and in population growth. Monte Alban temporarily relaxed its grip on the outlying territories and

Monte Alban urn

reduced the number of settlements it maintained. According to some estimates, the city's population shrank from 16,000 to 14,500 at this time.

Major construction was continued, however, and several new aspects of culture were introduced. There is some evidence that a new population group arrived, perhaps from Chiapas or from a region of Guatemala, and introduced new glyphs and new deities.

One structure built during this period (Mound J), in the southernmost part of the central axis of the city's plan, is distinct from both earlier and later architectural projects. It was designed in the shape of an arrow, pointing southwest. The other buildings of Monte Alban were aligned with the cardinal points. Mound J had a vaulted tunnel, a stairway on the northeast side and slabs incorporated into the walls. The glyphs used in these decorations denoted places, and some had calendric notations. They are thought to depict settlements incorporated into the city's territorial domain.

Geometric designs and flower themes were incorporated into construction, and human bones and trefoil ornaments were used. Statues of deities appeared as well, alongside male and female figures. The celebrated jade mask that depicted the Monte Alban bat god was created in this period, although some scholars date it to Monte Alban III. The mask was composed of 25 pieces of jade. The eyes and teeth were made of shells, and pendants made of slate were attached.

During the period known as Monte Alban III (c. A.D. 100–700), the Zapotec came to power in Monte Alban and in the region of Oaxaca, having been in that vicinity from 1500 B.C. Historians have divided this period into several ceramic phases, but the changes did not affect the general architecture of the city. Most surviving structures at Monte Alban date to this period.

The Great Plaza, which dates to the earliest times, was renovated in Monte Alban III. This plaza is now approximately 1,000 feet long and 650 feet wide. Several structures stand on its perimeter, including a platform. Carved stelae were incorporated into the base of the platform, some with glyphs. A structure called System M is composed of a four-tiered pyramid that had a columned temple on its topmost level. The North Platform also dates to Monte Alban III, with a sunken patio and stelae. The nearby tombs of the period had antechambers and niches for offerings.

Near the Great Plaza is the ball court, which reflected the Zapotec style. The court is reached by stairs, and there are platforms and other decorative additions, including some buildings that may have been used as residences. Included in this complex is a small shrine, which contained the famous jade mask already described.

The ball courts of Monte Alban probably were started in Monte Alban II but took their final form in the third period. These courts were designed in the shape of a capital I, and most had niches and circular center stones. The game played in these courts was called *lachi*, and the area itself was called *queya*. Players used the traditional hard rubber balls and wore helmets and knee pads. The ball games of Monte Alban, following the custom of other regions and other eras, were played for both religious and secular purposes.

One architectural style made famous in Monte Alban II was the *talud-tablero*. *Talud* is a sloping wall base, and *tablero* the slab placed above it. The *talud-tablero* style was derived from Teotihuacan. Carvings from Monte Alban III also used the serpent theme. In time the architects of Monte Alban's public buildings included terraces and courts in their designs. Residential districts were increased so that the city covered approximately 15 square miles. There were reportedly as many as 2,000 terraces on the slopes of Monte Alban's hills, with homes erected on the various levels. Ravines and ponds were incorporated into these terraces. An astronomical observatory was also built.

The tombs of this and later periods in Monte Alban were built in a similar style. Most were constructed of masonry and were situated below the courtyards. The more notable citizens were entombed under the public plazas. Some grave sites could be entered by stairs. The doors of the tombs contained niches for incense burners; similar compartments were introduced into the interiors for funerary offerings. These tombs usually were built for a single individual, and some were decorated with murals. One tomb has provided figurines depicting details on the mortuary rituals of Monte Alban. The corpse itself is depicted by a mask set on a pyramid. An orchestra and carved priests surround the mask.

Monte Alban experienced social and cultural changes in this era, influenced by Teotihuacan, which was emerging as a great power. An elite class is evident in the city, especially in the architectural projects. High-ranking families resided in vast and luxurious complexes removed from the common residential districts. Important personages were also depicted on monuments, such as the Lapida stela. These reliefs depict the rulers (called *caciques* by the Spanish) seated before the assembled ambassadors of other regions who have brought tribute to Monte Alban. The Old Man, a Monte Alban deity, was honored in the insignias of these *caciques*.

The ceramics of Monte Alban III included special pottery as well as wares for household use. The ceramics included polished gray, thin orange, and florero.

Vessels were globular or spouted jars, *tecomates*, conical bowls, dog effigies, *ollas* and cylindrical vases.

The religious aspects evidenced by the ceramics and by the monuments of Monte Alban III include ancestor worship and a pantheon of 39 gods, grouped into several major cosmogonical themes. One such theme was associated with rain and lightning. Cocijo was the rain god of Oaxaca, and the jaguar was also associated with this cosmogonical element. The maize god was Pitao, a bat. The great Sky Serpent, Quetzalcoatl, appears to have been worshipped in Monte Alban, as well as the "flayed god," Xipe Totec, associated with the Zapotec.

Both a priestly caste and a military caste held power in the city. The priests dominated the warriors, but sometimes their duties were entwined.

In Monte Alban IV, the empire forged by this complex collapsed. By A.D. 900, the city had fallen into ruins. There are several possible causes for the death of Monte Alban. The city could have been overpopulated, unable to sustain itself in face of urban stresses. Or there could have been an agricultural shortfall or even a military revolt against the authorities.

Evidence from Monte Alban V indicates that by A.D. 1350, Monte Alban was no longer inhabited. Burials were made there, as the city still maintained its ceremonial and religious impact. MITLA became the dominant Zapotec city in this era, and the Mixtec were gaining power. Zaachila was the heart of Zapotec renaissance and attempts to revive their ancient culture. In time the Zapotec were forced out of Oaxaca. One particular tradition, however, mentions the Zapotec return to Zaachila and their alliance with the Mixtec, especially confronted by Aztec aggression. Monte Alban was no longer a political or social force in the region. It remained in use as a religious and burial site, however, until A.D. 1521.

MONTE ALTO (FINCA) A Maya site near modern Guatemala City, now part of a large estate. Monte Alto is noted for a number of boulderlike sculptures. These are monolithic stones fashioned into barrel-shaped torsos topped with baby faces. Possibly of Pipil origin, and dating to c. A.D. 250 or earlier, the stones were discovered lying on their backs near the ceremonial mounds. These figures have wrap-around arms and legs. Some have feline features. Monte Alto has both Olmec and Itza influences. (See also BABY FORMS.)

MONTE NEGRO A site near the Valley of Oaxaca, dating to the Formative Period (2000 B.C.–250/290 A.D.). Two groups of monuments in Monte Negro extend from north to south, with another facing east. The buildings are single-terraced, with plain walls, built of white stone, bonded with red clay. Most are rectangular and surrounded by patios, but some Monte Negro structures are irregular in design. The monuments appear to have been constructed in association with astronomical positions. One rectangular structure has staircases on opposite sides. A building on the top contains two roofed vestibules, probably used in religious ceremonies. Residences were built nearby, generally consisting of three or four rooms opening onto a patio. Multiple columns, made of rubble and with a core of circular stones, were faced with smaller stones to form a cylinder. In the temples these tall columns were arranged in rows of 10. A drainage system served the site, with holes in the floors of the open patios, connecting them to the main conduits throughout the city. Some systems used clay pipes.

Monte Negro is listed as both a Zapotec and Mixtec site, but the original builders are unknown. It was influenced by Monte Alban and contained pottery and ceramics. The burial sites in the city are tombs or simple graves in the ground. The tombs were box-shape, with no entrances, and slab roofs. Pottery recovered from these graves are similar to Monte Alban I. Some records date Monte Negro to around 648 B.C. It does not seem to have developed into a Classic Period city.

MORELOS A highland region west of Puebla, reaching heights up to 4,500 feet, with vast plains and a temperate climate. Modern Cuernavaca in Morelos proves the year-round charm of the region. Open with pine and oak, forests, rivers and abundant rainfall attracted settlers to early sites, such as Gualupita. Influenced by the Olmec, the settlements of La Juana and San Pablo in Morelos give evidence of Olmec presence around 1300 B.C. The region area also served as the core for three distinct and heavily traveled trade routes for the Mesoamerican cultures. In many historical periods Morelos was thus linked to Puebla, Oaxaca and to

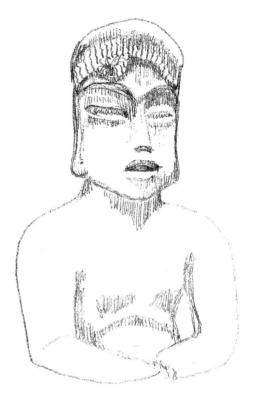

Morelos figure

the gulf regions, as well as to the Valley of Mexico and to Guerrero, via the Balsas River system.

MOQUIHUIX The ruler of the city of Tlatelolco, the sister city of Tenochtitlan on Lake Texcoco. He was on the throne during the reign of the Aztec emperor Axayacatl, married to the sister of the emperor. Supposedly he abused Axayacatl's sister, but he probably made threatening military or political gestures as well, posing a threat to Tenochtitlan. Axayacatl marched on Tlatelolco and slew Moquihuix on the steps of his own temple. Tlatelolco was then treated harshly as the Aztec began to assimilate the capital's population into Tenochtitlan.

MOSAIC ORNAMENTS A popular Aztec adornment, used for rituals or cultic ceremonies and depicting birds, fish and animals. Statues also had mosaic ornaments, and priests and warriors wore them as well. Mosaics with religious themes were popular. Wood was a common base for the mosaic, on which semiprecious stones were inlaid, as well as gold, bones and shells. Produced in Tenochtitlan, mosaics were also used on mirrors and on masks, evoking the styles of older cultures. (See MASSIVE OFFERINGS.)

MOTAGUA RIVER A waterway in the Chiapas and Guatemalan highlands that drains the regions and flows northeast to the Gulf of Honduras. A source of Maya jade, the Motagua River basin served as the setting for the cities of Copan and Quirigua.

MOTAGUA VALLEY A region in the Chiapas-Guatemala highlands at the base of the Minas Mountains. It is believed that jade was mined here, especially at Manzanai.

MOTECUHZOMA (Moctezuma) ILHUICAMINA I (The Elder)

Called the Lord That Shoots the Sky (or Heavens), the ruler of the Aztec from A.D. 1440 to 1469. He was the son of the emperor Huitzilhuitl and a mysterious princess from Cuernavaca brought back to Tenochtitlan after being wooed by Huitzilhuitl. He was also the younger brother of Itzcoatl, whom he served as a military commander and counselor. A gifted administrator who was adept in governing the growing Aztec domain, he began immediately to consolidate the Aztec claims on the sites in the Valley of Mexico that Aztec armies had won during the reign of Itzcoatl and the TRIPLE ALLIANCE, the league of the Mexica cities. He also started military units on a quest to find the fabled Aztlan, the homeland of the Aztec people, an endeavor that brought them into new regions and contact with other cultures. Military expansion resulted from these efforts and from campaigns conducted by Motecuhzoma. When he began rebuilding the Great Pyramid in Tenochtitlan, Motecuhzoma took laborers and materials from the cities and states that had been reduced to allied or vassal status. Chalco refused to take on any such responsibility and was attacked and subdued.

Working with the distinguished Nezahualcoyotl and other leaders of the Triple Alliance, Motecuhzoma moved into the Huaxtec area of Veracruz as punishment for the murder of Aztec traders, and then into the Mixtec domain, taking Coixtlahuaca, probably in 1458. The ruler of Coixtlahuaca was strangled and his family made slaves. Cotton, chili, salt, feathers, blankets, bead collars and red dye were brought back to Tenochtitlan by the Aztec, according to the Codex Mendoza. By the time Motecuhzoma died, the Aztec and other members of the Triple Alliance held lands south to Oaxaca, east to the Totonac domains, to Tuxpan in the Huaxtec realm and part of the northeastern highlands. His reign was not devoted entirely to military efforts, however, as he was the administrator of Tenochtitlan. During his reign the temple was transformed into a towering splendor. The city faced natural disasters, crippling blows that threatened its security and survival. In 1446 a locust plague wiped out many crops. In 1449 floods damaged the city and the agricultural lands. In 1450 the harvests failed, and a unique early frost mantled the capital, in 1451, 1452. Late frost and a drought damaged crops. Famine continued for a time, forcing in 1453 and 1454 Motecuhzoma to provide food for the people by opening tribute stores and importing crops.

Motecuhzoma initiated the FLOWER WARS, the battles that were used to advance the cause of the Aztec and the Triple Alliance and to acquire sacrificial victims for the altars of Tenochtitlan. He also designed a botanical garden at Oaxtepec, a site near Cuernavaca. The gardens, planted with exotic flowers and shrubs from other regions, had beds and terraces. Cypress trees adorned the retreat, in which medicinal herbs and plants were grown. A sophisticated irrigation system was installed to maintain the health of the trees and plants. The site is still popular because of its enduring beauty.

Motecuhzoma is also associated with the site of Achiotla, where a wondrous tree grew. Because the Tototepec refused to give the Aztec samples of the bark and flowers, Motecuhzoma attacked the tree. He was also known to have kept an aviary of exotic birds. The Aztecs thrived during Motecuhzoma I's reign.

MOTECUHZOMA (Moctezuma) XOCOYOTZIN II (The Younger)

Called the Angry Lord, the most celebrated Aztec ruler because of his ill-fated encounter with Hernando Cortez and the Spanish. He ruled the Aztecs from Tenochtitlan from A.D. 1502 to 1520. The successor to Ahuitzotl, chosen by the Aztec council, Motecuhzoma assumed the throne at a time when the political, economic, social and religious life of the Aztec was concentrated on the emperor. He had to revitalize the court and regulate the ranks and power of the nobles by restoring them to official posts over commoners while instituting social changes. So deified was the emperor at the time that he rode everywhere in a litter, took his meals behind gilded screens and walked on cloths covering the ground. Motecuhzoma was a notable warrior who enlarged the empire and maintained a firm grip on the lands the Aztec held from past reigns. Only the Tarascan and the Tlaxcalan were able to withstand his assaults. He fought four campaigns against Tlaxcala and Huexotzingo; the last one, in 1515, proved disastrous for the Aztec forces. Motecuhzoma also led his troops in campaigns in Oaxaca, Puebla, Guerrero, the old Chichimec domain and in the Isthmus of Tehuantepec.

A deeply religious man, he went to Teotihuacan on pilgrimage and retreated at times to his villa, called the Black House. One of his counselors, Nezahualpilli, predicted that dire events would cause the overthrow of the Aztec. The hesitation that Motecuhzoma displayed in his dealings with the Spanish may have resulted from those predictions.

Motecuhzoma kept beautiful aviaries in his palace compounds, with salt- and freshwater ponds. Hanging gardens displayed unique and rare plants, and he also kept a royal zoo.

Captured by Cortez, the emperor tried to calm his people and to allay the uprisings that eventually destroyed the capital city. He died while in custody. The Spanish recorded that he pined and grieved over the loss of Tenochtitlan, while the Aztec reported that their emperor was strangled by the Spanish. Motecuhzoma was succeeded by Prince Cuauhtemoc, who ruled only four months, and then by Prince Cuitlahuac, Motecuhzoma's brother, who took command of the armies and took up arms against the Spanish. Cuitlahuac and his small army confronted the Spanish and their allies and withstood a siege of 93 days. He was received graciously by Cortez when he surrendered, but he was hanged after three years in captivity.

According to scholars, the death of Motecuhzoma and the surrender of Cuitlahuac represent more than the collapse of the Aztec capital. Rather these events signaled the end of the civilizations of the entire Mesoamerican region, the demise of centuries of beauty and glory.

MOTUL DE SAN JOSE

A Late Classic Period (A.D. 600–900) ceremonial complex in the southern lowlands. The site is mentioned in texts recorded in Tikal and Seibal. Motul de San Jose was also the home of some women who married Bird Jaguar, the ruler of Yaxchilan. The city had a period of vitality before being abandoned. The Seibal records credit Motul de San Josas being an ancient capital.

MOUNTAIN-THAT-OPENS

A mysterious site in the region of the Mixtec in Oaxaca, dating to the start of the Post-Classic Period (c. A.D. 900). The rulers of this city were reported to have been slain by the Mixtec dynasty of Tilantongo after a military campaign.

MOYOCOYATZIN   An Aztec (Mexica) deity called the Lord Who Invented Himself or He Who Fashions Himself From His Own Thoughts. (See AZTEC GODS.)

MOYOTLAN   A district of the Aztec (Mexica) capital, Tenochtitlan, located in the southern part of the city. It was called the place of the Mosquitoes. This is probably in reference to its proximity to the swamplands of Lake Texcoco.

MOYOTZINCO   A site in the Puebla Valley, dating to 1300 B.C. This settlement contains houses, bottle-shape pits (*chultunes*) and small adobe platforms.

MOZATL   A Tepanec general who tried in vain to bring reserve troops to Atzcapotzalco to stem the advance of the Triple Alliance forces. The Aztec, Texcoco and Tlapacoyan slew Maxtla, the Tepanec king, and the city collapsed after a siege and campaign of 114 days.

MUL-CHIC   A Maya site in the Yucatan Peninsula near Uxmal. A six-tiered pyramid with stairs located on a plaza reveals several older interior structures. Part of the pyramid displays the Puuc style. Murals taken from the site are now on display in Merida and they depict the god Itzamna. The site dates to around A.D. 670–770.

MUYIL   A Maya site on the east coast of the Yucatan Peninsula. Twelve temples and ceremonial structures date to the Late-Classic Period (A.D. 1200/1250 to 1521).

N

NACASTE PHASE A cultural development in the Olmec city of San Lorenzo, on the Rio Chiquito in Veracruz. Dated to around 700 B.C., the phase is known for helmeted figures, punch-eyed figurines, animal effigies and torso statues.

NACO A Maya site in the Sula Plain, the region on the Gulf of Honduras in the Maya southern lowlands. Naco is believed to have had a population of 10,000. It was erected along the Chamelecon River and took part in the regional trade that flourished until the Spanish arrived. At one time Naco was an ally or a vassal of Copan. It was probably also controlled by the Chorti. There is also some evidence of Pipil habitation.

NACOXOC A Toltec ruler listed in the *Historia Tolteca Chichimeca*. He ruled from A.D. 718 to 770 according to this record.

NAGUALS Spirits revered by the Itza people. The *Naguals* were believed capable of becoming jaguars and other animals, walking about in the world of humans.

NAHUALPILLI A deity revered in the city of Xochimilco. This god was patron of the young.

NAHUAL (Nahua) A Mesoamerican people originating in the northern territories and in Chicomoztoc, the Land of the Seven Caves, who arrived in the Valley of Mexico in the Post-Classic Period (A.D. 900–1521) to become initiators of some of the great civilizations of Mesoamerica. The Aztec belong to this group. The Nahual spoke Nahuatl, a language belonging to the Uto-Aztecan family.

NAHUALATE RIVER A Guatemalan waterway that flows from the volcanic peaks of the highlands to the Pacific Ocean.

NAHUATL The language spoken by the Post-Classic Period (A.D. 900–1521) people entering the Valley of Mexico from Chicomoztoc, the Land of the Seven Caves, including the Aztec. Part of the Uto-Aztecan family, Nahuatl was the *lingua franca* of the Valley of Mexico in that historical period, and still is spoken today in some of the rural regions. The language has contributed many words to modern English, including:

chocolate—*chocolatl*	coyote—*coyotl*
cocoa—*cacao*	tamale—*tamalli*
copal—*copalli*	tomato—*tomatl*

Nahuatl place-names and the presence of Nahuatl words in modern Mesoamerica attests to the commonality of the language. (See MESOAMERICAN LANGUAGES.)

NAJ TUNICH A cave site located in the Peten (Putun) district of northern Guatemala, called the "stone house" in the local Maya dialect. Naj Tunich has historical importance because of the religious symbols of the Classic Maya there, dating from c. A.D. 1/250 to c. A.D. 400/900. The Maya used such caves for water resources in most regions. Caves were also considered the entrances to Xibalba, the Maya underworld. This association made caves appropriate sites for rituals of propitiation. Glyphs were incorporated into the wall decorations in Naj Tunich and were carved into the natural limestone formations. The "Chamber of the Crystal Columns" contains figures and glyphs concerning the Maya cult of the dead. Other chambers contain scenes of ball games, sacrifices and deities.

NANAHUATZIN A Teotihuacan deity called the Prurulent One. According to the cosmological traditions of the vast city-state of Teotihuacan, he threw himself into a fire to become the sun.

NARANJO RIVER A Guatemalan highland waterway that flows from the volcanic peaks to the Pacific Ocean. Maya cities were built near Naranjo, and the nobles of Caracol controlled the region for a time.

NATIVIDAD PHASE A cultural development associated with the Mixtec city of Coixtlahuaca, dating to A.D. 1000–1520/1525.

NAUCAMPATEPETL (Cofre de Perate) One of the major volcanic peaks in the Transverse Volcanic Axis on the Mesa Central of Mexico. (See MESOAMERICAN GEOGRAPHIC DIMENSIONS for details.)

NAUHYOTZIN I A Toltec ruler listed in the *Anales de Cuauhtitlan*. The document lists him as ruling from A.D. 983 to 997.

NAUTLA RIVER One of the major waterways of the gulf coastal lowlands, the setting for the recently discovered city of El Pital.

NAYARIT A region and modern state of Mexico between Guerrero and the Gulf of Mexico, with human habitation in the Early Formative Period (2000 B.C.–c. A.D. 250/290), recorded as the Nayarit, Jalisco and Colima cultures. Settlements at San Blas, Matachan and Ixtlan del Rio contained obsidian flakes, tools and some pottery dating to this period. San Blas had a shell-shape mound with some construction elements that date to 500 B.C. Ixtlan del Rio contained a remarkable series of lively figures and group ceramics in black, white and yellow, on a reddish background. One piece depicts four separate village residences with thatched roofs, set in a circle on a base. Fifty separate individual figures are included in this collection from Ixtlan del Rio, portraying men, women, lovers, dogs, children, musicians and their instruments. The entire scene vibrates with life and energy and is a complete rendition of the villages of the era. Other separate figures depict similar occupations or pasttimes, including a musician striking a turtle shell with a deer horn. Nayarit artists favored semicircular and circular themes and humor and realism are evident.

Some Nayarit figurines depict deformed individuals or people with physical defects. The Nayarit sites, including Penitas, Amapa, and Ixtlan del Rio, evidence crude petroglyphs as well as sophisticated figures. The Nayarit people worked in clay mostly, but many pieces were found fashioned from green stone, beads, obsidian and even alabaster. Nayarit ceramics include monochromes, bichrome and polychrome phases: red on orange, red, black and white on orange, slip and polished buff, slipped and polished brown, slip orange, dark brown ringed bases, red-rimmed orange, red-rimmed white and exterior red on buff. Besides figurines, the Nayarit craftsmen made elaborate stamps, whistles, effigy jars, spindle whorls and pottery with animal designs. Copper pieces, including needles, tweezers, pins, fish hooks and knives, were recovered in Amapa.

NEGRO RIVER A Guatemalan waterway that flows from the interior highlands to the Gulf of Campeche.

NEPOHUALCO Called the Place of the Count, a Chichimec site in the Valley of Mexico. It is believed to be the location of the first census taken in Mesoamerica. The census was conducted by Xolotl, the distinguished Chichimec ruler, sometime around A.D. 1240.

NEVADA DE TOLUCA (Xinantecatl) One of the major volcanic peaks in the Transverse Volcanic Axis in the Mesa Central of Mexico. (See MESOAMERICAN GEOGRAPHY for details.)

NEVADA PHASE A cultural development in the Valley of Mexico, dated from 1400 to 1250 B.C. The Nevada group left ceramic evidence, including *tecomates*, white wares and a variety of figurines. These statuettes, listed as in the *pilli* style, had Olmecoid features and possibly served as social or hereditary markers of rank.

NEW FIRE A ceremony conducted by the Aztec and other Mesoamerican groups, incorporating the traditions of earlier cultures and associated with astrology, cosmology and the calendar system. When the end of the various calendrical cycles came about, the Aztec looked upon the future with dread because they believed in the collapse of worlds as part of the calendric cycles. They believed that their world, called the Fifth Sun, was about to come to an end. All fires were extinguished throughout the empire, as the people awaited the ceremonies conducted on their behalf. The Hill of the Star (the Cerro de la Estrella or Citaltepec), a mountain east of Culhuacan, was the setting for such rituals. Aztec priests congregated there, anticipating the Pleiades, which crossed the meridian at exactly midnight on the appointed day. When the Pleiades made their fateful crossing, the priests could announce that disaster had been averted. The Fifth Sun would remain in place, sparing humanity. The alignment of various calendrical factors were involved in this determination of the New Fire observance, and it was a time of considerable fear and religious fervor among the Aztec and others.

The New Fire was lit on the Hill of the Star, usually ignited inside the cracked-open breast of a sacrificial victim. Seen by the people from great distances, the New Fire signaled salvation. The Aztec conducted New Fire ceremonies in their earliest historical periods, stopping while on their great trek toward the Valley of Mexico to celebrate the events. Their records indicate that they held a New Fire ritual in Coatepec in A.D. 1163.

NEXAPA RIVER A tributary of the great Balsas River system in western Mexico.

NEZAHUALCOYOTL Called the Sage of Anahuac, one of the most illustrious Mesoamericans, the ruler of Texcoco. Nezahualcoyotl influenced many cultures and was important in the Post-Classic Period in the Valley of Mexico, in the 1400s A.D. His father was Ixtlilxochtli, the ruler of Texcoco, who roused the ire of Tezozomoc, the king of the Tepanec. Taken by Ixtlilxochtli to a remote mountain retreat, Nezahualcoyotl faced the Tepanec who had trailed them. He was hidden by his father in a high branch of a tree, and told to remain there in silence. He then watched as Ixtlilxochtli turned on the Tepanec, who slew him. When the enemy had left, Nezahualcoyotl climbed down from the tree and sat with the body all night, waiting until family retainers arrived at dawn to give Ixtlilxochtli a proper burial. The retainers spirited the lad away, and Nezahualcoyotl began an adventurous life of avoiding Tepanec spies and assassins.

When Tezozomoc died, a power struggle ensued for the Tepanec throne. Maxtla won, taking up the hunt for Nezahualpilli in A.D. 1426. Maxtla also put to death Chimalpopoca, the ruler of the Aztec capital of Tenochtitlan, a deed that imbued Itzcoatl, Chimalpopoca's successor, and the Aztec people with the spirit of vengeance. Maxtla's harsh demands for tribute in A.D. 1428 led to the formation of the Triple Alliance, a confederation of Tenochtitlan, Texcoco and Tlacopan (Tacuba). These cities turned on Maxtla. Texcoco was already under siege, and the Aztec and their allied forces came to Nezahualcoyotl's assistance. Maxtla then blockaded Tenochtitlan but could not overcome the combined armies of his foes and was taken and slain. Maxtla and the Tepanec before him had tried unsuccessfully to murder Nezahualcoyotl, but he evaded them so often that he took on almost mythical dimensions among his contemporaries.

Revered as a sage and poet-king, Nezahualcoyotl drew a group of followers called the *tlamatine,* the "followers of truth." They were also called the Flower and Song Group because of their artistic bent. These men were philosophers, artists, musicians and sculptors who pursued their art in the court of Texcoco. Nezahualcoyotl was also something of a monotheist, honoring his god in a 10-level pyramidal temple. The roof of this shrine was gem-encrusted. No human sacrifices were permitted, only the offering of flowers and incense. He also established an academy of music and welcomed worthy entrants from all regions.

Nezahualcoyotl had close ties with the Aztec monarchy. When Motecuhzoma I erected a dike from Chapultepec to Tenochtitlan, Nezahualcoyotl advised him that such a dike was dangerous, prone to the floodwaters that would arrive with the seasonal changes. When the floods inundated Tenochtitlan, Nezahualcoyotl assisted the Aztec in establishing control systems. As a member of the Triple Alliance, Nezahualcoyotl took part in the wars conducted by the combined forces and received lands and tribute. He is credited with the rise of Texcoco's Golden Age, which brought scholarship and artistry to the city and set high standards that influenced other cultures. He wrote his *Lamentations,* a philosophical study of life. His palace, erected at Texcotzinco, had aqueducts, baths, gardens, stairways and over 300 separate chambers. Nezahualcoyotl ruled from a golden throne adorned with turquoise. Part of his duties took place in Tenochtitlan, where he was among the counselors choosing a successor to Motecuhzoma I. Nezahualcoyotl died in 1472 and was succeeded by Nezahualpilli.

NEZAHUALPILLI The heir to the celebrated Nezahualcoyotl of Texcoco. He was seven years old when Nezahualcoyotl died in 1472, and he was crowned at Tenochtitlan, with the Aztec emperor Axayacatl as his patron. Each year Axayacatl spent time with Nezahualpilli, educating him to rule. When Axayacatl died, Nezahualpilli was among the counselors who chose Tizoc as heir. He lectured the new Aztec emperor on the duties of the throne. A warrior and idealist, Nezahualpilli reconstructed palaces and shrines in his domain and lived in luxury with as many as 200 wives and concubines. When Tizoc died or was murdered, Nezahualpilli again joined the council that elected Ahuitzotl as the new Aztec emperor. He also instructed this successor on the duties of the throne. He remained active in Aztec affairs and elected Motecuhzoma as Ahuitzotl's heir. In talking with Motecuhzoma, Nezahualpilli predicted the collapse of the Aztec empire, a prophecy that influenced the emperor. Nezahualpilli was considered a powerful wizard. He died in 1515, and there is considerable speculation as to whether the Spanish invasion would have succeeded had he lived.

NICOYA A peninsula on the Pacific coast of Costa Rica, inhabited by the Maya by the sixth century A.D. The Maya there produced club heads of green stone representing animal and human heads and used polychrome techniques.

NIM LI PUNIT A Maya site dating to A.D. 700 to 800 in the southern part of Belize, allied in trade with nearby Lubaantun. The tallest stela ever found in Belize, standing some 30 feet, was discovered here with two dozen other stelae. A tomb was also found at the site. An unusual aspect of this site is that the masonry used contains no mortar.

NINE-WIND (1) The calendrical name given by the Maya for Quetzalcoatl, the Feathered Serpent, and the associated god Kukulcan. Masks discovered in the city of Cacaxtla in Puebla, Maya in style, depict the deity in this fashion. The deity appeared in Maya calendars.

NINE-WIND (2) A Mixtec deity, the god of the winds, a form of Ehecatl (Quetzalcoatl). The deity's temples were rounded to express his sweeping domain.

NIYOHUA The Zapotec deity of the hunt. This god appears to have had only local appeal, venerated in certain Zapotec districts.

NOCHIXTLAN VALLEY A region in Oaxaca, part of the Mixtec realm, dating to 1300 B.C. in the Early Formative Period. Civic architecture was begun there at an early time, and there is evidence of social castes in regional affairs. In the Ramos Phase, 200 B.C. to A.D. 500, the city of Yucuita came to power. In the Late Classic Period (A.D. 600–900), the Nochixtlan Valley is believed to have had a vast population, estimated as between 30,000 to 50,000.

NOGALES PHASE A cultural development in the Tamaulipas Sequence dating from c. 5000/4500 to 3000 B.C., found in the Sierra de Tamaulipas region, north of the Diablo Complex. A change in foods in Nogales is evident during this phase. Plant gathering appears to have supplied as much as 70 percent of the nutritional intake. The groups of this region and phase used millet, beans, gourds, chili peppers and squash. Basketry is evident, with knot designs. Large scrapers, nets, disk choppers and other tools were manufactured.

NOHMUL A Maya site in northern Belize near the modern border of Mexico that served as a regional ceremonial center. The site has two ceremonial complexes and a raised causeway. Nohmul was inhabited from 350 B.C., lasting until around A.D. 600 to 900. The name means "big mound."

NOHPAT A large, ruined Maya site, located in west-central Yucatan near the city of Uxmal. It was connected to Uxmal by a causeway and reflects Classic Puuc–style architecture. Two large structures are on the site. One has a vault, and the other once stood about 150 feet high.

NONOALCO A group of noted sculptors and artisans, probably related to the Toltec and originating in Veracruz and Tabasco. The Nonoalco are believed to have been associated at one time with the city of Teotihuacan. They are also recorded as having been brought from the gulf coast to Puebla to assist the Toltec construction of their capital of Tula. A second group is recorded in Michoacan. When Tula collapsed, the Nonoalco went into the Valley of Mexico.

They were described as wise and cultivated, a people who spoke several languages. The cities of El Tajin, Xochicalco, Teotihuacan and Monte Alban are associated with the Nonoalco in ceramic wares and other art forms. Their artistic abilities were much in demand during the Classic and Post-Classic Periods (c. A.D.1/250–900; 900–1521), and they appear to have traveled about to instruct various cultures in artistic projects. The Nonoalco were mentioned also in Spanish records. They may have been Pipil in origin, and their contemporaries called them "the Deaf and Dumb," an unexplained reference.

NOPALTZIN A Chichimec ruler, called the Revered Fruit of the Cactus, the son of the celebrated King Xolotl. Nopaltzin assisted his father in founding the Chichimec capital, Tenayuca. He inherited the throne in A.D. 1304, and introduced Toltec culture to his people. Nopaltzin's son Tlohtzins, the Hawk, continued his father's civilizing efforts.

NOPILOA A Late Classic Period (A.D. 600–900) site associated with the Remojada culture. Nopiloa was located in central Veracruz and served as a trade link between Teotihuacan, Kaminaljuyu and the Guatemalan highlands.

NUEVO (NEW) RIVER A Belize waterway near which the Maya ceremonial complex of Lamanai was constructed. The river formed a lake at Lamanai before joining the Belize and Hondo rivers. The city of Cerros was erected on the banks of the Nuevo.

O

OAXACA A valley on a high plateau that is now a modern state in Mexico. Oaxaca was the cradle for Mesoamerican groups, including the Mixtec and Zapotec. In the Balsas-Tepanec Depression, and containing the Sierra Madre del Sur and the Sierra Madre Coalcoman ranges, Oaxaca nurtured many cultures throughout the historical periods of Mesoamerican development. The region, a hilly expanse, is linked to Tlacula in the east and to Etla in the south. The Atoyac River, a tributary of the Balsas, drains Oaxaca. The vast peaks of the sierras and adjoining valleys and mesas offer a distinct environment for settlements. Human habitation here dates to the Paleo-Indian and Incipient Agriculture periods (11,000–7000 B.C.; 7000–c. 2000/2500 B.C.).

Volcanic activity formed much of Oaxaca, and streams pass through the region, which is ringed by steep slopes. Its climate is warm and temperate as well as semiarid. Habitations date to c. 7400/5500 B.C., continuing throughout the historical periods until 1300 B.C., when villages were established. The original settlements are evident in caves. Grain pollens dating to 7400–6700 B.C. have been discovered as well as bottle gourds and seeds that are older than those found in the Tehuacan region. The region was home to Monte Alban and its phases, as civic architecture and social structures and ranks developed there. The phases of development in Oaxaca include:

Espiridion c. 1400 B.C.–?
Tierras Largas 1400–1150 B.C.
San Jose Mogote 1400–850 B.C.
Guadalupe 850–700 B.C.
Rosario c. 700/650–500/450 B.C.
(See also MONTE ALBAN for associated phases.)

The coastal regions of Oaxaca were a blend of many cultures, with the earliest known settlements located beside lagoons and estuaries. Platform building did not begin there until c. 100 B.C. (See MIXTEC and ZAPOTEC for historical details.)

OAXTEPEC An Aztec site near Cuernavaca in the Valley of Mexico. Emperor Motecuhzoma (Moctezuma) I built a lavish garden retreat there, with carefully tended flowers on beds and terraces, all brought from other regions. Cypress trees adorned the retreat, which also had special sections for herbs and medicinal plants. A sophisticated irrigation system was installed to keep the vegetation healthy. The site remains popular today because of its enduring beauty.

OBSIDIAN A semiprecious stone favored when tinged with green. A volcanic glass, obsidian can be carved and shaped. Ixtepeque Volcano of Guatemala in the highlands region is a source of obsidian. A special market for obsidian objects was Quirigua, on the Motagua River. The Olmec and the Maya made use of obsidian. The Maya honed razor-sharp blades from the stone, for ritual blood-letting by the priests and nobles. Many Maya rulers controlled the obsidian supplies in their own regions. Maya sites associated with the stone include El Chayal, near modern Guatemala City, and Matapacan, which had Early Formative Period (c. 2000/1600–900 B.C.) obsidian workshops. In its own era, the city of Teotihuacan controlled a green variety of obsidian in Hidalgo. The city maintained hundreds of workshops where the stones were manufactured into items for trade. Obsidian points were always popular, and when the great empires of the Post-Classic Period (A.D. 900–1521) collected tributes, the stone remained a priority resource.

OBSIDIAN BUTTERFLY A Puebla earth goddess, called Itzpapalotl, honored by the Chichimec and others. The Obsidian Butterfly was worshipped in the city of Tenayuca.

OCAMPO A cave site in northern Mexico, in the Sierra Madres south of Monterey. The cave was occupied between 5000 to 3000 B.C. Food remains, baskets and mats were recovered there.

OCAMPO PHASE A cultural development in the Tamaulipas Sequence in the region of the Sierra de Tamaulipas, dated primarily from 500 B.C. to A.D. 500. During the phase from 70 to 80 percent foods of were from locally gathered vegetation. Domestic plant varieties made up a small part of the diet as well. Dart points, choppers, scrapers, nets and a variety of baskets have been traced to this era.

OCELOAPAN A site in the Sierra de Puebla region, probably Totonac in origin. Oceloapan is mentioned in Totonac records, but there is little documentation available on the site. Oceloapan may have been founded by a local group and then inhabited by the Totonac.

OCELOTL   The jaguar, representing a day sign in the Aztec variation of the *tonalpohualli,* the calendar system.

OCHPANIZTLI   Called the sweeping, an Aztec festival honoring the earth and vegetation. During the ceremonies of the feast a woman was ritually slain. Mock battles conducted by warrior groups were also part of the celebration.

OCOS PHASE   An important cultural development of Mesoamerica, taking place on the Pacific coastal plain (Soconusco), near the Mexican and Guatemalan border. The Ocos people were perhaps the oldest villagers in Mesoamerica. They built their shelters on a narrow coastal strip of savannas, crossed by rivers and containing with rain forests and gently sloping lands. The marine products available in this coastal region were staples in the diet, and included fish, clams, oysters, crabs and turtles.

The major Ocos site was La Victoria, where pole houses were covered with mud, built on mound platforms as a defense against tidal floods. There may have been many villages of this type in the region, as the lagoons, estuaries and alluvial fields offered considerable benefits to early inhabitants. Maize was grown at La Victoria, and the people hunted in the nearby mangrove swamps and in the forests. Of particular importance was the presence of salt *playas* (beaches), and a tree that they called *madresal,* the Mother of salt.

Ocos ceramics were sophisticated and included *tecomates* (neckless jars) and globular vessels. They also used rocker-stamped decorations on their flat bowls and plates. (Rocker stamping is a method of incising wet clay with the sharp edge of a shell or some other object, moving the edge back and forth. The way in which the shell edge is notched that determines the pattern, and the result is called dentated rocker stamping.) Ocos ceramic figurines include both stylish and grotesque human and animal forms.

The class system of the Ocos was based on the agricultural holdings in the region. In time a genuine aristocracy emerged. The Ocos also rose at a time when religious ceremonial complexes were being erected. This culture influenced the surrounding regions, as far as San Lorenzo in time. The Ocos are also associated with the Maya in Guatemala, c. 1500 to 850 B.C. The Cuadros Phase was contemporaneous.

OJOCHI PHASE   A cultural development on the gulf coast, associated with the Olmec site of San Lorenzo. It is dated to 1500 B.C., with the starting dates unknown and possibly continuing until 1350 B.C. A good number of ceramic wares have been recovered from sites of this phase. Ojochi villages were settled on the coast and on the banks of the Rio Chiquito. Ojochi villagers probably had a mixed economy of farming, fishing, hunting and gathering. It is believed that they cleared uplands for farms. Ojochi ceramics show an Ocos influence. Ojochi artisans produced *tecomates* (neckless jars), narrow-necked bottles and flat-bottom bowls with flaring sides. (See SAN LORENZO for accompanying cultural developments.)

OLMEC   Called People of Rubber by the Aztec and later cultures, one of the major civilizations of Mesoamerica,

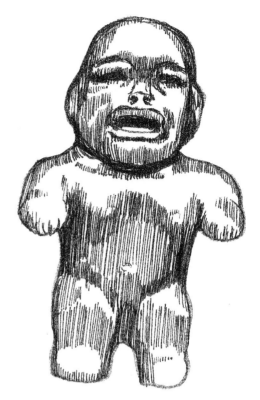

Olmec jade figure

influencing entire regions and peoples and considered by many to be the mother culture. The true origins of the Olmec remain obscure, and the name by which the Olmec were known to one another has been lost. They were once described as having appeared suddenly in Mesoamerica, having origins in other cultures. In time they were called the *Tenecelome,* the Jaguar-Mouthed People, and also the La Venta Culture, after one of their major sites. Their appearance was heralded by ceramic phases in the region, and they had associations with the Bajio cultural phase of San Lorenzo and with other developments. Some scholars call members of this culture who resided on the gulf coast the Metropolitan Olmec. They were associated, however, with many other sites under Olmec influence.

The Olmec are recorded as arriving in Mesoamerica sometime around 1500 B.C. While this appearance is historically correct, there is every reason to believe that it was not sudden. There are many indications of an earlier form of the great Olmec culture evolving in several remote sites in the Tuxtla Mountains. Their cultural beginnings can be traced accurately to the San Lorenzo site, located on the banks of the Rio Chiquito. This is now considered to have been the "heartland" of Olmec traditions and development, not only culturally but politically as well. As the Olmec prospered and began to set their own artistic and cultural goals, the products of their various industries began to appear in the marketplaces of other cultures. These ceramic wares and the jaguar motif, so characteristically Olmec, have been recovered from sites as far away as Oaxaca and the Valley of Mexico. When San Lorenzo collapsed, the site of La Venta on the gulf coast of Tabasco took on an importance. The cities of Chalcatzingo, in the far western part of the state of Morelos, and Oxtotitlan, a cave located in Guerrero, date to this early period as well.

Olmec society had two basic components: the aristocracy, who had political and religious power, and the commoners, who worked on farms or labored in various capacities in the settlements. The privileged Olmec resided in clusters of elaborate dwellings and public structures in the gulf coast region, in and around the great ceremonial complexes. Beyond these elite compounds the vast hordes of Olmec commoners toiled in the lowland farming communities.

As the well-born prospered from the agricultural economy, they developed complex trading enterprises, a process that had an impact on other societies. Trade was among the several factors that attracted other groups to Olmec society. The Olmec seem to have incorporated other cultures into their sphere, either through artistic or economic lures or by military suppression. The wares and products of these assimilated cultures flowed into districts of the privileged. The Olmec also established trading outposts that safeguarded various regions and were usually garrisoned. With these fortress cities they were able to insure the passage of raw materials into the Olmec domain and the exportation of manufactured goods in return. In some instances initial trade outposts became full-fledged colonies.

The Olmec decline was the paradoxical result of their own civilizing processes. In time other cities and other cultures, benefiting from the Olmec presence and learning quickly their ways, rose as competitors. The great centers of Olmec power faded as rituals arose at other sites and other regions.

The phases of Olmec development include Olmec I, II and III.

During Olmec I (1500–1200 B.C.), there were probably Olmec settlements before 1500 B.C. in the Tuxtlas Mountains, and links have been established with other settlements in the south. This is the period of their emergence in the region.

Olmec II (1200–c. 600/400 B.C.) is termed the San Lorenzo Phase in its earliest period. The Olmec were associated with the Valley of Mexico and Tabasco. Evidence of their presence was found in the Juxtlahuaca Cave and on the Chiapas coast.

In the La Venta period, which followed the San Lorenzo Phase, the Olmec conducted complex trade and manufacturing enterprises. Jade became popular because of their labors, and the Oxtotitlan murals were fashioned in Guerrero.

Olmec III (c. 600/400 B.C.–?) is termed by some the Post La Venta Phase, and clearly marks the decline of the Olmec civilization. The introduction of the Long Count can be traced to this period, and the site of Tres Zapotes emerged.

The land dominated by the Olmec has been called the Mesopotamia of the Americas and has been designated as encompassing from 6,200 to 7,200 square miles at the height of Olmec power. These lands included the swampy regions of Veracruz and neighboring Tabasco, which bordered on the gulf coast. This region is the Olmec "heartland," and most surviving Olmec sites have been discovered here. The region is actually a coastal plain, having low hills and bordered by the towering Tuxtla Mountains, the source of

basalt and one of the great remnants of the region's ancient volcanic activity.

The peculiar geological development of the region, particularly around the original Olmec site of San Lorenzo, and the climatic conditions gave rise to Olmec culture. Other great settlements, as at La Venta, were similarly formed by the landscape and by the conditions of the weather and the soil. Almost two-thirds of the Olmec domain was uplands, providing natural resources and raw materials. These highlands extended to the mountains of southern Oaxaca and with Olmec expansion eventually the Sierra Madre de Chiapas.

The rainfall in this region of Mesoamerica was abundant, with most of the precipitation occurring from late May through November. There was no actual dry season, as the winter months brought cold rains and mists. Flooding was the natural result of the rainfall, and the land received annual inundations and deposits of silt. The rivers, such as the San Juan and the Papaloapan, maintained fertility and formed natural levees upon which the mud built up from season to season. Lakes connected by the Limon and Cacique rivers offered stable water supplies, and in Tabasco there were swamps and marshes.

The Tuxtla Mountains rose out of Lake Catemaco, and a basin was formed between the Papaloapan and the Coatzacoalcos rivers. These lakes and streams were swollen with as much as 120 inches of rain every year. The agricultural prospects for the territory were thus high, and the climate and the configuration of the land fostered the growth of economies for a growing population.

OLMEC AGRICULTURE The slash-and-burn type of farming. People cleared the jungle by burning to create fields and drained the swamps in order to acquire more land. The drainage processes developed by the Olmec were new to Mesoamerica.

The *Milpas de ano*, the yearly techniques, provided methods of clearing the land. Trees and vegetation were cut down or hacked away in March. In May, after the clearing was completed, the entire region, including trees too large to be removed by hand, was set on fire in controlled burning. Everything blazed and then simmered until the vegetation was reduced to ash. The land was then somewhat cleared, with the fertilizing elements left. The land was sown in June and weeded continually, both for the crops being harvested in a short time and for the winter crops, which would need fertile and unchoked soil. Crops were harvested in November and December, and then the winter crop, the *tonamil*, was sown.

Several types of soil were available to the Olmec. The rich soil on the natural river levees, much prized, was called *tierra de prima*. The soil above flood levels was called *tierra de barreal*. *Tierra de grava*, the third type of soil, was nothing more than the deposits placed on the plateau of San Lorenzo. Clayey soil that would not support crops was called *tierra de potrero*, a reference to the vast savannas. The *tapachol*, the primary dry-season crop, was planted in the *tierra de primera* and in the *tierra de barreal*. In certain regions the fields showing secondary growth after clearing were called the *acahual*. Mulch and weeds were left to rot in fields of this type because they were usually too wet to burn properly. Along the rivers the grass was cut and maize was planted beside the grass roots, which did not interfere with the crop.

Because the soil was so rich and moisture laden, the erosive nature of the slash-and-burn technique did not do as much damage in the Olmec region as in other lands. The winter storms added to the wetness, as mists and rains swept across the region.

The Olmec raised maize, squash, beans, pumpkins and cotton. Their protein was derived mainly from fish, turtles and dog meat. Rivers offered an abundance of fish and turtles, and in the rainy season the savannas became large lakes, with islands and surrounding high crests. The Olmec fishermen used canoes, net, spears and harpoons. Animals hunted included the gopher, paca, deer, peccary, turkey and iguana. As in other cultures of the period, the agricultural endeavors of the Olmec served not only as an economic base but as a source of power for the aristocracy as well. Many fields were owned by aristocrats and worked by commoners.

OLMEC ARCHAEOLOGICAL SITES The documented locations that exhibit Olmec habitation and development. These are covered in separate entries, and they include Cerro Chalcatzinco, Cerro Cintepec, Cerro de las Mesas, Chalcatzinco, Las Bocas, Lagunas de Los Cerros, La Venta, Potrero Nuevo, Remolino, San Lorenzo, San Martin Paiapan Tenochtitlan Rio Chiquito, Tlapacoya, Tlatilco and Trez Zapotes.

Other sites were included in Olmec colonial expansion either militarily subjected to Olmec rule or part of the cultural alliance. Many of these sites were established by local groups but influenced by the Olmec and part of the development of their regions. Sites influenced by the Olmec are listed under separate headings. The inhabitants of those major Olmec sites were responsible for extensive territorial influence, and the trade enterprises of the culture brought other groups into their sphere. Some colonial regions were in the heartland of the Olmec domain while others were on frontier zones or trade outposts. In time some of these groups responded so well to Olmec influence that they were absorbed by the culture. Others were content to remain within the Olmec sphere but to maintain their own way of life and to pursue their own goals.

OLMEC ARCHITECTURE The buildings that expressed Olmec religious, cosmological and ceremonial ideals. Olmec architecture was influenced by that of neighboring cultures while developing those uniquely recognizable forms uncovered from their sites. The Olmec attempted to construct pyramidal platforms for ceremonial or religious structures early. Most of these structures were aligned on a north-south axis, obviously having some religious connotation. The building materials of the region were limited mostly to earth or adobe, although great stones were transported vast distances for the monumental forms. During early Olmec stages, few structures were adorned their architectural development, and the floors and walls were not stuccoed.

Olmec pyramids were solid mounds, designed as platforms. Alongside these structures Olmec sometimes constructed what is termed MASSIVE OFFERINGS. A massive offering is a trench, most often enormous, built for the sole purpose of being filled up again. Tons of serpentine, a semiprecious stone, were placed in designs on pavements, as in La Venta, and then covered with colored clays. The entire design was then reburied with earth and remained hidden. These trenches and their artistic treasures were probably some form of religious ritual concerned with offering the temple's deity a particularly enduring and artistically inspired devotional gift.

Olmec pyramids were also surrounded by plazas and courts, and the *talud-tablero* style were incorporated into the walls and designs. Such large solid structures demanded a vast labor force and considerable time in order to build. These massive monuments display the major elements of the Olmec style. They used formal lines, rounded at times, but always moving in fluid curves to achieve harmony. They define space, using it to give three-dimensional effect and to create tension. They developed the "slow-line" rhythm, in which no overloading of decorations distracted the eye or lessened the impact on the viewer. The massiveness and the solid qualities of the monuments prevailed, lending a formality and dignity to every structure.

Symbolism appearing on Olmec architecture lent mood and feeling to every monument. U-shaped elements, associated with early Mesoamerican concepts about earth monsters and caves, were defined in many structures, adding a cultic quality.

Courts were added to the massive structures in order to provide a stage or a setting to emphasize the massive slow-line rhythm. These courtyards were usually sunken and followed the same north-south axis, indicating strict architectural patterns and a canon for construction. Some courts had basalt blocks and serpentine layers, and many were adorned with the distinctive Olmec artistic embellishments.

OLMEC ART Sculptural and other forms created by Olmec that were varied and unique, reflecting distinct shapes and styles that exemplified clearly their cultural and religious ideals. The Olmec style, whether colossal heads, "baby faces" or the depiction of the jaguar, displays certain anthropomorphic aspects. The surviving pieces of Olmec art demonstrate not only the preoccupations of the artists of their era but reflect remarkable skill and technique.

The colossal heads found throughout the Olmec region of ancient Mesoamerica are emblematic of that culture today. Almost megalithic, these heads weigh several tons and stood as high as nine feet. Realistic, the faces carved into the massive heads were given broad, slightly flattened noses, thickened lips, slanted eyes and puffy cheeks. The heads, provided with helmets, may represent ball game players or kingly warriors. They could also be portraits of rulers or symbols of a religious function. Such heads have been found at sites of Olmec domination, including La Venta, San Lorenzo and Tres Zapotes, with smaller varieties at Laguna de los Cerros.

Figurines created by the Olmec include the "baby" forms, which portray squat, infantile creatures, carved to represent the fluid, chubby limbs of the young. Their combination of realism with an eerie mystical symbolism is startling. The babies are believed to be linked to the were-jaguar cult

Olmec were-jaguar

of the Olmec and other Mesoamerican cultures. The cult involved the religious worship of half-man, half-jaguar creatures that peopled part of the Olmec spiritual world. The infants have trapeziform mouths, slightly open, and swollen eyelids that make them not only beatific but also menacing.

Wrestler figurines, in contrast, are realistic renditions of the human form. The statues, detailed and lifelike, were usually small and depict older men, having shaved heads and beards. Details suggest the lines of the vertebrae and unique facial features. Each statue was carefully carved so that it may be viewed from all angles.

The jaguar or were-jaguar figurines were popular among the Olmec throughout their history. In religious art, the jaguar probably was a visible manifestation of the belief that sometime in the past a woman mated with a jaguar, giving birth to the hybrid form. The figures depicting this cat-child had a cleft head and a body suggesting neither sex. Some were-jaguars were depicted in the arms of women or young men. The jaguar was not the only animal glorified by Olmec artists. They also fashioned images of the harpy eagle, the cayman and the shark.

Celts, or ceremonial axes, were another form of Olmec art, used at times in conjunction with statues of human forms. A great number of celts were found at La Venta. These were ritual objects, carved of serpentine, and probably associated as well with the were-jaguar cult. They were small generally and easily carried. In some tombs the celts were combined with human forms in circular clusters. The La Venta cache of 16 figurines, surrounded by celts made

out of jade, is remarkable. The human forms, are made of jade and serpentine, have baby faces or the features of were-jaguars. They stand upright, with the celts forming a guardian wall around them.

Another Olmec art form was the stela. Carved from basalt or breccia, these stone slabs were from three to 17 feet high and were used for various commemorative purposes. They might be plain or with symbols. A favorite decoration was the jaguar form with renderings of humans in the jaws of the cats. Stelae have been found at most Olmec sites. One, Stela C from Tres Zapotes, carries the bar-dot symbols of the Long Count, the calender system that would come to flower during the Maya period.

Altars designed by the Olmec combined two separate Mesoamerican styles: the niche (in the *talud-tablero* fashion) and the Atlantean. In the niche style a cave was carved into the massive altar block, with a figure shown emerging from the block into the light. The Atlantean altar employed figures as support for the altar table. Discovered at Olmec ceremonial centers, these Atlantean altars are the first of their kind in Mesoamerica.

Stone boxes incised on four sides were another artistic form. Used for human hearts, some have lids and slight depressions in the center. An actual sarcophagus was found at La Venta, carved with unique jaguar symbols.

Masks were another popular form of Olmec artistic inventivness. These face coverings took on various purposes and styles, including the jaguar form, were-jaguars and ducks. Many masks were carved of jade and serpentine.

The Olmec also are noted for their remarkable cave paintings. At Oxtotitlan, in Guerrero, such paintings were discovered on a cliff wall and the walls of two shallow caves. The cliff painting shows a male figure seated in the head of a jaguar. The man's left leg is bent over the cat's head, and his right leg dangles before its face. The man holds an object in one hand, and the other is raised. His elaborate attire includes a helmet and a mantle edged with feathers. Other symbols accompany the painting, and the man resembles those portrayed at Chalcatzinco.

The cave paintings depict a flower with a human face, a man wearing a mask, a screech owl, a serpent and a man painted in black, except for his face, crown and enormous phallus. He is accompanied by a jaguar. An earth monster throne is part of this cave painting design.

At Juxtlahuaca, also in the state of Guerrero, a "Ritual Hall" was discovered in a cave. A painted panel there shows a standing figure, tall and bearded, attired luxuriously with a plumed headdress. His arms, legs and hands are covered with jaguar skin, as is the end of his loincloth. The figure is attached to a smaller man, as he holds a rope coiled about the second form. The second figure is painted black and has a prominent nose and a goatee. He is wearing a red tunic and a red and black headdress.

A second painted panel at Juxtlahuaca, in a room beyond the "Ritual Hall," depicts a serpent facing a jaguar. Both figures are painted in red.

Jade was a material favored for Olmec artistic endeavors. The English word is derived from the Spanish *Piedra ijada*, the stone of the loin. The more precise term is *lapis nephriticus*, the "stone of the kidney cures," so named because of a folklore legend concerning its healing powers. Nephrite

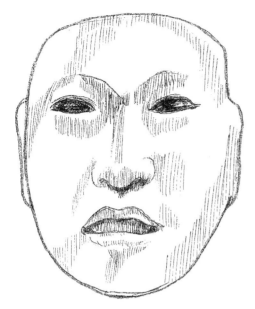

Olmec jade mask

jade is uniquely Chinese. The Mesoamerican variety, a silicate of sodium and aluminum, is jadite. The Olmec are the first people in Mesoamerica known to have worked in jade.

They were also noted for their jewelry, which included beads—discoidal, spherical, and tubular; bead balls; masks; pendants; pectorals; and waste plugs (Labrets).

The use of varied materials in Olmec art confirms the vast trade enterprises on which they embarked. Through trade, the Olmec could import luxury items and raw materials. Iron, for example, was brought into the Olmec territories, where the artists transformed it into the much sought after iron-ore mirrors used extensively throughout Mesoamerica. In time these mirrors became a major Olmec export. Obsidian was also imported, used for blades, flakes and dart points.

The Olmec had definite artistic sequences, during which time the listed ceramic style was prevalent.

Ojochi (1500–1350 B.C.)

Soft gray ware

Orange paste ware

Bajio (1350–1250 B.C.)

Large and hollow figures

Small and hollow figures

Solid heads

San Lorenzo (1150–900 B.C.)

Solid heads

Hollow heads

Solid dwarf forms

Ball players without headdress

Ball players with headdress

One-eyed gods

Obese forms

Animal effigies

Nacaste (900–700 B.C.)

Helmeted figures

"Punch-eyed" figures

Animal effigies

Torsos

Palangana (600–400 B.C.)

Heads

Villa Alta (A.D. 900–1100)

Animal effigies

Bird effigies

Hollow heads

OLMECA-XICALLANCA   A people not associated with the original Olmec of the Formative Period (2000 B.C.–c. A.D. 250/290) but given that name because of their Classic Period (c. A.D. 1/250–900) origins in the former territories of the Olmec in the southern gulf coastal regions. The Olmeca-Xicallancas were important traders and subdued some groups for a time, especially on the Puebla-Tlaxcala Plateau, the region of Cholula and Cacaxtla. They had definite ties to the Maya as well. Around A.D. 800, the Olmeca-Xicallanca reached the Valley of Puebla and became associated with the people of Cholollan. The group was reportedly ruled by two elders, one having charge of secular affairs and the other a priest-king. Other groups joined them, taking the name Chololtec. The citizens of Cholollan enlisted Chichimec warriors to stand off attacks by Xochimilco and other city-states. In time, the Chichimec absorbed them.

The Olmeca-Xicallanca built the city of Cacaxtla on a hillside in the Valley of Puebla, in the Tlaxcala region northeast of Cholula. Extraordinary murals have been found in a palace complex there, with patios and plazas, dated to the eighth or ninth centuries A.D. The architectural style of the city is similar to that of Xochicalco and Tula, but the paintings are Maya in style. Unfired clay was used in making Cacaxtla ceramics.

OLMEC CALENDAR   The method for the computation of time used by the Olmec culture that was initiated during the second phase of development (1200–c. 600/400 B.C.). This system required a basic knowledge of mathematics as well as a number system and the concept of zero. The stela discovered at Tres Zapotes which depicts the Long Count indicates that Olmec calendar skills were more advanced than had previously been supposed. In the past the Maya were credited with introducing the Long Count.

The Long Count is a specific method of keeping time. Throughout Mesoamerica the various cultures used two cyclical calendars: a 260-day calendar and a 365-day solar calendar. A day in one calendar would not coincide with a day in the other for 52 solar years. Knowing this, Mesoamericans could place any date within the cycle. The period of 52 years was called the Calendar Round.

The Olmec and their successors developed a lineal method of recording dates, a system that counted days from a definite starting point. The date chosen (as determined by archaeological research) was 13 August, 3114 or 3113 B.C. (correlated to the Gregorian calendar). Using this as a starting point, the Olmec and the Maya used cycles for computa-

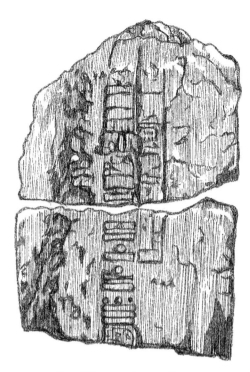

Tres Zapotes Long Count

tion. The longest period in this vigesimal (based on 20), system was 144,000 days, followed by 72,000, 360, 20 and then one. Such computations were expressed by bar-dot numerations, with the bars representing five and the dot one. An even earlier example of Olmec use of the Long Count than at Tres Zapotes was found in Chiapas.

OLMEC CERAMICS   The pottery wares evolving early in Olmec territories, used originally as utensils and then as trade items. The production of these wares was influenced by the techniques and skills of other regions, as trade allowed for a vast exchange among artisans. Some Olmec designs were unique to the individual regions, but many followed the traditional patterns. The ceramic industry of the Olmec region has been grouped into specific phases, called archaeological sequences and used to specify art items as well. The Olmec ceramic phases are (designs listed in decreasing order of numbers made):

Ojochi: 1500–1350 B.C.

Comano Coarse	Nanche Coarse
Moral Bluff	Cream
Chaya Punctuate	Achiotal Gray
Matalan Black and White	Amuchile Flesh
Chilpate Red on Cream	Cervelo Red-rimmed
Centavito Red	

Bajio: 1350–1250 B.C.

Camano Coarse	Hernandez Punctuate
Chaya Punctuate	Embarcadero Zoned
Nacahuita Red	Rosas Burnished
Rompido Black and White	Centavito Red
Aquatepec Thick	Achiotal Gray
Limon Carved-incised	Calzadas Carved

Tatagapa Red	Perdida Black and White
Tular Black and White	Majonera Black
La Mina Black	El Tigre Black
Ixtepec White	Xochiltepec White

Chicharras: 1250–1150 B.C.

Camano Coarse	Xochiltepec White
Ixtepec White	El Tigre White
La Mina White	Tatagapa Red
Achiotal Gray	Aguatepec Thick
Perdida Black and White	Tular Black and White
Majonera Black	

San Lorenzo: 1150–900 B.C.

Camano Coarse	Tatagapa Red
Yagua Orange	Macaya Scored
Calzados Carved	Limon Carved-incised
Xochiltepec White	La Mina White
El Tigre White	Ixtepec White
Conejo Orange (on white)	Perdida Black and White
Tular Black and White	Aguatepec Thick
Majonera Black	

Nacaste: 900–700 B.C.

Camano Coarse	Yagua Orange
Macaya Scored	Tacamichapa Hard
Tular Black and White	Majonera Black
Isletas Black	Remolino White
Camalate Black	

Palangana: 600–400 B.C.

Macayan Tan (to Black)	White-rimmed Black

Remplas: c. 300–100 B.C.

Tenochtitlan Red	Ixpuchuapa Incised
Cruz Incised	Chaparrito Red-on-Buff
Bernal Coarse	Dominquez White-rimmed Black

Villa Alta: A.D. 900–1100

Ceibal Coarse	Zapote Orange (to Gray)
Campameato Fine Orange	Tahil Plumbate
Jabi Black	Yual Fine Cream
Solerilla Red-on-Coarse	

(See MESOAMERICAN CERAMICS for a discussion of the evolution of these wares.)

OLMEC CEREMONIAL COMPLEXES   The sites reserved for religious or cultic ceremonies within the Olmec realm, where the construction and maintenance of pyramidal mounds, temples and monuments were carried out according to the practice demanded by local cults and styles. Such complexes were composed of temples and residences, and as a result varied in size and in importance. Such sites may have had limited populations, including only the priestly castes and the laborers who maintained the buildings and grounds. The suburban districts of the ceremonial complexes contained administrative offices for the regional government. They also served as burial places for Olmec of rank, particularly members of the ruling families. The tombs of such rulers took on prestige over the years, and their presence often gave the Olmec complexes long-lived importance which survived even after the culture lost its dominance in the region. Some Olmec ceremonial complexes were Chalcatzinco, Laguna de los Cerros, La Venta, San Lorenzo, Tonala, and Tres Zapotes.

OLMEC COSMOLOGY The creative legends of Olmec culture that are expressed in their artistic endeavors, with two themes dominant: the jaguar and the earth serpent. While Olmec tradition may have included a pantheon of cosmological deities, the Olmec creation concepts seem to emphasize the two animals. The earth serpent was believed to have explicit powers directly related to earthquakes and volcanoes, two natural forces that could devastate the Olmec region. Its design was incorporated into art forms found at the ceremonial complex at La Venta. The carvings discovered at Chalcatzinco are another example of this religious viewpoint. The earth serpent appears again in the cave paintings of Oxtotitlan. This serpent represented both a destructive force and a benevolent one. It provided fertility to the earth, the natural result of volcanoes and rivers, and was a symbol of divine intervention in Olmec life.

The jaguar also assumed importance in the Olmec religion, as it did in other Mesoamerican cultures. It was related to the Olmec beginnings in some mystical fashion, perhaps as the sire of humans or of the were-jaguars. The cult of the were-jaguar and the belief in half men, half jaguars stalking the earth were powerful images for the Olmec, represented again and again in their artistic renderings. Combined, the serpent and the jaguar were cosmological symbols and themes for religious ceremonies of the people.

OLMEC DEATH RITUALS Ceremonies and styles of burial that evidence the culture's belief in the afterlife. The grave offerings and the positions of the sites and corpses indicate that the Olmec dealt with concepts of eternity early on in their evolution. The establishment of tombs in the ceremonial complexes, such as La Venta, added a mythological aspect to death for the Olmec people. The were-jaguar mythology and the presence of the eternal earth serpent also indicate that the Olmec believed in a spiritual level of existence.

The grave offerings included in Olmec tomb sites verify this. While the actual meaning or function of the carved figures and celts discovered in such sites has not been determined, they were clearly part of a mortuary ritual provided for the Olmec deceased, especially those of greater rank. In some instances the personal effects of the deceased were included in the grave offerings, indicating a belief in the afterlife. Burials were probably performed under the platforms of the individual residences in most communities. The sites were then abandoned. In some Olmec sites vast numbers of graves were grouped together, with varied grave offerings.

The Olmec had three distinct grave styles, denoting the social caste or importance of the individuals and evidencing changes over the years in the mode of burial. The most basic graves were simple unadorned pits, probably dug into the household platforms or nearby. These pits held the

Olmec jade celt

corpses of deceased commoners. Some grave offerings have been found in these graves. The second type of Olmec grave was a pit in which stones were part of the ritual. These stones were discovered beside the remains. Their purpose is unknown. The third type of grave was the crypt, obviously reserved for those of rank in the Olmec regions because of the labor and the resources necessary for such construction. These burials required a great amount of stone. Such stone crypts were constructed by lining a pit with upright slabs of small stones to create a boxlike form. The box was then capped with additional stones. A tomb at La Venta was fashioned in this manner, using basalt. The districts housing those of rank were usually the site of such crypts. The grave offerings in such tombs were large and often costly.

OLMEC ECONOMY AND TRADE The bases established to insure stability of the state and for the expansion of the Olmec domain. The Olmec, like other Mesoamerican cultures, based their original economy on agriculture, as their farming techniques and their irrigation system was a direct result of the rich farmlands available to them. In time, however, trade became an important economic asset, having began quite early in the Olmec history. Agriculture, hunting, fishing and gathering could not sustain the growing populations of the Olmec settlements. The Olmec turned to trade and to import-export enterprises that provided additional economic strength and a source of wealth that could sustain the rapidly expanding domain. The far-flung Olmec communities, such as Tlatilco, depended on trade for stabilization and for transmitting the Olmec vision to older, indigenous populations. The political structure of these Olmec communities, part of an empire or confederation, has not been established. They may just have been part of a mutual and specialized system of trade.

In the beginning, the Olmec imported only raw materials that could be transformed by manufacture into wares. Those of rank amassed luxury items from other cultures, but commoners used only the raw materials brought into the Olmec lands. Iron ore, for example, could be transformed into mirrors, much in demand. The great stones used in making the colossal heads were brought into the Olmec heartland from distant sites. Other imported materials included andesite, chromite, cinnabar, jade, schist, seeds, and serpentine.

The rivers of the Olmec domain were natural highways and trade routes, and overland routes were established in Puebla, in the Valley of Mexico and in Morelos. Major markets were established or refurbished along these routes in time, to support the proliferation of goods in and out of the Olmec territories. Such markets were also outposts and watchtowers. Chalcatzinco, for example, was garrisoned and positioned to command various routes. Built into a natural amphitheater, the center had a three-dimensional view of the surrounding territories, safeguarding the movement of trade caravans. Later cultures probably established actual trade centers in the region, but such designated sites are not well documented in the Olmec period. Most likely the trade goods were delivered to the elite complexes and distributed from there along preferred routes or assigned to the various manufacturing industries.

OLMEC LANGUAGE The tongue spoken by the Olmec culture, thought by some scholars to be associated with the Huaxtec-Maya family or as a non-Maya group that came into the Huaxtec-Maya region and divided them. The language spoken by the Olmec is unknown, but some researchers have designated their history and words as being Mixe-Zoque, another linguistic family of the region. Still another theory put forth is that the Olmec spoke a form of Zapotec. Near metropolises the Olmec did associate with the Zapotec, but also with other groups. More evidence about the spoken Olmec language is necessary to define it further.

OLMEC RELIGION Deities and the Olmec practices of worship remain obscure and are only partially understood by modern scholars. Specific themes are evident in the religious customs of the Olmec and there is a certain pantheon and a cosmological basis for Olmec rituals and observances, but the origins of their religions practices are unknown. The great ceremonial complexes of the Olmec indicate that religion was essential there. The presence of Olmec priests, successors to the original shamans, also indicates that a temple hierarchical system had evolved over the years. The religious rites went through the same evolu-

tionary processes. The fact that the priests probably belonged to a special caste, designated for service in the various ceremonial complexes established strategically throughout the territories to serve the needs of regional population, points to an established religious system.

While little is known about what gave impetus to such religious observances, the most repeated symbol in Olmec religious practices was the jaguar. This animal and the earth serpent assumed monumental importance in all of the Olmec iconographic art forms. The jaguar was probably totemic in origin, stemming from myths and legends concerning the beginnings of the Olmec people. It also constituted a direct link between human beings and the natural world, as did the earth serpent. In Mesoamerica it was common for a people to claim a nonhuman ancestor, because such a link provided them with a primordial basis for their existence. The Olmec used the harpy eagle and the shark in the same manner. The totemic aspect of the jaguar in Olmec art is documented by the Rio Chiquito statue depicting sexual intercourse between a jaguar and a woman. The woman gave birth to a mutant form of the jaguar, now called the were-jaguar, hence providing all of his or her descendants with the stealth, ferocity and courage of the feline. The Olmec have been referred to as the Jaguar People, the *Tenocelome*, although whether they used that name for themselves is unknown.

The earth serpent, incorporated into artistic renderings and into the actual construction of Olmec sites, was another religious symbol. This creature was not a totem but the exemplification of the raw natural forces latent in Mesoamerican geological formations. Later the serpent was associated with earthquakes and volcanoes, the two most devastating forces unleashed in Mesoamerica throughout its history. The earth serpent was associated with caves, and in this capacity could be rendered with elaborate artistry as the seat of the powerful or as the entrance to the mysterious world belowground. Mesoamericans incorporated serpents into their artistic efforts throughout their history, but the Olmec endowed these creatures with mythological and cosmic attributes by linking them with the earth and with the convulsions that rocked their part of the world. Other gods included in the Olmec pantheon are known by names given for them in later eras and in later cultures. What the Olmec called them is unknown, but they worshipped Tlaloc, the rain deity; Chalchiuhtlicue, the water goddess; Xipe Totec, the flayed god; Quetzalcoatl, the feathered serpent, and the fire god.

The ceremonies conducted in Olmec temples and pyramidal complexes are not documented, but the sacrifice of slaves or captives was probably part of these rites. The recovery of sacrificial knives and blades adds evidence to the practice of human sacrifice, but no religious texts have shed light on the temple rituals or on the tenets underlying them. Cannibalism was also practiced, with spiritual elements symbolized by the rituals. The priests' role is not known either.

Several aspects of Olmec history, however, do give additional information about the religious functions. The discovery of great mosaic pavements, called "Massive Offerings" has led to speculation about the role of the individual in the Olmec system. The "Massive Offerings" were elaborate serpentine constructions that formed the diamond pattern on the snake. These designs were composed of hundreds of pieces of stone, which were then filled in with colored clay. When the designs were completed, the offering was covered with clay and adobe and then completely reburied. Thus the design remained a hidden offering to honor an individual buried nearby or to give a secret but everlasting homage to a deity.

The damage to recovered pieces of art in various abandoned ceremonial complexes has led to the belief that the statues were defaced or smashed by reformers, who desired changes in the cultic observances or in the direction of Olmec religion. Were-jaguar pieces were particularly vandalized at some sites, perhaps by reformers or by outside invaders.

The small groups of figurines, surrounded by jade or serpentine celts, discovered in tombs are certainly of religious importance. The figures are in communion, one with another. Most have baby faces or were-jaguar features. The celts, or ceremonial axes, guarded and protected the assemblage, but there is no indication of whether these figures are meeting in an earthly domain or in a heavenly sphere. Their distinct religious purpose is still to be determined.

OLMEC STATE   The complex social and political order within Olmec civilization, an institution that has not been documented. The Olmec form of government remains a mystery, as there is no indication of military organizations or a capital city in the Olmec territories. The Olmec complexes are in what is called a dispersed pattern. Only La Venta, clearly a ceremonial complex, contains any evidence that lesser sites were associated with it, even briefly. Most figurines recovered from Olmec lands indicate that a few Olmec governed or administered the affairs of these complexes, as the figures are portrayed with garments, ornaments or masks that clearly mark them as important. They may have functioned as priests, and they no doubt had a hand in the sudden emergence of Olmec culture in the various regions. It is obvious, however, that the Olmec civilization did not go through formative stages; thus there had to have been trained personnel on hand to direct the leaders there who could quickly educate people, resulting in relatively sudden artistic and architectural mastery. How these sites became associated with the Olmec is the mystery. There is little indication that armies of Olmec marched across the lands enslaving other cultures. Certainly there was warfare on the outer perimeters of Olmec territories, but it was probably conducted in defense of trade routes: actions taken against competitive trade enterprises or interference with the flow of goods by some outside agency. These trade cum military efforts were no doubt under the aegis of warriors, but it is unknown how the Olmec culture, with or without a warrior caste, administered so many regions and peoples.

The hierarchical nature of the Olmec state leads to theories that the rulers were priest-kings who had a force of architects, administrators, artists and as well as traders, merchants and peddlers. The city districts of the Olmec were probably a number of complexes grouped together for a common cause. These complexes could, in turn, enlist other

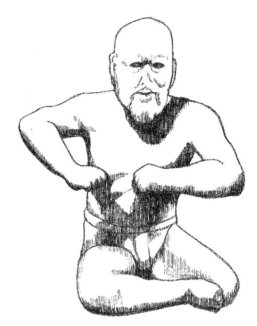
Olmec wrestler statue

groups having similar artistic goals and religious practices. Certainly few of the Olmec complexes were garrisoned or fortified, leading to the conclusion that they were built at a time of peace and calm, in a region where association between various groups was amicable and cooperative. The fact that such complexes were designed, built and thereafter maintained and administered is probably due to continued association and mutually shared interests, artistic visions and concerns.

Once a site was determined as vital to the Olmec political and social development, a nucleus of officials must have moved to inform the native populace by instructing them in the Olmec ways. The complexes that arose from the arrival of these influential people would have appeared suddenly and miraculously in the wilds. The more far-flung the sites, naturally, the less impressive the Olmec monuments, but there is no indication that the initial Olmec settlers and teachers met with any resistance. It would have been to the advantage of the local inhabitants to accept the benefits of aligning themselves with Olmec power.

At some sites Olmec style transformed everything to produce art entirely Olmec in design and manufacture. In other regions the Olmec influence was coupled with a sustained tradition of native style. Again there appears to have been no conflict in the development of the two concurrently. It is also likely that the trading caravans, coming by river or overland, met with curiosity only. The people in far-flung regions absorbed by the Olmec sphere through trade would have benefited from such contact. At the same time, the sight of a great contingent of distinguished and armed men would have discouraged any sudden or rash activity. Most cultures beyond the Olmec sphere would have heard rumors about their magnificent cities and the luxury in which they lived. The Zapotec, for example, benefited from Olmec cultural contacts, even as they maintained their own distinctive traditions.

The subject of an Olmec "empire" thus remains an enigma. There is little direct evidence of occupation by

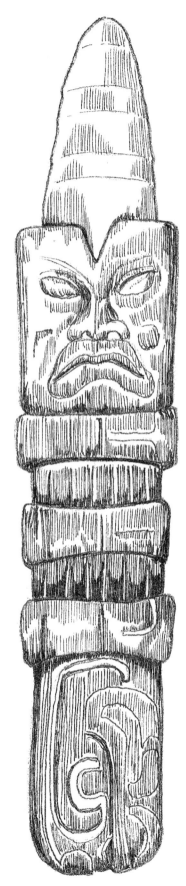

Olmec sacrificial knife

Olmec forces in any region, other than a flowering of art and architecture, as there is little direct evidence to confirm the presence of any garrisons or far-flung forts maintained by the Olmec other than their trade outposts. The role of the Olmec of rank is equally obscure, except for the fact that they drew their power and rank from agricultural riches and trade. These men of worth obviously congregated at certain sites and indulged in a way of life that was rare everywhere else in the Olmec region. They may have taken part in efforts to expose other groups to Olmec ways or else sponsored such expeditions. When those holding rank and power abandoned their metropolises, the Olmec complexes collapsed.

OLMEC TOOLS Implements necessary to agricultural and settlement activities, probably manufactured from raw materials. These following tools were made available for local use and for trade.

abrader saws	mortars
arrowshaft smoothers	needles, bone
awls	ovate stones
blades, obsidian	paint dishes
bowls	palettes, paint
engravers	pestles
knives	pestles, flat-iron
maize shellers	polishers, reamer
manos	polishing pebbles
mauls	scrapers
metates	smoothers
millstones	wedges

OLMEC WARFARE Military activities conducted in Olmec regions, undocumented because of the lack of evidence of warfare in Olmec art. There is little to suggest that the Olmec conducted wholesale military occupation of lands. Some of the sites associated with the Olmec bordered on those of other cultures, but there is no indication of hostilities or military adventures having occurred there. The types of military units employed by the Olmec thus remain unknown. Some artistic renderings suggest military efforts. Tres Zapotes has a battle scene incorporated in its designs, and a trophy head was recovered there. Captives are depicted in scenes at La Venta. It is known that the Olmec performed human sacrifices and practiced cannibalism, but how such victims were taken or chosen remains obscure. There are few records of warriors, and military associations are not depicted.

The Olmec civilization thus remains mysterious, with military expansion only guessed at. An artistic people, the Olmec appear to have been ready to transmit their knowledge, skills and traditions to all of the people in the region, thus enhancing the diverse segments of the local populace. Such a generosity and cooperative spirit are the marks of a complex culture, suggesting an intellectual and artistic superiority that served not only to encourage these traits in their region but provided later generations in Mesoamerica with foundations for emerging cultures.

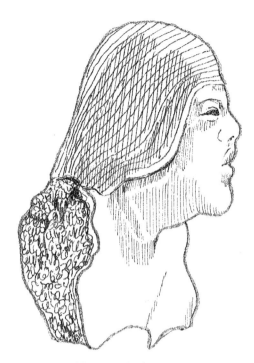

Olmec jade figurine

OMETECUHTLI A god worshipped in Tepoztlan, the patron of the liquor called *pulque.* (See also OMETEOTL.)

OMETEOTL The Aztec creator god, a deity of the sky, named the "navel of the world." The god was a combination of the male and female generative forces, associated with fire and maize and also called the Old Sorceror. As a female, the deity represented the earth and was addressed as Ometecuhtli or as Omecihuatl. The four sons of the god symbolized the earth's elements: earth, air, fire and water. Ometeotl headed an Aztec complex, a religious division honored in Tenochtitlan, and he presided over the highest heaven.

OMETEPEC A site in Guerrero near the border of Oaxaca, associated with the manufacturing of stelae and other monuments, used as accompanying pieces for pyramids and platforms. The site, noted for sculpture in the round, displays both Monte Alban and Teotihuacan influences.

ONE DEATH A Mixtec deity believed to have been a variation of the Aztec god Tonatiuh. The Tonatiuh cult was involved in solar sacrifices.

OPENO See EL OPENO.

OPOCHTLI An Aztec (Mexica) deity, the patron of fishing and aquatic hunting.

ORTICES PHASE A cultural development in the Formative Period (2000 B.C.–c. A.D. 250/290), associated with the culture of Colima and accompanied by other developmental periods. (See COLIMA for details.)

OTOLUM RIVER A natural waterway that served as the setting for the Maya ceremonial center of Palenque in the plain of Chiapas on the lower Usumacinta Valley.

OTOMI A group entering the Valley of Mexico in the Late Classic (A.D. 600–900) or Early Post-Classic (A.D. 900–c. 1200/1250) Period, following the Chichimec in the region. Called the Bird Hunters or the Bird Trappers by their contemporaries, the Otomi spoke an Oto-Manguean language. They attacked and burned Teotihuacan c. A.D. 650, and then settled in Xaltocan and in Cuauhtitlan c. A.D. 800. One branch joined the Toltec at Tula. Their ruler married a daughter of Xolotl, the Chichimec king. In time the Otomi went to Meztitlan, an independent city that eventually became a Tepanec vassal. The center of the Otomi population in the Early Post-Classic Period, however, was in Xaltocan, a city-state on the eastern shore of Lake Xaltocan. The Otomi were fierce warriors and tattooed their bodies and blackened their teeth, accompanying the Aztec on their military campaigns as expert bowmen. Some Otomi resided in Chiapas and in the Puebla highlands. The patron deity of the group was Otonticuhtli, a fire god who represented the souls of dead warriors.

OXKINTOK A Maya city called Three Day Flint, built on the scrub plains of western Yucatan, started c. 300 B.C. Oxkintok containing a glyph that dates to the Long Count, A.D. 475. This is the earliest example of the Long Count in the region. Just a short time before the glyph was made, the Maya undertook swift and increased efforts at expansion resulting in the construction of many such cities. The southern Maya moved steadily northward. The glyph, carved on a stone lintel, gives evidence of the Maya renaissance in this period. Oxkintok was a magnificent Maya city, and the site still contains pyramids and temples of architectural grace. The last dated monument here was around A.D. 849, and the city was abandoned around A.D. 1100.

OXOMOCO A grandmother diety of the Aztec, who lived with her consort, Cipactonal, in a sacred cave in Morelos. They were the oldest divine couple in the Aztec pantheon, and considered the grandparents of the god Quetzalcoatl.

OXTOTITLAN CAVE A site in Guerrero high on a hill, containing paintings from c. 900/700 B.C. The jaguar theme of the Olmec is evident here, and the artists who painted the murals were obviously familiar with the Olmec stone altars in the gulf coast ceremonial complexes. The interior paintings, in polychrome, were done in black and in red; they portray jaguars, baby faces and the earliest known representation of a speech scroll. The site is near the Juxtlahuaca Cave. Some scholars date Oxtotitlan to c. 1200–600/400 B.C., in the Olmec II phase era.

OXTOYAHUALCO Called the circle of caves, lying below the city of Teotihuacan. According to a tradition within the city, the sun and the moon emerged from these caves.

OWL A bird revered by the Maya as the messenger of Ah Puch, the god of death. The Maya also believed that the owl called the names of men and women about to die, summoning them to their graves. Owls were also portrayed in Teotihuacan murals, in association with military scenes.

OZOMATLI The monkey an Aztec day sign in their variation of the *tonalpohualli*, the calendar system.

OZTOPOLCO A group in the Valley of Mexico, believed to be the original inhabitants of the city of Tenayuca, west of modern Mexico City. In A.D. 1224, the Chichimec, led by their chief, XOLOTL (1), made Tenayuca their capital.

OZTUMA A Chontal Maya site caught in the Aztec onslaught led by Emperor AHUITZOTL (A.D. 1486–1502). The Chontal city of Alahuitzlan fell in this campaign, and Oztuma's population fled to other Maya strongholds to escape the Aztec wrath.

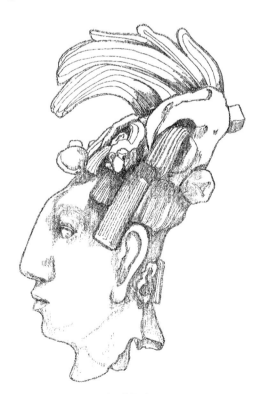

P

PACAL Called the Great, a ruler from A.D. 613/615 to 683 of the Maya city of Palenque, in the northeastern section of Chiapas. According to some records, he was the second ruler of that name in Palenque. His name means "shield." The Temple of the Inscriptions, his grave site, gives details of his reign. Among the temple's masterpieces of carving is Pascal's sarcophagus lid. His mother was Lady Zac-Kuk, a noblewoman of sufficient rank to be listed as a ruler in Maya accounts. His father was Kan-Bahlum-Mo, a nobleman who never ascended the throne. His sons, Chan-Bahlum II and Kan Xul II, followed him as rulers of Palenque. Pacal added to the prestige of Palenque, building temples and other buildings that reflect innovations in Maya architecture. Pacal was buried on his back, as if reclining. He wore a jade collar and jade cuffs, and a green headband was placed on his head to mark his status as a great ruler.

PACIFIC COAST Also called Soconusco, a region of Mexico that includes the Isthmus of Tehuantepec, the Chiapas highlands of Guatemala and the northern coasts. It is a

Pacal of Palenque

region composed of rocky inlets and bays. Human habitation there began as early as the Paleo-Indian Period (11,000–7000 B.C.). Agriculture, enhanced by the climate and the water resources, was developed by these early residents in the Incipient Agriculture and Formative Periods (7000–c. 2000/2500 B.C. and c. 2000/1600 B.C.–c. A.D. 250/290). Many sites arose there, continuing until the Post-Classic Period (A.D. 900–1521). Developmental phases are recorded in the region. (See MESOAMERICAN GEOGRAPHY for details; see also ALTAMIRA-BARRA CULTURE; CONCHAS PHASES I AND II; CUADROS; JOCATAL; OCOS PHASE.)

PACIFIC COASTAL LOWLANDS A narrow strip of verdant lands occupied in the early eras, containing the Altar Desert and many rivers. (See MESOAMERICAN GEOGRAPHY.)

PALANGANA PHASE A cultural development in San Lorenzo, an Olmec site on the Rio Chiquito in Veracruz. This phase dates to around 600 to 400 B.C. The ceramics associated with the Palangana Phase include Macayan tan to black wares and white-rimmed black pieces. (See also SAN LORENZO for details.)

PALENQUE A celebrated, elaborate Maya ceremonial complex located at the foot of a chain of forested hills in the northeastern portion of Chiapas, overlooking the Usumacinta plain. Rain forest surrounds the city, and a stream flows through it. Palenque was prominent in the Late Classic Period, abandoned c. A.D. 800–830. The name, given to it by the Spanish, translates as "palisade." The city was the Maya frontier, and it was thus constantly open to Mexica influence.

The Maya sculptural genius reached its height in this vast metropolis. The monuments of Palenque, called the loveliest of the Maya sites by some scholars, included religious structures, residences and mortuary buildings. These were constructed of calcareous stone, skillfully decorated with stucco.

The Palace of Palenque dominates much of the central portion, rising on a platform some 300 feet long, is 30 feet high and approximately 240 feet wide. The monument is actually a group of buildings gathered around four courtyards; the eastern, western and central courts, and the Court of the Temple. The north side of the platform is a pyramid having three tiers and a central stairway that measures almost 100 feet across, flanked by stucco heads and other decorations.

211

Pacal

its present 50 feet, the tower had three stories and skylights. In the center was a newel and a corridor.

The palace itself has T-shaped windows, vaulted roofs, niches, courtyards, galleries and sculptured panels. Its pillars were stuccoed and covered with reliefs, stucco masks and elaborate figures. Scenes and hieroglyphs were incorporated into the walls. The palace was built with a vaulted aqueduct that leads to a large eastern platform.

This eastern platform supported three temples, one in honor of the sun, another called the Temple of the Cross and a third, the Temple of the Foliated Cross. These shrines, and the Temple of Inscriptions, were constructed in the reign of the city's most illustrious ruler, Pacal (Shield), who ascended the throne in A.D. 615, supposedly at the age of 12. He ruled until his death in A.D. 683. His son and successor was Chan-Bahlum II (Serpent Jaguar), who began his reign in 684.

The Temple of the Inscription was built over Pacal's crypt, an elaborate tomb built 75 feet below the level of the temple. The 30- by 13-foot crypt was constructed with stone beams and a 23-foot-high vault. The walls are adorned with nine figures, probably the Maya Lords of the Underworld. The coffin within the tomb was covered with a stone slab, some 12 and a half feet long and seven feet wide. The slab, 10 inches thick, weighed five tons.

Pacal's remains, discovered within the coffin, were covered in jade, and the body was provided with a mosaic jade mask and a statue of the sun god. Jade stones were placed in the corpse's hands and mouth cavity.

The Temple of the Lion, also called the Temple of the Beautiful Reliefs, contains stucco reliefs on one wall, depicting a priest with a jaguar head.

A small but refined structure, the Temple of the Sun was built in five tiers on a platform measuring 75 feet on each side. The structure has two vaulted chambers and carved panels. These chambers are approximately 10 feet wide, with walls over three feet thick, with three openings on the facade. The rear chamber has a sanctuary set apart with a special vault. The Panel of the Sun, located on the wall opposite this vault, is a stone panel depicting an altar surmounted by a mask of the sun, surrounded by attendant priests and framed by columns of hieroglyphs. The structure was designed to honor the accession of Chan-Bahlum to the throne.

The Temple of the Cross was built in a similar fashion, with the tallest pyramidal base in Palenque. It contains a bas relief that was discovered in fragments. The Temple of the Foliated Cross is similar architecturally and contains a panel. The central motif is the cruciform, which was a Maya symbol of life and the earth. The quetzal bird, sacred to the Maya, surmounts this cross, with attendant priests and lateral hieroglyphic panels.

Pacal imbued Palenque with prestige and power throughout his lengthy reign. His son Chan-Bahlum II dedicated the Temple of the Inscriptions to his father. Other notable rulers were Chac Zutz, who began his rule in A.D. 722 and is commemorated on the Tablet of the Slaves, and Chaacal III, who ruled c. A.D. 721 and erected two temples. Kan Xul II, another son of Pacal, ascended the throne as Chan-Bahlum's successor.

The eastern courtyard is surrounded by four buildings. Vaulted chambers, walls with stucco bas reliefs, hieroglyphic panels and decorated stairways compose this complex. The western court opens onto a large structure having pillars and doorways and bas reliefs depicting a procession of nobles in elaborate dress. The central courtyard is connected to the Courtyard of the Tower by an elaborate structure with a relief of an owl engraved into its walls.

The Courtyard of the Tower was probably a Maya astronomical observatory. A glyph of the planet Venus was painted on one wall of the structure. The tower, to the north of the courtyard, stands on a platform that measures 13 feet high. Nine seated figures decorate the walls, and there is an altar on the south side. A stone in the tower bears the date (in glyphs) of A.D. 783. Once considerably larger than

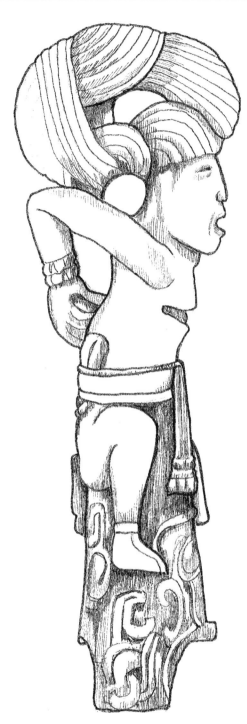

Palma of Veracruz

PALMA An elongated sculpted amulet, associated with Mesoamerican ball games. Carved at times as turkeys or other birds, and often with scenes or glyphs, the *palma* was worn on the players' belts. One such *palma* was found in the Totonac region, designed to depict a human skull, half alive and half dead. Considered a masterpiece, this *palma* reflects the Mesoamerican view of the transitory nature of human existence.

PALMILLAS PHASE A cultural development in the region of the Sierra de Tamaulipas and part of the Tamaulipas Sequence. Dating from 500 B.C. to A.D. 500, this phase gives evidence of agricultural expansion in the region and the emergence of stable settlements. (See TAMAULIPAS SEQUENCE.)

PALO BLANCO PHASE A cultural development associated with the Tehuacan Sequence and dating from 200 B.C. to A.D. 700. Agricultural innovations are the hallmarks of this period, and irrigation systems are evident. New products used by the people of the Palo Blanco Phase include tomatoes, peanuts, guavas and turkeys. Ceremonial complexes were thriving, with rudimentary pyramidal platforms fashioned out of stone, and plazas, ball courts and possibly the presence of priest-kings. Ceramics of the Palo Blanco Phase include the gray and the orange varieties. (See MESOAMERICAN CERAMICS AND CULTURAL DEVELOPMENTS.)

PANUCO RIVER A waterway in the gulf coastal lowlands of Mesoamerica.

PANUSCO An area settled by the Huaxtec soon after their arrival in northern Veracruz and in southern Tamaulipas, perhaps as early as 1500 B.C. Called the Place of the Crossing, Panusco received only some of the Huaxtec population entering the region. Others moved into the Tuxpan Basin.

PAPALOAPAN RIVER A waterway in the southern Mexican highland region, which joined the San Juan River to form a basin near Tehuacan. It is believed that the gold mines worked during the Aztec period in the Post-Classic Period (A.D. 900–1521) were near it. (See PAPALOAPAN-SAN JUAN BASIN.)

PAPALOAPAN-SAN JUAN BASIN A region some 100 miles north of La Venta. The city of Tres Zapotes was built here, on the banks of the Hueyapan River. The basin is near the plain of Tehuacan.

PAPER A material used for books and during rituals by the various Mesoamerican cultures in several historical periods. Priests and nobles punctured the soft tissue on their bodies and splattered their blood on papers that were then offered to the gods. Records and administrative accounts were also written on paper. Paper was made from the bark of the local fig trees (*Ficus cotinifolia* and *Ficus padifolia*). Stone beaters were used to prepare the bark. In some rituals, robes were made out of paper. This material was used in the Olmec city of San Lorenzo in the Early Formative Period (2000/1600–900 B.C.)

PAQUIME A site also called Casas Grandes, located near Nuevo Casas Grandes near the border town of Juarez. This was a frontier settlement, part of the trade system with North American Pueblo groups. A pyramid, a ceremonial center and over 130 structures have been uncovered in Paquime. Burial sites under former residences have yielded turquoise mosaics, copper bells, shells, pottery and other funerary offerings. The ceramic wares are black on white, with some geometric designs. (See TURQUOISE ROAD.)

PASION RIVER A waterway in the southern lowlands, a Maya territory, and the site of the Maya complex of Altar de Sacrificios. The Peten (Putun) Maya controlled this region by the Late Classic Period (A.D. 600–900). The Pasion joined the Usumacinta in Belize.

PATLACHIQUE PHASE A cultural development in Teotihuacan that endured from c. 100 B.C. to A.D. 1. Two settlements are evident in this phase. Ceremonial buildings, built in clusters, provided a setting for the religious ceremonies serving a population of about 5,000.

PATOLLI An Aztec game described in the *Codex Magliabecchiano*. Protected by the god Machulxochitl, *Patolli* was played on mats with cross-shape designs, marked off into 52 separate zones, equal to the sacred calendar cycles. Beans were thrown as dice might be. Colored stones were advanced according to count of the throw. The winner was the first player to return to the original square.

PATZCUARO (1) A Tarascan site on Lake Zirahuen, founded c. A.D. 1325 and serving for a time as the capital of that culture. No public monuments have survived on the site, but the ruins of King SICUIRANCHA's palace are still evident.

PATZCUARO (2) A division of the Tarascan empire under King Curatame, son of Tariacuari, the Tarascan national hero. Patzcuaro was called the Smoky Place. The other divisions were Ihuatzio and Tzintzuntzan.

PATZCUARO LAKE A water resource in Michoacan, associated with the Tarascan. Ihuatzio, a Tarascan capital, was built on the southeastern arm of the lake, near the island of Janitzio. The city of Tzintzuntzan, another capital, was erected on the rise of hill overlooking the northeastern arm of Lake Patzcuaro.

PAVACUME A Tarascan chief, probably from the Sierra region of Michoacan. He is recorded as marrying a lake-dwelling woman who bore him the great Tarascan national hero, TARIACUARI.

PEDREGAL An area of lava, broken, sooty and black, with sparse plants growing in crevices and cracks. The *pedregal*, a remnant of volcanic eruptions, is particularly striking just south of modern Mexico City, the original site of Cuicuilco.

PENITAS A site in the Nayarit region, a coastal culture dating to c. 2000 B.C. Penitas and other sites shows evidence of advances from crude petroglyphs to the accomplished figurines that are prized for their vibrance and energy. (See NAYARIT for details.)

PEOPLE OF THE SIERRAS The name given to the Tarascan by their contemporaries and by Spanish chroniclers.

PEREGRINATION PAINTINGS A form of narrative art, made by the Post-Classic Period (A.D. 900–1521) cultures, particularly the Aztec, depicting maps and accounts of mythical or actual journeys. They were found in temples and in manuscripts, particularly in Aztec codices. The *Codex Boturni* is called the *Tira de la Peregrination*.

PERIQUILLO PHASE A cultural development on the coast of Western Mexico, the Colima region. During the Formative Period (c. 2000/1600 B.C.–c. A.D. 250/290), this phase was associated with the hollow figures and effigies of Colima and with the Atlantean figures.

PETATES Twilled mats woven from yucca and agave from 6500 B.C. to 2000 B.C. in Tamaulipas and in "Desert Culture" regions.

PETEN (Putun) A region of Guatemala, home to the Classic Maya flowering. With neighboring regions, it is an extension of the Chiapas highlands. The Peten is also part of the Sierra de Ticul, stretching southward from the Yucatan Peninsula. A region of high temperatures and tropical rain forests, the Peten is well drained and provides a rich variety of wood and vegetation. The soil is scant, but the region is rich in natural resources, including limestone, obsidian and gold. The tropical forests and swamps also provide birds, peccaries, jaguars, ocelots, butterflies, copal, vanilla and rubber. The region was also a source of cacao in the Maya eras. Painted pottery and objects of prized wood, such as mahogany, ceiba and cedar, were trade items of the Peten merchants. The Classic Maya were at home in this rather forbidding place. Peten economic ties extended south and east, and ceremonial complexes arose there, especially around Lake Peten-Itza. (See MAYA; see also MAYA GROUPS; MAYA TRADE.)

PETEN-ITZA, LAKE See PETEN.

PEZELOA (Pezelao) A Zapotec priest credited by some sources as having founded the city of MITLA. This city benefited from royal patronage as a tomb site for kings. Many priests were prominent in Mitla's history.

PICO DE ORIZABA (Citlatepetl) A volcanic peak in the Transverse Volcanic Axis of the Mesa Central in Mexico. (See VOLCANOES.)

PIEDRAS NEGRAS A Maya ceremonial complex built on a rise on the northern bank of the Usumactina River in northwestern Guatemala, in the traditional Maya Lowlands. The city was dominant in the Classic Period, from A.D. 534 to 810. It is noted for its masonry pillars, especially in the palace structure. The artisans of Piedras Negras used wooden beams to support mortar roofs, with limestone 12 inches thick in some places. The city had temples, eight sweat baths (complete with stone hearths and drains) and residential structures, especially for the castes of rank. The stelae recovered from Piedras Negras were damaged by Mexica forces migrating into the region. The depiction of Tlaloc, the Mexica rain god, visible in some structures of the site suggests an early contact between the Mexica and the local Maya. Piedras Negras was deliberately abandoned with ritual desecration of the sacred portions of the complex, by the departing inhabitants. One wall panel, which originally depicted 15 separate individuals, of a ruler with his council, was deliberately vandalized. The head of each figure was hacked off. Six rulers led Piedras Negras for 174 years.

PILLI (1)   Aztec (Mexica) noblemen, called "the precious feathers from the wings of past kings." Such nobles served as imperial administrators, controlling land use and labor forces.

PILLI (2)   A style of figurines found in the Nevada Phase sites in the Valley of Mexico, 1400 to 1250 B.C.

PINTADERA   An Aztec sculpted device, so named by the Spanish. Actually a seal used to stamp designs on the human body. The Aztec employed stamped images for religious, festive and military purposes.

PIPIL   A people called *Tlamaquinime* by their contemporaries, a Nahual group associated with Teotihuacan. Their migratory routes, along the Pacific coast of Mesoamerica, coincide with the distribution of Teotihuacan tools, such as the yoke and the adze. The Pipil moved into Veracruz and Tabasco, along the coast, going then to Oaxaca and Guatemala. Some scholars suggest that the Pipil were actually Teotihuacan merchants. They were in Mesoamerica by A.D. 400, taking over markets in the cotton and cacao regions and linking them to Teotihuacan at the height of that city's power. The Pipil were more than traders in the regions of El Tajin and in Tabasco and Campeche. There they established an independent cultural development. When Teotihuacan fell in A.D. 650, the Pipil settled in Tabasco and Campeche but they are known to have entered Maya regions in the Toltec era. They used an art form called Cotzumalhuapa and spoke an archaic form of Nahuatl. There are Modern Pipil communities on the Pacific coast of Mexico and in the Motqua Valley of Guatemala.

From A.D. 700 to 900, the Pipil undertook another migration, going to Cholula, Xochicalco and Azcapotzalco. Some Pipil remained in El Tajin or joined the Maya on the gulf coast. The "Tajin-Teotihuacan" Pipil are thought to have been warlike and a factor in the destabilization of the Maya southern realm. The Pipil are also associated with the Toltec, living in El Salvador and Nicaragua. In A.D. 800, Pipil fled from the OLMECA-XICALLANCA. This culture also migrated from A.D. 1000 to 1200, joining the Toltec-Chichimeca groups. There are records of Pipil habitation in Cotzumalhuapa on the Pacific plain of Guatemala. (See NONOALCO.)

PITAO COZOBI   A Zapotec bat god, displayed in Monte Alban. The deity was the patron of maize and protected harvests and agricultural abundance.

PITAO HUICAANA   A Zapotec creator goddess, associated with the spirit of *Xee*. She represented as well the Zapotec cult of ancestor worship.

PITAO PEEZE   A Zapotec deity, the patron of traders and merchants. The god protected the vast Zapotec trade enterprises.

PITAO PEZELAO   A Zapotec deity of death, associated with the underworld, aiding Coqui Xee.

PITAO XICALA   A Zapotec deity, the patron of love, dreams and beauty.

PITAO XOO   The Zapotec deity of earthquakes, a part of the *Xee* that provides life to all things.

PITAO ZIJ   A Zapotec deity, the patron of the miserable and the lowly. Pitao Zij protected slaves, tenant farmers and prisoners of war.

PIT HOUSES   Abodes used during the Incipient Agriculture and Formative Periods (7000–c. 2000/2500 B.C.; c. 2000/1600 B.C.–c. A.D. 250/290) in the developing regions of Mesoamerica, such as the Tehuacan Valley. Pit houses were used seasonally, built on river terraces or beside caves, where subterranean levels could be dug. In time the pit houses became year-round abodes, as farming provided more of the people's dietary needs in the various regions.

PLACE OF THE HERONS   Called Aztlan, the legendary homeland of the Aztec (Mexica). (See AZTLAN.)

PLACE OF THE HUMMINGBIRDS   See TZINTZUNTZAN.

PLUGS   Special pieces of adornment used by several cultures and inserted in the nose or in the ear to denote rank. The Aztec wore plugs for their coronation ceremonies. Toltec era records indicate that plugs were used by the lords of Tula, not only for their own royal ceremonies but to honor rulers of other nations as well, denoting Toltec patronage. The Huaxtec were noted for their beautiful plugs, which were traded throughout Mesoamerica. (See EIGHT DEER.)

PLUMBATE   A type of ceramic, so-called because of its hard surface and its metallic iridescence. Plumbate was found from the region of Nayarit to Lake Nicaragua in the south. It was manufactured in colors, ranging from blue-gray to orange or reddish brown, and generally was lustrous and attractive. Plumbate, associated with the Toltec, was designed also for use as as effigies, censers, figurines and animal forms.

POCHTECA   The Aztec (Mexica) name for traders and merchants who served the empire not only by distributing wares and conducting trade across vast routes that brought contact with other city-states and cultures, but as administrators of some trade districts. The *pochteca* also served as intelligence agents in some eras of Aztec development. (See AZTEC TRADE for details.)

POKOMAN MAYA (Pokom)   See MAYA GROUPS, POKOMAN.

POKOMCHI MAYA   See MAYA GROUPS, POKOMCHI.

POLOCHIC RIVER   A Guatemalan highland waterway, flowing from the interior peaks to the Gulf of Honduras.

POPOCATEPETL A major volcanic peak in the Transverse Volcanic Axis of the Mesa Central of Mexico. The name translates as "Smoking Mountain." (See VOLCANOES.)

POPOLOCA An obscure cultural group associated in some accounts with the building of the city of TEOTIHUACAN. The Popoloca are also linked to the Olmec in the belief in *chaneque,* the ancient dwarves the Olmec depicted in their figurines. The Popoloca region was Puebla, where they were linguistically part of the Mixtec group, sharing artistic traditions as well.

POPOL VUH A Quiche Maya sacred document, actually a long epic poem, believed to have been written in the sixteenth century, also called *The Book of Counsel.* The religious, cosmological and spiritual traditions of the Maya are stressed in the work, as well as Maya achievement. The entire poem is set in a mythical landscape. The earliest extant copy of the *Popol Vuh* is in the Newberry Library in Chicago. Divided into three parts, the work records creation myths, the exploits of the Hero Twins and the Quiche Maya dynasties. (See MAYA LITERATURE.)

PORTRERO NUEVO A satellite site of the center of San Lorenzo, also associated with Tenochtitlan del Rio, on the banks of the Rio Chiquito. Originally built on a rise, the site contains two stone monuments, Olmec in design. One depicts a human holding a snake, and the other has a carved serpent. An Atlantean-style altar, probably brought from San Lorenzo, was found near the site. Portrero-Nuevo is now occupied by modern structures.

POST LA VENTA PHASE A cultural development also called Olmec III and dated to c. 600/400 B.C. The Long Count is reported to have emerged in this phase, and the city of TRES ZAPOTES was begun. (See MESOAMERICAN CERAMICS, and cultural developments; OLMEC.)

PROVIDENCIA MAJADA PHASE A cultural development concurrent the Miraflores Phase, dating from 300 B.C. to A.D. 200, associated with Kaminaljuyu and Izapa. During this phase pyramidal platforms were in use and Usulatan wares were evident. (See MESOAMERICAN CERAMICS AND CULTURAL DEVELOPMENTS.)

PUEBLA A vast region, a city and a modern state in the Mesa Central of Mexico. The Tehuacan Sequence developed in Puebla until around 7,000 B.C. The region is protected on the east by the Sierra Madres and is semiarid, requiring vast irrigation systems for farming. Several phases, including the Ajuereado, El Riego, Coxcatlan and Purron, are evident in Puebla. Pit houses were built there during the Abejas Phase, c. 3400 to 2300 B.C. In the Formative Period (c. 2000/1600 B.C.–c. A.D. 250/290), wares found in Las Bocas in Puebla reflected Olmec influence. The great city of Teotihuacan dominated the region. Cholula emerged, with its pyramidal structures dedicated to the god Quetzalcoatl. Cholula was taken in time by the OLMECA-XICALLANCA and then by the TOLTEC in A.D. 1292. The Tlaxcala cultural developments are also important in Puebla, and the site of Cacaxtla reflects Maya influences. Cacaxtla paintings are similar to those found in Seibal. A fragment of a mastodon pelvic bone, incised with images of camelids, tapirs and other animals, was discovered in Puebla in 1959. In the Post-Classic Period (A.D. 900–1521), Puebla was incorporated into the Mixtec domain. The Toltec also influenced regional development, and the Aztec Empire invaded the valley on many occasions. (See MESOAMERICAN GEOGRAPHY.)

PUERTO MARQUEZ A site in the Guerrero region of Mexico, near modern Acapulco, dating to the Formative Period (c. 2000/1600 B.C.–c. A.D. 250/290) or perhaps earlier. Shell middens found on this site give evidence of early habitation on the Pacific coast. Olmec ceramics and type of Formative Period ware were recovered here.

PUERTOSUELO A site in the Valley of Mexico, dated from A.D. 750 to 950. This was a ceremonial complex, probably independent, with a large population, estimated by some scholars at approximately 12,000.

PULQUE The intoxicating liquor made from the maguey plant and used in religious ceremonies and in festivities throughout Mesoamerica. Legends and myths concerning the deities in various cultures recount the use of *pulque.* Ce Acatl Topiltzin, called KULKULCAN (1) (Quetzalcoatl), was banished from the Toltec city of Tula because of *pulque.* The Huaxtec were forced to move to remote regions when their chief was discovered to have imbibed too much *pulque* and to have exposed himself.

PURRON PHASE A cultural development of the Tehuacan Sequence in the Puebla region, dating from 2300 to 1500 B.C. Some plant domestication took place during this phase, and maize cobs were recovered from sites associated with it. Gravel-tempered ceramics also emerged, similar to Abejas Phase wares. The Purron Phase is also evident in the Maya realms, where the people produced fired clay vessels and *tecomates,* neckless jars, as well as flat-bottomed wares.

PUTUN See PETEN.

PUUC (1) The Maya word for hill, especially in the regions of Campeche and Quintana Roo. The Puuc region in the Yucatan has a range of low hills. They form an inverted V across the Yucatan and Campeche. The Maya centers of Uxmal, Kabah and Sayil are in the Puuc area.

PUUC (2) A Maya art style developed in ceremonial complexes such as Labna, Chacmultun and UXMAL, dating to the Late Classic Period (c. A.D. 1200/1250–1521). The Puuc style use facades of thin squares of limestone placed over cement-rubble cores, boat-shape vaults, decorated cornices, rounded doorway columns, stone mosaics, latticework, balustrades, and cylindrical smooth walls with ornate friezes at the top, having broad moldings. These were modeled after the rope bindings used in earlier communities to secure the wooden structures of straw-thatched huts. In the Puuc region there was little surface water. The Maya called this area *zahcab,* the white earth, because it was rich in limestone. Limestone was used in the Puuc style and in the ceremonial complex of Mayapan.

PYRAMIDS See MESOAMERICAN ARCHITECTURE.

QUAUHTOCHCO A Totonac site in the Sierra de Puebla region where ruins were uncovered that show signs of Totonac and Toltec influence. A four-tiered pyramidal platform served as a temple base. Nail-shape stones were used on the summits, probably to represent the stars, an Aztec artistic innovation.

QUETZAL A bird highly prized by the Mesoamericans, indigenous to the Maya highlands of Chiapas, Mexico, Guatemala and Honduras. The Quetzal's elaborate tail feathers were much sought after. The bird is recorded as having only two front toes and no claws. Its four long, iridescent blue-green tail feathers were fashioned into ornaments. The Quetzal feathers were a trade commodity for the Maya. Killing a Quetzal was a capital offense among the Maya. The bird was depicted in Teotihuacan's military murals. Quetzal feathers were made into a headdress sent by the Aztec emperor Motecuhzoma II to Cortez, who had it delivered to Emperor Charles V of Spain. It was then given to Archduke Ferdinand of Tyrol and is now in a Vienna museum.

The Quetzal, shy and elusive, is protected in Guatemala today. The Quetzal Reserve in the Baja and Alta Verapaz areas has more than 2000 acres of cloud forests set aside as a sanctuary.

QUETZALCOATL The Feathered Serpent, the universal deity in Mesoamerica, having a major role in the cosmological traditions and religious ceremonies of the various cultures. The great pyramid of Cholula in Puebla, dating to the Middle Formative Period (900 B.C.–c. A.D. 250–290), honored this deity in his form as Ehecatl, the god of the wind. Quetzalcoatl also was honored as Ehecatl at Calixtlahuaca. The butterfly and other Quetzal symbols were popular. In Teotihuacan the god had a vast temple complex. Considered the creator and civilizer, Quetzalcoatl was shown as a feathered serpent, as Ehecatl or as an old man, painted black with a beard and robe. The abode of Quetzalcoatl was in the west.

This deity transformed himself into an ant in order to enter a sacred mountain to bring maize back to humans. He was also associated with the arts and with advances achieved by the various Mesoamerican cultures. Some groups honored Quetzalcoatl as the Morning Star. As Venus, the Evening Star, the god was depicted in a Tamuin statue fashioned by the Huaxtec. In this statue Quetzalcoatl was portrayed carrying his son on his back. Some groups considered him one of the offspring of the goddess Coat-

licue. The Maya called him Nine-Wind, a calendrical name.

Associated with astrology, astronomy, the arts and divination, Quetzalcoatl was also a patron of agriculture in some groups. In the Maya and Toltec traditions, Quetzalcoatl was provided with a human history as well. According to accounts in these cultures, the deity was a Toltec prince called Ce Acatl Topiltzin (One Reed, Our Prince), the son of the illustrious MIXCOATL. Reportedly born in Tepoztlan, Ce Acatl Topiltzin was educated at a shrine of the god Quetzalcoatl. In A.D. 935 or 947, Mixcoatl was murdered by a relative, probably a brother called Ihuitimal. Quetzalcoatl, exiled when Ihuitimal usurped the throne, grew up and slew the uncle, then proclaimed himself king. He proclaimed himself an incarnation of Quetzalcoatl and moved the Toltec capital to Tula in A.D. 968. The followers of the god Tezcatlipoca, a rival deity of the night sky, opposed Quetzalcoatl's supremacy and brought "the three demons of darkness" to confront him. He revolutionized Toltec society, banning human sacrifices, corruption and cruelty. The forces of the god Tezcatlipoca, however, did not end their opposition, and they succeeded in making Quetzalcoatl drunk one day, an act condemned by the Toltec. Therefore he was exiled from Tula in A.D. 999, leaving the Toltec at the mercy Tezcatlipoca's devotees.

Described in some accounts as being thin, fair in color, and having a black beard and long hair, Quetzalcoatl burned his palace, buried his treasure in the mountains and set out with a band of faithful followers to seek his destiny in exile. Before leaving Tula, however, he is reported to have turned the city's cacao plants into thorn bushes. Quetzalcoatl then went with his companions, including his favored dwarves, to "the Land of the Black and Red," toward the setting sun. Residing in Cholula for a time, Quetzalcoatl shared his magical arts with the local residents and endured many trials of faith. Deciding to end his mortal life, he placed himself on a fiery pyre and was cremated. When his body was reduced to ashes, he became Venus. According to the Maya tradition, however, Quetzalcoatl sailed to the Yucatan Peninsula, where he became Kukulcan, a popular form of the deity in that region. He is reported as arriving in the Yucatan in A.D. 987.

Quetzalcoatl, whose name is translated as bird (*quetzal*) snake (*coatl*), was called Tlahuizcalpantecuhtli in his role as Venus. Another Maya variation on the god's name combines the words *co* (serpent) and *atl* (the Nahuatl word for water). In all cultures, Quetzalcoatl was considered the bridge between humans and the divine, between humans and animals, and between humans and the stars. The god's symbols

Quetzalcoatl

were the butterfly, shells, the wind, the *atlatl* (the spear-thrower), jewels, feathers, a conical hat and hummingbirds. (See also TOLTEC RELIGION for details.)

QUETZALCOATZIN   The last recorded king of the city of Cholula in Puebla. Cholula, visited by Quetzalcoatl, was considered one of the holiest sites in Mesoamerica.

QUETZALPAPALOTL   The Palace of the Quetzal Butterfly, an important religious complex in the city of Teotihuacan, honoring the god Quetzalcoatl.

QUIAHUITL   The rain, an Aztec day sign in their version of the *tonalpohualli,* the calendar system.

QUIAHUITZLAN   A Totonac site in central Veracruz, dating to the Early Post-Classic Period (A.D. 900–c. 1200/1250). The site is renowned for its miniature temples, only four feet high but having columns, roofs and pyramidal platforms. These models have single doorways and may have been tomb sites originally. The city served as the meeting place for the Spanish and Aztec officials during the period of conquest (c. A.D. 1521).

QUICHE MAYA   At one time the most powerful of the Maya groups. The Quiche aristocracy filled all of the important posts in the political, military, and religious aspects of life in their region. They claimed descendance from the Toltec nobles and honored Toltec gods and the Toltec invested some of the Quiche lords with nose plugs, insignias of rank. There was an aristocratic kinship rank evident as well. The Quiche sometimes married noble women of the Cakchiquel, Tzutuhil, Mam and Itza. Sumptuous palaces were discovered in the Quiche area. (See MAYA GROUPS.)

QUIKAB   A Cakchiquel Maya king who led his people into a union with the Quiche Maya in the fifteenth century A.D. Soon after, however, Quikab was murdered in a Cakchiquel coup.

QUILAZTLI   A goddess honored in Xochimilco, called the Deer of Mixcatl, (Cihuacoatl) or Earth Mother.

QUINAMETZIN   Giants listed in the Toltec cosmological legends, recorded as populating the Second World or Sun. These giants failed tests imposed upon them by the god Tloque Nahuaque and were destroyed by earthquakes. (See TOLTEC COSMOLOGY for details about the suns.)

QUINATZIN   A Toltec-Chichimec ruler of Texcoco, who founded a new dynasty in that city. He imported laborers and artists and began construction of royal compounds and ceremonial complexes. During his reign the inhabitants of Texcoco accepted Nahual ways. As a result, Texcoco, became the "artistic capital of the Americas," called the Mesoamerican Athens. Quinatzin opened amicable relations with the Aztec and bequeathed not only his throne but his outlook to his heir, IXTLILXOCHTLI, when he died. (See IXTLILXOCHTLI and NEZAHUALCOYOTL for details about the Texcoco rulers.)

QUINTANA ROO   A region in the upper part of the Yucatan Peninsula. This flat, tropical plain broken by a series of hills, called *puuc* by the Maya, forms an inverted V on the landscape. The Maya used *cenotes,* the underground river systems that are exposed when their limestone crests collapse, extensively in Quintana Roo, where the soil is thin and rocky. Scrub palms, oak and palmettos thrive in the region. Many Maya centers were erected in Quintana Roo, including Chakalel.

QUIOTEPEC   A site in Oaxaca, set on a series of hills and dating from c. A.D. 100 to 900. The city, perhaps a vassal of MONTE ALBAN, had two large buildings around patios, with small side platforms. One plaza served as a ball court. Rectangular in style, with three stepped terraces, and having a staircase without balustrades, this monument was covered with thick plaster. A tomb uncovered in Quiotepec has a small stairway leading to an inner antechamber, decorated with cornices and panels. The one-room tomb is roofed with horizontal stone slabs. Two niches were carved into the walls, and the tomb has a door facade with cornices and panels.

QUIRIGUA   A Maya site on the Motagua River in modern Izabal, Guatemala, thirty miles from Copan. This site is on a fertile plain, once a rain forest. A prominent Maya trade center, specializing in obsidian and jade, Quirigua was dominated for a time by Copan and was ruled by the Sky dynasty as early as A.D. 724. Cauac Sky, who died in A.D. 784, transformed the city into a great ceremonial complex, erecting monolithic and zoomorphic monuments. He built at least seven such structures and laid out plazas. Five stelae there commemorate his memory. Because of his efforts, the city became dominant in the region, playing a well-defined role in politics and economics. In Quirigua three plazas were used as stages for ceremonial rituals, one containing the Great Turtle Altar. The major monumental groups incorporated three-dimensional sandstone stelae. One is believed to be the largest stone commemorative ever erected by the Maya, being approximately 35 feet tall and weighing 65 tons. Altars depicting sky deities were also incorporated into the architectural design of the site. A ceremonial temple containing zoomorphic carvings, mask panels and simple structures was uncovered here. There was a ruler on the throne of Quirigua as early as A.D. 455. Jade Sky is listed as ruling in A.D. 790.

QUIYAHUITZTECA   A group in the Valley of Mexico, part of the Chalco confederation called the Chalco-Amecameca.

RABINAL BASIN   A site located in the Sierra de Omoa in Guatemala, with the Cabulco and Salama basins, amid a fertile terrain. Jadeite is reported to have been mined in this region.

RAIN PARADISE   An eternal abode, the realm of Tlaloc, the rain deity of several Mesoamerican groups. This everlasting Eden is depicted in the city of Teotihuacan with jaguars, water spouts and a male human shown giving praise to the deity. (See TEOTIHUACAN; TLALOC.)

RAMOS PHASE   A ceramic development associated with the Mixtec city of Coixtlahuaca and dated from c. 200 B.C. to A.D. 500. The phase was evident also in the Nochixtlan Valley in Oaxaca. During the Ramos Phase, the Mixtec city of Yucuita, in the Nochixtlan Valley, was a thriving metropolis.

RELACION DE GENEOLOGIA   A document recording Toltec historical events, considered important because during his reign Aztec (Mexica) emperor Itzcoatl reportedly burned all other Toltec historical accounts.

RELACION DE MICHOACAN   One or more documents originating in the Tarascan language, translated by the Spanish. These histories records details of Tarascan life and the region of Michoacan, part of western Mexico.

REMOJADA   A site in the central region of Veracruz, on the Gulf of Mexico, dated from c. A.D. 1/250 to 900, in the Classic Period. Remojada represents as well one of the liveliest styles of pottery in Mesoamerica, and thousands of ceramics were discovered there, mostly hollow clay figurines having great natural vitality. These smiling forms were probably begun as an art form in the Late Formative Period (300 B.C.–c. A.D. 250/290), but developed fully in the Late Classic Period (A.D. 600–900). Definite Maya influences are visible, and the faces were fashioned from clay molds and decorated with black paint made from asphalt. The Remojada figures include males and females, standing or seated, as well as infants. All have smiling faces and some have filed teeth. Ball players, lovers and deities were depicted, with the gods Xipe Totec and Quetzalcoatl most often rendered.

The Remojada style was evident in the Veracruz lowlands also, where pottery, including deep bowls decorated with polychrome designs, was discovered in mounds. Depicted

as well were the *chiuateteo*, women who were deified after having died in childbirth. The best known of the Remojada figures are laughing boys and girls with upraised arms. These statuettes may represent the use of mushrooms or some other hallucinogenic drugs, with the smiling faces showing the drugs' effects. The Remojada culture was located near the city of Tajin, including the area around the Tecolutla River. Remojada figures were also found in Totonacapan on the gulf coast. (See EL TAJIN.)

REMOLINO   A site on the banks of the Rio Chiquito in the Olmec realm, one of the three cities discovered there, with Tenochtitlan del Rio and Portrero Nuevo. On the west bank of the river, Remolino was originally built near a whirlpool. Ceramic evidence links this site to San Lorenzo.

REMPLAS PHASE   A cultural development in the city of San Lorenzo, an Olmec site on the Rio Chiquito in southern Veracruz. This cultural development is dated to 100 B.C.

Remojada figure

MESOAMERICAN RIVERS

NAME	LOCATION	ROLE
Actopan	central Veracruz	site of Zempoala (Cempoala)
Amacuzac	Guerrero/Michoacan	forms modern state border
Amatzinac	eastern Morelos	site of Chalcatzinco
Arroyo-Yaxchilán	Chiapas	site of Yaxchilán
Atoyac	gulf coastal lowlands	drains northern Chiapas Valley
Balsas	Pacific coast/Tlaxcala/Puebla	vast water system
Belize	Belize	site of Maya centers
Blanco	gulf coast	site of Cerro de las Mesas
Bolanos	Zacatecas/Jalisco	part of Lerma river system
Cacique	Tuxtla Mountains	Olmec resource
Candelaria	gulf coastal lowlands	Chontal Maya resource
Chamelcon	Sula Plain	Maya trade route
Chiquito	Veracruz	site of San Lorenzo
Chixoy	Guatemalan highlands	flows to Campeche Gulf
Coatcalcoalcos	Gulf coastal lowlands	Olmec resource
Columbia	Belize	site of Lubaantúm
Copán	western Copán, Honduras	site of Copán
Coyolate	Guatemalan highlands	interior drainage system
Cuauhtla	Morelos/Guerrero	site of San Pablo Pantheon
Culiacan	Pacific coastal lowlands	flood and delta plains
Etla	Oaxaca Valley	served San José Mogoté
Fuerte	Pacific coastal lowlands	drains region
Grijalva	Chiapas/Guatemalan highlands	major regional waterway
Guayalejo	Sierra Madre Oriental	internal regional resource
Guayamas	northwestern Mexico	frontier regional resource
Hondo	Belize	frontier border marker
Hueyapan	Gulf coast	site of Tres Zapotes
Juchipala	Sierra Madre Oriental	part of Lemma river system
Lacanha	Guatemala	site of Bonampak
La Venta	Chiapas Valley	Grijalva tributary
Lerma	central Mexico	Chupicuaro regional resource
Limon	Tuxtla Mountains	Olmec resource
Maria Linda	Guatemala	drains interior
Mayo	Pacific coastal region	Delta, flood plains
Michatoya	Guatemala	flows to Pacific Ocean
Moctezuma	Sierra Madre Oriental	interior waterway
Moho	Belize	site of city of Pusilhá
Motagua	Chiapas	drains region
Nahualate	Guatemalan highlands	flows to Pacific Ocean
Naranjo	Guatemalan highlands	Maya resource
Nautla	Gulf coastal lowlands	major regional waterway
Negro	Guatemalan highlands	flows to Campeche Gulf
Nexapa	western Mexico	Balsas tributary
Nuevo (New)	Belize	site of Lamanai
Otolum	Chiapas	site of Palenque
Panuco	Gulf coastal lowlands	drains region
Papaloapan	southern Mexican highlands	region of gold mines
Pasión	southern lowlands	site of Altar de Sacrificios
Polochic	Guatemala	flows to Honduras Gulf
Rio Grande	northern Mexico	border between U.S./Mexico
Salado	Oaxaca	Zapotec domain
Salama	Guatemalan highlands	forms Salama Basin
Salinas	Guatemala	tributary of Pasión
San Juan	Nicaragua/Costa Rica	Maya trade route
San Juan	Valley of Mexico	site of Teotihuacan
San Pablo	Pacific coast	flood and delta plains
Santa Margarita	Guatemalan Pacific coast	Abaj Takalik site
Santiago	Pacific coast	drains region
Selequa	Guatemala	site of Zaculeu
Sinaloa	northwestern Mexico	early habitation region
Soatenco	Petén	site of Mirador
Solola	Guatemala	Maya trade route

NAME	LOCATION	ROLE
Suchiate	Guatemalan highlands	drains region
Tamesi	gulf coast	drains region
Tamuin	northern Veracruz	site of Tamuin
Tecoluta	Veracruz	resource of Remojada culture
Tejalpa	Toluca Valley	site of Calitlahuaca
Temesi	southern Veracruz	drains region
Tepalcatepec	Mexico/Michoacan	forms Tepalcatepec Basin
Tonala	gulf coast	site of La Venta
Tula	Hidalgo, Mexico	site of Tula
Tuncuilin	Panusco basin	Huaxtec domain
Tuxpan	gulf coast	Huaxtec domain
Ulua	Gulf of Honduras	drains region
Usumacinta	Guatemalan highlands	drains region
Verde	Sierra Madre Oriental	drains region
Yaqui	Pacific coastal lowlands	forms delta, flood plains
Zitacuaro	Yucatan	part of Balsas system

REPELO A site in the Sierra de Tamaulipas region that is part of the Tamaulipas Sequence in the Paleo-Indian Period (11,000–7000 B.C.). Skeletal remains were discovered there, wrapped in straw mats with evidence of basketwork. Bundles of maize ears were also included as grave offerings, an indication that wild maize was used in the region before the advent of ceramics there.

RESUMIDEROS Sinkholes in the Sierra Madre de Oriental region, found near limestone caverns.

RICHMOND HILL A site in northern Belize that contains evidence of tools and eroded low knolls. These crude tools and the flakes removed from them indicate that this Maya region was occupied possibly 10,000 to 20,000 years ago. No radiocarbon data is available.

RIO BEC B A site epitomizing a cluster of Maya sites bearing the same name in southern Quintana Roo and Campeche. Rio Bec B and the other sites are evidence of a Yucatan renaissance as the Maya declined in other regions due to Mexica advances. The style of the Rio Bec monuments is unique, designed more for exterior splendor than for functional use. Pseudopyramids were built in front of the temples with emphasis placed on artistic details and style. Rio Bec B is a small ceremonial site that symbolizes the artistic styles of the entire region. A temple discovered there has several levels, vaults and 10 chambers. The towers incorporated into the design of this shrine are 55 feet high, with rounded corners and narrow, false stairways. The towers are for design purposes only, having no ritual purpose; they could not be climbed. An elaborate stone roof comb and masks were also included. Rio Bec B also contained a remarkable female nude figure, having voluptuous lines and reflecting the sculptor's mastery of stone. The site and its companions define the Maya art style termed Rio Bec.

RIO BEC STYLE See MAYA ARCHITECTURE; RIO BEC B.

RIO CHIQUITO A waterway in Veracruz, the site of the great Olmec city of San Lorenzo. Tenochtitlan del Rio Chiquito and PORTRERO NUEVO were also erected on the banks of this river.

RIO GRANDE A waterway in northern Mexico, now the border between Mexico and the United States of America, actually north of the Mesoamerican region.

RIO GRANDE DE CHIAPAS A waterway in Chiapas, actually the Grijalva River, so called by those living there.

RIO TUNEL PHASE A cultural development associated with the Chalchihuites culture and dating from A.D. 950 to 1159. A unified ceramic industry was formed during this and related phases. Wares of the Rio Tunel phase include red-on-buff tripods, plain bowls and cloisonne decorations. Copper bells were also discovered in some sites related to this phase.

RITUAL OF THE BACABS (Bacabes) A document of Maya origin, recording the religious ceremonies concerning the cardinal points of the earth and their cosmological significance. The document also describes the roles of the BACABS and the ACANTUN, other beings associated with the calendar.

RIVERS OF MESOAMERICA The vast waterways in the region and another element in its varied terrain, vital to agricultural development and ensuing progress. The major systems, such as the Balsa and the Usumacinta, drained entire territories and created deltas and plains. These major waterways and other systems, served as transportation routes for the various cultures. In some historical periods trade depended on the rivers. A list of the Mesoamerican rivers and their roles begins at left. These rivers are cited individually in the text. See also trade sections in the major cultures for details about water use.

ROCK CRYSTAL A transparent, colorless form of quartz, highly valued by the Mesoamericans. The crystal was mined in Alta Vista, in the realm of the Chalchihuites culture. It was also prized on the Turquoise Road trade route, popular around A.D. 350. The rock crystals were used to fashion ornaments to be traded.

ROCKER STAMP   A tool used by artists of Mesoamerican cultures as a decorative device. The stamp was held in the hand and "walked" across the damp clay of a ceramic piece in order to press into the material the curved zigzag patterns popular among several groups. The Ocos culture is known for its use of rocker stamps. The tool was usually made from the edge of a cardium shell. Rocker stamping dates to Ajalpan in the Tehuacan Valley, as early as 1500 to 900 B.C.

ROSARIO PHASE   A cultural development in Oaxaca during the Formative Period, related to the Espiridion, Tierras Largas, Guadalupe and San Jose Mogote Phases. This period, dated to c. 700/600 B.C. to c. 500/450 B.C., witnessed the growth of San Jose Mogote as a ceremonial site and as a political power. The site of Huitzo was a smaller competitor, but San Jose Mogote had a large population. The cities of Etla, Zaachila-Zimatlan and Tlacolula were emerging in this period, and agricultural expansion and trade was on the rise. The great city of Monte Alban is believed to have arisen in the Rosario Phase. The ceramic period called Monte Alban I corresponds to Rosario ceramics. The Socorro fine gray vessels were being manufactured as well. Incised designs were developed and a form of burnished patterns appeared on wares. Negative painting was in use. The architectural patterns of the Rosario Phase were the basis for Monte Alban's splendor. Figures similar to the *danzantes* were emerging. The Rosario Phase was also evident in Tomatepec.

RUBBER *(Castilloa elastica)*   A pliable substance taken from tree trunks in latex form by the process of tapping. Rubber had a religious significance in Mesoamerican cultures. It and paper made from tree bark were used in rituals by many groups. Rubber balls were essential to the ball games conducted in Mesoamerican cities. Rubber was also spattered on paper during ceremonies. (See PAPER.)

S

SACAB A type of lime used by the Maya as a building material. The lime was probably stored in pits in the ceremonial complexes, especially in the *chultunes,* the bottle-shape reservoirs in the floors of plazas and shrines. *Chultunes* were also used for burials and as sweat baths.

SACHEOB See CAUSEWAY.

SAGE OF ANAHUAC See NEZAHUALCOYOTL.

SALADO RIVER A waterway in the Valley of Oaxaca that drains the area around Tlacolula. The river is located in the ancient realm of the Zapotec.

SALAMA BASIN A region formed by the Salama River in the highlands of Guatemala, associated with the Cabulco and Rabinal basins. Jadeite was mined there.

SALAMA RIVER A waterway in the Guatemalan highlands, flowing to the Pacific Ocean. The river forms a basin there. (See SALAMA BASIN.)

SALCAJA A Guatemalan highland site, dating to the Formative Period (2000 B.C.–c. A.D. 250/290) or perhaps even earlier. Habitation mounds were discovered in Salcaja, as well as storage pits, indicating permanent or seasonal habitation.

SALINAS LA BLANCA A site on the Pacific coast, associated with the Cuadros Phase culture and dated from 1000 to 850 B.C. Salinas La Blanca gives evidence of only seasonal occupation. The remains of *tecomates* and flat-bottom bowls with slanted sides and rocker stamp designs were found on the site, which indicates an Ocos influence. Shells and the remains of an early form of maize were also recovered there.

SALINAS RIVER A waterway in Guatemala that flows to the northwest to the Gulf of Campeche as a tributary of the Usumacinta River. The Salinas joins the Pasion River. The remains of Altar de Sacrificios is on its banks.

SAN BLAS A site on the Pacific coast between Guerrero and the Gulf of Mexico, associated with the Nayarit culture and dated to the Early Formative Period (2000–900 B.C.). San Blas has a shell-shape mound with elements dating to around 500 B.C. Obsidian flakes, pottery and tools were discovered there. The Nayarit culture is noted for distinctive ceramics.

SAN CRISTOBAL PLATEAU A region overlooking the central Chiapas Valley in the area of the Meseta Central. The plateau is associated with the Sierra de San Cristobal. (See also MESOAMERICAN GEOGRAPHY.)

SAN GERVASIO A Maya site in the northern central part of the island of Cozumel in the region of Quintana Roo. A *sacheob,* or Maya causeway, leads to San Gervasio. The *talud-tablero* (slab and table) architectural style was in use here.

SAN ISIDRO PIEDRA PARADA A region on the Pacific coast of Guatemala, dating to the Late Formative Period (300 B.C.–c. A.D. 250/290). Abaj Takalik, a Maya site, is nearby, on the banks of the Santa Margarita River.

SAN JOSE A small Maya ceremonial complex in west-central Belize. Four groups of ruins have been discovered in San Jose, each one containing a court with mounds. Pyramids as high as 40 feet accompany three courts. A two-story palace with 11 vaulted rooms and an interior staircase was also found. Another structure contains six rooms in two parallel rows and a seventh chamber in a transverse position. Objects reflecting the vast Maya trade enterprises throughout the Belize region and beyond were also recovered. San Jose structures used stucco designs.

SAN JOSE MOGOTE An important Formative Period (2000 B.C.–c. A.D. 250/290) site just northwest of Monte Alban in Oaxaca, reflecting a cultural development there. Several cultural phases were present in San Jose Mogote, with villages and as many as 700 inhabitants. The residences there were of the traditional Oaxaca style, with white-painted daub walls, and thatched roofs. Materials recovered there give evidence of including spinning, weaving, food preparation and farming. Agricultural products included maize, chili peppers and squash.

Several artistic features distinguish San Jose Mogote from its Formative Period neighbors. Imitating a style that had begun in an earlier phase, the people constructed a public square and promoted the first civic architecture. A double line of posts clearly mark the perimeter of this open-air plaza, which was designed to accommodate gatherings of local inhabitants. Stone slabs reinforce these posts. The square delineated probably dedicated to religious and social ceremonies conducted during this historical period.

In time this square was abandoned in favor of a one-room chamber, several of which are still on the site. It is believed that each was used on a separate occasion or perhaps in a particular era. They were made of cane bundles, daubed with clay. Platform-style foundations were also constructed, and the floors of these buildings were covered with lime stucco. Rectangular objects were found in these chambers, probably the first stages of altars for ceremonies. Storage pits were dug into the floors or positioned nearby, probably designed to hold powdered lime, which was used in construction for ceremonial purposes.

Another distinguishing aspect of San Jose Mogote's development was the concern for the welfare of the local artisans and their various industries. Workshops were operated for craftsmen, including a site from which iron ore mirrors have been recovered. Magnitite mirrors were a speciality of the San Jose Mogote artisans, coveted in other markets and a valued commodity on the trade routes of the region. Jade and greenstone ornaments were also manufactured there, indicating that the people of San Jose Mogote imported raw materials from other regions and produced items that could be traded locally or in other regions.

Two basic ceramic motifs were in use during the San Jose Mogote Phase. These were insignias used perhaps as competitive images by the various districts of the site. The fire serpent represented the eastern and western districts and suburbs, and the were-jaguar represented the north and south districts. Other nearby communities adopted one or the other and used them on their wares. The rise in population, brought about by the industries and trade, led to a increased agricultural demand as well as public project labor forces. Neighboring sites, such as Etzna, probably contributed services and goods in return for protection and participation in trade.

San Jose Mogote began a series of public constructions and stepped terraces, with adobe and stone facing. Based on analysis of the residential districts that were part of the urban building enterprises, it is apparent that social castes were already present in the local populations. The houses of families of higher rank were constructed of high-quality materials and contained shell ornaments and mica. These residences also had patios and additional structures, probably cooking areas. Individual domiciles used drainage canals and cisterns, decorated with animal-bone insignias. The burial sites at San Jose Mogote give more evidence of this social stratification, as the bodies recovered there show skull deformations, probably the result of customs to denote rank or social status within the community. The grave offerings accompanying these remains were ample. Stone slabs were also buried with the bodies.

SAN JOSE MOGOTE PHASE   See SAN JOSE MOGOTE.

SAN JUAN RIVER (1)   A waterway that marks the boundary between the countries of Nicaragua and Costa Rica. Merchants of the extensive Maya trade enterprises used this river to reach cities in the area, operating canoes, rafts, etc. over the water. Later cultures used the same trade route, and the San Juan River remained a link between the markets and products of Nicaragua and Costa Rica and the other Mesoamerican cultures. In time, during their imperial expansion, the Aztec sent trade expeditions to the San Juan River.

SAN JUAN RIVER (2)   A waterway in the Valley of Mexico, which forms a plain. The great city of Teotihuacan was erected on the plain, and the river served as a natural water resource for the developing city. The San Juan probably also was a means of transportation for the merchants of Teotihuacan, who were active in transporting their products and imported wares into the region.

SAN LORENZO   One of three Olmec sites on the Rio Chiquito in the Coatzalcos River basin in southern Veracruz. It is believed that San Lorenzo, along with Tenochtitlan Rio Chiquito and Portrero Nuevo, was settled by around 1500 B.C. The Olmec were on the site by c. 1200/1150 B.C., and the city was abandoned by 900 B.C. and then revived in a later era. The city is considered the oldest Olmec site known today. Designed originally as a vast ceremonial complex, San Lorenzo appears as a vast plateau rising some 160 feet above the surrounding savannas. Ridges cut into the plateau can be seen jutting out on the northwestern and southern sides. Mounds with linear designs were used in construction, and the central ceremonial complex was erected on a massive salt dome. The center also had access to a lagoon-estuary system, some formed naturally and others indicating they were man-made. The people of San Lorenzo added other innovative structures over the years, building a series of basalt conduits, using some 30 tons of stone to erect a 650-foot system. The conduits drained ponds of collected water and served as reservoirs, probably for religious or agricultural purposes. Several archaeological phases have been established at the site, including:

Ojochi: 1400–1300 B.C.

Bajio: 1300–1200 B.C.

Chicarras: 1200–1100 B.C.

San Lorenzo A: 1100–1000 B.C.

San Lorenzo B: 900 B.C.

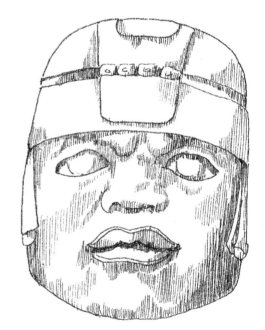

San Lorenzo head

Nacaste: 700 B.C.

Palanguan: 400 B.C.

Remplas: 100 B.C.

Villa Alta: A.D. 900

The San Lorenzo mounds were once thought to be products of natural erosion, but modern excavations demonstrate that some were constructed. The building of the mounds may predate Olmec domination or indicate earlier Olmec influence there. It is also possible that the mounds were a base for original residences, as some 200 have been discovered. The houses and mounds suggest a population of as many as 1,000 in San Lorenzo, despite the designation of the city as a ceremonial complex.

The central court of San Lorenzo, an essential aspect to all ceremonial complexes in Mesoamerica, contained ceramics from the Bajio, Chicarra and San Lorenzo A phases. In the Palanquan Phase mounds more ceramics were discovered, as were construction materials from the Nacaste era. A unique characteristic of the buildings is the presence of a *horno*, a tube fashioned of burned clay that might have served as a passageway for spirits or simply as a ventilation tube. In one area, human remains were found alongside animal bones, indicating that it was probably a dumping ground for the remains of victims of cannibalism, as irregular marks are evident.

The major monuments of San Lorenzo include eight colossal heads. Weighing many tons, these heads have negroid faces and are helmeted. They were probably quarried in the volcanic Cerro Cintepec, in the Tuxtla Mountains, more than 50 miles away. It is believed that the stones were dragged to navigable streams and then to the Coatzacoalcos River. Balsa rafts would have carried them to San Lorenzo, where the Olmec, using wooden rollers, would have transported them to designated mounds. The heads probably depicted Olmec rulers. The helmets were used both in the ball games and in battles. The city also contains a ceremonial ball court.

San Lorenzo was abandoned in 900 B.C., possibly as the result of an invasion or a civil revolution, although one theory suggests that water failure brought about an exodus. When the site was abandoned, the monuments were defaced or smashed and then buried in the drainage system. San Lorenzo was occupied again in the Villa Alta period, around A.D. 900. Some Olmec may have remained in the center even when it was abandoned by the general population.

Besides the colossal heads, animal figures carved out of basalt were discovered in San Lorenzo. An unusual piece is shaped like a sitting bird and had been called the duck fountain. Many seated figures, some with were-jaguar faces, were recovered, as well as a large basalt sphere and altar pieces showing the Olmec niche design. One circular ritual table was carved with stone bounds, and another has carved dwarf figures, Atlanteans, supporting the table. Of particular interest in the altars is a half-kneeling figure, thought to be an Olmec ruler wearing ball game armor.

SAN LORENZO PHASES A AND B   Cultural developments in Veracruz, associated with the Olmec center of San Lorenzo and dating from 1100 to 1000 B.C. and 900 B.C.

Evidence of Olmec habitation in these eras was also found in Juxtlahuaca Cave and on the Chiapas coast.

SAN LUIS POTOSI   A site on the Mesa del Norte of Mexico, located on an interior drainage system. In some historical eras, the Huaxtec dominated the region of San Luis Potosi. This site was also part of the Chichimec territories in other historical periods, and many cultures passed through the region as they invaded.

SAN MARTIN   A volcanic peak in southern Veracruz, located on the gulf coastal plain near Lake Catemaco, also of volcanic origin.

SAN MARTIN PAJAPAN   A small Olmec site near Lake Catemaco in Veracruz, dating to the San Lorenzo era (1500 B.C. to 900 B.C.). A jade statue was discovered on the site. Little excavation work has been done at San Martin Pajapan.

SAN MATEO   A small cultural group associated with the city of Cholula, dating to the Middle Formative Period (900–300 B.C.) in the Puebla region. Dominated by the great city of Teotihuacan, Cholula was occupied by several small groups that were assimilated into the population.

SAN PABLO PANTHEON   An Olmec site on the Cuautla River in Morelos that contains 200 graves. The oldest portion of the site is called La Juana, dating from 1100 to 900 B.C. Olmec figurines, rocker stamps and black wares were recovered in San Pablo Pantheon. The inhabitants of this site manufactured bottle forms and ceramics typical of the region in the Early Formative Period (2000–900 B.C.).

SAN PABLO RIVER   A waterway in the Pacific coastal lowlands, forming flood and delta plains for the regional inhabitants.

SAN PEDRO DE LOS PINOS   A Toltec site in western Mexico City in the Valley of Mexico. Several structures found within the precincts of San Pedro de los Pinos are believed to be royal palaces. The Toltec ruler Mixcohuatl (Mixcoac) is believed to have established the palace complex at the site.

SAN PEDRO ZACACHIMALPA   A site in the Valley of Puebla at Valsequillo, dating to the Paleo-Indian Period and evidencing habitation c. 11,000 to 7000 B.C.

SAN SEBASTIAN   A site in Jalisco, in Western Mexico, dated to the Early Formative Period (2000–900 B.C.). Two tombs were discovered there, containing skeletons and the remains of headless bodies. Hollow figurines, rectangular boxes with lids, polychrome bowls and dishes were also recovered from San Sebastian.

SANTA CECILIA   An Aztec (Mexica) site located north of modern Mexico City. This Chichimec city was taken by the Aztec and transformed into a religious conclave. A fully restored Aztec temple on a pyramidal base is on display here. A cobblestoned plaza faces the temple, providing a public arena for ceremonies. This major temple also contains evidence of four separate stages of construction. A plain stela and a drum-shape sculpture adorned the temple originally. The shrine is composed of carved stone with a single chamber on its summit. In some records the site is listed as Santa Cecilia Azcatitlan. In other records it is associated with the Chichimec city of Tenayuca.

SANTA CLARA PHASE   A cultural development associated with the great Miraflores Phase in the Maya cities of Izapa and Kaminaljuyu, dating to c. 900 to 300 B.C. This was a period of increased artistic and ceramic endeavors. The Santa Clara Phase was also associated with the Providence and Arenal cultural developments in the same cities.

SANTA ISABEL IZTAPAN   A site two miles from Tepexpan, near the old Lake Texcoco beds in the Valley of Mexico. Mammoth bones were recovered from deposits in Santa Isabel Iztapan in 1953. In these remains, discovered four feet below the surface, a flint spearhead was embedded in the mammoth's rib cage. Tools for preparing the carcass of the animal were found nearby: an obsidian scraper, a chalcedony dart point, another scraper and an obsidian knife blade. A second mammoth find, the species *Mammuthus Archidiskodon imperatur*, was located in a ditch at the same site. Both discoveries were designated geologically as belonging to the Upper Becerra Formation of the Terminal Pleistocene Period. The tools and weapons found at the site date to the Great American Plains Period, from 7000 to 5000 B.C. (See TEPEXPAN.)

SANTA LUCIA   A site in southern Veracruz, linked to preceramic habitations and to cultural development in the region.

SANTA MARGARITA RIVER   A waterway on the Pacific coast of Guatemala, a Maya domain. The city of ABAJ TAKALIK was located on the banks of the river.

SANTA MARTA CAVE   A site in the Chiapas highlands, west of the Grijalva Basin, where a rock shelter was occupied in the Incipient Agriculture Period (7000–c. 2000/2500 B.C.). Some evidence indicates that the cave was inhabited as early as 6700 B.C. Darts, scrapers, planes, pebble-style *manos* and gougers have been found. Burial sites discovered contained corpses covered with *metates*. Maize pollen on the site dates to the Early Formative Period (2000–900 B.C.), indicating prolonged use for the cave.

SANTA MARTA PHASE   Part of the Tehuacan Sequence in southern Puebla and in northern Oaxaca, dating to the Incipient Agriculture Period, c. 900 to 200 B.C. Villages and ceremonial complexes were emerging in this phase of cultural development. Full-time agriculture had become a way of life in the region, and settlements were formed to maintain the fields and the nearby hunting grounds. Hybrid plants also were developed by these early Mesoamerican farming communities. Tools were being refined for new roles, and grinding stones were used in food preparation. The ceramics of the period were white or gray, and bichromes were also being produced locally. The people left

remains of flat-bottomed bowls, water bottles and silhouette bowls. Incised patterns probably developed during this phase as well. It is believed that the slash-and-burn method of farming was developed at this time.

SANTA MARTA VOLCANO   A peak in southern Veracruz, in the gulf coastal lands, near San Martin Volcano and the volcanic Lake Catemaco.

SANTA RITA   A Maya site in northern Belize, overlooking the Caribbean Sea and inhabited around A.D. 300. Sculptured friezes and stucco murals were discovered there, along with a burial site. In one tomb, that of a local ruler and probably dating to A.D. 500, a skeleton was found covered with jade and other pieces of jewelry. Murals there show Maya and Mexica influences.

SANTA ROSA XTAMPAK   A Maya site in northeastern Campeche, on the edge of the Chenes region. It rivals nearby Uxmal in size and is equipped with some 60 *chultunes* in the limestone of the area. The site is on the modern Santa Rosa hacienda, or ranch. The palace, a large Chenes structure, rises in three stories, with many chambers and two stairways. A carved geometric design is visible there as well as the Chenes monster style. Another structure, called Building C, Serpent Mouth Facade, repeats the Chenes motif. Other structures form groups that show some Puuc and Rio Bec designs. An estimated 12,000 Maya lived there from 300 B.C. to A.D. 900. The city may have been deserted during many eras, reclaimed by roving Maya.

SANTIAGO RIVER   A waterway in the Pacific coastal lowlands that joined with other rivers to form flood and delta plains in the region. The Santiago links with the Lerma River in the Toluca Valley, draining the coastal portion of the Sierra Madre Oriental.

SAN VICENTE CHICOLOAPAN   A site in the Valley of Mexico, where a hearth dating to the Paleo-Indian Period (11,000–7000 B.C.) was discovered. Basalt implements were found on the site, including grinding stones, plus obsidian blades and projectile points. A human skeleton was recovered from San Vicente Chicoloapan as well.

SAPODILLAS   A tree that provides wood for the Mesoamerican region and a form of chewing gum.

SAYIL   A Maya site, considered a Puuc center, in the Yucatan Peninsula called "the Place of the Arts." Classic in style, Sayil was one of the cities established by the Maya who migrated into the Yucatan when their power declined in the south. It was abandoned c. A.D. 1000. The center is approximately 2½ square mile in diameter and was dominated by a three-story palace having a central staircase and recessed levels. The plazas had plaster floors, and underground cisterns were used. The palace, more than 275 feet wide, contains 75 separate chambers. The first level is dated to c. A.D. 850. The Mirador, so named by the Spanish, is another Sayil structure, erected on a pyramidal platform with stucco decorations. A large number of stelae were discovered near this building. Sayil also contains temples and an elaborate second royal residence, rectangular in design and adorned with banded columns. A ball court was discovered just beyond this palace which was believed to have served a population of around 9000. (See MAYA ARCHITECTURE, PUUC.)

SAYULA BASIN Region located in southern Jalisco, associated with the Zacoalco-Sayula archaeological zone there. It was inhabited in the Formative Period (2000 B.C.– c. A.D. 250/290). The Amacueca Phase is evident in there.

SAYULA PHASE A cultural development in southern Jalisco, part of the Zacoalco-Sayula archaeological zone and paralleling the rise of the city of Teotihuacan. Wares manufactured during this phase include Teotihuacan thin orange, red on buff and red on brown.

SCROLL AHAU JAGUAR The first historical ruler of the Maya city of TIKAL, depicted in a monument dated to A.D. 292. He claimed to be a descendant of Yax-Moch-Xoc, the founder of the TIKAL dynasty.

SEIBAL A Maya city on the Pasion River in the south-central part of the Peten region of Guatemala. The name is Spanish for the Ceiba Tree. The Xe culture was dominant in Seibal although the city was caught up in the expansion movement of Dos Pilas. Called *Sastanquiqui* originally, the city received an influx of population and engaged in construction around A.D. 851. Jade celts, associated with the Olmec, were discovered in the city. The city was abandoned from A.D. 500 to 690 and then resettled. Seibal was prominent from A.D. 830 to 890. More than 40 buildings have been discovered on the site, as well as fortifications, composed of extensive earthworks. The architectural style of Seibal is both Mexica and PETEN Maya, and the stelae recovered there are equally eclectic in design, reflecting the migration and invasions of the Maya lands in the Late Classic Period (A.D. 600–900). The remains of a pyramidal base contains four stairways and a temple having a corbeled vault. There is also a round building with a jaguar altar, associated with the cultic ceremonies of the region. The stelae, varied in style and content, are the most interesting aspects of Seibal's ruins.

SELEQUA RIVER A natural waterway in the Guatemalan highlands, the Maya domain. The river served as a resource for the Maya city of Zaculeu.

SERPENT COLUMNS A Toltec art form seen in their ceremonial complexes, such as CHICHEN ITZA. These columns, which stood as architectural complements or were incorporated into complex designs, depicted large serpents in stone, sometimes guarding temple entrances. The creatures' jaws jutted forward to form geometric lines. The upward-sweeping tails formed the lintels of the entrances.

SEVEN-FLOWER A Mixtec deity, believed to be a version of Xochipilli, the Aztec deity.

SEVEN-RAIN A Mixtec deity, believed to be a version of Xipe Totec, the Flayed God, patron of spring. Xipe Totec

Shield Jaguar and Lady Eveningstar

was universally revered throughout Mesoamerica. He is normally seen wearing a human skin.

SHIELD JAGUAR A Maya ruler, a member of the Jaguar dynasty of the city of Yaxchilan in Guatemala. Married to Lady Eveningstar, Shield Jaguar ruled until A.D. 742, when Bird Jaguar succeeded him. Shield Jaguar was born in A.D. 647 and ascended the throne of Yaxchilan in A.D. 742. It is possible that he was a usurper or perhaps a rightful heir forced to defend his rights. He is reported to have conducted a military campaign before assuming the rule of the city. Both Shield Jaguar and Lady Eveningstar were immortalized on a stela.

SICUIRANCHA A Tarascan ruler, the son of Hireticatame, called the Corpulent King by the Spanish. Hireticatame conquered the Tarascan lands around Lake Patzcuaro but was murdered during an internal feud. Sicuirancha began his rule from a palace on Lake Zirahuen, and the remains of that royal residence are still visible.

SIERRA ATRAVESADA A steep mountain chain bordering the Isthmus of Tehuantepec.

SIERRA CRUSILLAS A low-relief mountain chain in the gulf coastal lowlands of Mesoamerica.

SIERRA DE COALCOMAN   A mountain chain south of the Balsas River in the southern Mexican highlands. These sierras join with the Sierra Madre del Sur to form a mountainous region in Oaxaca.

SIERRA DE NAYARIT   A mountain range in the region of Nayarit in western Mexico, an extension of the Sierra Madre de Occidental.

SIERRA DE OMOA   A mountain range in Guatemala that forms highland regions, an extension of the Sierra Madre de Chiapas, with the Chuacan, Minas and Montana del Mico ranges. Having the Cabulco, Rabinal and Salama basins, the region is fertile. Jadeite was mined in this region.

SIERRA DE SAN CRISTOBAL   A mountain chain in the Chiapas highlands that form the *Sumidero*, a canyon site. This sierra extends into the Sierra Madre de Chiapas and then into Guatemala.

SIERRA DE TAMAULIPAS   A mountain chain with low-relief peaks in the gulf coastal lowlands, where various sites have been discovered and cataloged as part of a sequence of cultural development. (See TAMAULIPAS SEQUENCE for details.)

SIERRA DE TICUL   A ridge dividing the Yucatan plain and the Campeche highlands. In Guatemala this is part of the Peten region.

SIERRA MADRE DE CHIAPAS   A mountain range that formed the Pacific coastal region to the Bay of Honduras. The mountains overlook the ocean and stretch in a northeasterly direction to the central Chiapas Valley. This sierra forms the Chiapas and Guatemalan highlands.

SIERRA MADRE DE OAXACA   A low-relief mountain chain that serves as a barrier between the Oaxacan highlands and the Mexican highlands, and also to the coastal lowlands.

SIERRA MADRE DE SUR   A mountain chain extending from the Sierra Madre de Occidental to the Pacific coast in southern Mexico. The region has many rivers, marshes, lagoons, swamps, estuaries and a coastal plain. These peaks meet the Sierra de Coalcoman to form a rugged region in Oaxaca.

SIERRA MADRE DE OCCIDENTAL   A mountain range that forms the western or Pacific flank of the Mexican Plateau, with fertile plains and rugged crests. To the north is a narrow coastal plain, the terminal part of the Lerma-Santiago river system in the Roluca Valley of central Mexico. Within the towering crests, these mountains offer highland meadows, mesas and cliff habitations. The plains narrow and the coast becomes rugged and harsh. The deep canyons of these mountains are called *barrancas*. Gold and other metals are believed to have been mined in this region.

SIERRA MADRE DE ORIENTAL   The range of mountains and basins that stretches from north to south to form the eastern flank of the Mexican Plateau. These mountains give way to the Oaxaca highlands and blend into Chiapas, region altered by volcanic outpourings in Puebla and Veracruz. Elongated valleys, called *portreros*, are a distinctive feature of this region, as are *resumideros*, sinkholes. Limestone caverns formed over underground water systems offered resources to early inhabitants. The mountains are drained by rivers, including the Guayalejo, Verde and Moctezuma.

SIERRA SAN CARLOS   A low-relief mountain chain in Guatemala, in the gulf coastal lowlands.

SINALOA   A most northerly region of Mesoamerica, bordering on the American Desert Southwest. This region is located in the Fuerte River drainage system, and early habitation at certain sites is evident. The people of Sinaloa were competent agriculturalists and exploited the region's natural resources. There are recognizable cultural phases there, including the Chametla, Culiacan and Guasave, all associated with the Aztatlan Complex, which lasted until the Late Classic Period (A.D. 600–900). The Sinaloa artisans produced iron pyrite beads, onyx and alabaster vases, painted cloisonne mosaics, and pendants made of turquoise. Part of the Turquoise Road, the vast trade route that linked the Hohokam and Mogollon cultures of America's Southwest to those in Mesoamerica, Sinaloa was active in manufacturing wares out of local and imported materials. The industries collapsed, however, c. A.D. 1350, and the inhabitants moved to other regions.

SINALOA RIVER   A waterway in northwestern Mexico involved in Paleo-Indian Period (11,000–7000 B.C.) developments and cultural phases.

SISTEMA HUAUTLA   A 35-mile-long complex of limestone caverns in Oaxaca, now being explored. The caverns are 4,800 feet deep, filled in some places with water. No cultural artifacts have been recovered from the caverns, which have vast amounts of water channeled through them, but explorations continue.

SIX RABBITS   A deity honored in the city of Xochimilco and commemorated in a calendar stone. This god was a form of the Aztec Centeotl, called 400 Rabbits to denote the ways in which humans could become intoxicated. In Xochimilco, Six Rabbits was the patron of corn.

SKY XUL   A Maya ruler of Quirigua, on the Motagua River in Guatemala. He was the successor, probably son, of Cauac Sky, and he is listed as a member of the Sky dynasty. Middle age when he took the throne, Sky Xul reigned only 11 years.

SLIP WARES   A type of Mesoamerican ceramics that were given coats of water mixed with colored clay to create distinctive finishes. Brushes or the tails of small animals were used to apply the slip mixture in several coats, and then the ceramic was dried and polished using anything that would bring up the luster, including smooth stones and fiber materials.

SMOKE IMIX   A Maya ruler, the twelfth king of the city of Copan, in Honduras. His reign dated from A.D. 628 to June 665, when he died.

SMOKE MONEY The fourteenth Maya ruler of the city of Copan in Honduras. He is recorded as being somewhat retiring by nature, dependent on his nobles during his reign. He built a community house in Copan but left no other notable monuments.

SMOKE SHELL A Maya ruler of the city of Copan in Honduras. He was the successor to Smoke Money. Little documentation of his reign has survived, as Copan was in decline.

SMOKING ALTAR An image depicted in the murals discovered in the great city of Teotihuacan, begun in the Formative Period around 200 B.C. Such images evoked the religious doctrines behind the use of altars, both for sacrifices and for cremations.

SMOKING FROG A ruler of the Maya city of Uaxactun, in the Yucatan, believed to have been the brother of Great Jaguar Paw of Tikal. CURL SNOUT was recorded as being his nephew. Smoking Frog is depicted in some Maya accounts as a great military tactician and hero. His association with JAGUAR PAW (the Great) is part of this tradition.

SMOKING MIRROR See TEZCATLIPOCA (1).

SOATENCO RIVER A natural waterway in the northern Peten (Putun) region of Guatemala. The Maya city of Mirador was erected on its banks. Also called Rio de la Venta.

SOCONUSCO An alternative name for the Pacific coastal region of Mesoamerica, including the Isthmus of Tehuantepec. (See MESOAMERICAN GEOGRAPHY.)

SOLOLA Also called San Jose Chacaya, it overlooks Lake Atitlan in Guatemala. The site was occupied c. 2000 to 500 B.C. Associated with *Annals of the Cakchiquels*, Solola reflects the origins of the early highland Maya.

SPEECH SCROLLS An illustrative device used by the Maya to provide dialogue for figures. The scrolls represent and clearly state the speeches given by the individuals depicted or provide information about them. Such figures were usually of a divine or historical nature. The speech scrolls appeared in the center of Acanceh in the western Yucatan region c. A.D. 300/290, and they reflect the Izapa art style.

SQUASHES A variety of plants that were used in Mesoamerica in the earliest historical periods, one of the basic food sources for the emerging cultures. Such squashes include the pumpkin, crookneck (or warty) and the walnut squash, with other varieties appearing later.

STEAM BATHS Called *temazcalli* by some groups, a religious and social custom adopted by many cultures. Purification rituals involved steam baths, and the aristocrats used them for health reasons. Maxtli, the Tepanec ruler who attacked the Aztec and then found himself confronting the Triple Alliance, was dragged from his steam bath in his capital of Azcapotzalco in A.D. 1428 and executed.

STELA A slab or stone monument, used extensively in Mesoamerica, sometimes decorated with carvings, sometimes plain. Maya stelae, called the *te-tun,* the "tree stone," are studied because of their custom of dating stelae. These monuments, carrying specific information, provide details about the decline of the Maya realm in some regions. The oldest Maya stela discovered in Uaxactun is dated to A.D. 445. The earliest lowland Maya stela dates to A.D. 279. Some stelae are full-faced figures, standing 30 feet high. At first only one side of the stelae were carved, then details were engraved on all sides. The use of stelae in the Maya realms declined by A.D. 830. The last lowland stela, recovered from Tonina, is dated A.D. 909. (See MAYA ART.)

STONE OF TIZOC A monument discovered in the Great Temple of the Aztec (Mexica) capital of Tenochtitlan in the Valley of Mexico. The stone eight feet tall and two and one half feet thick, depicts the reign of the short-lived emperor, Tizoc (A.D. 1481–1486), probably murdered. This reign, however, is not portrayed as the simple mortal achievements of a temporal ruler but as a panorama of his role as the representative of the god Huitzilopochtli for the Aztec people. The stone is in the Museo Nacional de Anthopologia in Mexico City.

STORMY SKY A ruler of the Maya city of Tikal in Guatemala. He was the son and heir to Curl Nose, taking the throne in A.D. 426. Introducing Mexica traditions to Tikal, Stormy Sky also allowed Mexica immigrants into the city. A stela dated to A.D. 439 honors him. He was buried in the northern acropolis of the city.

SUCHIATE RIVER A waterway in the Guatemalan highlands, flowing south to the Pacific Ocean from the mountain peaks.

SUCHILQUITONGO A suburban district of the city of Huitzo, joined by a second residential district, Telixtlahuaca.

SULA PLAIN The Maya region on the Gulf of Honduras, an important trade area. Chetumal and other Maya cities were erected in this region to serve the Itza and Cocom nobles who came to trade. Cacao, obsidian, gold and feathers were important trade items. The Sula Plain, drained by the Motagua, Chamelecon and Ulua rivers, was part of the Maya southern lowlands. It served as a connecting link between the Maya and peoples to the south and east. One of the most prominent cities in the Sula Plain was NACO.

SWASEY CULTURE Also called Swazey, an artistic period associated with Maya history in the Belize region. The Swasey Culture dates from 2000 to 1000 B.C. and is evidenced in the city of Cuello in Belize. Plastered platforms were erected during this artistic phase, and the wares from the era are unusual in their sophistication. Domesticated crops were also used.

SWIDDEN See MESOAMERICAN AGRICULTURE.

T

TABASCO A region in the gulf coast lowlands, associated with early habitation dating to the Paleo-Indian Period (11,000–7000 B.C.) and with the emerging Olmec civilization during the Early Formative Period (c. 2000/1600–900 B.C.). The La Venta culture flourished there. Later cultures, such as the Peten Maya (Putun), traded in Tabasco, with cacao serving as a major trading commodity. The cacao crops of the region provided local groups with considerable wealth and power. Xicallanco was a center for the distribution of cacao and other products, and was occupied by the Aztec at times. The region was also noted for its ceramics, reflecting Olmec tradition and style. Fine orange wares from Tabasco remained a viable trading commodity throughout later periods of Mesoamerican expansion. It is believed that the region was named after a Maya prince called TABSCOOB.

TABLET OF THE SLAVES A Maya monument erected in A.D. 729 in Palenque. The tablet, a beautifully carved scene, commemorated the sixtieth birthday of Chac Zutz, who took the throne of Palenque in A.D. 722. He was the successor to Chaacal II.

TABSCOOB A Maya prince listed as ruling in the city of Comalcalco near Villahermosa in the modern state of Tabasco. Comalcalco was the westernmost Maya site. Prince Tabscoob may have the source of the name of modern TABASCO.

TACUBA See TLACOPAN.

TAJIN See EL TAJIN.

TALUD-TABLERO An architectural style notable in MONTE ALBAN but used widely by other cultures, including the great city of Teotihuacan. The *talud* is a sloping wall base with the *tablero,* a horizontal slab placed on top. Altars in the *talud-tablero* style were recovered in various sites, including Chalcatzinco, dating from 700 to 500 B.C. When used in large structures, a rectangular panel with an inset was placed over a sloping wall. In the city of Teotihuacan, the Temple of Quetzalcoatl is designed in the *talud-tablero* style, in six tiers. These tiers are decorated with images of the feathered serpent and the fire serpent. The great pyramid of Cholula consists of three superimposed *talud-tableros.* In Xochicalco, in western Morelos, the *taluds* are extremely high, sculpted with reliefs. The Monte Alban versions are somewhat modified.

TAMAULIPAS A region in the northeastern part of Mesoamerica, extending along the gulf coast on the west, having coastal plains, hills and a mountain range, the Sierra de Tamaulipas. This region, an archaeological treasure house, contains sites and evidence of Paleo-Indian Period (11,000–7000 B.C.) habitation and activity. Scholars have divided them into a sequence to explain the developmental processes of the region. (See TAMAULIPAS SEQUENCE.)

TAMAULIPAS SEQUENCE A term used to describe a series of sites that reflect the activities of the people who entered the Tamaulipas region and began the cultural and evolutionary processes on the various sites recorded. One of the most abundant regions of archaeological evidence in Mesoamerica, the Tamaulipas northern territory flanks the gulf coast and contains sites with materials as early as the Paleolithic Period, when microbands of hunters and gatherers entered the territory exploit the natural resources, including local game and vegetation. Seasonal campsites arose in caves and on cliffs; on the coast, lagoons and estuaries reveal evidence of habitation. This region was part of the change from the Paleo-Indian Period (11,000–7000 B.C.) to the Incipient Agricultural Period (7000–c. 2000/2500 B.C.), a time when early Mesoamericans discovered how to tame the environment and to set down roots in a single location. They also formed macrobands, which in time evolved to individual groups or cultures. The phases of the Tamaulipas Sequence are:

Diablo Cave Complex. Also called the Diablo Focus, a cultural development dated to c. 7000 B.C. This is the oldest stratification sequence of habitation in the arid caves of the Tamaulipas region. The Diablo Cave Complex predates the era of projectile history there. No projectile points were found, only scrapers, choppers, blades and crude bifacial tools.

Repelo. A site in the Sierra de Tamaulipas, dating to around 6800 B.C. Skeletal remains were discovered there, wrapped in straw mats and with evidence of basketwork. Bundles of maize ears were also included as grave offerings, an indication of the use of wild maize in the Tamaulipas region before the advent of ceramics.

Lerma. A site in the Tamaulipas region that lasted until around 6300 B.C. Hunting weapons were recovered from Lerma, including laurel-leaf projection points and the remains of deer and other animals that had been hunted and prepared for consumption. The weapons discovered in

Lerma are similar to those found in the Tehuacan Sequence in the same historical period, demonstrating cultural contacts and perhaps even trade.

Nogales. A Tamaulipas site and phase that is dated from 5000 to 3000 B.C. A change is evident in the diets of the hunters and gatherers who were in residence there. Plant gathering took on an additional value during this time, and it is estimated that around 70 percent of the food used by the local population was derived from plants. They used wild grains and beans, along with domesticated gourds, chili peppers and squashes or pumpkins. The Nogales groups were developing other skills and producing items for their own use. Basketry is evident, and strings were made with knots in the designs. Large scrapers, nets, disk choppers and scrapers were in their basic tool kits.

La Perra. A Tamaulipas Sequence phase that is dated from 3000 to 2000 B.C. The groups in the region appear to have hunted for only 15 percent of their dietary needs at this time, cultivating the rest or relying on wild varieties of plants. Domestic crops probably accounted for some 10 to 15 percent of their dietary needs. The early Nal-Tel maize seems to have been in use. Dart points, gouges, choppers, *manos,* scrapers, mats, baskets, nets and blankets were all recovered from sites of this phase, in fragmented condition.

Other phases of the Tamaulipas Sequence categorized from additional sites and studies include:

Infiernillos. A cultural development believed to be from 7000 to 9000 years old, providing ancient patterns of subsistence. Plant collecting in this phase accounted for as much as 50 to 70 percent of the dietary needs. Seasonal habitations are obvious, and macrobands were formed for communal labors during the hunting and gathering seasons. Projectile points, some attached to spear shafts or dart foreshafts, were also discovered. Planes, choppers, nets, scrapers, mats and baskets have also been recovered.

Ocampo. A phase dating from c. 5000 to 2200 B.C., from the Sierra Madre region. From 70 to 80 percent of the dietary needs were met by plant gathering. Domesticated vegetation also made up a small portion of the diet. Dart points, choppers, scrapers, nets and a variety of baskets were found there.

Flacco. Combined with the Almagre Phase, dated from 2200 to 1800 B.C. with evidence that agriculture had increased to meet 20 percent of the dietary needs in the region. The early Nal-Tel maize is evident here, located in a site called BAT CAVE. In the Almagre Phase there is evidence that the wattle-and-daub houses were being constructed.

Other phases in territories adjoining the Tamaulipas Sequence sites include Guerra, Laguna, Mesa de Guaje, and Pamillas.

TAMESI RIVER A waterway in the gulf coastal lowlands of southern Veracruz.

TAMIAMA A lagoon in the gulf coastal lowlands.

TAMIME A Chichimec group, called the "shooters of arrows," associated with the Teo-Chichimec. The Tamime were originally cave dwellers, taking up residence in gorges or rocky slopes. In time they built grass huts and took on the trappings of a more sophisticated civilization, including agricultural activities. The Tamime are reported as understanding both the Nahaul and Otomi languages. Some scholars consider them related to the Zapotec. These were a Post-Classic Period (A.D. 900–1521) people.

TAMOACHAN A legendary site used throughout Mesoamerican history. The name appears to be Maya in origin, meaning the "Land of Rain or Mist." The following are accounts from records concerning Tamoachan:

Tamoachan (1) A sacred site listed in Nahual poetry as having great religious significance, probably as a homeland associated in some accounts with Xomiltepec.

Tamoachan (2) A legendary source of the "Lords of Wisdom" of the great city of Teotihuacan.

Tamoachan (3) The legendary lands of the Olmec, supposedly in "the eastern sea."

Tamoachan (4) A site claimed by the Totonac as their sacred homeland.

Tamoachan (5) An alternate name for the Jade Shrine (Chalchiuhmomozoc) in the city of Chalco. (See JADE SHRINE.)

Tamoachan (6) The legendary Aztec paradise, a holy site, believed at one time to have comprised the present state of Morelos, possibly Xochicalco. The Aztec claimed Tamoachan as the source of the bones out of which humans were formed. Tamoachan belonged to the gods. There Xochiquetzal, the Earth Mother, called the Precious Flower, ruled a place of pleasure and delights. It was said also to be the abode of the Lord of Sustenance. The gods were created there, living on maize. It was a place of eternal summer and flowing water. A sacred tree, untouchable, grew there, where beautiful birds sang. The gods destroyed the tree and were exiled from Tamoachan.

TAMPICO A territory in the gulf coastal lowlands near the volcano Bernal de Horcasitas.

TAMUIN A Huaxtec capital, called the Place of the Bonfires and located near the coast in northern Veracruz, now modern San Luis Potosi, erected in the Post-Classic Period (A.D. 900–1521.) The Huaxtec abandoned their southern sites and took refuge in what they called Huaxteca Potosina, making the city their new capital. Tamuin was an enormous city for its time, located on the Tamuin River, a tributary of the Panuco. The ruins of a pyramidal mound in the city gives evidence of a monument of great height. A high hill was terraced on one side, nearest the center quadrangle, with an elevation of approximately 165 feet. Platforms built there were made from river boulders, carved to specification and then covered with plaster and decorative structures. The site of Tamuin was a typical ceremonial complex in design. Like other Huaxtec sites, this one had a circular architectural style, honoring Ehecatl, the god Quetzalcoatl as the wind; he was symbolized by round, endless curves.

A major plaza served as the public assembly area, where religious rituals were performed. This plaza was surrounded by buildings that opened onto it. A pyramidal platform, having an eastern staircase, was covered with plaster. The pyramid was decorated with stepped masonry and painted designs. A long bench and truncated conical altars stood at the foot of the pyramid's staircase. The altars, also round, were covered in plaster and red frescos. Several objects recovered from Tamuin include a statue called the "Adolescent," a form depicting the god Quetzalcoatl and his son, in the guise of the evening star. (See HUAXTEC and HUAXTEC ART for details.)

TAMUIN PLAIN   A site near the Tanchipa Mountain range, Huaxtec in origin but having definite Maya influence. A true truncated pyramid, measuring 66 feet in height, 197 feet in length and 66 feet in width, supports a sanctuary in the site. The usual staircase on the platform is designed as a ramp. Three altars stand nearby, on an east-west axis.

TANCAH   A Maya site on the shore of the Yucatan Peninsula, near Tulum. From c. A.D. 300 the site was continuously occupied until the Spanish Conquest. The surviving structures are believed to have been constructed between A.D. 300 and 500. A pyramid and murals distinguish the site, which was once a ceremonial center.

TANCITERO   One of the major volcanic peaks in the Transverse Volcanic Axis on the Mesa Central of Mexico. (See MESOAMERICAN GEOGRAPHY; VOLCANOES.)

TANCOL   A Huaxtec city site located in the Huaxtec Potosina in northern Veracruz. Remains of several pyramids are found there.

TANGAXOAN II ZINCHICHA   A Tarascan ruler, called the Old Shoe. He was the last Tarascan king, slain by the Spanish on the banks of the Lerma River.

TAPACHULA   A site in Chiapas on the Pacific coast founded by a group Zoquean Maya. The site was active in the Early Formative Period (A.D. 1/250 to 600), when the nearby settlement of Izapa was beginning.

TAPOSCOLULA   An archaeological zone in the Mixtec region of Oaxaca, dating to the Post-Classic Period (A.D. 900–1521). A plaza complex was discovered here, having terraces, fortified walls and a ball court.

TARASCAN   A culture of western Mexico, called the Lake People or the People of the Sierras. The Tarascan entered the region of Michoacan probably sometime c. A.D. 1000. They called themselves and their obscure language the *Pure'pecha*. Upon entering Michoacan, led by a chieftain called Ira Thicatame, one of an illustrious line of rulers, the people broke into separate groups, some going to the highlands and others to the lakes of the region: Patzcuaro, Zirahuen, Cuitzeo and Yurira. The *Pure'pecha* language remains a mystery because it is unique in Mesoamerica, not related to the local tongues and not akin to Nahuatl, the language of the major cultural groups in the Valley of Mexico in later eras. A Spanish history of the Tarascan, however, reports that the people around Lake Patzcuaro recognized the Tarascan tongue. Some scholars have suggested that there is a definite relationship between the

Tarascan bowl from Tzintzuntzan

Tarascan and the Quechua of South America, as reflected in their language. The Tarascan claimed to have originated at a site called Zacuba. Others place them in the Nahual Seven Caves region of Chicomoztec, which does not account for the separate language. It is possible that the Tarascan, hearing other groups boasting of Nahual origins, decided to claim Chicomoztoc as their own homeland in later periods.

The early history of the Tarascan is recorded as a time of rivalries and wars between the lake-dwelling groups and the Tarascan residing in the highlands. One Hireticatame, called by the Spaniards the Corpulent King, supposedly conquered the Tarascan who had settled at Lake Patzcuaro. He was subsequently murdered and succeeded by his son and heir, Sicuirancha, who appears to have ruled from a palace at Lake Zirahuen. A man called Pavacume, a Tarascan chief, probably from the sierra region, married the daughter of a lake-dwelling fisherman, and from this union came Tariacuari, the illustrious hero of the Tarascan nation. He unified the people, intrigued, fought and suffered defeats in order to weld a nation. His son, Curatame, with the support of relatives, completed the conquest of Patzcuaro and divided the kingdom into three separate portions: Patzcuaro, called the Smoky Place, Ihuatzio and Tzintzuntzan.

The Tarascan also initiated the beginning of their great empire, extending their domination and influence to the rest of Michoacan and Guerrero. In time they controlled portions of Colima and Jalisco as well, and their domain was said to have consisted of the lands between the Lerma and the Mezcala rivers. The capital of this empire was first at Patzcuaro, then at Ihuatzio and then at Tzintzuntzan, although all three may have functioned simultaneously in a governmental administrative capacity.

The Tarascan had great impact on their neighboring states; other cultures admired them for their artistic excellence and their craftsmanship. The Tarascan were especially known for their feather mosaics, metallurgy, textiles and delicate painted ceramics. They also maintained a standing army and went to war against the Aztec and others in swift response to any invasion or threat.

Overshadowed in the past by the vast empires of the Post-Classic Period, the Tarascan are now better understood. They established a unique and thriving culture that remained independent until the Spanish arrived. The Tarascan dominated vast parts of western Mexico, even though their nucleus remained at Patzcuaro. The lakes and the rugged sierras provided them with natural resources and with the opportunity to conduct their particular way of life, which appears to have been concentrated on village life. Settlements throughout the Tarascan realm were small and scattered, bound by common religious, social and administrative ideals that the rulers established early in the group's occupation of their lands. The Tarascan region was populated through the Formative Period (c. 2000/1600 B.C.–c. A.D. 250/290), and the Tarascan subdued local peoples when they arrived in new territory. It is believed that territories under Tarascan rule were united as early as A.D. 1250. The geographically diverse region encouraged a spirit of independence and agricultural living, and the people flourished. The entire Tarascan region included lakes and basins, but many of these were at elevations equal to those of the surrounding sierras. Most Tarascan lived in or near large coniferous pine and fir forests.

TARASCAN AGRICULTURE
Varied and unique forms of farming in a complex and widely diverse environment. Along the shore of the Michoacan lakes, the Tarascan planted fields of corn, cotton, and *chia* (a flax seed that could be made into a beverage or into oil). Tobacco was another product grown in the territory, used locally and then probably introduced as a trading commodity on the extensive trade routes of the region. Prized by many Mesoamerican cultures, tobacco could be transported long distances. The Tarascan used the local ceiba tree to make a type of down fabric. They combined this down with other materials, such as fibers, rabbit fur and feathers. Fishing was also a mainstay of the Tarascan economy. The Aztec called Michoacan the Place of the Masters of Fish, indicating the supremacy of the Tarascan in this regard. They caught fish with nets shaped like butterflies, spears, harpoons and hooks, and probably gathered other lake products from marshes, savannas and shallows. No doubt water fowls was plentiful as well.

The Tarascan probably used the *milpas* method of farming and slash-and-burn techniques. Due to the region's adequate rainfall, the irrigation problems of other regions would not have been a factor here.

TARASCAN ARCHAEOLOGICAL SITES
The settlements established by the Tarascan, listed as individual entries. These sites included Ihuatzio, Ixtepete, Janitzio, Patzcuaro, and Tzintzuntzin.

TARASCAN ARCHITECTURE
The style defining the construction of the culture's cities, emulating the traditions of other Mesoamerican groups while often innovative and unique. The Tarascan adopted the Mesoamerican custom of erecting pyramidal platforms for their temples and their

Tarascan bell

burial sites, but they also introduced a unique architectural style, one giving their cities individuality. This innovation was the *yacata*, a structure composed of three basic parts: a rectangular stepped pyramidal platform; a round stepped pyramidal platform attached to one side; and a stepped passageway connecting the two major portions of the monument.

All three portions of the structure formed the letter T when completed and joined. Made of rubble and stone slabs put together with mortar, the *yacatas* were faced with cut volcanic stones, called *xanamu*, similar to Inca structures. The *xanamu* were joined by mud mortar and had low-relief carvings. The interlocking methods used by Tarascan architects and builders were also Inkan.

TARASCAN ART
Esthetic expression that brought the group renown in the region, particularly in the field of metal ornamentations. The Tarascan handled metals by hammering, smelting, filigree, soldering, gilding and the lost wax techniques. Gold and copper alloys were treated with acids in the Tarascan metal workshops, so purer gold could be achieved in certain parts of the pieces. Other Mesoamerican groups highly prized this type of Tarascan work. Tarascan artistic products recovered include bells having the form of turtles, figurines, bracelets, earrings and plaques with turquoise decorations. Copper was available in Michoacan, silver in Jalisco and gold in Guerrero; thus the Tarascan had an ample supply of materials and fashioned their unique objects with amazing speed. They also carved obsidian in a special fashion, polishing it and shaping it into ornaments. Obsidian spool-shape ear plugs were discovered in Tzintzuntzan. The obsidian was so thin that it was almost transparent, and the plugs were decorated with turquoise. Lip plugs made of obsidian were also set with turquoise and gold. The delicacy of such pieces set the Tarascan apart as artistic masters. They also produced feather mosaics, turquoise mosaics and stone sculptures portraying coyotes. Some of these animal forms were manufactured as seats. Chac mool figures were produced as well, and masks of the rain god (probably Tlaloc) were popular. Textiles adorned with copper bells were a Tarascan speciality.

TARASCAN CERAMICS
Pottery that has been categorized into phases of development as evidenced in the capital of Tzintzuntzan. Included in these wares are bowls having human figures and negative and positive painted decorations. Spouted vessels, tripod bowls, double vessels,

pipes, squash-shape bowls and miniature polychrome pieces have also been recovered at the Tarascan sites.

TARASCAN DEATH RITUALS The burial ceremonies reflecting the religious and cosmological ideals of the culture. Burials of the Tarascan nobles and rulers were conducted in and around the *yacatas*, the monuments of their ceremonial complexes, and these rites were both solemn and elaborate. When a king died, his body was prepared for burial and then laid upon a platform. At that time the courtiers who would accompany the ruler into eternity were chosen. Seven women for each burial, and 14 artisans, servants and other courtiers were slain. When the king's grave was prepared, offerings were placed beside the body. Some burials were multiple, some single. Some individuals were buried in a flexed position. Skulls evincing cranial deformations were sometimes entombed separately. The grave offerings were generally ceramics, some "slain" by being smashed, copper pieces, gilt copper ornaments, gold and polished obsidian. The funerary ceramics were customarily decorated in black red or cream and gray, having geometric designs. *Ollas*, open bowls and plates were included in the offerings.

TARASCAN GOVERNMENT The administration of this culture based partly on defensive and military concepts and partly on the mixed society of the group. The Tarascan of pure lineage, those having had Tarascan ancestry, appear to have composed only about 10 percent of the overall population of the culture's territory. Other groups, including the Chichimec, entered the region to serve as vassals to the Tarascan aristocracy. Dominating the surrounding territories soon after their arrival in Michoacan, the original Tarascan expanded into the surrounding regions and conducted endless military campaigns to defend their realm. They confronted aggressive neighbors; the Aztec to the south and west and the Chichimec to the north. Establishing a series of fortresses on their borders and moving their capital to Ihuatzio, and then to Tzintzuntzan, the Tarascan were able to hand the Aztec and others stunning defeats. They also used a sophisticated spy system and intelligence agents posing probably as traders. These agents reported regularly and alerted the military units.

The military was an important facet of Tarascan society, although no special training school for Tarascan youths seems to have existed. It is not known if the Tarascans maintained special warrior orders or societies. The Tarascan king was the war chief as well as the administrator of internal and foreign affairs. He was called the *kansoni* and reportedly kept a large court, attended by many officials. He was informed by intelligence and the governors of the territories of Tzintzuntzan, Patzcuaro and Ihuatzio, the nation's three special provinces. The *kansoni* resided in one province while governors administered the other two. The king's palace was a handsome residence, staffed by officials who performed a great variety of tasks, including the maintenance of the royal zoo. Artists and craftsmen of the provinces were also represented at the court by their own officials.

Ruled by a strong line of kings, the Tarascan continued their state of military preparedness and waged war when-

ever necessary. In A.D. 1480, the Aztec ruler Axayacatl conquered the Valley of Toluca and attacked Tarascan holdings. After two battles, the Aztec withdrew from the region, humiliated. When the Aztec ruler Ahuitzotl returned with another force, the Tarascan king Zuanga met him on the field. The Aztec were routed again. Tarascan animosity toward the Aztec endured until the Spanish conquest, when the Tarascan ruler refused to support the city of Tenochtitlan in its efforts to fight off the invaders. When the Spanish turned on the Tarascan, they fought valiantly before being subdued.

TARASCAN RELIGION The pantheon and ceremonies reflecting this culture's spiritual values and worship. The presence of the Chichimec and other Nahua peoples in the Tarascan lands had an influence upon the religious rituals and concepts within the Tarascan kingdom. The Tarascan view of the universe, for example, was Nahual in its conception. Three separate realms were envisioned in this cosmos, each having its cardinal point of direction, patron deity and distinctive color. The Tarascan, also worshipped a pantheon of gods, and the national patron was Curicaueri, a fire god revered as the sun. The worship of the fire god and the moon reflected Inkan religious practices, and the Tarascan put particular stress on this aspect of worship. They maintained a calendar of religious observances and practiced human sacrifices in their ceremonial complexes. Self-mutilation, especially of the ear lobe, and the custom of splashing blood on altars and on offerings was common. The other deities honored by the Tarascans include Cueravaperi, the mother of the gods; Tariacuri, the god of the wind; Uinturopan, the goddess of corn, and Xaratanga, the goddess of fertility and subsistence.

The priests of the Tarascan temples were not celibate, and they carried tobacco gourds on their backs as insignias of their office. Tarascan temple hierarchy appears complex; a supreme high priest administered the religious affairs of the realm, in addition to secular administrators and military commanders.

TARASCAN TRADE The exchange of goods and their transport locally and with far-flung territories held by other cultures. The actual extent of Tarascan trade is unknown, but it is obvious that the artistic industries of the Tarascan were designed for markets other than their own. The intelligence system incorporated into trading practices by the Tarascan military was not unlike that of the Maya.

TARASCAN WARFARE The military campaigns and nature of the culture, evidenced by the supply of weapons uncovered and by the Tarascan reputation among contemporary cultures for military skill. The copper weapons and the ferocity of the Tarascan warriors allowed them to overcome the assaults of their more populous neighbors, particularly the Aztec. According to some scholars, the Tarascan overcame their enemies because they fought on their own terrain, thereby giving them the advantage. Military preparedness, maintained throughout Tarascan history, was another advantage, the military playing a distinct role in Tarascan society. Military intelligence was essential in various eras of Tarascan development, and provided an edge of a different kind. The full importance of military aspects of Tarascan culture has not been fully evaluated yet.

TARIACUARI A Tarascan national hero, the son of Pavacume, a local chief who married a lake-dwelling woman. Tariacuari unified his people, suffering personally in order to forge a nation. He had a son, Curatame, who continued his father's heroic efforts.

TARIACURI The Tarascan deity of the wind, honored in the temples and ceremonies of that culture.

TAYASAL A large Itza city in the Yucatan region, occupying five islands in Lake Peten and Ekixil. It was called *Noh Peten*, the Great Island, and was situated in Chol Maya territory. Twenty temples adorned the site, including a pyramid having nine steps, a retaining wall and a structure on the top level where a humanoid idol with squatting body and grimacing face stood. Another idol, having a rendering of the face of the sun outlined in mother-of-pearl with rays extending on all sides, as found in the pyramid as well. A half-rotted human shinbone hung from the ceiling of the temple dedicated to the god Kincanek on the pyramid. The bone was decorated with a crown emblem and was accompanied by a sack of bones on the floor. Censers and copal or maize leaves were stored there, as well as liquid amber. This appears to have been a temple reserved for the Itza nobility. The city was founded by refugee Itza after the fall of Chichen Itza, c. A.D. 1200. There were reportedly as many as 200 residences on the main island at one time. Ahau Canek, the ruler of Tayasal when it fell to the Spanish, had an elaborate government, including governors of the outlying districts. He was assisted by Kin Canek, his cousin, who was high priest. Tayasal dominated the region of Lake Peten-Itza.

TAYAUH Also called Quetzalayatzin, a son of King Tezozomoc of the Tepanec, named heir to the throne when his father died in A.D. 1426. He met opposition from his brother, Maxtla, who learned that Tayauh planned to strangle him at a banquet at the suggestion of Aztec king Chimalpopoca. Maxtla overpowered Tayauh, probably slaying him, and he then attacked Tenochtitlan, the Aztec capital, killing Chimalpopoca and the ruler of Tlatelolco as well.

TECALLI A white, onxylike stone used by Toltec artisans in fashioning highly prized ornaments. (See TOLTEC ART for details.)

TECAXIC See MATLATZINCA.

TECHOTLALATZIN A Chichimec ruler, the son of Quinatzin, who took the throne of Texcoco in A.D. 1337. Techotlalatzin welcomed groups entering the region and managed to advance the cause of Texcoco during his reign.

TECOLUTA RIVER A waterway in Veracruz, associated in some eras with the Remojada culture in the Classic Period (c. A.D. 1/250–900).

TECOMATE A small, neckless jar found in various ceramic phases. *Tecomates* were discovered in Ajalpan in the

Tehuacan Valley, dating from 1500 to 900 B.C., and in other early Mesoamerican sites. These vessels are also associated with the Maya Purron and Charcas/Phases.

TECPATL The flint, an Aztec day sign in their version of the *tonalpohualli,* the calendar system.

TEHUACAN A plain or depression that linked the Valley of Puebla to the Valley of Oaxaca in southern Mexico. Tehuacan is a treasure house of archaeological sites and materials, giving evidence of habitation and developmental processes, categorized in modern scholarship as the Tehuacan Sequence. (See TEHUACAN SEQUENCE.)

TEHUACAN SEQUENCE A series of cultural phases in the region of Tehuacan, a semiarid section of southern Puebla and northern Oaxaca. The sequence represents information spanning the artistic and cultural development in the region c. 7000 B.C. to A.D. 1520. As such it represents the evolutionary processes taking place from the hunter-gatherer periods to those of settled communities. The Tehuacan region was surrounded by caves and rocky shelters, and is an alluvial valley as well, encouraging agricultural development. The sequence includes nine phases.

Ajuereado. Dating to before 7000 B.C., a time in which small animals were hunted and wild plants were gathered as the basis of them.

El Riego. A phase that dates to just after 7000 B.C., containing evidence of plant domestication. Chili peppers, squash and avocados were harvested, and wild beans, seeds and a variety of amaranth gathered.

Coxcatlan. The phase dating from 5500 to 4500 B.C., and the period in which maize appears. The groups hunted small mammals and collected wild plants, fruits, seeds and pods and grew some crops. Mesoamericans of this era seem to have boiled or steamed their foods and consumed some substances raw. Flint points and flakes, scrapers, choppers and stone bowls were in use. Death rites had become part of the social structure, and included grave offerings.

Abejas. A phase in which pit houses were constructed, probably for seasonal habitation by microbands. Set on river terraces and alongside cave regions, the houses suggest evidence of some beginnings of crop domestication. The period is dated from 3400 to 2300 B.C. and is a time in which man domesticated dogs, as a food source and as hunting companions. Obsidian was in use, with stoneware and convex tools.

Purron. A phase dating from 2300 to 1500 B.C., giving evidence of food crops in the region. Accompany agricultural innovations and a change in local inhabitants' diets, as more and more domesticated products were available to them, are evident.

Ajalpan. A phase dating from 1500 to 900 B.C., when agriculture was firmly established in the Tehuacan region. Definite planting seasons were established, and villages were constructed close to the fields. It is believed that as many as 100 to 300 inhabitants lived in each village at the time. Female figurines carved in the region give evidence of developing religious practices. Male priests, shamans, were present, and women held certain rank. Pottery included the monochrome hematite red ware, including *teco-mates*. Rocker dentate stamps were used as tools to decorate ceramics.

Santa Marta Phase. Dated from c. 900 to 200 B.C., a period in which villages and the first ceremonial complexes were emerging in the region and elsewhere in Mesoamerica. Agriculture had become a way of life and the economic basis for cultures. Fields and hunting grounds were maintained, and hybrid plants were being developed. Tools and ground stones were refined and used in food preparation. The ceramics of the phase include monochrome white and gray, and some bichromes. Flat-bottomed bowls, silhouette bowls and bottles were made. The incised pattern of ceramic decoration was probably developed in this era. It is also believed that the *milpas* techniques of clearing the lands for farming originated at this time.

Palo Blanco. A phase dating from 200 B.C. to A.D. 700. Agricultural innovations, such as irrigation systems, are the hallmarks of this phase. New products consumed by Mesoamericans included tomatoes, peanuts, guavas and turkeys. Ceremonial complexes had residential districts annexed to them, and stone pyramidal platforms were being constructed, with ball courts and plazas. The phase ceramics included gray and orange varieties.

Venta Salada. The last phase of the Tehuacán Sequence, dating from c. A.D. 700/800 to 1520. A vast population inhabited the region, with some estimates ranging between 60,000 and 120,000 people. Intensive agricultural activity was under way, with the canal system of irrigation. Trade routes and enterprises were established and in use, and local products, such as salt, cotton and crafts, were valued. Kingdoms were emerging everywhere, as the cultures of the earlier periods began permanent settlements, permitting the development of sophisticated and complex systems of government in the region.

TEHUANTEPEC See ISTHMUS OF. (See also CERRO DE LAS MESAS; CHALCHUAPA; CHIAPAS DE CORZO; IZAPA; KAMINALJUYU; MAYA; OLMEC for details about trans-Isthmian cultures and their development.)

TEJALPA RIVER A waterway in the Valley of Mexico. The city of Calixtlahuaca was erected along its banks.

TELEMONES Toltec "Atlantean" warrior statues, colossal and geometric in design. (See ATLANTEAN [2]; TOLTEC ART.)

TELIXTLAHUACA See HUITZO.

TELOLOAPAN A Chontal Maya site in the frontier Maya lands, attacked by the Aztec emperor Ahuitzotl, with Alahuitzlan. The local Chontal Maya fled the region for safety in the traditional Maya domain.

TEMESI RIVER A waterway in southern Veracruz, associated with the cultural development of the gulf coastal lowlands.

TEMPLES See MESOAMERICAN ARCHITECTURE; see also under individual cultural group entries.

TENAYUCA A Chichmec city west of modern Mexico City, probably originating with a local culture called the Tenayucan or the Oztopolco. Called the Place Where Walls Are Made, the site was founded as a city c. A.D. 1224 by Xolotl and Nopaltzin, a Chichmec king and prince. The next rulers, Tlohtzin and Quinatzin, adopted Toltec customs. Tezozomoc ruled there before assuming the throne of Azcapotzalco. The city became the Chilchimec capital and was fortified and enclosed. At least six major construction phases were carried out until A.D. 1507, with Aztec influence visible by A.D. 1315. Some scholars believe the great pyramid of Tenayuca was the model for the Aztec temple in Tenochtitlan. It was a double pyramid, four-tiered, facing a plaza and decorated with long rows of serpents surrounding the base on three sides, forming a *coatepantli*, a serpent wall. The serpents, of mortar and stone, were originally plastered and painted various colors to honor the gods. Coiled serpent statues also were positioned at ground level on the north and south sides of the pyramid. Their crests identify them as Xiuhcoatl, the fire serpent, seen also in the older city of Teotihuacan. The pyramid also had a low platform and carved stone stairs. The low platform projected from the pyramid and was adorned with sculpted crossed skulls and bones. This monument, with its serpent wall, called a *coatepantli*, was no doubt dedicated to a sun cult. The gods Huitzilopochtli, Tlaloc, Mixcoatl, Itzapalatl, Chicomicoatl and Coatlique were worshipped there.

TENAYUCA PHASE A cultural development also called Aztec II, dated from A.D. 1200 to 1350. Black-on-orange wares were produced in this phase, decorated with stamps or irregular markings, including parallel lines and circular motifs.

TENECELOME The Jaguar-Mouthed People, a name given to the Olmec of the Formative Period (2000 B.C.–c. A.D. 250/290) in some records.

TENOCH The Aztec priest-king, the disciple of the god Huitzilopochtli, who led his people through the wilderness and through years of suffering. Tenoch was the ruler of the Aztec (Mexica) in A.D. 1325 when Tenochtitlan was founded as the group's capital. He encouraged the expansion of the city for 25 years. Because of Tenoch's revelations from Huitzilopochtli, Tenochtitlan was shown to the Aztec originally in a divine sign, which the priest-king predicted. The people were told to expect the image of an eagle perched on a prickly-pear cactus, devouring a serpent. Other omens mentioned by Tenoch included a white willow, a white field and a white frog. He also predicted that the heart of COPIL, the nephew of the god Huitzilopochtli, would mark the exact spot of the city. Copil had interfered in Aztec affairs during their original stay in Malinalco, and his heart was torn from his body and thrown "across the water," coming to rest in Tenochtitlan, on an island in Lake Texcoco. Throughout Tenoch's reign, the Aztec were vassal to other cities, especially to the Culhuacan and Tepanec. He died in A.D. 1376. (See TENOCHTITLAN.)

TENOCHAS   A name given to the Aztec by their contemporaries, an obvious reference to Tenochtitlan, the Aztec capital. At the same time, however, the Aztec had begun to refer to themselves as Mexica.

TENOCHTITLAN   The magnificent capital of the Aztec (Mexica), erected on an island near the western shore of Lake Texcoco in the Valley of Mexico at its founding in A.D. 1325. It is possible that the Aztec took over a site called Quanmixtitlan, already on the island. The name is derived from *tetl*, "rock;" *nochtli*, "cactus;" and *tlan*, a locative suffix. The city also may have been named in honor of Tenoch, the priest-king who prophetically announced the signs that would lead the Aztec to their eventual capital. He ruled the city for the first 25 years. Modern Mexico City now occupies that land. In 1473 A.D. Tenochtitlan was annexed to Tlaltelolco, which was a smaller, sister city on the same island. Both sites were linked by causeways and canals. The completed metropolis was so grand and immense that the Spanish, coming upon it, were struck speechless. Tenochtitlan extend to the marshes, merging into Lake Texcoco, and included Toltenco, the "place at the edge of the rushes"; Acatlan, "the place of the reeds"; Xihuitonco, "the meadow"; Atizapan, "whitish water"; Tepetitlan, "beside the hill"; and Amanalco, "the pool." In the first stages the capital was small, composed chiefly of a ceremonial complex and its surrounding residences. In time it would encompass all those places mentioned, extending east and west.

Because Tenochtitlan was a well-planned urban site, its streets were laid out in straight lines, leading to a central district. It was surrounded in time by a wall and a grid pattern was designed for both pedestrian and boat traffic, geometrically ordered and filled with fields, roads and canals of uniform size. Due to its island location, water traffic had to be guided skillfully. Originally, smaller mud islands were surrounded the main city, all of which were joined to the core. Tenochtitlan, is also translated as Place of the Prickly Pear, a reference to the Tenoch's prophecies. The city was the political heart of the Aztec Empire, a domain extending from the gulf coast to the Pacific, north to the deserts, south to the modern Mexican-Guatemalan border. The city had four major districts at its beginnings: Cuepopon, the northern district, was called "the place of the blossoming of the flowers"; Teopan, the eastern district, was called "the quarter of the god"; Moyotlan, the southern district, was called "the place of the mosquitoes"; and Aztacalco, the western district, was called "beside the house of the herons."

Causeways were constructed to link the city to the surrounding shores, and there were waterways, raised streets and expertly designed canals. Wooden bridges at the intersections over waterways could be removed in times of enemy attack. The causeways were in three of the four directions, linking the island at strategic points to the mainland. Dikes blocked the eastern side.

The ceremonial complex of Tenochtitlan was reported as having had more than 80 separate structures, surrounded by secondary complexes and rows of residences. This sacred precinct, called the *coatepantli*, was dedicated to the great religious ceremonies conducted throughout the year. The first temple erected here, probably during Tenoch's reign,

was a simple structure, called the *ayauhcalli*. As the city grew and the ceremonial complex became more elaborate and grand, the various precincts were enlarged. It is reported that as many as 8,000 men could dance in the temple plaza during religious rituals. The complex, built on a sumptuous scale, was designed to impress the populace with the power of the gods and of the state. The major temple was a double-pyramid shrine dedicated to Tlaloc and Huitzilopochtli. Other structures in this sector included ball courts, temples of Quetzalcoatl, the sun and the *tzompantli*, the skull wall.

The capital evolved slowly after the Aztec laid claim to the island in Texcoco. The lake extended southward to the freshwater resources of Lakes Xochimilco and Chalco. This landscape was subject to tides, floods and shallow marshes, and the Aztec and their neighbors used rafts to gather materials and to build embankments and waterworks for defense. Any original inhabitants of the islands were quickly absorbed into the Aztec community, becoming part of the Aztecs' *calpulli*-based society. Such *calpullis,* social groups or clans, were drawn on family groups, living in separate districts that provided administrative and governmental offices similar to the modern wards, precincts or districts. The *calpullis'* individual residences were laid out in precise geometric designs, generally single-storied, rectangular and having flat roofs and patios.

The palaces of the royal family, the nobles, priests and government officials were spacious and beautiful. The royal palace was a vast complex housing 1,000 guards, cooks, servants, nobles, courtiers and members of the king's harem. There were reportedly more than 600 nobles in attendance on the king at all times. As many as 300 men worked in the aviary and zoo of Tenochtitlan, a royal preserve. Garden estates, patterned after the ones in Texcoco, roof gardens and pavilions added beauty and magnificence to the royal household. In the compounds of the aristocracy, attached to the palace or nearby, there were palaces, residences, military housing and buildings for the warrior groups and the military orders. Priests had their own schools and training centers, and the temples of Tenochtitlan had similar attached buildings as well as arsenals and storehouses.

Tenochtitlan was founded in A.D. 1235, when the Aztec priest-king, TENOCH, led the Aztec to the island that would become their home. For 25 years Tenoch supervised the original building programs there, starting with the first small temple and mud-and-wattle residences. In the reign of ACAMAPICHTLI (A.D. 1376–c. 1391/96), stone buildings were erected. He also ordered religious ceremonies to be conducted and drew up laws and ordinances to govern the populace. During his reign the Aztec reportedly began wearing cotton clothing, having previously worn of maguey. Cotton came from the lowlands to the south and east.

At the time, the Aztec served as mercenaries for the more established city-states, particularly the Tepanec city of Atzcapotzalco. The Aztec involvement in Tepanec affairs reached its height under the Aztec ruler CHIMALPOPOCA, who reigned from A.D. 1415 to 1427. During this period the major religious complex of Tenochtitlan was enlarged. Chimalpopoca also laid out abundant *chinampas* for farming. According to one report, Tenochtitlan was invaded by a Tepanec force led by Maxtla, the heir to King Tezozomoc's throne. Chimalpopoca, who had been involved in the Tepanec power struggle after Tezozomoc's death, was slain.

In the reign of his successor, Itzcoatl (A.D. 1427–1440), the Tepanec besieged Tenochtitlan, but Texcoco and other allied city-states came to the support of the Aztec. The Triple Alliance was formed between Tenochtitlan, Texcoco and Tlacopan (Tacuba), with lesser city-states also involved. This Triple Alliance brought about the collapse of the Tepanec. Itzcoatl was advised by Motecuhzoma I and Tlacaelel. He began a revision of the Great Temple in Tenochtitlan and generally beautified the city.

In the reign of Motecuhzoma I (A.D. 1440–1469), Tenochtitlan and the Great Temple were transformed into splendors, the result of the expanding Aztec empire and tributes. Yet, Tenochtitlan also endured a series of natural disasters. In 1446 a locust plague destroyed many crops. In 1449 floods damaged the city and agricultural lands. Famine raged in the district for four years, and in 1450 the harvests failed and Tenochtitlan was struck by a snowstorm, which resulted in early frosts. Motecuhzoma strove to alleviate the suffering and to extend the empire. His successor, Axayacatl (A.D. 1469–1481), slew the ruler of Tlatelolco, Tenochtitlan's sister city, in 1473 and annexed that city. He also increased human sacrifices in the religious rituals.

During the brief reign of Tizoc (A.D. 1481–1486), the Great Temple was further enlarged. In the reign of his successor, Ahuitzotl (A.D. 1486–1502), the work on the Great Temple was completed, and the new shrine was dedicated. Rulers of many city-states arrived to take part in the festivities, and vast numbers of people were sacrificed over four days. All of the other temples in Tenochtitlan were refurbished for the occasion, and Ahuitzotl, a great military leader, brought tribute and captives back from his campaigns of imperial expansion. Thus the capital was vast and beautiful when Motecuhzoma II welcomed the Spanish into the city. (See AZTEC; entries on the individual rulers and AZTEC ARCHITECTURE and AZTEC ART for details.)

TENOCHTITLAN PHASE   A cultural development, also called Aztec III, dated from A.D. 1350 to 1450, having black-on-orange wares, including open bowls, plates, and tripod vessels. Lines, circles, animal forms and mystics symbols decorate these objects. The Aztec polychrome was also developed in this era, highly polished and sometimes painted inside.

TENOCHTITLAN RIO CHIQUITO   One of three Olmec sites on the Rio Chiquito near San Lorenzo, in the Olmec heartland region, southern Veracruz and Tabasco. The site, also called Tenochtitlan del Rio, honored the great Aztec capital by Lake Texcoco, was named by a local schoolteacher when discovered by an unknown individual in modern times. Tenochtitlan Rio Chiquito was a satellite of San Lorenzo and functioned in conjunction with Portrero Nuevo and Remolino. It is listed in some records as Tenochtitlan del Rio. The Olmec name for the site is unknown. Less than a mile long, Tenochtitlan Rio Chiquito extends in a north-south direction. Its structures are made of earth or clay. In the west group of mounds flanks long courts, one of which ends in a pyramidal mound, Olmec in design. It is believed that all ridges and mounds on the site were once

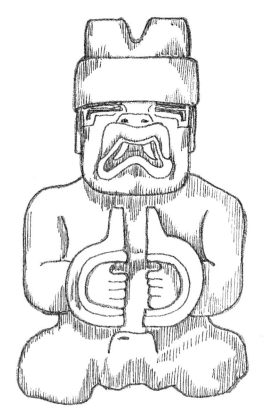

Olmec figure from Tenochtitlan del Rio

inhabited. A statue recovered there, called Monument I, depicts a woman lying on her back with a jaguar lying up on her, in the act of coupling. This statue is part of the Olmec were-jaguar cult.

TEOCALLI STONE   From *teocalli*, meaning "sacred house," this seat is believed to be an Aztec royal throne, shaped as a pyramid. The seat has stairs and hieroglyphic dates. A sun disk is above the seat or "altar," flanked by Huitzilopochtli, the Aztec national deity, and an image of Motecuhzoma I. The rear of the Teocalli Stone depicts an eagle on a prickly pear cactus, the sign augured by Tenoch for the founding of Tenochtitlan as the Aztec capital.

TEO-CHICHIMEC   Called the "true" Chichimec, the hunters and gatherers who wore animal skins, produced stone and feather objects, and used peyote as a hallucinogenic drug during religious rituals. Cave dwellers, the Teo-Chichimec were considered less advanced than the other Chichimec groups. They consumed rabbits, seeds and fruits, using yucca plant fibers for sandals. (See CHICHIMEC (1).)

TEOPAN   A district in the Aztec capital of Tenochtitlan, located in the eastern section. It was called the quarter of the god, a reference to ceremonial aspects of the city's public architecture.

TEOPANZALCO   A site within the city limits of Cuernavaca, Mexico, originally of Tlahuican control but taken over by the Aztec imperial forces. A pyramid, thought to be a replica of the Great Temple of Tenochtitlan in the Aztec capital, was erected at Teopanzalco. This pyramid had a double shrine on its summit, one dedicated to Tlaloc, the rain god, and the other to the titular Aztec deity, Huitzilopochtli. There are remains of earlier temples within the pyramid. Another temple in Teopanzalco was dedicated to the god Quetzalcoatl. Circular in design, therefore honors the deity in his form as Ehecatl, the wind. The city served as a crossroads for wandering groups and was called "the Place Where The Old Temple Stands." From A.D. 700, Teopanzalco was ruled by Xochicala, then by the Aztec.

TEOTENANCA A Nahual group, reportedly from the Aztlan region, the recorded original home of the Aztec (Mexica). The group moved to a site called Teotenanca, probably the modern Tenango del Valle in the Valley of Mexico. They fought as allies of the Toltec in some military campaigns conducted by that group. Six clans of Teotenanca migrated to Chalco at a later period.

TEOTIHUACAN A vast city located in a once-forested region adjacent to the Valley of Mexico, some 30 miles north of modern Mexico City. Begun in the Formative Period, c. 200 B.C., and enduring until c. A.D. 650/750, Teotihuacan was a planned metropolis that influenced the entire region of Mesoamerica, providing a model for artistic enterprise and urban sophistication. Its city-state government provided other groups with a cohesive and comprehensive pattern of unification and mutual benefits. The city maintained dominion over other territories. It linked vast cultural regions with trade and with a steady flow of arts and crafts that directed the development of local ceramic industries. Teotihuacan became a central marketplace and the heart of expansion and economic renaissance. It had an even greater influence on Mesoamerica in matters concerning religion and the ceremonial practices. By the time the Spanish arrived, the city was celebrated in Aztec literature as "the place where the gods convened," a reference to the city's cosmological outlook. The city was exalted to legendary status, and memories of its achievements endured long after it was abandoned.

The original setting for Teotihuacan, which eventually covered more than eight square miles, was a rich alluvial plain some 190 miles in diameter, surrounded by hills. Lakes and streams provided salt, fish and aquatic products, as well as lines of communication and routes for steadily increasing trade that the city developed and maintained as an essential to its economic base and its status of dominance over other cultures. Because of its unique location, Teotihuacan also had access to vast quantities of wood, to good clay and to nearby obsidian reserves, all of which were put to use in its various craft industries. The San Juan River flowed through Teotihuacan's plain, and nearby was the extinct volcano Cerro Gordo.

Teotihuacan was one of the largest cities constructed in the preindustrial world. In its final eras, in fact, the metropolis was vaster than that of Imperial Rome. The builders of the city, called the Lords of Wisdom by the cultures coming after them, appear to have attracted followers from the surrounding settlements, some of which were in decline due to changing environmental conditions and political upheavals. Such groups were welcomed in Teotihuacan,

Atetelco mural

occupying specific districts of the city. Even after Teotihuacan collapsed, the city was revered as a holy place and as the site upon which miracles of the human spirit had taken place. The Aztec (Mexica) emperor Motecuhzoma II made pilgrimages to Teotihuacan during his reign because of the ill omens that beset him just before the arrival of the Spanish and because of the city's lingering influence.

The city's Lords of Wisdom conducted its affairs and ceremonies honoring the deities Tlaloc and Quetzalcoatl. In time these administrators became cultural, religious, political and trade negotiators having far-flung influence. They were probably Nahua in origin, but other groups, such as the Zapotec, were known to have taken up residence in Teotihuacan as well. The Totonac also recorded a place in the construction eras of the site as it was an honor to share in the glories and fame of Teotihuacan.

The city's name means "the Place of the Gods" or "the Place Where Men Become Divine." In or around 200 B.C., the city served as a regional ceremonial complex. Cuicuilco, the neighboring site, began to decline at the time and by A.D. 150 was no longer a competitor. Probably many Cuicuilco craftsmen went to Teotihuacan to work. Five developmental stages have been recorded for the city:

Patlachique. A cultural development that lasted from c. 100 B.C. to A.D. 1. Two settlements were started in Teotihuacan at the time, and some of the ceremonial buildings around the Pyramid of the Moon were already in progress. According to some estimates of population in this phase, as many as 5,000 people inhabited the site. Teotihuacan was earning religious prominence, and settlers from surrounding territories came seeking intervention in various affairs, especially agriculture and human fertility.

Tzacualli. a cultural development that lasted from A.D. 1 to 150, a period of increasing population in Teotihuacan. Some estimates state that as many as 30,000 people inhabited the city in this phase. There is evidence that Oaxacan joined the new arrivals. The original Pyramid of the Sun was completed in this era, and the foundations for the Pyramid of the Moon and the Temple of Quetzalcoatl were laid.

Miccaotl. A developmental stage taking place from A.D. 150 to 250. This is the period of maximum expansion in Teotihuacan, when the resident population reached approximately 45,000. It was also a period of building and consolidation of the far-flung holdings of the city.

Tlamaimilolpa A developmental phase occurring from A.D. 300 to 500. The Ciudad was completed in this period, and the population is estimated at 65,000 to 100,000. The Temple of Quetzalcoatl was enlarged by a platform, in the *talud-tablero* style. The people of the city were in contact with other groups on the gulf coast, probably participating in trade with them there.

Xolalpan. This developmental period took place from A.D. 500 to 650, and is designated by continuing Teotihuacan prominence and by pottery innovations. The Teotihuacan artists also made designs in plano relief, symbolizing religious concepts in ornamentations and life-size figures. The ceramics of the period included thin orange, probably imported from Puebla.

In planning the city, the lords of Teotihuacan brought complex designs and innovations into play. The ceremonial complex was designated as a separate entity, with residential districts surrounding it. The city not only had to accommodate the religious aspects of a ceremonial complex but had to provide shelter and public worship stages for the thousands of pilgrims who streamed to the site for the scheduled observances. An administrative complex was also needed within the city. It is still a mystery as to how Teotihuacan came to hold such a pivotal role in Mesoamerican affairs of the time. The precise foundation for the city's ultimate power is undocumented. Religious, economic or even military might may have brought the city to its position of primacy, or perhaps a combination of all three. When Cuicuilco collapsed and was destroyed, Teotihuacan acquired control over that city's outlying regions and prospered. By this time it was involved in vast trade enterprises and had incorporated other territories into its sphere, through alliances, threats, intimidation or the simple hope of other cultures to share in Teotihuacan's vision of prosperity. The city's influential classes already controlled vast amounts of raw material and manufactured goods. In time, Teotihuacan would expand its economic influence into Morelos, Tlaxcala, Hidalgo, Tikal in the Maya domain and even into the vast ceremonial complexes of Kaminaljuyu and Cholula. The city had been originally provided with stages and complexes to meet all of these challenges. The grid map of the site indicates that it was the most systematically designed urban site in all Mesoamerica, laid out in a typical north-south axis, just 17 degrees east of true north. The primary purpose of this original axis, now called the Avenue of the Dead, is unknown. Markets, temples, plazas, palaces, apartments, waterways, reservoirs and a sophisticated drainage system were incorporated into the formal design. The Avenue of the Dead was intersected by an east-west axis and other streets. The east-west axis joined the Avenue of the Dead at the Citadel, the probable administrative core.

The natural resources of the San Juan River were used in the construction and original planning of Teotihuacan. The river water was channeled through the city, diverted first to the east and then to the west, flowing ultimately into a lake on the southeastern side. Channels were directed to the various districts of the city, and the river also served as

a large-scale irrigation system. A series of wells were dug to provide additional water systems.

The city districts were clearly delineated by walls, which may have been defensive in design or simply urban boundaries. *Chinampas* were located in the southwest and in the east. Other architectural innovations included the arrangement of temples so that the sun's rays emblazoned the structures at a given hour on a designated day of the year. *Talud-tablero* architecture dominated, but the *tablero*, the rectangular form, was always larger than the *talud*, the sloping base used as a support. The interiors of many structures were made of adobe, while the interiors were faced with volcanic stones set in clay and covered with lime. The builders used a mixture of *tezontle*, porous volcanic stone set into clay, mortar and gravel. The walls, ceilings and floors were covered with plaster, painted and then given a high-sheen polish. Roof beams were made of wood, as were the vertical supports, lintels and pilasters. Huge tree trunks were also used to support platforms. The buildings outside of the ceremonial complex were usually of one story, having flat roofs, decorated with ceramics. Spouts were used to drain the roofs. The buildings were designed with interior courtyards, as well as wide doorways and arcades.

During its period of domination, Teotihuacan was the creative center of Mesoamerica. Its inhabitants, and probably people of surrounding territories, believed that it was the seat of human existence, when the sun and the moon rose from the fire into which two deities had thrown themselves on behalf of humankind. Murals in Teotihuacan depict this and other legends. The city reflected the cosmological view that it thrived in the period in which time began in the fifth sun for humankind. The people of Teotihuacan believed in the fifth sun and derived energies from their faith. Its purpose was to keep the sun in the heavens, giving the city the status of a major shrine that attracted people from all districts. Later Mesoamerican cultures, especially the Aztec, would imitate the city in this regard as well. With this critical religious and symbolic role, Teotihuacan began to attract a vast population. It was governed by a hierarchical system of priests and rulers. The city became a pilgrimage site, and the state religion flourished. The rulers of Teotihuacan were able to point to the site itself as proof of their sacred claims. The Pyramid of the Sun stood above a cave, formed by a lava flow and ending in several chambers that were enlarged and embellished. Teotihuacan actually arose in a region abundant with such caves, called *Oxtoyahualco*, "the circle of caves" in Nahuatl. Such caves were held sacred as early as the time of the Olmec. They were thought to be the entrance to the underworld and the source of both the sun and the moon.

In order to maintain the religious standards that the city had encouraged and to accommodate pilgrims, the ceremonial complex was constructed on the Avenue of the Dead. The major monument of Teotihuacan faced west on the main axis. This temple stood on a pyramidal base and measured more than 200 feet, with a 700-foot base length. Four-tiered, the pyramid was probably of the *talud-tablero* design originally. The interior was of adobe brick and the exterior of volcanic stone with a lime coating. On the opposite end of the Avenue of the Dead was the building called the Pyramid of the Moon, four-tiered and having a platform with five steps. A plaza, designed as a companion structure and the site of many major ceremonies, held 10 shrines and 10 altars. The Pyramids of the Sun and the Moon thus set the standard for Teotihuacan's architectural masterpieces.

The temple of Quetzalcoatl, which also honored the god Tlaloc, was built during two separate phases in the Citadel. The outer portion, of the *talud-tablero* design, was built c. A.D. 300, with terraces that were probably covered with painted stucco. The inner temple, dating to an earlier period, was adorned with *tablero* panels of feathered serpents, stylized heads of the creatures forming a pattern, beside Tlaloc figures. A grand staircase with balustrades was decorated with more serpents, their eyes set with obsidian. The sculpture was painted, and seashells and water symbols were incorporated into its design. This structure was later built upon to allow a newer version. The Citadel, a rectangular complex with pyramidal bases and surrounded by raised areas on three sides, was at the junction of the Avenue of the Dead and the east-west axis formed by the well-regulated streets. This was the religious and administrative core of the city. A Great Compound, the city's marketplace, was across from the Citadel. Lesser temples were built in clusters surrounding small courtyards; among them were the Temple of Mythological Animals and the Temple of the Jaguar. The Plaza of the Four Temples was also erected there. All these sites had courts that probably served as stages for dances and rituals; some were depicted in murals in the city.

The palaces of the noble priests of Teotihucan are epitomized by the Palace of the Quetzal Butterfly (*Quetzalpapalotl*). This complex was designed to allow a central court to open onto porches, an arcade and three large chambers. The complex, rather formally structured, was probably used to accommodate audience or for administrative purposes. Separate apartments for the residents are situated at the rear of the court. The pillars, carved in relief, which adorn the court depict mythological creatures and water symbols. Some pieces of the design, which were of inlaid obsidian, were originally painted in polychrome. Inset panels above the pillars bear painted decorations, including the Teotihuacan year-sign. The lower walls were covered with murals.

The Jaguar Palace was joined by a courtyard to the Palace of the Quetzal Butterfly. A stairway incorporated into the design is carved with snake rattles. Murals of jaguars adorn the lower walls of the various rooms of this complex.

Those residential districts of Teotihuacan not intended to house royalty are the most striking examples of the architectural and planning skills of the Lords of Wisdom. Separate residential districts were erected for the growing population. These include Atetelco, Tepantitla, Tetitla, Tlamimilolpa, Xolalpan, and Zacuala.

Within these districts the city planners erected a vast array of apartment compounds. There were 2,000 such apartment compounds. They were generally one story and surrounded by high, windowless walls, which were made of stone and cement and covered with lime plaster. Some were small in size, but there were much larger apartments as well. The

Teotihuacan Butterfly Palace carving

interiors were divided into patios, rooms, porticos and passageways, and each compound had one temple platform, usually in a courtyard. Kitchen hearths provided room for ceramic stoves with three-pronged burners.

The interior walls of the apartments were made of stone or adobe, surfaced with concete and plaster. The floors were laid with the same durable materials. Patios had drains, and there were entire drainage systems beneath the floors of the residences. All of the apartment compounds were identical, and all had drains in place before the foundations were completed. Any apartment that was renovated because of wear or damage, followed the same design. The number of people who could live in the apartments is unknown, but they probably accommodated the entire population comfortably.

The Tlamimilolpa district was obviously designed for people of lower rank, and apartments there were small and less gracious. Teotihuacan also had certain districts that housed workshops for the obsidian markets and other artistic endeavors. Excavating more than 600 such workshops. These *barrios* were also home to a variety of ethnic groups who lived in Teotihuacan. Groups such as the Zapotec maintained their own religious rites.

Tlaloc mural from Teotihuacan

The statues of Teotihuacan were designed to enhance the architecture of the ceremonial structures. They were often massive, geometric in style and monumental in appearance. A colossal statue of a god was sculpted in the form of a square pillar carved on four sides in relief. The *talud-tablero* style dominated the carving, with the god's skirt and torso incorporated as an essential part of the design. The statue of the "Old God"—the deity of fire—however, is vibrant, having a remarkably sensitive face and clearly depicting the weight of the brazier on his head.

Teotihuacan artists were especially noted for masks, carrying on the Olmec tradition of working semiprecious stone. Small masks, are unusually realistic portraits, while the larger ones demonstrate the monumental, geometric grace of the statues in the city. The masks may portray gods, and some were made with holes so that they could be fastened onto a support and provided with accessories of cultic value. The masks were made of basalt or of white and green onyx. Sometimes they were covered with small fragments of coral or turquoise, for a mosaic effect. The eyes of the masks were often fashioned with inlaid mother of pearl, and obsidian was used as well. Teeth were made with shells.

The Teotihuacan artists excelled in the creation of murals. The surviving wall paintings demonstrate technical skill and a sureness of style and vision. The theme of these murals are mostly religious. There are static processions of deities, priests, mythical creatures and symbolic emblems. Very complex ritual offering scenes are accompanied by scenes depicting dances and games. Some of these scenes are set in the watery paradise of the god Tlaloc.

The murals were polychrome, with red serving as the dominant color. Other shades used were white, orange, pink, blue, green and yellow. The paintings were made in fresco style, with the colors put onto a wet lime base coat. The figures depicted are quite formal, emphasizing the rigidity of the wall and the confined space of each chamber. The backgrounds are often filled with creatures having animation and vibrancy thereby creating a sense of dimension.

The ceramics of Teotihuacan varied in design, shape and technique. They included jars, bottles and cylindrical tripod vases, well known in Mesoamerica, having conical covers. Decorations were incised, engraved, or were in relief, cloissone or champleve. Paintings were negative or positive, applied before and after firing. Thin orange was popular in the city. Teotihuacan also manufactured polychrome incense burners and candeleros as well as cream bowls. A variety of tools used by the artisans have been recovered. These included awls, knives, obsidian blades, and scrapers.

Teotihuacan had an impact on Mesoamerica because of its cosmological and religious life. Later cultures viewed the site as the source of creation, the origin of human existence. It was the stage for rebirth and resurrection among chosen souls. Several other religious themes evolved as well, displayed in murals and in other decorative art forms. These include rain god worship, the rain paradise, butterfly scenes, war scenes, smoking altars, and lightning scenes.

Butterfly Cluster. This religious theme, possibly depicting human souls with the god Quetzalcoatl, again reflects a promise of immortality. Women dying in childbirth in Teotihuacan were believed to have a special claim to eternal life.

Lightning Scenes. Images of jaguars blowing trumpets and of lightning flashes are found in lightning scenes. Thunder is demonstrated by scrolls bearing the symbols for noise. The association with Tlaloc is obvious, but these scenes also may revere other deities.

Rain God Worship. The adoration of Tlaloc, the god of rain, held an important place in Teotihuacan's ceremonial rites in the various districts. Murals depict Tlaloc with Zapotec scrolls, the artistic device used to demonstrate speech. The god's domain is also portrayed with jaguars, starfish, flowers, warriors and other religious symbols.

Rain Paradise. This religious theme born of Tlaloc's promise of a lovely eternal abode is depicted in many ways in Teotihuacan. In one scene water flows from a spout guarded by jaguars. A man in the scene has scrolls emanating from his mouth to demonstrate the praise he is offering to the god and his watery paradise.

Smoking Altars. The scenes of smoking altars depict offerings, pottery, food, doves and incense being burned. These paintings are of veneration and ceremony, but they also may depict the act of cremation in mortuary rituals.

War Scenes. Military activities were identified with the religious purpose of Teotihuacan because war was an opportunity to take victims for religious sacrifice. These scenes depict a possible military dynasty in the vast metropolis. Owls, arrows, shields and eagles serve as military symbols.

Teotihuacan maintained a clearly stratified social system. The city's architecture and urban planning strongly suggests a nucleus of power and authority, and the name ("the Place Where The Gods Convened") given the city by later civilizations indicates its important role. Public architecture of the scale found in Teotihuacan also indicates that an entrenched aristocracy had a limitless labor force at its disposal.

Teotihuacan ceramic jar

The murals of Teotihuacan also demonstrate its various societal levels. The parades of nobles and priests and the depictions of the military castes provide information about the city on a day-to-day basis. A unique aspect of the murals, however, is the fact that the smaller persons shown are not in obvious service to a noble, and no one is shown in servitude, except captives of military campaigns.

Teotihuacan's leaders were involved in both the administrative and the religious life of the city. They appear to have served two separate functions, and other social levels acted on their direction. The aristocracy was afforded palatial housing, and in keeping with the city's designated religious role, they were buried within the ceremonial complexes, called *teotl*, in their tombs. These aristocrats expected to rise again as gods; they were referred to in religious myths and Nahua literature as those who had gone to join the gods.

A sixteenth-century poem gave an account of the gatherings of the deities and the nobles in Teotihuacan. The theme of these spiritual encounters and their subsequent revelations permeated the city's art and architecture.

Below the nobility were the commoners, who were divided into five separate groups: farmers, craftsmen, merchants, bureaucrats, and foreigners.

Farmers lived within certain districts of Teotihuacan or else in nearby settlements, such as the site called Maquixco. There were apartment complexes in these communities, but poorer materials were used for their construction: adobe rather than concrete. While the apartments had fewer and smaller rooms, some were grouped around plazas, as in Teotihuacan. The farming communities were of vital importance to the city, because of the huge local population and because of its role as a pilgrimage destination.

Craftsmen maintained many workshops in Teotihuacan, and worked with obsidian. Craftsmen were in considerable demand to provide the goods needed to maintain a thriving trade. Craftsmen and artisans may have been recruited from such places as Oaxaca, which would have led to a population decline in these cities. Teotihuacan offered housing and a safe and stable environment. In most crafts skills

were hereditary, with parents passing them on to their own children.

Merchants were those people who took part in the vast trading enterprise of Teotihuacan. They were probably a hereditary group as well, answerable to the nobility for their profits and for the protection of the trade routes. These merchants and traders did not assume the importance of their later Maya or Aztec counterparts, but their presence provided Teotihuacan with certain economic stability.

Bureaucrats were a vital part of the administrative structure governing not only the city but surrounding territories. Learned and educated commoners could achieve positions of trust and considerable wealth as a result of their effort. Most answered to a director of higher rank, however, and the reins of the administrative and trade bureaucracies would have rested in the hands of the nobles. Some aristocrats also may have served as chiefs of small groups or ethnic leaders.

Foreigners consisted of culturally divergent groups inhabiting the city and maintaining their own traditions while working with other foreign elements within the city. Oaxaca and people from Monte Alban have left evidence of their presence in Teotihuacan, and some Maya ceramics were found there, perhaps from trade.

The cause and effect of the collapse of Teotihuacan c. A.D. 650/750 is under debate. The city could have declined as a result of dwindling resources, especially wood. Agricultural lands may have been exhausted, and irrigation problems may have arisen. Other city-states, such as Cholula, Xochicalco and El Tajin, were also on the ascent, perhaps becoming competitors. When Teotihuacan was abandoned, at least some of its inhabitants moved to the emerging cities. A legend tells that the *Tlamatinime*, the Lords of Wisdom or the great sages, left to follow their god to a more enlightened place. As many as 2,000 to 5,000, however, remained in various districts. Another legend recounts that the Lords of Wisdom remained to complete a spiritual work called the *Book of Dreams*. Whatever the cause for collapse or the numbers abandoning the site, Teotihuacan remains a remarkable interlude in the cultural development of Mesoamerica, having attaining spiritual and artistic heights that influenced an entire region and spurred other groups to further advances of their own.

TEOTIHUACAN MURALS   Unique art forms found in the great city of Teotihuacan that demonstrate artistic skill and portray religious themes. There are 40 separate structures with murals incorporating over 300 designs. The murals date to c. A.D. 500 and are studied in the following groups:

Atetelco Palace Murals.   Located in the Patio Blanco, these incorporate diamond borders. The murals depict the rain god, Tlaloc, with his traditional staff and spears, representing lightning. There is a coyote in serpentine form and a highly stylized jaguar in the panels.

Jaguar Palace.   Another grouping of murals, using a Tlaloc design border. Jaguars dominate the themes employed here. One such creature holds a conch shell, a depiction that is traditionally associated with the rising of the sun.

Palace of Quetzalpopolotl (the Palace of the Plumed or Feathered Butterfly). Located above the Temple of the Jaguar this palace contains more murals. Many designs here are continuations of other structures. The use of square columns with reliefs of butterflies and parrots is of particular interest.

Palace of Tepantitla, another Tlaloc-inspired set of murals. The god is represented along with his paradise, a recurring theme in Teotihuacan mythology. A ball game court is also depicted here.

Temple of Feathered Shells. Contains low relief carvings of plumed conches. Delicate flowers adorn the murals, with green parrots in provocative poses.

Tetitla Palace Murals. There are 56, quite formal in style. These murals use religious symbols and were painted on wet plaster with colors made out of various local mineral deposits. Elaborate and beautiful, the frescoes include depictions of priests, water birds, vultures, coyotes, jaguars and conch shells. Tlaloc is portrayed in one panel, designed to reflect his watery domain.

TEOTITLAN DEL CAMINO   A site on the Oaxaca and Tlaxcalan border, dating to the Post-Classic Period, A.D. 900–1521. The relation of the people of Teotitlan del Camino to the Aztec Empire is unknown.

TEPALCATEPEC BASIN   A region in Michoacan, bounded on the north, east and west by regional sierras. Apatzingan, a site in the basin, dates to the Early Classic Period (A.D. 250 to 600) and contains evidence of habitation and phases of ceramic development. Two other regional ceramic developments, the Chumbicuaro and the Delicias, preceded the Apatzingan Phase.

Chumbicuaro. A cultural development sparsely documented as a phase but offering red and gray ceramic wares having incised decorations. Bowls and ollas were recovered from this phase area.

Delicias. A cultural development exhibiting four types of ceramic wares: red on brown, red on buff, polished and plain. Other ceramics of the phase include cream to dark gray with a dull polish. *Ollas* were the basic forms uncovered. Some shell and pyrite ornaments were manufactured in this phase as well as pyrite mirrors. Two figurines were also discovered.

Apatzingan. A cultural development that included red-on-brown wares and plain ceramics in the shape of *ollas* and deep, in-rimmed bowls with flaring walls. Some red-on-brown pieces, incised, and a figurine were discovered dating to the Apatzingan Phase.

TEPALCATEPEC RIVER   A waterway that joined with the Balsas River to form a basin or depression in southern Mexico, separating the Mexican Plateau from the Oaxaca and Guerrero highlands. In southern Michoacan the river formed yet another depression, the Tepalcatepec Basin. (See TEPALCATEPEC BASIN.)

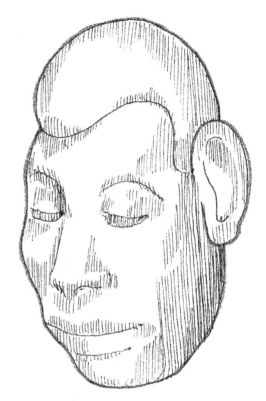

Ceramic Tepanec head

TEPANEC   One of the great nomadic people who entered the Valley of Mexico during the Late Classic Period, founding their capital, Azcapotzalco, c. A.D. 1250. The city endured until A.D. 1428. Xolotl, the king of the established Chichimec group in the Valley of Mexico, welcomed the Tepanec, who came from Chicomoztoc (the Land of the Seven Caves), home to the Aztec (Mexica) and others. Under their ruler, Acolnahuacatl, the Tepanec took over Azcapotzalco, called the Place of the Ant Hill of the People, the city may have been a vassal of Teotihuacan. In time the Tepanec emerged as one of the most powerful groups in the Valley of Mexico. They claimed to be the true descendants of the legendary king Matlaccoatl, grandfather of Acolnahuacatl. They also claimed to have come from Tamoachan, the mythical hill of special religious rites. The Tepanec were related to the Otomi people, using the same sort of weapons, tools and slings in their earlier stages. The sling remained a favorite Tepanec weapon in military campaigns.

Acolnahuacatl married a daughter of Xolotl (a Chichimec ruler c. A.D. 1200) named Cuitlaxochitzin, and he welcomed smaller groups to become part of the Tepanec development. When he died, his son Tezozomoc took the throne. Born in A.D. 1320, Tezozomoc was one of the more vigorous rulers in the Valley of Mexico, living past the age of 100. He had great impact upon the region and the emerging Aztec (Mexica) Empire. Ferocious in battle and cunning in diplomacy and statesmanship, Tezozomoc began to build an empire. He claimed the inheritance of Teotihuacan, residing in one of the vassal cities of that great metropolis, and then drew upon many Teotihuacan traditions. He overthrew the cities of Tenayuca and Culhuacan, absorbing their cultures, including that of the host Chichimec. The Aztec, newly arrived, became his vassals and were compelled to serve as mercenaries. In time the Tepanec dominated almost all of the Valley of Mexico, parts of the Valley of Toluca in the north, as well as portions of Morelos in the south, regions that provided the Tepanec with taxes and tribute. The city of Azcapotzalco thus was provided with abundant agricultural products, clothing, ornaments and featherworks, all made elsewhere. In time artisans from other cultures were brought to Azcapotzalco to maintain their industries under Tezozomoc's direct control.

Cuacuapitzhuac, a son of Tezozomoc, became the ruler of Tlatelolco, Tenochtitlan's sister city, established by the Aztec on an island in Lake Texcoco. In 1473 Tenochtitlan absorbed Tlatelolco. In Tezozomoc's time, however, the cities functioned separately, with Tlatelolco a major market place and the heart of the Aztec trade enterprise. With Cuacuapitzhuac on the throne, Tlaltelolco was spared many of Tezozomoc's harsh demands. The Tepanec king also gave one of his daughters to the Aztec king in Tenochtitlan, HUITZILIHUITL. The son of this union was CHIMALPOPOCA, who became Tezozomoc's favorite.

In A.D. 1395 Tezozomoc began a campaign against Xaltocan, destroying that city-state and giving the site and its resources to the Aztec. He also sent armies into the gulf region to subdue groups there. He was present when Chimalpopoca inherited the the throne of Tenochtitlan. Because of Tezozomoc's favoritism, the Tepanec nobles began a series of debates in the council, attacking Tezozomoc for his unfair tactics. Tezozomoc was reportedly so undone by this treatment of himself and his grandson that he died of grief in A.D. 1426. Before dying, however, he began a military campaign against the city-state of Texcoco. Ixtlilxochitl, Texcoco's ruler, claimed dominion over all of the former Acolhuan lands, which gave him equal status with Tezozomoc. Ixtlilxochitl was slain after a fierce war, and his son, the celebrated NEZAHUALCOYOTL, went into exile.

Tezozomoc's death unleashed some serious consequences for the region. Tayauh, Tezozomoc's son, was named heir to the throne, but he was challenged by another son, MAXTLA. Chimalpopoca, the Aztec ruler, became involved in the struggle and advised Tayauh to poison Maxtla or to strangle him at a banquet. When that was reported to Maxtla, he sent a force to Tenochtitlan. Chimalpopoca, learning of his impending doom, dressed himself as the Aztec ruler and faced his foes calmly. Maxtla succeeded in killing Tayauh and took the throne. Maxtla also slew Tlacateotl, the ruler of Tlatelolco.

The Tepanec ruler reserved his real hatred for Nezahualcoyotl, pursuing the young prince, who escaped the Tepanec assassins in almost magical fashion, thus enhancing his reputation. The new Aztec emperor, Itzcoatl, wary of Maxtla, began to plot his overthrow. As Maxtla began demanding tribute and services, the Aztec resolve deepened. Finally, in A.D. 1428, the Triple Alliance was born: The forces of Tenochtitlan, Texcoco and Tlacopan united with other allies. Bent on destroying Texcoco, Maxtla suddenly confronted a rebellion, and he attempted to blockade Tenochtitlan. The Triple Alliance, which endured for some 90 years, put Azcapotzalco under siege in return, and the

Tepanec endured continual assaults for 114 days. A Tepanec general, put forth a last valiant effort to conquer the Triple Alliance, but he failed to rout them. Maxtla was dragged from his steam bath and slain. As a result the Tepanec were then controlled by Tlacopan. In time, the Tepanec became part of the Triple Alliance empire. As a model for the Aztec, Tezozomoc and the Tepanec provided skills and leadership. Tezozomoc's reign was emblazoned the minds of later generations in the Valley of Mexico.

TEPEILHUITL An Aztec (Mexica) agricultural festival honoring mountains. The Aztec imperial domain contained many mountain ranges, which Mesoamericans considered to be the residence of Tlaloc, the rain god and his dwarvish rain brewers. On this festival, images of mountains were paraded through the plazas and streets, and during the religious rituals five women and one man were slain.

TEPETITLAN A district of the Aztec (Mexica) capital of Tenochtitlan, founded in A.D. 1325. The name means "beside the hill."

TEPEXPAN A site near the city of Teotihuacan, dating to the Paleo-Indian Period (11,000–7000 B.C.). In 1947 excavations unearthed the first fossilized human remains in Mexico. Sealed by a layer of caliche (a deposit of calcium carbonate), the remains were originally identified as a male and then as a female. Dated to an era c. 8,000 to 10,000 years ago, the remains are important. In 1945 a mammoth skull and other bones from an imperial mammoth (*Mammuthus Archidiskodon imperator*) were discovered nearby, related to the Paleo-Indian Period activities in the region. (See also TEQUIXQUIAC for more information on Paleo-Indian sites.)

TEPEYOLLOTL An Aztec jaguar deity, associated with Tezcatlipoca. Called the "heart of the mountain," the god was believed to reside in caves and to have a specific relationship to HUITZILOPOCHTLI and TLALOC. The deity was also associated with warriors and with calendars.

TEPOZTECATL A deity also called Ometecuhtli, the patron of *pulque,* the liquor distilled from the maguey plant. A pyramidal complex at the ceremonial site of Tepoztecatl, south of modern Mexico City, was dedicated to the god and contained a statue of him. The summit of the pyramid was called the Hill that Sheds Light.

TEPOZTECO A Nahua group related to the Aztec (Mexica) and others coming from Chicomoztoc, the Land of the Seven Caves. They are credited with the founding of the city of Tepoztlan in the Valley of Mexico with the Tlahuica. The city was conquered by the Aztec in the reign of Ahuitzotl.

TEPOZTLAN A site south of Mexico City, also called Tepozteco in some records, founded by the Tepozteco and the Tlahuica in the Late Post-Classic Period (c. A.D. 1200/1250–1521). The pyramidal complex of the city was dedicated to the god TEPOZTECATL, also called Ometecuhtli, the patron of *pulque.* The patron of the city was Centzon

Totochtin, or "400 Rabbits," a name that refers to the many forms of intoxication possible from imbibing *pulque*. The summit of the pyramidal base of Tepoztecatl's temple was called the Hill That Sheds Light. This "House of Tepoztecatl" is a massive pyramid about 30 feet high, with walls six feet thick. Two stuccoed pillars at the entrance were carved with sun motifs and figures. The temple is composed of two chambers, and narrow passages were constructed within the platform leading to two separate levels. Tepoztlan is associated with the god Quetzalcoatl (Kukulcan), as the Toltec prince Ce Acatl Topiltzin who became Kukulcan is reported to have been born there.

TEQUISTLANTECO   The name given for the Chontal Maya in some eras. (See MAYA GROUPS, CHONTAL.)

TEQUIXQUIAC   An important Paleolithic Period site in the Valley of Mexico, where a fossil bone carving was found in 1870. A large fragment of the vertebrae of an extinct camelid had been carved to resemble the head of a wolf or coyote, or possibly a peccary. The carving, the only example of art available from the Paleo-Indian Period (11,000–7000 B.C.) or earlier, was discovered some 40 feet below the surface at Tequixquiac. The remains of a mammoth (*Mammuthus Parelephas columbi*) also were discovered on the site. This type of mammoth appears to have been a common prey of nomadic Mesoamericans in the Paleo-Indian Period. This find is important because it helps to establish the presence of megafauna in the region. The Paleolithic hunters did use megafauna as a source of meat, although encounters between humans and mammoth were probably rare and an actual kill even rarer. Also uncovered at the site was evidence of stone and bone industries. These manufacturing processes were involved in making Paleolithic tool kits, those weapons and articles designed to prepare carcasses and other products for consumption. The Tequixquiac sites predates the site at San Isabel Iztapan. (See also TEPEXPAN.)

TETEOINNAN   A deity of the Aztec (Mexica), worshipped in Tenochtitlan, the patron of fertility, the earth, medicine, birth and flowers. (See AZTEC GODS.)

TETZAUHPILLI   A deity worshipped in the city-state of Xochimilco as the patron of flowers and rain.

TEXCOCO (Tezcoco, Tetzcoco)   A site in the Valley of Mexico, called the Place of the Large Rocks in Nahuatl. This city-state had a long and complex history, involving many cultures and spanning important Mesoamerican eras of development. Texcoco began with the entrance of the Acolhua people into the valley, around A.D. 1168, although the Toltec occupied the site earlier. The Acolhua's first capital was Coatlinchan, on the eastern shore of Lake Texcoco, a site that would always remain affiliated with Texcoco. Another Acolhua city was Huexotla. In Texcoco, a Toltec-Chichimec ruler founded a new dynasty. He took control over the city's inhabitants and was joined by other groups from Oaxaca, importing laborers and artists to build royal resi-

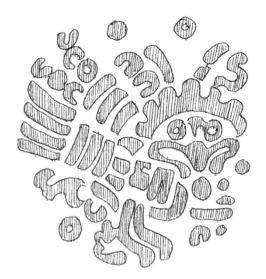

Texcoco owl stamp

dences and ceremonial complexes. The inhabitants of Texcoco appropriated Acolhuan and Toltec arts and customs. The refurbishing and building enterprises in Texcoco were so continuous and remarkable that in time the site would be called the Mesoamerican Athens. During this expansion and building era, the Texcoca became allied with the Aztec (Mexica), who were uneasy vassals of the Tepanec.

In A.D. 1418, the ruler of Texcoco, a man called IXTLIL-XOCHITL, the son of Quinatzin, declared himself the Acholhua emperor, on a political level with King Tezozomoc of the Tepanec in Azcapotzalco. The Tepanec, who had been watching the rise of Texcoco with concern, declared war. After a series of campaigns, Ixtlilxochitl took his son, NEZA-HUALCOYOTL, into the mountains, seeking refuge there. After hiding his son in the branches of a tree, Ixtlilxochitl met the pursuing Tepanec and was slain. When the Tepanec had left, Nezahualcoyotl climbed down from his hiding place and guarded his father's remains until retainers arrived to take them to a safe burial place. Nezahualcoyotl then fled into the wilderness; he later saw Texcoco given to the Aztec as part of their domain.

Nezahualcoyotl is one of the better-known Mesoamericans of the Post-Classic Period because of his own writings and influence. He spent so much of his youth evading Tepanec assassins that he gained a reputation for bravery and wizardry, as some of his escapes were miraculous. Once his retainers substituted a young man for him when escape seemed impossible, and another time he disappeared before his Tepanec pursuers in a cloud of smoke. After living for a time in Tenochtitlan, Nezahualcoyotl was allowed by the Aztec to return to Texcoco, and again the Tepanec tried to slay him. Itzcoatl, the successor to CHIMAL-POPOCA, the Aztec ruler slain by the Tepanec in the struggle for the Azcapotzalco's throne, taught Nezahualcoyotl and served as his patron. When Itzcoatl rebelled against the Tepanec in the wake of demands made by their ruler, Maxtla, Nezahualcoyotl and Texcoco served as valiant allies. Nezahualcoyotl went to the people of Tlaxcala and Huexotzinco for assistance. He also supported Tenochtitlan when it was placed under Tepanec blockade. By 1431, with the establishment of the Triple Alliance, which included Tenochtitlan, Texcoco and Tlacopan (Tacuba), and the destruction of Maxtla, Nezahualcoyotl began his reign in Texcoco.

Called the Sage of Anahuac by his contemporaries, Nezahualcoyotl was a poet king, drawing a brilliant circle about him called *tlamatini,* "the followers of truth." Making Texcoco a hub for the pursuit of the arts in the Valley of Mexico, he built a temple honoring a single god and forbade human sacrifice within its precincts. He established a music academy and opened his doors to artists from all groups. Nezahualcoyotl was also a counselor to the Aztec emperor Motecuhzoma I and took part in the Aztec wars of expansion. He is credited with the Golden Age of Texcoco, demonstrating a knowledge of law and the arts that influenced his neighbors and set high standards for workmanship and creativity. He wrote *Lamentations,* a philosophical treatise on values and meaning of existence. His immense palace at Texcotzinco had aqueducts, baths, gardens, stairways and over 300 rooms. Nezahualcoyotl also helped elect the successor to Motecuhzoma I, Axayacatl. When he died in 1472, his son and heir, NEZAHUALPILLI, was only seven. The boy was crowned in Tenochtitlan, with the Aztec emperor as his patron and guardian. Nezahualpilli assumed the same roles as his father in Texcoco and in Tenochtitlan. He helped elect Tizoc as heir to the Aztec throne when Axayacatl died. Both of these Aztec emperors had received stern lectures from Nezahualpilli, now the ruler of Texcoco, on the eve of their coronations. When Tizoc's short reign ended, Nezahualpilli again helped to elect the successor, Ahuitzotl. He remained at Ahuitzotl's side and supported his military campaigns and victories, benefiting from the Aztec imperial expansions. Few nations dared to stand against the armies of the Triple Alliance. Nezahualpilli also elected Motecuhzoma II as heir to the throne when Ahuitzotl died. The king of Texcoco, however, spent his declining years filled with dread, predicting the collapse of the great civilizations of the Valley of Mexico. Considered a sorceror with powers to predict the future, Nezahualpilli advised Motecuhzoma II to prepare for disaster. He died in 1515, just before the arrival of the Spanish and the destruction that he had foretold. His nephew, Cacama, was chosen by Motecuhzoma to succeed Nezahualpilli, and certain districts of Texcoco were ruled by other princes. This new administration was short-lived, as the city fell and Tenochtitlan fell to the Spanish forces.

TEXCOCO, LAKE A large body of water in the center of the Valley of Mexico, and the cradle for many civilizations throughout Mesoamerican history. Lake Texcoco is linked to Lakes Xoltocan and Chalco-Xochimilco. It has both saline and fresh water. Dikes and levees were used to promote irrigation on the lake, and *chinampas* (floating Islands) flourished there. Attempts by the Aztec (Mexica) to tame its floods, however, sometimes led to disaster. Causeways and canals were devised for the cities of Tenochtitlan and Tlatelolco as part of their original architectural designs. Lake Texcoco was called the Lake of the Moon by the Aztec and their contemporaries.

TEXCOTZINCO The site of King Nezahaulcoyotl's pleasure palace. This Texcoco ruler, called the Sage of Anhuac (Anahuac in some lists), erected his royal residence for his own use and to conduct meditations there with his followers, artists and musicians from all parts of Mesoamerica. The site, close to Texcoco, had aqueducts, baths, gardens and over 300 rooms.

TEXTILES The materials woven into clothing and other objects by Mesoamericans, who displayed a remarkable range of skills and excelled in the application of color and design. Little physical evidence exists for Mesoamerican textiles, as the materials have not survived. Images of the clothing worn by gods, rulers and participants in religious ceremonies, however, were reproduced on ceramics, in murals and on monuments. The Maya murals in Bonampak, for example, provide vivid reproductions of the elaborate costumes made by the textile industry of the region.

The manufacture of textiles probably began with the weaving of baskets and *petates,* the coiled mats of early Mesoamerican cultures. Cloth making is a complex process, demanding not only a knowledge of raw materials, such as cotton or wool, but the techniques of combing (untangling the raw material), softening and cleansing. Threads made by twisting or spinning the separate fibers could be dyed with prepared vegetable, mineral or animal substances. The backdrop loom and the spinning whorl were used. Some cultures spun by the drought-and-twist method. The cloth produced were decorated, painted, woven or embroidered, and brocading is evident in the Post-Classic Period (A.D. 900–1521). Such cloths however, has been dated to the Cotorra Phase in Chiapas de Corzo, c. 1500 to 1100 B.C.

Maguey fibers served as a stable textile material for the Tarascan and other groups. They made an exceptionally fine down from the fibers and added rabbit fur and feathers for elaborate styles. Cotton was a favorite material, dating in Mexico to 1700 B.C. Some groups also used ceiba fibers. In most groups the others used basic dress was elaborated upon in style and embellishment to denote rank and social standing. The Huaxtec were celebrated for their shirts, cloaks and mantles, and the Totonac for their embroidery. Dyes were obtained from the cochineal shellfish, alum, ferrous sulfates, vegetable roots, leaves, flowers and fruits. The textiles also ranged from white to brown cotton, and used yucca and agave fibers. Patron deities were granted the textile industries, and each group perfected styles to serve its needs. (See DRESS under individual cultures.)

TEZCATLIPOCA (1) A Toltec deity, called Smoking Mirror because of the black, magical mirror that he wore in place of a lost right foot. This god brought down plagues and disasters in the Toltec capital of Tula when Quetzalcoatl (Ce Acatl Topiltzin/Kukulcan) ruled there. For this reason he was called the bringer of grief, the destroyer. Obsidian was his symbol, reflecting darkness and gloom. The god had two doors in his chest, and brave souls could open these and take hold of his heart, thus gaining their "hearts' desires." Lesser souls were frightened to death by the doors. Tezcatlipoca is considered the originator of music in the Toltec world. He supposedly fell in love with the goddess

Xochiquetzal, the patron of flowers and love. When Quetzalcoatl was reborn in the form of Kukulcan, Tezcatlipoca collapsed into a shower of star dust.

TEZCATLIPOCA (2) An Aztec deity, obviously Toltec in origin, the head of a divine religious "complex" and considered omnipotent and omnipresent. This god was associated with the earth and the moon, and he was considered the patron of the north, the direction of the cardinal point.

TEZOZOMOC A Tepanec ruler, the son of King Acolnahuacatl, born in 1320 A.D. and one of the most influential leaders in the Valley of Mexico. He reportedly lived over 100 years and demonstrated statesmanship and the administrative genius that gained a vast empire for the Tepanec. Ferocious in battle and cunning in dealing with other cultures, Tezozomoc laid claim to Teotihuacan's heritage. In time, Tenayuca and Culhuacan became part of the Tepanec domain. Tezozomoc made the newly arrived Aztec (Mexica) his vassals and dominated all of the Valley of Mexico, part of the Valley of Toluca in the north and portions of Morelos in the south. A tribute system was used in these vassal states. His son, Prince Cuacuapitzhuac, became the ruler of Tlatelolco, the sister city of Tenochtitlan, and he married his granddaughter to Huitzilihuitl, the Aztec king. The son of this union, CHIMALPOPOCA, became Tezozomoc's favorite.

In A.D. 1395, Tezozomoc conducted a campaign against the city of Xaltocan, defeating the people there and giving the city's resources to the Aztec. Texcoco also became a target of Tezozomoc's wrath, and he sent troops to slay IXTLILXOCHITL and his son, NEZAHUALCOYOTL. The prince of Texcoco survived that and many other Tepanec assaults. Chimalpopoca's status as the favorite of Tezozomoc appears to have brought about a rebellion of sorts in Azcapotzalco, the Tepanec capital. Undone by the harsh treatment he received due to the complaints of the nobles, Tezozomoc took to his bed and died.

THRONES A royal symbol known throughout Mesoamerica from the Olmec to the Aztec. In some Maya murals, the ruling lords sat on elevated mats. In Kaminaljuyu around 600 to 300 B.C., rulers were attended by nobles or received obeisance from captives. At Palenque, Piedras Negras and other Maya centers, thrones were elaborate structures with reliefs and drawings depicting historic events or successes. The Aztec throne, epitomized by the Temple Stone of Motecuhzoma II, is an elaborate pyramidal structure created to observe the New Fire ceremony of A.D. 1507. This throne symbolized the role of the emperor as warrior and as divine mediator.

TICOMAN A cultural phase of the Formative Period in the Valley of Mexico, dating to c. 500 B.C. and named for a particular site in that region. The Ticoman style was unique and influenced developments in many regions. It was a pastoral phase, a return to simpler lines and forms. Ceramics of the Ticoman phase tended to be heavier than those of the past. These ceramics included pots and bowls of brown or red clay, with reinforced rims. The tripod was characteristic of the phase, having hollow supports that were made in the form of human female breasts or of swollen human legs.

The ceramics used as funerary offerings in the graves of the region during the Ticoman phase, included slipped red or white, highly polished pieces with some geometric designs. Most funerary vessels were decorated with black on red or with red or white on yellow. Some polychrome pieces have been recovered, including those decorated in black on red or white.

The figurines of the Ticoman phase were modeled, incised, gouged and covered with polished slip. Ticoman wares also are characterized by ear plugs, made of clay or volcanic stone. Cuicuilco, the great city-state arose in the Ticoman Phase. The architecture in Tlapacoya reflected Ticoman culture; the site has been called the most elaborate display of the artistic ideals of the period.

TIERRAS LARGAS A widespread ceramic complex, dating from 1400 to 1150 B.C. throughout the Oaxacan Valley and especially in its cave habitations. The vessels most frequently uncovered are jars and hemispherical bowls as well as *tecomates* and flat-bottomed vessels with convex curving sides. Most bowls were undecorated, but some had red bands at the rim or red chevron designs and red parallel stripes. Dentate rocker stamping was used as well, with the design incised in wet clay by shells or other tools rocked back and forth to bring about the intended pattern. A figurine belonging to the Tierras Largas phase was adorned with an elaborate headdress.

During the historical era in which the Tierras Largas complex dominated, buildings were being erected in Oaxaca out of pine posts, having walls of cane bundles, daubed with clay and roofed with thatch. Most inhabitants of these settlements added yards, storage pits, outdoor ovens, workshops and even burial plots to their property. The homes were generally constructed in clusters, with open spaces between them. These residences do not indicate any sort of social stratification. They are quite uniform and do not suggest rank or individual wealth. There were also no apparent distinctions made in the burials in this complex.

TIHOO The Maya site, now destroyed, upon which the Spanish city of Merida was built in the Yucatan, serving as the capital of the region.

TIKAL A Maya site, located about 12 miles south of Uaxactun in the northern part of the Peten (Putun) region of Guatemala. It was occupied as early as 600 B.C. and displays Chicanel Maya influences. Tikal has been called the supreme Maya ceremonial site, and it dominated the region in the Classic Period (c. A.D. 1/250–900). The structures of the ceremonial complex of Tikal covered more than six square miles, and there were vast areas for people to gather for religious rites and for sacrifices. Originally there were over 3,000 separate buildings in Tikal, with thousands more at lower levels, which were covered over in various phases of construction and renovation. An estimated 25,000 or more people lived there. The ruler Yax Moch Xoc is recorded as having founded the city's dynasty.

Earthworks were built on the city's perimeters to deflect possible advances from hostile groups from any direction. Tikal was graced by as many as 200 stelae and altars, which served to decorate the various ceremonial structures. Stela 29 recovered there is dated to 6 July, 292 A.D., according to the Western calendar. Tikal was erected near a large stand of breadnut trees, a popular staple of the region.

The heart of the city was the plaza, which was of the usual Maya design, and was the assembly point for the people. It was joined by the Northern Terrace and the Northern Acropolis. Four distinct floor surfaces have been uncovered in this Grand Plaza, the first dating to 150 B.C. and the last one to A.D. 700. The North Acropolis faces the plaza and is said to have contained approximately 100 separate structures, one layered beneath another. A temple dedicated to the jaguar god of the underworld faces the Grand Plaza, originally a structure 145 feet high, constructed of limestone. A stairway graces the exterior. The nearby Central Acropolis contains many structures, including a palace with five levels. Another palace was constructed beside it having a rear platform and a temple that is Teotihuacan in style. A ball court completes the design, as well as a second 125-foot-high temple.

The Western Plaza contains a temple 190 feet high, accompanied by the Plaza of the Seven Temples and a triple ball court. Nearby is another pyramid and palace, noted for its rows of windows. The palace appears to have been associated with the Maya bat cult. To the east is a temple that stood 185 feet high. The largest of all Tikal temples was erected just beyond, standing 212 feet, high it is one of the largest structures in pre-Columbian America. Another notable shrine is the Temple of the Inscriptions, which is covered with hieroglyphs. Panels of inscriptions were uncovered on the roof comb and on the accompanying stelae and altars. Causeways linked the various temples and plazas, and small commemorative monuments were placed beside the larger monuments for religious ceremonies. Tikal also had as many as 10 separate water reservoirs.

The history of Tikal includes the Mamon, Charcas and Tzakol phases and artistic horizons. Teotihuacan influences also are evident there. Throughout its history, the city had a single dynasty of rulers, begun in the Early Classic Period (c. A.D. 1/250–600) by Yax Moch-Xoc, who ruled sometime between A.D. 219 and 238. Scroll-Ahau Jaguar, Yax Balam, Zero-Moon Bird (who is depicted on the Leiden Plaque), Great Jaguar Paw and Ah-Cacau were among the vigorous rulers of the city. By the ninth century A.D., the stelae were no longer being dated; the last stela bearing a date is from A.D. 889. The population decline, although not sudden, was heavy, and Tikal began to recognize its own demise. When the city was abandoned c. A.D. 900, ritual destruction of its stelae and altars took place. A new group, reportedly the Eznab, entered Tikal to attempt to restore its past glories. Unable to sustain its artistic and architectural achievements, however, the Eznabs remained in the ruins of the city until the monuments' deterioration and the encroaching jungles forced them to move elsewhere.

TILANTONGO A site in the Mixteca Alta region of Oaxaca, the Mixtec capital, established around A.D. 859 or 875 and dominating the territory. Called Tilantongo Ilhuicacalli, "the Black Land, House of Heaven," the city was ruled by several powerful dynasties. The second royal line there included the famous Eight-Deer, who was born in A.D. 1011. Mixtec sculpture recovered from Tilantongo depicts the god Five-Death. Ceramics found on the site carried the same motif, and objects of gold and precious stones were reportedly looted from tombs there. A Mixtec group of the same name were part of the Mixtec confederation, active in the Mixteca Alta region.

TILCOATIN A Toltec king listed in the *Anales de Cuauhtitlan* as ruling from A.D. 1025 to 1046.

TITLACAUAN A Huaxtec deity of magic, personified in the legends concerning the fall of the Toltec city of Tula. Seen unclothed by a Toltec princess, Titlacauan married her and then was attacked by the Toltec. The god invited his enemies to a banquet—Toltec who did not recognize his divine nature—and he played music so beautiful that the Toltec were driven to suicide. Tula, according to the Huaxtec records, was thus ruined because of the loss of its aristocracy. This legend describes the Huaxtec had revenge on the Toltec for the suffering the Toltec had caused them.

TITLE OF THE LORDS OF TOTONICAPAN A Quiche Maya work from Guatemala, dated to c. A.D. 1554. This is an historical record of the Quiche Maya, offering parallels to the *Popol Vuh*. (See MAYA LITERATURE for details.)

TIZATLAN A site in central Tlaxcala on the heights of San Martin Texmelucan, that served as an artists' colony as well as a ceremonial city dedicated to music and to dance. The city, started c. A.D. 1348, was called the Place of the Chalk or the Place of White Stone, and welcomed many artists from various Mesoamerican regions. The site was designed to accommodate as many as seven *calpullis*, a designation of family units or "clan" districts. The ruins of a royal residence and a shrine in Tizatlan contain murals that portray the Tlaxcalans resisting an Aztec army. The gods, Tlaloc and Tezcatlipoca, are also depicted, along with eagles and jaguars. The murals are in the Cholula-Puebla style. A monolith was also recovered, made of fired brick. Four drums, called *teponztli*, were fashioned of wood and stone and positioned in the heart of the complex's shrines. The last ruler of Tizatlan is recorded as being a man called Xicotincatl.

TIZOC Called Leg of Chalk, the Aztec ruler from A.D. 1481 to 1486. The brother of Emperor Axayacatl, whom he succeeded, Tizoc was a military leader who attacked Toluca and possibly Oaxaca and Guerrero. He enlarged the Great Temple in Tenochtitlan, and the Stone of Tizoc was fashioned during his reign, recording his achievements and his role as mediator between humans and the gods. Tizoc's mysticism, however, and his reclusiveness made him un-

Tizoc glyph

popular. His reign ended abruptly, probably because he was murdered.

TIZOC STONE   See STONE OF TIZOC.

TLACAELEL   Called the mayor of the palace of Tenochtitlan, an Aztec priest and counselor to emperors Itzcoatl and Motecuhzoma I. He was the nephew of Itzcoatl and the brother of Motecuhzoma. In his role as high priest, he was called *Cihuacoatl*, the Woman Snake. Due to his counsel a series of reforms were made in Aztec society. It is also probable that he supported the forging of the Triple Alliance and the overthrow of the Tepanec. Tlacaelel burned any historical books that did not mention the Aztec, and under his guidance the people began to view themselves as the sole heirs to the Toltec tradition. He also encourage human sacrifices and the use of captives as victims in order to sustain the "world" or the "sun." The FLOWER WARS were begun during his lifetime. Tlacaelel also restored and revised the judicial, economic and political systems of the Aztec and counseled the refurbishing of Tenochtitlan. He is believed to have died c. A.D. 1475/80.

TLACAHUEPAN   An Aztec prince, a brother of Motecuhzoma I, who was taken prisoner by the Chalco-Amecameca confederation in 1459 or 1462. Honored by the Chalco, the prince refused a chiefdom in the enemy domain and killed himself. Records concerning the incident state that he leapt from the top of a high pole. His death inspired the

Aztecs to defeat the Chalco armies. (See also CHALCO and MOTECUHZOMA I.)

TLACATEOTL   The ruler of TLATELOLCO, the sister city of Tenochtitlan at the time of the Tepanec struggle and the rise of MAXTLA. The Aztec ruler of Tenochtitlan, CHIMALPOPOCA, was slain by Maxtla for interfering with his succession to the throne of Tezozomoc. The Tepanec also entered the city of Tlatelolco and hunted down Tlacateotl, although he apparently was not involved. Tlacateotl died at the hands of the Tepanec.

TLACOPAN   Also called Tacuba today after the modern village located there. This was a site on the western shore of Lake Texcoco in the Valley of Mexico, south of the Tepanec capital of Azcapotzalco. The city was connected to the Aztec (Mexica) capital of Tenochtitlan by a vast causeway, constructed by the Aztec to allow traffic to and from their island domain. Tlacopan was also associated with the Aztec politically by being a less important member of the Triple Alliance. This pact, formed between Texcoco, Tenochtitlan and Tlacopan when the Aztec and Texcoca rebelled against the Tepanec, endured 90 years and was successful in maintaining the peace among these cities as well as providing them with a united front against other groups. Because Tlacopan had remained neutral in the first stages of the revolt, it did not have an equal footing with Tenochtitlan and Texcoco as a member of the alliance. Tlacopan, however, did receive part of the tribute sent to the alliance. One record indicates that Tlacopan received one-fifth where the others received two-fifths each. The city also took part in the FLOWER WARS, military campaigns conducted against Tlaxcala, Cholula and Huexotzinco. The reported purpose of the battles, which seem to have occurred on the plains of Atlixco, was to obtain prisoners for human sacrifices and to provide the Triple Alliance forces with practice for imperial campaigns. With the arrival of the Spanish, Tlacopan suffered the same fate as its neighbors.

TLAHUICA   A Nahua group related to the Aztec (Mexica) and claiming the distinction of having come from Chicomoztoc, the Nahual homeland. This culture is credited with founding the city of Tepoztlan, with the Tepoztec. They are also associated with a structure in Cuernvaca, at a site called Teopanzalco. Located in the eastern part of the state of Morelos, in modern Cuernavaca, the site had a double pyramid, one built above the other. The pyramid faced a plaza, having a smaller platform on either side. Some circular platforms were also found, probably in honor of Ehecatl, Quetzalcoatl's manifestation as the wind. The Tlahuican in Cuernavaca were conquered by the Aztec in the reign of Ahuitzotl.

TLAHUIZCALPANTECUHTLI   Called "Lord of the Dawn," a Toltec deity adopted by succeeding Mesoamerican cultures. The god was associated with the threatening aspects of Venus. Tlahuizcalpantecuhtli hurled lightning balls at humans, maize and water. The god is evident at Chichen Itza and other Toltec sites, and Quetzalcoatl was believed to have been reborn in this deified form. Normally depicted as a man in an elaborate costume with five stars or white marks on his face, the deity was a skybearer, and was associated with Mixcoatl in some traditions or with the deity Itzlacoluihqui-Ixquimilli in others.

TLAILOTLAQUE A cultural group that inhabited the Chalco region in the southern part of the Valley of Mexico during the Paleo-Indian Period (11,000–7000 B.C.) The Tlailotlaque, with others, established a confederation called the Chalco-Amecameca.

TLALANCALECA A site on the edge of Puebla, a territory well populated between 800 and 300 B.C. Here are evidence of residences and agricultural practices. The *talud-tablero* style was also in use on the site, which had carved stelae and stone monuments.

TLALOC The Mesoamerican rain god, associated with Chac, the Maya rain deity. The Olmec worshipped Tlaloc, who was also honored in Teotihuacan. On the eastern shore of Lake Texcoco, in the city of Coatlinchan, a 23-foot statue of Tlaloc, weighing 180 tons, was discovered in a gulley. The Aztec (Mexica) made Tlaloc an important deity in Tenochtitlan, as the god was invoked in the agricultural practices of the city. The ritual murder of children was part of the Tlaloc rituals, held during certain festivals. (TLALOQUES and TLALCOLAN.)

TLALOCAN An Aztec paradise, the "Place of Tlaloc," supposedly located on a mountaintop amid rain clouds. The storm king ruled there and mortals went to Tlalocan only by invitation. Tlaloc favored the drowned, those struck by lightning, victims of skin diseases and dropsy. According to legend, such victims were given rare joys, including daily garlands of flowers. (See also CINCALCO.)

TLALOQUES Aztec deities, depicted as dwarves who were minions of the rain god, Tlaloc. The *Tlaloques* were Opochtli, Nappatecuhtli, Yauhqueme and Tomiyauhecuhtli. They were beings meant to have brewed the rain. In some Mesoamerican traditions they are associated with local mountain ranges.

TLALTECUHTLI An Aztec goddess, called the Earth Lady. Held to be eternal, she swam in the waters of chaos and was sometimes described as a huge toad with mouths at her joints, all bloodied. Trees and grasses came from her hair, flowers and short grasses from her skin, springs from her eyes, rivers and caverns from her mouth. Her shoulders became mountains and her nose valleys.

TLAMATINI Called the Followers of Truth, a group assembled by King NEZAHUALCOYOTL of Texcoco in his capital. Nezahualcoyotl, called the Sage of Anahuac, brought philosophers, musicians, artists, sculptors and craftsmen into his realm to enhance the cultural life there. The artists, who met regularly with the king, were also members of "the Flower and Song Group" at court.

TLAMATINIME The Lords of Wisdom of Teotihuacan, the great sages of that city who guided its construction and administration. When Teotihuacan was abandoned in c. A.D.

650/750, some sages migrated from the site while others remained to complete a spiritual work called *The Book of Dreams.*

TLAMIMILOLPA PHASE A cultural development associated with the city of Teotihuacan, lasting from A.D. 300 to 500. The Ciudad, part of the city's complex, was completed in this phase. The city's population increased. The Temple of Quetzalcoatl was enlarged and the trade enterprises were expanded.

TLAPACOYA A site located in the southeastern corner of the Valley of Mexico, occupied from 1500 B.C. and during the time of Olmec expansion, (Olmec II: 1200–c. 600/400 B.C.). Located across Lake Texcoco from the site of Tlatilco, Tlapacoya contained many examples of Olmec ceramics. The jaguar motif is especially evident there. Tlapacoya was probably not a trading depot, but in some respects it was associated with Olmec endeavors. An Olmec nucleus is believed to have lived in the ceremonial complex of the site, dominating the local culture. Tlapacoya is considered a transitional settlement between Cuicuilco and Teotihuacan and became a weaving center. The site also contained black ceramic wares, figurines, tools and other ornaments. It is believed that Tlapacoya served for a time as a regional ceremonial center. A pyramid was erected on a hill there, rising in several tiers and designed with several stairways. Three separate phases of construction are evident in the Tlapacoya pyramid. It was under repair from 400 to 200 B.C. Tombs were placed within the pyramid, with two vertical openings on the top level serving as entrances.

TLATECAHUAQUE A group involved in the development of the Chalco region in the southern part of the Valley of Mexico. Dated to the Paleo-Indian Period (11,000–7000 B.C.), this group was of the Chalco-Amecameca confederacy.

TLATELOLCO An Aztec (Mexica) city in the northern section of modern Mexico City, called Artificial Mound of Sand. The city is also called now the Plaza of the Three Cultures. Erected by the Aztec at the same time as Tenochtitlan, in A.D. 1325 or possibly as late as 1358, Tlatelolco was a rival of the major Aztec capital for a time. The name was probably derived from the word *tlatelli*, which meant "a built up mound of earth." It is possible that another local group was living on the site of Tlatelolco before the Aztec arrived there. The city became involved at an early stage in market and trade enterprises, all based on Maya and earlier cultural models. On market days the city's market attracted thousands of visitors; Spanish chroniclers stated that as many as 25,000 people came to trade there. The merchants, eventually becoming POCHTECAS, were valued members of society, serving as intelligence agents as well as traders. The city's market offered staples, local products and luxury goods from other regions. Each product had its designated place in the market.

Sharing the Lake Texcoco islands with Tenochtitlan, Tlatelolco was involved in the major Aztec affairs, including minor conflicts, wars and sieges. The founder of the city's ruling dynasty was Cuacuapitzahuac, "Pointed Horn," a son of Tezozomoc, the Tepanec king. When CHIMALPOPOCA, the Aztec ruler of Tenochtitlan, was slain by the Tepanec in A.D. 1427 TLACATEOTL, the ruler of Tlatelolco at the time, was also murdered. In 1473, however, Moquihuix, the Tlatelolco king, was accused of abusing his wife, the sister of the Aztec emperor Axayacatl. That accusation was one reason for the Aztec campaign against the city. It is probable that Moquihuix was also plotting politically, seeking more independence. Axayacatl marched on the city, slaying Moquihuix on the steps of his temple. The Aztec of Tenochtitlan treated the city's residents harshly for a time after annexing the site, incorporating Tlatelolco into Tenochtitlan. The city originally covered an area of 20 square miles; it had a double pyramid that dominated the ceremonial complex, with double balustrades. Smaller pyramids and temples were erected with platforms throughout the various districts. The Temple Calendrico, the Temple of the Calendar, is celebrated for its carved panels of dates, designs that decorated the first tier of the shrine on three sides. These panels are composed of 39 friezes.

TLALTELOLCO PHASE A cultural development also called Aztec IV (A.D. 1450–1521), offering largely black-on-orange wares. Tripod vases, ladles, plates and open bowls decorated with lines, circles, pictures of animals, symbols and other images were also manufactured during this phase. Birds, plants and fish were depicted naturalistically and the wares demonstrate a high standard in design.

TLATILCO An Early Formative Period (c. 2000/1600–900 B.C.) site in Oaxaca Valley, settled c. 1200 B.C. The site is very large, near Lake Teycoc and on a stream. Tlatilco's people fished, hunted deer, waterfowl and small animals. Bell-shape pots were used for the storage of maize. Some 340 burial sites were uncovered in Tlatilco, with extended skeletons recovered. Hollow figurines with red paint were also found. Some were large and some were small, solid and delicate. While there is evidence that the people of Tlatilco played ritual ball games, there is no evidence of a ball court on the site. Sinister masks were also produced, as well as hunchbacks, two-headed creatures and figures having three eyes. The ceramics of Tlatilco are advanced, and zoned rocker stamps (tools for making indented designs) were used.

Tlatilco is an important archaeological site because its finds demonstrate advances in ceramics during the Early Formative Period.

TLAXCALA (Tlaxcalla) A site in the Valley of Puebla, inhabited by the Olmeca-Xicallanca c. A.D. 1350, joined by the Teo-Chichimec within a few decades. The region had long been influenced by the great cities of Cholula and Teotihuacan. A battle took place in the regional foothills after the invasion, and the original inhabitants were displaced. Then a warrior claiming to be a descendant of the Aztec emperor Acamapichtli defeated the enemies and moved into the Cholula region, where he formed his own society and launched Tlaxcala on its progression to power and domination. Attacked by Huexotzinco, the Tlaxcala fought and won. They then erected a series of fortresses and towers to keep watch on their borders. They also constructed a massive wall, reported to have extended for two miles along the Otomi-Totonac-Tlaxcalan frontier, reportedly 10 feet wide and 20 feet thick. The Tlaxcala were autonomous in this site, having four lords to rule the region. Divisions within the society allowed merchants, judges and other officials to reside in their own districts. One of the four divisions, Tizatlan, served also as a ceremonial complex for artists. When the Tlaxcala were attacked, however, the independence of the various precincts ended abruptly, and they functioned as a confederated military force. This unified response to attacks maintained the Tlaxcala region, even when the Aztec tried repeatedly to subdue them. A deep enmity grew between Tlaxcala and Tenochtitlan. The Tlaxcala region also had a vast judiciary and economic bureacracy, with tax collection made on a territorial basis and tributes collected as well. Traders and merchants, probably deeply involved in the vast trade mechanisms of the region, were highly regarded in Tlaxcala. The history of the region, which was surrounded by the Triple Alliance forces, was reported in the *Lienzo de Tlaxcala*, a document written for the Spanish governor after the conquest. There were ceramic phases and artistic achievements within Tlaxcala, and Cacaxtla and Tizatlan remain sites of the Tlaxcala efforts.

TLAXCALTEC A group belonging to the OLMECA-XICALLANCA who journeyed to Zacatlan and then to the southern Acolhua domain, where they were challenged by the Tepanec and sent into retreat. They dispersed to Chalco and other regions.

TLAXIACO One of the confederated peoples of the Mixtec, living in the Sierras of Oaxaca, the Land of the Clouds. (See MIXTEC.)

TLAXOCHIMACO An Aztec festival related to agriculture. It was a time of of feasting and dancing and a celebration of flowers.

TLAZOLTEOTL A Valley of Mexico deity, identified with disease and filth. She was the purifier and the healer, and she is depicted with a broom. The Huaxtec portrayed her in their Veracruz centers, and she was probably adopted by the Aztec and other regional groups from that culture. In the codices, she is shown with spools of cotton in her headdress.

TLILPOTONQUI CIHUACOATL An Aztec noble, the son of the famed Tlacaelel, whom he succeeded as chief priest or Woman Snake in Tenochtitlan. He appears to have ruled for a rather short time, dying in 1503, succeeded by another brother, Miccacalcatl Tlaltetecuintzin Cihuacoatl.

TLOHTZIN A Chichimec ruler, the son of Nopaltzin and the grandson of the celebrated XOLOTL. He succeeded his father on the throne and became known for establishing Nahuatl as the official language of the Chichimec people. He is called the Hawk. His son, QUINATZIN, followed him to the throne and ruled until A.D. 1337.

TLOQUE NAHUAQUE A deity called the creator, worshipped in the great city of Teotihuacan. Adopting many Teotihuacan traditions, the Aztec (Mexica) also accepted Tloque Nahuaque, calling him Impalnemohuani, or the Giver of Life. Aztec priests also described Tloque Nahuaque as "the god of the near and the immediate."

TLOZOLTEOTL A Huaxtec deity, called Our Grandmother, perhaps reference to the Maya roots of this culture. This was a goddess of fertility and the patron of divination, childbirth, sexual love and ritual medicine. Under the title of *Tlaelquani*, which translates as "the Eater of Dirt," Tlozolteotel presided over the rituals concerned with the confession of sin, part of the Huaxtec ceremonial practices. The Aztec (Mexica) adopted this deity, honoring Our Grandmother in annual rituals. The Huaxtec conical headdress was worn in such rites, and Huaxtec music and ceremonies were adopted as part of the services dedicated to Tlozolteotl.

TOAD The *Bufo marinus,* a highly toxic animal, having poison in its skin. Toad remains were discovered in San Lorenzo and in other sites, indicating that the animals were used by many Mesoamerican cultures over the centuries as a source of drugs. Bufotinine, the toxic element of the toad's skin, is a hallucinogen and was probably valued for its psychical properties during rituals.

TOBACCO A plant *Nicotiana tabacun* L. and *Nicotania rustica* L. that was grown in Mesoamerica. *Nicotania rustica* was native to Mesoamerica, the other variety to South American regions. As the nicotine content of the plant was very high, tobacco was used ritually by some cultures.

TOCHTLI The rabbit or hare, used by the Aztec as a day sign in their version of the *tonalpohualli,* the calendar system.

TOHIL A Quiche Maya deity, depicted in the *Popol Vuh* as the patron of noble lineages. The god was associated with human sacrifices and was worshipped in the Quiche domain. He has been identified with God K in the Maya codices and his name has been associated with obsidian.

TOJOLABAL MAYA See MAYA GROUPS, TOJOLABAL.

TOLIMAN PHASE A cultural development in the Tuxcacuesco-Zapolitan archaeological zone in Jalisco and Colima, associated with Autlan wares. Red-on-brown ceramics were manufactured as part of this phase, as well as clay whistles, cylinder seals, stamps, stone mace heads and jewelry. The phase dates to the Formative Period (c. 2000/1600 B.C.–c. A.D. 250/290).

TOLLAN (1) The Toltec word for "the Place of the Rushes," also called *Tollin* or *Tullin.* The word probably represents the vast population of the Toltec, who appeared as numerous as the rushes along the lakes. The Toltec name is derived from this word.

TOLLAN (2) A name for the Toltec capital city of Tula. It is also used to designate other Toltec sites in some records.

TOLLAN (3) A term that refers to the original Toltec homeland, a site not identified but believed by some, to be

Tollan figure

near Jalisco or by others, Hidalgo, Mexico. Regions also suggested as the original Toltec homeland include Jalisco, the Mesa Central, Veracruz and Michoacan.

TOLLAN (4) A term used by Toltec contemporaries and later civilizations to represent the true source of legitimate royal power. The subsequent Mesoamerican cultures, particularly the Aztec (Mexica), laid claim to Toltec ancestry in order to solidify their imperial status and to bring their dynastic lines into conformity with the traditions accepted at the time.

TOLLAN (5) A name used to designate a mysterious site from which Mesoamerican groups either originated or sought as their ultimate destination. Having a mystical quality, this *tollan* represented power, fulfillment and a manifestation of destiny.

TOLLAN PHASE A cultural development in the Toltec capital city of Tula, in Hidalgo, Mexico. This phase dates from A.D. 900 to 1150, heralding the Toltec culture at its best. Plumbate ceramics, including Nicoya wares, and Fine Orange were manufactured during this cultural development.

TOLLAN ZUIVA See TULAN ZUIVA.

TOLTEC A major Mesoamerican culture that is credited with bringing about a true renaissance or a golden age to the region during the Early Post-Classic Period (A.D. 900–1200). The Toltec had a major impact on the emerging cultures of the Valley of Mexico and its environs and linked these groups with traditions of the past. The name Toltec is derived from the word *Tollan* (*tullin, tollin*), which means "the place of the rushes" and can refer to a multitude of people, congregating like rushes on the shore of a lake or sea. The term *Tollan* has been associated with the Toltec over the centuries but has also taken on some metaphysical implications. (See TOLLAN entries; TOLLAN PHASE.)

The Toltec, dominating both the era and the region in which they lived, ruled or influenced much of central and northern Mexico as well as territories in the Guatemalan

Toltec vase

highlands and in the Yucatan Peninsula, traditionally Maya realms. Wherever the Toltec settled, they introduced an artistic and social renaissance to the local populations, even those of advanced civilizations. Due to this impact on the various cultures, later groups claimed Toltec lineage for their royal dynasties. The succeeding civilizations also imitated to a great degree Toltec imperial methods and absorbed Toltec glorification of war and battle. So heavily did the newer cultures rely on Toltec military, social and governmental traditions, in fact, that some scholars classify them as Toltec "renaissance" groups.

The Toltec were called the *toltecoyotl*, the Great Artificers. They were also termed the *Toltical*, the many people, like rushes and the Lords of the House of Turquoise. Cultures that followed considered them all wise and all powerful, and the period in which they lived was looked upon as a golden age. The Aztec (Mexica), who emulated the Toltec and promulgated the Toltec outlook with the greatest success, called them the Master Builders, a reference to the cities of Tula and Chichen Itza.

The actual history of the Toltec is not derived from direct or interior sources, most of which were destroyed by the Aztec and by the Spanish. The material now available (other than data accumulated at excavations and studies at Toltec sites) is thus interwoven with legends and myths that have taken on a religious and metaphysical symbolism. The destruction of Toltec documents has been credited to the Aztec emperor Itzcoatl and Tlacaelel, his priest-counselor. For the purposes of study, therefore, outside sources are used to trace the Toltec historical development. These sources include the *Anales de Cuautitlan*, the *Relacion de Genealogia* and the *Memoria Breve de Chimapahin*.

The Toltec arrived on the Mesoamerican scene after the fall of the great city of Teotihuacan (A.D. 650/750), probably part of the Chichimec invasion of that era. Some scholars have suggested that the Toltec were from a phase of the Chalchihuites culture, incorporating other groups, including Nonoalco, Huaxtec and Chichimec. They entered the northern part of the Valley of Mexico and the central plateau region, led by their war chief, CE TECPATL MIXCOATL, which means "One Flint." Nahual in origin, the Toltec are called the Ancient Nahual; the Aztec are called "the New (or Young) Nahual." Mixcoatl and his people may have taken part in the burning of Teotihuacan, but this has not been documented. It is believed that he led the Toltec from a site beyond Jalisco. Other scholars point to an origin on the Mesa Central and still others to Veracruz or Michoacan.

The first migration was to Culhuacan, then called the Place of the Turning or the Place of the Bent Ancients. The Toltec may have entered the region on a simple military adventure that grew to become a lasting redeployment of the culture because of the resources and opportunities that presented themselves. They conquered the surrounding cultures rather quickly, including the Otomis, and then settled near the Cerro de la Estrella, the sacred mountain called the Hill of the Star. This era of Toltec history is documented in *Memoria Breve de Chimalpahin*, which shows their power in the region by A.D. 900.

Mixcoatl is reported to have married a Nahual woman who gave birth to his son and heir, Ce Acatl Topiltzin, whose name means "One Reed, Our Prince." This son and heir is more widely known as Quetzalcoatl or as Kukulcan. Mixcoatl directed the Toltec in the acquisition of a culture, and they began to clothe themselves and embarked on what were to become the agricultural and social traditions of their homeland. Their religious customs appear to have been shaped by Teotihuacan and the other ceremonial complexes of the region. Mixcoatl, however, was murdered in 935 or in 947. A relative, called Ihuitmal, slew him and took the throne, supposedly in the year that Ce Acatl Topiltzin was born. Ihuitmal continued his rule until Ce Acatl Topiltzin slew the usurper and claimed the throne as Mixcoatl's rightful heir. The king then proclaimed himself a reincarnation of the god Quetzalcoatl, having been instructed at this deity's shrine. In A.D. 968 he moved the capital to Tula, in Hidalgo, Mexico. The great capital was constructed according to Toltec architectural designs and became a great force in the region. Within the government, however, a great conflict was taking place, and Ce Acatl Topiltzin was attacked and defeated by his religious enemies.

Ce Acatl Topiltzin was driven from Tula, entering the realm of legend and becoming Kukulcan, the Quetzalcoatl of the Maya. Tezcatlipoca became the bringer of grief and destruction as the major deity of the Toltec, recorded in the histories as seducing princesses and transforming the empire into a miasma of indolence and evil. He probably represents the inevitable decline of the capital, as the nation turned from the light and the vitality of previous eras. Actually, Tula did not collapse but prospered and formed an empire of sorts. The basic provinces of this domain appear to have been in the northern and western parts of the Valley of Mexico and in Tula. Several complexes were open in this region and in Jalisco. The Toltec prevailed over other groups with their military might, and they were probably ruled by a single king, perhaps elected by a coalition of the participating national groups. How much power was in the hands of the priests is not known. One ruler, a woman named Xihuiquenitzin, reigned from A.D. 829 to 833, perhaps as a regent for a minor heir. Certain other rulers also give insight into the Toltec world. One, Mitl Tlaomihua, ruling from A.D. 770 to 829, perhaps the husband of Xihuiquenitzin, is mentioned in the *Historia Tolteca Chichimeca* and is associated with building the finer temples and pyramidal platforms that survive in Tula. Soon after his reign, the cult of Huitzilopochtli, the war god, was introduced into the Toltec lands.

Tula served as the Toltec capital until A.D. 1156, when it was overthrown by uncivilized groups or by some of the peoples who had been part of its population all along. The darkness of the god Tezcatlipoca, the "Smoking Mirror," had taken its toll, according to the chroniclers. Huemac, the ruler at the time, was overthrown and fled to Chapultepec. Some give this date as A.D. 1186. He committed suicide in his haven or was slain—the accounts of his death vary. The fall of Tula was swift and destructive, but it was apparently preceded by a gradual decline of Toltec authority in the various regions of their domination.

The Toltec had survived on the tribute system that they employed everywhere, the system by which certain regions were accountable for set quotas of particular products. The tribute might be agricultural, metals, clothing, feathers, ornaments or ceramic in nature. The Aztec and the members of the Triple Alliance would imitate the Toltec in this regard, sharing in the tribute collected from their domains throughout Mesoamerica. When the outlying regions under Toltec domination were threatened by a loss of population, poor crops, natural disasters or the presence of uncivilized hordes, the system was imperiled. A number of these strongholds arose in the region, and they would have brought pressure on the Toltec holdings. Even the failure or loss of the agricultural regions would have spelled disaster for the capital. Tula was abandoned by the bulk of its population and by its nobility, and the Toltec ceased to be a power in the Valley of Mexico. Their story does not end with the collapse of their fabled metropolis, however.

In the Yucatan Peninsula, long the domain of the Maya, the civilization called Puuc Maya was flourishing. Around 987 A.D. a man called Kukulkan, the Maya name for Quetzalcoatl, arrived with his followers. Again the chroniclers have personalized and have added religious dimensions to a historical fact. The Toltec invaded the Yucatan and are reported to have established colonies and to have penetrated deep into the region to occupy the Maya city of Chichen Itza, which they transformed.

Chichen Itza had been a Maya ceremonial center for the Yucatan, drawing offerings from as far away as the Valley of Mexico and Panama. It was built beside a vast *cenote*, an underground water reservoir, a Maya tradition. The Toltec who had fled with Quetzalcoatl perhaps arrived there as pilgrims originally, then settled in the region. They were not numerous, and they were accompanied by other groups, probably the Itza, who were returning to Chichen Itza. Using Maya workmanship, which was superior to anything seen in the northern regions of Mesoamerica at the time,

Toltec relief

the Toltec reached new heights at this new site. Many of the structures remaining there today date to the period of Toltec occupation. The round tower for the study of astronomy, for example, is Toltec in style, reflecting the Valley of Mexico designs. The Chac Mool and Atlantea figures were evident, miniature versions of those celebrated at Tula. Standing or seated figures "standard-bearers" are also Toltec. The bas reliefs, sculptured panels and processions of jaguars and coyotes also reflect Toltec style. The Maya historical records depict "a time of battle," probably heralding the Toltec arrival. A second Toltec invasion was also reported as having taken place in the Yucatan, this time because of the conditions in the Valley of Mexico. The Toltec, however, did not remain dominant, not even in Chichen Itza, they slowly become absorbed into the Maya way of life.

During their period of domination, the Toltec inhabited Hidalgo, north of the Valley of Mexico, and controlled the valley and portions of Bajio and Morelos. Their domain probably extended to the western slopes of the Sierra Madre Oriental, into Zacateca, Jalisco and Michoacan. This region is one of eroded hillsides, cacti, thickets and dust-filled plains. The valleys have alluvial soils and water for irrigation. Summer rainfalls were not adequate for agricultural needs, so dams were constructed to divert the necessary water. Strategically located canals were devised to bring the water into the fields. The Toltec realm was thus capable of supporting a sizable population, despite cold winter temperatures and the constant chance of freezing. Despite the chilling frosts, the climate in the region is actually mild.

TOLTEC AGRICULTURE The farming practices of the people, their economic base and support of the populations of the various urban districts within the Toltec domain. Not only food crops were essential to this support but fibers as well, including cotton, grown in the lowlands. Maize was the staple crop of the Toltec, in keeping with Mesoamerican tradition, and they also grew beans, chili peppers, amaranth and maguey. The Toltec used the maguey plant in many ways. Its heart was roasted as food. Its fibers were woven into various articles of clothing, and its sap was fermented and distilled as liquor. Maguey thorns became needles for sewing, and its leaves were burned as fuel. The Toltec also relied on a variety of seeds, to flavor food and as culinary accompaniaments. They also used persimmons, prickly pears and capulin. Animals raised or hunted include dogs, turkeys, bees, deer and two types of rabbit: the cottontail and the jackrabbit.

The *milpas* techniques were adapted, and farmers turned to fresh lands each year, setting aside fields to lie fallow for nourishment while new sites were cleared. Limited in growing seasons by the winter frosts and a single rainy season, the Toltec were heavily dependent on irrigation. They farmed in the spring and in the summer, and canals and earthwork dams were employed. Hillside terraces were carved into the more rugged terrains, and stone walls were put in place on the higher slopes to trap water. Individual Toltec families kept their own gardens, raising medicinal plants, herbs, condiments and maguey. Orchards were common, within the areas of the individual residences. All orchard and garden surplus could have been traded for luxury items or for necessities not available locally. Some agricultural products were given to Toltec officials as taxes.

TOLTEC ARCHAEOLOGICAL SITES The Toltec occupied many cities and established their own great capital, in Hidalgo, northwest of the Valley of Mexico. They are also associated with sites in the Maya domain. It is difficult, however, to establish the actual limits of the empire with any certainty. The following sites are listed in records as being associated with this culture:

Atasta	Ixtalapapa
Calixtlahuaca	San Pedro de los Pinos
Chalco Atempan	Tula
Chapultepec	Tulan Zuiva
Chichen Itza	Tulixlahuaca
Cincoc	Tuzapan
Coatepec	Xicco
Coatzalcoalcos	Xicuco
Comaltepec	Xippacayan
Huapacalli	Xochitlan

TOLTEC ARCHITECTURE The designs and structures of the culture that reflect not only the traditions of the region but a dramatic art form, obviously constructed rapidly. Tula, the Toltec capital, contains structures that are both ambitious and striking. The Toltec used massive horizontal lines, flat roofs with decorative profiles and rectangular panels to achieve monumental effects. Their construction techniques, however, were poor, and the materials used were sun-dried adobe and masonry composed of coarse stones and mud. Some contemporaries reported that when the Toltec took over a city, they covered niches and friezes with plain masonry, in order to clear away confusing or distracting lines within a monument. They employed geometric and cylindrical forms to advantage, not caring if the structures that they erected lasted for centuries. Massive horizontal lines were incorporated into the design of their ceremonial precincts, which were decorated with merlons,

pieces unique to their circular or starkly angled designs in architecture and in construction. The monumental effect achieved provided magnificent settings for Toltec ceremonies, architectural in time the Aztec also mastered the monumental architectural style.

In the design of their ceremonial complexes, the Toltec followed the Mesoamerican pattern, building pyramidal platforms having levels and stairways and with adjacent patios and plazas. One innovation included in Tula were vast colonnades, with decorated columns supporting roofs or providing the base for benches. They also incorporated the renowned Atlantean statues into their designs as well as platforms and daises. Murals once adorned the walls of the buildings of Tula, but these did not endure. Ceiling openings for skylights were also used.

Later civilizations revered Tula as the utopian center of the Master Builders, although little discovered there gives evidence of such achievements. The city was a masterpiece of grandeur and religious spectacle, but it was also imbued with militaristic nuances. No painted decorations remain on the structures; such decorations probably transformed the buildings, making the city appear haven for artistic ideals.

The Toltec also understood the acropolis effect. While geography and geology may have required the use of terraced ridges for important structures, the effect achieved was stunning and memorable. Only the acropolis section of Tula was surrounded and given defenses, although the entire city was constructed on a rather high site. The larger sections of Tula, which served as a ceremonial complex as well as the capital, were undefended. Perhaps the presence of Toltec units there, forces whose very reputation on the battlefield insured against rash attacks, allowed the luxury of such construction.

No discussion of Toltec architecture is complete without a reference to the Toltec innovations in the city of Chichen Itza, a site that had seen Maya and Itza builders. When the Toltec invaded the Yucatan and assumed control of Chichen Itza, they constructed a new city that represents the height of the Toltec culture. Serpent columns, Chac Mul reclining figures, skull racks, and bas reliefs of coyotes, jaguars and eagles are identical in both sites, as Chichen Itza took on the trappings of Tula. The Toltec also brought with them their devotion to the god Quetzalcoatl as Venus, as well as their military attitudes and their glorification of warriors. They demonstrate refinement and power at this site, as well as purity of lines and monumental splendor.

El Castillo, one of the important structures at Chichen Itza, rises in nine levels to 180 feet, having a wide ceremonial staircase. The present platform was built above an earlier Maya edifice. A Chac Mul figure was discovered in the antechamber of this temple, as was as the celebrated red jaguar throne. This throne, carved from a single piece of limestone and painted with red cinnabar, had inlaid teeth fashioned from pieces of carved flint. Its eyes were of jade. This was not merely the throne of an earthly Toltec king; it was meant to represent the seat of the sun. A solar disk, a small jade mask and a necklace of shells were also found on the throne. These were obviously ceremonial objects with religious significance.

TOLTEC ART   The expression of Toltec ideals and culture, represented in an important and enduring fashion by sculpture, which was the hallmark of the Toltec style. The pyramids of their cities have disappeared, as have the friezes that once adorned them, but the statues that formed part of the colonnaded porticos remain as evidence of Toltec religious and artistic horizons. Shafts of basalt and pillars once used to hold up roofs in the Tula ceremonial complex have been recovered, and some now stand on the pyramidal platform at the site. These statues, the Atlanteans, or *Telemones,* are 15 feet high, composed of four sections joined with mortise. They demonstrate the warrior aspects of Toltec life and their religious preoccupation with the worship of the god Quetzalcoatl. Armored and provided with the god's butterfly breastplates, these warrior statues have a uniformity, even of expression, that does not blunt the vigor and the strength of their geometric precision, which contrast with the massive horizontal lines employed in their settings. As headdresses the statues wear toques, bearing rows of disks, probably representing the stars, and crowned with rigid and geometrically precise plumes. The statues' swords are attached to belts that descend in front and are decorated in the rear with a fibula representing the sun and with disks adorned with four serpents. Details, even including a bag of copal, are used carefully within a geometric whole. The colossal forms were once painted, and they maintain a strangely realistic quality although designed as columns.

Toltec pillars used in various sites were about the same height as the Atlanteans, but they were placed on square bases and were carved in low relief. Warriors were again profiled, attired in the same armor as the Atlanteans and honoring Quetzalcoatl's cult, but they also wear carved nose ornaments. A serpent motif completes the design of the columns. Others were sculpted as snakes, and some shafts are believed to have been used in conjunction with the various temples. Small tables used within the temples were also decorated with miniature Atlanteans, a custom practiced by several earlier Mesoamerican cultures.

The Chac Mul statues not only demonstrate Toltec art form but demonstrate Toltec influence in given regions of Mesoamerica. The first was discovered at Chichen Itza, which accounts for its Maya name. It was once believed that these figures served as receptacles of human hearts. Now the Chac Muls are thought to represent various divinities, and their specific function relates to the cultic rites of the god depicted gods. Geometrically decorated, the Chac Muls bear the symbols of some deities. Their poses are precise and unyielding, contrasting sharply with the massive horizontal settings in which they have been placed and and are focal points of interest.

Serpent columns were another Toltec art form, elaborated into architectural components, as at Chichen Itza, or incorporated into individual complexes. These were stone sculptures of large serpents, used as columns as well for the temple entrances. The serpents' jaws jutted forward in geometric lines, and their tails swept upward to form lintels.

The Toltec are not renowned for their metalworks or for their jeweled ornaments, although there are some historical references to Toltec metalwares. Metals do not appear in Toltec remains, and there is no documented evidence that they excelled in the manufacture of such objects.

The Toltec appear to be the first in the region to have carved hieroglyphs. This was not a Teotihuacan tradition. A Toltec sign of Quetzalcoatl was found near the Cerro de la Malinche. The Aztec copied the form and used it throughout their history. These hieroglyphs, like the Toltec statues, were used chiefly in conjunction with the worship of Quetzalcoatl.

Telemone

TOLTEC CERAMICS   A pottery that reflects no relationship to the Teotihuacan Classic forms but does have much in common with later phases of that culture, especially regarding shape and in the application of various religious motifs. One of the common motifs evident in Toltec ceramics is the sectional designs of shells, which was the accepted symbol of Ehecatl, the wind deity. Ehecatl was believed to be a form sometimes taken by the god Quetzalcoatl, and the deity was incorporated into Toltec religious observances. Statues of the flayed god, Xipe Totec, the deity of spring, rebirth and rejuvenation, were also motifs common to Teotihuacan and earlier Mesoamerican sites. This god was popular throughout Mesoamerican eras.

The ceramic phases of the Toltec, as evidenced by the finds in the remaining Toltec sites in the region, have been designated to include Coyotlatelco and Mazapa.

Coyotlatelco.   This ceramic phase follows the Teotihuacan era in the Valley of Mexico, appearing in places at about the same time as the Corral and Mazapan ceramics. Coyotlatelco disappeared after the destruction of the city of Tula. It was characterized by bowls decorated with spiral or wavy designs between fine parallel lines. These decorations were painted in red on natural clay. Tripod vases of polished brown clay, with large, hollow legs, were decorated with wide bands and with incised designs. Bottles and flat figurines were also involved.

Mazapa (Corral Phase).   This ceramic period follows the Teotihuacan era in the Valley of Mexico and is simultaneous with the Coyotlatelco phase in some regions. Bowls and dishes were manufactured in this era, decorated with parallel wavy lines. Tripod bowls with heavy legs were decorated with blotches of red. Molded spindle whorls made their first appearance in the region, in this era, and flat figurines were also produced. The Mazapa-based groups produced large Tlaloc-faced braziers, hollow heads and figures of the gods.

Other ceramics in the Toltec period were the *molcajetes,* medium-size hemispherical bowls with tripod supports. Fine orange and plumbate were also contemporary with the Mazapan wares. Plumbate was found from Nayarit to Lake Nicaragua in the south. It is so called because of its surface of hard material and its metallic iridescence, in colors ranging from blue-gray to orange or reddish brown. It was usually lustrous and attractive. Plumbate wares included effigies, censors, figurines and animal forms.

The fine orange wares were found in the Yucatan and only rarely in Tula. The central gulf coast region was the source of these ceramics, which included tripod bowls and cups, effigy vessels and figurines.

At Chichen Itza the Toltecs were being absorbed into the Maya community there, and they employed Maya artisans and craftsmen who kept alive the great traditions of their own culture even in the period of Toltec domination. (See MAYA ARCHITECTURE for description of Chichen Itza, see also MAYA ARCHAEOLOGICAL SITES for discussion of the city.)

TOLTEC CODICES   See TOLTEC.

TOLTEC COSMOLOGY   The traditional Nahual concepts, common to other groups and elaborated upon in religious ceremonies and in evolving customs. The Toltec had precise concepts about the world and the universe as well as humankind's role. In his account of the Toltec cosmological ideals, Ixtlilxochitl reported that they believed in the existence of four separate periods of the world, each one a distinct creation with a beginning and a prescribed end. The Aztec and others adhered to this view of the universe and transitional worlds, elaborating upon them and adding new to human obligations to help sustain such worlds. The recorded Toltec worlds were the First, Second, Third and Fourth.

First World or Sun.   Created by Tloque Nahuaque and destroyed by that god some 1,700 years later with floods and lightning.

Second World or Sun.   Populated by the Quinametzin, the giants who failed in their tests to exhibit the proper attitudes toward the gods and were destroyed by earthquakes.

Third World or Sun.   The period in which the Olmec and others roamed the world to slay the surviving giants. Quetzalcoatl is recorded as appearing in this age, foretelling the destruction to come. When he left the world, winds came to destroy the sun and human beings were transformed into monkeys.

Fourth World or Sun.   The one in which the Toltec lived. Predictions about the end of this world foretold of a great consuming fire.

Their cosmological view and their view of human existence as transitory and subject to destinies imposed by the gods led the Toltec to take on the basic Nahual obligations

Toltec priest relief

of sacrifice and propitiatory ceremonies. The Aztec and others followed the religious implications and prescribed rituals, developing elaborate sacrificial ceremonies to mark the various aspects of the calendar and the worship of deities. The Toltec received much of their original religious impetus from Teotihuacan, which invoked the deity Quetzalcoatl and the rain god, Tlaloc. Warrior worship is evident in the murals and reliefs of Teotihuacan. Although secular and imperial in nature, the warriors of Teotihuacan and the Toltec cities were also implicated in the perpetuation of the religious aspect of their culture. War brought victims for sacrifice, and battle was a glorious exercise in supporting the gods who maintained the world or sun, thus insuring that both the people of Teotihuacan and the Toltec themselves would survive and prosper. (See TOLTEC RELIGION for details about Quetzalcoatl and ceremonies.)

TOLTEC DRESS The attire worn by this multiethnic group, which had links to the other Nahual cultures, including the Nonoalco and the Otomi. The Toltec described by their contemporaries are taller than most other Mesoamericans. They were also reported to have been hardier, able to run endlessly without tiring, an advantage in battle and in assaults. Warlike and distinctive in their ways, the Toltec did, however, assume the customs of their neighbors and wore much the same attire.

Men wore simple loincloths generally, with capelike garments and mantles during the winter. Women wore sarongs, wrap-around skirts, as well as the tunics common in the region. Some women did not wear tunics, preferring to remain nude. Toltec nobles wore styles similar to those of the commoners, but of finer materials, often decorated with feathers and semiprecious stones. Animal skins were worn as mantles, and the nobles also adorned themselves with metal ornaments and necklaces made of stones or shells. The Toltec warrior caste wore armor and elaborate headdresses, designed to designate military order. Coyote, jaguar or eagle insignias and motifs were used on shields and armors and on feathered helmets. Nose plugs were worn by the Toltec, probably as a symbol of rank. Such adornments were given to other vassal lords as well, promoting them in the region. The foreheads of Toltec babies were flattened by being tied to headboards, as that was considered a mark of personal beauty and was practiced throughout the Toltec domain.

TOLTEC GOVERNMENT The administration of this people, which remains as obscure as other aspects of their history because of the lack of internal documentation. Some specific kings are known by several lists that do not agree in details, and the Toltec tribute system, which was successful in the Toltec region and was adopted by succeeding civilizations, is also well documented. Specifically, however, the extent of the Toltec Empire is not certain. The manner in which vassal or subjugated states were treated also remains unknown, except for documents from those states. The Huaxtec, for example, who suffered much at the hands of the Toltec, had a specific site dedicated to the anguish of their people under the Toltec regime. One Huaxtec legend treats of divine revenge upon the Toltec nobles of Tula because of this treatment.

The actual Toltec Empire, lauded by succeeding cultures after the fall of Tula, remains an enigma, although some specific evidence is available. Toltec pottery, for example, has been discovered in Xochicalco, Michoacan, along the northeastern coast and in the region of Matlatzinca. It is also known that the Toltec founded colonies in Veracruz and in the Yucatan Peninsula. Toltec evidence is also visible in the city of Tajin, on the gulf coast of Mexico. Four bas relief slabs incorporated into the ball court there are Toltec in style. The serpent motifs and other Toltec architectural elements combine with Totonac influences in masterful displays. Statues recovered in Castillo de Teayo date to the Toltec period and reflect Toltec influence, as do some pieces in Tres Zapotes.

Whatever the size of the Toltec Empire in truth, and wherever the Toltec managed to establish colonies, alliances or vassal states, these sites were ruled by kings. Some members of royalty were elevated to semidivine status while on the throne or soon after their death. Mixcoatl, for example, the Toltec king who led his people into the region of Hidalgo, Mexico, was made the divine patron of hunters and warriors after his murder. His son, Ce Acatl Topiltzin, who slew the usurper to rightfully assume the throne, announced that he was an incarnation of the god Quetzalcoatl. When exiled from Tula at the instigation of worshippers of the god Tezcatlipoca, Quetzalcoatl became Kukulcan in the Yucatan.

Some records list the Toltec kings, and they established dynastic lines and confederations. They were served by a series of nobles, highly educated, well-trained individuals who took on the burden of imperial administration, both of Tula and for the vassal domains. In some eras the king may have ruled with a religious authority, or possibly was guided by the high priests of the ranking temples. Such sharing of power was in keeping with the traditions of the period. Military commanders would also have had a say in the day-to-day affairs of government, acting as counselors to the throne and obeying the ruler, who was their war chief.

Governors of the various Toltec regions were taken from the ranks of the nobles, who probably took part in the councils convened on the death of each king to determine the fitness of candidates hoping to be named heir. This was a usual Mesoamerican pattern in the historical era of the Toltec, one adopted by the Aztec and later cultures. These same aristocrats would also have been instrumental in the collection of tribute from the vassal or allied cities and regions. Such tribute was a hallmark of the Toltec Empire, providing increased economic stability. The tribute received from other groups was distributed as part of the wealth of the Toltec upper classes or provided to those in need in the lower ranks of society. Some tribute, however, was set aside as a resource to be utilized in the vast Toltec trade enterprises.

Since agriculture was basic to the Toltec economy, the farmers, although far removed in status from the aristocracy, were in the majority and were secure in their rights and privileges. Tula, the Toltec capital, held a diverse population throughout the Toltec era. Commoners in the capital would have come from other cultures and from allied or vassal states.

TOLTEC RULERS AND THEIR ERAS

HISTORIA TOLTECA-CHICHIMECA

Huemac—leads Toltec

Chalchiuhtlanetzin	A.D. 510–562
Ixtlilcuechahauac	562–614
Huetzin	614–666
Totepeuh	666–718
Nacoxoc	718–770
Mitl Tlaomihua	770–829
Xihuiquenitzin (queen)	829–833
Iztaccaltzin	833–885
Topiltzin (Quetzalcoatl)	885–959

ANALES DE CUAUHTITLAN

Micoamazatzin—leads Toltec

Huetzin	A.D. 869–?
Totepeuh	?–887?
Ihuitimal	887–923?
Topiltzin (Quetzalcoatl)	923–947
Matlacxochtli	947–983
Nauhyotzin I	983–997
Matlaccoatzin	997–1025
Tilcoatin	1025–1046
Huemac	1047–1122

Artists and craftsmen were especially valued and were a special force within the Toltec government, as were the merchants. Toltec priests and warriors made up the other castes in Toltec society. Generally the aristocratic ranks of the Mesoamerican cultures held the commanding positions, but within the priestly and warrior groups certain commoners, especially those who demonstrated courage, wisdom, intellect and the ability to lead, might advance certain levels of power. Restrictions were probably in force within the Toltec government to ensure that commoners did not exceed themselves beyond a certain point, but worthy candidates for less powerful offices were drawn from all ranks.

The status of slaves in the Toltec world is not documented. It is known, however, that the Huaxtec and others were carried weeping into Tula, possibly as victims for sacrificial ceremonies or as doomed chattel. The role of women remains equally obscure, although there is a record of one woman ruling the Toltec for a brief time. She possibly served as regent for an heir.

Two documents provide king lists for the Toltec—*Historia Tolteca-Chichimeca* and *Anales de Cuauhtitlan*. While they contradict in the order of kings and in dates, they offer a rare insight into the royal dynasties involved in Toltec government. These leaders are also listed under separate entries. The table above lists the rulers.

TOLTEC RELIGION   Belief in a pantheon of gods that was adopted by the Aztec in a later era, combined with Mesoamerican traditions and regional observances. The Toltec gods were associated with the Ometeotl complex, the aspects of a single celestial deity, bisexual and paternal. He was one of the ancient solar gods of Mesoamerica and also

Tezcatlipoca

represented the earth and its fertility. This complex, which included several other gods as well, was overshadowed by the particular deities whose mythic reputations were so interwoven in Toltec historical accounts as to become embodiments of particular periods or religious ideals. The two major deities on this level were Quetzalcoatl and Tezcatlipoca. The Aztec and Toltec-Chichimec worshipped both deities as their own in time, and city-states in the Valley of Mexico nurtured the traditions, which were also linked to the Maya realms in the more southerly domains of Mesoamerica. The Maya and the Nahual people held many beliefs in common, including cosmological views, religious concepts about humankind and about the ultimate destiny of humans with the gods. The Nahuals were called "those who speak with authority" by their Mesoamerican contemporaries, possibly suggesting a belief that they understood divine or spiritual matters, especially those concerning human responses to events and the will of the gods. Human sacrifice, cannibalism, blood-letting and self-mutilation were all aspects of the Toltec religion, mirroring other cultures in the region.

From a cosmological viewpoint, the Toltec adopted the Nahual ideals concerning world in balance. (These views are discussed in the entry on Toltec cosmology.) Their gods were drawn from the Mesoamerican pantheons, including Tlaloc, the rain deity. Two major gods appear to have held sway in Tula and in Chichen Itza: Quetzalcoatl and Tezcatlipoca.

Quetzalcoatl was a Toltec ruler, forced to flee the city and remembered in legends and traditions both in the original Toltec region and in the Maya domain, where he was called Kukulcan. Among the Toltec Quetzalcoatl was also worshipped as Venus, the Morning Star, then called Tlahuizcalpantecuhtli. He was honored as well as Ehecatl, the god of wind, whose rounded temples are unique at some sites.

Quetzalcoatl was the bridge for humans, linking them to animals, water and minerals. He is thought to have ascended into the stars and planets and even into the sun. The god discovered maize and led human beings to the artistic and cultural awareness that resulted in the great Mesoamerican civilizations. Among the Toltec he was a living being, having become reincarnated in their king, Ce Acatl Topiltzin. The god represented a major aspect of

Mesoamerican ideals: the creation of a heart filled with divine truth and a visage that truly expressed a refined inner spirit. In Tula Quetzalcoatl was a god-king. The Toltec worship of the sun and moon, brought from Teotihuacan, reflected the legends of Quetzalcoatl, wherein he rose to the heavens, received honors and then took upon himself the universal and everlasting moon and the stars as his symbols.

His symbols—the butterfly, shells, wind masks, the *atlatl*, jewels, feathers and a conical hat—were tangible representations of his spiritual signs: the mountain of the sun and the double peaks of the sunset and the evening star. He was the serpent that crawled upon the ground and the bird that flew in the sky. The hummingbird was another of his symbols. Born of Coatlicue, Quetzalcoatl had a twin, Xolotl, the dog, another representation of Venus, the Evening Star. With the sun and Coatlicue, Quetzalcoatl represented a trinity of harmony, stability and abundance for the Toltec and for subsequent cultures.

The god Tezcatlipoca was an opposite of Quetzalcoatl, both among the Toltec and other Mesoamerican cultures. He was called Smoking Mirror in a reference to the pyrite mirror that replaced his lost right foot. Obsidian was a symbol of Tezcatlipoca, as that stone represents darkness and gloom. A patron of the commoners of Tula, Tezcatlipoca was revered by the Chichimec groups that composed part of the capital's diverse population. He has been depicted as a truly evil force, probably representing the more violent aspects of nature, which remain neutral regarding humans and yet able to bring about grief and suffering.

Tezcatlipoca is recorded as having two doors on his breast. The brave souls who dared open these doors, meeting threats and terrors in the act, could grasp the god's heart, thus attaining their desires. Lesser beings attempting the same feat perished at the god's hands.

Much of this deity's activities concerned his relationship with Quetzalcoatl in Tula. Known among the Toltec as the creator of music in the world, Tezcatlipoca fell in love with Xochiquetzal, the goddess of flowers and love. He composed songs for her and sang of her beauty and her charm. His female counterpart in the Toltec pantheon was Itzpapalotl, called "the Obsidian Butterfly," the soul crystallized into rock.

The tradition concerning the treachery of followers of Tezcatlipoca and their success in exiling Quetzalcoatl, the heir to the throne, (Mixcoatl's son, Ce Acatl Topiltzin), demonstrates the effect of this deity. He is personified as evil in the conflict, symbolizing the decay and the problems within Toltec capital. When Quetzalcoatl was duped into a drunken state and then exposed as an unworthy monarch, Tezcatlipoca's followers achieved their enduring success. Toltec records state that the god brought about death and despair, ravishing maidens and turning brother against brother as the empire began to collapse in Tula. A magician and a sorceror, Tezcatlipoca existed in half truths only, residing in a cloudy realm of superstition, where he fed on emotional upheavals and chaos. Sowing discord everywhere, the god could also befriend the poor and the downtrodden. This poetic, dramatic tradition defines the civil problems of Tula that led ultimately to its collapse.

When Quetzalcoatl died and was reborn—or when he reappeared according to Maya tradition as Kukulcan—the

god Tezcatlipoca was no more. He was transformed into a shower of stardust, remaining visible only as stars in the night sky. The capital of Tula faded at the same instant.

TOLTEC SOCIETY See TOLTEC, TOLTEC GOVERNMENT, TOLTEC RELIGION, TOLTEC TRADE, and TOLTEC WARFARE.

TOLTEC TRADE Methods of exchange and barter that have not been documented entirely, as the exact perimeters of the empire have not been noted with any certainty. Many of their trade goods may have been tributes sent to Tula by vassal states within the empire. Because of the traditions in Mesoamerica at the time, however, and because of the

Toltec Pipil stela

vacuum left in trade by the fall of Teotihuacan, it is believed that the Toltec conducted vast mercantile enterprises. Their traders, who probably constituted a separate level in the social structure, traveled freely throughout Mesoamerica in search of products and markets. These hardy bargainers are believed to have followed distinct trade routes.

1. A trip through the region of Michoacan to the Lerma-Santiago drainage systems, and then north to the Pacific coastal regions where a variety of products were available.
2. A trip across the eastern Sierra Madre Occidental foothills, through Zacatecas and Durango, into the desert regions of the Northwest.
3. A trip east across the mountains into the tropical lowlands, which extended to the Gulf coast. This route would have linked the Toltec to the Maya of Tabasco and Campeche. It is considered the most important of the Toltec trade routes.

Products moved throughout the Toltec Empire included: cacao, cloaks and other textile materials, feather works, headdresses, maize, obsidian from Toltec-controlled Pachuca mines, plumbate ceramics (the most important item in Tula), Quetzal bird feathers from Maya territories, shields, and turquoise.

These products were not only traded along the routes listed; they were distributed in local markets in all of the regions Toltec merchants, reached and were sent to markets in other regions, including parts of the American Southwest. A trade link between the Toltec and the Hohokam has been established. Other possible trade goods that the Toltec distributed include adobe brick, animal skins, basalt, copper from Michoacan, incense burners, designed as the god Tlaloc, lime, rubber from the gulf coast, serpentine and other green stones, and yarn and woven goods.

The government regulated the marketplaces in the major Toltec settlements. Merchants and trading caravans had armed escorts, and the Toltec may have established garrisons to control and protect the various trade depots and major places of production. Obsidian, for example, was considered a vital product and was closely guarded, both at the mines and en route to the marketplace. It is possible that the Chichimec achieved control of the mining regions, thus hastening Tula's fall.

TOLTEC WARFARE A military system introduced by this group revolutionized war in Mesoamerica. Other cultures had used military force before the arrival of the Toltec, but they had not glamorized battles or warriors. The Toltec elevated warfare into a religious and state-controlled status in the region, which reached its peak in the Aztec military power in the centuries following the fall of Tula. Militarism was vital aspect of the Toltec Empire, one that carried distinction and honor and endowed an entire class of warriors. Such warriors were depicted in the Atlantean statues at Tula, fully armed with symbols of Quetzalcoatl distinguishing them as servants of the nation. (The Toltec fighters adopted Huitzilopochtli, the Nahua god of war, as a patron

after Quetzalcoatl left the capital of Tula.) A majority of Toltec sculptures, in fact, represent such warriors.

The Toltec initiated the great military orders that would flourish again at Tenochtitlan. These orders included the Knights of the Coyote, the Knights of the Eagle and the Knights of the Jaguar. In keeping with Nahua religious beliefs, warriors who fell in battle and those who died as sacrificial victims were destined for paradise. Women dying in childbirth the equivalent of battle for women at the time, also would attain paradise.

The Toltec were skilled in battle, ferocious and highly trained. A standing army, garrisons, forts and reserve units comprised a formidable weapon against inhabitants of regions coveted by the Toltec and against enemies. Because of their skill and their bravery in battle, the Toltec were able to instill enough awe and respect among their neighbors that cities such as Tula could be built without heavy defenses incorporated into their design.

The military orders were probably hereditary, and the Toltec no doubt raised up their commanders through the ranks, demanding long periods of service and training. These were descendants of as yet uncivilized tribes, known in the past for skill with bow and arrow and their ferocity on the battlefields of the region surrounding the Valley of Mexico and northern Mesoamerica.

The great warrior statues at Tula, the *Telemones*, provide a detailed picture of the sort of weapons and gear used by the Toltec warriors. The common soldiers probably went into battle with simple loincloths and few weapons, but the upper ranks of warriors probably wore the garb seen on the statues.

They wore cotton armor, heavily padded to deflect enemy, arrows and spears, with breastplates, probably in the form of the coyote, jaguar or eagle if the warrior belonged to the order of one of these animal totems. A round shield was carried into battle, and the swords were fastened with belts. A short kilt protected the lower half of the torso, and the legs and ankles were covered with sandals and straps. Quetzal plumes decorated warriors' helmets, and skins, plumage and other materials probably were used as emblems of the particular god or order that they served. The fact that the warriors depicted wore nose ornaments indicates that they were of noble rank. Some of the warriors wore beards. The separate military orders, which the Aztec later adopted, would have been fraternities for the education of the young, including special training in emulating their patrons and ancestors. To be received in such a military order meant success in the military establishment and access to those government posts open to veteran commanders. Usually of noble lineage, the members of the military orders were also prime candidates for government positions because of their years of specialized services.

TOLUCA A valley in central Mexico where the Lerma-Santiago river system rose. The region was also occupied by the Matlatzinca, with the Aztec in the east and the Tarascan in the west. Toluca was controlled by the Toltec during their eras of domination and then by the Aztec, taken during the reign of Axacayatl (A.D. 1469–1481). It is believed that Toluca was inhabited during the Formative

Toluca effigy

Period (c. 2000/1600 B.C.–c. A.D. 250/290). Calixtlahuaca and Malinalco are sites of note in the region.

TOMALTEPEC A site having cultural developments in the region of Oaxaca, during the Rosario Phase (c. 700/600–c. 500/450 B.C.) A pyramidal platform was used as a burial chamber there.

TOMIYAUH The wife of the Chichimec king Xolotl who wielded great authority during his reign. She was probably the mother of Nopaltzin, Xolotl's, heir who took the throne in A.D. 1304.

TONACATECUHTLI An Aztec deity, associated with the agricultural cycles and festivals. He was the patron of maize and called Lord of Our Sustenance, dwelling in the thirteenth heaven.

TONACATLAPAN A region in the Huaxtec domain, considered verdant and abundant. It was called the land of food.

TONALA A site on the side of a mountain in Chiapas, serving as a regional ceremonial center. The pyramidal temples there have central staircases with central paved ramps. Two stone altars, one shaped as a jaguar, one as an alligator, were discovered there, as well as Olmec-style stelae.

TONALA RIVER A gulf coastal waterway, the site of the Olmec city of La Venta, some 18 miles from the gulf coast in Tabasco.

TONALMATL The "Book of Days," used in the *tonalpohualli.* (See *TONALPOHUALLI.*)

TONALPOHUALLI The "count of days," a calendar used by the Aztec (Mexica) and other cultures, recorded in the *Tonalmatl,* the "Book of Days." Each of the 260 named days of this divinatory calendar was used in combination with the numbers one to 13. The various Mesoamerican cultures adapted this basic form to their own needs, with different divisions and assignments. Some scholars believe the *Tonalpohualli* was used solely or chiefly for astronomical or astrological purposes or for religious ceremonies and observances. Divination was practiced according to this calendar, and was considered are accurate method of foretelling the future. (See CALENDAR; see also calendar under each individual culture.)

TONATIUH An Aztec adopted deity associated with the primordial creative forces and with the sun and probably of Maya origin. The god, called He Who Goes Forth Shining, was offered blood sacrifices as a sun god capable of staving off the earthquakes the Aztec expected as to end the fifth sun, the world in which they existed. Tonatiuh was also called Nahui Ollin in some rituals and was called Yaomicqui at sunset. (See AZTEC GODS.)

TONINA A Maya site in the north-central part of the Chiapas portion highlands, powerful politically and economically during the Classic Period. Tonina was associated with Palenque in trade and ceremonial customs and suffered when Palenque declined. The last known Long Count date in the site was carved on a monument there in A.D. 909. Noted for its three-dimensional carvings, Tonina was called Stone House. The city was erected on a terraced hillside. Only the lower walls of the original foundation remain, fashioned from slablike stones. Four circular altars, carved with elaborate glyphs, were discovered in Tonina. Three-dimensional limestone stelae, depicting frontal-view figures, reflect the artistic styles of Copan and Quirigua. These figures are attired in elaborate costumes, and some stelae include the Maya bar-dot system with glyphs. An elaborate tomb was discovered, located in the lower terrace area, decorated with mask panels, similar to the Chac masks used elsewhere in the Maya domain. These panels are made of stone and stucco. Another mound, having similar decorations, had a stepped vault. A cache of jade was also found at the site. Among other regional wars, Tonina fought against Palenque, and its warriors captured Kan-Hok-Xul, the second son of the illustrious Pacal of Palenque. Due to its military skills, the city maintained power and rank for a time, even as the region around it was undergoing change. The dated monument of Tonina, a tree stone, signified that the city lasted longer than most of its neighboring sites. The monument was the last known inscribed art piece erected in the Maya southern lowlands.

TOPILTZIN (1) A Toltec king listed in the *Historia Tolteca Chichimeca* and in the *Anales de Cuauhtitlan.* He is recorded as ruling from A.D. 885 to 959 in the *Historia* and from A.D. 923 to 947 in the *Anales.*

TOPILTZIN (2) See CE ACATL TOPILTZIN; see also KUKULCAN; and QUETZALCOATL.

TOPOXTE A Maya ceremonial center dating to the mid-13th century, located in a group of islands in Lake Yaxha in the southern lowlands. The site has temples and a palace structure, with beam-and-mortar roofs instead of the traditional vaults. It is possible that Topoxte was occupied by the Itza from Chichen Itza. Such a presence would have stimulated the growth and progress of the center in a time when other Maya cities were in decline.

TOTEPEUH A Toltec king, listed in the *Historia Tolteca Chichimeca* as ruling from A.D. 666 to 718. Listed also in the *Anales de Cuauhtitlan*, he is recorded in this document as ruling from an unknown date until 887.

TOTOMIHUACAN A Puebla site occupied by the Chichimecs, probably during the reign of XOLOTL, who conducted an expansionist policy in the region around A.D. 1246. It is believed that Totomihuacan was autonomous but held to Chichimec cultural and religious traditions.

TOTONACOPAN A site on the gulf coast associated with the Remojada culture. Figures recovered on this site date to the Classic Period (c. A.D. 1/250–900) and reflect the Remojada styles. (See also TOTONAC.)

TOTONAC A group called the People Who Come From Where the Sun Rises, a Formative Period culture in north-central Veracruz. The Totonac also occupied part of the Sierra de Puebla, and they are believed to have migrated into the region c. A.D. 800. A sixteenth-century account states that the local inhabitants of the coastal region saw the Totonac "coming out of the sea." This was possibly one of several migrations of the group, as the Toltec were establishing colonies and displacing smaller cultures. Spanish and Aztec sources list the final region of Totonac occupation as Totonacopan, on the gulf coast. Supposedly as many as 10 Totonac chiefs ruled there for a span of 80 years.

Some contemporaries recorded that the Totonac were one of the most aristocratic, refined and elegant people of Mesoamerica. They were Nahual in origin, coming from Chicomoztoc, the Land of the Seven Caves—the site that was homeland of so many of the Post-Classic civilizations, including the Aztec. The Totonac claimed to have left the Chicomoztoc region long before other groups. Some scholars, who citing the fact that the Totonac spoke a form of the Macro-Penutian language, also link them to the Olmec.

In their own accounts, the Totonac state that they visited the great city of Teotihuacan and were part of the group that erected the massive pyramidal platforms there. From Teotihuacan, the Totonac journeyed to Zacatlan in the Sierra de Puebla region, a place distinguished by its scenic low, deep *barrancas* and by the yearly crops of vanilla beans harvested in the nearby lowlands. The Totonac established this region as their homeland and earned a reputation for being humble, just and kindly to neighbors and newcomers. In time they experienced the pressures of invaders. Wishing to avoid war, the Totonac withdrew to the coastal region. The sites of Aparicio, Ocelopan and Zempoala date to the period following their exodus from the Sierra de Puebla.

The Totonac apparently adapted quickly to the coastal environment, which they shared to some extent with the

Totonac figure

surviving Maya. Other Mesoamerican groups considered the Totonac and the Maya to be skilled navigators and daring seafarers. They maintained a sizable "merchant marine," a fleet of trading vessels that plied the coastal waters in marketing and trade ventures. The vanilla bean would have been of considerable value as a trade commodity. The extent of such trade, however, is unknown.

They used large floating rafts for some of their journeys, as well as long, narrow canoes manned by a single oarsman who stood in the center of the vessel. Larger Totonac crafts had curved prows and sterns and were relatively massive for the time. The Totonac made sails from palm leaves or rushes. Contemporary reports indicate that the Totonac and the Maya used a type of compass that always registered the direction of east and assisted them in navigation.

The Totonac discovered other Nahual cultures in the coastal regions of Veracruz and mingled freely with them, always expressing the hospitality and kindness for which

Totonac priest

they were famous. Supposedly, the Chichimec arrived during the reign of the second Totonac king. The term "Chichimec" was applied to any uncivilized group, without distinction. The actual designation of these newcomers has not been made. All that is known is that they were warlike nomads who probably straggled into the territory, exhausted by their journeys. The Totonac welcomed them, and the two groups were associated to some extent. Upon the death of the eighth Totonac king, his heirs, two sons, quarreled and allowed the Chichimec to intervene in the affairs of the nation. The extent of their intervention is not recorded. The Totonac survived the rivalry and the subsequent difficulties. As many as 25,000 Totonac were recorded as meeting with the Spanish at Zempoala (Cempoala). The king at the time was made famous by the Spanish, who called him the "Fat Cacique" (an Arawak Indian word that the Spanish had begun to use for rulers). Zempoala impressed the Spanish, who were amazed by the architecture and innovative hygiene systems there. The city was a vassal of the Aztec empire, as the Totonac and the Aztec had been in contact for some time. In the reign of Motecuhzoma I, the Aztec of Tenochtitlan had endured a series of natural disasters that brought famine to their domain. Many Aztec are reported to have fled to the Totonac for assistance, selling themselves or their children into temporary slavery in order to survive.

Like their Mesoamerican counterparts, the Totonac were an agricultural people who adapted their farming routines to their geological and climatic regions. Their communities had large populations generally, and most of them resided in houses constructed of adobe and lime. Each Totonac residence was provided with its own garden plot. The regularity and neatness of the Totonac communities apparently impressed their neighbors. Totonac clothing was also comfortable and distinguished by good materials, and adhered to the usual Mesoamerican styles of loincloths, tunics, skirts and mantles. Ornaments also appealed to the Totonac.

TOTONAC ARCHAEOLOGICAL SITES The cities and communities that were established by this culture, listed in separate entries. These sites include Aparicio, El Tajin, El Zapotal, Isla de Sacrificios, Las Higueras, Oceloapan, Quauhtochco, Quiahuitzlan, and Zempoala (Cempoala).

TOTONAC ARCHITECTURE AND ART A distinguished style long associated with the site of El Tajin, with the use of platforms and inverted *taluds*. El Tajin was influenced by the Totonac, but it had been an independent city-state at one time. Other Totonac sites reflect El Tajin influence, having similar communication tunnels. The Totonac used columns and friezes in high relief as decorations. All these elements are evident in the last two periods of construction in El Tajin. Flat stuccoed walls and highly polished cement panels or stones were another hallmark of the Totonac constructions. The use of cisterns and aqueducts with pipes to bring water to the various districts of their communities was an architectural and engineering feat, of which the Totonac were masters.

Unlike the Totonac's unique architecture, their art appears to have been influenced by many other sources. Totonac stone sculpture, laden often with mysterious symbols, took three major forms that reflected much of the art of Classic Veracruz. These forms included yokes, *palmas* and *hachas*.

Yokes are horseshoe-shape stone objects that are believed to represent the hip guard worn by ball players. The athletes' yoke was generally made of padded leather. Stone yokes may have been considered magical symbols. Many

Totonac head

yokes contain images of toads, owls and eagles, all associated with death rituals. Hieroglyphs are associated with the yokes, and some contain faces of men.

Palmas sometimes resemble palm fronds and again are associated with the ball games. They were worn as sacred amulets by the players. One such *palma* found in the Totonac region depicts a human skull, half living and half dead. It is considered a masterpiece and reflects the Nahua insistence on recognizing the transitory nature of human existence.

Hachas are objects used as ceremonial battle-axes throughout Mesoamerica. Often they are in the form of human profiles, but in many *hachas* the geometric motifs prevail, intertwined with human features. The axes all have sharp edges, and the motifs or the human heads were carved skillfully. One Totonac *hacha* portrays a human profile with great elegance. Other Totonac heads and figures display a realism and gentle grace that mirror the Veracruz style. Heads and female forms are associated with fertility, the gods and the religious traditions of the people.

TOTONAC CERAMICS   The wares that reflect the cultural development of Veracruz and the coastal regions. The following ceramics are listed in separate entries: Cerro Montoso; Fine Orange; Isla de Sacrificios, I, II, III; Quiahuiztlan I, II, III; Tres Picos I, II, III, and Zempoala. (See also MESOAMERICAN CERAMICS.)

TOTONAC DEATH RITUALS   Rites adhering to Nahua traditions and those of Veracruz. Several Totonac burial practices are involved. Square, oval or conical sites were chosen to bury the dead, usually pits placed within pyramidal platforms in the ceremonial complexes or within the stairs or even in the cores of these buildings. The graves' interiors were generally covered with a veneer made of stones or slabs of stones. The burials in these sites were usually collective, involving several corpses.

Another characteristic is the cruciform-style graves, which were also dug into the core of buildings or positioned at the foot of the pyramidal platform stairways.

Mausoleum-style graves were provided for later burials. Temples or structures designed to resemble houses were erected at Quiahuiztlan and elsewhere. Each one of these miniature temples was usually around four feet in height, having a rectangular base, a stepped terrace, stairs and a balustrade. Most had roofs decorated with merlons.

Little is known of the Totonac social or governmental practices. Other Mesoamericans extolled the Totonac as being forthright and kindly. Their language included reverential phrases and courtesy. The Totonac also observed the Mesoamerican *voladores*, the dance of death. Although thousands of Totonac were alive when the Spanish arrived, many died during an epidemic that struck soon after. In time even the great city of Zempoala (Cempoala) was decimated.

TOTOTEPEC   Also called Tototepec del Sur, an individual kingdom located in the coastal region of Oaxaca, identified in some records as the home of the Mixtec ruler Eight-Deer. The city of Tototepec arose after the collapse of the Toltec capital of Tula, A.D. 1156, and was a thriving city during the Aztec imperial age. The Tototepec were obviously related to the Mixtec but remained independent. The Tototepec site of Achiotla was famous throughout Mesoamerica for its beautiful tree that had rare and beautiful flowers and filled the area with a special perfume. When an Aztec ruler, identified in some records as Motecuhzoma II, heard about the tree, he sent a delegation to Achiotla, requesting samples. The Tototepec people refused to give the Aztec any part of the tree, and soon afterward the Aztec arrived with an army and uprooted the plant, killing it. The people of Tototepec attacked the Aztec as a result of this act. The Aztec never managed to subdue the Tototepec.

TOZOZTONTLI   An Aztec festival honoring the goddess Coatlicue, the patroness of flowers and gardeners. The Aztec were dedicated to raising flowers and ornamental plants, and large tracts of *chinampas* in Tenochtitlan and other Aztec sites were reserved for such seasonal crops. (See AZTEC AGRICULTURE.)

TRANSVERSE VOLCANIC AXIS   Called the *Cordillera Neo-volcanico*, an east-west range of volcanoes on the Mesa Central. Within the Transverse Volcanic Axis are the following major volcanoes, accompanied by lesser peaks: Citlatepetl, also called Orizaba; Ixtaccihuatl; Malinche, also called Matlalcueyetl; Naucampatepetl, also called Cofre de Perate; Popocatepetl; Tancitaro; Volcan de Colima; and Xinantecatl, also called Nevada de Toluca.

The Transverse Volcanic Axis is characterized by conical hills of cinder and explosion varieties and has craters and vents formed during the volcanoes' original eruptions. Some are still active. The axis goes through the Mesa Central and into the Sierra Madre Oriental, on the eastern rim of Mesoamerica. Another volcanic axis stretches from the Grijalva River region to the southern borders. Some volcanic peaks included in this axis reach 13,000 to 17,000 feet and keep the surrounding lands alive with tremors and eruptions that threaten entire populations. (See VOLCANOES.)

TRAPICHE-CHALAHUITE   An archaeological zone in Veracruz, in the Chalchalacas drainage basin. Two trenches dug in this region uncovered basalt plates, which give evidence of ceramic phases in the zone. The wares were fluted or striated in black and white. Natural bichromes were also plentiful. The figurines recovered in the Trapiche Chalahuite zone include depictions of idealized humans and deities. A yoke and tools were found in a mound, which included pellets for blowguns. The remains of rectangular and circular houses are either pit form in design or constructed as semisubterranean dwellings. These were erected on artificial mounds that were designed to avoid floods.

TREE OF THE WORLD   A mythic tradition adhered to some Mesoamerican groups, including the Maya. The *Wacab Chan*, the Tree of the World, with the celestial bird perched in its branches, stood at the center of the Maya world. The cardinal points are depicted on the four sides. Some stelae portray the Maya rulers as the *Wacab Chan*, with the celestial bird, depicting these lords as intermediaries between the people and divine forces.

TRES PICOS I, II, III   A series of ceramic phases associated with the Totonac in Veracruz. Polychrome wares from this phase were discovered, which paralleled the cultural developments at the Isla de Sacrificios. The Totonac ceramic phases, like their art and architecture, reflected the styles and the developments of the people of Veracruz and those of the coastal regions. (See TOTONAC CERAMICS; see also MESOAMERICAN CERAMICS.)

TRES ZAPOTES   An Olmec site in the hills of the Papaloapan-San Juan Basin, some 100 miles northwest of La Venta. The city measures little more than two square miles, and it was constructed on the banks of the Hueyapan River. Tres Zapotes is distinguished by 50 or more earthen mounds that stretch along the river's edge. An Olmec site, it was occupied as early as 1000 B.C. The composition of the city includes: Mound Group One, called Ranchito; Mound Group Two, called the Burned Mounds; and Mound Group Three, unnamed.

These earthen mounds are all that remain at Tres Zapotes, and the site has not been fully studied. It is known it was one of the last prominent Olmec sites, and the monuments discovered there have added to the mystery of the Olmec decline. Two finds at Tres Zapotes are of particular importance. Monument C is a badly broken stone box with a mask carved into its top center. The mask is so stylized in design that it is difficult to determine that it contains the typical were-jaguar Olmec motif. This box blends the Olmec culture with the rising Izapa influence in the region, and lends some credence to the concept that the Izapa culture arose from Tres Zapotes. Stela C, a basalt fragment also recovered on the site, depicts the Olmec jaguar motif on one side and a Long Count date on the other. The Long Count, once believed to be solely Maya, determined dates by counting the days elapsed from a chosen starting point, believed to have been 13 August 3114/13 B.C., according to the Gregorian calendar. Stela C's importance was confirmed when the missing fragment was recovered and restored. The presence of the bar-dot system in a site predating the Maya is of immense value. Other calendar finds have confirmed the Long Count at Tres Zapotes, one of the last vestiges of Olmec power.

TRIPLE ALLIANCE   A coalition between Aztec (Mexica), TEXCOCO and TLACOPAN (Tacuba) that came into existence during the reign of the Aztec emperor ITZCOATL (A.D. 1427–1440). The Aztec and Texcoco, ruled by the illustrious NEZAHUALCOYOTL, were rebelling against the demands of MAXTLA, the ruler of the Tepanec at Azcapotzalco. Maxtla had slain CHIMALPOPOCA, the Aztec emperor, in his attempt to claim the Tepanec throne. When Itzcoatl asked for support in defending Tenochtitlan against Maxtla's forces, Nezahualcoyotl marched with his troops and routed the Tepanec forces in Tenochtitlan. Now allied, Nezahualcoyotl and the Aztec began the siege of Azcapotzalco. Tlacopan joined this alliance, and after 114 days, Azcapotzalco collapsed and Maxtla was slain. Tenochtitlan, Texcoco and Tlacopan divided the Tepanec territories and wealth. The Aztec and the Texcocan received two-fifths each, and Tlacopan one-fifth. Warriors and rulers benefited the most from the division of the spoils. The Triple Alliance forces attacked other regions soon afterward, in order to acquire valuable

agricultural regions. Culhuacan, Xochimilco, Cuitlahuac and other sites were brought under the command of the Triple Alliance as result. The next target was the Tlahuica lands to the south. A vast army was assembled, and the region was subdued, as the Aztec and their confederates began imperial conquests in earnest. The *Codex Mendoza* details the success of such campaigns. While the three cities took part in such efforts, in time assisted by other groups, they alternated in taking the commanding role. Provinces were given to Alliance members as spoils of war. Although the cities made war as individual states, they responded to challenges to the Triple Alliance as a cohesive force, working together and dividing all gained lands, slaves and materials. Tribute was also shared.

In the reign of Axayacatl (A.D. 1469–1481), however, following the death of Nezahualcoyotl, the Triple Alliance showed signs of instability. When attacking Tlatelolco, the Aztec confronted an alliance of long-time enemies and had to fight to subdue the region. Axayacatl's defeat by the Tarascan in 1479 lowered the prestige of Tenochtitlan in the region. The Triple Alliance conducted FLOWER WARS against Huexotzingo, Atlixco and other Puebla Valley sites. The alliance lasted approximately 90 years, and changes occurred only only the deaths of the principals in Texcoco and Tlacopan. The alliance permitted Aztec imperial expansion and continuance of the political alignments of Mesoamerica that were in place when the Spanish arrived.

TUFF   Volcanic outpouring, a type of lava, used by Mesoamerican potters because of its ability to withstand relatively high firing temperatures.

TULA   Also called Tollan in some records, the capital of the Toltec Empire in Hidalgo, Mexico, north of Mexico City, covering an area of over five square miles, including the uninhabited El Salitre Swamp. Toltec chroniclers stated that the first building in the Tula region was at a village called Xicocotitlan, the forerunner of the capital. Some remains of stone serpents still stand vertically, with their heads in the ground. The actual capital of Tula was built on a limestone ridge above the Tula and Rosas rivers. The ancient name means "the Place of Rushes," the "Place Where People are Congregated Like Rushes," or simply "the City." The Aztec (Mexica) referred to the site as "Tula-Teotihuacan." The city maintained a diverse population, composed of various groups that had accompanied the Toltec into the region, including the OLMECA-XICALLANCA and the Nonoalco. Such alliances were common in the area during the Toltec period.

The history of the Toltec capital has been obscured by its name and by conflicting Toltec accounts. Study of the site has also been complicated because some structures have been burned and because other Mesoamerican groups, including the Aztec, carried off parts of the city. Studies conducted in Hidalgo, Mexico, however, located some 50 miles north of modern Mexico City, have allowed the establishment of the site's true name and purpose.

Tula was designed for defense, as it was surrounded on three sides by steep banks. Its site on a promontory added protection, probably a boon to earlier groups inhabiting the region. Tula was occupied from A.D. 800, perhaps even earlier, and it underwent several cultural and artistic phases, including the Corral Phase and the Tollan Phase.

Corral Phase. A cultural development dating to around A.D. 800, associated with Mazapan ceramics that were produced as monochromes and as bichromes, shaped into bowls, water jars and legged vessels.

Tollan Phase. A cultural development from A.D. 900 to 1150, heralding the Toltec Empire at its height. The estimated population of Tula is believed to have been 30,000 to 40,000 at the time. Plumbate ceramics are evident, as well as fine orange and Nicoya polychromes.

When the Toltec established Tula as their capital, they began a vast building program, although without the usual highland Mesoamerican designs and without the grid patterns clearly evident in other Mesoamerican metropolises. The location of the site on a promontory may have prohibited such patterns. The residences in and around Tula were built of stones, mud and adobe. Beam and mortar roofs were used, and the homes had additional areas for grinding and cooking, weaving and other crafts. A kiln was discovered in one of the housing districts. These residences, which appear to have been built for familial groups, included shrines and burial sites.

The Great Pyramid dominated Tula, which was probably a regional ceremonial complex as well as a site from which the region was administered. Much of the platform was vandalized by later cultures. It is known that the Aztec carried off statues and carved stone blocks to incorporate into their own capital of Tenochtitlan. The western lower levels have been restored on the platform. This pyramid was dedicated to the Toltec deity Tlahuizcalpantecuhtli, the form of the god Quetzalcoatl as the Morning Star Venus. A pillared portal was originally a major part of the structure, with three rows of 14 Atlantean statues, with a roof. This portal was closed off on one side by a wall and by the steps of the pyramid. A sculpted and painted bench was was discovered as well as a frieze.

The Great Pyramid measures 131 feet on each side at its base and was designed with five levels, giving it a height of almost 33 feet. It was decorated with sculpted panels, which resemble a frieze, depicting jaguars, pumas, eagles, vultures and Quetzalcoatl. The eagles are shown in profile, devouring human hearts, and Quetzalcoatl is depicted in the mouth of a serpent. The pyramidal platform is accompanied by a structure on its west side composed of several chambers, a central patio and a roof supported by more columns. One of these chambers was used for the New Fire rituals, and another was designed with a bench, decorated with low reliefs, along the entire walls. A procession of elaboratly garbed priests is depicted there, with rich attire and ornaments. Mixcoatl, the Cloud Serpent, the war chief who led the Toltec into the region and was then deified, is also portrayed in this building, which is designated by the Spanish as "the Burnt Palace" (*Palacio Quemada*). Tobacco pipes and other ceremonial objects indicate that this was probably not a royal residence but a ceremonial site reserved for the celebration of rituals. A Chac Mul statue was also recovered there, and some rooms were designed with central skylights in the ceilings.

The portal facing the Burnt Palace and the pyramid, called by some the Great Vestibule, contained the great Atlantean statues known as *Telemones*. These statues became one of the hallmarks of Toltec sculpture. They depicted Toltec warriors and were carved in four sections, standing 15 feet high and signifying also the appearance of Quetzalcoatl as Venus, the Morning Star. The statues were provided with full armor, elaborate headdresses, butterfly-shape breast plates (another Quetzalcoatl symbol) and ornamental aprons. Even the warriors' sandals were decorated, and each warrior holds an *atlatl* for throwing spears. The warriors' eye sockets were originally inlaid. The pyramid had five levels. When Tula was abandoned a ditch was dug alongside the lower levels, and the *Telemones* were placed in one and buried, thus insuring their preservation.

On the north side of the pyramid was a serpent wall (a *coateopantli*), composed of five separate sections. The wall was covered with elaborate bas reliefs and with open-work shells on the top. There was also a wall with serpent designs, ball courts, sunken and surrounded by vertical walls and platforms, and a palace that supposedly was the original home of Ce Acatl Topiltzin (Quetzalcoatl/Kukulcan). A procession of jaguars and coyotes, with profiles of eagles and jaguars, decorated the palace and its accompanying structures. A rounded Corral Temple is also associated with Tula, called Tula Chico, and this was probably dedicated to Quetzalcoatl in his form of the wind god, Ehecatl. An attached altar carries a frieze of skulls and crossed bones as well as portraits of Toltec warriors.

Tula was legendary in Mesoamerica as the site of wonders and splendor. The chief ceremonial complex, designed for public or civic ceremonies, was elevated like an acropolis on the southern edge of a major ridge in the area. It had artificially terraced slopes and is believed to have contained a vast mound. Walls from 50 to 60 feet surround this section of the capital, which otherwise was constructed with few defensive measures evident. Besides the major monuments, there were other colonnades and residences. Patios having altars, daises and benches were protected by arcades. Plastered firepits and incense burners were found among the structures as well as stone friezes and stone gaming boards. Dance platforms were also positioned strategically before the major shrines. The workmanship at Tula does not reflect the zenith of Toltec architecture, as it does at Chichen Itza. The buildings, made of poor materials, were not designed to endure. One complex that does possess a unique charm is the group of small temples located near the major canal. This is a shrine dedicated to Tlaloc, the rain deity, and it is surrounded by patios and colonnaded chambers. This shrine also contains a turtle carapace statue. (See TOLTEC for historical and cosmological details about Tula.)

TULA RIVER A waterway in Hidalgo, Mexico. The city of Tula, the capital of the Toltec, was constructed on its banks.

TULAN ZUIVA A Toltec site associated with the birth of the culture, called "Civan Tulan-Vucub Pec" or "Vucub Siwan." It may have been part of another group's holdings. The site was recorded as being in Tabasco.

TULIXLAHUACA A Toltec ceremonial site in the coastal region, listed in Toltec historical records but unidentified at this time.

TULUM   A Maya site located in the northeastern part of Quintana Roo, near Cozumel, called *Izama,* "the City of Dawn." It was a fortress, erected on a projecting piece of land that overlooks the Caribbean. Three sides of this small city are surrounded by water. A wall also served as possible defense, enclosing 15 acres and designed with watchtowers and five gateways. Tulum was an active trade depot for the Maya of that region, linked to the trade routes throughout the Maya domain. The site is noted for the murals that were discovered in a structure called the Temple of the Frescoes. These paintings date to the Classic Period (c. A.D. 1/250–900) and demonstrate skill in achieving depth and perspective. They depict rituals, costumes of the period, musical instruments, sacrifices and warfare. The temple is two story with columns in the central entranceway.

A stela found on the site, obviously brought from another city, is dated to A.D. 564. The Temple of the Descending God, called El Castillo by the Spanish, stands on a terrace and has multiple levels and a large central stairway. The walls are sloped and there are columns in the doorways as well. It is believed that as few as 2,500 people lived in Tulum, perhaps only 500. The wall may have been decorative, but the trade goods stored at the site might have prompted building it as a defense. There are two ruined structures outside the walls of Tulum, one located near a *cenote* (water reservoir).

TUMILCO   An archaeological zone in the basin of Veracruz, on the Tuxpan River. The zone contains mounds that date to the Formative Period (c. 2000/1600 B.C.–c. A.D. 250/290). Ceramics recovered there include the Chila black and whites.

TUNCUILIN RIVER   A river near the Panusco River Basin, associated with the Huaxtec people in their migrations. (See HUAXTEC for details.)

TURQUOISE ROAD   A route taken in the vast Mesoamerican trade venture, linking Alta Vista with the American New Mexico region. Turquoise, called *xihuitl,* or "solar year," was brought from the American Southwest to Alta Vista, where it was worked into mosaics and other adornments and then sent out as trade goods. Malachite, cinnabar, hematite and rock crystal were also mined in Alta Vista c. A.D. 350. In the region of Sinaloa, Aztatlan was also on the Turquoise Road trade route, producing iron pyrite, onyx and alabaster as objects for marketing. The Turquoise Road in Zacatecas was valuable to the city of Teotihuacan and was in use throughout the Classic Period. Over 750 mines are known to have existed in the region. People from Alta Vista may have traveled into the American Southwest to mine turquoise. When Alta Vista was abandoned, c. A.D. 900, La Quemada, a Chalchihuites city, became the controlling force on the Turquoise Road. Toltec customs and traditions appeared in the American Southwest through the Turquoise Road, which some scholars have equated with the Asian Silk Route.

TUTUTEPEC (1)   A site in the coastal region of Oaxaca, one of the four Mixtec capitals. Ceramic wares there were highly developed. Some of tombs associated with the site have been looted. A monolith was erected at Tututepec.

TUTUTEPEC (2)   A Mixtec group, part of the national confederacy. The Tututepec were active in the coastal regions. (see TUTUTEPEC (1); see also MIXTEC.)

TUXCACUESCO-ZAPOLITAN   An archaeological zone in southern Jalisco and in parts of Colima where three ceramic complexes were discovered, associated in part with Autlan wares. Dating to the Formative Period (c. 2000/1600 B.C.–c. A.D. 250/290), the zone includes the sites of Tuxcacuesco, Coralillo, and Toliman.

Tuxcacuesco is associated with the Colima Ortices Phase, especially large figures and red wares, some incised and then painted black on red. A hollow, polished dog figure was found at one site in this cultural development, and effigy flutes, ear spools, shell and stone ornaments were also recovered. Coralillo sites are associated with Mazapan wares, having ceramics painted red on buff and red on brown. Clay whistles were also recovered. Toliman sites have red on brown wares. Clay whistles, cylinder seals, stamps, pottery bracelets and stone mace heads were also recovered.

TUXPAN   Also called Tochpan, a basin beside the Tuxpan River on the gulf coast. The Huaxtec and Totonac were in the region, and the Aztec (Mexica) conquered it in the Late Classic Period during their eras of imperical expansion.

TUXPAN RIVER   See TUXPAN.

TUXTLA, LOS, MOUNTAINS   A volcanic range on the gulf coast of southern Veracruz, which is composed primarily of extinct cinder cones and large peaks. A *caldera,* called Catemaco, formed by one of the volcanoes in the chain, is in the Tuxtla region. Two major drainage basins flank the Tuxtla. The "Metropolitan" Olmec lived in this region and took advantage of the mountainous terrain. They are associated with Olmec development as early as Olmec I (1500–1200 B.C.), perhaps earlier. Some peaks reach 3,000 feet, and Tuxtla Mountains are visible for miles.

TUZAPAN   A Toltec fortress in central Veracruz. The site appears to have been related to the Mazapa and Coyotlatelco phases of Toltec development. Tuzapan may have been a Toltec trading depot.

TWINS, HERO   See HERO TWINS.

TZACUALLI PHASE   A cultural development in the city of Teotihuacan, lasting from A.D. 1 to 150. An estimated population of 30,000, including Oaxaca artisans, lived in the city at the time. The Pyramid of the Sun was completed in Teotihuacan during this period, and the foundations for the Pyramid of the Moon and the Temple of Quetzalcoatl were also laid down.

TZAKOL CULTURE   An Early Classic Period (c. A.D. 1/250–600) development in the Peten (Putun) and surrounding Maya region, lasting until around the end of that historical period. Artistic endeavors achieved new refinement during this period, and the classic Maya murals were made at that time. These paintings were found in Uaxactan and in the "Painted Tomb" of Tikal. Polychrome bowls, spouted jugs, tripod cylindrical vessels, elaborate grave offerings and pedestal bowls as well as polychrome figures are associated with the Tzakol culture. Some of these wares were discovered in the city of Teotihuacan.

TZELTAL MAYA   See MAYA GROUPS, TZELTAL.

TZINTZUNTZAN   A site called the Place of the Hummingbirds, associated with the Tarascan and located on the northeastern arm of Lake Patzcuaro in Michoacan. The site was a Tarascan capital, enduring until the Spanish conquest. The city was constructed on a terraced elevation above the lake and was dominated by a palace, large enough to house a staff and many nobles. Luxury goods were recovered from Tzintzuntzan, which was distinguished by the unique architectural innovation called *yacata*, a T-shaped structure. The *yacata* form was constructed as a series of large rectangular platforms, 1,400 feet long and 850 feet wide. Five *yacata* were built on a north-south axis in the capital, rising in stepped levels to more than 40 feet. Each had a staircase on the east side, opposite the rounded portions. Spiral carvings and other reliefs were incorporated into their design. The *yacata* were also burial sites for Tarascan nobles. Little else remains in Tzintzuntzan.

TZITZIMITL   An Aztec (Mexica) goddess, depicted as a skeleton with claws and mouths at each joint. The goddess wore human heads as earrings and a necklace of human hearts and hands.

TZOMPANTLI   A skull rack, found on Mesoamerican temple sites, having wide use especially in the Post-Classic Period (A.D. 900–1521) and found beside temples in the major ceremonial complexes of the major and minor Mesoamerican cultures of the time. The Toltec and Aztec (Mexica) complexes used the *tzompantli*. Such skull racks were also found in Calixtlahuaca and in Alta Vista, near Tula. Skull racks were designed as accompanying pieces for the temples. Some were elaborately carved.

TZONTECOMATL   An Acolhuan ruler who married a Toltec princess. He ruled Coatlinchan c. A.D. 1260 and may have increased the Acolhua realm during his reign.

TZOTZIL MAYA   See MAYA GROUPS, TZOTZIL.

TZUTZUMATZIN   The last ruler of the city of Coyoacan, slain by the Aztec (Mexica) emperor AHUITZOTL.

U

UAXACTUN   One of the most elaborate of the Chicanel Maya sites, located in the Peten (Putun) region of the Yucatan, north of the great ceremonial city of Tikal. The buildings in Uaxactun are so profusely decorated and the architecture so complex that the original scholars working in the region could not categorize them. Maya cosmological views were impetus for the edifices in the ceremonial clusters and vast acropolises. The platforms discovered in Uaxactun are from the Formative Period (2000 B.C.–c. 250-290 A.D.) or later. A stela on the site dates to A.D. 327. Some resemble keyholes, built in the rectangular or round style and having rectangular projections. Huts or other structures with thatched roofs once stood up on these platforms, which also bore elaborate decorative motifs dramatizing the religious ceremonies performed there.

The Chicanel Phase is evident in Uaxactun, dating from 100 B.C. to A.D. 130. In the Early Classic Period (c. A.D. 1/ 250–600), the city appears to have been influenced by the Tzakal culture. There are certain Olmec traces as well.

The cosmological theme that dominates in some of the acropolises is that of the sacred mountain, called the *Witz*, that was believed to rise through the layers of the universe. A monster guarded this mountain and was also portrayed with the *Witz*. Massive stucco sculptures decorate the panels and terraces of the platforms and structures. Individual rulers were also depicted, and masks of the *Witz* monster are extensive and decorative adjuncts to the palaces and pyramids.

A body found in a tomb in Uaxactun was buried with its skull between its knees. The facial bones of the skull had been removed, a Cocom tradition. Stelae recovered at the site offer vast amounts of information concerning the city and its populace. The last such stela is dated A.D. 889. Although Uaxactun had a rather powerful dynasty of rulers and managed to control a large portion of the Yucatan, it fell victim to the ambitions of Jaguar Paw, called the Great, the ruler of Tikal whose army was led by Smoking Frog. In A.D. 378, Tikal overthrew Uaxactun, slaying the king and reducing the city to vassal status.

UINTUROPAN   A Tarascan deity, worshipped as the patroness of maize. As such, the goddess was associated with the agricultural traditions of the Tarascan and honored in various festivals throughout the year.

ULUA RIVER   A natural waterway located in the Sula Plains, an area on the Gulf of Honduras. The Ulua serves to drain the interior regions.

UPPER BECERRA FORMATION   A geological term used to explain the particular location of certain discoveries at Santa Isabel Iztapan and Tepexpan. The term denotes a stratum associated with the Terminal Pleistocene Period. The Upper Becerra Formation is also evident in other regions of the Valley of Mexico and in the Puebla Valley.

USUKUNKYUM   The brother of the god Ah Kinchil, called Kinich Ahau in the Yucatan. Usukunkyum protected his brother deity from the evil spells of the god Kisin (Cizin) in Xibalba, the Maya underworld. Such divine intervention was necessitated in the cosmological battle between good and evil in the Maya tradition.

USULATAN CERAMICS   Highly prized wares that are associated with the ceramic phases of several regions and valued goods in the major trade ventures of Mesoamerica. They are believed to have originated in the ceramic industry of El Salvador and are indicative of the Late Formative Period (300 B.C.–c. A.D. 250-290) at Maya sites. Usulatan ceramics were made using the lost wax technique, in which wax or thin clay was applied to a vessel, darkened in a reducing fire and then removed to leave an imprint of wavy, yellowish lines on a darker orange or brown background. The wares have been found in the Chul Phase (400 B.C.–A.D. 200), in the Chicanel Phase in Uaxactun and Tikal (100 B.C.–A.D. 130) and in the Caynac Phase (400 B.C.–A.D. 200). There is some speculation that Chalchuapa, a Maya frontier site near El Salvador, was the source of the Usulatan wares. Chalchuapa is dated from 400 B.C. to A.D. 200. In El Salvador, Usulatan wares were associated with the Miraflores Phase.

USUMACINTA RIVER   A waterway in the Guatemalan highlands, joined by the Pasion the Salinas and the Chixoy rivers at the site of Altar de Sacrificios. The name is derived from the Aztec Nahuatl language, meaning "Place of Small Monkeys." The great Maya ceremonial complex Bonampak utilized the Usumacinta River as a water resource. In the Chontal region, the Usumacinta joins the Grijalva River to form a vast water system. These streams and deltas are abundant, and it is called the Place of Canoes, denoting that the Usumacinta and its many tributaries are used widely, especially in regional trade ventures.

UTATLAN   The capital of the Quiche Maya, located on the Pacific coast of modern Quatemala. Utatlan was said to have been built on a series of plateaus covering more than six square miles. The site included palaces and temples an urban grid plane and monumental architecture. The city had three sections, each with its own ceremonial centers. Three Quiche noble families served in the government. During the Classic Period (c. A.D. 1/250–900) Kukulcan, the god Quetzalcoatl in his Maya form of Kukulcan, was the dominant deity worshipped in the region. Utatlan was also associated with the great Classic Maya epic, the *Popol Vuh.* It is believed that the *Popol Vuh* was written in Utatlan during the sixteenth century A.D.

UXBENKA   A Maya site in southern Belize, erected on a ridge overlooking the Maya Mountains. Called the Old Place, the center provided more than 20 stelae and dates to the Early Classical Period (A.D. 1/250 to 600). Little documentation is available for this site.

UXMAL   A Maya ceremonial in the west-central part of the Yucatan Peninsula, demonstrating Puuc, Mexican and Chenes influences and recorded as participating in the the Classic Period (c. A.D. 1-250–900) conflicts struggles in the region. The name is believed to represent a Maya term for "three times." Uxmal, which in its time held considerable sway over the surrounding region, contains evidence of foreign elements, perhaps enclaves of Mexica. The Xiu dynasty also is associated with the ceremonial complex, a later noble house but a royal line that participated in the wars and rivalries of the historical period. Uxmal is believed to have had as many as 200,000 inhabitants at the height of its power, mostly immigrants from the southern Maya lands, then in a state of decline. These immigrants would have brought their own traditions and customs with them. The ceremonial complex thus reflects, in many ways, the decline of the Maya sites and the rivalries and the unrest caused by Mexica intrusion into the region and by the introduction of competing cultures.

Uxmal collapsed soon after A.D. 900, the date on the last monument there. Throughout its history, the city's design incorporated both religious and administrative structures. These structures are divided into six major clusters, with the Palace of the Governor probably housing the local ruler. Built on a terrace, the palace has three stairways and originally stood 65 feet high. A stairway having three landings and a ramp leads to a platform 319 feet long and almost 40 feet wide. Vaulted corridors divide the chambers on this level, and the entire building is architecturally splendid. The House of the Turtle, a rectangular structure about 94 feet long, stands on the platform with the palace. A ball court and a large pyramid complete the cluster. The city is

considered by some to reflect the peak of Maya urban planning.

The second cluster of buildings in Uxmal is composed of a structure called the Nunnery by the Spanish and the Temple of the Adivino. The Nunnery Quadrangle stands on a platform having a southern stairway. This complex is actually composed of four buildings surrounding a central courtyard, which is more than 250 feet long and 210 feet wide. The southernmost building in the complex forms the facade of the Nunnery, with a wide vaulted entrance and two large chambers, each divided into eight separate sections. The front rooms have doorways, and those in the rear open onto the courtyard. Two symmetrical additions built later form a block 260 feet long. Trelliswork decorates the walls above the doors in this section. The northern building, resting on a platform 325 feet long, has a stairway 88 feet wide. This structure is divided into two large parallel rooms, each having 11 chambers with separate doors. The walls above the doors in this edifice are decorated with human figures, birds and geometric designs. There are also small carved symbols above each door. The eastern building has two large rooms also, divided into 10 separate sections having five openings. Trelliswork replaces reliefs in this structure. The western structure is 175 feet long and consists of seven rooms, reached by a stairway. A throne with a canopy was discovered in this edifice, and a figure once graced the chamber as well.

The Temple of the Adivino, so named by the Spanish in reference to as the residence of "the Magician," has an oval base measuring about 227 feet along its north-south axis and 162 feet along its east-west axis. It is three-tiered, showing evidence of having been constructed during five separate periods. There are temples on the various levels; the one at the top is rectangular, with three chambers.

The Pigeon House Cluster has platforms, stairways and vaults. A roof comb surmounted the wall originally. Also discovered on the site was the Great Pyramid, which measured 260 feet along one side and stood 93 feet high. A collection of ruins called the Cemetery Group, also include another pyramid. At the southeastern end of Uxmal is the Pyramid of the Old Woman, so called by the Spanish, which stands on a rectangular base. This structure refers to a legend concerning a dwarf hatched from an egg and cared for by an old woman. The dwarf built the Temple of the Adivino in one night to avoid punishment by the local people. The western and northern clusters are in ruins. Uxmal is also noted for the Platform of the Stelae and the Temple of the Phalli. (See MAYA ARCHITECTURE; MAYA CEREMONIAL COMPLEXES; YUCATAN.)

$$V$$

VALLEY OF MEXICO   See MEXICO, VALLEY OF.

VALSEQUILLO   A site in the Valley of Puebla, where objects recovered date to the UPPER BECERRA FORMATION of the Terminal Pleistocene Period. A reservoir, Valesquillo has yielded vast quantities of data concerning the emerging groups in that region of Mesoamerica. One piece of charcoal recovered from a Valesquillo site dates to around 36,000 B.C. Tools and weapons were also uncovered, as well as an incised pelvic bone of a large elephant. The bone fragment is believed by some to depict bison, mammoths and a tapir, animals of the megafauna of the earlier Mesoamerican eras. The finds at Valsequillo offer valuable information concerning the evolution of the region. The site is located in the San Pedro Zacachimalpa Barranca, beside the Atoyac River.

VENTA SALADA PHASE   A cultural development of the Tehuacan Sequence, in the Incipient Agriculture Period (7000–c. 2000/2500 B.C.). The Venta Salada was the last phase of the sequence in southern Puebla and northern Oaxaca, dating from A.D. 700/800 to 1520. A vast population, estimated between 60,000 to 120,000, was engaged in agriculture and used canals for irrigation during this developmental stage. Trade was also undertaken, as more advanced cultures came to have influence on the region. Salt, cotton and local crafts were traded in this phase. Aristocratic dynasties emerged as well, and borders were being established among the city-states.

VERACRUZ   A region in the gulf coastal lowlands, where hills dominate the landscape in the north and the low coastal plains offer hospitable living conditions. In southern Veracruz the volcanic Los Tuxtla Mountains tower over a plain between two rivers, the habitation of the Metropolitan Olmec. Nearby is Lake Catemaco, a *caldera*, also volcanic in origin. The San Martin and Santa Marta volcanoes are also here. Veracruz underwent the typical Paleo-Indian and Formative development, and in the Classic Period (c. A.D. 1/250–900) the region was the home of major cultures and independent city-states. El Tajin was in the north, and Cerro de las Mesas, the most important archaeological site in Veracruz after the Olmec collapse, was in the south. Maya and Izapa influences were present, as were the various ceramic phases of the city of Teotihuacan. About 800 ceramic pieces were recovered at Cerro de Las Mesas. Another site, Matapacan, was located in the mountains and contained Teotihuacan wares as well as objects from the city of Kaminaljuyu. It is believed that Matapacan might

have linked Teotihuacan and the coastal plains of Guatamala and Kaminaljuyu in trade. Nopiloa was also important to trade, as was El Zapotal. Shrines made of molded clay and stacks of skulls distinguished these sites, which contain ceramics from Teotihuacan. In the Post-Classic Period (A.D. 900–1521), Veracruz was inhabited by Olmec remnant groups and by the Totonac, Huaxtec and Nahual clans. The Toltec entered the region during the era of their expansion, forcing the Totonac back to the coastal plains. Zempoala and other Totonac cities flourished in Veracruz for a time. Quiahuiztlan, another Totonac site, was the scene of negotiations between Spanish invaders and Aztec officials following the Europeans' arrival in the region.

VERDE RIVER   A waterway in the Sierra Madre Oriental that drains the interior and serves as a natural resource.

VERDIA PHASE   A ceramic development associated with the Zacoalco-Sayula archaeological zone in southern Jalisco, dating to the Formative Period (2000 B.C.–c. A.D. 250/290). Some unique wares were produced during this phase.

VILLA ALTA PHASE   A cultural development in San Lorenzo, a former Olmec site on the Rio Chiquito, dating to A.D. 900, when the site was reoccupied by other groups. Abandoned at the time of the Olmec collapse, c. 400 B.C., the city had a brief population renewal in this later period as new groups moved into area.

Veracruz stamp

273

VISION SERPENT See WORLD TREE.

VOLADORES A "dance of death," a religious ritual practiced by the Totonac, Huaxtec and other Mesoamerican groups to ensure good fortune. On certain festival days, a platform was attached to a gigantic pole that was firmly positioned in the ground. Five men climbed to this platform. One remained in the center, blowing on a reed instrument to provide musical accompaniment and to rotate the platform slowly. The four other men, representing the cardinal points of the earth, tied ropes to their ankles and dropped off the platform at the corners to swing in arcs above the spectators' heads. With each turn of the platform the ropes slowly unwound, lowering the men to the ground. This whirling, dangerous and dramatic performance had religious significance. The Totonac are reported as performing the *Voladores* in modern times.

VOLATILES Glyph signs used by the Aztec in their calendar system, accompanying the numbers given to the various days. The *volatiles*, usually represented by birds, were included with the Lords of the Day on Aztec calendars.

VOLCAN DE COLIMA One of the major volcanic peaks in the Transverse Volcanic Axis in the Mesa Central of Mexico. (See VOLCANOES.)

VOLCANOES Natural formations brought about by upheavals blow the earth's surface and acting as vents for pressure built up within the levels of magma and other elements. Volcanoes were abundant in Mexico and Guatemala. Some formed the Pacific edge of the region from the Mexican-Guatemala border into Costa Rica. The Transverse Volcanic Axis on the Mesa Central of Mexico is the most impressive of the Mesoamerican volcanic ranges, following the Mesa Central and entering the region of the Sierra Madre Oriental on the eastern rim. Another volcanic axis extends from the Grijalva River to the southern borders. These volcanic formations destroyed some Mesoamerican cities, including Cuicuilco (now part of modern Mexico City). That city was buried by lava from Xictli Volcano in A.D. 100, leaving the site preserved to some extent. Such volcanic outpourings decimated regions but also formed fertile highlands for subsequent generations of Mesoamericans. Actually, the regions with volcanic activity, both in Mexico and in Guatemala, maintained rather dense populations throughout historic periods.

The traditional volcanic formations still evident in Mesoamerica include cinder and explosion conical hills, craters, vents and lakes. Such formations were generated by the original eruptions of the volcanoes and, in some regions, were altered over the centuries by continued volcanic activ-

MESOAMERICAN VOLCANOES
MEXICO

Cofre de Perate
Ixtaccihuatl
Malinche
Nevada de Toluca
Orizaba, Pico de (Citlatepetl)
Popocatepetl
Tancitero
Volcan de Colima

GUATEMALA

Atitlan
Cerro Quemada
San Pedro
Santa Maria
Tacana
Tajunmulco
Toliman
Zunil

ity. In the Tarascan domain, situated around Lake Patzcuaro, as many as 800 volcanoes exist. Some volcanic peaks, including Pico de Orizaba (Citlatepetl), Popocatepetl and others, are between 13,000 and 17,000 feet high. These volcanoes are considered still active. The table lists the major volcanic peaks in Mexico and Guatemala. (See also MESOAMERICAN GEOGRAPHY and under separate entries.)

VUCUB CAQUIX A Maya deity taking the form of a vulture and associated with death and with the Lords of the Night, who ruled Xibalba the Maya underworld. In the Maya cosmological traditions concerning good and evil, this god was slain by the Hero Twins in their adventures on behalf of humankind as recorded in the *Popol Vuh*. He was also called Seven Macaw, and had a body made out of gold, silver and precious stones. The death of Vucub Caquix was celebrated in the Maya realms and was associated in some records with the Maya ball games. (See TWINS, HERO.)

VULTURE A species of bird widespread in Mesoamerica. The king vulture (*Sarcoramphus papa*) is very large and well known outside of the Valley of Mexico. The turkey vulture (*Cathartes aura*) and the black vulture (*Coragypes atratus*) are found throughout the entire region. The Maya depicted the god of Xibalba, Vucub Caquix, as a vulture. The Zapotec and other cultures venerated vulture deities.

WARRIOR LANDS An Aztec (Mexica) agricultural division, possibly related to Toltec customs concerning distribution of resources. These lands were estates granted to military veterans, especially those who took part in imperial military campaigns for the acquisition of new Aztec lands. The emperors gave portions of the lands won in battle to veterans, particularly those who had distinguished themselves. Aztec military training encouraged men to seek such distinction and the rewards that ensued.

The warrior lands were not actual land grants; the veterans could use the land in the conquered territories during their lifetimes but, if they died without an heir, the land reverted to the state government. Such land allotments allowed the Aztec to maintain entire territories and to enforce their style of government and rule on newly acquired domains. The conquered populations, stripped of ownership, worked the warrior lands under the surveillance of the Aztec veterans.

WARRIOR SOCIETIES See KNIGHTS.

WATER LILY PERSONS A Maya term, *Ah Nob*, used to denote nobles among the various aristocratic clans. The term reflects the natural environment of much of the Maya domains, especially the lowlands. These had rivers and wetlands, as in Peten and parts of Belize. The lily plant signifies abundance, alluding to the essential role of the noble clans in providing for the rulers of the Maya centers.

WATER, LORD See LORD WATER.

WERE-JAGUAR The cosmological mystical being and a symbol in Olmec religious tradition and art. The were-jaguars were products of the legend that an Olmec woman once mated with a jaguar, producing offspring with the characteristics of both. The were-jaguars were thus portrayed having somewhat puffy infantlike features. They had infant limbs and snarling mouths and fangs. Most were-jaguar heads were cleft at the top.

Were-jaguars were generally portrayed as genderless and in the arms of women or alone. The exact purpose of the were-jaguar cult is undetermined. It is known, however, that were-jaguars were believed to represent humans inheriting feline traits and characteristics. The jaguar cult was popular in Olmec territories, as the animal embodied the virtues of courage, cunning and stamina, all of which were extolled during cult ceremonies. By linking themselves to such a powerful predatory force in nature, the Olmec praised these virtues and impressed upon new generations the relationship between humans and their environment. Statues depicting a woman mating with a jaguar were widespread in the Olmec domain.

WHEELS Wheeled toys have been discovered in Veracruz and elsewhere. There were, however, no beasts of burden in the region so wheels were not employed with transportation vehicles. The terrain limited the type of transportation available; porters were most commonly used. Horses were introduced into the area by the Spanish c. A.D. 1521.

WITZ MONSTER A Maya religious symbol depicting a living mountain. This mountain has eyelids and a cleft in the center of its forehead. The mouth, usually agape, was the entry to the mountain. When the Witz Mountain portrayed a particular mountain, the name of that peak was painted on the face of the symbol.

WOMAN OF TIKAL A Maya noblewoman, the daughter of Lord Kan Boar, who was buried in Tikal. Her tomb, one of the few elaborate grave sites for women in the Maya realm, is the object of considerable interest. She was buried with a spider monkey, possibly her pet.

WORLD TREE (see TREE OF THE WORLD).

X

XALAPOZCO   A dry volcano cinder cone formed in the Valley of Mexico and in the Puebla Basin. *Axalapozcoes*, cinder cones with small lakes, also are present in these regions. (See VOLCANOES.)

XALPANECA   A Nahua group from Chicomotoz, the Land of the Seven Caves, the legendary home of the Aztec (Mexica) and others. The Xalpaneca are believed to have accompanied the Totonac in their initial migration to the city of Teotihuacan. The group broke away from the Totonac at some stage and disappeared.

XALTOCAN   A powerful city-state on some islands in the lake, located on the eastern side of Lake Xaltocan-Zumpango as well as in the Valley of Mexico in an area inhabited by the Otomi and the Chichimecs. Founded sometime around A.D. 1230, Xaltocan apparently had a mixed population, as the Otomi were reported living there, among others. In time the city dominated the Valley of Toluca, making the Mazahua, a people called Those Who Have Deer, their vassals. The city also exerted influence on the emerging civilizations in the region. In time the site was taken by the Tepanec, led by their king, Tezozomoc, who had imperial ambitions and a trained military force. Xaltocan fell to the Tepanec in A.D. 1395. Survivors of the assault fled to Texcoco, a rival city-state. There they received land grants and were offered a safe haven. The Aztec never managed to completely subdue the region.

XALTOCAN-ZUMPANGO LAKE   A water resource in the Valley of Mexico, linked to Lakes Texcoco and Chalco-Xochimilco. The city of Xaltocan was erected on the eastern bank of this lake and on some islands within it.

XAMEN EK   A Maya name for the planet Venus, which was also called Ah Chac Mitan Ch'oc. The planet was called Xamen Ek when it was revered as a brother of the great deity Itzamna. (See MAYA ASTRONOMY; MAYA GODS.)

XARATANGA   A Tarascan goddess, revered by that culture as the patronness of fertility and nurturing.

XAYACAMACHAN   Aztec ruler of the powerful city-state of Huexotzingo during the Aztec rebellion against the Tepanec. Huexotzingo had a unit in the Aztec forces, supposedly led by Xayacamachan. His empire was in the Puebla-Tlaxcala Valley. Huexotzingo captured no prisoners or booty from the raid.

XE CULTURE   A Maya lowlands development, evident on the Pasion River and dating to around 1000 B.C. The Xe may or may not have been true Maya, but they pioneered settlements in regions that would one day compose part of the Maya realm. Such Xe settlements have been found to include small villages built on the ground, generally located near ancient agricultural sites. The Xe farmers tended a variety of domesticated plants. Xe ceramics indicate a well-developed skill. The Xe manufactured the *tecomate* (neckless jar) and flat pans used as cooking or storage vessels. They do not appear to have used ceremonial ceramics. Some solid ceramic figures were discovered in Xe settlements, but there is no evidence of shamanistic activity.

Most Xe communities consisted of less than 100 people, and they thrived on the river products available to them as well as on plants and animals in the surrounding marshes and jungles. The Xe region teemed with serpents, deer, wild pigs, rodents and jaguars.

It is believed that the Xe migrated into the region along the Pasion River from the gulf coast. They appear to have been related to highland cultures in Guatemala. In time, the Maya culture dominated all of the Xe settlements, imposing its own cultural ideals. The Xe apparently did not participate in the developmental processes undertaken by the Maya. (See XE PHASE.)

XE PHASE   A Maya ceramic development evident in the Maya cities of Altar de Sacrificios and Seibal. This phase, which dates to c. 900 B.C., is associated in some records with the Mamon, Ocos, Barra and Swasey cultural developments.

XIBALBA (1)   "The Place of Fright," the Maya underworld, celebrated in Maya religion and in their literature and believed located south of the Peten. The underworld was also called the Maw. Venus, as the Evening Star was believed to rise from Xibalba. Xibalba was ruled by beings called the Nine Lords of the Night, the *Bolontiku*. The Maya deity Ah Kin (Kinich Ahau) descended into Xibalba each night to confront Ah Puch and the forces of death and evil. Tales of this cosmological journey had wide appeal in Mesoamerica, as in ancient cultures in other parts of the world. Ah Puch, the emaciated god of death, ruled the lowest level of the underworld. He was the foe of the benevolent deities of the Maya, playing out the duality of good and evil and the eternal combat between these forces. When Ah Kin descended into Xibalba each night, his brother Usukunkyum protected him from evil spells and dangers, as Ah Puch and the Nine Lords of the Night had ferocious

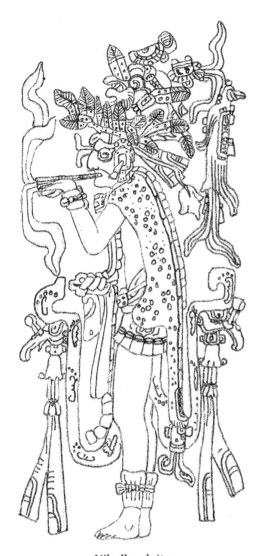

Xibalba deity

allies and weapons. The *Popol Vuh*, the great Maya literary masterpiece, records that Lady Blood, a princess of Xibalba, gave birth to the Hero Twins, who battled the forces of darkness and death on behalf of humankind. (See MAYA COSMOLOGY; MAYA GODS; see also TWINS, HERO.)

XIBALBA (2) According to Maya religious traditions, the other world reserved for kings and priests, who spend eternity there in an enraptured state. Replete with natural wonders, Xibalba was a paradise. At sundown Xibalba became the night sky visible from the earth.

XICALLANCO (Xicalanco) An important port site located in southern Campeche. The port was originally founded by the Maya and dominated by the Peten (Putun) Maya in time. It became a trading center of considerable renown in the region. The name translates as "the land of the calabashes," which are a type of gourd. In the Late Classic Period (c. A.D. 1200/1250–1521), Xicallanco had ties with the major trade systems of many Mesoamerican cultures, as the Maya extended their markets and routes to adapt to growing populations elsewhere. It is believed that Xicallanco had been the original home of the OLMEC-XICAL-LANCA, who claimed in their own records to have originated there.

In the later eras, however, the merchants of the port acted quite separately from the Maya or any older culture. They made their own alliances and set their own standards for marketing products. They are known to have conducted trade activities on the Yucatan Peninsula, which had large populations in the ceremonial complexes, but they also traveled to what is now Honduras. Many of their trade ventures occurred by river or sea, as the merchants were skilled seafarers. Hugging the coastline, the merchants sailed in all directions to trade the diverse assortment of wares available from the northern territories. The large merchant fleets made these sea rounds on a regular basis, and the people of Xicallanco, with the Totonac, employed rafts, canoes and large vessels having curved prows and sterns. Sails were made from palm leafs and reeds. Some reports credit these merchants with having compasses that pointed to the east, a great boon for navigation. The merchants of Xicallanco earned the name of the Phoenicians of the Americas. In time the Aztec began to use the region to further their imperial trade systems.

XICOTENCATL A Chichimec ruler recorded as starting the city of Tlaxcala in A.D. 1348. The Tlaxcalan were a rare group that remained free of Aztec (Mexica) domination. The city of Tozatlan, a Tlaxcalan site, has murals depicting the wars between the Tlaxcalan and Aztec.

XICCO A city founded on a island in Lake Chalco-Xochimilco in the Valley of Mexico. The founders of Xicco were reportedly the survivors of the fallen city of Tula, the Toltec capital. As the heirs of this culture, the people of Xicco maintained the traditions of Tula and were said to be associated with the Mazapan ceramic and cultural phases. Xicco was an important site in the Valley of Mexico as the Post-Classic (A.D. 900–1521) civilizations were emerging. It transmitted older traditions and artistic ideals to the newcomers, influencing architectural and artistic style. According to legend, the original site predates the fall of Tula and was taken over by Toltec fleeing the fall of their capital. The god-king, Quetzalcoatl (Ce Acatl Topiltzin), was reported as using a cave there as a hiding place from his enemies, the followers of the god Tezcatlipoca. These enemies drove Quetzalcoatl from Tula. One of Quetzalcoatl's sons, Xilotzin, was captured near Xicco, while a second son, Pochotl, escaped. (See QUETZALCOATL; TOLTEC).

XICUCO A hill near the Toltec capital of Tula, which was associated with religious ceremonies honoring the god Quetzalcoatl in the Post-Classic Period (A.D. 900–1521).

XIHUIQUENITZIN A Toltec queen, listed in the *Historia Tolteca-Chichimeca* as ruling from A.D. 829 to 833.

XIHUITL The chronological system of 365 days, as calculated by the Aztec, divided into 18 months, having 20 days each and five epagomenal days, called *nemontemi*. This is also a solar year calendric account, called Year Bundle. The months were called *meztli;* their count is the *metlipohualli.* The *Xiuhmolpilli* (the century) was part of this count.

XIHUITONCO   Called the meadow, a district of the Aztec capital of Tenochtitlan, begun in A.D. 1325 in Lake Texcoco.

XILONEN   An Aztec goddess of maize. Her festivals were *Hueytecuilhuitl* and *Ochpaniztli,* celebrated in the capital of Tenochtitlan and in other Aztec (Mexica) imperial holdings.

XINANTECATL   Also called Nevada de Toluca, one of the major volcanic peaks in the Transverse Volcanic Axis in the Mesa Central. (See MESOAMERICAN GEOGRAPHY DI; VOLCANOES.)

XIPE BUNDLE   A city site in the Mixtec region of Oaxaca, either Mixtec in origin or a local community with Mixtec ties. The city was dominant at the start of the Mixtec empire, with the Tilantongo dynasty in control. In time Xipe Bundle was reduced to vassal status.

XIPE TOTEC   The "Flayed God," a deity worshipped in many Mesoamerican cultures, usually depicted as a young man wearing a human skin. The god was revered in Teotihuacan and in Monte Alban. Tlaxcala and other regions maintained the cult, which came to prominence in the Aztec (Mexica) era. (See AZTEC for legends concerning this god.)

XIPPACAYAN   A Toltec site near Tula, once a settlement of that group. The site, now called San Lorenzo, is mentioned in Toltec records.

XITLE VOLCANO   A peak located south of modern Mexico City in the Valley of Mexico. Xitle erupted violently around A.D. 100. Sending off clouds of dust and ash, the volcano shook the surrounding region with warning tremors and then underwent a full-scale eruption that sent lava into the city of Cuicuilco. It is estimated that as many as 140,000 people were affected by the explosions and the lava flow. The lava from Xitle buried Cuicuilco's cemetery called Capilco, an important archaeological site today.

XIU   See MAYA DYNASTIES.

XKICHMOOK (Kichmo or Kich Moo)   A Maya site near Uxmal in western central Yucatan that has rather elaborate buildings in Late Classic Period (A.D. 1200/1250 to 1521) Puuc and Chenes styles. The palace in Xkichmook has Chac masks and columns, as well as rosette designs on the buildings. The site may have been involved in Uxmal trade and religious worship.

XLAPAK (XLABPAK)   A Maya site named "Old Walls," located in the Puuc area of the Yucatan between Tayil and Labna. The ruins of the site contain a building with a plain lower facade and highly decorated upper levels. There are tiers of masks and geometric designs on this structure.

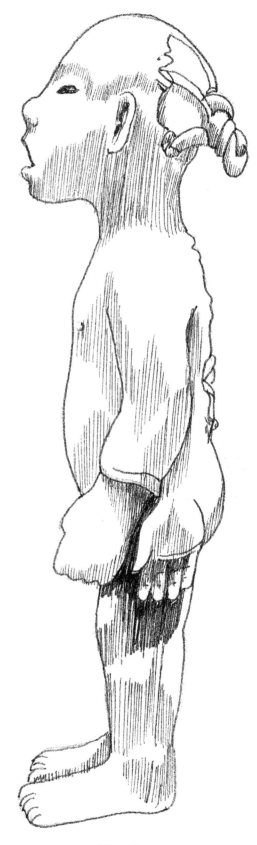

Xipe Totec

XIUHCOATL The "fire serpent," depicted at the Great Pyramid of Tenayuca. Statues of this god were usually crested. Xiuhcoatl was also honored in relief on the *coatepantli*, the serpent wall designed to accompany the pyramid.

XIUHTECUHTLI A Mesoamerican fire god, especially invoked in the ceremonies of the New Fire and in rituals concerning the calendar. He was called the Turquoise Year Lord and was chief in an Axtec religious division called a complex. Usually depicted as an old man and then called Huehueteotl, Xiuhtecuhtli was associated with Xitle Volcano in the Valley of Mexico. In Zapotec temples, the fire god was portrayed as a young man. The god received the first sacrifices at festivals.

XOCHICALCO A site located in the Morelos foothills, southwest of Cuernavaca. Xochicalco was a major marketplace and city that sponsored religious, cultural and technical activities, as well as the arts. The name means "the Place of the Flower House," reflecting the rich and verdant Morelos region. Cotton was a major local crop, traded along the important routes that connected the Valley of Mexico to the various Balsas River sites to the west and to the south. The city was founded after the fall of Teotihuacan and in A.D. 650 drew a group of sages from major Mesoamerican cultures. These sages are reported to have adopted a new calendar for the entire region. The mathematical and astronomical skills of the priests and scholars gathered in Xochicalco provided guidance for these calculations and decisions. The Xochicalco inherited Maya lore, as Maya influence is quite evident in the city. The city prevailed during the Classic and Post-Classic periods, maintaining the traditions and artistic ideals of Teotihuacan and other ceremonial cities.

Xochicalco was constructed on a series of hills overlooking a verdant plain. These hills were connected by a series of causeways, and the entire metropolitan complex was linked to other regions by cement roads. The Acropolis, the ceremonial complex of Xochicalco, was built on one hill, on a series of stepped terraces, estimated at around 3,900 feet from north to south and 2,280 feet from east to west. La Malinche and other residential enclaves and institutions were constructed on another hill, which included a ball court.

The elevation of the city, some 430 feet above the plain, and its deliberate fortification and defense, including ditches, ramparts and moats, were the result of the continued presence of invading groups in the region, including the Olmec-Xicallanca. Because of the elaborate measures taken in construction and design, Xochicalco has been called by some the first fortress in the Americas. Some earlier Maya cities, however, were designed with fortifications and unique defenses. Xochicalco was a refuge for the peoples of the surrounding lands, who fled there in times of crisis and could be assured of ample room. Originally it was inhabited by an unidentified culture, possibly the Mixtec-Puebla.

Xochicalco had a dramatic access road leading to its terraced heights. The most imposing section of the city was the Acropolis, which was surrounded again by walls. A traditional Mesoamerican plaza was laid out as the focal point in the center, serving as the gathering place of the people, as the stage for the religious dances and choirs and for the sacrificial aspects of worship. The plaza was provided with a low rectangular platform, stelae and stairways.

A pyramid mound and called the Chamber of Offerings faced the plaza. The base of the pyramid was double-tiered and had a broad stairway. The temple, called the Place of Three Stelae, was nearby. There erect, free-standing stelae were discovered in a hidden chamber. They were five feet high, carved of stone, two of which were rose colored. These stelae were elaborately carved and skillfully executed, depicting images of the god Quetzalcoatl in human form and as Venus, the Morning Star. A third stela depicted Tlaloc, the god of rain throughout Mesoamerica, called Chac by the Maya.

The dominant structure on the plaza was the Temple of the Feathered or the Plumed Serpent. This was dedicated to Quetzalcoatl and was composed of a pyramidal base with a staircase, leading to a temple with a single room on its summit. Besides the religious rituals in honor of Quetzalcoatl, the temple was also the shrine for New Fire ceremonies. The temple was elaborately adorned with exterior carvings. Eight fork-tongued reptiles coiled in stone over the walls, and there were designs of shells and friezes depicting processions of chieftains and warriors. Also shown were priests, seated in Buddha-like poses. Serpent scales, birds and animals completed the displays. Each of these figures was supplied with a glyph that included dates in the Maya bar-dot system, and the Nahua and Mixtec forms as well. An eclipse scene, crosses and circles were included. It was reported that in A.D. 900 at a time of threatened invasion, the Temple of the Feathered Serpent was covered in cinnabar.

On the other hill the Temple of La Malinche was built on another pyramidal mound. This shrine was also constructed on an artificial summit, and stone pedestals lined the road and the paths to other pyramids, all having chambers, columns, courts, plazas and porticos. In keeping with the pursuit of astronomy, Xochicalco sages maintained a number of observatories in nearby caves. One such cave contains an astronomical sighting shaft and a stucco floor. Xochicalco also included institutions for priests and schools for noble youths. It is believed that Ce Acatl Topiltzin (Quetzalcoatl/Kukulcan) was raised there, imbued with the prevailing religious principles.

Xochicalco was a remarkable city, holding sway over the hearts and minds of Mesoamericans and linking them to older cultures. As newer civilizations emerged in the region, Xochicalco lost its dominant position, although trade continued with Cholula, and other cities.

XOCHIMILCO A site on the southern end of Lake Xochimilco, south of modern Mexico City, in the Valley of Mexico. The name means "the Field of Flowers" and may have been a reference to the many *chinampas* that the people of Xochimilco utilized in their agricultural practices. The Xochimilcos were a Nahua group, originating in Chicomoztoc, the Land of the Seven Caves, where the Aztec (Mexica) and others originated. The people of Xochimilco originally went to a site in Puebla, called Tochmilco, which they called the Place Where Our God Dwells. They maintained contact with Puebla but traveled to Xochimilco with a priest called Huetzalin. After choosing a mountain ridge beside the lake as their home, the people began to build. Their domain extended across the ridge, and in time they incorporated other sites into their holdings. These included:

Chimalhuacan	Tlactotepec
Ehecatzinco	Tlamimilulpan
Ocuituco	Tlayacapa
Temoac	Totlapa
Tepetlixan	Xumiltepec
Tepoztlan	Zacualpa
Tetelaneyapan	

In the early eras the war chiefs ruled Xochimilco, but in A.D. 1256, a man called Acatonalli came to the throne. Xochmilco dates as a city to his accession. He built temples and constructed the residential districts, instituting a system of *chinampas.* Thereafter the people of Xochimilco elected their rulers, dependent solely upon the character of the individual and his ability to provide public service. Any ruler committing misdeeds or abusing power could be removed. The rise of the Tepanec and other cultures of the region drew Xochimilco into the changing times, as rivalries between the Tepanec, Culhua and the newcomers, the Aztec (Mexica), led to strife. When the Triple Alliance was made c. 1427/1430 A.D., Xochimilco refused to support the Tepanec king, Maxtla, in his battle against Tenochtitlan, Texcoco and Tlacopan (Tacuba). Later, when the Aztec began their imperial campaigns, the people of Xochimilco, aware that they would soon be drawn into battle, sat down to an elaborate feast. The food on the plates, however, turned into parts of the human body, and the priests announced that the city was doomed. After a series of unpleasant exchanges, Xochimilco did confront the Aztec forces and lost the war. The Aztec, however, did not sack the city; they were content to reduce Xochimilco to vassal status and to demand that tribute and services be provided annually. Xochimilco's people constructed a vast causeway to link their city with Tenochtitlan, the Aztec capital. They also were forced to take part in Aztec colonization in the region of Oaxaca, and their holdings in some regions were taken from them. When the Spanish arrived in the region, however, Xochimilco was thriving. The city then had three separate districts, each with its own ruler. The last of these, a man called Apochquiyauhtzin, ruled under Spanish auspices.

Noted as stone workers, the people of Xochimilco built the causeway on Lake Texcoco that is still visible today, bearing petroglyphs and carvings of humans and serpents. Another rock discovered on the site, reportedly a memorial to Huetzalin, recounts the arrival of the culture there. A calendar stone honoring another deity was also found. In a cemetery adjacent to the city, more petroglyphs were uncovered. One, called Las Flores, is beautifully carved in a likeness of the goddesses of the four corners of the earth. In one called La Primavera by the Spanish, the god Xochipilli, the patron of beauty, dance and love is depicted. This carving was made on the side of a hill. A pyramidal mound,

called El Huacel or Huetlalcueye, contained stone maps, slabs and religious portraits. The people of Xochimilco were the guardians of the Earth Mother, Quilaztli, the Deer of Mixcoatl. Other deities of the city include Amimitl and Atlahuac, patrons of canals and gardens; Centeotl, patron of maize; Chicomecoatl (Chantico), patronness of the hearth; Chiconahuizcuintl, deity of the aged; Macuilcalli, patron of virgins; Nahualpilli, patron of the young; Tetzauhpilli, patron of rain and farmers; Xochipilli, god of beauty, dance and love; and Xochiquetzalli, goddess of labor, harvests and the New Fire rites.

The shrines of the Xochimilco people had strange chambers, one of which included a "solar eye" as well as a map depicting the ancient Nahua homeland and the old highways. Xochimilco sages maintained an observatory to the south of the city, a site called El Adoratorio by the Spanish.

XOCHIMILCO LAKE   A water resource in the Valley of Mexico, joined to Lake Chalco, then to Lakes Texcoco and Xaltocan-Zumpango. The great city of Xochmilco was constructed on its shores and remains an active city today.

XOCHIPALA PHASE   A cultural development in Guerrero, dating to the Formative Period (c. 2000/1600 B.C.–c. A.D. 250/290). Wares produced during this phase include tripod vases with human faces and serpent heads, fashioned of green stone and demonstrating Maya influence.

XOCHIPILLI   Called the Flower Prince by the Aztec (Mexica), the god of maize, flowers, feasting, pleasures and the patron of feather workers. He was worshipped in the city of Xochipilli as the patron of beauty, dance and love. With Centeotl, Xochipilli was a solar deity who headed the Aztec complex bearing their name. Mesoamerican ball games in the Valley of Mexico are reported to depict the battle of Xochipilli against Centeotl. This god was also worshipped in Xochimilco and other sites.

XOCHIQUETZAL   "Flower Quetzal," an Aztec goddess serving as patroness of weavers, childbirth, pregnancy and motherhood. Shown as a beautiful young woman in elaborate dress, she received the sacrifice of a human virgin in her honor each year. The people confessed their sins to her and performed bloodletting exercises in her honor.

XOCHIQUETZALLI   A Xochimilco goddess of labor, harvests and the New Fire rituals.

XOCHITLAN   A Toltec site, located east of Tula but undocumented. The site is mentioned in Toltec records.

XOCHTEC   A group involved in the development of the Chalco region, in the southern part of the Valley of Mexico. They belonged to the confederation called the Chalco-Amecameca.

XOCHTL   The flower, an Aztec (Mexica) day sign in their version of the *tonalpohualli,* the calendar system.

XOLALPAN PHASE   A cultural development associated with the city of Teotihuacan, dated from A.D. 500 to

650. Pottery innovations appear during this phase, as well as plano reliefs and life-size figures. Ceramics of the Xolalpan Phase include thin orange wares imported perhaps from Puebla.

XOLOITZCUINTLI   A type of hairless dog, not the modern Chihuahua but an earlier breed. Larger than the Chihuahua, Xoloitzcuintli was believed to be the original breed of the region. Nearly extinct by modern times, the Xoloitzcuintli was saved by an Englishman who began to breed surviving pairs, and the line is now popular in Mexican kennel groups.

XOLOTL (1)   A Chichimec ruler of considerable distinction, called the Monster. He is recorded as having his people into the Valley of Mexico sometime around A.D. 1200, part of the vast migration into the region at the time. Xolotl routed the last Toltec there and then consolidated his gains by marrying a local heiress. After wandering through various locales, the Chichimec settled in Tenayuca, making that city their capital. Xolotl gave his daughter to Acolnahuacatl, the Tepanec king, and he allowed the Tepanec to settle on Chichimec lands. Xolotl's son was Nopaltzin, called the Revered Fruit of the Cactus, and he succeeded his father. Nopaltzin's son, Quinatzin, acquired Texcoco in his return. Xolotl also gave one of his daughters to the chief of the Otomi people when they arrived in his domain. He appears to have welcomed many cultures, and others claimed association with him whenever possible.

XOLOTL (2)   The mystical twin of the god Quetzalcoatl. Xolotl was represented by a dog, and he was the symbol of Venus as the Evening Star. The god was honored for his service to Quetzalcoatl and to humans but was associated with filth and immorality and thus was shown as a dog.

He was a patron deity of deformities and diseases. In the Aztec tradition, Xolotl was part of the fifth sun. (See TOLTEC RELIGION; see also CE ACATL TOPILTZIN; QUETZALCOATL.)

XOMILTEPEC   A Nahua homeland, listed in some records with Tamoachan as the original site of the various cultures entering the Valley of Mexico in the Classic and Post-Classic Periods, including the Aztec (Mexica). In time these cultures journeyed to Chicomoztoc, the Land of the Seven Caves, a site that was the place of origin for those vast numbers migrating into the Valley of Mexico.

XONAXI QUECUYA   A Zapotec goddess, the patron of the underworld and death. She was revered in Zapotec ceremonies as the consort of the god Pitao Pezelaco. (See ZAPOTEC GODS.)

XPUHIL   A Maya city in Quintana Roo called Place of the Cattails, constructed in the Rio Bec architectural style c. A.D. 875. Towers of the temple in Xpuhil are decorative only, in the Rio Bec design with rounded corners and banded tiers. (See MAYA ARCHITECTURE; see also RIO BEC B.)

XUNANTUNICH   A Maya site, called the Stone Lady, located in Belize and dated to c. A.D. 150–900. The major monument on the site, called El Castillo by the Spanish, is 135 feet high. This temple was designed with a stucco frieze and is accompanied by three ceremonial plazas. Three carved stelae were also recovered in Xunantunich, which appears to have suffered an earthquake that destroyed part of the city. The site is now called Benque Viejo.

XUX EK   A Maya name for the planet Venus when revered as the brother of the god Itzamna. (See also AH CHAC MITAN CH'OC.)

Y

YACATA A Tarascan architectural innovation, in use in the cities of this culture as temple forms. *Yacatas* were constructed on large rectangular platforms, usually about 1,400 feet long and 850 feet wide. Made of rubble and stone slabs, the *yacatas* were put together without mortar and faced with volcanic stone. Three separate elements were incorporated into their construction: the rectangular platform, a round stepped pyramidal platform attached to one side and a stepped passageway connecting the major portions of the monument. *Yacatas* formed the shape of the letter T, with a short stem and a rounded base. Most were decorated with reliefs and spiral carvings. They served as burial sites for the Tarascan nobles. Remains of these monuments exist at the site of Tzintzuntzan.

YAGUL A Zapotec site, called *Gui-y-Baa* originally, believed by some scholars to be the ancient Tlacolula, a renowned Zapotec city. Yagul is located in the central portion of Oaxaca and was originally a vast and highly complex metropolis. There is evidence of occupation in the region before the Zapotec arrived sometime c. 500 to 200 B.C, in a historical period called Monte Alban I. Carbon dating indicates that some parts of Yagul existed as early as 390 B.C., but it is possible that a local culture was in residence at that time. Yagul was constructed on a plain, at the base of a hill that was artificially leveled to build an acropolis today called the Great Fortress.

This fortified structure was constructed out of stone and mud, resembling a similar building discovered in Mitla, a city located just a few miles away. The fortifications and the provisions for a garrison indicate that the people of Yagul confronted the threat of hostilities from neighbors or nomadic tribes. Yagul is believed to have been a place of refuge for the surrounding region in time of attack or natural disaster. The southern slope upon which the site was built contained the chief ceremonial complex as well as administrative buildings. Pyramidal mounds, palaces, shrines and a ball court were all constructed there, probably dating to the era of Yagul's ascendancy. The Palace of the Six Patios was located in this major complex. One structure there contained five floors, with evidence of widespread superimposed construction having taken place as well. Each succeeding generation apparently added to the original structure. Ceramics covering a prolonged period were also recovered on the site.

The tombs uncovered in Yagul were constructed of adobe, generally located beneath patios. Mural decorations and carved stepped-fret designs were incorporated into the tombs, as three-dimensional carved heads. These perhaps represented those buried in the tombs or some of the Zapotec deities associated with the death rites. A *brasero*, or incense burner, was also found, as well as a tripod vase having the supports carved as human heads, an unusual ceramic innovation not duplicated in other Mesoamerican regions. Considerable grave offerings were included in these tombs, usually placed on the floor beside the skeletal remains. In one tomb there is evidence of cremation. The corpse does not appear to have been burned in the tomb, however; that chamber was used only as a receptacle for the ashes after ritual incineration.

Yagul had a council hall elaborately decorated with stone mosaics, with geometric designs incorporated into the forms. One panel, of a stepped-fret style, was over 120 feet long, similar to those found in Mitla. No stone lintels were used in construction in this council hall, or in other buildings of Yagul, hence the extensive deterioration of the site's remains. The Zapotec occupied Yagul but then surrendered it to the Mixtec.

YAHUI Mixtec divine beings believed to be demon companions of sorcerers. As such they are associated with lightning and thunder. The Yahui are depicted as flying creatures, wearing serpent headdresses with turtle shells and tails and carraying flint and conch shells.

YANHUITLAN A site in the Nochixtlan Valley in western Oaxaca, believed to have been founded in the Formative Period (c. 2000/1600 B.C.–250/290 A.D., although Paleo-Indian Period (11,000–7,000 B.C.) hearths and tools have been recovered from the site as well. A ceremonial complex with palaces, called the *Loma de Ayuxi*, is associated with Yanhuitlan, which was an independent city-state, part of the Mixtec confederation. Stable for centuries under ruling nobility, Yanhuitlan participated in trade and was or city of the Natividad Phase.

YAQUI RIVER A waterway in the Pacific coastal lowlands, forming delta and flood plains.

YAXCHEELCAB Stone columns erected by the Itza, representing the "First Tree of the World." These columns were thus symbols of both the Maya and Izapa religious traditions. The Itza inhabited Chichen Itza and in other Maya regions. (See TREE OF THE WORLD.)

YAXCHILAN A major Maya ceremonial complex on the banks of the Usumactina River in the southern lowlands of Chiapas. The name means "Green Stones," taken from a form of algae visible in the nearby Arroyo-Yxchilan River. The center was founded in 320 A.D. by Yat-Balam (Progenitor Jaguar), and his dynasty ruled there for some 500 years. An enormous metropolis, Yaxchilan had beautifully constructed temples and pyramids. The upper facades and the roof combs of these structures were ornamented in stone or in stucco. Mansard roofs, roof combs and the facades of Yaxchilan resemble those in the Maya city of Palenque. Some temples and patios were erected on the slopes of hills while others were constructed along the riverbank.

The carved lintels of the ceremonial complex are widely known, depicting historical personages and events. These lintels contain some of the most complete documentation of the political panorama of the Maya. Yaxchilan was a capital of the region in the Late Classic Period. Bird Jaguar Shield Jaguar and two of its rulers, father and son, reigned in the city from A.D. 681 to 771. Lady Xoc, Shield Jaguar's wife, appears to have wielded considerable political power as well. Yaxchilan festivals drew aristocrats from Bonampak, Piedras Negras and Tikal. In time, during the reign of Bird Jaguar, Bonampak was forced to become vassal to Yaxchilan.

Yaxchilan offers evidence of the presence of the Mexica in the Maya region. It also reflects a Yucatan influence. Yaxchilan ended construction of its public architecture c. A.D. 840, but remained vibrant and powerful amid the general Maya decline in the region.

YAXHA A Maya site in the Peten region, modern Guatemala. Yaxha is believed to have been one of the largest ceremonial centers in the region. Like Tikal, it is known for a twin pyramidal religious complex. Ceremonial temple groupings with pyramids, platforms and traditional acropolis-style structures were found at the site. The city also constructed a solstice observatory of considerable note. Yaxha, a close neighbor of Tikal, shared the trade and cultural systems of the region. Yaxha, as with other southern lowland Maya centers, is essentially a Classic Period (A.D. 1/250 to 900) center.

YAX KIN CA'AN CHAC A Maya ruler of the city of Tikal in the Peten region of modern Guatemala. He was a son of Ah Cacau and assumed the throne of Tikal in A.D. 734. Yax Kin Ca'an Chac was memorialized on a wooden lintel in Tikal. A stela was also raised in his honor.

YAX K'UK MO A Maya ruler, listed in the records as founder of the ceremonial city of Copan. He took the throne of that city in July A.D. 763.

YAX-MOCH-XOC A Maya ruler, actually the founder of the Tikal dynasty. He ruled sometime between A.D. 219 and 238. The dynasty that he founded ruled Tikal for centuries. Each of his successors listed their rank and number in the dynasty.

YAXUNA A Maya ceremonial city located in the eastern Yucatan, some 62 miles from Coba. Temples discovered at this site are 197 by 427 feet in diameter. A causeway from Yaxuna led to Coba indicating Coba's influence in the region as an areal capital. The city, located 12 miles south of Chichen Itza, started public architectural works as early as the start of the Classic Period (c. A.D. 1/250) and there is evidence of sophisticated planning and construction.

YESTLA-NARANJO A site in the Sierra Madre del Sur region of Guerrero, associated with the Formative Period (c. 2000/1600 B.C.–c. A.D. 250/290) cultural development. (See MESOAMERICA for details.)

YICH'AK BALAM A ruler of the Maya city of Seibal, depicted in the Dos Pilas Stela 2 as the defeated victim of the regional wars conducted by Maya aristocrats.

YOKE (1) A horsehoe-shape stone object that is believed to represent the hip guards worn by the Mesoamerican ball players. The Tepanec and others wore stone yokes as amulets, designed to ward off evil spirits and unfortunate or harmful events. Many were carved with images of toads, owls and eagles, all associated with death rituals. Hieroglyphs and portraits also were carved in the stones. Yoke amulets were prized by Mesoamericans and were manufactured for trade.

YOKE (2) U-shape belts having carved designs that were worn by the players of ball games in various Mesoamerican cultures. Yokes and other protective gear were necessary to ensure the players' safety, as the balls used were heavy, some weighing as much as seven pounds. Representations as these protective belts, when carved in stone, served as amulets.

YOPE A warrior group of Mesoamerica, living in the region of Guerrero during the Post Classic Period (A.D. 900–1521). The Yope were attacked by the Aztec (Mexica) during their campaigns of imperial expansion but managed to feud off Aztec advances into their territory. As a result, the Aztec honored the Yope for their valor and military skill and invited them to Tenochtitlan for celebrations. The Yope arrived in the Aztec capital bearing lavish gifts of precious stones, gold and pelts. Impressed, the Aztec feted the Yope. This warrior group is recorded as worshipping Xipe Totec, the Flayed God. (See YOPITZINCO.)

YOPITZINCO The homeland of the Yope people, located in southern Tlaxcala. The Yope, a warrior group, were actually a confederation of small cultures. They defended Yopitzinco successfully against Aztec raids. Legend records that Xipe Totec, the Flayed God, originated in this region. The Aztec were unable to incorporate Yopitzinco into their empire because of the courage of the Yope.

YUCATAN PENINSULA The origin of Maya civilization, once called the *Antillean Foreland* and a geological

Yucatan dish

region that emerged in the Pleistocene Period. The Yucatan formation includes the Sierra de Ticul, a major ridge lying between Campeche and Merida. The ridge dominates the surrounding territories and divides the Yucatan plain and the hills of Campeche, which are located to the north. This chain continues into Guatemala. Along the peninsula's eastern side, the Maya Mountains consist of limestone ridges, swamps and marshlands, once home to nomadic groups during the Paleo-Indian Period (11,000–7000 B.C.). Later the region was inhabited by the emerging Maya.

Geologically the Yucatan Peninsula is termed *karstic*, which means that the area does not have much surface water available; the light seasonal rain every year is absorbed by the porous rock and is maintained only in deep, underground channels. To the Maya, such channels or sinkholes, or *cenotes*, were gifts of the gods and a symbols of nourishment. *Cenotes* also were settings for fertility ceremonies and incentives for the construction of their great ceremonial complexes and residential communities. Two types of *cenotes* are prevalent in the Yucatan; the true *cenote*, a round or oval well having vertical walls; and the *resumidero*, a funnel-shape well.

Another source of water in the Yucatan region is the *aguada*, a shallow depression that fills with temporary water reserves at certain times of the year. The water does not remain; it is burned off by the intense sun. The Maya learned how to locate *aguadas* and how to use their water effectively for agriculture and settlements. The Yucatan also offers a series of caves, warm and dry in all seasons, some quite vast and multichambered. These caves were used in the earliest periods and throughout Maya cultural development. Even after the great ceremonial cities were established, the caves were still maintained as refuges in time of attack, as storage centers and as sites for religious ceremonies. Of particular value as well are the Yucatan *hayas*, which

are pockets of soil made fertile by rainfall. These pockets are found in the rocky ridges and depressions of the peninsula. They are particularly prominent in the Sierra de Ticul region and in the northeastern hill region of Campeche. The Maya term for hill, *puuc*, in time also came to signify more than a geological or geographic phenomenon. A Maya art form called the *puuc* arose, with such cities as Labna and Uxmal exhibiting the style.

The Peten (Putun) region of the Yucatan Peninsula covers most of northern Guatemala and consists of rolling hills, *aguadas* and conical volcanic formations. Depressions in the southern area are normally filled with lakes or swamps and tropical rain forests. The northern and northwestern sections of the Yucatan form barrier beaches that enclose lagoons and tidal swamps rich in sea life. These lagoons once served as sites where earlier inhabitants of the peninsula could collect salt. The eastern coast is a cliffed shoreline, having beaches and headlands. The northeastern region has always been faulted, showing the scars of erosion and weather damage. Cozumel, the Maya island ceremonial complex, was separated from the mainland as a direct result of the geological activity in the Yucatan Peninsula. A dense coral reef extends from the northeastern corner of the Yucatan Peninsula to the Gulf of Honduras. In time the Peten (Putun) and Totonac traders sailed fleets of merchant ships through these waters, connecting the region to other parts of Mesoamerica in the Classic and Post-Classic periods (c. A.D. 1/250–900; 900–1521). The Maya called the Yucatan the Land of the Turkey and the Deer. The northern portion of the peninsula includes Quintana Roo, Campeche, Belize and the Peten. At the end of the Post-Classic Period, the Maya of the Yucatan had divided into 16 politically autonomous districts, and there was a strong Aztec (Mexica) presence in the region as well.

YUCATEC MAYA   See MAYA GROUPS, YUCATEC.

YUCUITA   A Mixtec site that dominated the Nochixtlan Valley and is considered the earliest settlement in this area of Oaxaca. Established around 200 B.C., the city probably was founded by a local culture but became Mixtec and was important in trade and manufacture. About two square miles in diameter, Yucuita had several hundred buildings and as many as 1,000 inhabitants. It served as a major urban site in the Late Formative Period (300 B.C.–c. A.D. 250/290). Ten major civic complexes have been uncovered there. The city is also associated with the Ramos Phase, from 200 B.C. to A.D. 500. An estimated population of 4,000 to 7,000 occupied Yucuita during some eras.

YUCUNDAHAI   A Mixtec capital city, located in the Nochixtlan Valley of western Oaxaca, established in the Las Flores Phase era of the Late Classic Period (600–900 A.D.). A well-planned urban section on an L-shaped ridge, Yucundahai had sculpted monuments and residential districts built on terraces, with ceremonial complexes and palaces. A Classic Period tomb was discovered at the site. Teotihuacan and Maya ceramics, as well as a Mixtec year sign, the symbol for the solar ray, were also recovered there. A temple of the rain god, a residential structure called Mogote Grande and a ball court (constructed on a north-south axis and shaped like a capital I) were uncovered. The Classic Period tomb, which has an intact wooden roof, is in an isolated mound. The tomb has five steps, two antechambers and a large vault. There was red plaster on the walls. The site was called "Cloud Mountain" by the Mixtec and is associated with Chachoapan as a possible origin of the Mixtec culture.

YUM KAAX   See AH MUN.

YURIRA LAKE   A water resource in the region of Michoacan, associated with the Tarascan culture in some eras.

Z

ZAACHILA (1) A Zapotec site in Oaxaca, originally called Teozapotlan, or the "Sky Dragon," and the last Zapotec capital. The region around Zaachila, called Zaachila-Zimitlan, was well populated as early as the Formative Period (c. 2000/1600 B.C.–c. A.D. 250/290) and perhaps in earlier historical eras. Zaachila gained ascendancy during the Zapotec occupation of the city of Monte Alban, c. A.D. 100 to 700. It is believed to have been ruled by a prince of the Zapotec royal family, a designated administrator of the entire region. The city was taken by the Mixtec in A.D. 1200 but reclaimed by the Zapotec king Cosihuesa, who made a treaty with the Mixtec and the Spanish. His daughter, Princess Donaji, was buried in the Spanish church in Zaachila under the name Maiona Cortez.

Few remains of Zaachila have survived, including a rectangular patio having adobe walls. Two tombs were discovered beneath this patio, and one contained a doorway fret design. Sculpted figures on the walls were marked with calendrical names, and there are images of the Mixtec god

Zaachila relief

of death, Mictlantecuhtli, in connection with the tombs. This deity figure represents the earliest stage of Mixtec occupation of the site. Grave offerings recovered represent some of the finest pottery in Mesoamerica, products of both Zapotec and Mixtec artisans. Objects fashioned from gold and carved bones were also recovered, as well as 80 ceramic pieces. Included in this cache is the notable polychrome vessel, small and delicately colored, with a blue hummingbird on its rim. This vessel is believed to be of Mixtec origin.

ZAACHILA (2) A Zapotec dynasty ruling the cities of Zaachila, Mitla and Tehuantepec. Spanish historians included the following rulers in this royal line:

Zaachila I. The founder of the dynasty at Zaachila, ruling in the late fourteenth and early fifteenth centuries. He is listed as a warrior king who defended Zapotec lands from Mixtec raids.

Zaachila II. A ruler ascending the Zaachila throne in A.D. 1415, probably not actually called Zaachila. He made a truce with the Mixtec and was noted for his intelligence and quickness. This king ruled for almost 40 years.

Zaachila III. Called the Deceiver by the Zapotec, succeeding Zaachila II in A.D. 1454. He was a contemporary of the Aztec (Mexica) emperor Ahuitzotl, and his nickname was derived from his association with the Mixtec at Huitzo. He made an alliance with the Mixtec but then led the Aztec by a secret trail to ambush the Mixtec in battle. Zaachila III died in A.D. 1487, to be succeeded by Cosihuesa.

ZACALEU See ZACULEU.

ZACAPU PHASE A cultural development in Michocan, dated to the Formative Period (c. 2000/1600 B.C.–c. A.D. 250/290). The ceramic industry of this phase flourished in Michoacan in El Openo and in Jaquilipas.

ZACATECA (1) A Mesoamerican group belonging to the Uta-Aztecan language family, called the Teo-Chichimec by the Aztec (Mexica). The Zacateca lived on the rocky plateau of northern Mexico, flanked by the Sierra Madre Oriental and the Sierra Madre Occidental. The heirs of the "Desert Culture," the Zacateca were unable to farm because of the aridity of the land, relying on hunting and gathering for survival. The group was seminomadic, living in caves and in reed huts. It is believed that the Zacateca culture had ties to the American tribes of the Southwest. (See ZACATECAS-DURANGO.)

ZACATECA (2) A group, Olmec in origin, from Cholollan and Tlaxcala. With their Chichimec neighbors, they settled in the Zacatlan territory of the Sierra de Puebla, the eventual domain of the Totonac. This group may have been related in part to the Zacateca culture in northern Mexico.

ZACATECAS-DURANGO The northern frontier regions of Mesoamerica in northern Mexico, the wild and desolate terrain that was the origin of some of the "Desert Culture" groups. Zacatecas-Durango was included in the Turquoise Road, the route over which turquoise was brought from what is now New Mexico in America to the Chalchihuites workshops. The region extended from San Luis Potosi through Zacatecas-Durango, along the Sierra Madre Occidental to the region of Sinaloa by A.D. 1000. Some of the "Desert Culture" groups, called Zacateca, were related to the Chichimec. They did not migrate south but remained on the northern frontier until the Spanish arrived. Distinct phases or cultural developments can be defined in Zacatecas-Durango, and certain sites or groups of sites are associated with it, including: Bolanos-Juchipala, Chalchihuites, Loma San Gabriel, Malpaso.

ZACATENCO See ZACATENCO-ARBOLILLO.

ZACATENCO-ARBOLILLO An archaeological zone with sites located on Lake Texcoco in the Valley of Mexico. These sites date to c. 1100 B.C. in the Zacatenco region and to c. 1350 B.C. in Arbolillo, although there were probably

Zacatenco figurine

earlier populations in both regions. Zacatenco-Arbolillo experienced ceramic phases and cultural developments that kept pace with agricultural pursuits. Hunters and gatherers who entered the regions established villages and initiated agricultural practices in time, cultivating the arable lands and utilizing natural resources. Burial customs indicate that the people wrapped their dead and made grave offerings. In Zacatenco one body was discovered wrapped in a thick cloth, possibly a straw mat. Flat stone slabs had been placed on top of the burial pit, which was then covered with earth. Some burial pits were finished with gravel flooring. In several instances the dead were covered with cinnabar, indicative of respect and possibly the burial of a member of the local aristocracy. Animals, stone tools, pottery and clay figurines were the usual grave offerings recovered.

During the Formative Period (c. 2000/1600 B.C.–A.D. 250/290), the Zacatenco-Arbolillo region gained population, but building and administrative practice did not increase greatly. The zone remained a farming community without cities or ceremonial complexes of note. Figurines recovered from this period were hand-molded generally and mass-produced for trade. Mother and child figurines were popular, and a variety of such statuettes depicted the act of childbirth, of religious significance throughout Mesoamerica. Some scholars believed that the Zacatenco-Arbolillo archaeological zone is associated with the advances made during the Ticoman Phase.

ZACATLAN A region in the Sierra de Puebla, the origins of the Totonac. A scenic terrain of low hills, Zacatlan was the source of vanilla beans, prized by Mesoamerican cultures and traded by the Totonac.

ZAC KUB A Maya noblewoman, called the White Quetzal Bird. She was the mother of Lord Pacal of Palenque, the great Maya ceremonial city. In some records she holds the rank of a Maya ruler, although she does not appear to have served as a regent for Pacal at any time. Her husband, Kan Bahlum Mo', apparently was of aristocratic rank but did not rule in Palenque. Zac Kub and other royal women maintained their rank because of their ancestry. She and her husband are both depicted in reliefs discovered in the Pacal's tomb in Palenque.

ZACOALCO-SAYULA An archaeological zone in the Sayula Basin of Northern Jalisco. There was activity in the zone during Formative Period (c. 2000/1600 B.C.–c. A.D. 250/290) when hunters and gathers began agricultural plots and maintained communities and settlements there. Zacoalco-Sayua underwent several cultural developments, including Verdia, Sayula, and Amacueca.

Verdia is a cultural phase dating to the earliest eras and noted for the production of local, unique ceramic wares. The Sayula cultural phase parallels the rise of the city of Teotihuacan, with Teotihuacan thin orange ware present. Also discovered were red-on-buff and red-on-brown wares. Amacueca is a cultural phase related to the polychrome wares known today as Autlan.

ZACUBA A region claimed by the Tarascan as their place of origin, but not documented as to location.

ZACULEU A Mam Maya site in in the highlands of Guatemala, surrounded by mountains reaching 6,500 feet, Zaculeu was a ceremonial center that once covered about three acres. It was fortified and its site chosen because mountains ringed three sides. Ravines acted as moats, providing added protection. The city was in a fertile valley with considerable rainfall. Water was also available from the Selequa River, and wood was plentiful. Zaculeu had plazas and buildings representative of the architectural patterns of most Maya ceremonial cities of the time. Begun in the Early Classic Period (c. A.D. 1/250–600), Zaculeu's last temple was erected in the Early Post-Classic Period (A.D. 900–c. 1200/1250). In time the Mam gave way to the Quiche Maya in the area. This temple is a single-chambered structure, rectangular, having a large opening on one side. Two single columns divide the opening into three entrances. A plain rectangular altar was discovered against one wall of the temple chamber. Other buildings include two-room structures and one with a circular chamber. Their roofs were made of thatch, beams and mortar. Also recovered in Zaculeu were tooth-shape jade pendants.

ZAMORA A type of ceramic ware found at early Michoacan sites, dated to the Formative Period (c. 2000/1600 B.C.–c. A.D. 250/290). The ceramic industry of Michoacan in demand for, was located in El Openo and Laquilipas.

ZAPATLAN EL GRANDE See CIUDAD GUZMAN.

ZAPOTEC The people called the *Ben Zaa,* or the *Binii Gula'sa,* which can be translated as the Cloud People. The Zapotec were a prominent and historically important group in Mesoamerica from c. 1500 B.C. to after A.D. 1200, which means that they participated in critical developments from the Formative Period to the Late Post-Classic Period. Their origins were in the Valley of Oaxaca, forming part of the Proto-Otomanguean language family there. Their historical development indicates that they were closely related to the Mixtec and the Otomi. Some scholars believe that they were once united with the Mixtec, breaking away as early as 4100 to 3500 B.C., initiating their own settlements in the Oaxaca region. The Zapotec and Mixtec were always associated, however, occupying the same sites throughout their history and competing with one another in achievements.

The Zapotec village was extant in the Oaxaca region by 1350 B.C., and the San Jose Mogote culture traded as far as the Pacific coast to the northern domains of Mesoamerica, sponsored by various groups and maintained in good times and in bad. During the Rosario Phase, the Zapotec carved *danzantes,* the relief figures found in the city of Monte Alban. By the Late Formative Period (300 B.C.–c. A.D. 250/290), the Zapotec had evolved to a great Mesoamerican state, holding Oaxaca domains and other regions. They were evident in Etla, Yagul and Zaachila-Zimitlan (the region around the city of Zaachila). In time their influence extended to the Sierra Madre Oriental to the north and to the Tlacolula Mountains in the southeast. The Zapotec also inhabited Tehuacan in Pueblo and portions of northwestern Guerrero. The modern name of the group, Zapotec, is believed to have been derived from the *zapote* or *zapate,* a tree that grew in abundance in their domain.

Unlike the other nomadic groups that invaded Mesoamerican territories, the Zapotec had a definite historical presence in their local regions. Linked to the Mixtec in their various stages of development, they nevertheless maintained their own heritage and traditions and evolved in pursuit of their own specific ideals.

It is believed that the Proto-Zapotec-Chatino, the possible ancestors of the Classic Zapotec, separated from the Proto-Mixteca-Cuicatec sometime c. 4100 to 3700 B.C. These hunters and gatherers were then moving toward agriculture as a means of survival. The cosmological aspects of the Zapotec religion is rooted in the nation's agricultural beginnings, and the unique concept of *pee* or *pitao,* the creative life force sustaining all life. As population increased, so did the pace of development. In this stage, Oaxaca contained as many as 500 to several thousand people, especially in the valleys. The Zapotec took advantage of the highland water reserves in the Oaxaca region and began farming communities.

By 850 B.C., Oaxaca had a defined stratified society with aristocrats and commoners, and over the decades some regions acquired dominance. At the same time, however, outside cultures had an impact on Zapotec regions, isolating various groups and influencing them with their diverse approaches to architecture and other arts. Stone and adobe buildings were erected, and the loom was used, as was the 260-day calendar.

The Formative Period saw the rise of the Zapotec state in the Valley of Oaxaca. By 500 B.C., the people there had formed a true historical Zapotec society. San Jose Mogote's culture and Rosario Phase communities had large populations, and they were linked to outlying settlements, beginning the cohesive pattern of metropolises. Monte Alban was begun in this period, whether by direct Zapotec intervention or as the result of a related group that in time gave way to the Zapotec. Other mountaintop communities emerged as ceremonial cities, and the Zapotec aristocracy was active in setting a pattern of domination.

The Zapotec entered Monte Alban during the Late Formative Period (300 B.C.–c. A.D. 250/290) but met with almost immediate changes that threatened their advance around c. A.D. 600 to 1100. The city of Teotihuacan collapsed during this period, allowing the Zapotec to extend their power until Monte Alban was reduced to the same fate. The Zapotec appear to have had close ties to Teotihuacan, as did many other groups in the region. With the collapse of that great unifying metropolis and the arrival of the warrior Toltec, the Zapotec withdrew. At the same time, however, they strengthened their smaller cities and prepared for the Toltec onslaught. The Zapotec were held together by the rigid social structures they had developed over the centuries, and they survived upheavals resulting from Chichimec invasions from the north. When the Aztec (Mexica) replaced the Toltec as the dominant force in the region, and as the Triple Alliance began imperial campaigns of expansion, the Zapotec found themselves confronting the Mixtec, who had been forced out of their own lands. The Zapotec fled, leaving Oaxaca and retiring to the southeast. They established a new capital at Mitla. After that city fell to the forces of the Triple Alliance in A.D. 1494, the Zapotec constructed a mountainside fortress at Guiengola, in Tehuantepec. This garrisoned retreat had double walls 10 feet high and six feet wide. A palace and other structures were also erected there.

Cosihuesa, the Zapotec ruler at the time, attacked the Aztec allies. Because of his victories, he was given an Aztec princess, Pelaxilla, in marriage. Pelaxilla betrayed her father, Emperor Ahuitzotl, who had expected her to open the Zapotec gates to him and his armies. When he arrived in the territory he was met by Zapotec forces and escorted from the region. Cosihuesa and Pelaxilla's son governed Tehuantepec. Their daughters, Penopua and Donaji, were both heroines in the Zapotec tradition. Some records indicate that Cosihuesa eventually retook Zaachila, the original Zapotec capital, where he died in 1529.

The Zapotec region, the Valley of Oaxaca, is shaped like a wishbone. It is drained by the Atoyac River, which flows from north to south. The Etla side of the valley is on the north, and the Tlacolula side on the southeast, drained also by the Salado River. The Zaachila region has the broadest and lowest territories. On the east the Sierra Madre del Sur borders the valley, with the Mixteca Alta, the Nochixtlan Valley, bordering as an archaeological zone. Streams keep the region well drained. The Oaxaca Valley is semiarid, with a rainy season from May through September. Farmers at the higher elevations met with frosts when they planted after the summer months. The lowlands were more temperate. Forests of willow and alder, ferns and low shrubs cover much of the terrain, with evergreens in the higher elevations and thorn shrubs and mesquite elsewhere.

ZAPOTEC AGRICULTURE   Following the traditional *milpas* farming practices, the Zapotec raised abundant crops of maize in the lowlands and temperate zones. The annual rainfall in the Zapotec region is from two to 10 inches, and the soil is rich, even at the higher elevations, irrigated by the rivers and the high water tables, although some portions are dry. In the temperate zones, several crops could be grown each year. Effluvium deposited by the river systems during the flood seasons provide natural fertilization, and the Zapotec rotated crops and developed vast farmlands. They were not obliged to rely upon the vast man-made irrigation systems of other regions. Ponds and the natural rainfall provided abundant water. The staple crops of the Zapotec consisted of maize, squash, curcurbits and the various seed plants readily available. They terraced when necessary and hunted a wide variety of game was available in the region, as well as fish.

ZAPOTEC ARCHAEOLOGICAL SITES   The complexes and cities constructed by the Zapotec, covered in individual entries. These include Dainzu, Huitzo, Lambityeco, Mitla, Monte Alban, Monte Negro, Yagul, and Zaachila.

ZAPOTEC ART AND ARCHITECTURE   The creative expression represented in Monte Alban buildings and sculpture. Having occupied that site from A.D. 100 to 700, the Zapotec took pains to incorporate the highly stylized Oaxaca artistic traditions of the past with the innovations and advances of the period, achieving a unified whole. The celebrated *danzantes* figures, for example, predate the Zapotec occupation but reflect forms that used in Oaxaca

for centuries. The early pyramidal platforms of Monte Alban also reflect Zapotec and Oaxacan expressions.

Other Zapotec architectural monuments in Monte Alban include the tombs dating to the period of their occupation of the city. These tombs are underground residences, a Zapotec architectural innovation. They were constructed of dressed stone and included corridors, elaborately decorated single chambers and doorways having carved stone slabs, usually surrounded by stone blocks that, in turn, often were surmounted by niches and by elaborate urns depicting deities.

The Classic Period monuments of Monte Alban, again reflecting Zapotec architectural style, had few carved decorations. Massive lines and structural uniformity were ideals exemplified in the buildings. The builders seldom allowed used excess carving or embellishments on exterior surfaces. Balustrades to accompany stairways, tiers and the stairs themselves provided sufficient variety while maintaining the harmonious balance desired.

Many monuments designed by the Zapotec, however, were accompanied by fine stone structures, in the form of stelae, pillars, columns and lintels, all carved in detailed low relief. The Zapotec did not carve sculpture in the round, and even the *danzantes* carvings lacked the fluidity and natural quality of older Monte Alban figures. The Zapotec handled figures symbolically, adding hieroglyphs and their scrolls, which emanate from the mouths of the figures portrayed and are symbolic of words being spoken. The costumes of these figures were detailed, having elaborate headdresses clearly indicating their rank and the role in Zapotec society. The figures carved in the reliefs are solid and formal in pose, of rigid appearance.

Zapotec art is visible not only in the carvings, stelae, geometric designs and details on the walls of the monuments but in urns, braziers and other commemorative pieces dedicated to the deities or to a concept of religious import in their world. The bat god was a symbol of wide appeal, as were jaguar signs. Figures without apparent designations on a monument are called *accompanantes* and were found in Zapotec ruins. The bat, the corn god and a warrior figure with the head of a bird were uncovered.

Murals were another expression of Zapotecan art, and again the formality of the style is evident, using specific insignias and motifs. Murals were painted in white, red, yellow, ochre, green, turquoise, blue and black. Tomb walls were decorated with figures and glyphs painted in these hues. Mosaics also had wide appeal and were produced in jade, greenstone, quartz, obsidian and mica. Shell ornaments have been recovered from Zapotec sites. The renowned bat god jade mask of Monte Alban is a vivid example of Zapotec skill. They also produced jade figurines and whistles.

ZAPOTEC BURIAL RITES   The process of entombment, a gradual evolution in Monte Alban, beginning with small stone boxes and evolving into the use of complex cruciform sites having niches, separate chambers and sculpted entrance corridors. The Zapotec tombs of Mitla, which was actually a ceremonial complex and burial ground for the Zapotec royal lines, reflect the same sort of development. Funerary urns and mural paintings completed the mortuary decorations. Images of personages were accompanied by glyphs. The Zapotec rulers were buried with family members interred nearby. This custom reflected the Zapotec belief in ancestor worship. Zapotec burials invoked the patronage of the gods and the reception of the deceased into the arms of those who had gone before. It is not known if cremation was practiced. Royal tombs do not reflect this generally, containing only a few remains reduced to ashes, obviously at the result of cremation conducted prior to burial.

ZAPOTEC CALENDAR   The calculation of time included in a ritual calendar of 260 days and the 365-day agricultural calendar.

The Zapotec, arriving, and occupying the city of Monte Alban, accepted the traditions of the site but added their own concept of "infinity," symbolized by Caqui Xee or Pijetao, "the great time." Each Zapotec received a calendrical name at birth as well as an animal, plant or bird form. The people also conducted their affairs according to the rituals recorded in a sacred book, the 260-day calendar, which assisted priests in their divinations. This calendar was linked as well to the cosmological traditions of the nation.

Some scholars believed the Zapotec calendar is one of the oldest used in Mesoamerica. Called the *pije* or *piye*, translated in Nahuatl as *tonalpohualli*, this calendar consisted of 260 days divided into four separate periods of 65 days each. These divisions were assigned a sign or a planetary insignia, also called a *pije* or *piye*. The insignias designated the duration of each division. The 65 days of each division were again divided into five parts of 13 days each, called *tobicocij*. These parts corresponded to the modern month. Each day in the calendar was given its own insignia in the Zapotec system. The four planets that presided over the major calendrical divisions appear as the ultimate causes of events in the world and in the affairs of mankind. For this reason they were provided with blood offerings and with prayers designed to appease and placate them. Each 65-day period was called by the name of the 13-day unit that began the period.

The Zapotec also employed a calendar of 365 days, called the *yza*. This was an agricultural calendar, evolved from the seasonal year and the economy on which the group relied. This calendar is believed to have consisted of 18 separate months, called *peo*, which is the Zapotec word for moon. Each month contained 20 days each. This calendar, returning to its original combination of numbers, day signs and months every 52 years, was observed in conjunction with the *pije*, or the 260-day calendar. Such a custom was traditional throughout Mesoamerica. This calendar's 52-year cycle was also a widespread tradition throughout the region in almost every historical era.

The Zapotec calendar, with its day signs and its elaborate pattern patron deities or planets, is known by scholars today because a list of nine day-name deities survived. These day-name deities represented the natural forces and the elements in the Zapotec world. The list actually corresponds to the Lords of the Night in their *tonalpohualli* of the Aztec (Mexica). The Zapotec calendar use was also based on the numbers nine, 13, 20 and 200. All of these numerical designations were sacred in Mesoamerican cultures, utilized in rituals and calendars throughout the region.

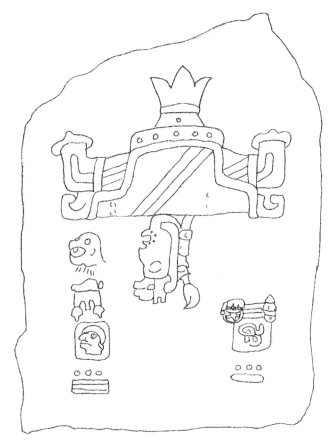

Zapotec sign of conquest

Zapotec calendars recovered in Monte Alban are illustrated by glyphs on the carvings of the *danzantes* figures. These carvings and glyphs represent a hallmark of Zapotec culture. They indicate clearly that this culture produced a sophisticated calendar and had mastered the art of writing at the same time.

ZAPOTEC CERAMICS   Pottery that reflects not only Zapotec artistry but the ceramic traditions of the region of Oaxaca and those of the city of Monte Alban as well. As the Zapotec were indigenous to the region, not having originated in a distant homeland as other Mesoamerican groups had, their ceramics reflect the evolution of their own advances in art. In time the Zapotec were especially noted for their gray wares and for other distinctive ceramic products, which included coarse gray, conical gray, figurines, Florero-olla gray, hemispherical bowls, Tiger-claw vases, and Zapotec olla.

All of these Zapotec ceramic wares reflected Oaxaca processes and phases, from the early Naquitz (8900–6700 B.C.) to the Post-Classic Period (A.D. 900–1521). As the lords of Monte Alban and Oaxaca, the Zapotec, when they were not moving on to avoid migrating and invading groups, adopted new techniques and elaborated upon them.

ZAPOTEC COSMOLOGY   The explanation for the existence of the culture in the world and universe in which they found themselves. The Zapotec of each generation were raised hearing accounts that attempted to explain their origins and relationship to the universe. Some held that the Zapotec had sprung from the rocks of Oaxaca or had been born by pumas and ocelots. While the Spanish and others thought that the Zapotec had originated in the Nahual Land of the Seven Caves (Chicomoztoc), their languages, customs and their history in the Oaxacan regio belie this.

The Zapotec viewed the material world as being dominated at all times by a spiritual force called *pee*. *Pee* imbued nature and all life, including the elements and even the deities who served as intermediaries between human beings and the cosmos. This view was borne out in the complex societal arrangement that prevailed throughout the Zapotec domains, in which one group endowed with power was always shielded by a maze of agents, servants or representatives. The lords of each Zapotec community, whether in the capital or in outlying regions, were isolated in their particular role and status and might be approached only by designated intermediaries.

The supreme force in the Zapotec cosmology was Coqui Xee, or Coquixilla, a deity accepted as omnipotent, omnipresent and everlasting. He was the personification of an abstract concept held by the Zapotec concerning infinity and the participation humankind in that realm. The deity was also unknowable as a god, invisible and unhampered by any natural or limiting form. For this reason Coqui Xee was approachable only through the divine intermediaries who understood his attributes and were designated as those who could sustain contact with him. Thus the lesser deities served as simple agents of Coqui Xee, who remained the principal or vital force, one not subject to human manipulation.

Pee, also called *pitao*, existed in all living, moving things, granting them supernatural qualities and elevating them to exalted status. Everything that the Zapotec observed was believed to contain this vital force. *Pitao* can be translated as "the great breath" or as "the great spirit." The concept was not confined to a single deity or site but moved in the world as the life force. In some sense this concept approaches monotheism. Coqui Xee was creator of all natural and supernatural forces in the Zapotec world.

The Zapotec, however, also maintained cultic practices in their religion. Both lesser deities and ancestors were aspects of their traditions. When they arrived in the Zapotec realm, Spanish conquerors destroyed statues of ancestors of a particular royal line or group, having mistaking them for idols.

The Zapotec could recognize *pee* or *pitao* in certain elements. Lightning was one aspect of Coqui Xee, containing *pee* or *pitao*. The lightning bolt was *cocijo*, and the thunder that resulted from the lightning was called *xoo cocijo*, meaning "the earthquake of lightning." Lightning flashes in the skies, sometimes resulting in disastrous fires, were visible manifestations of the vital principle. Lightning also accompanied rain, needed for the agricultural growth. For this reason lightning, as a manifestation of the god, was included as a force in the Zapotec calendar. Clouds were important as well, not only as the partners of lightning and thunder but as manifestations of the ancestors of the Zapotec people. The Zapotec believed they returned to the skies as clouds when they died, thus uniting with Coqui Xee and with his visible manifestations for future generations. (See ZAPOTEC GODS; ZAPOTEC RELIGION.)

ZAPOTEC GODS Deities designated as intermediaries between the Zapotec people and the great creative force, Coqui Xee. These gods were stratified in rank and purpose in the Zapotec pantheon that was honored in the regional ceremonial complexes. This stratification was reflected in the Zapotec world as well. The gods were believed to serve as agents for humankind and the creative force that alone represented eternity and the unknowable in the universe. The following list cites Coqui Xee, the first principle, followed by less-exalted divine beings who attended him and interceded for humans.

Coqui Xee	Also called *Pijetao Xee* in some records, the Zapotec creative force; unseen, present in all things, the sustainer and life gives, served by less-exalted gods and by the Zapotec people. Coqui Xee was made manifest to humans by lightning, thunder and clouds, all divine aspects of nature to the Zapotec. Coqui Xee endowed all animate beings and nature with "the great breath," *pee*.
Bat god	Associated with fertility and an ancient unnamed deity.
Cocijo	The Zapotec deity of rain and lightning, possibly another manifestation of Coqui Xee. Cocijo has obvious influences from other Mesoamerican cultures, where rain gods were worshipped because of the need for rain. Cocijo was the lightning, and the thunder that followed was called *xoo cocijo*.
Copijcha	The god of the sun and the patron of warriors and battle.
Laxee	The god of sorcery and magic.
Lera Acuece	The Zapotec god of medicine and the healing arts.
Niyohua	The god of the hunt, a regional deity not worshipped by all Zapotecs; his worship probably confined to certain eras.
Pitao Cozobi	The Zapotec deity of maize, the patron of yearly harvests and of abundance.
Pitao Huicaana	A creator goddess, associated with the spirit of Coqui Xee but also revered in the Zapotec cult of ancestor worship.
Pitao Peeze	The patron of Zapotec traders and merchants as well as of trade itself that served Zapotec and linked the area to other city-states.
Pitao Pezelao	The god of the underworld and of death, who was an aide to Coqui Xee and the patron of ancestors.
Pitao Xicala	The god of love and dreams and all things of beauty.
Pitao Xoo	The god of earthquakes, partial essence of the *pee* that endowed all things with life.
Pitao Zij	The god of the miserable, probably of slaves, tenant farmers and prisoners of war.

Xipe Totec	The Flayed God, the deity of spring. This cult was ancient in Mesoamerica. Xipe Totec, worshipped by many of the region's cultures over the centuries, was depicted as a child wrapped in human skin.
Xiuhtecuhtl	The god of fire, depicted as a young man, whereas the god was represented by the Zapotec in other Mesoamerican cultures as an aged man.
Xonaxi Quecuya	The goddess of the underworld and of death, the consort of Pitao Pezelao.

ZAPOTEC GOVERNMENT AND SOCIETY The administration and community structure that provided each individual with clearly defined roles and obligations. A caste system of nobility and commoners existed in most Zapotec communities. The nobility consisted of the first rank (the priestly caste), called the *Tijacoqui*, or the second rank or the secular nobility, called the *Tijajoana* or *Tijajonanahuini*. Both men and women in Zapotec society could inherit or achieve rank through marriage, as no gender distinction was made. Noblewomen were called *Coquitao xonaxi* if they were members of the ruling dynasty and *Xonaxi xinijoana* if they were members of one of the secondary noble lines. A similar distinction was made in the case of men. All nobles were aware of the various ranks and social levels within their own castes and were vigilant in guarding them.

These Zapotec aristocrats inherited their titles, which endowed them with wealth and certain privileges. In some eras, however, the records indicate that certain Zapotec who had distinguished themselves in some fashion or those with innate abilities and talents could attain high positions. Because of the hereditary nature of their caste system, Zapotec nobles maintained rigid standards for marriages and arranged them for obvious political advantage, never permitting those of lower rank to enter their circle through marriage. The lines of familial rank were traced through the female as well as through the male lineages, so the Zapotec noblewomen were as highly regarded as the males when it came to choosing a mate.

Each of the Zapotec regions claimed at least one noble clan, most of them dating to the early eras of the city-state's development. In these formative periods the nobility emerged slowly, basing their claims to status generally on lands they had accumulated within a given district. These nobles ruled the region, usually in the name of the king. They held administrative posts and military commands and answered to regional governors or to the council chosen by the monarch. The complex system of attaining power and rank within each class was part of the life of the aristocracy, and nobles worked within specific regulations concerning how far they might venture to gain audience with an overlord or how avidly they could pursue a particular course of action. Even aristocrats were bound by the custom of those of superior rank remaining isolated from petitioners or underlings.

The rules concerning commoners were also complex, and those born into this social strata were obliged to follow the customs that were accepted by society. The commoners were grouped in the following designations: chiefs of individual settlements, farmers, artisans, and merchants.

The leaders of various Zapotec districts were called *piniqueche* and were vassals of the ranking lord. They administered their own offices, paying tribute and taxes to the local aristocrats, who gave tribute, in turn, to those of higher rank and to the temple priests. The heads of the local districts were generally a distinguished clan who claimed certain rights and holdings, not elevated enough to claim status in the nobility but possessing a certain degree of power within their own circle.

The farmers were tied to the land and lived in simple pastoral communities near or beside their fields. Most owned the land or held it in common with other members of their families. Tenant farming also may have been practiced in some Zapotec regions. The farmers generally worked independently in their own fields and gardens, but they combined their efforts for the seasonal clearings and for irrigation projects vital to an arid region or necessitated by a failure of rain in the proper season.

Zapotec artisans, adhering to the Mesoamerican pattern for craftsmen and valued workers, applied their craft in the larger cities, especially those sites that were important to Zapotec trade or regional commercial enterprises. Zapotec artists, sculptors, masons and metalworkers performed the various tasks assigned to them based on the needs of local groups and the demands of trade. Musicians were held in high esteem, as the Zapotec, like their Mesoamerican neighbors, appreciated music and incorporated it into their religious and secular celebrations. The rank of artisan also included diviners and fortune-tellers, those who did not hold temple rank but served the various rural communities.

Zapotec merchants, in keeping with Mesoamerican tradition, were drawn from the ranks of both nobles and commoners. The nobles, often powerfully traders in their own right, holding vast quantities of products and directing both local and the long-distance trade enterprises that kept manufactured goods and raw materials moving throughout the region, administered most trading ventures. Merchant commoners especially those who demonstrated ability, worked for these nobles, although many achieved distinction and privileges because of their own efforts. On the lowest rung of this class were the rural hawkers, local peddlers who sold their wares at markets or went through the farming communities with goods on their backs.

Zapotec priests were a special caste in the social structure in most regions. They were generally sons of lesser nobles who were given to the temples as small children because they were not in line to inherit noble rank. These boys were trained by the priests to serve the temples and to maintain the shrines. Some spent only seven years in the priesthood, returning to secular pursuits after having given their allotted time. Others, especially those who demonstrated aptitude and ambition, probably dedicated their lives to the temples.

The Zapotec priesthood was regulated by certain traditional customs and restrictions. During their terms of office, most priests might not enter into legal marriages. Whether this celibacy extended to other relationships is not known. They were also banned from drinking *pulque*, the heady liquor distilled from the maguey plant and consumed avidly throughout Mesoamerica. Other regulations depended on the attributes of the particular god served and the temple requirements. In some instances violation of the more stringent rules carried a death penalty.

The priestly roles in the Zapotec temple ceremonies were generally inherited, or at least confined to a particular noble clan. Entire families supported the worship of a particular god and participated in temple. These roles included *Huipatoo* or *heujatao,* called the Great Seer, the High Priest of the cult; *Cope-vitoo,* the priests who served as guardians of the various temples and shrines, probably required in most ceremonial complexes during the time when pilgrimages brought an influx of celebrants from outlying regions; and *Neza-eche,* attendants upon ritual sacrifices. Other priests studied astronomy and astrology, taught the young, advised the various ruling councils, worked with the tribute collectors, designed new shrines and cult buildings and performed the routines of any Mesoamerican institution. Most Mesoamerican cultures had a number of these priests, each assigned a title and a specific task.

Slaves were held of the lowest rank in the Zapotec social structure, and during religious celebrations, they were sacrificed. Others served in the palace residences, worked in the caravans for traders and probably in the fields held by the temples.

Zapotec dress and way of life depended very much on social distinctions. The aristocrats wore cotton mantles and loincloths, with feathered decorations and with jewelry and other, sometimes expensive, ornamentations. Commoners wore clothes made of various fibers from local plants. They used shells and other small stones as ornamentations. Their diets were equally different. The aristocrats consumed the grains and fruits that were staples of the commoners' diets, but they also ate turkeys, deer, hares, rabbits and other mammals, and the drink cacao, all of which were denied commoners except on special feast days or if granted dispensation.

Despite the fact that the Zapotec influenced vast territories, including much of Oaxaca, the single community on the local level remained the political reality. Each city or hamlet was integrated into an harmonious whole, with each inhabitant working toward the common good and pursuing the activities required of him or her. This sort of contribution to the common good began in the family, when sons and daughters were early advised of their obligations. In their roles in the community, the Zapotec worked for the betterment of the entire population, in keeping with the requirements set by a chief and then a governor, representing the king.

Zapotec lords were the authorities in the regions placed under their control. These nobles reserved for themselves all weighty decisions. Sometimes, if the region was large or complex or included a large number of smaller communities, the lords took on a considerable number of assistants, some of whom were assigned to distant places and handled the affairs of a limited territory. Such assistants were called *colaabachina.*

Tributes levied on each particular district, labor units and materials for public projects could be drafted or demanded by the governing noble and his assistants. In turn, however, each local administrator had to provide the Zapotec king with military forces, labor groups and tributes. Administrators in the more troubled regions of the Zapotec domain were usually campaign veterans or men trained in military skill and discipline. Military life held the respect of the Zapotec people, as those who served were their defense against constantly threatening neighbors and maintained the unity of diverse populations.

This system, employing people in all walks of life and on all levels of society, did not allow for individual participation in government but did allow each Zapotec man and woman to play a clearly defined role that increased the general good. From the king to the governors, and from the governors to the chiefs, the favors, rights and protection given demanded loyalty and generosity in return. Thus the average Zapotec, guided by this complex state mechanism, benefited from its administration but did not have a voice in government on a regional or even local level.

Zapotec Royalty

The early Zapotec dynasties are unknown. Only those who ruled at Zaachila and later at Mitla and Tehuantepec are named. The information about royalty was gathered by the Spanish historians. The rulers mentioned by the Spanish include:

Zaachila I. Founder of the Zapotec dynasty at Zaachila, ruling at the end of the fourteenth century and in the first years of the fifteenth century. He was listed as a warrior king, who led his armies against the incursions of the Mixtecs in the region.

Zaachila II. Ascending the throne in A.D. 1415, probably not actually called Zaachila. He is reported to have withdrawn his forces to make a truce with the Mixtec. Noted for his intelligence and swift decisions in taking advantage of situations, he supposedly ruled for almost 40 years.

Zaachila III. Called the Deceiver by the Zapotec, he succeeded to the throne on the death of Zaachila II c. A.D. 1454. This made him a contemporary of the Aztec (Mexica) ruler AHUITZOTL. He made an alliance with the Mixtec but then led Ahuitzotl and the Aztec army by a secret trail to attack the Mixtec. Zaachila III is recorded as dying in A.D. 1487.

Cosihuesa (Cocijoesa). The son of the Deceiver, Zaachila III, whose name means Lightning Creator. He is probably the best documented of the Zapotec kings. Cosihuesa defended the Isthmus of Tehuantepec against the Aztec, aligning his troops with those of the Mixtec. The battle that took place at Guiengola ended in a truce, and the Aztec gave Cosihuesa an Aztec princess, Pelaxilla (called Coyolicatzin in Nahuatl), as his wife. Expected to betray the Zapotec and open the gates for the Aztec, Pelaxilla took the part of her husband and his people. The son of this royal marriage was Cocijopii, who became the ruler of Tehuantepec. Both Cosihuesa and his son, however, confronted change and conflict.

Cosihuesa had five legitimate children, including two pure Zapotec sons, Bitoopa and Natippa. His daughters were Penopias, who was made patron of Tehuantepec after her death because of her piety, and Donaji, who married a Mixtec prince and became a Christian.

Cocijopii. The son of the Zapotec king Cosihuesa and the Aztec princess Pelaxilea. He was born in 1502 and was called Lightning Wind because of a diviner's prediction that he would achieve great power and fame and then be humbled. Named ruler of Tehuantepec at the age of 16, eventually he was forced to become a vassal of the Spanish. Devoutly religious, Cocijopii was brought before the Spanish Inquisition because of his adherence to the old ways. He cleared his name but died soon after effecting his release.

ZAPOTEC HIEROGLYPHS One of the four major regional systems of writing in Mesoamerica, initiated by this culture at Monte Alban during the Formative Period (c. 2000/1600 B.C.–c. A.D. 250/290), making it the oldest writing form. The other four systems were those of the Maya of southern Mexico, Belize, Guatemala and Honduras; the Aztec (Mexica) system of central Mexico, and the Mixtec writing system. The Zapotec hieroglyphs appeared as early as 600 B.C. in Oaxaca as relief inscriptions on tomb walls. Some 500 Zapotec inscriptions have been found in the region of Oaxaca, although Zapotec writing is the least studied of the four Mesoamerican systems. Part of the difficulties in deciphering and evaluating Zapotec hieroglyphs lies in the fact that these people were members of the Otomanguean language family, quite distinct from the Maya and the Aztec, and few examples of the language are available today.

Some Zapotec hieroglyphs concerned their secular and religious calendars, both innovations that predate those of other cultures. Each day in the Zapotec religious calendar was designated by one of 20 separate day-name glyphs, combined with a number between one and 13, so that the combination would allow for 260 days of the sacred cycle.

The Zapotec made glyphs to represent particular sites as well. Other inscriptions were made that provided accounts of the lives of the ruling families of the various colonies. Such inscribed glyphs appeared in Oaxaca in the Rosario Phase (700–500 B.C.) just before the rise of Monte Alban. Zapotec culture dominated the city during its third phase, but there is evidence that this culture influenced it before then. The earliest known Zapotec carving was discovered at San Jose Mogote, this representation of a nude male figure contained a glyph, *xoo*, which denotes motion or earthquake. The hand-compound style of glyphs, representing parts of the hands in figures, was developed by the Zapotec at Monte Alban after the end of the Rosario Phase, when San Jose Mogote was in decline.

The conquest slabs erected in Monte Alban carry the significance of the glyph even further. Each slab represents the subjugation of a particular town or city nearby. These slabs contain glyphs describing the location and name of each site. Heads inscribed upside-down attached to the insignias probably represent the slain former chieftains of the territories.

Later Zapotec inscriptions trace the genealogies of individuals in their tombs, providing details of their family lives in glyphs. A register of the 13 day signs and their numerical counterparts were made on Zapotec calendric tablets, and one particular slab related to the historical name of the culture, depicting the presence of sacred clouds.

ZAPOTEC LANGUAGE The tongue spoken by the Otomanguean group, which included, among others, Chinatecan, Manguean, Mixtecan, and Otomian.

A dialect called Chatino, which dates to the earliest eras of Oaxaca development, is part of the Zapotec language. The dialect is still spoken in the southwestern portion of the region. The Otomanguean group had definite links with other Mesoamerican languages, believed to date to c. 7000 to 5000 B.C. Zapotec is a tonal language, in which the meaning of a word can be determined by the pitch of the voice used in pronouncing it. The language employs *tonemes*, tones required to distinguish certain meanings. It thus has a musical or harmonious character. At the present time, the Zapotec language is spoken in Oaxaca, Tehuantepec, Villa Alta and in the southern Sierra region.

ZAPOTEC MARRIAGE The institution recognized by Zapotec of all castes and especially among the nobility, whose unions could affect the inheritance of ranks and estates. The royal and most noble families engaged in alliances to consolidate power and resources. Such unions also provided the nation with royal dynasties and aristocrats of pure lineage. The *caciques*, as the Spanish called this nobility, practiced polygyny, with some men marrying as many as 20 women during their lifetimes. All these wives were aristocrats, as children born of unions between nobles and commoners were considered illegitimate, and were denied all ranks.

Marriages in the upper classes were arranged by intermediaries who represented the grooms in consultation with the bride's family. If the marriage was approved by both parties, and if the diviners decreed that such a union would not bring about misfortune for the offspring, an agreement concerning gifts was reached. These gifts varied, and in some cases, such as a marriage between a prince and a princess, the groom might be given an entire city. The marriage ceremony itself was simple. The bride and groom were brought together and seated on a mat in the presence of their families. They drank *pulque* from cups and then had their cloaks tied together to symbolize their union.

Common marriages were generally monogamous. It has been recorded that the Zapotec male commoners did not marry early, and they too consulted diviners. Virginity was prized by commoners, and young women had to submit to examinations before the ceremony, which was also a simple one. After the ceremony the groom took the bride to his home and consummated the union.

Zapotec marriages could end in divorce, and various charges could be brought to obtain one. If there was a difference in rank, particularly involving a woman of high rank and a lower-caste male, a divorce was granted quickly. If a couple remained childless, the union was also dissolved. If the names of the couple were linked numerically indicating misfortune for the offspring, the marriage could also be ended. If a couple fought on a continual basis, or if the man abused his wife enough to stir her to action, a divorce could be arranged. Adultery might be a criminal offense at times. Any adultery involving the male could be grounds for divorce. An adulterous woman could be killed and cannibalized or returned to her parents to live in isolation. Marriage linked the clans of the Zapotec world, provided documented lineage and was the method by which the ranks and the privileges of the various castes could be preserved. Lineage in the Zapotec cities was documented based on both the male and the female ancestors of the family.

ZAPOTEC RELIGION   The belief and practices that reflected the Zapotec view of their world and brought unity and stability to its people. The Zapotec worshipped the usual pantheon of Mesoamerican deities, but they also acknowledged a supreme force, unknowable and unapproachable. Called the Cloud People, the Zapotec incorporated the concept of returning to the cloud realms after death. They also believed in an underworld and practiced ancestor worship. Other Zapotec tradition decreed that the people originated from Oaxaca rocks or were given birth by puma and ocelots. Later the idea that the Zapotec originated in Chicomoztoc, the Land of the Seven Caves, the Nahua origin, was circulated, but the language and customs of the Zapotec culture belie this theory.

The Zapotec constructed temples for religious rites that celebrated various events and the legendary pursuits of their pantheon. Priests served in these temples, and ceremonies that were conducted for the populace included bloodletting, self-immolation, sacrifices and ritualistic cannibalism. Such services reflect the general Mesoamerican religious practices of the times. The ceremonial complexes of the Zapotec cities were stages for the enactment of these rituals and for the religious processions and festivals that celebrated the themes of the various cults.

Like Zapotec society, however, the religious practices of this culture were carried out with local variations. In each city, whether a princedom or governed by a representative of the Zapotec nobility, a patron deity presided over the cultic ceremonies. In some instances this divine being was not only a god but considered the ancestor of the local inhabitants. The rituals varied, but most included intoxication, dancing, sacrifices and offerings.

With the celebration of the local deity's honors or life, the community demonstrated its unity. Each god, however, served as well as a protector of various walks of life in the Zapotec world. Some were responsible for earthquakes, wind, rain and the other natural elements. Some were agricultural in origin and represented fertility. The god of death and the underworld, with his consort, presided over the end of all Zapotec lives. Others were patrons of daily activities, such as the practice of medicine, hunting, farming, fishing, love, dreams, trade and childbearing.

All these gods were manifestations of the one supreme force: Coqui Xee, who could not be seen and could not be approached by human beings. The gods were thus intermediaries to the great Xee, and only chosen priests might approach these deities in turn. Thus a stern hierarchy was superimposed on all aspects of human existence; divine beings were elevated and approachable only by those few who were endowed to make such encounters by birth and by rank. The religious calendar adopted by the Zapotec, the first in Mesoamerica, provided each individual member of society with a calendrical name and with a spirit companion. Both specified the destiny of the individual, which was union with the divine. This religious calendar, read as a book by the Zapotec priests and sages, included sections on cosmic awareness, the role of the universe and the ties that bound humankind to the supernatural.

ZAPOTEC TRADE   An active enterprise that evolved early in Oaxaca, with specialization its hallmark, the result of the geographical and climatic conditions, including varying degrees of altitude. The Zapotec had a vast array of products and resources available to them. Early on, they welcomed trade and the marketplace to supplement their regional products, and they established trade routes, depots and marketplaces in their communities. All of these regional markets functioned on specific days and offered products brought from distant sources. Salt, for example, was found in some Zapotec regions, such as Mitla, but it was also brought there from Tehuacan, with cotton, fruits, furs and gems. In return, the Zapotec provided woven materials, tobacco, medicinal herbs and other products.

ZAPOTEC WARFARE   The military actions that distinguished the Zapotec and provided them with defense throughout their history. Most Zapotec men were warriors or militarily trained, as such skills were considered a vital aspect of the aristocratic and priestly life. The fact that military campaigns were waged continuously added to the necessity of having military leadership. The Zapotec were confronted by Mixtec and other foes throughout their history, and for a time they appear to have waged war upon one another as well. Local chiefs set out to right wrongs or to halt the trespass of strangers. Zapotec warriors conducted auguries before going into battle, and they generally marched into the campaign behind the image of a deity, possibly a deceased ancestor of note. Officers wore padded cotton armor and used shields made of cane. The common soldier wore a loincloth. Weapons included the wooden broadsword, edged with obsidian, the bow and arrow, the lance and the sling.

The first prisoner taken in any Zapotec battle was sacrificed to the patron deity of the campaign, and the rest were taken as slaves. The prisoner's own bow was tied around his genitals and in that condition he was led away. The Zapotec maintained fortifications, and they relied on hills and man-made structures as defensive measures. Mitla and other cities were walled, and Huitzo was a mountain fortress. While being militarily active, however, especially in the last stages of their civilization, the Zapotec were also known to practice deception and diplomacy at the same time.

ZAPOTEL, EL   A site near Nopiloa, in southern Mexico, dating to the Late Formative Period (300 B.C.–c. A.D. 250/ 290) as a coastal cultural development. Villages are evident in its remains, and smiling figures were also recovered from local mounds. A multiple burial site offered grave relics and smiling figures of the Remojada variety. An ossuary was also discovered, containing some 80 skulls without bodies, which were deposited in a pit.

ZEMPOALA (Cempoala)   A Totonac city near the gulf coast in Veracruz, meaning "20 Waters." This was a reference to the region's vast river system. Zempoala was located between the Actopan and San Carlos Chachalacas rivers. It was built c. A.D. 1200, following the Toltec exodus from their original homeland in the Sierra de Puebla. Highly fortified and covering approximately two square miles, Zempoala was designed with 10 separate districts, into which familial housing units were placed. Most Totonac cities involved a mixed population. Each district also had administrative, military and ceremonial sectors. Eleven defense systems are also evident, and the buildings were made of highly polished stone. Thick walls, covered with stucco and cemented with seashell lime and sand, were then painted red and yellow, separating these precincts. The buildings within the districts were surrounded by pyramidal platforms and residences. Elaborate stone aqueducts provided water for the structures, using pipes and angled formations to reach the individual cisterns. These cisterns, in turn, were kept free of debris and clutter. Canals also served the precincts and the adjoining fields.

Dominating Zempoala was the Great Temple, which stood in the northern part of the city. It was erected on a large pyramidal base reaching 25 feet, with three platforms and with a central stairway. Columns adorned the temple, as well as Totonac architectural accompaniaments called merlons, stone decorations in the shape of triangles. These were called *almenas* in the region. A wall having merlons surrounded the major ceremonial complex, which included the traditional plaza. This plaza faced the pyramid and was used either as a dance platform or as an altar; it was elevated and had stairs on all four sides, in honor of the cardinal points. Two circular structures were built nearby, again employing the merlon designs. Circular structures in Mesoamerican cities were generally built in honor of Quetzalcoatl as Ehecatl, the wind god. The circle was unending, representing the spirit form of the god. Several smaller pyramids were built along the sides of the plaza to provide additional ceremonial sites and to complete the symmetry of the complex. A semicircular extension was added to one of the smaller edifices.

On the east side of the plaza the Temple of the Chimneys was discovered. Called *Las Chimneas* by the Spanish, the temple was so named because of columns that stood on either side. Walls and columns were polished and shining and there was a temple pyramid with stairs and seven levels. Much of Zempoala was celebrated for its whiteness and polished cement stones. The city was made vassal to the Aztec (Mexica) empire in the reign of Motecuhzoma II. Another record states that it was given to King Nezahualpilli of Texcoco, as a member of the Triple Alliance.

ZERO MOON BIRD   A Tikal Maya ruler, depicted in the Leiden Plaque, which was made to commemorate his accession to the throne in 320 A.D..

ZINCANTAN   A Tzotzil Maya trade center in the western highlands. A prosperous commercial area, the city was attacked by the Aztec but they were unable to establish a foothold there. The city worshipped Chac as the Earth owner. The Aztec considered the traders of Zinacantan dangerous and used disguises when travelling there. When the Aztec did manage to involve themselves in regional trade, the city of the Chiapanec rose as a rival to Zinacantan. Disputes over valuable salt deposits led to confrontations.

ZIRAHUEN LAKE   A water reserve in Michoacan, associated with the Tarascan culture. Patzcuaro, a Tarascan regional capital, was erected on the banks of Lake Zirahuen by King Sicuirancha.

ZITACUARO RIVER   A waterway that forms a tributary of the vast Balsas River system in the Yucatan Peninsula.

ZOQUE   See MAYA GROUPS, ZOQUE.

ZUANGA   A Tarascan ruler who led his military forces against the attacking Aztec (Mexica), under the command of Emperor Axayacatl. After two attempts to penetrate the Tarascan defenses, the Aztec withdrew in humiliation.

Appendix I

MESOAMERICAN DEITIES

Acantun Maya demons associated with the religious rituals of the cardinal points of the earth (the four directions); also associated with the *Bacabes.*

Ah Chac Mitan Ch'oc A Maya deity, representing the planet Venus. (See also *Xamen Ek.*)

Ah Kinchil A Maya deity, associated with agricultural efforts and with planting ceremonies.

Ah Mun A Maya god of maize, also called Yum Kaax in some regions.

Ah Puch A Maya deity associated with death; called God A in some codex references.

Ahuiateteo A group of five Aztec deities concerned with pleasure and with the punishments that come from a lack of moderation.

Amimitl A deity of Xochimilco, the patron of canals and gardens.

Ancestors, Divine The creator parents, depicted on an aged couple, worshipped by the Maya and by the civilizations in the Valley of Mexico.

Atlahuac A god of Xochimilco, worshipped in rituals with Amimitl. The deity was called Atlahua by the Aztec.

Atlahua An Aztec deity associated with fishing and aquatic hunts.

Bacab Maya demons corresponding in some rites to the *Acantun.*

Bolom Dz'acab A Maya deity serving as the patron of aristocrats and ancestral lineages, a vital aspect of Maya society; in some lists called God K.

Bolontiku The underworld deities of the Maya, nine in number, called the Lords of the Night.

Camazotz A Maya vampire bat god, involved with the Hero Twins in Xibalba, noted as vicious and blood thirsty.

Ce Acatl An Aztec god associated in ceremonies with Quetzalcoatl, probably from Toltec origins.

Ce Acatl Topiltzin The Toltec prince associated historically with Quetzalcoatl in Tula and with the Maya Kukulcan.

Celestial Bird A Maya religious image associated with the World Tree.

Celestial Monster A Maya religious being that resembles a dragon.

Centeotl An Aztec god called 400 Rabbits, a derivation from the numerous methods of becoming intoxicated; associated with flowers, magic, feasting and drink.

Chac The Maya deity of rain, comparable to the Aztec Tlaloc, associated with the Cardinal Points.

Chac Mool (Mul) A deity form, used in Maya and Toltec ceremonial centers, such as Chichen Itza, copied by the Aztec.

Chalchiuhtlicue An Olmec goddess of water, also revered in Teotihuacan and by the Aztec.

Chicomicoatl A goddess honored in Xochimilco and in other Valley of Mexico sites as a maiden corn deity and as patroness of the hearth; also called Chantico.

Chiconahuizcuintl A Xochimilco god, the patron of the aged.

Cihuacoatl A deity associated with the ball game in many cultures and a popular goddess in the Valley of Mexico, patroness of midwives.

Cipactli An Aztec goddess, believed to personify the unformed earth and chaos; broken into two parts to form earth and sky.

Cipactonal The oldest male divine being, husband of Oxomoco and grandfather of Quetzalcoatl, honored by many cultures.

Citlalatonac An Aztec deity associated with the Milky Way; the husband of Citlalinicue and called Starshine.

Citlalinicue An Aztec goddess ruling the Milky Way, (the consort of Citllalatonac) called Star Skirt.

Cizin (Kisin) A Maya deity of death, revered in the Yuczatan; also honored as an earth god in Chiapas.

Coatlicue An Aztec goddess of the earth, sun and moon, and the mother of Quetzalcoatl.

Cocijo   An Oaxaca rain deity, related to the Maya rain god, Chac and worshipped by the Zapotec and in Monte Alban.

Copil   An Aztec divine being, the son of Malinalxoch and nephew of Huitzilopochtli; associated with the founding of Tenochtitlan.

Coyolxauhqui   An Aztec goddess, the sister of Huitzilopochtli, who slew their mother.

Cueraveraperi   A Tarascan deity, called the mother of the gods.

Curiacaveri   A Tarascan deity, associated with solar rituals.

Diving God   A Huaxtec deity with a monster face, depicted in Tepetzintla reliefs in a diving position; also a Maya deity in the Yucatan.

Earth Moon Goddess   A Huaxtec deity, shown as a young woman.

Ehecatl   A popular form of Quetzalcoatl, honored in many cultures; the god of the wind, with round temples, reflecting the sweeping, boundless nature of the god.

Ek Chuah   A Maya deity of trade and markets, and a patron of war and cacao.

Fat God   A Teotihuacan deity, associated with *pulque* and festivals; also worshipped by the Maya; representing gluttony.

Fire God   A variety of deities, under different names, worshipped almost universally in Mesoamerica.

Fire Serpent   A being revered by many Mesoamerican cultures as a form of Quetzalcoatl.

Five-Death   A Mixtec deity, unknown as to purpose or role.

Four Hundred Rabbits   A Tepoztlan deity of intoxication. Also see Centeotl.

Gucumatz   A Maya deity worshipped in Guatemala, called the Feathered Serpent, possibly a form of Quetzalcoatl.

Hapay Can   A Maya deity called Sucking Snake.

Huehueteotl   A Huaxtec fire deity, patron of volcanoes.

Huitzilopochtli   The Aztec patron deity.

Hunhau   A Maya god of death, associated with Ah Puch.

Hun Hunahpu   one of the Maya Hero Twins, patron of cosmological rites.

Hurakan   The Maya deity of storms.

Ikil   An Aztec goddess of the Milky Way.

Ilamatecuhtli   A popular deity associated with ball games in many cultures.

Ipalnemohuani   An Aztec creator deity.

Itzamna   A Maya deity associated with creation.

Itzlacoyoliuhqui-Ixguimilli   A god of the Valley of Mexico, representing stones and cold.

Itzpapaleotl   A Toltec/Aztec/Zapotec goddess called Obsidian Butterfly, associated with dark forces.

Ixbalanque   A Maya Hero Twin, involved in creation traditions.

Ix Chel   A Maya goddess of suicides.

Ixlilton   A Mesoamerican deity associated with ball games in many cultures.

Ixtab   A Maya goddess, the patronness of suicides.

Jaguar Baby   A Maya divine being, the patron of Tikal and other sites.

Kan-cross Water Lily Monster   A Maya religious symbol associated with the foliated cross.

Kukulcan   The Maya Quetzalcoatl, worshipped in the Yucatan.

Lady Blood   A Maya divine being, the mother of the Hero Twins.

Laxee   A Zapotec deity, the patron of magic.

Lera Acuece   A Zapotec god of medicine.

Macuilxochitl   An Aztec god, patron of games, gambling, and associated with Xochipilli.

Malinalxoch   The Aztec sister of Huitzilopochtli and mother of Copil. She was abandoned by the Aztec.

Mam   A Huaxtec deity called Our Grandfather, patron of *pulque* and the earth.

Mayahuel   A Toltec and Aztec deity, patroness of maguey and *pulque.*

Mictlantecuhtli   A death god worshipped by the Aztec and other cultures, viewed as an enemy of Quetzalcoatl.

Mixcoatl   An Aztec deity called Cloud Serpent, worshipped in solar rituals, probably introduced by the Chichimec and popular.

Mixitli   An Aztec deity associated with the earth.

Moyocoyatzin   An Aztec creation god, called the Lord who Invented Himself.

Naguals   Spirits worshipped by the Itza, capable of becoming jaguars.

Nahualpilli   A Xochimilco god of youth.

Nanahuatzin   A Teotihuacan deity, involved in solar and cosmological traditions; becoming the sun.

Nine-Wind   A Mixtec divine version of Ehecatl.

Niyohua   A Zapotec god of the hunt, whose rituals were limited to certain regions of that culture.

Obsidian Butterfly (Itzpapolotl)   A Chichimec earth goddess.

Ometecuhtli   A Tepoztlan deity, patron of *pulque.*

Ometeotl   An Aztec creator deity, called the navel of the world.

One Death   A Mixtec deity, considered a variation of the Aztec god Tonatiuh.

Opochtli   An Aztec god associated with fishing and aquatic hunts.

Oxomoco   A grandmother deity of the Aztec, consort of Cipactonal, dwelling in a cave in Morelos.

Pitao Cozobi   An ancient Zapotec bat god.

Pitao Huicaana   A Zapotec creator goddess.

Pitao Peeze   A Zapotec deity, patron of trade and merchants.

Pitao Pezelao   A Zapotec deity of death.

Pitao Xicala   A Zapotec deity of love.

Pitao Xoo   A Zapotec deity of earthquakes.

Pitao Zij   A Zapotec deity of slaves.

Quetzalcoatl   The most popular deity in Mesoamerica, worshipped in Maya centers as Kukulcan.

Quilaztli   A Xochimilco goddess, an earth mother.

Quinametzin   Toltec giants, part of the Second World.

Seven-Flower   A Mixtec god, considered a variation of the deity Xochipilli.

Seven-Rain   A Mixtec god, considered a variation of the deity Xipe Totec.

Six Rabbits   A Xochimilco deity, patron of corn.

Tariacuri   A Tarascan god of the wind.

Tepeyollotl   An Aztec jaguar deity, associated with the god Tezcatlipoca.

Tepoztecatl   A Valley of Mexico god associated with *pulque*, the liquor made from the maguey plant.

Teteoinnan   An Aztec deity of fertility, birth and medicine.

Tetzahuitl   An Aztec deity of the lunar cults, very ancient.

Tetzaupilli   A Xochimilco deity of flowers and rain.

Tezcatlipoca   A Toltec deity of magic; honored by the Aztec as a god of the earth and moon.

Titlacauan   A Huaxtec deity of magic, traditionally involved in the of Tula.

Tlahuizcalpantecuhtl   The Toltec deity called the Lord of the Dawn.

Tlaloc   A Mesoamerican rain deity, worshipped by many cultures.

Tlaloques   Aztec dwarves that served Tlaloc and were associated with mountains.

Tlalteuchtli   An Aztec goddess called the Earth Lady, a creative power.

Tloque Nahuaque   A Teotihuacan deity of life and creation.

Tlozolteotl   A Huaxtec goddess of creation and purification, also called Tlaelquani in some forms, and referred to as "Our Grandmother."

Tonacatecuhtli   An Aztec deity of sustenance, an earth creator; father of the gods.

Tonatiuh   An Aztec god of primordial creation, called the Eagle.

Tzitzimitl   Aztec divine beings; demons of the night involved in the ending of the world and eclipses.

Uinturopan   A Tarascan goddess, patroness of maize.

Usukunkyum   A Maya deity, brother of Ah Kinchil, who aided good in the battle of Xibalba.

Vucub Caquix   A Maya deity of death, sire of the earthquake gods.

Were-Jaguar   An Olmec jaguar cult being.

Witz Monster   A Maya deity, a living mountain symbol.

Xamen Ek   The Maya Venus.

Xaratang   A Tarascan goddess, patroness of fertility.

Xilonen   An Aztec goddess of maize.

Xipe Totec   The "Flayed God," popular in Teotihuacan and in other cultures.

Xiuhcoatl   The fire serpent of Tenayuca.

Xiuhtecuhtli   The Aztec "Lord of the Year."

Xochipilli   An Aztec deity, patron of maize, called the Flower Prince, and depicted in the Valley of Mexico ballgames.

Xochiquetzal   An Aztec goddess of weavers, called Flower Quetzal.

Xochiquetzalli   A Xochimilco goddess of harvests and the New Fire.

Xolotl   A Toltec deity, the twin of Quetzalcoatl.

Xonaxi Quecuya   A Zapotec goddess of death, the consort of the god Pitao Pezelaco.

Xux Ek   A Maya name for the planet Venus when honored as the divine brother of the god Itzamna.

Yahui   Mixtec spirits serving as companions to sorcerors.

APPENDIX II
MESOAMERICAN CULTURAL GROUPS

NAME	REGION	ERA
Abasalo	Tamaulipas	11,000–7000 B.C.
Acolhua	Valley of Mexico	A.D. 1260/1168
Acozac	Lake Texcoco	A.D. 1200/1250
Acxotec	Chalco	2000–900 B.C.
Ah Canul	Yucatan	A.D. 1450
Aztec	Valley of Mexico	A.D. 1300–1521
Chachapa	Cholula	900–300 B.C.
Chalchihuites	northern Mexico	c. A.D. 1/250–600
Chalco-Amecameca	Chalco	A.D. 600–900
Chalco-Chichimec	Valley of Mexico	A.D. 1156–1168
Chantuto	Chiapas	3000–2000 B.C.
Chichimec	Valley of Mexico	A.D. 1200
Chimalpanec	Texcoco	A.D. 900–1200/1250
Chocho-Popoloca	Puebla	A.D. 800
Choltec	Valley of Mexico	A.D. 1200
Chontal	Oaxaca	A.D. 1200–1521
Coatlinchan	Texcoco	A.D. 900–1200/1250
Coixtlahuaca	Mixteca Baja	1300 B.C.–A.D. 1521
Couixca	Valley of Mexico	A.D. 1/250–900
Colcolca	Chalco	A.D. 600–900
Contec	Chalco	A.D. 900–1200/1250
Costa Grande	Guerrero	300 B.C.–A.D. 600
Couixca	Valley of Mexico	c. A.D. 1/250–900
Cuadros	Pacific coast	1000–840 B.C.
Cuanalan	Valley of Mexico	c. 1300 B.C.
Cuauhtinchan	Puebla	c. A.D. 1200
Cuauhtitlan	Valley of Mexico	A.D. 1200–1521
Cuernavaca	Valley of Mexico	A.D. 900–1521
Cuicuilco	Valley of Mexico	900 B.C.–A.D. 300/400
Culhua	Valley of Mexico	A.D. 1200–1521
Desert Culture	Desert regions	7000–c. 2000/2500 B.C.
Huaxtec	Veracruz/Tamaulipas	1800 B.C.–A.D. 1521
Huexotzinco	Puebla	A.D. 1/250–900
Huitznahua	Valley of Mexico	A.D. 900–1200
Itzá	Tabasco	A.D. 900–1521
Ixtapaluca	Valley of Mexico	1250–900 B.C.
Izapa	Chiapas	2000 B.C.–A.D. 290
Jalieza	Oaxaca	A.D. 250–450
Jalisco	Western Mexico	2000 B.C.–A.D. 290
Loma San Gabriel	Durango	7000–2500 B.C.
Malpaso	Zacatenco	c. A.D. 1/250–600
Manzanilla	Puebla	900–300 B.C.
Matlatzinca	Valley of Mexico	A.D. 1200–1521
Maya	Mayan domains	2500 B.C.–A.D. 1521
Mazahua	Northern Mexico	A.D. 600–900
Mexiti	Valley of Mexico	A.D. 900–1521
Mihuaque	Valley of Mexico	A.D. 600–900
Mixiti	Valley of Mexico	A.D. 900–1521
Mixtec	Oaxaca	2000 B.C.–A.D. 1521
Monte Albán	Oaxaca	500 B.C.–A.D. 900
Monte Negro	Oaxaca	2000 B.C.–A.D. 290
Moyotzinco	Puebla	1300 B.C.
Nayarit	Valley of Mexico	2000 B.C.–A.D. 290
Nonoalco	Veracruz/Tabasco	c. A.D. 1/250–1521
Ocós	Pacific Coast	1500–850 B.C.
Ojochi	Gulf coast	1500–1350 B.C.
Olmec	Gulf coast	1500–c. 600/400 B.C.
Olmeca-Xicallanca	Gulf coast	2000 B.C.–A.D. 900
Otomí	Valley of Mexico	A.D. 100–1521
Oztopolco	Valley of Mexico	c. A.D. 1224

NAME	REGION	ERA
Pipil	Oaxaca/Guatemala	A.D. 400–1521
Popoloca	Teotihuacan	c. 900–300 B.C.
Quiyahuitzteca	Valley of Mexico	A.D. 600–900
Remojada	Veracruz	300 B.C.–A.D. 900
San José Mogoté	Oaxaca	2000 B.C.–A.D. 290
San Mateo	Puebla	900–200 B.C.
Santa Isabel Iztapan	Valley of Mexico	7000–5000 B.C.
Swasey	Belize	2000–1000 B.C.
Tamaulipa	Sierra Tamaulipas	11,000–1800 B.C.
Tamime	Valley of Mexico	A.D. 900–1521
Tarascan	Western Mexico/Michoacan	A.D. 1000–1521
Tehuacan	Puebla/Oaxaca	7000 B.C.–A.D. 1521
Teotenanca	Valley of Mexico	A.D. 900–1200
Teotihuacan	Valley of Mexico	2000 B.C.–A.D. 750
Tepanec	Valley of Mexico	A.D. 1250–1428
Tepexpan	Valley of Mexico	11,000–7000 B.C.
Tepozteco	Valley of Mexico	A.D. 1200–1521
Tequixquiac	Valley of Mexico	11,000–7000 B.C.
Ticoman	Valley of Mexico	c. 500 B.C.
Tierras Largas	Oaxaca	1400–1150 B.C.
Tlahuicas	Valley of Mexico	A.D. 900–1521
Tlailotlaque	Valley of Mexico	11,000–7000 B.C.
Tlatecahuaque	Valley of Mexico	11,000–7,000 B.C.
Tlatilco	Oaxaca	2000–900 B.C.
Tlaxcaltec	Puebla	A.D. 1350–1521
Toltec	Valley of Mexico	A.D. 900–1200
Totonac	Veracruz/Puebla	A.D. 800–1521
Tototepec	Oaxaca	A.D. 1150–1521
Valsequillo	Puebla	36,000 B.C.–?
Xalpaneca	Veracruz	c. A.D. 800
Xochicalco	Morelos	A.D. 650–1521
Xochimilco	Valley of Mexico	A.D. 1200–1521
Xochtec	Chalco	A.D. 600–900
Yope	Guerrero	A.D. 900–1521
Zacateca	Northern Mexico/Puebla	A.D. 900–1521
Zapotec	Oaxaca	1500 B.C.–A.D. 1521

GLOSSARY

accompanates Stone figures created by the Zapotec, usually in the form of bats, deities or warriors, used as part of the architectural designs of temples and ceremonial complexes.

actun A Maya-region limestone cave.

aguada A small pond formed by rainwater and used by the Maya, who established ceremonial centers near such natural reservoirs.

adobe Sun-dried clay, formed into bricks and serving as materials for building throughout Mesoamerica.

apoztles Sieves designed and used by the Mixtec for cleaning maize.

Atlantean A style of statuary used by the Olmec and the Toltec, incorporated into altars or standing as monuments.

amaranth A grain and pot herb used by many Mesoamerican cultures to make drinks and as an alternate crop to maize.

atlatl A form of spear thrower invented early in Mesoamerica and used throughout the region in all eras.

axalapazco A form of volcanic cinder cone, containing a lake.

baja A field in the Maya region, raised in sections from flat or level ground and formed by agriculturists to protect crops.

barranca a steep-sided gorge, formed by a river.

biface A term used to describe double-sided chipped stone tools.

cacao (*Theodroma cacao*) A crop nurtured in Mesoamerican regions, originally grown wild. Cacao beans were used as currency or ground into drinks for the regional aristocrats.

calmecac An architectural complex in various cultures, and a term used by the Aztec to denote regional schools.

calpulli A term used to specify Aztec social groupings and land divisions.

camelid (*Camelidae*) A family of animals including llamas, alpacas, vicunas and guanacos; once common in Mesoamerica but today confined to the Andes Mountains.

canada A flat-topped mesa with terraced hills.

canitas A type of figurine dating to the pre-Olmec period.

cardinal points The four directional regions of the earth, having great religious importance for Mesoamerican cultures.

cartouche A term in Mesoamerica denoting the enclosing frame used in Maya glyphs.

caryatid A supporting column, fashioned in human form, such as the Olmec and Toltec Atlantean figures.

celt A religious, carved object used by the Olmec; also a grooved stone ax or a woodworking tool.

cenote A natural well or underground river exposed when the limestone coverings collapsed; used by the Maya in the Yucatan.

chamfer Horizontal moldings, intaglio in effect, used in Maya religious structures.

cire perdue The lost wax technique, used in casting metallic objects, such as those of the Maya, Tarascan and other cultures.

chinampa Called a floating islands, a specially devised agricultural bed that was anchored in canals and lakes and kept fertile.

chultun A Maya architectural innovation used as a tomb chamber or as a storage area.

coa A digging stick used in many Mesoamerican cultures.

coatepantli A wall of stone serpents in the pyramid of Tenayuca, surrounding the temple on three sides.

complex A division of deities and corresponding religious rites used by the Aztec.

corbel arch A Maya architectural form used in ceremonial centers, fashioned by carrying the faces of the walls inward by overlapping stone courses until the gap between the walls is bridged.

danzante An unusual carved relief figure discovered in Monte Alban, normally a nude male, Olmecoid in style.

doble escapulario The double recessed architectural style of the city of Monte Alban.

excising A Mesoamerican ceramic technique for making grooved patterns in objects or making relief designs.

fresco a form of painting on a wet stucco or plaster surface.

freize A band of sculpted or painted decorations on walls or on ceramic wares.

glyph A unit of Mesoamerican writing, such as the Maya form; also a term designating the emblems found at Monte Alban and in Olmec sites.

hacha A stone marker used in Mesoamerican ball games; also a thin stone blade, a ceremonial battle-axe, usually with a human profile.

haya A thin pocket of soil found in arid Maya territories, used for farming.

horno A tube fashioned out of burned clay and incorporated into Olmec tomb constructions.

ideogram A symbol of representing an idea, used by the Aztec and by the Maya.

incensario An incense burner used in Teotihuacan and other cities; some represented deities and assumed complex, sophisticated forms.

inscription A term used to describe hieroglyphic writing on stone or on wood.

Jaguar Baby An Olmec figure and a Maya form involved in the complex jaguar cult of these cultures.

Kukulcan The Maya form of the god Quetzalcoatl.

llano A grass-covered territory in Chiapas.

maguey A plant used throughout many regions of Mesoamerica; the fibers are made into various products and the juice into *pulque*.

mano A hand-held stone used to grind maize and other grains.

mercadore A stone ring used in the Mesoamerican ball game arenas.

metate A flat stone mortar used as the base for the *mano*.

midden A refuse area denoting prior human habitation.

negative painting A process that covers a ceramic with gum or wax before firing; the slip used in the process becomes colored by the fire, whereas the covered area is cleared.

obsidian A highly prized natural glass formed by volcanic activity; used for blades.

palma Sculptured forms used in the ball game and in religious rituals; its name is derived from its shape.

pedregal An arid area of volcanic debris.

potrero An elongated valley with grassy plains.

projectile point A term used to denote a stone weapon point, also called arrowhead.

pulque Intoxicating liquor made from the maguey plant.

pyramid A structure used in Mesoamerican centers, solid or hollow, sometimes on a base, serving as a ceremonial stage.

resumidero A sinkhole found in the region of the Sierras, normally near limestone caverns, sometimes funnel shaped.

sacab A type of lime used by the Maya in building.

sacheob A Maya causeway, a constructed avenue elevated over swampy region to connect centers or areas within cities.

stela A columnar stone monument used by the Olmec, Maya, Zapotec and other cultures.

talud-tablero An architectural and design style introduced by the Olmec and others, using a sloping wall base (*talud*) and a slab placed above the base (*tablero*).

tecomate A small, neckless jar developed in early ceramic phases.

terra cotta Glazed or unglazed fired clay.

tzompantli A skull rack used as an architectural component in Toltec, Aztec and other ceremonial temples.

voladore The "dance of death," a ritual of acrobatic displays performed by the Totonac and others on high poles.

xalapazco A dry volcanic cinder cone in the Valley of Mexico and in Puebla.

yoke The U-shape stone piece, sometimes carved, associated with the Olmec and with Mesoamerican ball games.

zoomorphic A term denoting animal qualities exemplified in Mesoamerican religious art forms.

BIBLIOGRAPHICAL NOTE

There are numerous accessible volumes on pre-Columbian America for the general reader. The *Atlas of Ancient America*, by Michael Coe, Dean Snow, and Elizabeth Benson (Facts On File, 1986), provides a good introduction to the many cultures that rose and fell in this region; see also *Mysteries of the Ancient Americas: The New World Before Columbus* by Reader's Digest editors (Reader's Digest, 1986); *The Art of Mesoamerica* by Mary E. Miller (Thames & Hudson, 1986); *Pre-Columbian Art* by Jose Alcina Franch (Abrams, 1983); and *Sweat of the Sun and Tears of the Moon: Gold and Silver in Pre-Columbian Art* by Andre Emmerich, (Hacker, 1977). More advanced are Muriel P. Weaver's *Aztecs, Maya and Their Predecessors: Archaeology of Mesoamerica* (Academic Press, 1981); Richard E. Blanton's *Ancient Mesoamerica: A Comparison of Change in Three Regions* (Cambridge University Press, 1982); *Ancient North Americans, Ancient South Americans,* edited by Jesse D. Jennings (Freeman, 1983, 2 vols.); and *Archaeology of West and Northwest Mesoamerica,* edited by Michael S. Foster (Westview Press, 1985). The definitive text, at least in scope, is the 16-volume *Handbook of Middle American Indians* edited by Robert Wauchope (University of Texas Press, 1964–1975).

To learn more about the Olmec, Mesoamerica's first complex culture, see Roman Pina Chan's *Olmec: Mother Culture of Mesoamerica* (Rizzoli, 1989); Ignacio Bernal's *Olmec World* (University of California Press, 1969); Robert J. Sharer's *The Olmec and the Development of Formative Mesoamerican Civilisation* (Cambridge University Press, 1989); and the two-volume *Land of the Olmec* by Michael D. Coe and Richard A. Diehl (University of Texas, 1980), which focuses specifically on recent archaeological excavations in Tenochtitlan.

For more on the Toltec culture, which served almost as an inspiration to the Aztec, Richard A. Diehl's *Tula: The Toltec Capital of Ancient Mexico* (Thames & Hudson, 1983) and Nigel Davies's *The Toltec Heritage: From the Fall of Tula to the Rise of Tenochtitlan* (University of Oklahoma Press, 1980) are useful.

There is no lack of books on the Aztec themselves, and the reader is referred to these volumes: *The Aztecs* by Eduardo Matos Moctezuma (Rizzoli, 1989); *Daily Life of the Aztecs on the Eve of the Spanish Conquest* by Jacques Soustelle (Stanford University Press, 1961); *The Aztec Empire: The Toltec Resurgence* by Nigel Davies; (University of Oklahoma Press, 1987); *The Aztec Arrangement: The Social History of Pre-Spanish Mexico* by Rudolf van Zantwijk; (University of Oklahoma Press, 1985); and *Aztec Thought and Culture: A Study of the Ancient Nahuatl Mind* (University of Oklahoma Press, 1982).

The incredible bureaucracy and structure of the Inca is covered in detail in Sally F. Moore's *Power and Property in Inca Peru* (Greenwood Press, 1973) and *The Inca and Aztec States, Fourteen Hundred to Eighteen Hundred: Anthropology and History* (Academic Press, 1982), edited by George Collier. The scholar Burr Cartwright Brundage has written numerous studies of Mesoamerican cultures including *Empire of the Inca* (University of Oklahoma, 1985) and *Lords of Cuzco: A History and Description of the Inca People in Their Final Days* (University of Oklahoma Press, 1985). For a comparative study, see *Two Earths, Two Heavens: An Essay Contrasting the Aztecs and the Incas* (University of New Mexico Press, 1975).

To learn more about the Maya, see *Blood of Kings: Dynasty and Ritual in Maya Art* by Linda Schele and Jeffrey H. Miller (Braziller, 1986), which includes important information on the deciphering of the Maya hieroglphyic code in 1960; *Lords of the Underworld: Masterpieces of Classical Mayan Ceramics* by Michael D. Coe (Princeton University Press, 1978); *Ceremonial Centers of the Maya* by Roy C. Craven, Jr., William R. Bullard, Jr., and Michael E. Kapne (University of Florida Press, 1974); and *The Ancient Maya* by Sylvanus G. Morley and George W. Brainerd (4th ed. revised by Robert J. Sharer, Stanford University Press, 1983).

A fuller appreciation of many early cultures can be gained through a study of their religious beliefs. This is especially true of the Aztec, though their reliance on human sacrifices and blood offerings may be too grim for some readers. See Ake Hultkrantz's *Religions of the American Indians* (University of California Press, 1979) and *Belief and Worship in Native North America,* edited by Christopher Vecsey (Syracuse University Press, 1981); *North American Indian Mythologies* by Cottie Burland (P. Bedrick Books, 1985); *Olmec Religion: A Key to Middle America and Beyond* by Karl W. Luckert (University of Oklahoma Press, 1978); *The Fifth Sun: Aztec Gods, Aztec World* by Burr C. Brundage (University of Texas Press, 1979); *The Aztec Cosmos* by Tomas Filsinger (Celestial Arts Publishing Company, 1984); and *Archaeoastronomy in the New World; American Primitive Astronomy* edited by A.F. Aveni (Cambridge University Press, 1982). In pre-industrial cultures, medicine and religion often go hand in hand, and the shaman's herbal collections and lore have ritualistic as well as healing purposes. For more on this relationship, see *The Smoking Gods: Tobacco in Maya Art, History, and Religion* by Francis Robicsek; (University of Oklahoma Press, 1978); *Plants of the Gods: Origins of Hallucinogenic Use* by Richard Schultes and Albert Hofmann (Van der Marck, 1987); and *Hallucinogens and Shamanism,* edited by Michael J. Harner

(Oxford University Press, 1973). *The Pre-Columbian Mind* by Francisco Guerra (Seminar Press, 1971), presents a good overall view of how these cultures saw their world.

The general reader who wants to get an idea of what day-to-day life was like for the pre-Columbian Indian should consult Jeremy A. Sabloff's excellent *Cities of Ancient Mexico: Reconstructing a Lost World* (Thames and Hudson, 1989). Also, Dorset Press has a very readable Everyday Life Series, of which three titles are relevant here: *Everyday Life of the Aztecs* by Warwick Bray (1987); *Everyday Life of the Maya* by Ralph Whitlock (1987); and *Everyday Life of the North American Indians* by Jon Manchip White (1988); the latter includes a separate chapter on reservation life.

For a taste of pre-Columbian literature, several translations exist of early texts. The Maya account of the creation of the world is beautifully related in *Popol Vuh: The Mayan Book of the Dawn of Life,* translated by Dennis Tedlock (Simon & Schuster, 1985). The *Codex Magliabechiano,* the sixteenth-century Aztec pictorial manuscript, is reproduced in the two-volume *Book of the Life of the Ancient Mexicans* with text and commentary by Zelia Nuttall and Elizabeth Hill Boone (University of California Press, 1982). Also, a number of early American creation myths are included in *This Country Was Ours: A Documentary History of the American Indian* edited by Virgil J. Vogel (Harper & Row, 1972), and *Voices of the Winds: Native American Tales* by Margot Edmonds and Etta E. Clark (Facts On File, 1989).

Serious students who contemplate reading some of the existing Mesoamerican texts in the original are referred to *Maya Glyphs* (University of California Press, 1989), by S.D. Houston; *An Outline Dictionary of Maya Glyphs* by William Gates (Dover Publications, 1978); *Mayan Language Dictionary* by Robert W. Blair (Garland Publishing, 1981); and *A Dictionary of the Huazalinguillo Dialect of Nahuatl with Grammatical Sketch and Readings* by Geoffrey Kimball (Tulane University Press, 1980).

Contemporary Spanish accounts of the conquest are numerous; see Bernal Diaz del Castillo's *Conquest of New Spain* (Penguin, 1963), translated by John M. Cohen; Bernardino de Sahagun's *War of Conquest: How It Was Waged Here in Mexico,* translated by Arthur J. Anderson and Charles E. Dibble, (University of Utah Press, 1978), and the 13-volume *Florentine Codex: A General History of the Things of New Spain,* also translated by Anderson and Dibble and published by the University of Utah Press, 1982; Garcilaso de la Vega's *Florida of the Inca,* edited by John and Jeannette Varner (University of Texas Press, 1957), and *Royal Commentaries of the Incas,* translated and edited by Clements R. Markham (B. Franklin, reprint of 1869 edition).

The relationship between Old and New World cultures and the inevitable comparisons—the similarity of the pyramids of Egypt to those in Mesoamerica, for instance—has inspired a number of trans-Atlantic colonization theories, which date back at least to the nineteenth century: Lord Kingsborough (*Antiquities of Mexico*) believed the Maya to be descended from the 10 lost tribes of Israel, while Augustus Le Plongeon (*Maya-Atlantis; Queen Moo and the Egyptian Sphinx*) argued that the Maya colonized the Nile. In more modern times, Thor Heyerdahl has demonstrated that reed boats of the type commonly used in Egypt could withstand the rigors of ocean travel, and his experiences are well documented; Heyerdahl's own account is contained in *RA Expeditions* (Chronica Botanica India, 1971). Harvard professor Barry Fell has carried Heyerdahl's ideas a step further in books like *America B.C.* (Simon & Schuster, 1989), which places ancient Phoenicians in Iowa and Celtic Druids in Vermont.

For information about the effects of Spanish exploration on the ancient native civilizations, the catalog to an extensive exhibition mounted at the Florida Museum of Natural History, *First Encounters: Spanish Explorations in the Caribbean & the United States, 1492–1570,* edited by Jerald T. Milanich and Susan Milbrath (University of Florida Press, 1990), is an up-to-date survey. The reader should see also *The Columbian Exchange: Biological and Cultural Consequences of 1492* by Alfred W. Crosby (Greenwood Press, 1973). Bernardine de Sahagun's multivolume *Florentine Codex: General History of the Things of New Spain* (University of Utah Press, 1982), and Diego De Landa's *Yucatan Before and After the Conquest* (Dover, 1978), are near-contemporary accounts from the Spanish perspective.

The best way to study anything, of course, is firsthand, and those lucky enough actually to visit ancient sites of importance to pre-Columbian Americans should carry along Joyce Kelly's *Complete Visitor's Guide to Mesoamerican Ruins* (University of Oklahoma Press, 1982), C. Bruce Hunter's *Guide to Ancient Maya Ruins* (University of Oklahoma Press, 1974), or Arnold Marquis's *A Guide to America's Indians: Ceremonials, Reservations and Museums* (University of Oklahoma Press, 1975).

INDEX

This index is designed to be used in conjunction with the many cross-references within the A-to-Z entries. The main A-to-Z entries are indicated by **boldface** page references. The general subjects are subdivided by both descriptives and A-to-Z entries. Page references in *italic* indicate illustrations; page references followed by "t" indicate tables; page references followed by "g" indicate glossary items.